T0202665

Lecture Notes in Computer Science 14861

Founding Editors

Gerhard Goos
Juris Hartmanis

The series Lecture Notes in Computer Science (LNCS), including its subseries Lecture Notes in Artificial Intelligence (LNAI) and Lecture Notes in Bioinformatics (LNBI), has established itself as a medium for the publication of new developments in computer science and information technology research, teaching, and education.

LNCS enjoys close cooperation with the computer science R & D community, the series counts many renowned academics among its volume editors and paper authors, and collaborates with prestigious societies. Its mission is to serve this international community by providing an invaluable service, mainly focused on the publication of conference and workshop proceedings and postproceedings. LNCS commenced publication in 1973.

Serge Vaudenay · Christophe Petit
Editors

Progress in Cryptology - AFRICACRYPT 2024

15th International Conference on Cryptology in Africa
Douala, Cameroon, July 10–12, 2024
Proceedings

 Springer

Editors
Serge Vaudenay 🆔
Ecole Polytechnique Fédérale de Lausanne
Lausanne, Switzerland

Christophe Petit 🆔
University of Birmingham
Birmingham, UK

Université libre de Bruxelles
Bruxelles, Belgium

ISSN 0302-9743   ISSN 1611-3349 (electronic)
Lecture Notes in Computer Science
ISBN 978-3-031-64380-4   ISBN 978-3-031-64381-1 (eBook)
https://doi.org/10.1007/978-3-031-64381-1

Preface

This volume contains the papers accepted for presentation at AFRICACRYPT 2024, the 15th International Conference on the Theory and Application of Cryptographic Techniques in Africa. The aim of this series of conferences is to provide an international forum for practitioners and researchers from industry, academia, and government agencies for a discussion of all forms of cryptography and its applications. The initiative of organizing AFRICACRYPT started in 2008 and it was first held in Morocco. Subsequent yearly events were held in Tunisia, South Africa, Senegal, Morocco, and Egypt. In 2024, AFRICACRYPT was organized for the first time in Cameroon, jointly by the University of Bamenda and the National Agency for Information and Communication Technologies (ANTIC) in cooperation with the International Association for Cryptologic Research (IACR). It was held in Douala, during July 10–12.

We received 35 submissions authored by researchers from countries from all over the world. After a double-blind reviewing process that included online discussion and involved 55 Program Committee members and 17 external reviewers, we decided to accept 19 papers. All submitted papers received at least three and often four reviews. We early settled on EasyChair for our submission and review system, and we never regretted our choice.

The paper "Quasi-Optimal Permutation Ranking and Applications to PERK" by Alessandro Budroni, Slim Bettaieb, Marco Palumbi, and Décio Luiz Gazzoni Filho was selected among all accepted papers for the best paper award. The selection was made by the chairs based on nominations by program committee members among a preselection of three papers that had received the best evaluations during the review process. The above paper was selected for its novelty, potential future application, and high editorial quality.

We were honored to host Betül Durak, Atsuko Miyaji, and Luca De Feo as invited speakers. They respectively talked on "Security and Privacy Balance of Anonymous Tokens and Its Applications", "Privacy-preserving Machine Learning Framework", and "The Isogeny Toolbox". We thank them for agreeing to come and deliver their keynote talks at the conference. The abstracts of their presentation are included in the present proceedings. The program also included a poster session and a cultural session.

Acting as program chairs for AFRICACRYPT 2024 was a privilege. We thank the Program Committee and the external reviewers for their diligent work and fruitful discussions. We also thank our General Chairs, Emmanuel Fouotsa from the University of Bamenda and Boris Fouotsa from École Polytechnique Fédérale de Lausanne, for organizing the conference locally and for the smooth collaboration.

The conference received generous financial support from the Technology Innovation Institute Abu Dhabi, the Belgian Académie de recherche et enseignement supérieur (ARES) through a Training Project for the South between Université libre de Bruxelles and the University of Bamenda, as well as École Polytechnique Fédérale de Lausanne and Osaka University.

Many thanks also go to the authors of all submitted papers for their contribution to the conference, and to all those people who helped us make this conference a big success.

May 2024   Christophe Petit
                                                    Serge Vaudenay

Organization

Program Committee

Gora Adj	Technology Innovation Institute, UAE
Riham Altawy	University of Victoria, Canada
Elena Andreeva	TU Wien, Austria
Hatem M. Bahig	Ain Shams University, Egypt
Hussain Ben-Azza	Moulay Ismail University, Morocco
Olivier Blazy	École Polytechnique, France
Sébastien Canard	Télécom Paris, France
Céline Chevalier	University Paris-Panthéon-Assas and DI/ENS, PSL University, France
Daniel Collins	EPFL, Switzerland
Tingting Cui	Hangzhou Dianzi University, China
Joan Daemen	Radboud University, The Netherlands
Luca De Feo	IBM Research Zürich, Switzerland
Christoph Dobraunig	Intel Labs, Austria
Sylvain Duquesne	University Rennes 1, France
Laila El Aimani	University of Cadi Ayyad, Morocco
Nadia El Mrabet	SAS - CGCP – EMSE, France
Muhammad ElSheikh	National Institute of Standards, Egypt
Emmanuel Fouotsa	University of Bamenda, Cameroon
Tony Ezome	École Normale Supérieure Libreville, Gabon
Georgios Fotiadis	Foundation, Luxembourg
Tako Boris Fouotsa	École Polytechnique Fédérale de Lausanne, Switzerland
Gina Gallegos-Garcia	Instituto Politécnico Nacional, Mexico
Essam Ghadafi	Newcastle University, UK
Loubna Ghammam	ITK Engineering GmbH, Germany
Satrajit Ghosh	IIT Kharagpur, India
Javier Herranz	Universitat Politècnica de Catalunya, Spain
Akinori Hosoyamada	NTT Social Informatics Laboratories, Japan
Sorina Ionica	Université de Picardie Jules Verne, France
Tetsu Iwata	Nagoya University, Japan
Samuel Jaques	University of Waterloo, Canada
Muhammad Rezal Kamel Ariffin	Universiti Putra Malaysia, Malaysia
Juliane Krämer	University of Regensburg, Germany

Péter Kutas	University of Birmingham, UK and Eötvös Loránd University, Hungary
Marine Minier	LORIA, Nancy, France
Mainack Mondal	Indian Institute of Technology, Kharagpur, India
Abderrahmane Nitaj	LMNO, Université de Caen Normandie, France
Yanbin Pan	AMSS, Chinese Academy of Sciences, China
Sikhar Patranabis	IBM Research, India
Christophe Petit	University of Birmingham, UK and Université libre de Bruxelles, Belgium
Divya Ravi	University of Amsterdam, The Netherlands
Joost Renes	NXP Semiconductors, USA
Yann Rotella	Paris-Saclay University, France
Simona Samardjiska	Radboud University, The Netherlands
Palash Sarkar	Indian Statistical Institute, India
Ali Aydin Selçuk	TOBB University, Turkey
Dave Singelee	Katholieke Universiteit Leuven, Belgium
El Mamoun Souidi	Mohammed V University in Rabat, Morocco
Pantelimon Stanica	Naval Postgraduate School, USA
Hervé Tale Kalachi	École Nationale Supérieure Polytechnique de Yaoundé, Cameroon
Patrick Towa	Aztec Labs, Switzerland
Gilles Van Assche	STMicroelectronics, Belgium
Serge Vaudenay	École Polytechnique Fédérale de Lausanne, Switzerland
Fernando Virdia	Universidade NOVA de Lisboa, Portugal
Vanessa Vitse	Université Grenoble Alpes, France
Amr Youssef	Concordia University, Canada

Additional Reviewers

Ismail Afia	Nimish Mishra
Thomas Aulbach	Anisha Mukherjee
Souhayl Ben El Haj Soulami	Protik Kumar Paul
Bhuvnesh Chaturvedi	Amit Singh Bhati
Benne de Weger	Abdullah Talayhan
Loïs Huguenin-Dumittan	George Teseleanu
Murat Burhan Ilter	Cihangir Tezcan
Zhen Liu	Violetta Weger
Nascimo Madieta	

Steering Committee

Abdelhak Azhari	École Normale Supérieure, Casablanca, Morocco
Hatem M. Bahig	Ain Shams University, Egypt
Abderrahmane Nitaj	Université de Caen Normandie, France
Djiby Sow	Cheikh Anta Diop University of Dakar, Senegal
Amr Youssef	Concordia University, Canada

General Chairs

Emmanuel Fouotsa	University of Bamenda, Cameroon
Tako Boris Fouotsa	EPFL, Switzerland

Abstract of Invited Talks

Security and Privacy Balance of Anonymous Tokens and Its Applications

F. Betül Durak

Microsoft Research, Redmond, WA, USA
betul.durak@microsoft.com

On the one hand, the web needs to be secured from malicious activities such as bots or DoS attacks; on the other hand, this should not justify services tracking people's activities on the web. Anonymous tokens provide a nice tradeoff. These tokens define a protocol between three types of parties: a client, an issuer, and a redeemer. The client wishes to obtain tokens from an issuer and then to present them to a redeemer. The issuer determines the trustworthiness of clients and issues tokens; and the redeemer verifies the tokens.

There has been significant industry interest recently in anonymous tokens. These protocols are used to transfer trust signals without compromising users' privacy. They are anonymous in that the token issuance and redemption are unlinkable, in the sense that the issuer and redeemer cannot tell which of the issued tokens was used in any given redemption. However, to balance the security and privacy can be tricky at times. In this talk, we will look at two cases where the privacy needs to be balanced to protect the security of the services.

The presentation will be based on recent publications. We first look at how to build anonymous tokens from algebraic MACs instead of oblivious pseudorandom functions [1, 2]. Then, we show how to add non-transferability to prevent a token owner from selling it to another client [5, 6]. Finally, we present an application for a reputation system in direct communication [3, 4].

References

1. Chase, M., Durak, F.B., Vaudenay, S.: Anonymous Tokens with Hidden Metadata Bit From Algebraic MACs. Cryptology ePrint Archive, Report 2022/1622 (2022). https://eprint.iacr.org/2022/1622.pdf.
2. Chase, M., Durak, F.B., Vaudenay, S.: Anonymous tokens with stronger metadata bit hiding from algebraic MACs. In: Handschuh, H., Lysyanskaya, A. (eds.) CRYPTO 2023. LNCS, vol. 14082, pp. 418–449. Springer, Cham (2023). https://doi.org/10.1007/978-3-031-38545-2_14
3. Durak, F.B., Laine, K., Langowski, S., Moreno, R.C.: Sandi: A System for Accountability and Applications in Direct Communication. CoRR, abs/2401.16759 (2024)

4. Durak, F.B., et al.: Sandi: A System for Accountability and Applications in Direct Communication (extended abstract). CoRR, abs/2311.04861 (2023)
5. Durak, F.B., Marco, L., Talayhan, A., Vaudenay, S.: Non-Transferable Anonymous Tokens by Secret Binding. ACM CCS (2024, to appear)
6. Durak, F.B., Marco, L., Talayhan, A., Vaudenay, S.: Non-Transferable Anonymous Tokens by Secret Binding. Cryptology ePrint Archive, Paper 2024/711 (2024). https://eprint.iacr.org/2024/711

Privacy-Preserving Machine Learning Framework

Atsuko Miyaji

Graduate School of Engineering, Osaka University, Suita, Japan
miyaji@comm.eng.osaka-u.ac.jp

Abstract. With the spread of IoT devices, various data about our lives are being collected, such as heart rate, physical activity, number of steps, pulse, oxygen intake, calorie consumption, etc. If these data can be analyzed, it will be possible to learn the signs of disease. However, it is dangerous for a person's activity status to be managed on an external server with the view of privacy. Generally, privacy in machine learning requires consideration of the following two aspects In general, there are two aspects of privacy that should be protected in machine learning.

1. (Data Privacy) Privacy protection of training or testing data
2. (Model Privacy) Privacy protection from model

Differential Privacy provides (DP) privacy protection in the context of a trusted server (TTP) collecting and managing data. The attacker in DP is the user of the machine learning model. In other words, DP achieves *model privacy* but does not consider *data privacy* for the server. Local Differential Privacy (LDP) protects the privacy by adding noise when the data provider sends data to the server. LDP protects both data privacy and model privacy. However, machine learning with using LDP-data faces accuracy degradation issues.

In this talk, we will present privacy-preserving machine learning frameworks that protect privacy from both data and model privacy perspectives. While ensuring privacy by LDP is certainly important, it degrades the usefulness of the analysis of LDP-data. We will investigate how to reduce performance degradation in machine learning while protecting privacy.

The Isogeny Toolbox

Luca De Feo

IBM Research Europe, Zürich, Switzerland

When I was invited to give a presentation at AfricaCrypt 2017, isogeny-based cryptography could still fit in a single talk. Seven years later, through ups and downs, it has grown into a rich and diverse field, with plenty of algorithms, protocols and cryptanalytic techniques.

An interesting subplot is the evolution of the algorithms for computing isogenies. It is André Weil who, in the '50s, laid the foundations of the modern theory of elliptic curves and isogenies. But, until Vélu's seminal work in the '70s, we did not even know a generic tool to compute isogenies.

The growth of elliptic curve cryptography in the '90s, and in particular research on point-counting algorithms, motivated the development of new algorithms for isogeny computation. Elkies was the first to give an algorithm to compute an isogeny from its domain and codomain curves, then improved by Bostan, Morain, Salvy and Schost, while Charlap, Coley, Robbins, Couveignes, Lercier and others proposed several alternative algorithms.

The inventions of SIDH and CSIDH brought forward a paradigm shift in isogeny-computation algorithms. Indeed with these cryptosystems it became apparent that the usual representation of isogenies was redundant: parties in a cryptosystem needed to evaluate isogenies *exponentially faster* than what it took to write them down. Important developments in this direction were the so-called *strategies*} for evaluating isogenies of prime-power degree in quasi-logarithmic time, and the so-called $\sqrt{\text{élu}}$ (*Vélu-square-root*) algorithm to evaluate prime-degree isogenies in quasi-square-root time.

With more and more complex protocols being developed, more tools were invented to efficiently evaluate isogenies even more generally. Based on the theory of complex multiplication, or on the so-called *Deuring correspondence*, these tools gave alternative representations of isogenies, and efficient tools to evaluate them, becoming the basis of signature schemes such as CSI-FiSh and SQIsign.

Unexpectedly, the recent attacks on SIKE added a new tool to the isogeny computation toolbox. By *embedding* isogenies of elliptic curves into isogenies of higher-dimensional Abelian varieties, new representations with efficient algorithms became available. These representations are being used today to generalize and improve schemes, with some remarkable results.

In my talk I will review the history of isogeny computations from its beginnings until these very recent developments, and showcase some notable results.

Contents

Lattice-Based Cryptography Cryptanalysis

Symmetric Key Cryptography

On the Double Differential Uniformity of Vectorial Boolean Functions

Said Eddahmani[1](✉) and Sihem Mesnager[1,2]

[1] Department of Mathematics, University of Paris VIII, LAGA, University Sorbonne
Paris Nord, CNRS, UMR 7539, 93430 Paris, France
`said.eddahmani@etud.univ-paris8.fr`, `smesnager@univ-paris8.fr`
[2] Telecom Paris, 91120 Palaiseau, France

Abstract. We introduce the double differential distribution table (DDDT) and the double differential uniformity of a vectorial Boolean function to study the security of an S-box to differential attacks. We study several properties of the DDDT and the double differential uniformity and present their explicit values for three of the most practical vectorial Boolean functions: the inverse function, the Gold function, and the Bracken-Leander function. The double differential uniformity is an extension of the differential uniformity and the Feistel boomerang uniformity. It can be used as a distinguisher, and a new criterion for the security of an S-box derived from a vectorial Boolean function against differential attacks.

Keywords: Boolean Function · Differential Uniformity · Double Differential Distribution Table

1 Introduction

Let m and n be positive integers. The finite field with 2^n elements is denoted $\mathbb{F}_{2^n}$ and the n-dimensional vector space over $\mathbb{F}_2$ is denoted $\mathbb{F}_2^n$. An (n, m)-vectorial Boolean function is a function F from $\mathbb{F}_{2^n}$ to $\mathbb{F}_{2^m}$. Vectorial functions play a central role in the design of block ciphers such as the Advanced Encryption Standard (AES) [7,11]. Various attacks have been proposed to test a block cipher's resistance, leading to several criteria to be satisfied by the vectorial Boolean functions. Differential [3], linear [10], and boomerang [14] attacks are the major tools which are applied to most vectorial Boolean functions. Specifically, the differential criteria on vectorial Boolean function F is measured by its differential uniformity δ_F, which is defined by [12]

$$\delta_F = \max_{\substack{(a,b)\in\mathbb{F}_{2^n}\times\mathbb{F}_{2^m} \\ a\neq 0}} \#\{x \in \mathbb{F}_{2^n} | F(x + a) + F(x) = b\}.$$

Vectorial Boolean functions with low differential uniformity have been extensively studied(see [8,12]). For ciphers following a Feistel construction, Boukerrou

S. Vaudenay and C. Petit (Eds.): AFRICACRYPT 2024, LNCS 14861, pp. 3–20, 2024.
https://doi.org/10.1007/978-3-031-64381-1_1

et al. [4] presented a criterion from which the Feistel Boomerang Connectivity Table (FBCT) is constructed, where entry at $(a, b) \in (\mathbb{F}_{2^n})^2$ is defined by

$$\mathrm{FBCT}_F(a, b) = \#\{x \in \mathbb{F}_{2^n} | F(x) + F(x + a) + F(x + b) + F(x + a + b) = 0\}.$$

The Feistel boomerang uniformity of F is defined by

$$\beta^{\mathrm{Feistel}}(F) = \max_{a,b \in \mathbb{F}_{2^n}, ab(a+b) \neq 0} \mathrm{FBCT}_F(a, b).$$

For a randomly chosen vectorial Boolean function F, the value $F(x) + F(x + a) + F(x + b) + F(x + a + b)$ is expected to take all possible values with the same probability. As a consequence, this can be used as a distinguisher if the values $F(x) + F(x + a) + F(x + b) + F(x + a + b)$ are not equiprobable. For this reason, we introduce the *double differential uniformity*, a new criterion to be satisfied by vectorial Boolean functions to ensure improved security against differential attacks. First, for an (n, m)-vectorial Boolean function F, we introduce the double differential distribution table (DDDT) in which the entry at position $(a, b, u) \in \mathbb{F}_{2^n} \times \mathbb{F}_{2^n} \times \mathbb{F}_{2^m}$ is defined by

$$\mathrm{DDDT}_F(a, b, u) = \#\{x \in \mathbb{F}_{2^n} | F(x + a + b) + F(x + a) + F(x + b) + F(x) = u\}.$$

We observe that if $ab(a + b) = 0$, then for all $x \in \mathbb{F}_{2^n}$, we have $F(x + a + b) + F(x + a) + F(x + b) + F(x) = 0$. This leads to defining the double differential uniformity Δ_F of F as

$$\Delta_F = \max_{\substack{(a,b,u) \in \mathbb{F}_{2^n} \times \mathbb{F}_{2^n} \times \mathbb{F}_{2^m} \\ ab(a+b) \neq 0}} \mathrm{DDDT}_F(a, b, u).$$

The double differential uniformity can be seen as an extension of the differential and Feistel boomerang uniformity.

We study the basic properties of the DDDT and the double differential uniformity and give their explicit values for three families of power functions.

- For the inverse function, we show that the possible values for the DDDT are $0, 4, 8, 2^n$, and the double differential uniformity is 8 for $n \geq 4$. A specific example is obtained with $n = 7$ for which the double differential uniformity is $\Delta_F = 8$ while the differential uniformity is $\delta_F = 2$.
- For the Gold function G defined over $\mathbb{F}_{2^n}$ by $G(x) = x^{2^k+1}$ where $1 \leq k < n$, $\gcd(k, n) = d$, and $\frac{n}{d}$ is odd, we show that the possible values for the DDDT are 0 and 2^n and that the double differential uniformity is $\Delta_F = 2^n$. This result is independent of the differential uniformity of the Gold function for which $\delta_F = 2^d$. This shows that the Gold function is unsuitable for building secure S-boxes for block ciphers regarding the DDDT criterion.
- For the Bracken-Leander function F defined over $\mathbb{F}_{2^n}$ by $F(x) = x^{2^{2k}+2^k+1}$ with $n = 4k$, we show that the possible values for the DDDT are 0, 2^{2k}, and 2^n. We also show that the double differential uniformity of the Bracken-Leander function is $\Delta_F = 2^n$.

Notice that Aubry and Herbaut [1] have investigated the second order derivatives for generic polynomials and have proved a density result which is related to such polynomials.

2   Preliminaries

Let n and m be positive integers, and let $\mathbb{F}_{2^n}$ denote the finite field with 2^n elements. An (n, m)-vectorial Boolean function is a mapping F from $\mathbb{F}_{2^n}$ to $\mathbb{F}_{2^m}$.

Definition 1. *Let n and d be two integers with $d < n$ and $d | n$. The trace function $Tr_d^n(x)$ of an element $x \in \mathbb{F}_{2^n}$ is given by*

$$Tr_d^n(x) = x + x^{2^d} + x^{2^{2d}} + \cdots + x^{2^{n-d}}.$$

If $d = 1$, one sets $Tr_d^n = Tr$.

The trace function satisfies the following properties [9]

1. $Tr_d^n(x) \in \mathbb{F}_{2^d}$ for all $x \in \mathbb{F}_{2^n}$.
2. $Tr_d^n\left(x^{2^d}\right) = Tr_d^n(x)$ for all $x \in \mathbb{F}_{2^n}$.
3. $Tr_d^n(ax + by) = aTr_d^n(x) + bTr_d^n(y)$ for all $a, b \in \mathbb{F}_{2^d}$, and all $x, y \in \mathbb{F}_{2^n}$.

Definition 2. *Let $F : \mathbb{F}_2^n \to \mathbb{F}_2^m$ be an (n, m)-vectorial Boolean function and $a \in \mathbb{F}_2^n$. The derivative of F with respect to a is the (n, m)-vectorial function $D_a F$ satisfying*

$$D_a F(x) = F(x + a) + F(x),$$

for all $x \in \mathbb{F}_2^n$.

Definition 3. *Let $F : \mathbb{F}_2^n \to \mathbb{F}_2^m$ be an (n, m)-vectorial Boolean function. The differential distribution table of F is an $n \times m$ table whose components are defined for $a \in \mathbb{F}_2^n$ and $b \in \mathbb{F}_2^m$ by*

$$\text{DDT}_F(a, b) = \#\{x \in \mathbb{F}_2^n \mid F(x + a) + F(x) = b\}.$$

The differential uniformity δ_F of F is defined by [12]

$$\delta_F = \max_{\substack{(a,b) \in \mathbb{F}_{2^n} \times \mathbb{F}_{2^m} \\ a \neq 0}} \text{DDT}_F(a, b).$$

The following results are useful in the present paper.

Lemma 1 (Proposition 1 of [13]). *Let $a, b, c \in \mathbb{F}_{2^n}$. The equation $ax^2 + bx + c = 0$ has*

(i) *One root if and only if $b = 0$.*
(ii) *Two roots if and only if $b \neq 0$ and $Tr\left(\frac{ac}{b^2}\right) = 0$.*
(iii) *No root if and only if $b \neq 0$ and $Tr\left(\frac{ac}{b^2}\right) = 1$.*

Lemma 2 ([6]). *Let k and n be positive integers such that $k < n$. Let $d = \gcd(k, n)$, $m = \frac{n}{d} > 1$, and $\beta_{m-1} = Tr_d^n(b_0)$. Then, the trinomial $f(X) = X^{2^k} + X + b_0$ has no root if $\beta_{m-1} \neq 0$, and has 2^d roots in $\mathbb{F}_{2^n}$ if $\beta_{m-1} = 0$.*

3   Double Differentials

For an (n, m)-vectorial Boolean function F, and for any $a \in \mathbb{F}_{2^n}$, the simple derivative is defined by

$$D_a F(x) = F(x + a) + F(x).$$

For any $a \in \mathbb{F}_{2^n}$ and any $b \in \mathbb{F}_{2^n}$, the double derivative is defined by

$$\begin{aligned} D_{a,b} F(x) &= D_a D_b F(x) \\ &= D_b F(x + a) + D_b F(x) \\ &= F(x + a + b) + F(x + a) + F(x + b) + F(x). \end{aligned}$$

The differential distribution table (DDT) of F is a $2^n \times 2^m$ table in which the entry at the position $(a, u) \in \mathbb{F}_{2^n} \times \mathbb{F}_{2^n}$ is given by

$$\mathrm{DDT}_F(a, u) = \#\{x \in \mathbb{F}_{2^n} | F(x + a) + F(x) = u\}.$$

For a cipher with a Feistel structure, Boukerrou et al. [4] proposed to study its Feistel boomerang connectivity table (FBCT), defined for the vectorial Boolean function F by the entry at $(a, b) \in \mathbb{F}_{2^n}$ as

$$\mathrm{FBCT}_F(a, b) = \#\{x \in \mathbb{F}_{2^n}, \ F(x) + F(x + a) + F(x + b) + F(x + a + b) = 0\}.$$

The Feistel boomerang uniformity of F is then defined by

$$\beta^{\mathrm{Feistel}}(F) = \max_{a, b \in \mathbb{F}_{2^n}, ab(a+b) \neq 0} \mathrm{FBCT}_F(a, b).$$

To extend the double derivative and the Feistel boomerang connectivity table, we define the double differential distribution table (DDDT).

Definition 4. *Let F be an (n, m)-vectorial Boolean function. The double differential distribution table is an $2^n \times 2^n \times 2^m$ table in which the entry at position $(a, b, u) \in \mathbb{F}_{2^n} \times \mathbb{F}_{2^n} \times \mathbb{F}_{2^m}$ is defined by*

$$\mathrm{DDDT}_F(a, b, u) = \#\{x \in \mathbb{F}_{2^n} | F(x + a + b) + F(x + a) + F(x + b) + F(x) = u\}.$$

Notice that if $ab(a + b) = 0$, then $F(x + a + b) + F(x + a) + F(x + b) + F(x) = 0$ holds for all $x \in \mathbb{F}_{2^n}$, and $\mathrm{DDDT}_F(a, b, u) = 2^n$. This leads us to define the double differential uniformity.

Definition 5. *Let F be an (n, m)-vectorial Boolean function. The double differential uniformity of F is*

$$\Delta_F = \max_{\substack{(a,b,u) \in \mathbb{F}_{2^n} \times \mathbb{F}_{2^n} \times \mathbb{F}_{2^m} \\ ab(a+b) \neq 0}} \mathrm{DDDT}_F(a, b, u).$$

The function is said Δ-double differentially uniform if $\Delta_F = \Delta$.

It is known that the minimum possible value for the differential uniformity δ_F of a function is 2. The following results concern the double differential uniformity.

Proposition 1. *Let F be an (n, m)-vectorial Boolean function. The double differential uniformity of F satisfies $\Delta_F \geq 4$.*

Proof. For $a, b \in \mathbb{F}_{2^n}$ with $ab(a+b) \neq 0$, define the function $G : \mathbb{F}_{2^n} \to \mathbb{F}_{2^m}$ by $G(x) = F(x) + F(x+a) + F(x+b) + F(x+a+b)$. For any $u \in \mathbb{F}_{2^m}$, if $G(x) = u$, then $G(x+a) = G(x+b) = G(x+a+b) = u$. This implies that $\Delta_F \geq 4$. $\quad\square$

The following result concerns the double differential uniformity of extended affine equivalent functions.

Definition 6. *Two vectorial Boolean functions $F : \mathbb{F}_{2^n} \to \mathbb{F}_{2^m}$ and $G : \mathbb{F}_{2^n} \to \mathbb{F}_{2^m}$ are extended affine equivalent if $G = A \circ F \circ B + C$ where A is an affine permutation of $\mathbb{F}_{2^m}$, B is an affine permutation of $\mathbb{F}_{2^n}$, and $C : \mathbb{F}_{2^n} \to \mathbb{F}_{2^m}$ is an affine function.*

Proposition 2. *Let F and G be two extended affine equivalent (n, m)-vectorial Boolean functions with $G = A_2 \circ F \circ A_1 + A$. Then $\Delta_F = \Delta_G$. and*

$$\mathrm{DDDT}_G(a, b, u) = \mathrm{DDDT}_F(A_1(a), A_1(b), A_2^{-1}(u)),$$

Proof. Suppose that F and G are extended affine equivalent. Then there exist a permutation A_1 of $\mathbb{F}_{2^n}$, a permutation A_2, of $\mathbb{F}_{2^m}$, and an affine function $A : \mathbb{F}_{2^n} \to \mathbb{F}_{2^m}$ such that $G = A_2 \circ F \circ A_1 + A$. We have

$$
\begin{aligned}
&G(x + a + b) + G(x + a) + G(x + b) + G(x) \\
&= A_2\left(F \circ A_1(x + a + b) + F \circ A_1(x + a) + F \circ A_1(x + b) + F \circ A_1(x)\right) \\
&= A_2(F(A_1(x) + A_1(a) + A_1(b)) + F(A_1(x) + A_1(a)) + F(A_1(x) + A_1(b)) \\
&\quad + F(A_1(x))) \\
&= A_2(F(x' + a' + b') + F(x' + a') + F(x' + b') + F(x')),
\end{aligned}
$$

where $x' = A_1(x)$, $a' = A_1(a)$, and $b' = A_1(b)$. Hence, if $F(x' + a' + b') + F(x' + a') + F(x' + b') + F(x') = u'$, then $G(x + a + b) + G(x + a) + G(x + b) + G(x) = u$ where $u = A_2(u')$. Then

$$\mathrm{DDDT}_G(a, b, u) = \mathrm{DDDT}_F(A_1(a), A_1(b), A_2^{-1}(u)).$$

and, since A_1 and A_2 are two permutations, we get

$$\max_{\substack{(a,b,u) \in \mathbb{F}_{2^n} \times \mathbb{F}_{2^n} \times \mathbb{F}_{2^m} \\ ab(a+b) \neq 0}} \mathrm{DDDT}_G(a, b, u) = \max_{\substack{(a',b',u') \in \mathbb{F}_{2^n} \times \mathbb{F}_{2^n} \times \mathbb{F}_{2^m} \\ a'b'(a'+b') \neq 0}} \mathrm{DDDT}_F(a', b', u').$$

that is $\Delta_G = \Delta_F$. $\quad\square$

For power functions, the following result gives a specific expression for the double differential uniformity.

Proposition 3. *Let F be a power function defined over $\mathbb{F}_{2^n}$ by $F(x) = x^d$ where $d \leq 2^n - 2$. The double differential uniformity of F satisfies*

$$\Delta_F = \max_{\substack{(a,u)\in\mathbb{F}_{2^n}\times\mathbb{F}_{2^n} \\ a\neq 0,1}} \text{DDDT}_F(a,1,u).$$

Proof. For $b \neq 0$, we have

$$F(x+a+b) + F(x+a) + F(x+b) + F(x)$$
$$= (x+a+b)^d + (x+a)^d + (x+b)^d + x^d$$
$$= b^d\left[\left(\frac{x}{b}+1+\frac{a}{b}\right)^d + \left(\frac{x}{b}+\frac{a}{b}\right)^d + \left(\frac{x}{b}+1\right)^d + \left(\frac{x}{b}\right)^d\right]$$
$$= b^d\left[(x'+1+a')^d + (x'+a')^d + (x'+1)^d + x'^d\right]$$
$$= b^d(F(x'+a'+1) + F(x'+a') + F(x'+1) + F(x')),$$

where $x' = \frac{x}{b}$, and $a' = \frac{a}{b}$. Hence,

$$\Delta_F = \max_{\substack{(a,b,u)\in\mathbb{F}_{2^n}\times\mathbb{F}_{2^n}\times\mathbb{F}_{2^n} \\ ab(a+b)\neq 0}} \text{DDDT}_F(a,b,u) = \max_{\substack{(a,u)\in\mathbb{F}_{2^n}\times\mathbb{F}_{2^n} \\ a\neq 0,1}} \text{DDDT}_F(a,1,u).$$

This terminates the proof. □

4   The Double Differential Distribution Table of the Inverse Function

In this section, we give the inverse function's explicit values of the DDDT. The following result will be used in the computation.

Lemma 3. *For any $a,b \in \mathbb{F}_{2^n}$,*

$$\text{Tr}\left(\frac{ab}{(a+b)^2}\right) = 0,$$

under the convention that $\frac{ab}{a^2+b^2} = 0$ if $a = b$.

Proof. If $a = b$, then with the convention $\frac{ab}{a^2+b^2} = 0$, we have

$$\text{Tr}\left(\frac{ab}{a^2+b^2}\right) = \text{Tr}(0) = 0.$$

Suppose that $a \neq b$. Then the equation $(x+a)(x+b) = x^2 + (a+b)x + ab = 0$ has two different solutions, namely a and b. Hence, according to Lemma 1, we get

$$\text{Tr}\left(\frac{ab}{(a+b)^2}\right) = 0.$$

This terminates the proof. □

Theorem 1. *Let F be the inverse function defined by $F(0) = 0$ and $F(x) = \frac{1}{x}$ for $x \neq 0$. For $a, b, u \in \mathbb{F}_{2^n}$ with $abu \neq 0$, let z_1, $z_2 = z_1 + 1$ be the solutions of $z^2 + z + \frac{a+b}{abu} = 0$. Then*

$$
\mathrm{DDDT}_F(a, b, u) =
\begin{cases}
2^n & \text{if } ab(a+b) = 0, u = 0, \\
8 & \text{if } u = \frac{a^2+ab+b^2}{ab(a+b)} \neq 0,\ Tr\left(\frac{a^2+b^2}{a^2+ab+b^2}\right) = 0, \\
& Tr\left(\frac{abz_1}{a^2+b^2}\right) = 0, \\
4 & \text{if } (a, b, u) \in I_1 \cup I_2 \cup I_3 \cup I_4, \\
0 & \text{otherwise,}
\end{cases}
$$

where

$$I_1 = \left\{(a, b, u) : u = \frac{a^2+ab+b^2}{ab(a+b)} \neq 0,\ Tr\left(\frac{a^2+b^2}{a^2+ab+b^2}\right) = 0,\ Tr\left(\frac{abz_1}{a^2+b^2}\right) = 1\right\},$$

$$I_2 = \left\{(a, b, u) : u = 0, ab(a+b) \neq 0, a^2+ab+b^2 = 0\right\},$$

$$I_3 = \left\{(a, b, u) : u = \frac{a^2+ab+b^2}{ab(a+b)},\ Tr\left(\frac{a^2+b^2}{a^2+ab+b^2}\right) = 1\right\},$$

$$I_4 = \left\{(a, b, u) : u \neq \frac{a^2+ab+b^2}{ab(a+b)},\ Tr\left(\frac{a+b}{abu}\right) = 0,\ Tr\left(\frac{abz_1}{a^2+b^2}\right) = 0\right\}.$$

Proof. For $(a, b, u) \in \mathbb{F}_{2^n} \times \mathbb{F}_{2^n} \times \mathbb{F}_{2^m}$, consider the equation

$$F(x + a + b) + F(x + a) + F(x + b) + F(x) = u, \tag{1}$$

in $x \in \mathbb{F}_{2^n}$.

Case 1. Suppose that $u = 0$. If $ab(a + b) = 0$, then the Eq. (1) is satisfied for all $x \in \mathbb{F}_{2^n}$. Hence, if $ab(a + b) = 0$, we have

$$\mathrm{DDDT}_F(a, b, 0) = 2^n.$$

Case 2. Suppose that $u = 0$, $ab(a + b) \neq 0$, and $a^2 + ab + b^2 = 0$. For $x \in \{0, a, b, a + b\}$, we have

$$F(x + a + b) + F(x + a) + F(x + b) + F(x) = \frac{1}{a} + \frac{1}{b} + \frac{1}{a+b} = \frac{a^2+ab+b^2}{ab(a+b)} = 0.$$

For $x \notin \{0, a, b, a + b\}$, the Eq. (1) becomes

$$\frac{1}{x} + \frac{1}{x+a} + \frac{1}{x+b} + \frac{1}{x+a+b} = 0,$$

or equivalently $ab(a + b) = 0$ which is impossible. Hence, in the case $u = 0$, $ab(a + b) \neq 0$, and $a^2 + ab + b^2 = 0$, we have

$$\mathrm{DDDT}_F(a, b, 0) = 4.$$

Case 3. Suppose that $u = 0$, $ab(a + b) \neq 0$, and $a^2 + ab + b^2 \neq 0$. We observe that for $x \in \{0, a, b, a + b\}$, we have

$$F(x + a + b) + F(x + a) + F(x + b) + F(x) = \frac{1}{a} + \frac{1}{b} + \frac{1}{a + b} = \frac{a^2 + ab + b^2}{ab(a + b)} \neq 0.$$

For $x \notin \{0, a, b, a + b\}$, the Eq. (1) can be rewritten as

$$\frac{1}{x} + \frac{1}{x + a} + \frac{1}{x + b} + \frac{1}{x + a + b} = 0,$$

or equivalently $ab(a + b) = 0$ which is impossible. Hence, in the case $u = 0$, $ab(a + b) \neq 0$, and $a^2 + ab + b^2 \neq 0$, we have

$$\text{DDDT}_F(a, b, 0) = 0.$$

Case 4. Suppose that $u \neq 0$, and $ab(a + b) = 0$. Then

$$F(x + a + b) + F(x + a) + F(x + b) + F(x) = 0 \neq u,$$

and the Eq. (1) is never satisfied. Hence, in this case, for $u \neq 0$, we have

$$\text{DDDT}_F(0, b, u) = \text{DDDT}_F(a, 0, u) = \text{DDDT}_F(a, a, u) = 0.$$

Case 5. Suppose that $ab(a + b) \neq 0$ and $u = \frac{a^2 + ab + b^2}{ab(a + b)} \neq 0$. Then, if $x \in \{0, a, b, a + b\}$, we get

$$F(x + a + b) + F(x + a) + F(x + b) + F(x) = \frac{1}{a} + \frac{1}{b} + \frac{1}{a + b} = \frac{a^2 + ab + b^2}{ab(a + b)} = u,$$

and the Eq. (1) is satisfied. Now, suppose that $x \notin \{0, a, b, a + b\}$. Then, the Eq. (1) becomes

$$\frac{1}{x} + \frac{1}{x + a} + \frac{1}{x + b} + \frac{1}{x + a + b} = \frac{ab(a + b)}{x(x + a)(x + b)(x + a + b)} = u.$$

Using $u = \frac{a^2 + ab + b^2}{ab(a + b)}$, this is equivalent to

$$\left(a^2 + ab + b^2\right) x^4 + \left(a^2 + ab + b^2\right)^2 x^2 + ab \left(a^3 + b^3\right) x + a^2 b^2 \left(a^2 + b^2\right) = 0.$$

If we set $y = x(x + a + b)$, the former equation can be rewritten as

$$\left(a^2 + ab + b^2\right) y^2 + ab \left(a^2 + ab + b^2\right) y + a^2 b^2 \left(a^2 + b^2\right) = 0. \tag{2}$$

Since $ab \left(a^2 + ab + b^2\right) \neq 0$, then multiplying (2) by $\frac{1}{a^2 b^2 (a^2 + ab + b^2)}$ gives

$$\left(\frac{y}{ab}\right)^2 + \left(\frac{y}{ab}\right) + \frac{a^2 + b^2}{a^2 + ab + b^2} = 0.$$

Setting $z = \frac{y}{ab}$, this can be rewritten as

$$z^2 + z + \frac{a^2 + b^2}{a^2 + ab + b^2} = 0. \tag{3}$$

Case 5.1. If $\mathrm{Tr}\left(\frac{a^2+b^2}{a^2+ab+b^2}\right) = 1$, then, by Lemma 1, the Eq. (3) has no solution. In this case, we get

$$\mathrm{DDDT}_F(a, b, u) = 4.$$

Case 5.2. If $\mathrm{Tr}\left(\frac{a^2+b^2}{a^2+ab+b^2}\right) = 0$, then the Eq. (3) has two solutions z_1 and $z_2 = z_1 + 1$. In turn, the equations $\frac{y}{ab} = z_1$ and $\frac{y}{ab} = z_2$ lead to the equations $x^2 + (a + b)x + abz_1 = 0$ and $x^2 + (a + b)x + abz_2 = 0$. By Lemma 3, we have

$$\mathrm{Tr}\left(\frac{abz_2}{a^2 + b^2}\right) = \mathrm{Tr}\left(\frac{abz_1}{a^2 + b^2}\right) + \mathrm{Tr}\left(\frac{ab}{a^2 + b^2}\right) = \mathrm{Tr}\left(\frac{abz_1}{a^2 + b^2}\right).$$

If $\mathrm{Tr}\left(\frac{abz_1}{a^2+b^2}\right) = 1$, then the former equations have no solution, and, consequently

$$\mathrm{DDDT}_F(a, b, u) = 4.$$

If $\mathrm{Tr}\left(\frac{abz_1}{a^2+b^2}\right) = 0$, the equation $x^2 + (a+b)x + abz_1 = 0$ has two solutions x_1 and $x_2 = x_1 + 1$. Similarly, the equation $x^2 + (a+b)x + abz_2 = 0$ has two solutions x_3 and $x_4 = x_3 + 1$. We note that the solutions x_1, x_2, x_3, x_4 are pairwise distinct, and do not belong to the set $\{0, a, b, a + b\}$. As a consequence, we have

$$\mathrm{DDDT}_F(a, b, u) = 8.$$

Case 6. Suppose that $u \neq 0$, $ab(a + b) \neq 0$, and $u \neq \frac{a^2+ab+b^2}{ab(a+b)}$. Then $0, a, b, a + b$ are not solutions of the Eq. (1), which can be rewritten as

$$\frac{1}{x} + \frac{1}{x + a} + \frac{1}{x + b} + \frac{1}{x + a + b} = \frac{ab(a + b)}{x(x + a)(x + b)(x + a + b)} = u,$$

or equivalently

$$ux^4 + u\left(a^2 + ab + b^2\right)x^2 + abu(a + b)x + ab(a + b) = 0.$$

If we set $y = x(x + a + b)$, we get

$$uy^2 + abuy + ab(a + b) = 0.$$

Since $abu \neq 0$, then, multiplying by $\frac{1}{a^2b^2u}$, this can be rewritten as

$$\left(\frac{y}{ab}\right)^2 + \left(\frac{y}{ab}\right) + \frac{a + b}{abu} = 0,$$

which is equivalent to

$$z^2 + z + \frac{a + b}{abu} = 0, \tag{4}$$

where $z = \frac{y}{ab}$.

Case 6.1. If $\mathrm{Tr}\left(\frac{a+b}{abu}\right) = 1$, the Eq. (4) has no solution, and, for this case, we have

$$\mathrm{DDDT}_F(a, b, u) = 0.$$

Case 6.2. If $\mathrm{Tr}\left(\frac{a+b}{abu}\right) = 0$, the Eq. (4) has two solutions z_1 and $z_2 = z_1 + 1$. The equations $\frac{y}{ab} = z_1$ and $\frac{y}{ab} = z_2$ lead to $x^2 + (a + b)x + abz_1 = 0$ and $x^2 + (a+b)x + abz_2 = 0$. Again, by Lemma 3, we have $\mathrm{Tr}\left(\frac{abz_1}{a^2+b^2}\right) = \mathrm{Tr}\left(\frac{abz_2}{a^2+b^2}\right)$. If $\mathrm{Tr}\left(\frac{abz_1}{a^2+b^2}\right) = 1$, the former equations have no solution. Consequently

$$\mathrm{DDDT}_F(a, b, u) = 0.$$

If $\mathrm{Tr}\left(\frac{abz_1}{a^2+b^2}\right) = 0$, the equation $x^2 + (a+b)x + abz_1 = 0$ has two solutions x_1' and $x_2' = x_1' + 1$. Similarly, the equation $x^2 + (a+b)x + abz_2 = 0$ has two solutions x_3' and $x_4' = x_3' + 1$. We note that the solutions x_1', x_2', x_3', x_4' are pairwise distinct, and that do not belong to the set $\{0, a, b, a + b\}$. As a consequence, we have

$$\mathrm{DDDT}_F(a, b, u) = 4.$$

This completes the proof.   □

The following result is a direct consequence of Theorem 1.

Corollary 1. *The double differential uniformity of the inverse function F defined by $F(0) = 0$ and $F(x) = \frac{1}{x}$ for $x \neq 0$ is $\Delta_F = 8$.*

Example 1. Note that in contrast to the differential uniformity of the inverse function defined over $\mathbb{F}_{2^n}$ by $F(0) = 0$ and $F(x) = \frac{1}{x}$ for $x \neq 0$ which satisfies (see [5,8])

$$\delta_F = \begin{cases} 4 & \text{if } n \text{ is even,} \\ 2 & \text{if } n \text{ is odd,} \end{cases}$$

and depends on the parity of n, the double differential uniformity depends on n regardless of its parity. In Table 1, we list the double spectrums and the double differential uniformities of the inverse function over $\mathbb{F}_{2^n}$ for $n = 2, 3, 4, 5, 6, 7, 8$.

Example 2. In this example, we consider the inverse function defined over $\mathbb{F}_{2^6}$ by $S(0) = 0$ and $S(x) = \frac{1}{x}$ using the primitive polynomial $x^6 + x + 1$. The table of S is presented in Table 2. The spectrum of the DDDT of S is $\{0, 4, 8, 64\}$ as stipulated by Proposition 1. In Table 3, we list the distribution of the DDDT.

Table 1. The spectrums of the DDDT and the double uniformity of the inverse function over $\mathbb{F}_{2^n}$

n	2	3	4	5	6	7	8
Double Spectrum	$\{0,4\}$	$\{0,8\}$	$\{0,4,16\}$	$\{0,4,32\}$	$\{0,4,8,64\}$	$\{0,4,8,128\}$	$\{0,4,8,256\}$
Δ	4	8	4	4	8	8	8

Table 2. Table of the inverse function over $\mathbb{F}_{2^6}$

x	0	1	2	3	4	5	6	7	8	9	10	11	12	13	14	15
S(x)	0	1	33	62	49	43	31	44	57	37	52	28	46	40	22	25
x	16	17	18	19	20	21	22	23	24	25	26	27	28	29	30	31
S(x)	61	54	51	39	26	35	14	24	23	15	20	34	11	53	45	6
x	32	33	34	35	36	37	38	39	40	41	42	43	44	45	46	47
S(x)	63	2	27	21	56	9	50	19	13	47	48	5	7	30	12	41
x	48	49	50	51	52	53	54	55	56	57	58	59	60	61	62	63
S(x)	42	4	38	18	10	29	17	60	36	8	59	58	55	16	3	32

Next, we give numerical examples of all cases in the proof of Proposition 1.

1. **Case 1.** For all $a \in \mathbb{F}_{2^n}$, we have

$$\mathrm{DDDT}_F(a,0,0) = \mathrm{DDDT}_F(0,a,0) = \mathrm{DDDT}_F(a,a,0) = 2^n.$$

2. **Case 2.** Let $a = 1$, and $b = 58$, then $a^2 + ab + b^2 = 0$, and

$$\mathrm{DDDT}_F(a,b,0) = 4.$$

3. **Case 3.** Let $a = 56$, and $b = 10$, then $a^2 + ab + b^2 \neq 0$, and

$$\mathrm{DDDT}_F(a,b,0) = 0.$$

4. **Case 4.** Let $u \in \mathbb{F}_{2^n}$ with $u \neq 0$. For all $a \in \mathbb{F}_{2^n}$, we have

$$\mathrm{DDDT}_F(a,0,u) = \mathrm{DDDT}_F(0,a,u) = \mathrm{DDDT}_F(a,a,u) = 0.$$

5. **Case 5.1.** Let $a = 59$, $b = 16$, and $u = 2$. Then $u = \frac{a^2+ab+b^2}{ab(a+b)}$, $\mathrm{Tr}\left(\frac{a^2+b^2}{a^2+ab+b^2}\right) = 1$, and

$$\mathrm{DDDT}_F(a,b,u) = 4.$$

Table 3. Spectrum of the DDDT of the inverse function over $\mathbb{F}_{2^6}$

$DDDT_S(a,b,u)$	0	4	8	64
$\#\{(a,b,u)\}$	199836	61740	378	190

6. **Case 5.2.** Let $a = 53$, $b = 3$, and $u = 50$. Then $u \neq \frac{a^2 + ab + b^2}{ab(a+b)} = 28$, and $\text{Tr}\left(\frac{a^2 + b^2}{a^2 + ab + b^2}\right) = 0$. Also, the Eq. 3 has two solutions $z_1 = 4$, and $z_2 = 5$ with $\text{Tr}\left(\frac{abz_1}{a^2 + b^2}\right) = 1$. In this example, we have

$$\text{DDDT}_F(a, b, u) = 4.$$

An alternate example for this case is $a = 47$, $b = 16$, and $u = 52$. Then $u \neq \frac{a^2 + ab + b^2}{ab(a+b)} = 14$, and $\text{Tr}\left(\frac{a^2 + b^2}{a^2 + ab + b^2}\right) = 0$. Here, the Eq. 3 has two solutions $z_1 = 22$, and $z_2 = 23$ with $\text{Tr}\left(\frac{abz_1}{a^2 + b^2}\right) = 0$, and we have

$$\text{DDDT}_F(a, b, u) = 8,$$

as expected.

7. **Case 6.1.** Let $a = 45$, $b = 11$, and $u = 23$. Then $u \neq \frac{a^2 + ab + b^2}{ab(a+b)} = 25$, and $\frac{a+b}{abu} = 48$ with $\text{Tr}(48) = 1$. The Eq. 3 becomes $z^2 + z + 48 = 0$, and has no solutions. For this example, we have

$$\text{DDDT}_F(a, b, u) = 0.$$

8. **Case 6.2.** Let $a = 37$, $b = 51$, and $u = 9$. Then $\frac{a^2 + ab + b^2}{ab(a+b)} = 21 \neq u$, and $\frac{a+b}{abu} = 3$ with $\text{Tr}(3) = 0$. Also, the Eq. 3 has two solutions $z_3 = 28$, and $z_4 = 29$ with $\text{Tr}\left(\frac{abz_3}{a^2 + b^2}\right) = 1$. For this example, we have

$$\text{DDDT}_F(a, b, u) = 0.$$

An alternate example for this case is $a = 37$, $b = 51$, and $u = 31$. Then $\frac{a^2 + ab + b^2}{ab(a+b)} = 21 \neq$, and $\frac{a^2 + b^2}{abu} = 25$ with $\text{Tr}(25) = 0$. Here, the Eq. 3 has two solutions $z_1 = 14$, and $z_2 = 15$ with $\text{Tr}\left(\frac{abz_1}{a^2 + b^2}\right) = 0$, and we have

$$\text{DDDT}_F(a, b, u) = 4,$$

as expected.

5   The Double Differential Distribution Table of the Gold Function

The double differential distribution table of the Gold function is straightforward.

Theorem 2. *Let G be the Gold function defined by $F(x) = x^{2^k + 1}$. Then*

$$\text{DDDT}_G(a, b, u) = \begin{cases} 2^n & \text{if } u = ab\left(a^{2^k - 1} + b^{2^k - 1}\right), \\ 0 & \text{if } u \neq ab\left(a^{2^k - 1} + b^{2^k - 1}\right). \end{cases}$$

Proof. For $(a, b, u) \in \mathbb{F}_{2^n} \times \mathbb{F}_{2^n} \times \mathbb{F}_{2^m}$, consider the equation $G(x + a + b) + G(x + a) + G(x + b) + G(x) = u$, that is

$$x^{2^k+1} + (x + a)^{2^k+1} + (x + b)^{2^k+1} + (x + a + b)^{2^k+1} = u,$$

in $x \in \mathbb{F}_{2^n}$. Expanding the former equation, we get

$$ab\left(a^{2^k-1} + b^{2^k-1}\right) = u,$$

which has either 2^n or 0 solutions according to $u = ab\left(a^{2^k-1} + b^{2^k-1}\right)$ or not. □

The following result is a direct consequence of Theorem 2.

Corollary 2. *The double differential uniformity of the Gold function F defined by $F(x) = x^{2^k+1}$ is $\Delta_F = 2^n$.*

6 The Double Differential Distribution Table of the Bracken-Leander Function

In this section, we give an explicit of the DDDT of the Bracken-Leander function over the finite field $\mathbb{F}_{2^n}$.

Theorem 3. *Let $n = 4k$ where k is a positive integer. Let F be the Bracken-Leander function defined over $\mathbb{F}_{2^n}$ by $F(x) = x^{2^{2k}+2^k+1}$. For $b \neq 0$, let $c = \frac{a}{b}$, and $v = \frac{u}{b^{2^{2k}+2^k+1}}$. The DDDT of F satisfies*

$$\text{DDDT}_F(a, b, u) = \begin{cases} 2^n & \text{if } a \in b\mathbb{F}_{2^k}, u = a(a + b)b^{2^{2k}+2^k+1}, \\ 2^{2k} & \text{if } (a, b, u) \in I_1 \cup I_2, \\ 0 & \text{otherwise,} \end{cases}$$

where

$$I_1 = \left\{(a, b, u) \; : \; c \in \mathbb{F}_{2^{2k}} \backslash \mathbb{F}_{2^k}, u \in b^{2^{2k}+2^k+1}\mathbb{F}_{2^{2k}}\right\},$$

$$I_2 = \{(a, b, u) \; : \; c \in \mathbb{F}_{2^n} \backslash \mathbb{F}_{2^{2k}}, \text{Tr}_{2k}^{4k}(B) = 0,$$
$$\left(c^{q^3} + c^{q^2} + c^q + c\right)D + \left(c^{q^3} + c\right)B^q + (c^q + c)^{q^2}B = 0\},$$

with

$$B = \frac{((v + c)^q + v + c)^q}{(c^q + c)^{q^2+1}} + \frac{c^{q^3+q} + c^{q^3+1} + c^{q^2+q} + c^{q^2+1} + c^{q^2} + c}{(c^q + c)^{q^2+1}},$$

$$D = \frac{c^{q^2+q} + c^{q^2+1} + c^{q^2} + c^{q+1} + c^q + c + v}{(c^q + c)^{q+1}}.$$

Proof. Let $a, b, u \in \mathbb{F}_{2^n}$ and $F(x) = x^{2^{2k}+2^k+1}$ be the Bracken-Leander function defined over $\mathbb{F}_{2^n}$. We set $q = 2^k$ so that $F(x) = x^{q^2+q+1}$. Our objective is to count the number of solutions of the equation

$$F(x) + F(x + a) + F(x + b) + F(x + a + b) = u. \tag{5}$$

We consider several cases.

Case 1. Suppose that $a = 0$, or $b = 0$, or $a = b$. Then the Eq. (5) is valid for any $x \in \mathbb{F}_{2^n}$ if $u = 0$, and no solution if $u \neq 0$. Hence

$$\mathrm{DDDT}_F(a, b, u) = \begin{cases} 2^n & \text{if } ab(a + b) = 0, u = 0, \\ 0 & \text{if } ab(a + b) = 0, u \neq 0. \end{cases}$$

Case 2. Suppose that $ab(a + b) \neq 0$. We set $y = \frac{x}{b}$ and $c = \frac{a}{b}$. Then

$$F(x) + F(x + a) + F(x + b) + F(x + a + b)$$
$$= x^{q^2+q+1} + (x + a)^{q^2+q+1} + (x + b)^{q^2+q+1} + (x + a + b)^{q^2+q+1}$$
$$= b^{q^2+q+1} \left(y^{q^2+q+1} + (y + c)^{q^2+q+1} + (y + 1)^{q^2+q+1} + (y + c + 1)^{q^2+q+1} \right).$$

Setting $v = \frac{u}{b^{q^2+q+1}}$, the Eq. (5) transforms into

$$y^{q^2+q+1} + (y + c)^{q^2+q+1} + (y + 1)^{q^2+q+1} + (y + c + 1)^{q^2+q+1} = v. \tag{6}$$

The expansion of $(y + c)^{q^2+q+1}$ gives

$$(y + c)^{q^2+q+1} = y^{q^2+q+1} + cy^{q^2+q} + c^q y^{q^2+1} + c^{q+1} y^{q^2} + c^{q^2} y^{q+1}$$
$$+ c^{q^2+1} y^q + c^{q^2+q} y + c^{q^2+q+1}.$$

Similarly, the expansion of $(y + 1)^{q^2+q+1}$ gives

$$(y + 1)^{q^2+q+1} = y^{q^2+q+1} + y^{q^2+q} + y^{q^2+1} + y^{q^2} + y^{q+1} + y^q + y + 1.$$

Finally, the expansion of $(y + c + 1)^{q^2+q+1}$ gives

$$(y + c + 1)^{q^2+q+1} = y^{q^2+q+1} + (c + 1)y^{q^2+q} + (c^q + 1) y^{q^2+1}$$
$$+ \left(c^{q+1} + c^q + c + 1\right) y^{q^2} + \left(c^{q^2} + 1\right) y^{q+1}$$
$$+ \left(c^{q^2+1} + c^{q^2} + c + 1\right) y^q + \left(c^{q^2+q} + c^{q^2} + c^q + 1\right) y$$
$$+ c^{q^2+q+1} + c^{q^2+q} + c^{q^2+1} + c^{q^2} + c^{q+1} + c^q + c + 1.$$

Combining the former expansions, the Eq. (6) is equivalent to

$$(c^q + c) y^{q^2} + \left(c^{q^2} + c\right) y^q + \left(c^{q^2} + c^q\right) y$$
$$+ c^{q^2+q} + c^{q^2+1} + c^{q^2} + c^{q+1} + c^q + c = v. \tag{7}$$

We consider the following cases.

Case 2.1: Assume that $c \in \mathbb{F}_q \setminus \{0, 1\}$. Then $c^{q^2} = c^q = c$, and Eq. (7) reduces to

$$c^{q^2+q} + c^{q^2+1} + c^{q^2} + c^{q+1} + c^q + c = c^2 + c = v.$$

This is possible only if $v = c^2 + c$, that is $u = b^{q^2+q+1}\left(c^2 + c\right) = a(a+b)b^{2^{2k}+2^k-1}$. This gives

$$\mathrm{DDDT}_F(a, b, u) = \begin{cases} 2^n & \text{if } \frac{a}{b} \in \mathbb{F}_q \setminus \{0, 1\}, u = a(a+b)b^{2^{2k}+2^k-1}, \\ 0 & \text{if } \frac{a}{b} \in \mathbb{F}_q \setminus \{0, 1\}, u \neq a(a+b)b^{2^{2k}+2^k-1}. \end{cases}$$

Case 2.2: Assume that $c \in \mathbb{F}_{q^2} \setminus \mathbb{F}_q$. Then $c^{q^2} = c$, $c^q \neq c$, and the Eq. (7) becomes

$$\left(c^q + c\right) y^{q^2} + \left(c^q + c\right) y + c^2 + c^q = v.$$

This is equivalent to

$$y^{q^2} + y + \frac{v + c^2 + c^q}{c^q + c} = 0. \tag{8}$$

We apply Lemma 2 with $b_0 = \frac{v+c^2+c^q}{c^q+c}$, $n = 4k$, $d = \gcd(2k, 4k) = 2k$, and $m = \frac{4k}{2k} = 2$. This gives

$$\beta_{m-1} = \mathrm{Tr}_{2k}^{4k}\left(\frac{v + c^2 + c^q}{c^q + c}\right)$$

$$= \frac{v + c^2 + c^q}{c^q + c} + \left(\frac{v + c^2 + c^q}{c^q + c}\right)^{q^2}$$

$$= \frac{v + v^{q^2}}{c^q + c}.$$

Hence, if $v \notin \mathbb{F}_{q^2}$, then $\beta_{m-1} \neq 0$, and the Eq. (8) has no solution, and if $v \in \mathbb{F}_{q^2}$, then $\beta_{m-1} = 0$, and the Eq. (8) has $2^{q^2} = 2^{2k}$ solutions. As a consequence, for this case, we have

$$\mathrm{DDDT}_F(a, b, u) = \begin{cases} 2^{2k} & \text{if } c \in \mathbb{F}_{q^2} \setminus \mathbb{F}_q, v \in \mathbb{F}_{q^2}, \\ 0 & \text{if } c \in \mathbb{F}_{q^2} \setminus \mathbb{F}_q, v \notin \mathbb{F}_{q^2}. \end{cases}$$

Case 2.3: Assume that $c \in \mathbb{F}_{2^n} \setminus \mathbb{F}_{q^2}$. Then $c^{q^2} \neq c$, and $c^q \neq c$. We raise (7) by q and get

$$\left(c^{q^2} + c^q\right) y^{q^3} + \left(c^{q^3} + c^q\right) y^{q^2} + \left(c^{q^3} + c^{q^2}\right) y^q$$
$$+ c^{q^3+q^2} + c^{q^3+q} + c^{q^3} + c^{q^2+q} + c^{q^2} + c^q = v^q. \tag{9}$$

Next, we raise (7) by q^2 and get

$$\left(c^{q^3} + c^{q^2}\right) y + \left(c + c^{q^2}\right) y^{q^3} + \left(c + c^{q^3}\right) y^{q^2}$$
$$+ c^{1+q^3} + c^{1+q^2} + c + c^{q^3+q^2} + c^{q^3} + c^{q^2} = v^{q^2}. \tag{10}$$

Finally, we raise (7) by q^3 and get

$$\left(c + c^{q^3}\right) y^q + \left(c^q + c^{q^3}\right) y + (c^q + c) y^{q^3}$$
$$+ c^{q+1} + c^{q+q^3} + c^q + c^{1+q^3} + c + c^{q^3} = v^{q^3}. \tag{11}$$

Adding the Eqs. (7), (9), (10), and (11), we get

$$c^{q^3} + c^{q^2} + c^q + c = v^{q^3} + v^{q^2} + v^q + v, \tag{12}$$

or equivalently $\mathrm{Tr}_k^{4k} (v + c) = 0$. Hence, if $\mathrm{Tr}_k^{4k} (v + c) \neq 0$, then the Eq. (7) has no solution and

$$\mathrm{DDDT}_F(a, b, u) = 0.$$

Now, suppose that $\mathrm{Tr}_k^{4k} (v + c) = 0$. Then

$$(v + c)^{q^3} + (v + c)^{q^2} = ((v + c)^q + v + c)^{q^2}$$
$$= (v + c)^q + v + c,$$

This implies that $(v + c)^q + v + c \in \mathbb{F}_{q^2}$. If we add the Eqs. (9) and (10), we get after rearrangement

$$(c^q + c) (y^q + y)^{q^2} + (c^q + c)^{q^2} (y^q + y) + (c^q + c) \left(c^{q^3} + c^{q^2} + 1\right)$$
$$= v^q + v^{q^2}. \tag{13}$$

Since $c^q + c \neq 0$, then dividing by $(c^q + c)^{q^2+1}$, this can be rewritten as $z^{q^2} + z + B = 0$, where

$$z = \frac{y^q + y}{c^q + c},$$
$$B = \frac{((v + c)^q + v + c)^q}{(c^q + c)^{q^2+1}} + \frac{c^{q^3+q} + c^{q^3+1} + c^{q^2+q} + c^{q^2+1} + c^{q^2} + c}{(c^q + c)^{q^2+1}}.$$

Since $(v + c)^q + v + c \in \mathbb{F}_{q^2}$, then, a straightforward calculation shows that $B + B^{q^2} = 0$. Since $y^q = y + (c^q + c) z$, then

$$y^{q^2} = y^q + (c^q + c)^q z^q = y + (c^q + c)^q z^q + (c^q + c) z.$$

Plugging these values in (7), we get

$$(c^q + c)^{q+1} z^q + (c^q + c)^{q+1} z + c^{q^2+q} + c^{q^2+1} + c^{q^2} + c^{q+1} + c^q + c + v = 0.$$

Since $c^q + c \neq 0$, then dividing by $(c^q + c)^{q+1}$, we get

$$z^q + z + D = 0,$$

where

$$D = \frac{c^{q^2+q} + c^{q^2+1} + c^{q^2} + c^{q+1} + c^q + c + v}{(c^q + c)^{q+1}}.$$

Hence $z^{q^2} + z^q + D^q = 0$, and combining with $z^{q^2} + z + B = 0$, we get

$$B = D^q + D.$$

We can apply Lemma 2 to the equation $z^q + z + D = 0$ with $b_0 = D$, $n = 4k$, $d = \gcd(4k, k) = k$, $m = \frac{4k}{k} = 4$, and $q = 2^k$. We have

$$\mathrm{Tr}_k^{4k}(D) = (D^q + D)^{q^2} + D^q + D = B^{q^2} + B = 0.$$

Consequently, the equation $z^q + z + D = 0$ has $2^d = 2^k$ solutions z_i, $i = 0, \ldots, 2^{k-1}$. For each solution z_i, consider the equation $y^q + y + (c^q + c) z_i = 0$. This equation has no solution if $\mathrm{Tr}_k^{4k}((c^q + c) z_i) \neq 0$, and 2^k solutions if $\mathrm{Tr}_k^{4k}((c^q + c) z_i) = 0$. Using $z^{q^2} + z + B = 0$, we get

$$\mathrm{Tr}_k^{4k}((c^q + c) z_i) = (c^q + c)^{q^3} z_i^{q^3} + (c^q + c)^{q^2} z_i^{q^2} + (c^q + c)^q z_i^q + (c^q + c) z_i$$
$$= \left(c^{q^3} + c^{q^2} + c^q + c\right)(z_i^q + z_i) + \left(c^{q^3} + c\right) B^q + (c^q + c)^{q^2} B$$
$$= \left(c^{q^3} + c^{q^2} + c^q + c\right) D + \left(c^{q^3} + c\right) B^q + (c^q + c)^{q^2} B.$$

Set

$$E = \left(c^{q^3} + c^{q^2} + c^q + c\right) D + \left(c^{q^3} + c\right) B^q + (c^q + c)^{q^2} B.$$

If $E = 0$, then the equation $y^q + y = (c^q + c) z_i$ has 2^k solutions, and the Eq. (7) has $2^k \times 2^k = 2^{2k}$ solutions. In these cases, we have

$$\mathrm{DDDT}_F(a, b, u) = \begin{cases} 2^{2k} & \text{if } \mathrm{Tr}_{2k}^{4k}(B) = 0 \text{ and } E = 0, \\ 0 & \text{if } \mathrm{Tr}_{2k}^{4k}(B) \neq 0 \text{ or } E \neq 0. \end{cases}$$

This terminates the proof.   □

The following result is a direct consequence of Theorem 3.

Corollary 3. *The double differential uniformity of the Bracken-Leander function F defined by $F(x) = x^{2^{2k}+2^k+1}$ is $\Delta_F = 2^n$.*

7   Conclusion

In this paper, we have introduced the notion of a double difference distribution table of a vectorial Boolean function and its double differential uniformity. We studied their properties and gave the explicit entries of the double difference distribution table of three power vectorial Boolean functions: the inverse function, the Gold function, and the Bracken-Leander function. The double difference distribution table is an extension of the difference distribution table, the Feistel boomerang connectivity table. The double differential uniformity can be used as a distinguisher, and a criterion for the security of a block cipher derived from a vectorial Boolean function. Finally, we believe that the notion introduced and studied here for some crucial families of vectorial power functions could be explored in another framework in symmetric cryptography leading to novel applications in this domain. We leave such investigations in future work.

References

1. Aubry, Y., Herbaut, F.: Differential uniformity and second order derivatives for generic polynomials. J. Pure Appl. Algebra **222**, 1095–1110 (2017)
2. Bar-On, A., Dunkelman, O., Keller, N., Weizman, A.: DLCT: a new tool for differential-linear cryptanalysis. In: Ishai, Y., Rijmen, V. (eds.) EUROCRYPT 2019. LNCS, vol. 11476, pp. 313–342. Springer, Cham (2019). https://doi.org/10.1007/978-3-030-17653-2_11
3. Biham, E., Shamir, A.: Differential cryptanalysis of DES-like cryptosystems. J. Cryptol. **4**(1), 3–72 (1991)
4. Boukerrou, H., Huynh, P., Lallemand, V., Mandal, B., Minier, M.: On the Feistel counterpart of the boomerang connectivity table: introduction and analysis of the FBCT. IACR Trans. Symmetric Cryptol. **020**(1), 331–362 (2020)
5. Carlet, C.: Characterizations of the differential uniformity of vectorial functions by the Walsh transform. IEEE Trans. Inf. Theory **64**(9), 6443–6453 (2018)
6. Coulter, S., Henderson, M.: A note on the roots of trinomials over a finite field. Bull. Austral. Math. Soc. **69**, 429–432 (2004)
7. Daemen, J., Rijmen, V.: The Design of Rijndael: AES - The Advanced Encryption Standard. Springer, Heidelberg (2002). https://doi.org/10.1007/978-3-662-04722-4
8. Eddahmani, S., Mesnager, S.: Explicit values of the DDT, the BCT, the FBCT, and the FBDT of the inverse, the gold, and the Bracken-Leander S-boxes. Cryptogr. Commun. **14**, 1301–1344 (2022)
9. Lidl, R., Niederreiter, H.: Introduction to Finite Fields and Their Applications. Cambridge University Press, Cambridge (1986)
10. Matsui, M.: Linear cryptanalysis method for DES cipher. In: Helleseth, T. (ed.) EUROCRYPT 1993. LNCS, vol. 765, pp. 386–397. Springer, Heidelberg (1994). https://doi.org/10.1007/3-540-48285-7_33
11. National Institute of Standards and Technology: Federal Information Processing Standards Publication 197: Announcing the Advanced Encryption Standard (AES). http://csrc.nist.gov/publications/fips/fips197/fips-197.pdf
12. Nyberg, K.: Differentially uniform mappings for cryptography. In: Helleseth, T. (ed.) EUROCRYPT 1993. LNCS, vol. 765, pp. 55–64. Springer, Heidelberg (1994). https://doi.org/10.1007/3-540-48285-7_6
13. Pommerening, K.: Quadratic equations in finite fields of characteristic 2, February 2012. http://www.staff.uni-mainz.de/pommeren/MathMisc/QuGlChar2.pdf
14. Wagner, D.: The boomerang attack. In: Knudsen, L. (ed.) FSE 1999. LNCS, vol. 1636, pp. 156–170. Springer, Heidelberg (1999). https://doi.org/10.1007/3-540-48519-8_12

TooLIP: How to Find New Instances of FiLIP Cipher with Smaller Key Size and New Filters

François Gérard$^{(\boxtimes)}$, Agnese Gini$^{(\boxtimes)}$, and Pierrick Méaux$^{(\boxtimes)}$

University of Luxembourg, Esch-sur-Alzette, Luxembourg
{francois.gerard,agnese.gini,pierrick.meaux}@uni.lu

Abstract. In this article, we propose a new tool to evaluate the security of instances of FiLIP cipher. TooLIP is user friendly, it automatically evaluates the cost of several attacks on user-defined Boolean functions. It allows to test new families of filters that are more homomorphic friendly for recent techniques of evaluations, and is designed to easily add new attacks, or change parameters in the considered attacks. To demonstrate our tool we apply it in three contexts. First we show how the keysize can be reduced for former instances with XOR-Threshold functions when the amount of encrypted plaintext obtained by the adversary is limited. Then, we use TooLIP to determine secure instances with filters in less variables for two new families of Boolean functions, leading to a more efficient evaluation and/or a reduced bandwidth. Finally, we apply it to find other instances with filters where we know only (bounds on) the algebraic immunity and resiliency.

Keywords: Automatic tool · Stream ciphers · FiLIP cipher · Boolean functions

1 Introduction

With the growing interest of practical Fully Homomorphic Encryption (FHE), in the last decade multiple symmetric ciphers have been designed to be efficient in the context of Hybrid Homomorphic Encryption [NLV11] (HHE). After considering standard symmetric ciphers such as AES [GHS12, CLT14] or SIMON [LN14], dedicated symmetric schemes have been introduced in the context of HHE since traditional ciphers are hard to efficiently evaluate homomorphically. For example, the first of these ciphers, LowMC [ARS+15] has a drastically reduced number of multiplications to be more FHE-friendly. The cipher FLIP [MJSC16] introduces a new stream cipher paradigm where a significant part of the cipher evaluation can be performed without homomorphic cost. This strategy has been generalized with extendable output functions and is common in recent ciphers for HHE such as in *e.g.* [DEG+18, CHK+21, HKL+22, HKC+20, DGH+21, CHMS22, HMS23]. All these designs for HHE are still recent and improvable, as witnessed recently

S. Vaudenay and C. Petit (Eds.): AFRICACRYPT 2024, LNCS 14861, pp. 21–45, 2024.
https://doi.org/10.1007/978-3-031-64381-1_2

with improvements on building blocks of the symmetric scheme [HL20, CIR22] or new techniques of homomorphic evaluation [CDPP22, MPP23].

In this article we focus on FiLIP, introduced in [MCJS19b]. FiLIP is a binary stream cipher following the improved filter permutator paradigm, extending the paradigm of FLIP. The main advantage of this cipher is that both its security and performance when it is homomorphically evaluated depend on a sole Boolean function, the one used as filter. On the homomorphic side, it allows to obtain a small latency in the context of HHE, as experimented in [MCJS19b], and more recently in [HMR20] and [CDPP22] reaching a latency of only 2.62ms, using the multiples progresses on the so-called third generation of FHE schemes such as FHEW [DM15], TFHE [CGGI16] and FINAL [BIP+22]. On the symmetric security side, in addition to the security analysis relying on the cryptographic criteria of the filter, the security of the filter permutator has been studied in an idealized model in [CT19]. Moreover, the design is similar to a popular pseudorandom generator design by Goldreich [Gol00] which asymptotic security has been thoroughly investigated e.g. [AL16, AL18, CDM+18, YGJL22, Üna23].

In [MCJS19b], FiLIP is instantiated using two families of functions, i.e. direct sum of monomials and XOR-Threshold functions. The security of these instances is determined by a procedure bounding the complexity of different attacks via cryptographic criteria (namely, the algebraic immunity, resiliency, and nonlinearity). Producing an efficient algorithmic implementation of this procedure is not trivial, because it requires to evaluate the parameters of all the sub-functions that are obtained by fixing up to λ variables[1], together with their probability. In fact, the authors needed to introduce specific optimisations to compute the suggested parameters for aforementioned families. Therefore, a major bottleneck for finding alternative instances of FiLIP is evaluating their security. Our work aims to facilitate this task by introducing a tool designed exactly for this purpose.

Having an automated tool to assess the security of constructions is always a plus to help the community in broadening the field of cryptography. Indeed, when designers of schemes, protocols, or any cryptographic application propose something new, they often face the challenge of finding secure parameters. While sometimes, an ad-hoc security evaluation has to be performed due to the specificity of the proposal, it is often the case that the new construction simply relies on well-known assumptions or designs with unusual parameters. Then, it greatly simplifies the task of the designers if they can solely specify those parameters to a tool and get a security estimation. A notable example in the field of lattice-based cryptography is the estimator first proposed in [APS15a]. Not only a common tool helps for simplicity, but it also importantly sets a common ground for everyone. Indeed, estimating the cost of an attack for an adversary is often made under specific assumptions on parameters of the attack, this might lead to unfair comparisons between works that were both analyzed in good faith. Because attacks, as well as the accuracy of their bounds, might evolve over time, a unified tool is often a collaborative effort and should also evolve, this is why

---

[1] λ being the security parameter.

the current ePrint version of [APS15a] ([APS15b]), starts with a disclaimer to warn the reader that the state of the art advanced since its initial publication.

Our Contributions. In this article, we propose straightforward Python scripts to estimate the security of FiLIP when used with a given filter function and register size. The code has been written with user-friendliness in mind. The goal is that the user who wishes to study a new function can simply write a new Python class with a specific interface to evaluate the cost of well-known attacks. This new piece of code must provide methods that compute () Boolean criteria such as algebraic immunity, resiliency, and nonlinearity and also what are the direct descendants of the function obtained when fixing an input variable to 0 or 1. While testing new functions on fixed attacks is probably the simplest use case of the tool, it is also possible to implement new attacks or to modify the existing one by changing parameters such as the number of ciphertexts that the adversary can observe. Since we put emphasis on user-friendliness and re-usability, the scripts are written in pure Python. This naturally comes with a performance penalty. However, this has not been problematic for the functions we tested and should not be a problem unless the security parameter is severely increased. Since the tool is quite modular, it should be possible to rewrite and integrate optimized code for some parts if efficiency is the bottleneck.

More precisely our contributions are the following. First, based on [MCJS19a], we describe a general framework in which the security of FiLIP can be bounded for a given filter function and register size N. Then, we propose a user-friendly tool called TooLIP that automatically runs several attacks on user-defined functions. The tool can be used to test new families of filters that are more homomorphic friendly for recent techniques of evaluations. To demonstrate the applicability of the tool, we use it in three contexts:

- First, we consider the improvements on XOR-THR filters, which are studied in [MCJS19a] and used in the context of HHE in [HMR20] and [CDPP22]. We show that for the same functions the register size N can be significantly reduced when we take into consideration a limit on the quantity of encrypted plaintext ($2^{\lambda/2}$ for our examples). A reduced N leads to bandwidth improvements in HHE. Then, we exhibit filters with fewer variables in the same family for the same security level, which would lead to better HHE general performances.
- We determine secure instances for two new families of filters, XOR-QUAD-THR and XOR-THR-THR functions. First we investigate the Boolean criteria of these two families, then we exhibit new instances of FiLIP with smaller register sizes as for XOR-THR functions or direct sum of monomials as used in [MCJS19b]. For example, we propose several instances with N lower than 500 for 80-bit security and lower than 1000 for 128-bit security.
- Finally, we investigate instances with arbitrary filters: functions in n variables such that the main cryptographic parameters are known but not the specific structure of the functions nor its descendants. For example we show that a

512-variable function with optimal algebraic immunity in direct sum with a 196-variable XOR function is sufficient for 128-bit security since $N \geq 2500$.

The implemented tool is available at github.com/agnesegini/TooLIP.

2   Preliminaries

Additionally to usual notations we denote the set of integers $\{1, \ldots, n\}$ by $[1, n]$, and use $+$ instead of $\oplus$ for the addition in $\mathbb{F}_2$.

2.1   Boolean Functions and Cryptographic Criteria

We give some preliminaries on Boolean functions and their cryptographic criteria, for a deeper introduction on these notions we refer to the book of Carlet [Car21].

Definition 1 (Boolean Function). *A Boolean function f in n variables is a function from $\mathbb{F}_2^n$ to $\mathbb{F}_2$. The set of all Boolean functions in n variables is denoted by $\mathcal{B}_n$.*

Definition 2 (Balancedness and Resiliency). *A Boolean function $f \in \mathcal{B}_n$ is said to be balanced if $|f^{-1}(0)| = |f^{-1}(1)| = 2^{n-1}$. The function f is called k-resilient if any of its restrictions obtained by fixing at most k of its coordinates is balanced. We denote by $\mathsf{res}(f)$ the maximum resiliency (also called resiliency order) of f and set $\mathsf{res}(f) = -1$ if f is unbalanced.*

Definition 3 (Nonlinearity). *The nonlinearity $\mathsf{NL}(f)$ of a Boolean function $f \in \mathcal{B}_n$, where n is a positive integer, is the minimum Hamming distance (d_H) between f and all the affine functions in $\mathcal{B}_n$: $\mathsf{NL}(f) = \min_{g, \deg(g) \leq 1} \{d_H(f, g)\}$, where $g(x) = a \cdot x + \varepsilon$, $a \in \mathbb{F}_2^n, \varepsilon \in \mathbb{F}_2$ (where $\cdot$ is an inner product in $\mathbb{F}_2^n$, any choice of inner product will give the same value of $\mathsf{NL}(f)$).*

Definition 4 (Algebraic Normal Form (ANF), degree and monomials). *We call Algebraic Normal Form of a Boolean function f its n-variable polynomial representation over $\mathbb{F}_2$ (i.e. belonging to $\mathbb{F}_2[x_1, \ldots, x_n]/(x_1^2 + x_1, \ldots, x_n^2 + x_n))$: $f(x_1, \ldots, x_n) = \sum_{I \subseteq [1,n]} a_I \left(\prod_{i \in I} x_i\right)$ where $a_I \in \mathbb{F}_2$.*
The (algebraic) degree of a non-zero function f is $\deg(f) = \max_{I \subseteq [1,n]} \{|I| \mid a_I = 1\}$. If $f = 0$, $\deg(f) = 0$.
Each term $\prod_{i \in I} x_i$ is called a monomial, and we refer to monomial functions as the ones having only one coefficient $a_I = 1$ in their ANF.

Definition 5 (Algebraic Immunity [MPC04], annihilators and $\Delta_{\mathsf{AN}}(f)$). *The algebraic immunity of a Boolean function $f \in \mathcal{B}_n$, denoted as $\mathsf{AI}(f)$, is defined as: $\mathsf{AI}(f) = \min_{g \neq 0} \{\deg(g) \mid fg = 0 \text{ or } (f+1)g = 0\}$.*
The function g is called an annihilator of f (or $f+1$). Additionally we denote $\mathsf{AN}(f) = \min_{g \neq 0} \{\deg(g) \mid fg = 0\}$, and $\Delta_{\mathsf{AN}}(f) = |\mathsf{AN}(f) - \mathsf{AN}(f+1)|$.

Definition 6 (Fast Algebraic Immunity, e.g. [Car21] page 94). *The fast algebraic immunity of a Boolean function $f \in \mathcal{B}_n$, denoted as $\mathsf{FAI}(f)$, is defined as: $\mathsf{FAI}(f) = \min\{2\mathsf{AI}(f), \min_{1 \leq \deg(g) < \mathsf{AI}(f)} \deg(g) + \deg(fg)\}$.*

Families of Boolean Functions. We give the definition of families of Boolean functions that are used to build FiLIP filters, and we recall their parameters.

Definition 7 (XOR function). *For any positive integers k, XOR_k is the k-variable Boolean function such that for all $x = (x_1, \ldots, x_k) \in \mathbb{F}_2^k$*

$$\mathsf{XOR}_k(x) = \sum_{i=1}^{k} x_i.$$

Definition 8 (QUAD function). *For any positive integers q, Q_q is the $2q$-variable Boolean function such that $\forall x = (x_1, \ldots, x_{2q}) \in \mathbb{F}_2^{2q}$*

$$\mathsf{Q}_q(x) = \sum_{i=1}^{q} x_{2i-1} x_{2i}.$$

Definition 9 (Threshold function). *For any positive integers d and n such that $d \leq n + 1$ we define the Boolean function $\mathsf{T}_{d,n}$ as follows:*

$$\forall x = (x_1, \ldots, x_n) \in \mathbb{F}_2^n, \quad \mathsf{T}_{d,n}(x) = \begin{cases} 0 & \text{if Hamming weight } \mathsf{w_H}(x) < d, \\ 1 & \text{otherwise.} \end{cases}$$

Definition 10 (Direct sum). *Let f be a Boolean function of n variables and g a Boolean function of m variables, the direct sum h of f and g is defined by $h(x, y) = f(x) + g(y)$ where $x \in \mathbb{F}_2^n$ and $y \in \mathbb{F}_2^m$.*

Property 1 (Direct sum properties (e.g., [MJSC16] Lemma 3)). Let h be the direct sum of two functions f, in n variables, and g, in m variables. Then h has the following cryptographic properties:

1. Resiliency: $\mathsf{res}(h) = \mathsf{res}(f) + \mathsf{res}(g) + 1$.
2. Nonlinearity: $\mathsf{NL}(h) = 2^m \mathsf{NL}(f) + 2^n \mathsf{NL}(g) - 2\mathsf{NL}(f)\mathsf{NL}(g)$.
3. Algebraic Immunity: $\max(\mathsf{AI}(f), \mathsf{AI}(g)) \leq \mathsf{AI}(h) \leq \mathsf{AI}(f) + \mathsf{AI}(g)$.

We focus on subfamilies obtained by the direct sum construction:

Definition 11 (Direct Sum of Monomials and Direct Sum Vector [MJSC16]). *Let f be a non constant n-variable Boolean function. We call f a Direct Sum of Monomials (or DSM) if the following holds for its ANF:*

$$\forall (I, J) \text{ such that } a_I = a_J = 1, \ I \cap J \in \{\emptyset, I \cup J\}.$$

In other words, in the ANF of such functions, each variable appears at most once. We define its direct sum vector (DSV)$\mathbf{m}_f = [m_1, m_2, \ldots, m_k]$, of length $k = \deg(f)$, where m_i is the number of monomials of degree i, $i > 0$, in the ANF of f: $m_i = |\{I \subset [n]\}; a_I = 1 \text{ and } |I| = i\}|$.

Definition 12 (XOR-THR Function). *For any positive integers k, d and n such that $d \leq n + 1$ we define $\mathsf{XOR}_k + \mathsf{T}_{d,n}$ for all $z = (x_1, \ldots, x_k, y_1, \ldots, y_n) \in \mathbb{F}_2^{k+n}$ as follows:*

$$(\mathsf{XOR}_k + \mathsf{T}_{d,n})(z) = x_1 + \cdots + x_k + \mathsf{T}_{d,n}(y_1, \ldots, y_n) = \mathsf{XOR}_k(x) + \mathsf{T}_{d,n}(y).$$

The XOR and QUAD functions are common functions in different areas and their properties are considered as folklore. The cryptographic properties of threshold and Xor-Threshold functions have been characterized in [CM19, CM22]. We summarize the parameters they reach in the following:

Property 2. Let $k \in \mathbb{N}$, then $f = \mathsf{XOR}_k$ has the following properties: $\mathsf{res}(f) = k - 1, \mathsf{NL}(f) = 0$, and $\mathsf{AI}(f) = 0$ if $k = 0$, 1 otherwise.

Let $q \in \mathbb{N}$, then $g = \mathsf{Q}_q$ has the following properties: $\mathsf{res}(g) = 0$, $\mathsf{NL}(g) = 2^{2q-1} - 2^{q-1}$, and $\mathsf{AI}(g) = 0$ if $q = 0$, 1 if $q = 1$, 2 otherwise.

Let $d, n \in \mathbb{N}^*$ and $k \in \mathbb{N}^*$ such that $d \le n + 1$ the function $h = \mathsf{XOR}_k + \mathsf{T}_{d,n}$ has the following properties:

1. Resiliency: $\mathsf{res}(h) = \begin{cases} k & \text{if } n = 2d - 1, \\ k - 1 & \text{otherwise.} \end{cases}$

2. Nonlinearity:

$$\mathsf{NL}(h) = \begin{cases} 2^{n+k-1} - 2^k \binom{n-1}{(n-1)/2} & \text{if } d = \frac{n+1}{2}, \\ 2^k \sum_{i=d}^{n} \binom{n}{i} & \text{if } d > \frac{n+1}{2}, \\ 2^k \sum_{i=0}^{d-1} \binom{n}{i} & \text{if } d < \frac{n+1}{2}. \end{cases}$$

3. Algebraic Immunity: if $k = 0$, $\mathsf{AI}(h) = \min(d, n - d + 1)$ otherwise:

$$\mathsf{AI}(h) = \begin{cases} \frac{n+1}{2} & \text{if } d = \frac{n+1}{2}, \\ \min(d + 1, n - d + 2) & \text{otherwise.} \end{cases}$$

4. $\Delta_{\mathsf{AN}}(h)$: $\Delta_{\mathsf{AN}}(h) = |n - 2d + 1|$ if $k = 0$, 0 otherwise.

We recall the notion of descendant functions [MJSC16] introduced to study the guess and determine attacks on FLIP [DLR16], and the concept of bit-fixing stable functions.

Definition 13 (Depth-ℓ descendants). *Let $f(x_1, \ldots, x_n)$ be a n-variable function with $n > 1$ and $\ell \in \mathbb{N}$ such that $0 \le \ell < n$. Let S_ℓ be the collection of subsets $I = \{i_1, \ldots, i_\ell\} \subseteq \{1, \ldots, n\}$ such that $|I| = \ell$. The depth ℓ descendants $\mathcal{D}_\ell(f)$ is the set of functions in $n - \ell$-variables that can be obtained by setting $x_{i_j} = b_j$ for $j = 1, \ldots, \ell$ and $x_j \in I$ for every possible pair of $(I, b_1, \ldots, b_\ell) \in S_\ell \times \mathbb{F}_2^\ell$.*

For I in $\{1, \ldots, n\}$ and $b \in \mathbb{F}_2^{|I|}$ we denote by $f_{I,b}$ the descendant of f where the variables indexed by I are fixed to the values of b.

Definition 14 (Bit-fixing stability). *Let $\mathcal{F}$ be a family of Boolean functions, $\mathcal{F}$ is called bit-fixing stable, or stable relatively to guessing and determining, if for all functions $f \in \mathcal{F}$ such that f is a n-variable function with $n > 1$, all its (depth-ℓ) descendants are such that $f_{I,b} \in \mathcal{F}$, or $f_{I,b} + 1 \in \mathcal{F}$, or $\deg(f_{I,b}) = 0$.*

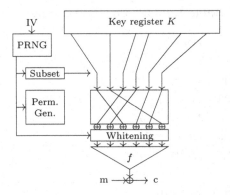

Fig. 1. Improved filter permutator paradigm.

2.2 Improved Filter Permutator and FiLIP

FiLIP is a family of stream ciphers following the Improved Filter Permutator paradigm (IFP) [MCJS19b], represented in Fig. 1.

The IFP is composed of 6 parts, a register where the key is stored, a forward secure PseudoRandom Number Generator (PRNG) initialized with a public IV, a generator of wire-cross permutations a generator of subsets, a generator of binary strings called whitenings, and a filter function which produces the keystream.

For a security parameter λ, to encrypt $m \leq 2^{\frac{\lambda}{\kappa}}$ bits under a secret key $K \in \mathbb{F}_2^N$, the public parameters of the PRNG are chosen and then the following process is executed for each keystream bit b_i (for $i \in [m]$):

- The PRNG is updated, its output determines the subset S_i of n-out-of-N elements, the permutation P_i from n to n elements at time i, and the whitening w_i, that is a n-size binary vector,
- the subset is applied to the key,
- the permutation is applied,
- the whitening is added,
- the keystream bit b_i is computed, $b_i = f(P_i(S_i(K)) + w_i)$ through the n-variable Boolean filter f.

FiLIP [MCJS19b] stream cipher family is an instantiation of the IFP paradigm. The PRNG is instantiated with the forward secure PRG construction from [BY03] using AES as the underlying block cipher. So far, two kinds of instances have been introduced, with DSM functions, and with Xor-Threshold functions in the long version [MCJS19a], we recall them in Table 1.

Table 1. FiLIP instances [MCJS19a].

n	N	XOR$_k$ + T$_{d,m}$	λ
144	2048	$113, 16, 31$	80
144	2048	$81, 32, 63$	80
256	1536	$129, 64, 127$	80
512	1024	$257, 128, 255$	80
256	8192	$129, 64, 127$	128
512	4096	$257, 128, 255$	128
n	N	DSM with $\mathbf{m}_f$	λ
512	16384	$[89, 67, 47, 37]$	80
430	1792	$[80, 40, 15, 15, 15, 15]$	80
320	1800	$[80, 40, 0, 20, 0, 0, 0, 10]$	128
1216	16384	$[128, 64, 0, 80, 0, 0, 0, 80]$	128
1280	4096	$[128, 64, 0, 0, 0, 0, 0, 0, 0, 0, 0, 0, 0, 0, 0, 64]$	128

2.3   Attacks Applying on IFP

In this part we recall the attacks studied on the IFP and FiLIP so far, necessary to understand the functions implemented in the tool, we refer to [MCJS19b, MCJS19a] for the security analysis of the cipher. In a nutshell, the attack considered are adaptations of the ones applying on filtered Linear Feedback Shift Register (LFSR) as considered for FLIP [MJSC16], combined with guess and determine attacks, since these attacks been shown efficient on filter permutator designs [DLR16].

An IFP produces keystream bits by applying first linear operations and then a filter Boolean function. The usage of a PRNG avoids biases in the intermediate operations, *i.e.* subset selection, permutation and whitening, and leaves as principal target for the security analysis the filter function. Méaux *et al.* [MCJS19b] observed that resemblance to filter generators may expose IFPs to the attacks developed for these stream ciphers. Namely, they described a framework to bound the security of IFPs by analyzing the impact of known key-recovery attacks and their combinations, based on the evaluation of complexities via the estimation of Boolean criteria. The authors identify three main types of attack in the known-ciphertext model: algebraic-type attacks, correlation-type attacks, and guess-and-determine strategies. While the first two kinds of attack exploit properties of a given function, the guess-and-determine strategies consists in first guessing a few key bits and determining the security in such case, *i.e.* by using properties of functions in less variables. In fact, guess-and-determine strategies include algebraic and correlation type attacks as building blocks and profit from a time/data complexity trade-off.[2]

---

[2] Notice that in this context time complexity refers to the expected running time of the algorithm, while data complexity refers to the size of the keystream bits' sample.

More precisely, let us consider an n-variable Boolean function and a fixed subset set of ℓ variables. Then, guessing ℓ bits of the input corresponds to pre-set those ℓ-variables and produce 2^ℓ *descendants*, *i.e.* 2^ℓ Boolean functions in $n-\ell$ variables. Hence, each descendant can be independently studied and contributes to the full strategy according to the impact of the chosen type of attack on the descendant itself. Therefore, to claim a level of security λ for a specific filter function, one has to take into account both data and time complexities of all the possible classes of descendants up to $\ell \leq \lambda$.

We will thoroughly explain the procedure to compute the complexity of a guess-and-determine strategy associated with one or more attacks in Sect. 3. While we summarise here the algebraic-type and correlation-type attacks that we will use as building blocks. For both classes we consider a few significant algorithms, as suggested in [MCJS19b], and we identify the suitable Boolean criteria for estimating the data and time complexities.

Algebraic-Type Attacks. We refer to algorithms generating systems of equations from the key-stream and using algebraic techniques to retrieve the secret key as algebraic attacks. Algebraic attacks [CM03], fast algebraic attacks [Cou03a] and use of Gröbner bases, *e.g.* [Fau99, Fau02], belong to this class. For simplicity, we take into account the first two types as representative of this class.

Following [CM03], the so called *algebraic attack* (AA) aims to solve an over-defined system of equations, possibly via linearization, previously processed to reduce the degree. In fact, if f is the n-variable input Boolean function, one can find a non null function g such that the algebraic degree of gf is lower. Hence, since the equations in the system have form $f(y_i) = b_i$ where y_i is a linear transformation of the original variables, by multiplying the equations by g the degree system decreases and consequently the cost of the algorithm. The minimal reachable degree is determined by $\mathsf{AI}(f)$ the algebraic immunity of f (Definition 5), since for instance by multiplying by a non null annihilator g we obtain an equation $g(y_i)b_i = f(y_i)g(y_i) = 0$.

The linearization of a multivariate system of degree $\mathsf{AI}(f)$ in n variables produces a linear system in $D = \sum_{i=0}^{\mathsf{AI}(f)} \binom{n}{d}$ variables. The AA consists in solving such reduced system. Then, we consider a bound for the time complexity and the data complexity $O(D^\omega)$ and $O(D/\binom{n}{\mathsf{AI}(f)})$, respectively, where we denote by ω the constant of linear algebra.

Relaxing the condition on the minimality of the degree and introducing inter-mediate elimination steps can improve the attack's performance. This variation was proposed by Courtois in [Cou03a], we refer to it as *fast algebraic attack* (FAA). The main idea is to consider also functions g of degree $e < \mathsf{AI}(f)$ and such that gf has low degree d, and later remove monomials of degree larger than e, via Berlekamp-Massey algorithm. We refer to [Cou03a, ACG+06] for details. Letting $E = \sum_{i=0}^{e} \binom{n}{i}$ and $D = \sum_{i=0}^{d} \binom{n}{i}$, for filter functions we consider in this context we expect the time complexities of the algorithm to be $O(D \log_2(D) + ED \log_2(D) + E^\omega)$ and the data complexities being $O(D/\binom{n}{d})$. In our tool we will consider only $e = 1$, *i.e.* $E = n + 1$, and $d = \mathsf{AI}(f)$, which is always giving a lower bound of the complexities, and in this case the Boolean criterion to take into account remains the algebraic immunity.

Correlation-Type Attacks. We refer to algorithms exploiting properties of the distribution's outputs as correlation-type attacks. More precisely, these attacks aim to distinguish the key-stream from a random sequence to learn properties of the functions and later apply more specific algorithms. Among the possible attacks we consider here those which take advantage of either proximity to affine functions or non balancedness of the filter function. In fact, we can characterize the effectiveness of the related attacks by studying its *nonlinearity* and *resiliency* of the filter function, respectively.

More precisely, if we consider the higher order correlation attack with XL algorithm [Cou03b], its complexity grows with the degree. Then an attacker would rather prefer working with functions of low degree if possible. If the filter function f has high degree, to reduce the complexity of this approach, one can search for a low degree approximation, *i.e.* a function g that has a low algebraic degree d and such that $f(x) = g(x)$ with probability $1 - \varepsilon$ for a real $\varepsilon \in [0, 1]$, and apply the XL algorithm to the system associated to this new function. We call this attack (HCA) and refer to [Cou03b] for the details. In particular, an affine approximation ($d \leq 1$) results into an attack having time complexity at least $O(n^\omega (1-\varepsilon)^{-n})$ and data complexity $O((1-\varepsilon)^{-n})$, (using the lower bounds from [MCJS19a] Sect. 9.1). Since the distance to the closest affine function is the nonlinearity, we consider $\varepsilon = \mathsf{NL}(f)/2^n$.

Furthermore, we recall that the resiliency of a Boolean function is the maximum value k such that every restrictions of f obtained by fixing at most k of its coordinates is balanced. If a function is unbalanced, the keystream generated can be distinguished from one uniformly at random by comparing the expectations of the output. If the function is balanced, we can similarly analyze descendants at level its resiliency plus one, to distinguish the distributions. The quantity of bits necessary to determine the presence of a bias in the keystream depends on the value is $O(\delta^{-2})$ where

$$\delta(f) = \frac{1}{2} - \frac{\mathsf{NL}(f)}{2^n} \tag{1}$$

We consider as lower bound from the time and data complexity of this simple correlation attack (CA) $2^{\mathsf{res}(f)}\delta(f)^{-2}$ and $\delta(f)^{-2}$, respectively (and refer to [MCJS19a], Sect. 9.1 for more details).

Remark 1. We explained in this section a few algorithms and determined "safe" (but meaningful) bounds on their complexity in order to evaluate the security of IFP. In the following, we will use the results about the algebraic and correlation-like attacks algorithms as building blocks inside the main guess-and-determine strategy. Although the list of algorithms we consider is not exhaustive, the design of the tool allows to plug other algorithms. Hence, different and future attack can also be included in the security evaluation.

3 Tool's Description

3.1 Attacks and Profiles

The problem of bounding the security of IFP was first addressed in [MCJS19a]. We recall the suggested procedure in this section. Previously, we discussed several attacks for which the complexity can be evaluated by computing the parameter of the filter function relatively to a criterion of Boolean functions. In practice, a well-know strategy is to perform guess-and-determine. In our case, instead of computing the complexity only on the initial function, one can first find a descendant (See Definition 13) by guessing a few bits of the input and then determine the complexity on this smaller instance of the problem. Since a single guess might not to lead to a significantly simple instance[3], one likely has to repeat the process multiple times and target a weakness that various descendants share. As the number of smaller instances is exponential in the number of guessed variables of the Boolean function, evaluating the complexity on all of them independently is unfeasible for concrete security parameters.

Nevertheless, we can optimize this computation by merging equivalent descendants. For instance, consider $f_n(x_1, \ldots, x_n) = \mathsf{XOR}_n = x_1 + x_2 + \cdots + x_n$. By setting any variable to 0, we always obtain a descendant of the form $f_{n-1}(y_1, \ldots, y_{n-1}) = y_1 + y_2 + \cdots + y_{n-1}$. Namely, we get n equivalent descendants. Similarly, after ℓ guesses we can have only two types of descendant $f_{n-\ell}$ and $f_{n-\ell} + 1$. While in this example the number of descendant stays moderate, for other functions it might not be the case. In fact, the merging procedure has a major impact on the running time of the algorithm evaluating the security.

Furthermore, one can group descendants according to a specific criterion since all the attacks' complexities depend only the number of variables and some criterion[4]. See Sect. 2.3. For the function f_n considered above, it actually means that all descendants at depth ℓ (that is to say, after fixing ℓ variables) are equivalent since the values of the criteria considered in the attacks are the same for $f_{n-\ell}$ and $f_{n-\ell} + 1$.

Eventually, the crucial point for evaluating the impact of an attack on the security of IFP, via this guess-and-determine strategy, is to compute the distribution of selected Boolean criteria over the set of all descendants up to the security level. Indeed, the core of the strategy consists in running the attack on the initial function and descendants that are obtained by guessing some bits. This implies that we have to consider the probability to find by guessing descendants leading to a certain complexity. For instance, a descendant at depth ν might be easy to attack but the probability of guessing it could be only $2^{-\nu}$, i.e. making this attack unpractical.

Since the probability of getting an object with a certain Boolean criterion (or criteria) is relevant to the computation of the expected complexity, we define the following:

---

[3] In terms of being subject to one of the consider attacks.

[4] If the complexity of the attack depends on more than one criterion, one has to categorize the function according to all of them. The overall strategy remains unchanged.

Definition 15 $((\pi, \ell)$-**profile**)**.** *Let π be a function defined over the set of all Boolean functions to an ordered discrete set. Let $p_j : \pi(\mathcal{D}_j(f)) \to [0,1]$ be probability distribution function $p_j(a) = P(\pi(g) = a | g \in \mathcal{D}_j)$. The (π, ℓ)-profile of f is the sequence $C_0, \ldots, C_\ell$ of the cumulative functions of $p_0, \ldots, p_\ell$, respectively.*

For instance, if π is the function outputting the algebraic immunity, $\pi(\mathcal{D}_j)$ is the set of all possible values of the AI. Then, the (AI, ℓ)-profile at index $i \le \ell$ contains the probability that a depth-i descendant picked uniformly at random has an AI of at most k for $k \in \pi(\mathcal{D}_i)$. The practical computation of the profile is discussed in Sect. 3.2.

To evaluate the complexity of an attack relatively to an IFP with filter function f in n variables and register size N, we guess L bits of the key register. Then, we also have to take into account the probability of ℓ out of L guessed bits actually being selected as input for the filter function, *i.e.*

$$P_{L=\ell} = \frac{\binom{L}{\ell} \cdot \binom{N-L}{n-\ell}}{\binom{N}{n}}.$$

Hence, for every value of the set of criteria $k \in \bigcup_{\ell=0}^{L} \pi(\mathcal{D}_\ell(f))$ the probability of getting a descendant with at most such k is $P(k, L) = \sum_{\ell=0}^{L} P_{L=\ell} \cdot C_\ell(k)$ For instance, if π is the algebraic immunity, this is the probability of getting a descendant with AI at most k by guessing L bits of the key.

Therefore, to analyze, up to λ bits of security, the guess-and-determine strategy with a building block attack associated to a function π encoding a set of criteria, time complexity function $\mathtt{time}(\cdot)$ and data complexity function $\mathtt{data}(\cdot)$ we do the following operations: for every $L \in \mathbb{N}$ such that $0 \le L \le \lambda$ and for each value $k \in \bigcup_{\ell=0}^{\lambda} \pi(\mathcal{D}_\ell(f))$ we compute:

– the time complexity given by $\mathtt{t}_{k,L} = 2^L \cdot \mathtt{time}(\cdot)$;
– the data complexity is affected by the probability of getting a descendant $g \in \bigcup_{\ell=0}^{L} \pi(\mathcal{D}_\ell(f))$ having such that $\pi(g) \le k$, *i.e.* $P(k, L)$, so we set it to $\mathtt{d}_{k,L} = P(k, L)^{-1} \cdot \mathtt{data}(\cdot)$. Furthermore, since the adversary is limited to observe λ/κ ciphertexts, this complexity can actually be scaled by κ.

Finally, the lower bound on the guess-and-determine strategy is given by

$$\min_{k,L} \left\{ \max \left\{ \mathtt{t}_{k,L}, \kappa \cdot \mathtt{d}_{k,L} \right\} \right\}. \tag{2}$$

An algorithmic description can be found in Algorithm 1.

Algorithm 1. Guess-and-determine attack

Require: A filter function f, a profile P, a depth λ a range for the criterion $[min_C, max_C]$ and a scaling factor κ modeling the limited amount of queries of the adversary.

Ensure: Complexity c

1: $lowest\_complexity \leftarrow \infty$
2: **for** $L = 0$ to λ **do**
3:     $c \leftarrow min_C$
4:     **while** $c \leq max_C$ **do**
5:         $time\_complexity \leftarrow L + \mathtt{time}(\cdot)$
6:         $proba \leftarrow 0$
7:         **for** $\ell = 0$ to L **do**
8:             $proba_\ell \leftarrow \binom{L}{\ell} \cdot \binom{N-L}{n-\ell} / \binom{N}{n}$
9:             $proba \leftarrow proba + proba_\ell \cdot P[\ell][c]$
10:            **if** $proba \neq 0$ **then**
11:                $data\_complexity \leftarrow \mathtt{data}(\cdot)/proba$
12:                $complexity \leftarrow \mathtt{max}(\kappa \cdot data\_complexity, time\_complexity)$
13:                $lowest\_complexity \leftarrow \mathtt{min}(complexity, lowest\_complexity)$
14:            **end if**
15:        **end for**
16:        $c \leftarrow c + 1$
17:    **end while**
18: **end for**
19: **return** $lowest\_complexity$

3.2 Implementation

We provide Python scripts to evaluate the security of new parameters for FiLIP. The code aims to be easy to modify and reuse to study new instances. In particular, the user simply has to describe new functions in order to study their security when used as filter in FiLIP. The code has three main components: the profiling module, the attack module and the function objects.

Function Objects. New families of functions are created by writing a class following a given interface. While it would be natural to have a hierarchy with an abstract class at the top representing a generic Boolean function, we do not provide one since we felt that it is unnecessary and describing the interface is enough. A documented blank class is provided as template for the user to create new functions with all the required methods. In a nutshell, the class will contain methods to evaluate the criteria used in the attacks (Algebraic Immunity, Resiliency and Nonlinearity), to compute the direct descendants of the function that are obtained by fixing a variable to 0 or 1 (as well as their probability) and to compare with other functions in order to compare instances. Instances of the class represent functions object with concrete parameters. For example `f = XOR_TR(2,5,10)` will create an object corresponding to $XOR_2 + T_{5,10}$ and `f.AI()` will return its Algebraic Immunity.

Profiling Module. The profiling module is computing the different profiles corresponding to each criterion of a function. A profile is represented by a matrix for which columns are indexed by the different values that can be taken by the criterion. The row i contains at index j the probability that descendants obtained by fixing i variables have a value below or equal to j for the given criterion. Hence, in the first row, where only the initial function is considered, all the indexes will have value 0, except the ones that are superior or equal to the criterion (in this case we have a 1). We note that if an attack depends on n criteria, we need a $n + 1$ dimensional array. In our case we mostly consider matrices since most attacks depend on one criterion, the only exception is the attack depending on the Resiliency and Nonlinearity.

The profiling phase starts with the creation of a profile of appropriate size for each criterion. In most of the cases, the maximum value for the criterion is known without exploring the descendants. Indeed, Algebraic Immunity can only decrease and δ and ϵ are in the interval $[0, 0.5]$. The exception is resiliency that can increase when fixing a bit and thus the size of the array must correspond to the maximum resiliency among all descendants.

Then, up to a maximal depth in the (rooted directed) graph of descendants equal to the security parameter, we compute the descendants of each node at the current level, their probability, and update the profile accordingly by computing the criteria on each descendant. Since we want each row of the profile for criterion C to contain at index i the probability $Pr[C \leq i]$ and not $Pr[C = i]$, we need to eventually accumulate the values in each row.

Since, for a given function, two descendants are obtained by fixing a variable to 0 and 1, their amount should grow exponentially at each level. Obviously, this would make the computation of the profile impossible since we have to explore the descendants up to fixing a number of variables equal to the security parameter. This is why an important aspect of profiling is to detect when two descendants are equivalent[5] and merge their node (this is why all the descendants form a graph and not a tree). In the implementation, we rely on Python dictionaries to store descendants while detecting collisions. This forces us to define the hashing operator on function objects in order to use the hash map structure offered by the dictionary.

Attack Module. Once the profiling phase is finished, the complexities of the attacks can be evaluated. All the attacks are very similar and a generic code could be written to implement the guess and determine strategy. For the sake of simplicity, and to potentially add some tweaks, we separated them in different classes having the same interface. Each instance of an attack requires a profile, a function and a register size. Being associated to one or several criteria, it requires methods to obtain data and time complexities with respect to

---

[5] See Sect. 3.1.

the criteria. The main method actually computing bounds for the complexities implements Algorithm 1.

Configuration. Since we want the code to be flexible in terms of modelling the attack scenario, we added a small configuration file containing the main constants. In particular, the user can easily modify

- κ the ratio between the security parameter,
- the granularity of the discretization for the criteria depending on the non-linearity,
- the value ω used in some algebraic and correlation attacks.

4 Candidate Secure Functions

In this section, we discuss new functions that can be used to instantiate FiLIP as well as concrete parameters at various security levels. All of the results were obtained by using the tool presented in Sect. 3.

4.1 Former Instances with Smaller Key Size

Unlike in [MCJS19a], we decided to limit the amount of ciphertext data that the adversary can obtain while mounting the attack. In practice, we bound the number of queries to the square root of the computational capabilities of the adversary. For example, if the targeted security parameter λ is equal to 80, we only consider as successful attacks that require less than 2^{40} ciphertexts. This correspond to setting the κ parameter to 2 in Algorithm 1. Thus, it was natural to have a second look at some of the instances that were described in [MCJS19a] and to propose new parameters that would either reduce the register size or speed up the homomorphic evaluation of the filter. The results are presented in Table 2.

For a security of $\lambda = 80$ bits, we can obtain a function in 144 variables with a register size as small as $N = 530$, this size is almost four times smaller than what was proposed in [MCJS19a]. However, this requires a threshold function in more variables, that might be more expensive to evaluate. Thus we also propose an alternative with $N = 982$ and a threshold function in less variables.

For a security of $\lambda = 128$ bits, several trade-offs can be made depending on what the user of the filter finds convenient. In the table, we highlighted two functions $f_1 = \mathsf{XOR}_{65} + \mathsf{T}_{32,63}$ and $f_2 = \mathsf{XOR}_{58} + \mathsf{T}_{35,70}$ which both have a minimal number of variable ($n = \lambda$). Surprisingly, f_1 also exhibits a register size that is almost twice as small as the smaller register size possible for this value of λ in [MCJS19a].

Reducing the value of N can lead to a significant save in practice, for example, in the framework of [CDPP22], the bandwidth is directly proportional to the register size since they encrypt separately each key bit of FiLIP. In their case, this comes with no penalty cost on the runtime since it is mainly driven by the threshold size s which stays the same. In fact, f_1 will even be slightly faster to evaluate since less additions are required for the threshold part.

Table 2. For N and n the function $\mathsf{XOR}_k + \mathsf{T}_{d,s}$ provides λ-bit of security.

k	d	s	n	N	λ
40	52	104	144	530	80
100	24	44	144	982	80
65	32	63	128	2560	128
58	35	70	128	4096	128

k	d	s	n	N	λ
80	260	520	600	1200	128
70	93	186	256	1499	128
65	96	191	256	1461	128
70	61	122	192	1777	128
160	48	96	256	1987	128

4.2   Instances with New Families of Direct Sum of Threshold Functions (DST)

We remarked that both kind of filters previously used to instantiate FiLIP belong to a larger family, that we call direct sum of thresholds, or DST. Indeed, a degree d monomial corresponds to the threshold function $\mathsf{T}_{d,d}$, hence DSM functions are the direct sums of multiple threshold functions of highest threshold. The Xor-Threshold functions are the sum of many thresholds $\mathsf{T}_{1,1}$ and one high threshold in more variables, usually a majority function. Considering direct sums of threshold for FiLIP filters has different interest. First, threshold function can be efficiently evaluated homomorphically (*e.g.* [HMR20, CDPP22, MPP23]), then the resiliency and nonlinearity can be exactly determined based on the properties of threshold functions, finally these functions are bit-fixing stable. We focus on two new subfamilies, interesting for their cryptographic properties and mainly for their friendliness regarding homomorphic evaluation.

Definition 16 (XOR-QUAD-THR function). *For any positive integers k, q, d and n such that $d \leq n+1$ we define $\mathsf{XOR}_k + \mathsf{Q}_q + \mathsf{T}_{d,n}$ for all*
$$v = (x_1, \ldots, x_k, y_1, \ldots, y_{2q}, z_1, \ldots, z_n) \in \mathbb{F}_2^{k+2q+n} \text{ as:}$$

$$(\mathsf{XOR}_k + \mathsf{Q}_q + \mathsf{T}_{d,n})(v) = x_1 + \cdots + x_k + \sum_{i=1}^{q} y_{2i-1}y_{2i} + \mathsf{T}_{d,n}(z_1, \ldots, z_n)$$
$$= \mathsf{XOR}_k(x) + \mathsf{Q}_q(y) + \mathsf{T}_{d,n}(z).$$

Definition 17 (XOR-QUAD-THR function). *For any positive integers k, d_1, d_2, n_1 and n_2 such that $d_1 \leq n_1+1$ and $d_2 \leq n_2+1$ we define $\mathsf{XOR}_k + \mathsf{T}_{d_1,n_1} + \mathsf{T}_{d_2,n_2}$ for all*
$$v = (x_1, \ldots, x_k, y_1, \ldots, y_{n_1}, z_1, \ldots, z_{n_2}) \in \mathbb{F}_2^{k+n_1+n_2} \text{ as:}$$

$$(\mathsf{XOR}_k + \mathsf{T}_{d_1,n_1} + \mathsf{T}_{d_2,n_2})(v) = x_1 + \cdots + x_k$$
$$+ \mathsf{T}_{d_1,n_1}(y_1, \ldots, y_{n_1}) + \mathsf{T}_{d_2,n_2}(z_1, \ldots, z_{n_2})$$
$$= \mathsf{XOR}_k(x) + \mathsf{T}_{d_1,n_1}(y) + \mathsf{T}_{d_2,n_2}(z).$$

Using Property 1 and Property 2 we can compute the resiliency, nonlinearity and a lower bound on the algebraic immunity of these functions. Since the AI value is often the bottleneck for the security, we rely on a better bound that we derive using a result from [Méa22] using the parameter $\Delta_{\mathsf{AN}}(f)$ (see Definition 5).

Property 3 ([Méa22], Corollary 3). Let $n, m \in \mathbb{N}^*$, $f \in \mathcal{B}_n$, $g \in \mathcal{B}_m$, and ψ the direct sum of f and g, the following bound holds on its algebraic immunity:

$$\mathsf{AI}(\psi) \geq \max\left(\mathsf{AI}(f) + \min\{\Delta_{\mathsf{AN}}(f), \mathsf{AI}(g)\}, \mathsf{AI}(g) + \min\{\Delta_{\mathsf{AN}}(g), \mathsf{AI}(f)\}\right).$$

We detail the property of these two subfamilies in the following proposition:

Proposition 1 (Properties of *XOR-QUAD-THR* and *XOR-THR-THR* functions). *Let $k, q, d, n > 0$, and $d \leq n$, then the function $f = \mathsf{XOR}_k + \mathsf{Q}_q + \mathsf{T}_{d,n}$ has the following properties:*

1. *Resiliency:* $\mathsf{res}(f) = \begin{cases} k & \text{if } n = 2d - 1, \\ k - 1 & \text{otherwise.} \end{cases}$

2. *Nonlinearity:* $\mathsf{NL}(f) = 2^{n+k}(2^{2q-1} - 2^{q-1}) + 2^{2q}\mathsf{NL}(\mathsf{XOR}_k + \mathsf{T}_{d,n}) - (2^{2q} - 2^q)\mathsf{NL}(\mathsf{XOR}_k + \mathsf{T}_{d,n}).$

3. *Algebraic Immunity:* $\mathsf{AI}(f) \begin{cases} \geq \frac{n+1}{2} & \text{if } n - 2d + 1 = 0, \\ \geq \min(d+1, n-d+2) & \text{if } |n - 2d+1| = 1, \\ = \min(d+2, n-d+3) & \text{otherwise.} \end{cases}$

    Let $k, d_1, d_2, n_1, n_2 > 0$, $d_1 \leq n_1$ and $d_2 \leq n_2$, then the function $g = \mathsf{XOR}_k + \mathsf{T}_{d_1,n_1} + \mathsf{T}_{d_2,n_2}$ has the following properties:

1. *Resiliency:* $\mathsf{res}(g) = \begin{cases} k+1 & \text{if } n_1 = 2d_1 - 1 \text{ and } n_2 = 2d_2 - 1, \\ k-1 & \text{if } n_1 \neq 2d_1 - 1 \text{ and } n_2 \neq 2d_2 - 1,, \\ k & \text{otherwise.} \end{cases}$

2. *Nonlinearity:* $\mathsf{NL}(g) = 2^{n_2}\mathsf{NL}(\mathsf{XOR}_k + \mathsf{T}_{d_1,n_1}) + 2^{k+n_1}\mathsf{NL}(\mathsf{T}_{d_2,n_2}) - 2\mathsf{NL}(\mathsf{XOR}_k + \mathsf{T}_{d_1,n_1})\mathsf{NL}(\mathsf{T}_{d_2,n_2}).$

3. *Algebraic Immunity:*

$$\begin{aligned}
\mathsf{AI}(g) \geq \max\{ &\min(d_1, n_1 - d_1 + 1) \\
&+ \min(|n_1 - 2d_1 + 1|, \min(d_2, n_2 - d_2 + 1) + \varepsilon_g), \\
&\min(d_2, n_2 - d_2 + 1) \\
&+ \min(|n_2 - 2d_2 + 1|, \min(d_1, n_1 - d_1 + 1) + \varepsilon_f)\}.
\end{aligned}$$

where $\varepsilon_g = 1$ if $n_2 \neq 2d_2 - 1$, 0 otherwise, and $\varepsilon_f = 1$ if $n_1 \neq 2d_1 - 1$, 0 otherwise.

Proof. For the resiliency and nonlinearity, the exact number are directly derived from Property 1, and Property 2, using the direct sum with $\mathsf{XOR}_k + \mathsf{T}_{d,n}$ and Q_q for f, $\mathsf{XOR}_k + \mathsf{T}_{d_1,n_1}$ and T_{d_2,n_2} for g.

    Then we show the bounds on the algebraic immunity of $f = \mathsf{XOR}_k + \mathsf{Q}_q + \mathsf{T}_{d,n}$. If $n - 2d + 1 = 0$ then $\min(d, n - d + 1) = d = (n+1)/2$ and using Property 1 Item 3, $\mathsf{AI}(f) \geq \mathsf{AI}(\mathsf{T}_{(n+1)/2,n})$, that is $\mathsf{AI}(f) \geq (n+1)/2$ using Property 2 Item 3. For the two other cases, we use Property 3, considering the direct sum of $\mathsf{T}_{d,n}$ and $\mathsf{XOR}_k + \mathsf{Q}_q$. If $|n - 2d + 1| = 1$ then $\mathsf{AI}(\mathsf{T}_{d,n}) = \min(n, n - d + 1)$

and $\Delta_{\mathsf{AN}}(\mathsf{T}_{d,n}) = 1$ (by Property 2), then the bound gives $\mathsf{AI}(f) \geq \min(n, n - d + 1) + \min(1, \mathsf{AI}(\mathsf{XOR}_k + \mathsf{Q}_q))$. Since $\mathsf{XOR}_k + \mathsf{Q}_q$ is not a constant function its AI is at least 1, therefore in this case $\mathsf{AI}(f) \geq \min(n + 1, n - d + 2)$. For the last case, $|n - 2d + 1| > 1$, using the same reasoning $\mathsf{AI}(f) \geq \min(n, n - d + 1) + \min(2, \mathsf{AI}(\mathsf{XOR}_k + \mathsf{Q}_q))$. Since by definition $k > 0$ and $q > 0$, the function $\mathsf{XOR}_k + \mathsf{Q}_q$ is the direct sum of $\mathsf{XOR}_1 + \mathsf{Q}_1 = \mathsf{XOR}_1 + \mathsf{T}_{2,2}$ and another function. Since $\mathsf{XOR}_1 + \mathsf{T}_{2,2}$ has algebraic immunity 2 using Property 2 Item 3, applying Property 1 Item 3 we get $\mathsf{AI}(\mathsf{XOR}_k + \mathsf{Q}_q) \geq 2$, allowing us to conclude $\mathsf{AI}(f) \geq \min(d + 2, n - d + 3)$. In this case we have $\mathsf{AI}(f) = \min(d + 2, n - d + 3)$ since $\mathsf{AI}(f) \leq \mathsf{AI}(\mathsf{T}_{d,n}) + \mathsf{AI}(\mathsf{XOR}_k + \mathsf{Q}_q)$ using the upper bound of Property 1 Item 3 since $\mathsf{AI}(\mathsf{T}_{d,n}) = \min(d, n - d + 1)$ and $\mathsf{AI}(\mathsf{XOR}_k + \mathsf{Q}_q) = 2$ since it is a degree 2 function (of AI greater than 1).

Finally, we demonstrate the bounds on the algebraic immunity of $g = \mathsf{XOR}_k + \mathsf{T}_{d_1,n_1} + \mathsf{T}_{d_2,n_2}$. Using Property 3 with T_{d_1,n_1} and $\mathsf{XOR}_k + \mathsf{T}_{d_2,n_2}$ we obtain (also using Property 2 Item 3 and 4)):

$$\mathsf{AI}(g) \geq \mathsf{AI}(\mathsf{T}_{d_1,n_1}) + \min(\Delta_{\mathsf{AN}}(\mathsf{T}_{d_1,n_1}), \mathsf{AI}(\mathsf{XOR}_k + \mathsf{T}_{d_2,n_2}))$$
$$\geq \min(d_1, n_1 - d_1 + 1) + \min(|n_1 - 2d_1 + 1|, \min(d_2, n_2 - d_2 + 1) + \varepsilon_g).$$

Similarly, using Property 3 with T_{d_2,n_2} and $\mathsf{XOR}_k + \mathsf{T}_{d_1,n_1}$ we obtain:

$$\mathsf{AI}(g) \geq \min(d_2, n_2 - d_2 + 1) + \min(|n_2 - 2d_2 + 1|, \min(d_1, n_1 - d_1 + 1) + \varepsilon_f),$$

which allows us to conclude.   □

Remark 2. First, we note that XOR-QUAD-THR functions have already been suggested as filters for FiLIP, as mentioned in [MCJS19a] Section 9.2, but with no concrete instantiation up to our knowledge. Second, for functions using more threshold functions of different degrees more general results from [Méa22] could be used to improve the lower bound on the AI of direct sums, such as Lemma 6 and Theorem 1. We did not find improvements for the two subfamilies we consider.

We studied the security of several concrete functions in the two families with TooLIP. Table 5 shows results for XOR-THR-THR. The practical goal of studying XOR-THR-THR was mainly to assess the impact of splitting a threshold in two thresholds of half the size. It is thus natural to compare Table 5 and Table 2. We can see that for non minimal values of n, splitting the threshold opens the possibility to reduce the register size N. However, XOR-THR functions that were obtained by setting $n = \lambda$ seems to still offer better register size. That being said, having two smaller threshold to evaluate could be an efficiency gain (depending on the method of homomorphic evaluation). For $\lambda = 80$, we have a straightforward improvement.

Tables 3 and 4 gives secure parameters for XOR-QUAD-THR functions. The idea was to add quadratic terms to heavily increase the nonlinearity without adding too many variables. Since this could have a negative impact on the evaluation time of the function depending on the evaluation technique used, we

Table 3. For N and n the function $\mathsf{XOR}_k + \mathsf{Q}_{10} + \mathsf{T}_{d,s}(n)$ provides λ-bit of security.

k	q	d	s	n	N	λ
40	10	52	104	164	329	80
100	10	21	44	164	329	80
70	10	93	186	276	789	128
65	10	96	191	276	780	128
70	10	61	122	212	834	128
160	10	48	96	276	864	128

Table 4. For N and n the function $\mathsf{XOR}_k + \mathsf{Q}_q + \mathsf{T}_{d,s}(n)$ provides λ-bit of security.

k	q	d	s	n	N	λ
60	20	85	170	270	541	128
60	20	65	150	250	873	128
50	40	80	160	290	617	128
50	60	65	150	320	640	128
60	40	65	150	290	581	128
60	60	50	100	280	560	128
60	60	60	120	300	600	128
160	15	60	120	310	5000	256
140	20	60	120	310	4800	256

first tried to (arbitrarily) limit the number of quadratic terms in QUAD to 10 (see Table 3). Then, to broaden the result, we allowed the number of terms in QUAD to grow further (see Table 4). We can see that this eventually lead to even smaller register size than the one we had with XOR-THR and XOR-THR-THR. While 10 quadratic terms seems not enough to significantly improve over the XOR-THR-THR construction, 20 QUAD offers 128 bits of security for a register size of only 541. This is approximately 7 times smaller than the smallest function proposed in [MCJS19a]. Furthermore, it also allows us to propose 256-bit secure instances for a reasonable number of variables.

Table 5. For N and n the function $\mathsf{XOR}_k + \mathsf{T}_{d_1,s_1} + \mathsf{T}_{d_2,s_2}$ provides λ-bit of security.

k	d_1	s_1	d_2	s_2	n	N	λ
40	26	52	26	52	144	360	80
100	11	22	11	22	144	397	80
54	19	38	19	38	130	6500	128
54	22	45	23	45	144	3072	128
70	30	61	31	61	192	841	128
65	47	95	48	96	256	830	128
70	46	93	47	93	256	736	128
60	26	53	27	53	166	1229	128
160	24	48	24	48	256	913	128

4.3   FiLIP with Arbitrary Filter

We consider instances of FiLIP with arbitrary functions, in this case functions given by the their number of variables, algebraic immunity, resiliency and non-linearity only. We use that "arbitrary" functions is a bit-fixing stable family (Definition 14), and we can track the parameters of the descendants using the following proposition.

Proposition 2 (Parameter degradation by bit-fixing). *Let $n \in \mathbb{N}^*$ and f be an n variable Boolean function, for all $i \in \{1, \ldots, n\}$ and $\varepsilon \in \{0,1\}$ the following bound applies on the properties of $f_{i,\varepsilon}$:*

- *Resiliency:* $\mathsf{res}(f_{i,\varepsilon}) \geq \mathsf{res}(f) - 1$.
- *Algebraic immunity:* $\mathsf{AI}(f_{i,\varepsilon}) \geq \mathsf{AI}(f) - 1$.

Proof. First, we show the result on the resiliency. By contradiction we assume there exists i and ε such that $\mathsf{res}(f_{i,\varepsilon}) < \mathsf{res}(f) - 1$. By the definition of resiliency, it means that after fixing $\mathsf{res}(f) - 1$ variables, $f_{i,\varepsilon}$ is not balanced anymore, hence fixing $\mathsf{res}(f) - 1 + 1 = \mathsf{res}(f)$ variables (the ones for $f_{i,\varepsilon}$ and the i-th variable to ε) of f gives an unbalanced function, which leads to a contradiction.

Then, we prove the bound on the AI. By contradiction we assume there exists i and ε such that $\mathsf{AI}(f_{i,\varepsilon}) < \mathsf{AI}(f) - 1$. Therefore there exists an annihilator of $f_{i,\varepsilon}$ (respectively $f_{i,\varepsilon} + 1$), g_i, non null, of degree lower than $\mathsf{AI}(f) - 1$. Then we take the function $h = (\varepsilon + x_i) \cdot g_i$ which is not null since, and of degree at lower than $\mathsf{AI}(f)$. Since $(\varepsilon + x_i)f = f_{i,\varepsilon}$ we have that h is an annihilator of f (respectively $f + 1$), leading to a contradiction.   □

Moreover, for the nonlinearity we use a lower bound derived from the AI given by Lobanov [Lob09]:

Property 4 ([Lob09]). Let f be an n variable Boolean function, then the following bound applies on its nonlinearity:

$$\mathsf{NL}(f) \geq 2 \sum_{i=0}^{\mathsf{AI}(f)-2} \binom{n-1}{i}$$

We consider two kinds of functions for our tests in this part. First, we use TooLIP on functions which are the direct sum of a XOR function and an arbitrary function with high algebraic immunity and no resiliency. Since a random function have high algebraic immunity and low resiliency with high probability (see [Did06]), this test gives an idea on the number of variables necessary to have a secure instance of FiLIP by taking a random function and adding it in direct sum with a XOR function. Then, we consider a type of function having both optimal algebraic immunity and resilience, a dahu, whose existence is conjectured and investigated in [DMR21]. The advantage of using such function is that no direct sum is necessary with a XOR function to reach a high resiliency.

Definition 18 (Dahus, adapted from [DMR21] Definition 14). *Let $n \geq 3$, we call dahu an n-variable Boolean function such that:* $\mathsf{AI}(f) + \mathsf{res}(f) + 1 = n$ *and* $\mathsf{AI}(f) = \lfloor (n+1)/2 \rfloor$.

Setting λ to 128, we obtain the following result:

- Writing $f[\alpha, n]$ an arbitrary function f in n variables with $\mathsf{AI}(f) = \alpha$ and $\mathsf{res}(f) = 0$, we fulfill the security goal for a function $f[213, 450] + \mathsf{XOR}_{256}$ and key register size $N = 6000$. For the function $f[256, 512] + \mathsf{XOR}_{196}$ we obtain the same result since $N \geq 2500$.
- A dahu in 512 variables, that is to say with algebraic immunity 256 and resiliency 255 is a secure filter for $N = 2500$. For $n = 450$ the same result apply for $N \geq 3000$.

5   Conclusion and Open Questions

In this article, we discussed new instances for FiLIP by studying the security of different families of filter functions. To automate this process, we propose a tool called TooLIP that runs several existing attacks on user defined functions. While the functions studied in this article are already implemented in the tool, it should be simple for an user to add new ones as long as computing (bounds on) the criteria and the descendant is feasible. In particular, we focused on XOR-THR-THR and XOR-QUAD-THR which gave instances that are more efficient in terms of bandwidth and/or evaluation time when FiLIP is used in an HHE protocol. We also provided results for arbitrary filters in case the function used as some unknown properties. These different contributions enable to easily update the state of the art on the attacks, and determine secure instances in new families of functions that become more homomorphic friendly.

Two main open questions arose during this work. First, in [MCJS19b] various modifications are performed on the algorithm to determine instances with DSM functions since the number of descendants prevents to use the generic algorithms. It would be interesting to see if similar improvements could be implemented generically with the tool, such as simplifying the graph of descendants by merging sub-paths when descendants with worse properties are identified. Second, the throughput of FiLIP is less competitive than its latency compared to other symmetric ciphers used in HHE due to the fact that it produces its keystream bit by bit. A multi-bit output version of FiLIP could have a better throughput, and it raises the question of the tool to be adaptable to such generalizations.

Acknowledgments. The authors were supported by the ERC Advanced Grant no. 787390.

References

[ACG+06] Armknecht, F., Carlet, C., Gaborit, P., Künzli, S., Meier, W., Ruatta, O.: Efficient computation of algebraic immunity for algebraic and fast algebraic attacks. In: Vaudenay, S. (ed.) EUROCRYPT 2006. LNCS, vol. 4004, pp. 147–164. Springer, Heidelberg (2006). https://doi.org/10.1007/11761679_10

[AL16] Applebaum, B., Lovett, S.: Algebraic attacks against random local functions and their countermeasures. In: Wichs, D., Mansour, Y. (eds.) 48th ACM STOC. ACM Press (2016)

[AL18] Applebaum, B., Lovett, S.: Algebraic attacks against random local functions and their countermeasures. SIAM J. Comput. 52–79 (2018)

[APS15a] Albrecht, M.R., Player, R., Scott, S.: On the concrete hardness of learning with errors. J. Math. Cryptol. 9(3), 169–203 (2015)

[APS15b] Albrecht, M.R., Player, R., Scott, S.: On the concrete hardness of learning with errors. Cryptology ePrint Archive, Paper 2015/046 (2015)

[ARS+15] Albrecht, M.R., Rechberger, C., Schneider, T., Tiessen, T., Zohner, M.: Ciphers for MPC and FHE. In: Oswald, E., Fischlin, M. (eds.) EUROCRYPT 2015. LNCS, vol. 9056, pp. 430–454. Springer, Heidelberg (2015). https://doi.org/10.1007/978-3-662-46800-5_17

[BIP+22] Bonte, C., Iliashenko, I., Park, J., Pereira, H.V.L., Smart, N.P.: FINAL: faster FHE instantiated with NTRU and LWE. In: Agrawal, S., Lin, D. (eds.) ASIACRYPT 2022. LNCS, vol. 13792, pp. 188–215. Springer, Cham (2022). https://doi.org/10.1007/978-3-031-22966-4_7

[BY03] Bellare, M., Yee, B.: Forward-security in private-key cryptography. In: Joye, M. (ed.) CT-RSA 2003. LNCS, vol. 2612, pp. 1–18. Springer, Heidelberg (2003). https://doi.org/10.1007/3-540-36563-X_1

[Car21] Carlet, C.: Boolean Functions for Cryptography and Coding Theory. Cambridge University Press, Cambridge (2021)

[CDM+18] Couteau, G., Dupin, A., Méaux, P., Rossi, M., Rotella, Y.: On the concrete security of Goldreich's pseudorandom generator. In: Peyrin, T., Galbraith, S. (eds.) ASIACRYPT 2018, Part I. LNCS, vol. 11273, pp. 96–124. Springer, Cham (2018). https://doi.org/10.1007/978-3-030-03329-3_4

[CDPP22] Cong, K., Das, D., Park, J., Pereira, H.V.L.: SortingHat: efficient private decision tree evaluation via homomorphic encryption and transciphering. In: ACM SIGSAC Conference on Computer and Communications Security, CCS 2022, pp. 563–577 (2022)

[CGGI16] Chillotti, I., Gama, N., Georgieva, M., Izabachène, M.: Faster fully homomorphic encryption: bootstrapping in less than 0.1 seconds. In: Cheon, J.H., Takagi, T. (eds.) ASIACRYPT 2016, Part I. LNCS, vol. 10031, pp. 3–33. Springer, Heidelberg (2016). https://doi.org/10.1007/978-3-662-53887-6_1

[CHK+21] Cho, J., et al.: Transciphering framework for approximate homomorphic encryption. In: Tibouchi, M., Wang, H. (eds.) ASIACRYPT 2021. LNCS, vol. 13092, pp. 640–669. Springer, Cham (2021). https://doi.org/10.1007/978-3-030-92078-4_22

[CHMS22] Cosseron, O., Hoffmann, C., Méaux, P., Standaert, F.-X.: Towards case-optimized hybrid homomorphic encryption - featuring the Elisabeth stream cipher. In: Agrawal, S., Lin, D. (eds.) ASIACRYPT 2022. LNCS, vol. 13793, pp. 32–67. Springer, Cham (2022). https://doi.org/10.1007/978-3-031-22969-5_2

[CIR22] Cid, C., Indrøy, J.P., Raddum, H.: FASTA – a stream cipher for fast FHE evaluation. In: Galbraith, S.D. (ed.) CT-RSA 2022. LNCS, vol. 13161, pp. 451–483. Springer, Cham (2022). https://doi.org/10.1007/978-3-030-95312-6_19

[CLT14] Coron, J.-S., Lepoint, T., Tibouchi, M.: Scale-invariant fully homomorphic encryption over the integers. In: Krawczyk, H. (ed.) PKC 2014. LNCS, vol. 8383, pp. 311–328. Springer, Heidelberg (2014). https://doi.org/10.1007/978-3-642-54631-0_18

[CM03] Courtois, N.T., Meier, W.: Algebraic attacks on stream ciphers with linear feedback. In: Biham, E. (ed.) EUROCRYPT 2003. LNCS, vol. 2656, pp. 345–359. Springer, Heidelberg (2003). https://doi.org/10.1007/3-540-39200-9_21

[CM19] Carlet, C., Méaux, P.: Boolean functions for homomorphic-friendly stream ciphers. In: Gueye, C.T., Persichetti, E., Cayrel, P.-L., Buchmann, J. (eds.) A2C 2019. CCIS, vol. 1133, pp. 166–182. Springer, Cham (2019). https://doi.org/10.1007/978-3-030-36237-9_10

[CM22] Carlet, C., Méaux, P.: A complete study of two classes of Boolean functions: direct sums of monomials and threshold functions. IEEE Trans. Inf. Theory **68**(5), 3404–3425 (2022)

[Cou03a] Courtois, N.T.: Fast algebraic attacks on stream ciphers with linear feedback. In: Boneh, D. (ed.) CRYPTO 2003. LNCS, vol. 2729, pp. 176–194. Springer, Heidelberg (2003). https://doi.org/10.1007/978-3-540-45146-4_11

[Cou03b] Courtois, N.T.: Higher order correlation attacks, XL algorithm and cryptanalysis of toyocrypt. In: Lee, P.J., Lim, C.H. (eds.) ICISC 2002. LNCS, vol. 2587, pp. 182–199. Springer, Heidelberg (2003). https://doi.org/10.1007/3-540-36552-4_13

[CT19] Cogliati, B., Tanguy, T.: Multi-user security bound for filter permutators in the random oracle model. Des. Codes Cryptogr. **87**(7), 1621–1638 (2019)

[DEG+18] Dobraunig, C., et al.: Rasta: a cipher with low ANDdepth and Few ANDs per bit. In: Shacham, H., Boldyreva, A. (eds.) CRYPTO 2018. LNCS, vol. 10991, pp. 662–692. Springer, Cham (2018). https://doi.org/10.1007/978-3-319-96884-1_22

[DGH+21] Dobraunig, C., Grassi, L., Helminger, L., Rechberger, C., Schofnegger, M., Walch, R.: Pasta: a case for hybrid homomorphic encryption. IACR Cryptol. ePrint Arch. 731 (2021)

[Did06] Didier, F.: A new upper bound on the block error probability after decoding over the erasure channel. IEEE Trans. Inf. Theory **52**(10), 4496–4503 (2006)

[DLR16] Duval, S., Lallemand, V., Rotella, Y.: Cryptanalysis of the FLIP family of stream ciphers. In: Robshaw, M., Katz, J. (eds.) CRYPTO 2016, Part I. LNCS, vol. 9814, pp. 457–475. Springer, Heidelberg (2016). https://doi.org/10.1007/978-3-662-53018-4_17

[DM15] Ducas, L., Micciancio, D.: FHEW: bootstrapping homomorphic encryption in less than a second. In: Oswald, E., Fischlin, M. (eds.) EUROCRYPT 2015, Part I. LNCS, vol. 9056, pp. 617–640. Springer, Heidelberg (2015). https://doi.org/10.1007/978-3-662-46800-5_24

[DMR21] Dupin, A., Méaux, P., Rossi, M.: On the algebraic immunity - resiliency trade-off, implications for Goldreich's pseudorandom generator. IACR Cryptol. ePrint Arch. 649 (2021)

[Fau99] Faugère, J.-C.: A new efficient algorithm for computing Groebner bases. J. Pure Appl. Algebra **139**, 61–88 (1999)

[Fau02] Faugère, J.C.: A new efficient algorithm for computing Grobner bases without reduction to zero. In: Workshop on application of Groebner Bases 2002, Catania, Spain (2002)

[GHS12] Gentry, C., Halevi, S., Smart, N.P.: Homomorphic evaluation of the AES circuit. In: Safavi-Naini, R., Canetti, R. (eds.) CRYPTO 2012. LNCS, vol. 7417, pp. 850–867. Springer, Heidelberg (2012). https://doi.org/10.1007/978-3-642-32009-5_49

[Gol00] Goldreich, O.: Candidate one-way functions based on expander graphs. Electron. Colloquium Comput. Complexity (ECCC) **7**(90) (2000)

[HKC+20] Ha, J., et al.: Masta: an he-friendly cipher using modular arithmetic. IEEE Access **8**, 194741–194751 (2020)

[HKL+22] Ha, J., Kim, S., Lee, B., Lee, J., Son, M.: Rubato: noisy ciphers for approximate homomorphic encryption. In: Dunkelman, O., Dziembowski, S. (eds.) EUROCRYPT 2022. LNCS, vol. 13275, pp. 581–610. Springer, Cham (2022). https://doi.org/10.1007/978-3-031-06944-4_20

[HL20] Hebborn, P., Leander, G.: Dasta - alternative linear layer for rasta. IACR Trans. Symmetric Cryptol. **2020**(3), 46–86 (2020)

[HMR20] Hoffmann, C., Méaux, P., Ricosset, T.: Transciphering, using FiLIP and TFHE for an efficient delegation of computation. In: Bhargavan, K., Oswald, E., Prabhakaran, M. (eds.) INDOCRYPT 2020. LNCS, vol. 12578, pp. 39–61. Springer, Cham (2020). https://doi.org/10.1007/978-3-030-65277-7_3

[HMS23] Hoffmann, C., Méaux, P., Standaert, F.-X.: The patching landscape of Elisabeth-4 and the mixed filter permutator paradigm. IACR Cryptol. ePrint Arch. 1895 (2023)

[LN14] Lepoint, T., Naehrig, M.: A comparison of the homomorphic encryption schemes **FV** and **YASHE**. In: Pointcheval, D., Vergnaud, D. (eds.) AFRICACRYPT 2014. LNCS, vol. 8469, pp. 318–335. Springer, Cham (2014). https://doi.org/10.1007/978-3-319-06734-6_20

[Lob09] Lobanov, M.S.: Exact relations between nonlinearity and algebraic immunity. J. Appl. Ind. Math. **3**(3), 367–376 (2009)

[MCJS19a] Méaux, P., Carlet, C., Journault, A., Standaert, F.-X.: Improved filter permutators: combining symmetric encryption design, Boolean functions, low complexity cryptography, and homomorphic encryption, for private delegation of computations. Cryptology ePrint Archive, Report 2019/483 (2019)

[MCJS19b] Méaux, P., Carlet, C., Journault, A., Standaert, F.-X.: Improved filter permutators for efficient FHE: better instances and implementations. In: Hao, F., Ruj, S., Sen Gupta, S. (eds.) INDOCRYPT 2019. LNCS, vol. 11898, pp. 68–91. Springer, Cham (2019). https://doi.org/10.1007/978-3-030-35423-7_4

[Méa22] Méaux, P.: On the algebraic immunity of direct sum constructions. Discret. Appl. Math. **320**, 223–234 (2022)

[MJSC16] Méaux, P., Journault, A., Standaert, F.-X., Carlet, C.: Towards stream ciphers for efficient FHE with low-noise ciphertexts. In: Fischlin, M., Coron, J.-S. (eds.) EUROCRYPT 2016. LNCS, vol. 9665, pp. 311–343. Springer, Heidelberg (2016). https://doi.org/10.1007/978-3-662-49890-3_13

[MPC04] Meier, W., Pasalic, E., Carlet, C.: Algebraic attacks and decomposition of Boolean functions. In: Cachin, C., Camenisch, J.L. (eds.) EUROCRYPT 2004. LNCS, vol. 3027, pp. 474–491. Springer, Heidelberg (2004). https://doi.org/10.1007/978-3-540-24676-3_28

[MPP23] Méaux, P., Park, J., Pereira, H.V.L.: Towards practical transciphering for FHE with setup independent of the plaintext space. IACR Cryptol. ePrint Arch. 1531 (2023)

[NLV11] Naehrig, M., Lauter, K.E., Vaikuntanathan, V.: Can homomorphic encryption be practical? In: CCSW, pp. 113–124. ACM (2011)

[Üna23] Ünal, A.: Worst-case subexponential attacks on PRGs of constant degree or constant locality. In: Hazay, C., Stam, M. (eds.) EUROCRYPT 2023. LNCS, vol. 14004, pp. 25–54. Springer, Cham (2023). https://doi.org/10.1007/978-3-031-30545-0_2

[YGJL22] Yang, J., Guo, Q., Johansson, T., Lentmaier, M.: Revisiting the concrete security of Goldreich's pseudorandom generator. IEEE Trans. Inf. Theory **68**(2), 1329–1354 (2022)

Best Paper Award

Quasi-optimal Permutation Ranking and Applications to PERK

Slim Bettaieb[1], Alessandro Budroni[1]([✉]), Marco Palumbi[1],
and Décio Luiz Gazzoni Filho[2,3]

[1] Cryptography Research Center, Technology Innovation Institute, Abu Dhabi, UAE
{slim.bettaieb,alessandro.budroni,marco.palumbi}@tii.ae
[2] Instituto de Computação, Universidade Estadual de Campinas (UNICAMP),
Campinas, Brazil
decio.gazzoni@ic.unicamp.br
[3] Department of Electrical Engineering, State University of Londrina, Londrina,
Brazil
dgazzoni@uel.br

Abstract. A ranking function for permutations maps every permutation of length n to a unique integer between 0 and $n! - 1$. For permutations of size that are of interest in cryptographic applications, evaluating such a function requires multiple-precision arithmetic. This work introduces a quasi-optimal ranking technique that allows us to rank a permutation efficiently without needing a multiple-precision arithmetic library. We present experiments that show the computational advantage of our method compared to the standard lexicographic optimal permutation ranking. As an application of our result, we show how this technique improves the signature sizes and the efficiency of PERK digital signature scheme.

Keywords: Efficient Compression · PERK · Permutation ranking ·
Post-quantum Cryptography

1 Introduction

Permutations have been employed in Cryptography in various scenarios, including the construction of block ciphers and hash functions. Some of the fundamental hard problems in Post-quantum Cryptography, e.g., Permutation Code Equivalence [Leo82] and Permuted Kernel Problem [Sha90], guarantee a hardness based on the application of a secret permutation on certain geometrical or algebraic structures. Motivated by the ongoing standardization initiatives led by the authorities of different countries, such as NIST [NIS17,NIS23] and CACR [fCR20], several new cryptosystems featuring public-key encryption, key-encapsulation mechanisms and digital signatures have been proposed. Some of these introduced new technical and engineering challenges related to permutations such as efficient permutation sampling and composition. This work addresses the challenge of efficiently compressing a permutation.

The PERK signature scheme [ABB+23a] is a new digital signature whose security relies on a variant of the Permuted Kernel Problem, and it is currently

S. Vaudenay and C. Petit (Eds.): AFRICACRYPT 2024, LNCS 14861, pp. 49–65, 2024.
https://doi.org/10.1007/978-3-031-64381-1_3

one of the candidates for round 1 of the NIST post-quantum competition for additional signatures [NIS23]. Essentially, the signature scheme functions as a zero-knowledge proof of knowledge, leveraging the Multi-Party Computation in-the-Head (MPCitH) paradigm [IKOS07]. Subsequently, the Fiat-Shamir transform [FS87], is employed to transition the interactive proof into a signature within the random oracle model. PERK provides three sets of parameters, to meet the different security levels I, III, and V defined by NIST [NIS23]. For each security level, there are two trade-offs: the first involves parameters labeled *short* aiming to reduce signature's size, and the second involves parameters labeled *fast* focusing on minimizing computational costs to achieve faster signature computation. The authors announced an updated version of the scheme [ABB+23b] a few months after the first submission. Here, a novel compression technique was introduced specifically for the *short* parameter sets based on a ranking/unranking algorithm for permutations. While this strategy achieves optimal permutation compression sizes, leading to an approximate 5% reduction in the overall size of *short* PERK signatures, it comes with the trade-off of increased compression time and a requirement for a multiple-precision arithmetic library. Notice that the percentage of PERK signatures occupied by compressed permutations ranges from 15% to 25%. Hence, any substantial improvement in the compression technique for permutations would translate into an improvement in the whole signature sizes.

Contributions. In this work, we introduce a new permutation compression technique that offers simultaneously three significant advantages with respect to previously known compression techniques:

- it gives quasi-optimal compression sizes, that is, a few bits only larger than the best compression possible,
- both compression and decompression routines are highly efficient to compute and easily parallelizable,
- it does not require heap-memory allocations or a multiple-precision arithmetic library, making it portable to resource-constrained devices.

We implement our novel compression method both in pure C and with AVX2 optimization.[1] We show that, by applying it to the PERK signature scheme, we obtain the following improvements:

- we reduce the signature sizes for the *fast* parameter sets by around 5%, at the price of a negligible increase in execution time,
- while maintaining equivalent signature sizes for the *short* parameter sets, we drop the dependency from heap-memory allocations and the GMP library for multiple-precision arithmetic. Moreover, we obtain a speed-up of about 2%.

The above considerations significantly increase PERK's code portability. Because of the simplicity of our implementation, we expect our contribution to be even more impactful on resource-constrained devices.

---

[1] The implementation is available at
https://github.com/marco-palumbi/quasi-optimal_ranking.

Paper Organization. We give in Sect. 2 the necessary background to understand our work. We introduce our quasi-optimal ranking and unranking methods in Sect. 3 and present the impact on PERK together with the results of our experiments in Sect. 4. Finally we give our conclusions in Sect. 5.

2 Preliminaries

Let $\mathbb{N}$ and $\mathbb{Z}$ denote the sets natural and integer numbers respectively. Let $[n]$ represent the set of integers $\{0, 1, \ldots, n-1\} \subset \mathbb{Z}$, and $\mathcal{S}_n$ denote the group of permutations of $[n]$ with the operation of permutation composition. We write permutations $\pi \in \mathcal{S}_n$ using the so-called *one-line* representation,

$$\pi = (\pi(0), \pi(1), \ldots, \pi(n-1)),$$

that is, as the resulting list of the elements of the ordered set $[n]$ after the permutation is applied.

We define the function that gives the minimum number of bits to represent an integer as

$$\texttt{bitlen} : \mathbb{N} \to \mathbb{N}, \qquad x \mapsto \begin{cases} 1 & \text{if } x = 0 \\ \lceil \log_2(x+1) \rceil & \text{otherwise} \end{cases}.$$

2.1 Ranking/Unranking of Permutations

In the context of permutations, we call *ranking* a bijective function from $\mathcal{S}_n$ to $\{0, 1, \ldots, n! - 1\}$. The reverse function is called *unranking*. Ranking algorithms typically rank permutations in lexicographic ordering [Leh60, Bon08], but others using a different order also exist [MR01].

Ranking. The ranking of $\pi \in \mathcal{S}_n$ in lexicographic order is computed as follows. Consider the list of integers $(d_0, d_1, \ldots, d_{n-1})$, where

$$d_{n-i-1} = \sum_{j=i+1}^{n-1} \mathbb{1}_{\pi(j) < \pi(i)}, \quad \text{for } i = 0, \ldots, n-2, \qquad d_0 = 0, \qquad (1)$$

where $\mathbb{1}_{\pi(j) < \pi(i)}$ is the characteristic function that returns 1 if $\pi(j) < \pi(i)$, 0 otherwise. The list of d_i is known as the *factorial representation* of the permutation. Notice that $d_i \in \{0, \ldots, i\}$, for $i = 0, \ldots, n-1$. The ranking of π is defined as

$$r : \mathcal{S}_n \to \{0, \ldots, n! - 1\}, \quad r(\pi) \mapsto \sum_{i=1}^{n} d_i \cdot i!. \qquad (2)$$

An equivalent but recursive expression for $r(\pi)$ is

$$r(\pi) = d_0 + 1 \cdot (d_1 + \cdots + (n-2) \cdot (d_{n-2} + (n-1) \cdot d_{n-1}) \cdots) \qquad (3)$$

The sequence $(d_0, d_1, \ldots, d_{n-1})$ is different for every $\pi \in \mathcal{S}_n$, and it is the factorial base representation of $r(\pi)$. It follows that $r(\cdot)$ is a bijection and so the ranking of each permutation is unique.

We report the complete ranking procedure in the variant using Eq. 2 in Algorithm 1. Note that Eq. 1 has an asymptotic cost of $O(n^2)$. However, Bonet provided an equivalent algorithm with an asymptotic cost of $O(n \log n)$ [Bon08]. For permutations of length $n > 20$, computing $r(\pi)$ requires, in practice, a multiple-precision arithmetic library. Equation 3 comes with the practical advantage, w.r.t. Equation 2, of allowing computation of $r(\pi)$ by performing multiplications by factors $< n$. Certain libraries (e.g., GMP [Pro23]) come with efficient and dedicated bignum multiplications by 32-bit integer types (e.g., uint32_t), and so this formula is preferred in this case. On the other hand, Eq. 2, paired with a look-up table for the precomputed factorials, might be a better option when such an optimized function is not available.

Algorithm 1: Ranking of a permutation

Input: permutation $\pi \in \mathcal{S}_n$
Output: Rank $0 \le r(\pi) < n!$
1 $R \leftarrow 0$;
2 **for** $i \leftarrow 0, \ldots, n-1$ **do**
3 $\quad$ $c \leftarrow 0$;   // Equation 1
4 $\quad$ **for** $j \leftarrow i+1, \ldots, n-1$ **do**
5 $\quad\quad$ **if** $\pi(i) < \pi(j)$ **then**
6 $\quad\quad\quad$ $c \leftarrow c+1$;
7 $\quad$ $R \leftarrow R + c \cdot i!$;   // Equation 2
8 **return** R

Unranking. The unranking procedure is the inverse of ranking, i.e., from an integer $R \le n! - 1$, one obtains the unique permutation $\pi \in \mathcal{S}_n$ such that $r(\pi) = R$. We report this procedure as Algorithm 2. Similarly to Algorithm 1, there exists a variant that makes use of a recursive formula to obtain the indexes d_i. Furthermore, its asymptotic complexity is $O(n^2)$. However, also in this case, Bonet proposed an equivalent algorithm that runs in time $O(n \log(n))$ [Bon08].

2.2 Permutation Compression in PERK

According to the specifications of PERK (see Table 2 [ABB+23b]), the signature includes a set of τ compressed permutations of length n aimed at reducing the overall size of the signature. There are two compression approaches optimized for *fast* and *short* parameters, respectively. In the following sections, we detail these techniques, starting with the compression tailored for *fast* parameters and

---

Algorithm 2: Unranking of a permutation

Input: rank $0 \leq R < n!$
Output: permutation $\pi \in \mathcal{S}_n$

1 used $\leftarrow [false : \textbf{for } i \leftarrow 0, \ldots, n-1]$;
2 **for** $i \leftarrow 0, \ldots, n-1$ **do**
3       $d_{n-i-1} = \left\lfloor \frac{R \mod (i+1)!}{i!} \right\rfloor$;
4       $c \leftarrow 0$;
5   **for** $j \leftarrow 0, \ldots, n-1$ **do**
6   **if** *not* used[j] **then**
7               $c \leftarrow c+1$;
8   **if** $c == d_{n-i-1}+1$ **then**
9               $\pi(i) \leftarrow j$;
10   used[j] = *true*;
11   *break*;

12 **return** π

---

followed by the one designed for *short* parameters. Table 1 provides a breakdown of the compressed permutation sizes within the signature for all PERK parameter sets, and the relative percentage over the whole signature size.

Pack-in-Pairs Permutation Compression. Let $\pi \in \mathcal{S}_n$ be a permutation. Instead of representing π, with the one-line notation, as a list of elements of $[n]$, one packs its elements in pairs and represents it as a sequence of $\lceil n/2 \rceil$ elements in $[n^2]$. This is possible when

$$\lceil \log_2(n^2) \rceil \leq 2 \lceil \log_2(n) \rceil ,$$

which is true for $n \leq 181$, covering all PERK's parameters. More specifically, let us denote by L the list of $\in n \cdot \tau$ coefficients of all permutations to compress. The packing procedure works as follows. Let $A = \lfloor 2^b \rfloor$, where $b = 6.5$ for Level I, $b = 7$ for Level III, and $b = 7.5$ for Level V. For any two consecutive coefficients $L(i)$ and $L(i+1)$ of L, the compact representation cp is set as $cp = A \cdot L(i) + L(i+1)$. Subsequently, the resulting compact representations cp, comprising $2 \cdot b$ bits each, are concatenated and stored as a byte string. The aggregate size of the compressed permutations within the signature, employing these techniques, is $(2 \cdot b) \cdot \frac{n \cdot \tau}{2}$ bits. The unpacking procedure, is done by computing $L(i) = \lfloor \frac{cp}{A} \rfloor$ and $L(i+1) = cp \mod A$.

Optimal Permutation Compression via Ranking. For each permutation, one computes its ranking $r(\pi)$ in lexicographic order. Specifically, the algorithm by Bonet [Bon08] is implemented using the gmp library for multiple-precision computations. In the ranking procedure, the recursive formula from Eq. 3 is used to exploit the fast multiplication times a uint32_t available in gmp. On

Table 1. The fourth column presents the sizes of permutations in bytes as components of the overall signature for all parameter set. The fifth column gives the percentage over the whole signature size covered by compressed permutations.

Parameter Set	n	τ	size of permutations	%
PERK-I-fast3	79	30	1926 B	23.0
PERK-I-fast5	83	28	1889 B	24.0
PERK-I-short3	79	20	980 B	15.7
PERK-I-short5	83	18	936 B	16.2
PERK-III-fast3	112	46	4508 B	24.0
PERK-III-fast5	116	43	4365 B	24.3
PERK-III-short3	112	31	2356 B	16.5
PERK-III-short5	116	28	2240 B	17.0
PERK-V-fast3	146	61	8350 B	25.0
PERK-V-fast5	150	57	8016 B	25.3
PERK-V-short3	146	41	4346 B	17.3
PERK-V-short5	150	37	4070 B	17.7

the other hand, when unranking, the standard unranking subroutine to obtain the factorial base representation (line 3 of Algorithm 2) is used in pair with a look-up table for storing the pre-computed factorials $0!, 1!, \ldots, (n-1)!$. This kind of permutation compression is *optimal*, i.e., each permutation is represented uniquely by the minimum number of bits possible, equal to $\texttt{bitlen}(n!-1)$, the resulting size of compressed permutations in the signature is $\tau \cdot \texttt{bitlen}(n!-1)$ bits.

3 Quasi-optimal Permutation Ranking

A major drawback of compressing permutations through ranking is that it requires performing arithmetic operations between integers of up to $\texttt{bitlen}(n!-1)$ bits. As already mentioned, the sizes of permutations in PERK make the use of a library for multiple-precision integer operations necessary. Consequently, the compression algorithm is relatively slow, and the portability of the implementation is reduced, especially when targeting resource-constrained devices.

This section, presents a *quasi-optimal* ranking approach for permutations that extends the optimal ranking method outlined in Sect. 2.1. Specifically, we map permutations uniquely to a set of integers with a maximum bit-size slightly exceeding $\texttt{bitlen}(n!-1)$. This slight increase in size facilitates the ranking evaluation in one fundamental aspect: all computations are performed using only 32-bit words, eliminating the need for a multiple-precision arithmetic library.

3.1   Quasi-optimal Ranking Routine

Let $\pi \in \mathcal{S}_n$ be a permutation and let $(d_0, d_1, \ldots, d_{n-1})$ be its factorial base representation (see Eq. 1). Let N be the target word-size for our computations (e.g., $N = 32$ bits). The strategy that we follow here consists of dividing $d_0, d_1, \ldots, d_{n-1}$ into ℓ subsequences and considering them as ℓ separate factorial bases such that the corresponding integers are smaller than 2^N.

Let us assume that $n < 2^N$ and let $j_1 < j_2 < \ldots < j_\ell$ be the largest integers possible such that

$$j_0 = 0, \quad \frac{j_k!}{j_{k-1}!} < 2^N, \quad j_\ell = n, \quad \text{for every } k = 1, \ldots, \ell. \tag{4}$$

Define the following integers

$$s_k = \sum_{i=j_{k-1}}^{j_k - 1} d_i \cdot \frac{i!}{j_{k-1}!}, \quad k = 1, \ldots, \ell. \tag{5}$$

Equivalently, analogously to Eq. 3, the following recursive formula holds:

$$s_k = d_{j_{k-1}} + (j_{k-1} + 1) \cdot (d_{j_{k-1}+1} + \cdots + (j_k - 2) \cdot (d_{j_k-2} + (j_k - 1) \cdot d_{j_k-1}) \cdots).$$

Notice that $s_k \le j_k!/j_{k-1}! - 1$, an so $s_k < 2^N$ for every $k = 1, \ldots, \ell$. Let

$$M = \sum_{k=1}^{\ell} \texttt{bitlen}\left(\frac{j_k!}{j_{k-1}!} - 1\right),$$

and define the following function

$$s : \mathcal{S}_n \to \{0, 1\}^M, \quad s(\pi) \mapsto (s_1 \| s_2 \| \cdots \| s_\ell).$$

The image of $s()$ is as follows

$$\mathrm{Im}(s) = \{s(\pi) : \forall \pi \in \mathcal{S}_n\} = \{(x_1 \| x_2 \| \cdots \| x_\ell) : x_k \le j_k!/j_{k-1}!\} \subset \{0, 1\}^M.$$

To determine whether an element x of $\{0, 1\}^M$ is in the image of $s()$, one should check whether its dissections x_i are within the corresponding bound. In particular, one can see that $\mathcal{S}_n$ is bijective to $\mathrm{Im}(s)$ via $s()$. Indeed, if two permutations π_1, π_2 are mapped to the same element in $\mathrm{Im}(s)$, then they must have the same factorial base representation, meaning that $\pi_1 = \pi_2$.

Our compression method represents the permutation π as $s(\pi)$, and is displayed as Algorithm 3. In general, the bit size of the compression M is (slightly) larger than $\log_2(n!)$, the size obtained with the compression via ranking. However, since every s_k is bounded by 2^N, each one of them can be computed using only N-bit size registers. Choosing $N = 16$, 32, or 64 allows compressing permutations of a certain length without requiring a multiple-precision arithmetic library. In practice, to produce a code portable to several different architectures; in this work, we consider $N = 32$.

Algorithm 3: Quasi-optimal ranking of a permutation

Input: permutation $\pi \in S_n$; j_k as in Eq. 4
Output: Rank $0 \leq r(\pi) < 2^M$

1 **for** $i \leftarrow 0, \ldots, n-1$ **do**
2 | **for** $j \leftarrow i+1, \ldots, n-1$ **do**
3 | | **if** $\pi(i) < \pi(j)$ **then**
4 | | | $d[i] \leftarrow d[i] + 1$;

5 **for** $k \leftarrow 0, \ldots, \ell - 1$ **do**
6 | $s[k] \leftarrow 0$;   `// Equation 5`
7 | **for** $i \leftarrow j_{k+1} - 1, \ldots, j_k$ **do**
8 | | $s[k] \leftarrow s[k] \cdot i + d[i]$;

9 $R \leftarrow s[0] \parallel s[1] \parallel \ldots \parallel s[\ell - 1]$;   `// pack compactly`
10 **return** R

3.2   Quasi-optimal Unranking Routine

To invert the quasi-optimal ranking procedure detailed in Sect. 3.1, one first must obtain the factorial representation $d_1, \ldots, d_{n-1}$ of the permutation π, as follows.

$$d_{j_{k-1}+j_k-i-1} = \left\lfloor \frac{s_k \mod (i+1)!/(j_{k-1})!}{i!/(j_{k-1})!} \right\rfloor, \quad \text{for } i = j_{k-1}, \ldots, j_k - 1, \quad (6)$$

for $k = 1 \ldots, \ell$. Then, one obtains the one-line permutation representation from the factorial representation using, for example, the sub-routine line 4–11 of Algorithm 2, or Bonet unranking algorithm [Bon08, Figure 4]. We display this idea as Algorithm 4.

An additional advantage of our proposed method, when compared to optimal ranking, lies in its facilitation of vectorization (SIMD instructions) in both ranking and unranking processes. This is made possible by utilizing 32-bit registers only for all computations.

3.3   Further Improvements

One can obtain some further improvements in size thanks to the following idea. Let us consider the factorial

$$n! = 1 \cdot 2 \cdots (n-1) \cdot n.$$

Then we have that

$$\log_2(n!) = \log_2(1) + \log_2(2) + \cdots + \log_2(n-1) + \log_2(n).$$

Following the approach outlined in Sect. 3.1, one could pack such number as follows

$$\underbrace{1 \cdot 2 \cdots (j_1 - 1)}_{s_1} \cdot \underbrace{j_1 \cdots (j_2 - 1)}_{s_2} \cdots \underbrace{j_{\ell-1} \cdots n}_{s_\ell},$$

Algorithm 4: Quasi-optimal unranking of a permutation

Input: rank $R = s[0] \parallel s[1] \parallel \ldots \parallel s[\ell - 1]$ $(0 \le R < 2^M)$
Output: permutation $\pi \in \mathcal{S}_n$

1   **for** $k \leftarrow 0, \ldots, \ell - 1$ **do**
2   **for** $i \leftarrow j_k + 1, \ldots, j_{k+1}$ **do**
3       $d[n - 1 - i] \leftarrow s[k] \bmod i$;   // Equation 6
4       $s[k] \leftarrow \lfloor s[k]/i \rfloor$;

5   **for** $i \leftarrow 0, \ldots, n - 1$ **do**
6     $c \leftarrow 0$;
7   **for** $j \leftarrow 0, \ldots, n - 1$ **do**
8   **if** *not* used$[j]$ **then**
9         $c \leftarrow c + 1$;
10   **if** $c == d[n - i - 1] + 1$ **then**
11         $\pi(i) \leftarrow j$;
12   used$[j] = true$;
13   *break;*

14 **return** π

---

and so one has that

$$\texttt{bitlen}(n!) \le \texttt{bitlen}(s_1) + \texttt{bitlen}(s_2) + \cdots + \texttt{bitlen}(s_\ell). \tag{7}$$

However, such an attempt to maximize $s_1, s_2, \ldots, s_\ell$ (subject to $\texttt{bitlen}(s_k) < N$) in this order is unlikely to result in a minimal packing. Instead, we propose using the well-known A* search algorithm [RN09][Sec. 3]. Given the small size of n in the cases of our interest, and using the bit-size of the remaining factors to be packed as the heuristic in the A* search algorithm (which is easily seen to be admissible), a packing of the factors that minimizes the overall size can be quickly found. Nevertheless, we choose to introduce additional constraints that lead to a faster implementation when using vectorization (and specifically the AVX2 instruction set):

- the number of words is chosen as either 16, 24, or 32 depending on n, which is a multiple of 8 (the 256-bit vector length of AVX2 divided by $N = 32$);
- we bound the minimum and maximum number of indexes per word and introduce heuristic penalties to seek a balanced distribution between words, especially within the natural 8-lane boundaries of AVX2.

A further generalization of this concept would be to dispense with the requirement of consecutive indexes within each word. This would immensely increase the search space, making it likely that packings that are either optimal or within very few bits of it are found; however, non-consecutive indexes would also complicate the implementation, and thus, we chose not to pursue this idea.

Example 1. Let us compute the compression size of a permutation π of length $n = 79$, as in PERK-I-fast3 and PERK-I-short3. We choose the word length of $N = 32$ bits. In Table 2, we report the values for the indexes j_k and the size in bits for each s_k, for $k = 1, \ldots, 78$. The total size in bits of our quasi-optimal ranking is $M = \mathtt{bitlen}(s(\pi)) = 394$. Note that the size in bits of the optimal ranking is $\mathtt{bitlen}(r(\pi)) = 389$. Therefore, our compression is only 5 bits larger than the compression via optimal ranking, a small price to pay ($\approx 1.3\%$) for the benefit of being able to perform all computations more efficiently using 32-bit registers only.

Table 2. Quasi-optimal permutation compression parameters and sizes for $n = 79$ and $N = 32$. Note that $d_0 = 0$ always, hence there is no need to encode it.

k	factorial base subsequence	j_k	$\mathtt{bitlen}(s_k)$
1	d_1, d_2, d_3, d_4, d_5	6	10
2	$d_6, d_7, d_8, d_9, d_{10}$	11	16
3	$d_{11}, d_{12}, d_{13}, d_{14}$	15	15
4	$d_{15}, d_{16}, d_{17}, d_{18}, d_{19}$	20	21
5	$d_{20}, d_{21}, d_{22}, d_{23}$	24	18
6	$d_{24}, d_{25}, d_{26}, d_{27}, d_{28}$	29	24
7	$d_{29}, d_{30}, d_{31}, d_{32}, d_{33}$	34	25
8	$d_{34}, d_{35}, d_{36}, d_{37}, d_{38}$	39	27
9	$d_{39}, d_{40}, d_{41}, d_{42}, d_{43}$	44	27
10	$d_{44}, d_{45}, d_{46}, d_{47}, d_{48}$	49	28
11	$d_{49}, d_{50}, d_{51}, d_{52}, d_{53}$	54	29
12	$d_{54}, d_{55}, d_{56}, d_{57}, d_{58}$	59	30
13	$d_{59}, d_{60}, d_{61}, d_{62}, d_{63}$	64	30
14	$d_{64}, d_{65}, d_{66}, d_{67}, d_{68}$	69	31
15	$d_{69}, d_{70}, d_{71}, d_{72}, d_{73}$	74	31
16	$d_{74}, d_{75}, d_{76}, d_{77}, d_{78}$	79	32
Total			394

3.4   Comparison

We report in Table 3 the comparison of our sub-optimal permutation against the other two methods used in PERK, for the relevant values of n. One can see that our method gives compression sizes very close to *optimal*, while beating significantly *pack-in-pairs*.

Table 3. Amount in *bits* required to compress a permutation. The second and third columns are the values resulting in PERK's *fast* and *short* parameter sets respectively. The last column represent the values of our novel compression method.

n	pack-in-pairs	optimal ranking	sub-optimal ranking
79	514	389	394
83	540	414	421
112	784	606	615
116	812	633	643
146	1095	845	860
150	1125	873	889

4   Experiments and Applications to PERK

In this section, we give the details regarding the C implementation of our algorithm, the results of our benchmark tests, and the impact of our work on PERK signature both computationally and on the signature size. To start, we describe our testing environment.

4.1   Testing Environment

We preformed all experiments presented in this section on a machine with 96GB of memory and an Intel® Core™ i7-13700K CPU @ 3.40 GHz. As a compiler, we used clang (version 17.0.2), and the version of the GMP multiple-precision library installed on the machine is 6.3.0. Especially when testing the integration of our algorithms on the full PERK scheme, we expect the impact to be relatively small and hard to detect if the testing environment is not adequately set. Hence, we took the following countermeasure to reduce possible noise in benchmarks, not only due to hardware and OS factors but also because of issues such as code and data layout [MDHS09], as this noise is of similar magnitude to the improvements we are trying to measure on full scheme benchmarks.

On the hardware and OS side, we disabled HyperThreading and TurboBoost CPU features, installed Ubuntu's low-latency Linux kernel, set the scaling governor to performance mode, isolated a CPU and pinned our benchmarks to run on it while masking interrupts to avoid running on that CPU, used Linux's NOHZ feature to reduce tick interrupts and disabled address space layout randomization. Before running the benchmarks, we turned off WiFi and Bluetooth and removed the Ethernet cable. The machine is placed in a temperature-controlled room, and its cooling system is adequate to ensure clock speed is not throttled.

On the software side, we employed a feature of the lld link, which randomizes the order of functions in the binary, one of the factors explicitly pointed out by [MDHS09]. We also renamed the binary before each run with a differently-sized name (varying this over a range of 64 consecutive sizes), which has the effect of realigning the stack memory for the process, another effect discussed by [MDHS09]. We set code alignment to 64 bytes to match the cache line size of the CPU. We ran each test with 8 different randomized linking orders and 64 consecutive alignments; for the full-scheme benchmarks, each routine was run 12 times, discarding the first 2 results, which serve as a warm-up for the CPU's branch predictor and its caches.

We also perform a statistical hypothesis test (Student's independent two sample t-test) to determine whether speedups/slowdowns between the baseline and our proposed implementation are statistically significant at the $p = 0.05$ level.

4.2 Implementation of Our Compression/Decompression Algorithms

We implemented the compression and decompression algorithms presented in Sect. 3 in pure C without any external library dependency. In addition, we have developed an AVX2-optimized implementation, the details of which are provided below in this section. The code is available under an open-source license at https://github.com/marco-palumbi/quasi-optimal_ranking.

We report in Table 4 the results of our experiment that compares the quasi-optimal ranking implementation against the compression from PERK version 1.1. To do so, we imported the compression and decompression algorithms from the official repository of PERK [ABB+23b]. The code has been compiled with compilation flags `-O3 -funroll-loops -march=native -mavx2` to make the comparison fair against our AVX2 implementation, and to highlight that this achieves vectorizations undetected by the compiler. Looking at Table 4, the first consideration is that our approach is always considerably faster than the optimal ranking method. Then, one can notice that, due to its simplicity, *pack-in-pairs* is still the fastest compression method in general. The pack-in-pairs implementation displays non-linear scaling for compression and decompression for the cases $n = 112, 116$, and as such, our AVX2 compression implementation is actually faster in these cases. The reason for such scaling is unclear, but may be related to code alignment issues or compiler heuristics not being satisfied for these particular values. For the other cases, our AVX2 implementation gives timings quite close to *pack-in-pairs* while providing much shorter compression sizes. Finally, our AVX2 code gives a speed-up against our pure C implementation of 5.6–6.9× in compression and 9.6–13.3× in decompression.

Details of Our AVX2 Optimization. At a high level, our AVX2 implementation is a straightforward translation of the C code, exploiting the considerable parallelization opportunities presented by the algorithm itself within a single compression or decompression. We wrote *compact* and manually *unrolled* versions of the code, but as the latter performed consistently better, we choose to present performance results only for it.

We employ vectors with 8 elements of 32 bits each for ranking and unranking. Referring to the example of Table 2, we operate first on $k = 1, \ldots, 8$, processing each "column" in sequence, and then $k = 9, \ldots, 16$. As can be seen, our A* search strategy ensures that vectors are fully utilized due to the choice of the number of words as 16, 24, or 32 depending on n. On the other hand, since, in general, $8 \nmid n$, it is inevitable that there will be some gaps in the distribution of indices, as seen in the cases $k = 3$ and 5 in Table 2. In these cases, we still process the full vector (therefore using invalid data for the gaps) but use the AVX2 `blend` instruction to choose whether to include the result (in the example, for the cases $k = 1, 2, 4, 6, 7, 8$) or not (for $k = 3$ and 5).

We note that the loads in the ranking algorithm map well to the `gather` instructions of AVX2, whereas the stores in the unranking algorithm are a clear use case for `scatter` instructions, which, unfortunately, are unavailable on AVX2, only AVX-512. Thus, we expect that an AVX-512 implementation of decompression could perform even better.

For computing the factorial representation, we employ vectors with 32 elements of 8 bits each, which is sufficient as $n \leq 150$. For the first iteration of the algorithm, the number of vectors required varies from $\lceil 79/32 \rceil = 3$ to $\lceil 150/32 \rceil = 5$ across PERK parameter sets. This number decreases as the algorithm restricts itself to progressively shorter ranges of the full array of indexes. We ensure that computations are performed only on the minimum number of vectors required at each iteration. If the length of the current range is k, then we use $\lfloor k/32 \rfloor$ full vectors and a partially masked vector, using only $k \bmod 32$ out of the 32 available lanes. As with ranking and unranking, we still process the entire vector and conditionally select only the lanes performing useful work, this time using masks and the bitwise AND operator.

We expect that a batched implementation, compressing or decompressing multiple permutations at once, opens up possibilities for further instruction-level parallelism and better utilization of 32-byte vectors for computing the factorial representation. This should lead to more considerable speedups in exchange for more complex code. We leave such an investigation to future work.

4.3   On the Impact of Our Work on PERK Signature Scheme

To assess the impact of the compression technique presented in Sect. 3 to PERK [ABB+23b], we have integrated it into PERK's official implementation and conducted experiments. In order to not introduce any vulnerability to PERK, we included in our decompression algorithm (Algorithm 4) a check that each $s[k] \leq \frac{j_k!}{j_{k-1}!}$, for $k = 1 \cdots, \ell$, to ensure that the compression is bijective and one cannot easily generate another valid signature. If the bound does not hold, the signature gets rejected. Note that constant-time code is not required in our case, as we compress and decompress public data.

We start by reporting in Table 5 a comparison of the signature sizes of PERK when using the compression explained in Sect. 3 compared to PERK version 1.1. One can see that our quasi-optimal ranking increases the signature sizes of PERK by a negligible fraction (never more than 0.25%) for the *short* parameter sets. On the other hand, it always reduces the sizes of PERK's *fast* parameter sets by more than 5%.

Table 4. Comparison in CPU cycles of the compression and decompression routines from PERK version 1.1 and the one introduced in Sect. 3. The results of each parameter set were obtained by computing the mean from $64 \cdot 64 \cdot 10{,}000 = 40{,}960{,}000$ random instances.

n	Pack-in-pairs	Optimal	Quasi-optimal	Quasi-optimal AVX2
Compression				
79	309	11307	2606	411
83	330	11995	2792	419
112	887	17775	4271	623
116	920	18582	4508	649
146	652	25772	6172	1086
150	694	26552	6408	1130
Decompression				
79	280	30586	7172	743
83	292	33048	7838	773
112	824	54572	13219	1104
116	873	58013	14101	1140
146	601	89232	21226	1670
150	606	93817	22902	1718

In Tables 6 and 7, we present the CPU-cycle performance on the aforementioned benchmark platform when utilizing various compression methods for each parameter set of PERK across both reference and optimized (AVX2) implementations. For the reference version, there are generally small slowdowns for the *fast* parameters and small speedups for the *short* parameters, on the order of <1% for signing and <3% for verification. The optimized version compares better: there are a few slowdowns, most of which are negligible (≤0.35%, with the exception of verification for PERK-V-fast5 at 0.88%). On the other hand, there are speedups for all *short* parameters, and even for some *fast* parameters, of up to 2.9%.

Summarizing the results of Tables 5, 6 and 7, PERK would get the following impact from our compression:

- significantly smaller signature sizes for *fast* parameter sets, for a negligible computational cost increase,
- equivalent signature sizes for the *short* parameter sets, with either equivalent or slightly faster signature and verification algorithms,
- more straightforward and more portable code, free of any dependency from a multiple-precision arithmetic library. In addition, our compression drops the need for any heap-memory allocation required by GMP, which is a critical issue for resource-constrained devices; indeed, the pqm4 project [KKPY24], mirroring best practices in the embedded industry, excludes any implementations that perform dynamic memory allocations.

Table 5. Signature size gain and loss using quasi-optimal ranking for compressing permutations compared to PERK version 1.1 [ABB+23b]. For each row, we write in bold the compression that gives the shortest signatures. The last column reports the gain/loss in percentage of our method against PERK version 1.1.

Parameter Set	PERK v. 1.1 Signature Size	PERK + Section 3 Signature Size	gain/loss %
PERK-I-fast3	8345 B	**7897 B**	−5.37
PERK-I-fast5	8026 B	**7611 B**	−5.17
PERK-I-short3	**6251 B**	6256 B	+0.08
PERK-I-short5	**5780 B**	5792 B	+0.21
PERK-III-fast3	18820 B	**17849 B**	−5.16
PERK-III-fast5	17968 B	**17060 B**	−5.05
PERK-III-short3	**14280 B**	14308 B	+0.20
PERK-III-short5	**13164 B**	13175 B	+0.08
PERK-V-fast3	33339 B	**31547 B**	−5.37
PERK-V-fast5	31664 B	**29983 B**	−5.30
PERK-V-short3	**25141 B**	25203 B	+0.25
PERK-V-short5	**23040 B**	23082 B	+0.18

Table 6. Performance in millions of CPU-cycles of the quasi-optimal ranking for compressing permutations compared to the reference implementation of PERK version 1.1 [ABB+23b]. The results of each parameter set were obtained by computing the mean from $8 \cdot 64 \cdot 10 = 5120$ random instances. Speedups in bold indicate statistically significant results at the $p = 0.05$ significance level.

Parameter set	PERK v. 1.1		PERK + Sec. 3		Speedup	
	Sign	Verify	Sign	Verify	Sign	Verify
I-fast3	20.7	10.2	20.8	10.5	**−0.65%**	**−2.46%**
I-fast5	20.4	9.90	20.5	10.2	**−0.76%**	**−2.81%**
I-short3	111	55.6	110	54.6	**0.53%**	**1.91%**
I-short5	106	52.2	105	51.2	**0.85%**	**1.98%**
III-fast3	49.9	25.2	50.1	25.9	**−0.50%**	**−2.45%**
III-fast5	48.5	24.2	48.8	24.8	**−0.45%**	**−2.48%**
III-short3	268	136	268	135	**0.09%**	**0.68%**
III-short5	252	127	252	125	**0.22%**	**1.51%**
V-fast3	104	54.9	104	55.9	**−0.16%**	**−1.79%**
V-fast5	99.9	52.4	100	53.7	**−0.43%**	**−2.35%**
V-short3	556	297	557	296	**−0.03%**	**0.63%**
V-short5	519	274	517	271	**0.31%**	**1.03%**

One additional benefit is that PERK could use the same compression algorithm (and code) for both *short* and *fast* parameter sets.

Table 7. Performance in millions of CPU-cycles of the AVX2 quasi-optimal ranking for compressing permutations compared to the optimized implementation of PERK version 1.1 [ABB+23b]. The results of each parameter set were obtained by computing the mean from $8 \cdot 64 \cdot 10 = 5120$ random instances. Speedups in bold indicate statistically significant results at the $p = 0.05$ significance level.

Parameter set	PERK v. 1.1		PERK + Section 3		Speedup	
	Sign	Verify	Sign	Verify	Sign	Verify
I-fast3	7.53	5.07	7.53	5.08	−0.02%	−0.22%
I-fast5	7.21	4.91	7.21	4.92	−0.07%	−0.35%
I-short3	39.4	26.9	39.2	26.3	**0.46%**	**2.13%**
I-short5	36.0	24.6	35.8	24.0	**0.56%**	**2.27%**
III-fast3	15.9	12.2	15.8	12.2	**0.57%**	−0.10%
III-fast5	15.4	11.7	15.3	11.7	**0.39%**	−0.06%
III-short3	83.2	65.1	82.6	64.2	**0.75%**	**1.52%**
III-short5	77.4	59.5	76.8	57.8	**0.77%**	**2.90%**
V-fast3	36.4	27.5	36.4	27.8	−0.14%	−0.88%
V-fast5	34.9	26.5	34.5	26.4	**0.99%**	0.40%
V-short3	193	146	192	142	**0.57%**	**2.73%**
V-short5	179	133	178	130	**0.59%**	**2.62%**

5   Conclusions

We introduced a quasi-optimal permutation ranking that, unlike its optimal counterpart, allows it to be computed without using a multiple-precision arithmetic library. This allowed us to define a new permutation compression technique. Our experiments suggest that our technique achieves the best trade-off of efficiency and compression size for the permutation sizes considered in this work. We applied our result to the digital signature PERK, obtaining a considerable improvement in the signature size for the *fast* versions of the scheme and an overall more straightforward and more portable code. Moreover, we expect our code to yield significant improvements in efficiency for implementations of PERK on resource-constrained devices since the GMP library cannot be ported there.

Additionally, we believe that our result might be useful also outside the realm of Cryptography, in applications such as heuristic search, combinatorial optimization and data structure indexing.

References

[ABB+23a] Aaraj, N., et al.: PERK version 1.0. NIST's post-quantum cryptography standardization of additional digital signature schemes project (round 1) (2023). https://pqc-perk.org/

[ABB+23b] Aaraj, N., et al.: PERK version 1.1 (2023). https://pqc-perk.org/resources.html

[Bon08] Bonet, B.: Efficient algorithms to rank and unrank permutations in lexicographic order. In: Workshop on Search in Artificial Intelligence and Robotics - Technical Report (2008)

[fCR20] Chinese Association for Cryptographic Research. National cryptography algorithm design competition (2020). https://www.cacrnet.org.cn/site/content/854.html

[FS87] Fiat, A., Shamir, A.: How to prove yourself: practical solutions to identification and signature problems. In: Odlyzko, A.M. (ed.) CRYPTO 1986. LNCS, vol. 263, pp. 186–194. Springer, Heidelberg (1987). https://doi.org/10.1007/3-540-47721-7_12

[IKOS07] Ishai, Y., Kushilevitz, E., Ostrovsky, R., Sahai, A.: Zero-knowledge from secure multiparty computation. In: Proceedings of the 39th annual ACM symposium on Theory of computing (STOC) (2007)

[KKPY24] Kannwischer, M.J., Krausz, M., Petri, R., Yang, S.-J.: pqm4: benchmarking NIST additional post-quantum signature schemes on microcontrollers. Cryptology ePrint Archive, Paper 2024/112 (2024). https://eprint.iacr.org/2024/112

[Leh60] Lehmer, D.H.: Teaching combinatorial tricks to a computer. Combin. Anal. 179–193 (1960)

[Leo82] Leon, J.: Computing automorphism groups of error-correcting codes. IEEE Trans. Inf. Theory **28**(3), 496–511 (1982)

[MDHS09] Mytkowicz, T., Diwan, A., Hauswirth, M., Sweeney, P.F.: Producing wrong data without doing anything obviously wrong! ACM Sigplan Not. **44**(3), 265–276 (2009)

[MR01] Myrvold, W., Ruskey, F.: Ranking and unranking permutations in linear time. Inf. Process. Lett. **79**(6), 281–284 (2001)

[NIS17] NIST. Post-quantum cryptography standardization (2017). https://csrc.nist.gov/projects/post-quantum-cryptography

[NIS23] NIST. Post-quantum cryptography: Digital signature schemes (2023). https://csrc.nist.gov/Projects/pqc-dig-sig/round-1-additional-signatures

[Pro23] The GNU Project. GMP: The GNU Multiple Precision Arithmetic Library (2023). https://gmplib.org/. [version 6.2.1]

[RN09] Russell, S., Norvig, P.: Artificial Intelligence: A Modern Approach, 3rd edn. Prentice Hall Press, USA (2009)

[Sha90] Shamir, A.: An efficient identification scheme based on permuted kernels (extended abstract). In: Brassard, G. (ed.) CRYPTO 1989. LNCS, vol. 435, pp. 606–609. Springer, New York (1990). https://doi.org/10.1007/0-387-34805-0_54

Advanced Primitives (I)

CDLS: Proving Knowledge of Committed Discrete Logarithms with Soundness

Sofia Celi[1]([⊠]) [iD], Shai Levin[2] [iD], and Joe Rowell[3]

[1] Brave Software, Lisbon, Portugal
cherenkov@riseup.net
[2] University of Auckland, Auckland, New Zealand
shai.levin@auckland.ac.nz
[3] Royal Holloway, University of London, Egham, UK
Joe.Rowell.2015@live.rhul.ac.uk

Abstract. The works of CRYPTO '18 [1] and SAC '21 [15] exist in the Σ-protocol setting in order to prove knowledge that a commitment to a scalar is the discrete logarithm of the commitment to an elliptic curve point. While the former, original work [1] is inadequately specified so that detailed analysis can be performed, we show that the latter follow up work, the Σ-protocol of *ZKAttest* [15], suffers from soundness issues that invalidate its security proof. Further, we also provide a practical attack on *ZKAttest*'s public implementation, and point out other flaws in it that differ from the paper's specification. Lastly, we introduce two new protocols, **CDLSS** and **CDLSD**, which are sound, provably secure, have concrete security bounds, and perform favourably in comparison to the prior works when the soundness issue is taken into account.

Keywords: Sigma-protocols · Zero-Knowledge · PoK · Elliptic-Curves

1 Introduction

Non-interactive zero knowledge proofs of knowledge (NIZKPoK) [4] are protocols that allow provers to convince verifiers, in a non-interactive setting, that they possess knowledge of a secret witness for a decisional statement without directly revealing such a witness. The paradigm allows for the construction of secure identification protocols and signature schemes.

In 1999, Nguyen *et al.* [23] proposed the first general construction of zero-knowledge "proofs of possession" for digital signatures. In their proposal, they construct a NIZKPoK which convinces a verifier that a prover possesses a valid signature for a given message and public key. Their construction is realised in the discrete logarithm setting over the group $\mathbb{Z}_p^\times$ by proving that the openings to a commitment to a secret exponent α and a commitment to the representation of a group element h satisfy the relation $h = g^\alpha$. The proof of Nguyen *et al.*, however, applies only to the group $\mathbb{Z}_p^\times$, and does not extend to arbitrary groups, such as, in particular, the groups of points of an elliptic curve.

S. Vaudenay and C. Petit (Eds.): AFRICACRYPT 2024, LNCS 14861, pp. 69–93, 2024.
https://doi.org/10.1007/978-3-031-64381-1_4

In order to extend the idea to the elliptic curve group setting, one considers the following problem: given a public base point P, a commitment to a secret coefficient α, and a commitment to the affine coordinates of the elliptic curve point αP, prove, non-interactively, that the committed value of α is the discrete logarithm (to the base P) of the commitments to αP.

In CRYPTO'18, Agrawal *et al.* [1, Fig. 2] introduced a protocol, ddlog, for this setting which works using a composition of Σ-protocols techniques (seen in [9]) and range proofs (seen in [5,7,8]). Internally, they also use an inner 'Proof of Knowledge of the Sum' which proves that the commitments of three elliptic curve points satisfy an additive relation. However, the protocol included in [1] is inadequately described. In particular, it is not clear how they obtain a challenge for the internal proof of knowledge of the sum, as this is either done non-interactively or the challenge is obtained in an additional round (making it a 5 round protocol). Note that neither of these solutions yields a Σ-protocol. In this work, we avoid further analysis of ddlog due to the lack of clarity in its description, but we focus on follow-up work building on top of it.

Follow-up work, published in the proceedings of SAC'21 [15], proposed *ZKAttest* (which we describe in Sect. 3.1), which resolves the prior presented ambiguity in description by clearly stipulating how the inner challenges are obtained (in the verifier's challenge phase of a three round protocol). Beyond this, they also modify the previous underlying commitment scheme to improve efficiency, and include an additional verification check with the aim of fixing the original proof of security. However, we show that their protocol's proof of security is flawed, and their protocol is, hence, not sound.

In order to prove a Σ-protocol is *knowledge sound*, or a "Proof of Knowledge" (PoK), one relies on proving the 2-special-soundness (or n-special soundness) property. That is, given two (or n) transcripts with identical first rounds and different challenges, one can efficiently recover a witness for the instance. The knowledge error of a Σ-protocol is dependent on the number of transcripts needed to extract a witness and the size of the challenge set, but can be boosted through parallel composition of protocol instances. We show that the Σ-protocol of *ZKAttest* does not satisfy *special-soundness* (or n-special soundness for any reasonable n). In particular, a witness cannot be extracted for all possible pairs of transcripts with distinct challenges. Moreover, the authors make an ad-hoc choice, for efficiency reasons, of only performing verification on a random subset of the parallel repetitions of their protocol, which leads to a practical attack on their implementation, described in detail in Sect. 3.2.

Unfortunately, it is difficult to comment on the soundness issues that may or may not be present in the protocol of [1]: it is likely to suffer from the same issue of an inadequete special soundness extractor that *ZKAttest* suffers. As such, this protocol should be considered with caution.

Contributions. We contribute the following results in our work:

- We show that the extractor used in the proof of special soundness of *ZKAttest*'s proof of committed discrete logarithm [15] does not extract a witness for all possible colliding transcript pairs. As a consequence, the protocol is not knowledge sound, and hence there is no guarantees about the unforgeability of accepting proofs.

- We show that *ZKAttest*'s choice of only performing verification on a random subset of 20 out of the 128 repetitions, as performed in their implementation, leads to a practical and "cheap" forgery attack.
- We propose an optimized and sound Σ-protocol for 'Proof of Knowledge of the Sum', CDLSS, which proves an additive relation between the commitments to the coordinates of three elliptic curve points. This protocol can be internally used by any proof of committed discrete logarithm.
- We introduce a new Σ-protocol for proving knowledge of a committed discrete logarithm, CDLSD, which is provably perfectly complete, 2-special sound and statistically honest-verifier zero-knowledge. By doing this, we resolve the soundness misdesign of prior works. Performing λ repetitions of the protocol and applying the Fiat-Shamir transform, yields a NIZKPoK for committed discrete logarithms with knowledge error $2^{-\lambda}$ and statistical zero-knowledge.
- We provide an efficient, open-source Rust implementation for our scheme and our interpretation of *ZKAttest*, with benchmarks comparing their performance. Aside from resolving security issues, our implementation yields an order of magnitude improvement to performance when compared to the Typescript implementation of *ZKAttest* [15].

2 Preliminaries

2.1 Notation and General Definitions

As a small note first, in this section, we refer to group operations multiplicatively, but due to the concrete instantiation of groups as elliptic curves, we opt to refer to group operations additively in the sections after this one.

We refer to the set $\{1,\ldots,n\}$ as $[n]$. We denote negligible functions in a security parameter λ as $\mathsf{negl}(\lambda)$. We use the standard Landau notation $O(\cdot)$ for asymptotics and we use $\tilde{O}(n)$, which hides logarithmic factors in the parameter n. For any $q \in \mathbb{Z}$, $\mathbb{Z}_q = \mathbb{Z}/q\mathbb{Z}$ denotes the ring of integers modulo q. We refer to a prover as $\mathcal{P}$ and a verifier as $\mathcal{V}$, which are probabilistic polynomial time machines (PPTs); to a polynomial-time simulator as Sim and to polynomial-time algorithm extractor as Ext. We say that two probability ensembles (X_n, Y_n), which are families of distributions over a finite set of size n, are:

- *perfectly indistinguishable*, written as $X_n \equiv Y_n$, if they are identically distributed.
- *statistically indistinguishable*, with negligible advantage ϵ, if for any computationally unbounded distinguisher D,

$$\left| \Pr[D(X_n) = 1] - \Pr[D(Y_n) = 1] \right| \leq \epsilon(n)$$

which is written as $X_n \overset{s}{\equiv} Y_n$.

2.2 NP Relations and Proofs of Knowledge

The concept of proof of knowledge (PoK) was initially formalised by Feige, Fiat and Shamir [16,18]. The construction allows for $\mathcal{P}$ to convince $\mathcal{V}$ that they know a witness, w, which is computationally related to a common input, x. That is, given an NP language $\mathcal{L}$, w allows a decision algorithm to determine if $x \in \mathcal{L}$ in a polynomial number of steps. We define the relation of instance-witness pairs for a given language as a set $\mathcal{R}$. Loosely, a proof of knowledge with *knowledge error* κ has probability $\kappa(\lambda)$ of a cheating $\mathcal{P}$ successfully convincing $\mathcal{V}$ that $x \in \mathcal{L}$ without knowing the corresponding w. The correlated language $\mathcal{L}(\mathcal{R})$ is the set of all x such that there exists a w, where $(x, w) \in \mathcal{R}$. Fiat and Shamir [18] showed that one can transform a 3-round interactive PoK into a non-interactive one, preserving knowledge soundness.

2.3 Sigma Protocols

A Sigma protocol (Σ-protocol) is a three-move protocol between two parties: $\mathcal{P}$ and $\mathcal{V}$. Σ-protocols are Arthur-Merlin protocols [3], which means that $\mathcal{V}$'s randomness is public. We give a brief description below, but for more details, see [14,21,22].

Given a common input, where both $\mathcal{P}$ and $\mathcal{V}$ have x, and $\mathcal{P}$ has a value w (the witness) such that $(x, w) \in \mathcal{R}$, a Σ-protocol for a relation $\mathcal{R}$ works as follows:

Round 1 (Commit): $\mathcal{P}$ sends a message Comm to $\mathcal{V}$.
Round 2 (Challenge): On receiving Comm, $\mathcal{V}$ sends a random t-bit string Chall.
Round 3 (Response): $\mathcal{P}$ receives the challenge and sends a reply Resp to $\mathcal{V}$.
Verification: At the end of the interaction, $\mathcal{V}$ receives Resp and decides to accept or reject based solely on seen data: (Comm, Chall, Resp). $\mathcal{V}$ outputs 1 if it accepts; otherwise, 0.

We assume that $\mathcal{P}$'s only advantage over $\mathcal{V}$ is that they know the private witness w. We stress that the parties use independent randomness for generating their messages in every execution. Given this, Σ-protocols must satisfy the following properties:

Completeness. If $(x, w) \in \mathcal{R}$, and $\mathcal{P}$ and $\mathcal{V}$ follow the protocol honestly, on common input x and $\mathcal{P}$'s private input w, then $\mathcal{V}$ accepts with probability 1.

Special Honest Verifier Zero-Knowledge (HVZK). When given a statement x and a challenge, Sim outputs a valid transcript (Comm, Chall, Resp) that is (perfectly) indistinguishable from a real transcript (with the same probability distribution as those between an honest $\mathcal{P}$ and a honest $\mathcal{V}$ on common input x). Note that the challenge being randomly sampled implies that $\mathcal{V}$ behaves honestly. If Sim's output distribution is only statistically indistinguishable with advantage ϵ from the real transcript distribution, the protocol is said to be *statistically* HVZK with advantage ϵ.

Special Soundness. When given any x and any pair of accepting distinct transcripts $[(\mathsf{Comm}, \mathsf{Chall}, \mathsf{Resp}), (\mathsf{Comm}, \mathsf{Chall}', \mathsf{Resp}')]$ for x, where $\mathsf{Chall} \neq \mathsf{Chall}'$, Ext outputs w so that $(x, w) \in \mathcal{R}$.

Special soundness [12] is restricted to the case where *two* colliding transcripts are necessary and sufficient for extracting w. However, this property can be relaxed to "n-special soundness", where Ext needs $n > 2$ colliding transcripts to extract w. We state this relaxed definition below.

n-Special Soundness [2, Defn. 7]. When given a statement x and n valid distinct transcripts $[(\mathsf{Comm}_i, \mathsf{Chall}_i, \mathsf{Resp}_i)_{i \in [n]}]$ where $\mathsf{Comm}_i = \mathsf{Comm}_j$ (with a common first message), $\mathsf{Chall}_i \neq \mathsf{Chall}_j$ for all $1 \leq i < j \leq n$, Ext outputs w such that $(x, w) \in \mathcal{R}$. An n-special sound Σ-protocol with a t-bit challenge space has knowledge error $\frac{n-1}{2^t}$ [2, Eqn. 1]. It is known that n-special-soundness for Σ-protocols implies knowledge soundness and thus renders PoKs.

The stated properties of Σ-protocols hold under parallel repetition, where the parties run the same protocol multiple times with the same input in parallel. Given a Σ-protocol with challenge length t, $\mathcal{V}$ samples a random challenge of length rt where r is the number of repetitions. $\mathcal{P}$ replies to each repetition using a different t-bit challenge. $\mathcal{V}$ accepts all iff it accepts in each repetition. Σ-protocols are also invariant under AND-composition. Given two Σ-protocols for different relations, by running parallel executions of the two protocols under the same challenge, one obtains a Σ-protocol for product relation. Furthermore, given a Σ-protocol with challenge length t, one can construct a Σ-protocol for the same relation, with challenge length s for all $s \leq t$, by restricting the challenge space to a subset of the original challenge space of size 2^s [14, Lemma 2].

As briefly touched upon, the Fiat-Shamir transform [18] allows for converting a interactive Σ-protocol into a non-interactive one by replacing $\mathcal{V}$'s challenges with the output of a random oracle query on the protocol transcript. In the random oracle model (ROM), the transformation preserves knowledge soundness and the protocol is perfect (resp. statistical) Zero-Knowledge (ZK) if the underlying Σ-protocol is perfect (resp. statistical) HVZK.

2.4 Commitment Schemes

We assume the reader is familiar with the definitions of commitment schemes, Comm, but we remind them of two important properties of variants of them:

Computationally Binding. Comm is computationally binding if for all PPT adversary's $\mathcal{A}$, $\Pr[(x \neq x') \land (\mathsf{Comm}(x, r) = \mathsf{Comm}(x', r')) \mid (x, x', r, r') \leftarrow \mathcal{A}] \leq \mathsf{negl}(\lambda)$, where λ is the security parameter of the commitment scheme.

Perfectly Hiding. A commitment scheme Comm is perfectly hiding if for all distinct messages (x, x'), $\{\mathsf{Comm}(x, R)\} \equiv \{\mathsf{Comm}(x', R)\}$, where R is the uniform distribution on the randomness set sampled for the commitments.

Pedersen Commitments (PC) [24]. Let (g, h) be generators of some group $\mathbb{G}$ of order q and let α be a secret value. We denote a *Pedersen commitment* to α with randomness r as $C = \text{Com}_q(\alpha, r) = g^\alpha h^r$. In settings where it is convenient to ignore the random value r, we shall simply omit it and write $C = \text{Com}_q(\alpha)$. Pedersen commitments are perfectly hiding, additively homomorphic and computationally binding assuming the hardness of the underlying group's discrete logarithm problem [24], and that the discrete logarithm of h with respect to g (and vice versa) is unknown.

2.5 Σ-Protocols for Proving Arithmetic Relations Between PCs

The heart of many PoK constructions rely on Σ-protocols proving arithmetic relations between different PC. Related protocols (e.g. Schnorr [25], Chaum-Pedersen [11] and Fujisaki-Okamoto [19]) can be used to construct the schemes. In this paper, we use the proofs of [27, App. A] due to their efficiency, and we formalise Construction 2.4, which is folklore.

Proving Knowledge of an Opening of a PC. Given commitment C to a message x with randomness r, $\mathcal{P}$ may convince $\mathcal{V}$ that they possess knowledge of x and r by engaging in the following Construction 2.1.

Construction 2.1: Opening Proof(C)

Public parameters: $g, h \in \mathbb{G}$ where $\text{ord}(g) = \text{ord}(h) = q$ for a prime q.
Inputs: C such that $C = g^x h^r$, and $\mathcal{P}$ knows $x, r \in \mathbb{Z}_q$.

1. $\mathcal{P}$ samples $\alpha_1, \alpha_2 \leftarrow\$\ [q-1]$ and sends $t \leftarrow g^{\alpha_1} h^{\alpha_2}$.
2. $\mathcal{V}$ sends challenge $c \leftarrow\$\ [q-1]$.
3. $\mathcal{P}$ sends $s_1 \leftarrow xc + \alpha_1$ and $s_2 \leftarrow rc + \alpha_2$.
4. $\mathcal{V}$ verifies that $g^{s_1} h^{s_2} = C^c t$.

Theorem 1. *Construction 2.1 is a Σ-protocol for the relation:*

$$\mathcal{R} = \{((C, g, h, q), (x, r)) \mid C = g^x h^r\}.$$

Proof. It follows from [25].

Proving Equality of PCs Under the Same Base. The proof works to attest the equality of PCs under the same base group elements. Given commitments (C_1, C_2) to the same message x under different randomness (r_1, r_2), $\mathcal{P}$ may convince $\mathcal{V}$ of this fact by engaging in Construction 2.2. We do not apply this construction in our schemes, including it to account for existing works. Observe that if C_1 and C_2 do not open to the same message, there is still a satisfying witness to the relation in Theorem 2. Taking advantage of it, however, requires a malicious $\mathcal{P}$ to solve a discrete logarithm of $C_1 C_2^{-1}$ to the base h, which is computationally infeasible.

Construction 2.2: EqualityProof(C_1, C_2)

Public parameters: $g, h \in \mathbb{G}$ where $\text{ord}(g) = \text{ord}(h) = q$ for a prime q.
Inputs: (C_1, C_2) such that $C_1 = g^x h^{r_1}$, $C_2 = g^x h^{r_2}$, and $\mathcal{P}$ knows $z \in \mathbb{Z}_q$ such that $z = r_1 - r_2$.

1. $\mathcal{P}$ samples $\alpha \leftarrow_\$ [q - 1]$ and sends $t \leftarrow h^\alpha$.
2. $\mathcal{V}$ sends challenge $c \leftarrow_\$ [q - 1]$.
3. $\mathcal{P}$ sends $s \leftarrow c(r_1 - r_2) + \alpha$.
4. $\mathcal{V}$ verifies that $h^s \overset{?}{=} t(C_1 C_2^{-1})^c$.

Theorem 2 (Folklore). *Construction 2.2 is a Σ-protocol for the relation:*

$$\mathcal{R} = \{((C_1, C_2, g, h, q), (z)) \mid C_1 C_2^{-1} = h^z\}.$$

Construction 2.3: MulProof(C_1, C_2, C_3)

Public parameters: $g, h \in \mathbb{G}$ where $\text{ord}(g) = \text{ord}(h) = q$ for a prime q.
Inputs: $C_1 = g^x h^{r_1}, C_2 = g^y h^{r_2}, C_3 = g^{xy} h^{r_3}$ where $\mathcal{P}$ knows x, y, r_1, r_2, r_3.

1. $\mathcal{P}$ samples $\alpha_1, \ldots, \alpha_5 \leftarrow_\$ [q - 1]$ and sends

$$t_1 \leftarrow g^{\alpha_1} h^{\alpha_2} \qquad t_2 \leftarrow g^{\alpha_3} h^{\alpha_4} \qquad t_3 \leftarrow C_1^{\alpha_3} h^{\alpha_5}$$

2. $\mathcal{V}$ sends challenge $c \leftarrow_\$ [q - 1]$
3. $\mathcal{P}$ sends response:

$$s_1 \leftarrow \alpha_1 + cx \qquad s_2 \leftarrow \alpha_2 + cr_1 \qquad s_3 \leftarrow \alpha_3 + cy$$
$$s_4 \leftarrow \alpha_4 + cr_2 \qquad s_5 \leftarrow \alpha_5 + c(r_3 - r_1 y)$$

4. $\mathcal{V}$ checks that

$$t_1 C_1^c \overset{?}{=} g^{s_1} h^{s_2} \qquad t_2 C_2^c \overset{?}{=} g^{s_3} h^{s_4} \qquad t_3 C_3^c \overset{?}{=} C_1^{s_3} h^{s_5}$$

Proving Multiplicative Relationships Between Committed Values.
Given $C_1 = Com(x) = g^x h^{r_1}$, $C_2 = Com(y) = g^y h^{r_2}$, $C_3 = Com(z) = g^z h^{r_3}$, $\mathcal{P}$ may engage in Construction 2.3 to convince $\mathcal{V}$ that $z = xy$.

Theorem 3. *Construction 2.3 is a Σ-protocol for the relation:*

$$\mathcal{R} = \{((C_1, C_2, C_3, g, h, q), (x, y, r_1, r_2, r_3)) \mid C_1 = g^x h^{r_1}, \ C_2 = g^x h^{r_2}, C_3 = g^{xy} h^{r_3}\}.$$

Proof. It follows from [27, Thm. 10].

Proving PC Opens to a Non-zero Value. Given a commitment $C = Com(x) = g^x h^r$, $\mathcal{P}$ may engage in Construction 2.4 to convince $\mathcal{V}$ that $x \neq 0$.

Construction 2.4: NonZeroProof(C)

Public parameters: Generators $g, h \in \mathbb{G}$ of prime order q.
Inputs: $C = g^x h^r$, $x \neq 0$, where $\mathcal{P}$ knows x, r.

1. $\mathcal{P}$ samples $\alpha_1, \ldots, \alpha_4 \leftarrow\!\!\$ \, [q-1]$ and sends

$$t_1 \leftarrow g^{\alpha_1 x} \qquad\qquad t_2 \leftarrow C^{\alpha_2} h^{\alpha_3} \qquad\qquad t_3 \leftarrow g^{\alpha_4}$$

2. $\mathcal{V}$ sends challenge $c \leftarrow\!\!\$ \, [q-1]$
3. $\mathcal{P}$ sends response:

$$s_1 \leftarrow \alpha_2 + c\alpha_1 \qquad s_2 \leftarrow \alpha_3 - c\alpha_1 r \qquad s_3 \leftarrow \alpha_4 + c\alpha_1 x$$

4. $\mathcal{V}$ checks that

$$t_1 \neq 1 \qquad\qquad t_1^c t_3 \overset{?}{=} g^{s_3} \qquad\qquad t_1^c t_2 \overset{?}{=} C^{s_1} h^{s_2}$$

Theorem 4. *Construction 2.4 is a Σ protocol for the relation:*

$$\mathcal{R} = \{(C, (x, r)) \mid C = Com(x, r), \ x \neq 0\}.$$

Proof. Completeness. Observe that $x \neq 0 \implies t_1 \neq 1$ and the other verification equations hold. Hence, $\mathcal{V}$ accepts an honest $\mathcal{P}$ with probability 1.

Special Soundness. Suppose $(\mathsf{Comm}, \mathsf{Chall}, \mathsf{Resp})$, $(\mathsf{Comm}', \mathsf{Chall}', \mathsf{Resp}')$ are two accepting transcripts where $\mathsf{Comm} = \mathsf{Comm}'$, and $\mathsf{Chall} \neq \mathsf{Chall}'$. Denote $\mathsf{Resp}, \mathsf{Resp}'$ as (s_1, s_2, s_3) and (s_1', s_2', s_3'), respectively. We define the output of an extractor to be (α_1', x', r') where:

$$\alpha_1' = \frac{s_1 - s_1'}{c - c'} \qquad x' = \alpha_1'^{-1} \frac{s_3 - s_3'}{c - c'} \qquad r' = \alpha_1'^{-1} \frac{s_2' - s_2}{c - c'}$$

We argue x', r' is a valid witness to the relation in Theorem 4. First, given the following equations:

$$t_1^c t_3 = g_3^s \qquad \text{and} \qquad t_1^{c'} t_3 = g^{s_3'}$$

we divide the first by the latter, obtaining

$$t_1^{c-c'} = g^{s_3 - s_3'}$$
$$\implies t_1 = g^{(s_3 - s_3')/(c - c')} \tag{1}$$

which implies that the discrete logarithm of t_1 is $(s_3 - s_3')/(c - c')$. Second, we consider the equations:

$$t_1^c t_2 = C^{s_1} h^{s_2} \qquad \text{and} \qquad t_1^{c'} t_2 = C^{s_1'} h^{s_2'}.$$

By dividing the two equations, we obtain

$$t_1^{c-c'} = C^{s_1 - s_1'} h^{s_2 - s_2'}$$
$$\implies \quad t_1 = C^{\alpha_1'} h^{(s_2 - s_2')/(c-c')}. \tag{2}$$

By Eqs. (1), (2), first we prove that $\alpha_1' \neq 0$ (i.e. s_1, s_1' are distinct). If $\alpha_1' = 0$, then

$$g^{(s_3 - s_3')/(c-c')} = h^{(s_2 - s_2')/(c-c')}$$

Hence, either the discrete logarithm relation between g and h may be recovered, or both $s_2 = s_2'$ and $s_3 = s_3'$. The former case contradicts the hardness assumption, and the latter case implies that $t_1 = 1$, which contradicts the first verification equation. Therefore, it must be the case that $\alpha_1' \neq 0$, and we have the following:

$$C^{\alpha_1'} h^{(s_2 - s_2')/(c-c')} = g^{(s_3 - s_3')/(c-c')}$$
$$\implies \quad C^{\alpha_1'} = g^{(s_3 - s_3')/(c-c')} h^{(s_2' - s_2)/(c-c')}$$
$$\implies \quad C = g^{\alpha_1'^{-1}(s_3 - s_3')/(c-c')} h^{\alpha_1'^{-1}(s_2' - s_2)/(c-c')}$$
$$\implies \quad C = g^{x'} h^{r'}.$$

Last, we show that if $x' = 0$, the first verification equation cannot be satisfied. Observe that
$$t_1 = g^{(s_3 - s_3')/(c-c')} = g^{\alpha_1' x'} = g^0 = 1$$

Hence, the extractor's output is valid.

Honest Verifier Zero-Knowledge. On input Chall, for a a given commitment C, Sim does the following:

1. Samples uniformly random values $s_1, s_2, s_3, \alpha \leftarrow\$ [q - 1]$, then computes:

$$t_1 = g^\alpha \qquad\qquad t_2 = \frac{C^{s_1} h^{s_2}}{t_1^c} \qquad\qquad t_3 = \frac{g^{s_3}}{t_1^c}.$$

2. Outputs the transcript $((t_1, t_2, t_3), c, (s_1, s_2, s_3))$.

By the choice of t_1, t_2, t_3, the transcript satisfies the verification equations above. We show that over uniformly distributed challenges, Sim outputs transcripts which are identically distributed with transcripts between an honest $\mathcal{P}$ and $\mathcal{V}$. Fix an instance C and challenge c. Observe that a real protocol execution is determined by $\mathcal{P}$'s random coins $\alpha_1, \ldots, \alpha_4$, while, on the other hand, a simulated transcript is uniquely determined by Sim's random coins s_1, s_2, s_3, α. Since both are sampled from the same probability space, and uniquely determine the resulting transcripts, we show that there exists bijection from the random coins of an honest $\mathcal{P}$ to the random coins of Sim that yields identical transcripts for a fixed instance challenge pair. Consider the bijection:

$$(\alpha_1, \alpha_2, \alpha_3, \alpha_4) \mapsto (\alpha_2 + c\alpha_1, \alpha_3 - c\alpha_1 r, \alpha_4 + c\alpha_1 x, \alpha_1 x)$$

By inspection, this map is both injective and surjective (and, hence, bijective), and when Sim picks random coins $(\alpha_2 + c\alpha_1, \alpha_3 - c\alpha_1 r, \alpha_4 + c\alpha_1 x, \alpha_1 x)$, it produces a transcript identical to that of an honest $\mathcal{P}$ who uses random coins $(\alpha_1, \alpha_2, \alpha_3, \alpha_4)$. Both of these events occur with equal probability. Therefore, over every possible transcript, the distributions between the transcripts of a simulator and honest protocol executions are identical.   □

3   ZKAttest's Proofs of Knowledge and Soundness Misdesign

ZKAttest (henceforth referred to as ZKA) is a protocol designed in [15]. The authors introduce the scheme as a way to build both a privacy-preserving ECDSA PoK and a ring signature, which require *pre-existing* signatures and their associated public key as input. Hence, the core primitive in ZKA is a NIZKPoK for proving knowledge of a valid *ECDSA signature* under a committed public key. Additional properties can be attested, such as proving that the commitment to the public key is a value on a list of valid public keys (a ring signature).

Theorem 3.1: Point addition

Let $P = (a_x, a_y)$, $Q = (b_x, b_y)$, $(P, Q) \in E(\mathbb{F}_t)$ where E is an elliptic curve of short weierstrass form $E : y^2 = x^3 + ax + b$ for some $a, b \in \mathbb{F}_t$. Given that $P \neq \pm Q$ and P, Q are non-identity elements, $(t_x, t_y) = P + Q$ is given by:

$$t_x = \left(\frac{b_y - a_y}{b_x - a_x} \right)^2 - a_x - b_x \tag{3}$$

$$t_y = \left(\frac{b_y - a_y}{b_x - a_x} \right) (a_x - t_x) - a_y \tag{4}$$

Under the hood, ZKA builds on top of the 'Proof of Knowledge of Double Discrete Logarithm (DLog)' (PKDLog) scheme given by [1], which aims to prove *the equality of a committed value and the discrete logarithm of another committed value* when working in elliptic curve groups (the known techniques for double discrete logarithm proofs do not work for this case [10,23], as a group element cannot be naturally interpreted as a field element). For this, [1] and ZKA first internally prove that the commitment of two points sum to the commitment of another ('Proof of Knowledge of the Sum').

In the subsections below, we briefly explain the schemes given by [1] and, then, how they are extended for ZKA. Note that internally all these protocols rely on Constructions 2.1 to 2.3 for opening, equality and multiplication proofs, respectively. Note that we fix the steps that were omitted or missing, which we incorporate for clarity and completeness. We introduce, and explain misdesigns and attacks to the constructions designed by both papers.

3.1 Proofs of Knowledge in ZKA [15]

Proof of Knowledge of the Sum (ZKAPointAddition):

Construction 3.1: ZKAPointAddition

Given $C_1 = \text{Com}_q(a_x)$, $C_2 = \text{Com}_q(a_y)$, $C_3 = \text{Com}_q(b_x)$, $C_4 = \text{Com}_q(b_y)$, $C_5 = \text{Com}_q(t_x)$, $C_6 = \text{Com}_q(t_y)$, prove that $T = A + B$, where $A = (a_x, a_y)$, $B = (b_x, b_y)$, $T = (t_x, t_y)$, $(A, B, T) \in E(\mathbb{F}_q)$.

1. $\mathcal{P}$ computes:

$$C_7 = C_3 - C_1 = \text{Com}_q(b_x - a_x) \quad C_8 = \text{Com}_q((b_x - a_x)^{-1}),$$

$$C_9 = C_4 - C_2 = \text{Com}_q(b_y - a_y) \quad C_{10} = \text{Com}_q\left(\frac{b_y - a_y}{b_x - a_x}\right),$$

$$C_{11} = \text{Com}_q\left(\left(\frac{b_y - a_y}{b_x - a_x}\right)^2\right) \quad C_{12} = \text{Com}_q(a_x - t_x),$$

$$C_{13} = \text{Com}_q\left(\left(\frac{b_y - a_y}{b_x - a_x}\right)(a_x - t_x)\right).$$

2. $\mathcal{P}$ engages with $\mathcal{V}$ in the following Σ-protocols *in parallel* (note that $\mathcal{V}$ can compute C_7 and C_9 from the public values of C_1, C_2, C_3, C_4):
   ⋆ Multiplication proofs via Construction 2.3:

   $$\text{MulProof}(C_7, C_8, \text{Com}_q(1)), \quad \text{MulProof}(C_8, C_9, C_{10}),$$
   $$\text{MulProof}(C_{10}, C_{10}, C_{11}), \quad \text{MulProof}(C_{10}, C_{12}, C_{13}).$$

   ⋆ Equality proofs via Construction 2.2:

   $$\text{EqualityProof}(C_5, C_{11} - C_1 - C_3), \quad \text{EqualityProof}(C_6, C_{13} - C_2).$$

This PoK aims to prove that the commitments to three elliptic curve points P, Q, T satisfy a valid point addition such that $P + Q = T$. We state the point addition formulae in Theorem 3.1 given by [26]. Given the family of curves $\mathcal{E}$ defined by $y^2 = x^3 + ax + b$ (where $a, b \in \mathbb{F}_t$), we have a point addition relation of the form shown in Theorem 3.1.

The above relations given for point addition can be proven by using Σ-protocol techniques for arithmetic relationships; but, as the point addition formulae is over $\mathbb{F}_t$, the commitments to the coordinates have to be in a group of order t, which is not necessarily the same as the order of the group $E(\mathbb{F}_t)$. [1] solve this problem by rearranging the point addition formulae so that Σ-protocols for polynomial relationships among committed values [9] and range proofs [5,7,8] can be used on the intermediate commitments. The proof is expanded to handle all the cases for point addition by using OR composition [13].

ZKA introduces a different strategy. They resolve the need for range proofs by proving relations among commitments which have a message space of matching order. Note that the point addition computation is done over the base field, so the commitments to the coordinates of each point can be done in $\mathbb{F}_q \cong \mathbb{Z}_q$, which is not the same as the order p of $E(\mathbb{F}_q)$. The authors rely on the method given by Bröker [6] to find elliptic curve groups of prescribed order q. Recall that the method takes $\tilde{O}(\log q)^3$ steps, and since it need only be run *once*, with this consideration in mind, it is sufficiently practical.

With elliptic curves of prescribed order q, ZKA prove the relations of Theorem 3.1 (note that their paper incorrectly stated the addition formulae for elliptic curve points: we use the correct formulae here) and create the proof seen in Construction 3.1.

We highlight some corrections we made to this proof:

- We fix several equations as highlighted in Construction 3.1. These mistakes stem from either incorrectly copying the point addition formulae or from arithmetic mistakes.
- We emphasise that all "internal" proofs have to be run in parallel, as is standard in the parallel composition of Σ-protocols. The implementation [15] of ZKAPointAddition composes them sequentially, which does not preserve special-soundness [17,20].

Note that this proof does not handle exceptional cases, where the public input is commitment to points A, B, T such that $A = \pm B$. It also does not guarantee that the given coordinates correspond to valid curve points, but if A and B are on the curve, so is T, as we note in Remark 1. If the points A, B are randomly chosen, the probability that $A = \pm B$ is $2/|E(\mathbb{F}_q)|$. If this occurs when ZKAPointAddition is invoked in ZKADlog (see Sect. 3.1), $\mathcal{P}$ can run the entire protocol again, but this admits an issue with perfect completeness. We stress that in ZKADlog, this issue can be resolved without the need for extending the point addition proof. Nevertheless, the ZKA paper (but not in its implementation) does propose an extension to handle exceptional cases at the cost of efficiency. Note that the protocol guarantees that $((a_x - b_x) \neq 0)$ by verifying it has an inverse in the first inner multiplication proof. This can be extended to the case when $((a_x - b_x) = 0)$, which corresponds to $P = \pm Q$, and is either a case of point doubling or addition to the point at infinity (observe below, that the latter is still disregarded). Theoretically, the authors propose handling of exceptional cases by using AND and OR composition of Σ protocols: $(a_x - b_x \neq 0 \wedge t = a + b) \vee (a_x = b_x \wedge a_y = b_y \wedge T = 2P)$ if represented in affine coordinates. This protocol, which would require a subroutine for proving the satisfiability of the doubling formulae (which is unspecified), would be complete provided $A \neq -B$, but still does not account for when $A = -B$, since the points are represented in affine coordinates.

Remark 1. Note that in ZKAPointAddition above, and later in Sect. 4.1, it is assumed that at least two of $\mathcal{P}$'s input point coordinates (A, B, T) are indeed valid points on a given curve E. If at least two points are valid, then following the point formulae, it follows that the third must be as well. In applications, as $\mathcal{V}$ should be convinced of this fact in outer protocols, this seems to be sufficient.

Proof of DLog (ZKADlog): As stated, [1] builds a proof of the equality of a committed value ω and the discrete logarithm to the public base point P of another committed value ωP. Extending this approach, ZKA introduces a ZKADlog that works by internally using the ZKAPointAddition proof. The protocol can be seen in Construction 3.2, where solid boxes represent the values sent by a party. For a given instance (C_1, C_2', C_3'), the witness is the tuple (ω, r_1, r_2, r_3) such that $(x, y) = \omega P$, $C_1 = \mathsf{Com}_p(\omega, r_1)$, $C_2' = \mathsf{Com}_q(x, r_2)$ and $C_3' = \mathsf{Com}_q(y, r_3)$.

It is worth noting that, as pointed out by ZKA, the proof from [1] fails to verify C_1, the commitment to the secret value ω. ZKA presents the corrected version of this proof with this verification. But even with this correction, the proof does not achieve special soundness. In short, this is due to the non-standard approach used in the composition of sigma protocols.

Below, we discuss the issues with ZKA's proof of security for this PoK. We note that the PoK is indicated to be a Σ-protocol and it is specified (by the number of repetitions) to have a knowledge error of $\frac{1}{2}$, and perfect HVZK. We explore the failures of the properties that ZKADlog should provide.

Completeness. We remark that the protocol described in Construction 3.2 does not satisfy perfect completeness. If $\alpha \in \{0, \omega, 2\omega\}$, then the inner ZKAPointAddition will fail, since it does not handle point doubling, inverse addition (without its extension), and addition by the identity. This failure, in turn, means that the outer protocol will fail, and we note that these exceptional cases occur with probability $\frac{3}{p}$. A solution to this completeness issue would be to have an honest prover sample from $\mathbb{Z}_p \backslash \{0, \omega, 2\omega\}$. As a trade-off, doing so leads to a protocol that is honest verifier *statistical* zero-knowledge.

Special Honest Verifier Zero-Knowledge. The proof of SHVZK provided in the final version of ZKA is missing details, but it can be shown that their protocol satisfies statistical HVZK, as they state, using a simulator similar to the one given in the proof of Theorem 6.

Construction 3.2: ZKADlog

Given $C_1 = \mathsf{Com}_p(\omega) = \omega P + r_1 Q$, $C_2' = \mathsf{Com}_q(x) = xP' + r_2 Q'$, $C_3' = \mathsf{Com}_q(y) = yP' + r_3 Q'$, for q equal to the modulus of the base field of E, prove that $S = (x, y)$ is equal to ωP, where $P, Q \in E$ are public elements of prime order p, and (P', Q') are points in E' of prime order q.

1. The **prover**::
   * chooses a random $\alpha, \beta_1 \in \mathbb{Z}_p$, and $\beta_2, \beta_3, \ \beta_4, \beta_5 \ \in \mathbb{Z}_q$,
   * sets $(\gamma_1, \gamma_2) = \alpha P$, and
   * sets $(u, v) = (\alpha - \omega)P$

   They, then, compute the following values:
   $$a_1 = \mathsf{Com}_p(\alpha) = \alpha P + \beta_1 Q,$$
   $$a_2 = \mathsf{Com}_q(\gamma_1) = \gamma_1 P' + \beta_2 Q', \qquad a_3 = \mathsf{Com}_q(\gamma_2) = \gamma_2 P' + \beta_3 Q',$$
   $$C_4' = \mathsf{Com}_q(u) = uP' + \beta_4 Q', \qquad C_5' = \mathsf{Com}_q(v) = vP' + \beta_5 Q'.$$

   sending $\boxed{a_1, a_2, a_3, C_4', C_5' , \mathsf{Comm}'}$ to $\mathcal{V}$ as Comm,

   where Comm' is for ZKAPointAddition on $(C_2', C_3', C_4', C_5', a_2, a_3)$.

2. The **verifier**:
   – chooses a challenge string $c = (c_0, c_1)$, where c_0 is a single random bit $\in \{0, 1\}$ and $c_1 \in \mathbb{Z}_q$ is a challenge for the ZKAPointAddition. They send $\boxed{c}$ as Chall.

3. The **prover** receives c:
   * If $c_0 = 0$, computes $z_1 = \alpha$, $z_2 = \beta_1$, $z_3 = \beta_2$, $z_4 = \beta_3$.
   Sends the tuple $\boxed{(z_1, z_2, z_3, z_4)}$ as Resp.

   * If $c_0 = 1$, computes $z_1 = \alpha - \omega$, $z_2 = \beta_1 - r_1$, $z_3 = \beta_4$, $z_4 = \beta_5$.
   Then, they compute the response for ZKAPointAddition:
     • Given $T = z_1 P = (u, v)$,
     • Compute Resp' with $\mathsf{Chall}' = c_1$. which verifies that $T = (\gamma_1, \gamma_2) - (x, y)$ $(T = \alpha P - S)$.

   Sends the tuple $\boxed{(z_1, z_2, z_3, z_4 , \mathsf{Resp}')}$ as Resp.

4. Upon receiving Resp, the **verifier** performs the following:
   * If $c_0 = 0$, computes $(t_1, t_2) = z_1 P$. Then, verifies that $a_1 \overset{?}{=} z_1 P + z_2 Q$, $a_2 \overset{?}{=} \mathsf{Com}_q(t_1, z_3)$ and $a_3 \overset{?}{=} \mathsf{Com}_q(t_2, z_4)$.
   * If $c_0 = 1$, computes $(t_1, t_2) = z_1 P$. Then, verifies that $a_1 \overset{?}{=} z_1 P + z_2 Q + C_1$, that $C_4' \overset{?}{=} \mathsf{Com}_q(t_1, z_3)$ and $C_5' \overset{?}{=} \mathsf{Com}_q(t_2, z_4)$, and sequentially verifies the point addition proof $\pi = (\mathsf{Comm}', c_1, \mathsf{Resp}')$.

Special-Soundness. The proof of special-soundness in ZKA is flawed due to inherent misdesign. First, note that in the original protocol specification and implementation $\mathcal{P}$ does not construct the commitment phase for the point addition protocol until after the challenge has been received[1], and their implementation computes challenges for the subroutines of the point addition proof on the fly. Sending a challenge before the commitment phase leads to a trivial attack where one can forge a valid point addition proof in the same way the HVZK simulator for ZKAPointAddition behaves. In their published version, they correctly include commitment phase for ZKAPointAddition in the first round, but this issue is present in their open source implementation at the time of publication.

The authors of ZKA claim the protocol is 3-special-sound, and construct an extractor which takes as input three transcripts, $(\mathsf{Comm}_i, \mathsf{Chall}_i, \mathsf{Resp}_i)_{i \in [3]}$, where $\mathsf{Chall}_1 = (0, a)$, $\mathsf{Chall}_2 = (1, b)$, $\mathsf{Chall}_3 = (1, c)$ with $b \neq c$ and $a, b, c \in \mathbb{Z}_q$. Such an accepting transcript would allow for the extraction of the witness since:

- Given that ZKAPointAddition is 2-special sound, Ext can invoke the extractor of this internal proof with transcripts for the challenges b, c. This would yield x, y, r_2, r_3 as output.
- Ext may take $\mathsf{Resp}_1 = (z_1, z_2, z_3, z_4)$ and $\mathsf{Resp}_2 = (z_1', z_2', z_3', z_4', \pi)$, and deduce $\omega = z_1 - z_1'$ and $r_1 = z_2 - z_2'$.

We note that for this specific input, the witness extracted above is valid. For further justification, see the proof of the fixed protocol in Sect. 4.2. However, Ext is still flawed. In particular, there is no way to extract the witness given the following cases with these transcript triples (with $a, b, c \in \mathbb{Z}_q$):

1. $(\mathsf{Comm}_i, \mathsf{Chall}_i, \mathsf{Resp}_i)_{i \in [3]}$ where $\mathsf{Chall}_1 = (0, a)$, $\mathsf{Chall}_2 = (0, b)$, $\mathsf{Chall}_3 = (1, c)$ for $a \neq b$. We explain this extractor fault first since it is the easiest to correct. In this case, Ext may recover the values ω, x, y, r_1, but not the randomness r_2, r_3. In particular, if we modify the protocol to run ZKAPointAddition independently of c_0, such that $\mathcal{P}$ engages in it for both $c_0 \in \{0, 1\}$, then, this case can yield a valid witness extraction.
2. $(\mathsf{Comm}_i, \mathsf{Chall}_i, \mathsf{Resp}_i)_{i \in [3]}$ where $\mathsf{Chall}_1 = (1, a)$, $\mathsf{Chall}_2 = (1, b)$, $\mathsf{Chall}_3 = (1, c)$ for $a \neq b \neq c$. In this case, Ext may recover part of the witness by invoking the extractor of ZKAPointAddition, but the extractor cannot recover ω, only the openings of C_2', C_3'. There is no clear solution that allows Ext to recover ω in this setting.
3. $(\mathsf{Comm}_i, \mathsf{Chall}_i, \mathsf{Resp}_i)_{i \in [3]}$ where $\mathsf{Chall}_1 = (0, a)$, $\mathsf{Chall}_2 = (0, b)$, $\mathsf{Chall}_3 = (0, c)$ for $a \neq b \neq c$. In this case, it follows that Ext can learn nothing about the witness, since $\mathsf{Resp}_1 = \mathsf{Resp}_2 = \mathsf{Resp}_3$. If we perform the same modification to the proof as in the first case, we still remain with the same issue as in the second case, where it is not possible to extract ω.

Note that the definition of 3-special soundness requires Ext to succeed in extracting the witness for *any* 3 accepting transcripts. Therefore, the scheme is

---

[1] This is likely also the case in [1], however the specification of the protocol is not sufficiently detailed.

not 3-special sound. Furthermore, the claim that the protocol above has soundness error $\frac{1}{2}$ is left unjustified. Recall that an n-special sound protocol of challenge space C has knowledge error $\frac{n-1}{|C|}$. If the scheme was 3-special sound, it would have knowledge error $\frac{2}{2q}$ (since $C = \mathbb{Z}_2 \times \mathbb{Z}_q$), which is unrealistic for this construction.

3.2 A Practical Attack on ZKA's Implementation

In addition to the above concerns, the authors of ZKA implemented the non-interactive protocol with the Fiat-Shamir transform applied on 128 repetitions. However, as an efficiency measure (as stated in Sect. 8 of their paper), the verification is only performed on a random subset of 20 of the repetitions. This ad-hoc choice reduces the probability of a forged proof being accepted to at least 2^{-20} (we note this bound is not tight due to the soundness issues above), but may also allow for a further reduction to security. Note that:

A malicious $\mathcal{P}$ may construct the commitment phase for $c_0 = 0$ in the same fashion as the HVZK simulator, ZKSim, for the 128 repetitions, and compute the resultant challenge, which is a hash of the concatenation of these commitments. Then, they arbitrarily select the transcript of a single repetition. They will replace the commitment to C_4' in this repetition in order to change the output of the resulting challenge hash. This can be done as this commitment is never opened for the verifier and should be uniformly distributed in the point-set of $E'(\mathbb{F}_{q'})$. For i steps, the malicious prover sets C_4' to a random point[2] in $E'(\mathbb{F}_{q'})$ until the resultant hash yields a challenge string which contains at least m challenges which have $c_0 = 0$. Call these the 'good' challenges. For the 'good' challenges, they complete their proofs as in the ZKSim, and for 'bad' challenges they output uniformly random values as response.

For $m = 115$, the probability that a verifier chooses repetitions which have 'good' challenges, and accepts the forged proof, is roughly 2%. We make some heuristic assumptions as to the practicality of this attack. The expected number of attempts to find a hash which has at least 115 zeroes is $i \approx 2^{70}$. This takes 2^{70} hash computations. Now, assuming each increment's hash only requires a single SHA-256 execution and basing the cost of SHA-256 computations on the revenue of Bitcoin mining[3], the approximate cost of the attack is 1500 USD.[4] Even with the counter-measure of rate-limiting, this "cheap" attack is sufficiently practical if launched in a distributed fashion. Alongside the other issues, the authors of ZKA have been made aware and acknowledged this attack.

---

[2] Using the common compressed representation for elliptic curve points, which is the x-coordinate along with a parity bit, one does not need to evaluate the curve equation each time.

[3] See https://charts.woobull.com/bitcoin-hash-price/, which places the value of 10^{12} SHA-256 hashes at approximately 10^{-6} USD, assuming modern ASICs can be set up to handle arbitrary fixed length input.

[4] For the calculations of these estimates, see the attached Sage script as seen in https://github.com/brave-experiments/CDLS.

4   Sound Proofs of Knowledge: CDLS

In this section, we consider several solutions to the issues faced with the flawed security proof of ZKA's ZKADlog for proving knowledge of an elliptic curve discrete logarithm. Recall that in our context, we are interested in protocols which operate in the elliptic curve setting, where [23] does not apply.

In Sect. 4.1, we propose an optimized Σ-protocol for proving that the coordinates of a committed elliptic curve point is the sum of two others, which we call CDLSS. In Sect. 4.2, we propose a Σ-protocol with knowledge error $\frac{1}{2}$, for a proof of committed discrete logarithm, which we call CDLSD.

4.1   Proof of Knowledge of the Sum: CDLSS

A key insight that yields optimisation beyond [1,9,15], is that only multiplication and a small number of opening proofs are necessary in the process of proving a polynomial relation. In particular, linear combinations of commitments can be obtained without any interaction from $\mathcal{P}$. As an example, consider a $\mathcal{P}$ who wishes to convince $\mathcal{V}$ that taking the product of the opening of two commitments $X = \text{Com}(x)$, $Y = \text{Com}(y)$ is a linear combination of n other committed values, such that for $Z_i = \text{Com}(z_i)$, $i \in [n]$,

$$xy = \sum_{i \in [n]} a_i z_i$$

In this example, $\mathcal{P}$ may verify the relationship holds by having $\mathcal{V}$ compute $T = \prod_{i \in [n]} Z_i^{a_i}$, and engaging them with $\text{MulProof}(X, Y, T)$. This holds since T is a valid commitment for the linear combination. The opening proofs are needed to allow an extractor to recover the openings for the individual commitments given an opening for the linear combination.

Proving Knowledge of the Sum. Given $C_1 = \text{Com}_q(a_x)$, $C_2 = \text{Com}_q(a_y)$, $C_3 = \text{Com}_q(b_x)$, $C_4 = \text{Com}_q(b_y)$, $C_5 = \text{Com}_q(t_x)$, $C_6 = \text{Com}_q(t_y)$, prove that $T = A + B$, where $A = (a_x, a_y)$, $B = (b_x, b_y)$, $T = (t_x, t_y)$, $(A, B, T) \in E(\mathbb{F}_q)$.

Recall the elliptic curve addition formulae (stated in Theorem 3.1). We may rearrange this formula into a system of equations, by adding an additional variable τ (note that $\tau = \frac{b_y - a_y}{b_x - a_x}$):

$$(b_x - a_x)\tau = b_y - a_y \tag{5}$$

$$\tau^2 = a_x + b_x + t_x \tag{6}$$

$$\tau(a_x - t_x) = a_y + t_y \tag{7}$$

With this rearrangement, $\mathcal{P}$ will send the commitment $C_7 = \text{Com}_q(\tau)$ along with the previously defined commitments $(C_1, \ldots, C_6)$ in the commitment phase of CDLSS. $\mathcal{P}$ engages $\mathcal{V}$ on the instance $(C_1, \ldots, C_6)$. Note that $\mathcal{V}$ can compute the commitment to any linear combination of known commitments (including C_7) due to the linearity of Pedersen commitments. They perform the following proof interactions in parallel:

- MulProof($C_3 - C_1, C_7, C_4 - C_2$) which verifies that Eq. (5) holds,
- MulProof($C_7, C_7, C_1 + C_3 + C_5$) which verifies that Eq. (6) holds,
- MulProof($C_7, C_1 - C_5, C_2 + C_6$), which verifies that Eq. (7) holds.
- OpeningProof(C_2), which allows the extractor to fully recover a witness.
- NonZeroProof($C_3 - C_1$), which verifies that the $b_x - a_x \neq 0$ (i.e. $A \neq \pm B$).

We note that without the final non-zero check, the prover may maliciously choose points A, B such that $A = -B$. This unconstrains the value of τ, and thus the prover can choose any t_x, t_y and τ such that Eqs. (6), (7) hold.

As an abuse of notation, we write the elliptic curve group operations above additively, instead of multiplicatively as in Constructions 2.1 and 2.3. $\mathcal{V}$ accepts if all of the above protocols are accepting.

Theorem 5. *The protocol described above is a Σ-protocol for the relation $\mathcal{R} =$*

$$\left\{ \left(\begin{pmatrix} C_1, C_2, \\ C_3, C_4, \\ C_5, C_6 \end{pmatrix}, \begin{pmatrix} a_x, a_y, b_x, b_y, \\ t_x, t_y, r_1, r_2, \\ r_3, r_4, r_5, r_6 \end{pmatrix} \right) \middle| \begin{array}{c} A + B = T \text{ where } A \neq \pm B, A, B \neq \mathcal{O} \\ A = (a_x, a_y), B = (b_x, b_y), \ T = (t_x, t_y) \\ \text{Each commitment } C_i \text{ is valid} \\ \text{with randomness } r_i \end{array} \right\}$$

assuming the coordinates of at least two of the points correspond to valid points on an elliptic curve.

Proof. We show the protocol satisfies *completeness*, *honest verifier zero-knowledge* and *special-soundness*.

Completeness. Due to the correctness of the point addition formulae, the multiplication proofs will be accepted, since the coordinates of the points must satisfy Eqs. (5) to (7), given that $A \neq \pm B$, and neither points correspond to the identity element. It is worth highlighting the following two cases: i) if A or B are maliciously chosen such that $A = \pm B$, $\mathcal{V}$ will reject the non-zero check. ii) if A, T are chosen such that $A = \pm T$, then Eq. (7) implies that $a_y = -t_y$ and hence that $A = -T$, which is a valid case (in particular, $B = -2A$). Since the system of equations is symmetric in the choice of A and B, the same holds for $B = \pm T$.

Honest Verifier Zero-Knowledge. On input $(C_1, \ldots, C_6)$, and challenge c, the simulator samples random $(a, b) \leftarrow\!\!\$ \ [q]$, and sets $C_7' = \mathrm{Com}_q(a, b)$, adding it to the commitment phase of the transcript. The simulator then invokes the simulators for the three inner multiplication proofs and opening proof where C_7' is used as input in lieu of C_7. The scheme is perfect HVZK due to the perfect hiding property of the commitment C_7', and the perfect HVZK of the underlying inner multiplication and opening proofs.

2-Special Soundness. Given two accepting transcripts for the protocol, Ext invokes the sub-extractor for the three multiplication proofs, respectively. In particular, Ext learns the quantities $b_x - a_x$, $a_x + b_x + t_x$ and $a_x - t_x$. Note that Ext also recovers $b_y - a_y$, $a_y + t_y$, $r_4 - r_2$ and $r_2 + r_6$ from the extractors of the multiplication proofs.

To recover the x-coordinates and associated randomness, Ext solves a system of 3 linear equations in three unknowns and recovers a_x, b_x, and t_x. The randomness r_1, r_3, r_5, which satisfies the same system of equations, is extracted similarly. To recover the y-coordinates and associated randomness, Ext invokes the sub-extractor for the opening proof of C_2, learning a_y and r_2. Having the y coordinate and the associated randomness, Ext can recover b_y, t_y and r_4, r_6 by substituting the known values for a_y and r_2.

Note that the committed values satisfy the affine point coordinate equations, since $A \neq \pm B$ by the non-zero check. Further, neither A nor B can correspond to the identity since they are represented in affine coordinates. Hence, Ext recovers a valid witness.   □

4.2   Fixing ZKA: Σ-Protocol for Committed Discrete Logarithms: CDLSD

Due to the flawed extractor in ZKADlog, we propose reducing the challenge space of the inner point addition protocol. The intuition behind this choice, is that the outer ZKADlog has knowledge error of at least $\frac{1}{2}$, and thus the inner ZKAPointAddition (which has knowledge error of $\approx \frac{1}{q}$) cannot be utilised properly. Moreover, instead of running the point addition proof conditionally on the response of the verifier, we choose to run it in parallel. Lastly, we also differentiate between the base of the discrete logarithm, R, and the parameter P used as a parameter in PC, as these need not necessarily be equal.

CDLSD: Sigma Protocol with Binary Challenges. We show CDLSD in Construction 5.1.

Theorem 6. CDLSD *(Construction 5.1) is a Σ-protocol for the relation $\mathcal{R} =$*

$$\left\{ ((C_1, C_2', C_3'), (\omega, r_1, r_2, r_3)) \;\middle|\; \begin{array}{c} (x, y) = \omega R, \; C_1 = Com_p(\omega, r_1), \\ C_2' = Com_q(x, r_2), \; C_3' = Com_q(y, r_3) \end{array} \right\}$$

assuming $\omega \neq 0$ and the instantiations of PCs Com_p, Com_q are perfectly hiding and computationally binding.

Proof. We aim to prove *completeness, HVZP* and *Special-Soundness.*

Completeness. If $\mathcal{P}$ knows the witness w, and samples an α such that $\alpha - \omega \notin \{0, \omega, -\omega\}$, then the inner CDLSS will accept with probability 1, the equalities in Step 4 of Construction 5.1 will hold, and $\mathcal{V}$ will always accept.

Honest Verifier Zero-Knowledge. We construct a simulator for an accepting transcript which is *statistically indistinguishable* from a real accepting transcript. On input challenge c, $\mathcal{P}$ does the following:

- If $c = 0$, the simulator randomly samples $z_1 \in \mathbb{Z}_p \backslash \{0\}$, $z_2 \in \mathbb{Z}_p$, $z_3, z_4, u, v \in \mathbb{Z}_q$, and sets $(s,t) = z_1 R$. The simulator computes $C_4 = z_1 P + z_2 Q$, $C_5' = sP' + z_3 Q'$ and $C_6' = tP' + z_4 Q'$, and sets C_7', C_8' as commitments to the random values (u, v).
- If $c = 1$, the simulator randomly samples $z_1 \in \mathbb{Z}_p \backslash \{0\}$, $z_2 \in \mathbb{Z}_p$ and $z_3, z_4, s, t \in \mathbb{Z}_q$, and sets $(u, v) = z_1 R$. The simulator computes $C_4 = z_1 P + z_2 Q + C_1$, $C_7' = uP' + z_3 Q'$, $C_8' = vP' + z_4 Q'$ and C_5', C_6' as the commitments to the random values (s, t).

In both cases, the simulator invokes the inner simulator for CDLSS with input $(C_2', C_3', C_7', C_8', C_5', C_6')$ and the binary challenge c. We show that real and simulated transcripts are *statistically indistinguishable* given that the simulator of CDLSS outputs a transcript that is perfectly indistinguishable from a real transcript and considering the outer messages sent by $\mathcal{P}$. Observe that if $c = 0$ (resp. $c = 1$), z_1 in the real transcript is a uniformly random value in $\mathbb{Z}_p \backslash \{0, \omega, 2\omega\}$ (resp. $\mathbb{Z}_p \backslash \{0, -\omega, \omega\}$) and z_1 in the simulated transcript is a uniformly random value in $\mathbb{Z}_p \backslash \{0\}$. Call the real sampling distribution X_q and the simulated sampling distribution Y_q (resp. Y_q'). Note that the statistical distance:

$$\Delta(X_q, Y_q) = \frac{1}{2} \sum_{x \in \mathbb{Z}_q \backslash \{0\}} |\Pr[X_q = x] - \Pr[Y_q = x]|$$

$$= \frac{1}{2} \left(2\left|0 - \frac{1}{q-1}\right| + \sum_{x \in \mathbb{Z}_q \backslash \{0, \omega, 2\omega\}} \left|\frac{1}{q-3} - \frac{1}{q-1}\right| \right)$$

$$= \frac{1}{q-1} + \frac{1}{q-1}$$

$$= \frac{2}{q-1} \quad (= \Delta(X_q, Y_q') \text{ by a similar argument})$$

is statistically indistinguishable, since we require that $q = \exp(\omega)$, which is negligible in ω. Furthermore, both in the real and simulated proofs, z_2, z_3, z_4 is uniformly random in their respective domains ($z_2 \in \mathbb{Z}_p$ and $z_3, z_4 \in \mathbb{Z}_q$). If $c = 0$ (resp $c = 1$), the verification equations uniquely determine C_4, C_5', C_6' (resp. C_4, C_7', C_8') conditioned on $(z_1, z_2, z_3, z_4, C_1)$ and that the remaining commitments are to uniformly random inputs in $\mathbb{Z}_q$. Since the commitment scheme is perfectly hiding, the commitments in the real and simulated transcripts are perfectly indistinguishable. Hence, the distribution of the real and simulated transcripts are statistically indistinguishable, where an unbounded distinguisher has at most negligible advantage.

2-Special Soundness. Given two accepting transcripts for the protocol for challenges $c = 0$ and $c' = 1$, the extractor invokes the extractor for the inner CDLSS, which renders r_2, r_3 as openings to the commitments C_2', C_3'.

Let $(z_1, z_2, z_3, z_4), (z'_1, z'_2, z'_3, z'_4)$ be the responses for c and c', respectively. By the verification equations, we know that C'_5, C'_6 and C'_7, C'_8 are valid commitments to the coordinates of points $z_1 P$ and $z'_1 P$, respectively. Furthermore, since both the transcripts are accepting, CDLSS must correspond to a valid instance, and thus we know that the commitments to the coordinates of ωR, $z_1 R$ and $z'_1 R$ must satisfy the equation $\omega R + z'_1 R = z_1 R$. Lastly, we know by the verification equations, that $C_4 - C_1 = \text{Com}_p(z'_1, z'_2)$ and $C_4 = \text{Com}_p(z_1, z_2)$, and hence we can recover the opening to C_1 as $\omega = z_1 - z'_1$, and $r_1 = z_2 - z'_2$. Hence, the extractor recovers ω, r_1, r_2, r_3. By the point addition proof, and the consistency of the commitments of $z_1 = \alpha, z'_1 = \alpha - \omega$, we must have that for $(x, y) = (z_1 - z'_1)P$, $C'_2 = \text{Com}_q(x, r_2)$ and $C'_3 = \text{Com}_q(y, r_3)$. □

Remark 2. Constructing a 5-round protocol was considered, where in the first round, $\mathcal{P}$ would open one of the points and verify the consistency of the point multiplication commitments. In the second, $\mathcal{P}$ would run the point addition protocol (conditional on the first challenge being 1). We believe such an interactive protocol would be secure, with the techniques described in [2]. However, in the analysis of [2], the authors claim knowledge error loss when Fiat-Shamir transform is applied to parallel repetitions of a multi-round protocol. In this case, the security loss would be quadratic in the number of random oracle queries of an attacker. Since the 5 round protocol would offer very few benefits if provably secure as a $(2, q)$-special-sound protocol, with expected proof lengths roughly $\frac{1}{3}$ shorter than the protocol above in the best case, we opt to remain in the more secure setting of 3-round protocols.

4.3 Transforming to Non-Interactive Zero-Knowledge Proof of Knowledge

To boost the soundness of CDLSD, we run λ parallel repetitions, and apply the Fiat-Shamir transform [18] to obtain a NIZKPoK with knowledge error of $2^{-\lambda}$. There is still a healthy margin for the statistical zero-knowledge parameter. Given λ repetitions, a real and simulated transcript can be distinguished by an unbounded distinguisher with advantage at most $\frac{2\lambda}{2^{2\lambda}-1} \leq 2^{-\lambda}$ (for $\lambda \geq 3$).

5   Implementation and Benchmarks

In this section, we discuss the implementation details and evaluation of the CDLS protocols. All timings and results in this section were produced using our prototype Rust implementation[5] on a Macbook M1 with 8 GB of memory. The timings presented in this section were produced as the average of 100 iterations.

We implemented both the PoKs of CDLS and ZKA in around 4700 lines of Rust code. We note that our re-implementation of ZKA, which still suffers from soundness issues, is primarily for the sake of fair comparison: ZKA's original implementation is written in Typescript, which suffers from a lack of direct

---

[5] https://github.com/brave-experiments/CDLS.

hardware access making it less efficient than Rust. We note that we did not re-implement the subset checking algorithm used in ZKA due to security concerns.

Construction 5.1: CDLSD

Given $C_1 = \mathrm{Comp}_p(\omega) = \omega P + r_1 Q$, $C_2' = \mathrm{Com}_q(x) = xP' + r_2 Q'$, $C_3' = \mathrm{Com}_q(y) = yP' + r_3 Q'$, for q equal to the modulus of the base field of E, prove that $S = (x, y)$ is equal to ωR, where $R, P, Q \in E(\mathbb{F}_q)$ are public points of prime order p; $P', Q' \in E'(\mathbb{F}_{q'})$ are public points of prime order q and (P, Q), (P', Q') instantiate Com_p and Com_q respectively.

1. **The prover:**
   (a) chooses a random $\alpha, \beta_1 \in \mathbb{Z}_p$, and $\beta_2, \beta_3, \beta_4, \beta_5 \in \mathbb{Z}_q$, such that $\alpha \notin \{0, \omega, 2\omega\}$.
   (b) sets $(s, t) = \alpha R$ (the x and y coordinates of αR),
   (c) sets $(u, v) = (\alpha - \omega)R$ (the x and y coordinates of $((\alpha - \omega)R)$),
   Then, they compute commitments to α, and to the coordinates of αR and $((\alpha - \omega)R)$ $((s, t), (u, v)$, respectively) in the following way:

$$C_4 = \mathrm{Comp}_p(\alpha) = \alpha P + \beta_1 Q,$$
$$C_5' = \mathrm{Com}_q(s) = sP' + \beta_2 Q', \qquad C_6' = \mathrm{Com}_q(t) = tP' + \beta_3 Q',$$
$$C_7' = \mathrm{Com}_q(u) = uP' + \beta_4 Q', \qquad C_8' = \mathrm{Com}_q(v) = vP' + \beta_5 Q'.$$

Then, they send $C_4, C_5', C_6', C_7', C_8'$ to $\mathcal{V}$. In parallel, they send the commitments for the inner CDLSS (as in Section 4.1), with binary challenge space, and input $(C_2', C_3', C_7', C_8', C_5', C_6')$ that will be used to verify that $\alpha R = \omega R + ((\alpha - \omega)R)$.
2. **The verifier** chooses a random challenge $c \in \{0, 1\}$ and sends it to $\mathcal{P}$.
3. **The prover** receives c and performs the following:
   (a) If $c = 0$, sends $(z_1, z_2, z_3, z_4) = (\alpha, \beta_1, \beta_2, \beta_3)$.
   (b) If $c = 1$, sends $(z_1, z_2, z_3, z_4) = (\alpha - \omega, \beta_1 - r_1, \beta_4, \beta_5)$.
   (c) They send the response to the inner CDLSS with challenge c.
4. Upon response, **the verifier** performs the following:
   (a) If $c = 0$, computes $(s', t') = z_1 R$ and check that $C_4 \overset{?}{=} \mathrm{Comp}_p(z_1, z_2)$, $C_5' \overset{?}{=} \mathrm{Com}_q(s', z_3)$ and $C_6' \overset{?}{=} \mathrm{Com}_q(t', z_4)$.
   (b) If $c = 1$, computes $(u', v') = z_1 R$ and check that $C_4 - C_1 \overset{?}{=} \mathrm{Comp}_p(z_1, z_2)$, $C_7' \overset{?}{=} \mathrm{Com}_q(u', z_3)$ and $C_8' \overset{?}{=} \mathrm{Com}_q(v', z_4)$.
   (c) In parallel, verifies the response for the point addition proof with binary challenge c.

In terms of complexity, the cost of the ZKADlog is dominated by the inner ZKAPointAddition proof, which, in turn, is dominated by the number of field multiplications and field inversions. Since the prover only provides the response to the point addition protocol with probability $\frac{1}{2}$, the expected cost for a single execution of ZKADlog is 46 point multiplications for $\mathcal{P}$, 24 point multiplications for $\mathcal{V}$, and a proof size of length 24 elliptic curve points and 15 field elements. Our point addition protocol, CDLSS, incurs in 26 point multiplications for $\mathcal{P}$, 34 point multiplications for $\mathcal{V}$, and proofs contain 14 elliptic curve points and 20 field elements. Our committed discrete log proof, CDLSD, incurs 37 point multiplications for $\mathcal{P}$, 30 point multiplications for $\mathcal{V}$, and a proof length of 19 elliptic curve points and 24 field elements. Note that $\mathcal{V}$'s complexity is reduced in CDLSS as binary challenges reduce the number of point multiplications required.

Table 1. $\mathcal{P}$ and $\mathcal{V}$ timings (average of 100) for the PoKs with 256-bit curves.

Protocol	ZKA		CDLS	
	Prover (ms)	*Verifier (ms)*	*Prover (ms)*	*Verifier (ms)*
Sum PoK.	4.20	3.07	3.32	2.70
DLog PoK.	5.75	3.79	4.80	3.41
DLog PoK. (128 rep.)	737	298	616	456

Table 1 summarise $\mathcal{P}$ and $\mathcal{V}$'s time for PoK of the Sum, PoK of DLog and repeated PoK of DLog for a 256-bit curve. It shows that CDLS performs favourably compared to ZKA, achieving a speed-up for $\mathcal{P}$'s times and with similar times for verification. These timings also show that the subset checking technique used in ZKA is entirely unnecessary, as, even when checking all commitments, our verification timings are comparable to those originally given by ZKA. Note that our $\mathcal{P}$ times are around a factor of ten faster than those reported in ZKA [15].

Table 2. Size of the proof for ZKA and CDLS on 256-bit and 384-bit curves, where the security parameter λ is 128 and 192 respectively.

Protocol	256-*bit curve*		384-*bit curve*	
	ZKA (kB)	CDLS (kB)	ZKA (kB)	CDLS (kB)
Sum PoK.	1.50	1.30	2.23	1.94
DLog PoK.	1.62	1.50	2.52	2.23
DLog PoK. (λ rep.)	164.8	178.7	364.0	400

6 Conclusion

In this work, we have highlighted and resolved security misdesigns in the Σ-protocols presented in ZKA [15] and, to an extent, in Agrawal *et al.* [1]. These issues stem from implementations which are not faithful to their source paper, and security proofs which miss cases, both of which can be prevented when a protocol description is sufficiently detailed.

References

1. Agrawal, S., Ganesh, C., Mohassel, P.: Non-interactive zero-knowledge proofs for composite statements. In: Shacham, H., Boldyreva, A. (eds.) CRYPTO 2018, Part III. LNCS, vol. 10993, pp. 643–673. Springer, Cham (2018). https://doi.org/10.1007/978-3-319-96878-0_22
2. Attema, T., Fehr, S., Klooß, M.: Fiat-Shamir transformation of multi-round interactive proofs. In: Kiltz, E., Vaikuntanathan, V. (eds.) TCC 2022, Part I. LNCS, vol. 13747, pp. 113–142. Springer, Heidelberg (2022). https://doi.org/10.1007/978-3-031-22318-1_5
3. Babai, L.: Trading group theory for randomness. In: Proceedings of the Seventeenth Annual ACM Symposium on Theory of Computing, STOC 1985, pp. 421–429. Association for Computing Machinery, New York (1985). https://doi.org/10.1145/22145.22192
4. Blum, M., Feldman, P., Micali, S.: Non-interactive zero-knowledge and its applications. In: Proceedings of the Twentieth Annual ACM Symposium on Theory of Computing, STOC 1988, pp. 103–112. Association for Computing Machinery, New York (1988). https://doi.org/10.1145/62212.62222
5. Boudot, F.: Efficient proofs that a committed number lies in an interval. In: Preneel, B. (ed.) EUROCRYPT 2000. LNCS, vol. 1807, pp. 431–444. Springer, Heidelberg (2000). https://doi.org/10.1007/3-540-45539-6_31
6. Broker, R.: Constructing elliptic curves of prescribed order. Ph.D. thesis (2006)
7. Bünz, B., Bootle, J., Boneh, D., Poelstra, A., Wuille, P., Maxwell, G.: Bulletproofs: short proofs for confidential transactions and more. In: 2018 IEEE Symposium on Security and Privacy, pp. 315–334. IEEE Computer Society Press (2018). https://doi.org/10.1109/SP.2018.00020
8. Camenisch, J., Chaabouni, R., Shelat, A.: Efficient protocols for set membership and range proofs. In: Pieprzyk, J. (ed.) ASIACRYPT 2008. LNCS, vol. 5350, pp. 234–252. Springer, Heidelberg (2008). https://doi.org/10.1007/978-3-540-89255-7_15
9. Camenisch, J., Michels, M.: Proving in zero-knowledge that a number is the product of two safe primes. In: Stern, J. (ed.) EUROCRYPT 1999. LNCS, vol. 1592, pp. 107–122. Springer, Heidelberg (1999). https://doi.org/10.1007/3-540-48910-X_8
10. Camenisch, J., Stadler, M.: Efficient group signature schemes for large groups. In: Kaliski, B.S. (ed.) CRYPTO 1997. LNCS, vol. 1294, pp. 410–424. Springer, Heidelberg (1997). https://doi.org/10.1007/BFb0052252
11. Chaum, D., Pedersen, T.P.: Wallet databases with observers. In: Brickell, E.F. (ed.) CRYPTO 1992. LNCS, vol. 740, pp. 89–105. Springer, Heidelberg (1993). https://doi.org/10.1007/3-540-48071-4_7
12. Cramer, R.: Modular design of secure yet practical cryptographic protocols. Ph.D. thesis (1997)
13. Cramer, R., Damgård, I., Schoenmakers, B.: Proofs of partial knowledge and simplified design of witness hiding protocols. In: Desmedt, Y.G. (ed.) CRYPTO 1994. LNCS, vol. 839, pp. 174–187. Springer, Heidelberg (1994). https://doi.org/10.1007/3-540-48658-5_19

14. Damgård, I.: On sigma-protocols (2010). https://www.cs.au.dk/~ivan/Sigma.pdf. https://www.cs.au.dk/~ivan/Sigma.pdf
15. Faz-Hernández, A., Ladd, W., Maram, D.: ZKAttest: ring and group signatures for existing ECDSA keys. In: AlTawy, R., Hülsing, A. (eds.) SAC 2021. LNCS, vol. 13203, pp. 68–83. Springer, Cham (2022). https://doi.org/10.1007/978-3-030-99277-4_4
16. Feige, U., Fiat, A., Shamir, A.: Zero-knowledge proofs of identity. J. Cryptol. 1(2), 77–94 (1988). https://doi.org/10.1007/BF02351717
17. Feige, U., Shamir, A.: Witness indistinguishable and witness hiding protocols. In: 22nd ACM STOC, pp. 416–426. ACM Press (1990). https://doi.org/10.1145/100216.100272
18. Fiat, A., Shamir, A.: How to prove yourself: practical solutions to identification and signature problems. In: Odlyzko, A.M. (ed.) CRYPTO 1986. LNCS, vol. 263, pp. 186–194. Springer, Heidelberg (1987). https://doi.org/10.1007/3-540-47721-7_12
19. Fujisaki, E., Okamoto, T.: Statistical zero knowledge protocols to prove modular polynomial relations. In: Kaliski, B.S. (ed.) CRYPTO 1997. LNCS, vol. 1294, pp. 16–30. Springer, Heidelberg (1997). https://doi.org/10.1007/BFb0052225
20. Goldreich, O., Krawczyk, H.: On the composition of zero-knowledge proof systems. In: Paterson, M.S. (ed.) ICALP 1990. LNCS, vol. 443, pp. 268–282. Springer, Heidelberg (1990). https://doi.org/10.1007/BFb0032038
21. Hazay, C., Lindell, Y.: Sigma protocols and efficient zero-knowledge[1]. In: Hazay, C., Lindell, Y. (eds.) Efficient Secure Two-Party Protocols. ISC, pp. 147–175. Springer, Heidelberg (2010). https://doi.org/10.1007/978-3-642-14303-8_6
22. Krenn, S., Orrù, M.: Proposal: σ-protocols (2021). https://docs.zkproof.org/pages/standards/accepted-workshop4/proposal-sigma.pdf
23. Nguyen, K.Q., Bao, F., Mu, Y., Varadharajan, V.: Zero-knowledge proofs of possession of digital signatures and its applications. In: Varadharajan, V., Mu, Y. (eds.) ICICS 1999. LNCS, vol. 1726, pp. 103–118. Springer, Heidelberg (1999). https://doi.org/10.1007/978-3-540-47942-0_9
24. Pedersen, T.P.: Non-interactive and information-theoretic secure verifiable secret sharing. In: Feigenbaum, J. (ed.) CRYPTO 1991. LNCS, vol. 576, pp. 129–140. Springer, Heidelberg (1992). https://doi.org/10.1007/3-540-46766-1_9
25. Schnorr, C.P.: Efficient signature generation by smart cards. J. Cryptol. 4(3), 161–174 (1991). https://doi.org/10.1007/BF00196725
26. Silverman, J.H.: The geometry of elliptic curves. In: Silverman, J.H. (ed.) The Arithmetic of Elliptic Curves. GTM, vol. 106, pp. 41–114. Springer, New York (2009). https://doi.org/10.1007/978-0-387-09494-6_3
27. Wahby, R.S., Tzialla, I., Shelat, A., Thaler, J., Walfish, M.: Doubly-efficient zkSNARKs without trusted setup. In: 2018 IEEE Symposium on Security and Privacy, pp. 926–943. IEEE Computer Society Press (2018). https://doi.org/10.1109/SP.2018.00060

Cryptographic Accumulators: New Definitions, Enhanced Security, and Delegatable Proofs

Anaïs Barthoulot[1]([⊠]), Olivier Blazy[2], and Sébastien Canard[3]

[1] Université de Montpellier, LIRMM, Montpellier, France
anais.barthoulot@lirmm.fr
[2] École Polytechnique, Palaiseau, France
olivier.blazy@polytechnique.edu
[3] LTCI, Télécom Paris, Institut Polytechnique de Paris, Palaiseau, France
sebastien.canard@telecom-paris.fr

Abstract. Cryptographic accumulators, introduced in 1993 by Benaloh and De Mare, represent a set with a concise value and offer proofs of (non-)membership. Accumulators have evolved, becoming essential in anonymous credentials, e-cash, and blockchain applications. Various properties like *dynamic* and *universal* emerged for specific needs, leading to multiple accumulator definitions. In 2015, Derler, Hanser, and Slamanig proposed a unified model, but new properties, including *zero-knowledge* security, have arisen since. We offer a new definition of accumulators, based on Derler *et al.*'s, that is suitable for all properties. We also introduce a new security property, *unforgeability of private evaluation*, to protect accumulator from forgery and we verify this property in Barthoulot, Blazy, and Canard's recent accumulator. Finally we provide discussions on security properties of accumulators and on the delegatable (non-)membership proofs property.

Keywords: Cryptographic accumulators · Dual pairing vector spaces · Security reductions

1 Introduction

Cryptographic Accumulators. In 1993, Benaloh and De Mare [15] introduced the concept of a one-way accumulator as a family of one-way hash functions satisfying the *quasi-commutative* property. Later, Baric and Pfitzmann [11] extended the definition, characterizing accumulators as schemes enabling the concise representation, termed the accumulator, of a finite set of values. A cryptographic accumulator provides membership proofs for elements in the set. Some accumulators require an additional element, called the *witness*, for generating a membership proof, classifying them as *asymmetric* accumulators; those without this requirement are *symmetric* accumulators. This work focuses on asymmetric accumulators, comprising four algorithms Setup, Eval, WitCreate, Verify. Specifically, Setup establishes accumulator parameters, Eval accumulates values, WitCreate generates membership witnesses, and Verify verifies membership. As for security, accumulators must satisfy the *collision resistance*

© The Author(s), under exclusive license to Springer Nature Switzerland AG 2024
S. Vaudenay and C. Petit (Eds.): AFRICACRYPT 2024, LNCS 14861, pp. 94–119, 2024.
https://doi.org/10.1007/978-3-031-64381-1_5

property, preventing adversaries from finding an element not in the set and producing a fraudulent witness for this element.

Uniform Modeling. From this basic property, the literature has been very prolific in terms of additional functionalities and/or properties. We can mention the *dynamic* or the *universal* properties, which respectively allow the addition or removal of elements to the accumulated set and efficient updates to witnesses, as well as the generation of witnesses to prove the absence of certain elements. Most of these new properties were introduced to satisfy a specific (and sometimes unique) need, thus they do not help in having a global picture of cryptographic accumulators and their properties, with some rare exceptions [7,26,28]. In the asymmetric setting, we consider that the most relevant paper on such issues is the one by Derler *et al.* [26] in 2015, who proposed a uniform model for dynamic universal cryptographic accumulators, regrouping existing properties. We use this paper model's in this work. Recently, [9] proposed the first universally composable treatment of cryptographic accumulators. However, due to its limited adoption in the literature, we opt for a property-based definition of accumulators rather than a universally composable treatment.

Instantiations and Related Primitives. Since their introduction, several accumulators were built. The original ones were based on the RSA assumption [11,15], and many works used variants of it to build their own scheme [19,27,54]. In [45], Nguyen proposed an accumulator based on pairings, and others followed [4,5,18,25,30, ...]. Recently, a few works presented accumulators based on lattices, such as [36,41,48] and [6,44] proposed a code-based scheme. We can then divide existing accumulator instantiations in five categories: hash-based accumulators, lattice-based accumulators, pairing-based, code-based, and number theoretic accumulators. Several works studied the relations between cryptographic accumulators and other primitives: [30] showed that zero-knowledge sets implies zero-knowledge accumulators, which itself implies primary-secondary-resolver membership proof systems, [22] proved that vector commitment can be used to build dynamic accumulators, and later [37] proved that functional commitments for linear functions implies cryptographic accumulators with large universe (i.e., domain size can be exponential in the security parameter).

Applications. Cryptographic accumulators are versatile tools with diverse applications. Originally used for timestamping and membership testing [15], they have found utility in various areas such as fail-stop signatures [11], ID-based ring signatures [45], and distributed public key infrastructure [51]. However, their central focus today is on protecting individual privacy, especially in membership revocation for group signatures, direct anonymous attestations [19], and anonymous credentials [2,4]. Accumulators play a crucial role in authenticated data structures, addressing the challenge of authenticating set operations [30,37,49]. Operations on sets, including subset and disjointness, can be directly performed on sets represented by an accumulator [53]. Additionally, accumulator-based representations support fundamental set operations such as union, intersection, and set difference [30,49]. Furthermore, in the context of blockchain and digital cash systems, accumulators serve crucial roles. In blockchain, they streamline transaction verification by proving membership in valid transactions while preserving privacy. They also contribute to data compression in blockchain states, reducing storage needs and improving scalability. In digital cash systems, accumulators provide efficient methods for verifying transaction validity while safeguarding user anonymity [5,21]. As a result, they play an indispensable role in ensuring both security and privacy in digital financial transactions across various applications.

Our Contributions. In this work, we present a new definition of cryptographic accumulators along with an overview of accumulator properties and features,that complements [26]'s model. Additionally, we engage in several discussions on accumulators properties. Specifically:

- We introduce a novel definition of cryptographic accumulators, representing the primary contribution of this work. For the sake of clarity, our scheme is static (*i.e.* not dynamic) and non-universal, but a definition for a dynamic universal scheme, as presented in [26], can easily be derived. This new definition offers flexibility as it serves as a foundational framework to incorporate all existing properties and functionalities of accumulators, thereby extending the model proposed by [26]. Furthermore, it aims to establish a standard in the field of cryptographic accumulators, thereby providing a unified framework for describing accumulators and their properties. To demonstrate the usability of our definition, we present a (informal) comprehensive and up-to-date overview of all accumulator properties, in Sect. 2.
- In Sect. 3, we focus on security properties of accumulators. First, we delve into a discussion on the property called *undeniability* within a specific scenario known as the trusted setup model. Then, we engage a discussion on a recently introduced security property, *obliviousness*. Finally, we explore the existing relations between these properties and establish new relations.
- In Sect. 4, we present the second contribution of this work: the introduction of a novel security property, called *unforgeability of private evaluation*. This property states that the scheme is resistant to attempts to forge or create false accumulators using the secret key. We also establish that the recent accumulator proposed in [12] satisfies this new security property. The latter operates in the asymmetric bilinear setting and employs dual pairing vector spaces [47], and to demonstrate that this scheme satisfies our new security property, we introduce a novel security assumption named *fixed argument dual pairing vector spaces inversion*. This assumption, constituting an auxiliary contribution, can be reduced to *computational Diffie Hellman* assumption and represents the first computational assumption for dual pairing vector spaces and may hold independent significance for future works.
- We conclude this paper with a discussion on a property known as delegatable (non-) membership proofs. In greater detail, we explore the requirements necessary to achieve this property with the aim of presenting a generic construction.

2 Cryptographic Accumulators

In this section, we formally introduce cryptographic accumulators and provide an exhaustive list of definitions, functionalities, and properties associated with this primitive. In line with our paper's introduction, we emphasize modern accumulator definitions over the original one by Benaloh and De Mare [15]. Throughout the remainder of our work, we focus on asymmetric accumulators, with the understanding that many of the properties apply to symmetric accumulators as well. We opt for asymmetric accumulators due to their improved efficiency: in the accumulators literature, it is admitted that symmetric accumulators cannot have a size less than linear in the number of accumulated elements, while asymmetric schemes can produce accumulators of constant size.

2.1   Our New Definition

We propose a definition of accumulators based on the definition given by Derler *et al.* [26] (that we slightly simplify), and based on proof systems as the definition given by Acar and Nguyen [1]. The motivation behind introducing this new definition stems from the absence of a sufficiently modular definition that can adapt to various properties. Currently, defining an accumulator scheme for a specific property requires a tailored approach, resulting in the need to redefine the accumulator to align with specific requirements. Our proposed definition addresses this limitation, offering a modular framework that can be applied universally across different properties. We start by giving the definition of proof system and its associated properties.

Definition 1. *Proof System* [1]. *Let* $\mathcal{R}$ *be an efficiently computable relation of* $(\mathsf{Para}, \mathsf{Sta}, \mathsf{Wit})$ *with setup parameters* Para, *a statement* Sta, *and a witness* Wit. *A non-interactive proof system for* $\mathcal{R}$ *consists of 3 PPT algorithms: a* Setup, *a prover* Prove, *and a verifier* Verif. *A non-interactive proof system* $(\mathsf{Setup}, \mathsf{Prove}, \mathsf{Verif})$ *must be* complete *and* sound. *Completeness means that for every PPT adversary* $\mathcal{A}$, *the following is negligible*

$$\left| \Pr \left[\begin{array}{c} \mathsf{Para} \leftarrow \mathsf{Setup}(\lambda); (\mathsf{Sta}, \mathsf{Wit}) \leftarrow \mathcal{A}(\mathsf{Para}); \mathsf{Proof} \leftarrow \mathsf{Prove}(\mathsf{Para}, \mathsf{Sta}, \mathsf{Wit}): \\ \mathsf{Verif}(\mathsf{Para}, \mathsf{Sta}, \mathsf{Proof}) = 1 \ if \ (\mathsf{Para}, \mathsf{Sta}, \mathsf{Wit}) \in \mathcal{R} \end{array} \right] - 1 \right|.$$

Soundness means that for every PPT adversary $\mathcal{A}$, *the following is negligible*

$$\left| \Pr \left[\begin{array}{c} \mathsf{Para} \leftarrow \mathsf{Setup}(\lambda); (\mathsf{Sta}, \mathsf{Proof}) \leftarrow \mathcal{A}(\mathsf{Para}): \\ \mathsf{Verif}(\mathsf{Para}, \mathsf{Sta}, \mathsf{Proof}) = 0 \ if \ (\mathsf{Para}, \mathsf{Sta}, \mathsf{Wit}) \notin \mathcal{R}, \forall \mathsf{Wit} \end{array} \right] - 1 \right|.$$

We now present our new definition of accumulators, based on proof systems.

Definition 2. *Cryptographic Accumulator* [15,26]. *A cryptographic accumulator scheme is a tuple of efficient algorithms defined as follows:*

- $\mathsf{Gen}(\lambda)$: *the generation algorithm takes as input a security parameter* λ. *It returns a key pair* $\mathfrak{K} = (\mathsf{sk_{acc}}, \mathsf{pk_{acc}})$, *where* $\mathsf{pk_{acc}}$ *contains the setup parameters* Para *of* $\mathcal{R}$, *an efficiently computable relation.* Gen *can also be seen as the* Setup *algorithm of a proof system* $(\mathsf{Setup}, \mathsf{Prove}, \mathsf{Verif})$ *for* $\mathcal{R}$.
- $\mathsf{Eval}(\mathfrak{K}, \mathcal{X})$: *the evaluation algorithm takes as input the accumulator key pair* $\mathfrak{K}$ *and a set* $\mathcal{X}$ *to be accumulated. It returns an accumulator* $\mathsf{acc}_{\mathcal{X}}$ *together with some auxiliary information* aux. *Notice that* $(\mathsf{acc}_{\mathcal{X}}, \mathsf{aux})$ *form a statement* Sta *for* $\mathcal{R}$.

- WitCreate($\mathfrak{K}, \mathcal{X}, \text{acc}_\mathcal{X}, \text{aux}, x$): *the witness creation algorithm takes as input the accumulator key pair $\mathfrak{K}$, an accumulator $\text{acc}_\mathcal{X}$, the associated set $\mathcal{X}$, auxiliary information* aux, *and an element x. If $x \in \mathcal{X}$ it outputs a witness $\text{wit}_x^\mathcal{X}$, otherwise it outputs a reject symbol $\bot$. Note that $\text{wit}_x^\mathcal{X}$ forms a witness* Wit *for $\mathcal{R}$.*
- CompProof($\text{pk}_\text{acc}, \text{acc}_\mathcal{X}, \text{aux}, \text{wit}_x^\mathcal{X}, x$): *the proof computation algorithm takes as input the accumulator public key pk_acc that contains the proof system parameters* Para, *an accumulator $\text{acc}_\mathcal{X} = $* Sta *and associated auxiliary information, a witness $\text{wit}_x^\mathcal{X} = $* Wit, *and element x. It runs the proof system prover algorithm* Prove(Para, Sta, Wit) *and outputs the result* Proof.
- Verify($\text{pk}_\text{acc}, \text{acc}_\mathcal{X}, \text{aux}, \text{Proof}$): *the verification algorithm takes as input the accumulator public key pk_acc that contains the proof system parameters* Para, *an accumulator $\text{acc}_\mathcal{X} = $* Sta *and associated auxiliary information* aux, *and a proof* Proof. *It runs the proof system verification algorithm* Verif(Para, Sta, Proof). *If* (Para, Sta, Wit) $\in \mathcal{R}$ *(meaning that $\text{wit}_x^\mathcal{X}$ is correct and thus that $x \in \mathcal{X}$) it returns 1, otherwise it returns 0.*

Note 1. The algorithm Gen is ran by a third party, called sometimes accumulator manager. We will come back on the trust of this party in Sect. 2.2.

We now present the two fundamental properties of accumulators, *correctness* and *collision resistance*. We start with the former that states that for all honestly generated keys, computed accumulators and witnesses, the Verify algorithm always return 1.

Definition 3. Correctness. *A cryptographic accumulator is said to be* correct *if for all security parameter λ, all set of values $\mathcal{X}$, and all element x such that $x \in \mathcal{X}$:*

$$\Pr \left[\begin{array}{c} \mathfrak{K} = (\text{sk}_\text{acc}, \text{pk}_\text{acc}) \leftarrow \text{Gen}(\lambda), (\text{acc}_\mathcal{X}, \text{aux}) \leftarrow \text{Eval}(\mathfrak{K}, \mathcal{X}), \\ \text{wit}_x^\mathcal{X} \leftarrow \text{WitCreate}(\mathfrak{K}, \mathcal{X}, \text{acc}_\mathcal{X}, \text{aux}, x) \\ \text{Proof} \leftarrow \text{CompProof}(\text{pk}_\text{acc}, \text{acc}_\mathcal{X}, \text{aux}, \text{wit}_x^\mathcal{X}, x) : \\ \text{Verify}(\text{pk}_\text{acc}, \text{acc}_\mathcal{X}, \text{Proof}) = 1 \end{array} \right] = 1$$

Regarding security of cryptographic accumulators, several notions were introduced such as *undeniability* [38], *indistinguishability* [26] or *zero-knowledge* [30] for example. We here only formally present the property of *collision resistance*, but in Sect. 2.2 we give an exhaustive list of all accumulator security properties and a (informal) definition for all of them. Informally a cryptographic accumulator is said to be *collision resistant* if it is hard for an adversary to forge a witness for an element that is not in the accumulated set.

Definition 4. Collision resistance [11,26]**.** *An accumulator scheme is said to satisfy collision resistance[1] if all PPT adversaries $\mathcal{A}$, the following advantage is negligible:*

$$\text{Adv}_\mathcal{A}^{CR}(\lambda) := \Pr \left[\begin{array}{c} \mathfrak{K} = (\text{sk}_\text{acc}, \text{pk}_\text{acc}) \leftarrow \text{Gen}(\lambda), (\mathcal{X}, \text{wit}_x^\mathcal{X}, x) \leftarrow \mathcal{A}^\mathcal{O}(\text{pk}_\text{acc}) \\ (\text{acc}_\mathcal{X}, \text{aux}) \leftarrow \text{Eval}(\mathfrak{K}, \mathcal{X}) \\ \text{Proof} \leftarrow \text{CompProof}(\text{pk}_\text{acc}, \text{acc}_\mathcal{X}, \text{aux}, \text{wit}_x^\mathcal{X}, x) : \\ \text{Verify}(\text{pk}_\text{acc}, \text{acc}_\mathcal{X}, \text{Proof}) = 1 \land x \notin \mathcal{X} \end{array} \right]$$

---

[1] In some works, "collision resistance" is called "collision freeness", "soundness" or "set binding" [22]. We will only use the terms *collision resistance* in the following.

where $\mathcal{O} = \{\mathcal{O}^E, \mathcal{O}^W\}$ *and* $\mathcal{O}^E, \mathcal{O}^W$ *represent the oracles for the algorithms* Eval *and* WitCreate *respectively. An adversary is allowed to query them an arbitrary number of times. If* $\mathcal{O}^W$ *is queried for an element not in the provided accumulator, it outputs a reject symbol.*

The following theorem establishes that correctness and collision resistance of the accumulator scheme hold if completeness and soundness of the underlying proof system hold respectively.

Theorem 1. *If the proof system* (Setup, Prove, Verif) *is respectively* complete *and* sound, *then the accumulator* (Gen, Eval, WitCreate, CompProof, Verify) *is respectively* correct *and satisfies* collision resistance.

We prove the theorem in two steps, corresponding to the following lemmas.

Lemma 1. *If the proof system* (Setup, Prove, Verif) *is* complete, *then the accumulator* (Gen, Eval, WitCreate, CompProof, Verify) *is* correct.

Proof. First, let us see the correctness property as a game between a challenger and an adversary. The aim of the adversary is to find a set $\mathcal{X}$ and an element x such that $x \in \mathcal{X}$ but Verify($\mathsf{pk}_{\mathsf{acc}}, \mathsf{acc}_{\mathcal{X}}, \mathsf{Proof}$) = 0, where ($\mathsf{acc}_{\mathcal{X}}, \mathsf{aux}$) $\leftarrow$ Eval($\mathfrak{K}, \mathcal{X}$), $\mathsf{wit}_x^{\mathcal{X}} \leftarrow$ WitCreate($\mathfrak{K}, \mathcal{X}, \mathsf{acc}_{\mathcal{X}}, \mathsf{aux}, x$) and Proof $\leftarrow$ CompProof($\mathsf{pk}_{\mathsf{acc}}, \mathsf{acc}_{\mathcal{X}}, \mathsf{aux}, \mathsf{wit}_x^{\mathcal{X}}, x$). In this case, we say that the accumulator is *correct* if the advantage of an adversary to win the game is negligible. Now, we prove the lemma by proving the contrapositive. Let $\mathcal{B}$ be an adversary that breaks the accumulator scheme correctness property with non negligible advantage. We build $\mathcal{A}$ an adversary that breaks the completeness property of the proof system. Let $\mathcal{C}$ be a challenger. $\mathcal{A}$ is given Para and λ from $\mathcal{C}$. She runs Gen(λ) and gives $\mathsf{pk}_{\mathsf{acc}}$ to $\mathcal{B}$. $\mathcal{B}$ sends ($\mathcal{X}, x$) to $\mathcal{A}$. The latter computes Sta = ($\mathsf{acc}_{\mathcal{X}}, \mathsf{aux}$) $\leftarrow$ Eval($\mathfrak{K}, \mathcal{X}$), Wit = $\mathsf{wit}_x^{\mathcal{X}} \leftarrow$ WitCreate($\mathfrak{K}, \mathcal{X}, \mathsf{acc}_{\mathcal{X}}, \mathsf{aux}, x$) (as she knows $\mathfrak{K}$) and Proof = Prove(Para, Sta, Wit = wit_x). As $\mathcal{B}$ wins the correctness security game, we have that Verify($\mathsf{pk}_{\mathsf{acc}}, \mathsf{acc}_{\mathcal{X}}, \mathsf{Proof}$) = 0 while $x \in \mathcal{X}$, which corresponds to Verif(Para, Sta, Proof) = 0 while (Para, Sta, Proof) $\in \mathcal{R}$. As $\mathcal{B}$ wins with non negligible advantage, then so does $\mathcal{A}$.

Lemma 2. *If the proof system* (Setup, Prove, Verif) *is* sound, *then the accumulator* (Gen, Eval, WitCreate, CompProof, Verify) *satisfies* collision resistance.

Proof. We prove the contrapositive. Let $\mathcal{B}$ be an adversary that breaks the accumulator scheme collision resistance property with non negligible advantage. We build $\mathcal{A}$ an adversary that breaks the soundness property of the proof system, using $\mathcal{B}$. Let $\mathcal{C}$ be a challenger. $\mathcal{A}$ is given Para and λ from $\mathcal{C}$. She runs Gen(λ) and gives $\mathsf{pk}_{\mathsf{acc}}$ to $\mathcal{B}$. As $\mathcal{A}$ knows $\mathsf{sk}_{\mathsf{acc}}$ she can answers to all of $\mathcal{B}$'s oracle queries. At some point, $\mathcal{B}$ sends ($\mathcal{X}, \mathsf{wit}_x, x$) to $\mathcal{A}$. The latter computes Sta = ($\mathsf{acc}_{\mathcal{X}}, \mathsf{aux}$) $\leftarrow$ Eval($\mathfrak{K}, \mathcal{X}$) and Proof = Prove(Para, Sta, Wit = wit_x). As $\mathcal{B}$ wins the collision resistance security game, we have that Verify($\mathsf{pk}_{\mathsf{acc}}, \mathsf{acc}_{\mathcal{X}}, \mathsf{Proof}$) = 1 while $x \notin \mathcal{X}$, which corresponds to Verif(Para, Sta, Proof) = 1 while (Para, Sta, Proof) $\notin \mathcal{R}$. As $\mathcal{B}$ wins with non negligible advantage, then so does $\mathcal{A}$.

Note 2. In the rest of the paper, a witness $\mathsf{wit}_x^{\mathcal{X}}$ will be written wit_x for short, if there is no ambiguity on the associated set $\mathcal{X}$.

2.2 Overview

As mentioned earlier, accumulators have evolved over time to serve various purposes, with new properties and functionalities being added to align with these objectives. However, these additions have often been made in isolation, leading to multiple definitions of accumulators accompanied by core algorithm modifications. That makes it complicated to have an overview of accumulators and their properties. That is why in 2015, Derler *et al.* [26] proposed a unified formal model, dealing with most of existing accumulators' properties. Their work became a reference when working with accumulators. However, since 2015 new properties of accumulators have been introduced, and some functionalities, were not taken into account in the work of Derler *et al.*. In this section we present an up-to-date (informal) overview of accumulators properties following our definition for accumulators. We first list the features of accumulators, except for the *correctness* property which was already defined in Sect. 2.1.

Trapdoorless: an accumulator scheme is said to be *trapdoorless* if the generation algorithm Gen outputs a single public key pk_{acc} instead of a key pair $\mathfrak{K} = (sk_{acc}, pk_{acc})$. Therefore, all algorithms taking as input $\mathfrak{K}$ now take as input pk_{acc}.

Note 3. Accumulators based on collision-resistant hash functions are trapdoorless.

Evaluation: in Definition 2, the evaluation algorithm takes as input the key pair $\mathfrak{K}$. If Eval takes as input sk_{acc} (resp. pk_{acc}) solely, we say that the accumulator has *private evaluation* (resp. *public evaluation*).

Witness Generation: regarding the way witnesses are generated in WitCreate, the literature gives four possibilities: **i)** only using the *public key* [37], in this case the accumulator is said to have *public witness generation*, **ii)** using the *secret key* [41], in this case the accumulator has *private evaluation*, **iii)** using the public key or in a more efficient way using the secret key [4,26], **iv)** using a specially created private key, called the *evaluation key* [30].

Note 4. In the case of trapdoorless accumulator, the evaluation and the witness generation are obliviously publicly made.

Trusted, Semi-Trusted and Non-Trusted Setup [26]: the knowledge of the accumulator secret key sk_{acc} allows an adversary to break the security of the accumulator scheme, such as the collision resistance property. Therefore a natural question arise: should we trust the third party that runs the generation algorithm Gen? Obliviously there is no need for a trusted setup in the case of trapdoorless accumulators. The question is more tricky for other accumulators, such as those based on number theoretic assumptions. Two models are defined: the *trusted* setup model in which a trusted third party runs the generation algorithm Gen and discards sk_{acc} afterwards; the *non-trusted* model in which such trusted third party does not exist. There exists another model, proposed by Lipmaa [38]: the *semi-trusted* setup model. The idea is to divide the generation algorithm Gen into two algorithms: Gen and Setup. In this model, the adversary can control the randomness used in Setup (thus knows the secret key sk_{acc}) but she can neither access or influence the randomness of the Gen algorithm. Notice that this model still requires a partially trusted setup, and is not generally applicable (for example it does not fit the known order group setting, refer to [26] for more details). Therefore, when considering the state of the art it seems most reasonable (regarding the efficiency of the schemes) to define a security model with respect to trusted setup as [26] did and as we will do subsequently. We emphasize that this model is compatible with all existing constructions.

Sizes Requirements [18]: accumulator and witness sizes should be independent of the number of accumulated elements. More formally, for $N \in \mathbb{N}$ that represents the size of the set $\mathcal{X}$ represented by the accumulator $\text{acc}_\mathcal{X}$, then we would like that $|\text{acc}_\mathcal{X}| \notin O(N)$ and for any $x \in \mathcal{X}$, $|\text{wit}_x| \notin O(N)$.

Boundedness [5]: an accumulator scheme (Gen, Eval, WitCreate, Verify) is said to be *bounded* if the generation algorithm Gen takes as additional input $b \in \mathbb{N}$, such that for all set $\mathcal{X}$ given as input of the evaluation algorithm Eval, $|\mathcal{X}| \leq b$.

Note 5. In some definitions, such as in [26], the parameter b belongs to $\mathbb{N} \cup \infty$ and is always given as an input of Gen. An accumulator is then said to be *bounded* if $b \neq \infty$.

Dynamic [19]: an accumulator that additionally provides efficient algorithms (Add, Delete, WitnessUpdate) that respectively adds/removes elements from the accumulated set and the accumulator, and updates the witness accordingly. More formally, the algorithms are defined as follows:

- Add($\mathfrak{K}, \text{acc}_\mathcal{X}, \text{aux}, y$): this algorithm takes as input the accumulator key pair $\mathfrak{K}$, an accumulator $\text{acc}_\mathcal{X}$ for a set $\mathcal{X}$, associated auxiliary information aux and an element y to be added. If $y \in \mathcal{X}$, it returns $\bot$. Otherwise it returns the updated accumulator $\text{acc}_{\mathcal{X}'}$, with $\mathcal{X}' = \mathcal{X} \cup \{y\}$, along with updated auxiliary information aux'.
- Delete($\mathfrak{K}, \text{acc}_\mathcal{X}, \text{aux}, y$): this algorithm takes as input the accumulator key pair $\mathfrak{K}$, an accumulator $\text{acc}_\mathcal{X}$ for a set $\mathcal{X}$, associated auxiliary information aux and an element y to be removed. If $y \notin \mathcal{X}$, it returns $\bot$. Otherwise it returns the updated accumulator $\text{acc}_{\mathcal{X}'}$, with $\mathcal{X}' = \mathcal{X} \setminus \{y\}$, and updated auxiliary information aux'.
- WitnessUpdate($\mathfrak{K}, \text{wit}_x, \text{aux}, y$): this algorithm takes as input the accumulator key pair $\mathfrak{K}$, a witness wit_x to be updated, auxiliary information aux and a value y that was added (resp. removed) to (resp. from) the accumulator, where aux indicates addition or deletion. It returns updated witness wit'_x on success, and $\bot$ otherwise.

Note 6. If the accumulator scheme only provides Add (resp. Delete) and WitnessUpdate algorithms, then we say that the scheme is *additive* (resp. *subtractive*).

Publicly Updatable [26]: a dynamic (or additive or subtractive) accumulator in which updates (of the accumulators and witnesses) are performed without the secret key.

Universal [35]: witnesses can be generated to prove membership or non-membership. The accumulator scheme now relies on two proof systems, one for proving membership and one for proving non-membership. The witness creation, the proof computation and the verification algorithms take an additional input, a boolean Type that indicates membership (Type $= 0$) or non-membership (Type $= 1$). More formally, an accumulator (Gen, Eval, WitCreate, CompProof, Verify) is said to be *universal* if the syntax of the witness creation, the proof computation algorithm, and the verification algorithms are as follows: WitCreate($\mathfrak{K}, \mathcal{X}, \text{acc}_\mathcal{X}, y, \text{Type}$), CompProof($\text{pk}_{\text{acc}}, \text{acc}_\mathcal{X}, \text{wit}_x, x, \text{Type}$) and Verify($\text{pk}_{\text{acc}}, \text{acc}_\mathcal{X}, y, \text{wit}_y, \text{Type}$). The witness creation algorithm outputs mwit_y for membership witness and nmwit_y for non-membership witness. When given as input Type $= 0$, the algorithms CompProof and Verify run respectively the Prove and Verif algorithms of the membership proof system. Given as input Type $= 1$, they run the non-membership proof system algorithms Prove and Verify.

Note 7. In some works, an accumulator scheme supporting only membership (resp. non-membership) proofs is said to be *positive* (resp. *negative*).

Delegatable Non-membership Proofs [1]: it is possible for a user to give to another entity the ability to prove non-membership of the former's element, without the latter knowing the concerned element. More formally, an accumulator with delegatable non-membership proofs has four extra algorithms (Dele, Vali, Rede, CompNMProof) such that Dele outputs a delegation key Del_y associated to element y; Vali verifies if a delegation key is valid; Rede computes a new delegation key from one given as input; and CompNMProof computes a non-membership proof from the delegation key of element y (Del_y) for an accumulator given as input. See Sect. 5 for more details.

Note 8. **i)** A witness for an element x is related to the accumulated set but not to the witness, whereas a delegation key is related to the x only and not the accumulated set. **ii)** Defining the delegatable property when using the [26] model is kinda complicated. The first thing to do is to separate the verification algorithm into two algorithms: the first one computes some values from the accumulator and the witness, and the second verifies if a given relation between those values is satisfied. However, defining formally for any accumulator what these values are and what is the relation to verify is not an easy task. Our definition is more suitable as it already propose two algorithms for the verification, and formally introduced and highlight the proof system used in the accumulator.

Subset Query [27,30,37] **and Batching** [28,55]: in an accumulator scheme with *subset query*, witnesses can be generated for a subset of the accumulated set rather than individual elements. In this case, the syntax of the witness generation algorithm is the following one WitCreate($\mathfrak{K}, \mathcal{X}, \text{acc}_\mathcal{X}, \text{aux}, \mathcal{I}$), where $\mathcal{I} \subset \mathcal{X}$. Sometimes, direct generation is not possible thus the accumulator is using *batching* techniques [16][2]. For example, *witness aggregation* [16] is a batching technique: first it computes individual witnesses for all elements of the subset, then aggregates the witnesses.

Multiset Setting [16,30,39]: sets that can be accumulated can be multisets. Each element is associated to a count (belonging to $\mathbb{N}$), that is equal to 0 when the element is not accumulated. More formally, any set $\mathcal{X}$ that is accumulated is composed of tuples

---

[2] Applying a single action applied to n items instead of one action per item.

of the form (x_i, k_i) for $i = 1, \cdots, |\mathcal{X}|$, where x_i is the element to accumulated and $k_i \in \mathbb{N}$ represents the multiplicity of the element in the set.

Asynchronous [52]: the accumulator satisfies both **low update frequency** and **old accumulator compatibility**. An accumulator satisfies *low update frequency* if it is dynamic, and witnesses do not have to be updated at each update of the accumulator (for witnesses associated to elements not added in the accumulator). An accumulator satisfies *old accumulator compatibility* if it is dynamic, and verification still holds with an updated witness and an old (not updated) accumulator, for an element already present in the old accumulator.

Note 9. We present the asynchronous property for an additive, non-universal scheme, as done in [52]. One can easily extend this property to a dynamic universal scheme.

Accumulators and Zero-Knowledge Proofs: some works (such as [4,19,34,46]) complete cryptographic accumulator with *zero-knowledge proof-of-knowledge protocols*: a client that knows his value x is (or is not) in $\mathcal{X}$, can efficiently prove to a third-party that his value is (resp. is not) in the set, without revealing x or its associated witness. Some accumulators are designed to be checked by a SNARK system efficiently, such as [20]. In this case we refer to such accumulators as *SNARKs-friendly*. Recently, Lipmaa introduced a new type of accumulator, called *determinantal* [40], that has a structure that support a special type of NIZK, called CLPØ [24].

Note 10. The formal definition of an accumulator scheme with zero-knowledge proofs, the one of a SNARK-friendly scheme, and the one of a determinantal scheme can easily be derived from our Definition 2 by replace the proof system by the appropriate NIZK. Again we here prove the modularity of our definition.

Dually Computable [12]: an accumulator with two evaluation algorithms, one that takes as input only the scheme's secret key, while the other takes as input the public key solely. Outputs of both algorithms are distinguishable. More formally, an accumulator $(\mathsf{Gen}, \mathsf{Eval}, \mathsf{WitCreate}, \mathsf{CompProof}, \mathsf{Verify})$ is said to be *dually computable* if **i)** the syntax of the evaluation algorithm is $\mathsf{Eval}(\mathsf{sk}_{\mathsf{acc}}, \mathcal{X})$, **ii)** there is a second evaluation algorithm, with syntax $\mathsf{PublicEval}(\mathsf{pk}_{\mathsf{acc}}, \mathcal{X})$, **iii)** for any set $\mathcal{X}$, $\mathsf{Eval}(\mathsf{sk}_{\mathsf{acc}}, \mathcal{X}) \neq \mathsf{PublicEval}(\mathsf{pk}_{\mathsf{acc}}, \mathcal{X})$, and **iv)** the witness creation, the proof computation and the verification algorithms work with the outputs of both evaluation algorithms.

We now list all security properties found in the literature. A fundamental requirement for a secure cryptographic accumulator is collision resistance, as already presented in Sect. 2.1. Various definitions have been proposed in the literature, and we discuss them for both dynamic and universal accumulators. In case of static (resp. non-universal) scheme, just omit the dynamic (resp. universal) related parts. Throughout this paper, we assume adversaries are "Probabilistic Polynomial Time" (PPT).

Note 11. In Definition 4, we use a static non-universal accumulator scheme. In the case of a dynamic universal accumulator, the property can be defined similarly: the adversary gains access to an oracle for acquiring membership and non-membership witnesses, as well as an oracle for adding or deleting elements from an accumulator. The winning condition remains consistent with the previous definition: meeting the condition from before or discovering an element x' in $\mathcal{X}$ to forge a non-membership witness[3].

One-Wayness [15]: informally it is hard for an adversary who is given a set $\mathcal{X} = (x_1, \cdots, x_N)$, its accumulation result $(\mathrm{acc}_{\mathcal{X}}, \mathrm{aux})$, and another value $x \notin \mathcal{X}$ (resp. $x \in \mathcal{X}$) to output a value wit such that $\mathsf{Verify}(\mathsf{pk}_{\mathrm{acc}}, \mathrm{acc}_{\mathcal{X}}, \mathsf{Proof}, 0) = 1$, where $\mathsf{Proof} \leftarrow \mathsf{CompProof}(\mathsf{pk}_{\mathrm{acc}}, \mathrm{acc}_{\mathcal{X}}, \mathrm{aux}, \mathrm{wit}, x, 0)$ (resp. $\mathsf{Verify}(\mathsf{pk}_{\mathrm{acc}}, \mathrm{acc}_{\mathcal{X}}, \mathsf{Proof}, 1) = 1$, $\mathsf{Proof} \leftarrow \mathsf{CompProof}(\mathsf{pk}_{\mathrm{acc}}, \mathrm{acc}_{\mathcal{X}}, \mathrm{aux}, \mathrm{wit}, x, 1)$).

Strong One-Wayness [11]: informally, given $\mathcal{X} = (x_1, \cdots, x_N)$ and $\mathrm{acc}_{\mathcal{X}}, \mathrm{aux}$, it is hard for an adversary to output $x \notin \mathcal{X}$ (resp. $x \in \mathcal{X}$) and wit such that $\mathsf{Verify}(\mathsf{pk}_{\mathrm{acc}}, \mathrm{acc}_{\mathcal{X}}, \mathsf{Proof}, 0) = 1$, where $\mathsf{Proof} \leftarrow \mathsf{CompProof}(\mathsf{pk}_{\mathrm{acc}}, \mathrm{acc}_{\mathcal{X}}, \mathrm{aux}, \mathrm{wit}, x, 0)$ (resp. $\mathsf{Verify}(\mathsf{pk}_{\mathrm{acc}}, \mathrm{acc}_{\mathcal{X}}, \mathsf{Proof}, 1) = 1$, where $\mathsf{Proof} \leftarrow \mathsf{CompProof}(\mathsf{pk}_{\mathrm{acc}}, \mathrm{acc}_{\mathcal{X}}, \mathrm{aux}, \mathrm{wit}, x, 1)$).

Undeniability [38]: informally, it is hard for an adversary to output an accumulator acc^*, a value x and two witnesses mwit and nmwit such that $\mathsf{Verify}(\mathsf{pk}_{\mathrm{acc}}, \mathrm{acc}^*, \mathsf{Proof}, 0) = 1$ and $\mathsf{Verify}(\mathsf{pk}_{\mathrm{acc}}, \mathrm{acc}^*, \mathsf{Proof}', 1) = 1)$ hold, where $\mathsf{Proof} \leftarrow \mathsf{CompProof}(\mathsf{pk}_{\mathrm{acc}}, \mathrm{acc}_{\mathcal{X}}, \mathrm{aux}, \mathrm{mwit}, x, 0)$ and $\mathsf{Proof}' \leftarrow \mathsf{CompProof}(\mathsf{pk}_{\mathrm{acc}}, \mathrm{acc}_{\mathcal{X}}, \mathrm{aux}, \mathrm{nmwit}, x, 1)$. Notice that the adversary has access to oracles $\mathcal{O}^E, \mathcal{O}^A, \mathcal{O}^D, \mathcal{O}^W$ that respectively represent the oracle for the algorithms Eval, Add, Delete and WitCreate.

One-Way-Domain [27]: informally, the accumulator is collision resistant, and the set of values that can be accumulated is the span of a one-way function. Hence, it is computationally intractable to find witnesses for random values in the accumulator's domain. More formally, there exists a relation $\mathfrak{R}$ over $\mathcal{D}$ (the accumulator domain)$\times \mathfrak{A}$, where $\mathfrak{A}$ is another set, called the antecedent set, such that:

- (efficient verification): there exists an efficient algorithm $\mathfrak{D}$ that on input $(y, a) \in \mathcal{D} \times \mathfrak{A}$, returns 1 if and only if $(y, a) \in \mathfrak{R}$.
- (efficient sampling): there exists a probabilistic algorithm W that on input λ returns $(y, a) \in \mathcal{D} \times \mathfrak{A}$ such that $(y, a) \in \mathfrak{R}$. We refer to a as pre-image of y.
- (one-wayness): it is computationally hard to compute any pre-image a' of an element y that was sampled with W. Formally, for any PPT adversary $\mathcal{A}$: $\Pr\left[(y, a) \leftarrow W(\lambda); a' \leftarrow \mathcal{A}(\lambda, y) : (y, a') \in \mathfrak{R}\right] = \epsilon(\lambda)$, where $\epsilon(.)$ is a negligible function.

Indistinguishability [26]: informally, given the public key, the adversary chooses two sets $\mathcal{X}_0$ and $\mathcal{X}_1$ and obtain the evaluation of one of the two. It has to decide which one. Note that the adversary has access to oracles $\mathcal{O}^E, \mathcal{O}^A, \mathcal{O}^D, \mathcal{O}^W$ that represent the oracles for the algorithms Eval, Add, Delete and WitCreate respectively. An adversary is allowed to query them an arbitrary number of times. However, there are some restrictions regarding the oracles to prevent a trivial win by the adversary: $\mathcal{O}^A$ can only be

---

[3] [55] introduced the *chosen element attack* (CEA) to characterize collision resistance in dynamic accumulators. Notice that this term has been discontinued or abandoned.

ran on elements $x \notin \mathcal{X}_0 \cup \mathcal{X}_1$, $\mathcal{O}^D$ can only be ran on elements $x \in \mathcal{X}_0 \cap \mathcal{X}_1$, $\mathcal{O}^W$ when queried for Type $= 0$ (*i.e.* membership) can only return witnesses for elements that belong to $\mathcal{X}_0 \cap \mathcal{X}_1$, while when queried for Type $= 1$ (*i.e.* non-membership) can only return witnesses for elements that do not belong to $\mathcal{X}_0 \cup \mathcal{X}_1$.

Zero-Knowledge Accumulator [30]: informally, an accumulator is *zero-knowledge* (ZK) if accumulated value, and (non-)membership witnesses leak nothing about the accumulated set at any given point in the security game (even after insertions and deletions, if the accumulator is dynamic).

Note 12. **i)** One requirement for ZK accumulator is to have *ephemeral* proofs, meaning that a proof generated before an update should not be valid after an update. With this condition, it is easy to see that a ZK accumulator scheme cannot be asynchronous. **ii)** In the two above definitions, the adversary is not given the auxiliary information. **iii)** Accumulators with *zero-knowledge proof-of-knowledge protocols* satisfy a privacy notion that is different from the *zero-knowledge* notion of [30] in which the entire protocol execution (as observed by a curious client or an external attacker) leaks nothing.

Obliviousness [10]: the accumulator satisfies both **element hiding** and **Add-Del indistinguishability**. An accumulator satisfies *element hiding* if publicly available auxiliary information aux output by update algorithms (Add or Delete) and associated to an accumulator does not lead any information about the elements in the accumulated set. An accumulator satisfies *Add-Del indistinguishability* if no adversary given publicly available information aux output by update algorithms (Add or Delete) can learn if an operation is an addition or a deletion.

3 Discussions on Accumulators Security

This section presents several discussions on the security properties of accumulators. First, we delve into the undeniability security property within the trusted model setup. Following that, we discuss the obliviousness property. Finally, we summarize existing relations between these properties and introduce new connections. It is worth noting that we did not specifically address the relationships between certain properties of accumulators and functionalities, as this aspect has already been explored in existing works [8].

3.1 Discussion About Undeniability in the Trusted Setup Model

According to [30], in the trusted setup model undeniability provides more than what is necessary in terms of security. We formalize this statement, and we prove it.

Theorem 2. *In the trapdoor setting, trusted model setup, if the evaluation is done privately, then the undeniability is an overkill; the collision resistance property is enough.*

Proof. In the undeniability security game, when the only way for the adversary $\mathcal{A}$ to compute acc* is to request the challenger (private evaluation) by giving a set $\mathcal{X}^*$ we need to consider both cases:

- If $x^* \in \mathcal{X}^*$, then $\mathsf{Verify}(\mathsf{pk}_{\mathsf{acc}}, \mathsf{acc}_{\mathcal{X}^*}, \mathsf{Proof}, 0) = 1$, by definition, where $\mathsf{Proof} = \mathsf{CompProof}(\mathsf{pk}_{\mathsf{acc}}, \mathsf{acc}_{\mathcal{X}^*}, \mathsf{aux}, \mathsf{mwit}_{x^*}, x^*, 0)$, $\mathsf{mwit}_{x^*} \leftarrow \mathsf{WitCreate}(\mathfrak{K}, \mathcal{X}^*, \mathsf{acc}_{\mathcal{X}^*}, \mathsf{aux}, x^*, 0)$. To win, $\mathcal{A}$ must find a non-membership witness nmwit_{x^*}' such that $\mathsf{Verify}(\mathsf{pk}_{\mathsf{acc}}, \mathsf{acc}_{\mathcal{X}^*}, \mathsf{Proof}', 1) = 1$, where $\mathsf{Proof}' = \mathsf{CompProof}(\mathsf{pk}_{\mathsf{acc}}, \mathsf{acc}_{\mathcal{X}^*}, \mathsf{aux}, \mathsf{nmwit}_{x^*}', x^*, 1)$. Thus $\mathcal{A}$ wins if she wins the collision resistant game.
- If $x^* \notin \mathcal{X}^*$, $\mathsf{Verify}(\mathsf{pk}_{\mathsf{acc}}, \mathsf{acc}_{\mathcal{X}^*}, \mathsf{Proof}, 1) = 1$, by definition, where $\mathsf{Proof} = \mathsf{CompProof}(\mathsf{pk}_{\mathsf{acc}}, \mathsf{acc}_{\mathcal{X}^*}, \mathsf{aux}, \mathsf{nmwit}_{x^*}, x^*, 1)$, $\mathsf{nmwit}_{x^*} \leftarrow \mathsf{WitCreate}(\mathfrak{K}, \mathcal{X}^*, \mathsf{acc}_{\mathcal{X}^*}, \mathsf{aux}, x', 1)$. To win the game, $\mathcal{A}$ must find a membership witness mwit_{x^*}' such that $\mathsf{Verify}(\mathsf{pk}_{\mathsf{acc}}, \mathsf{acc}_{\mathcal{X}^*}, \mathsf{Proof}', 1) = 1$, where $\mathsf{Proof}' = \mathsf{CompProof}(\mathsf{pk}_{\mathsf{acc}}, \mathsf{acc}_{\mathcal{X}^*}, \mathsf{aux}, \mathsf{mwit}_{x^*}', x^*, 0)$. This means that $\mathcal{A}$ wins if she wins the collision resistant game.

In both cases, collision-resistance is enough, and then undeniability is not required.

Note 13. If the evaluation is done publicly, *i.e.*, without the knowledge of $\mathsf{sk}_{\mathsf{acc}}$, then undeniability is required. Also (and obliviously) in the non-trusted setup model this property is also required.

3.2   Discussion on Obliviousness

Before the recent work of Baldimtsi *et al.* [10], only two privacy-preserving properties existed for accumulators: *indistinguishability* and *zero-knowledge*. Both demand that the adversary lacks access to the accumulator's auxiliary information aux, crucial for preventing leaks about the accumulated set. This precaution is essential because auxiliary information could potentially disclose details about the accumulated set, particularly when the latter is included in the auxiliary information or when the auxiliary information after an update reveals the added/removed element. Obliviousness [10] goes further, ensuring that publicly available information doesn't disclose anything about the set, including its size. This property focuses on enhancing privacy during update algorithm execution (*i.e.*, aux'). The authors introduced some secret information during the Add algorithm to hide the added element, which is also used in witness generation and verification. However, in accumulator schemes, verification should rely on public elements alone, making it challenging for an oblivious accumulator scheme. While acknowledging the importance of protecting information leaked by aux, we remain unconvinced that the proposed solution effectively addresses this concern.

3.3   Relations Between Security Properties

Looking at accumulators' security properties, we classify them into two categories: those that protect the witness (i.e., preventing forgery of witnesses), and those that protect the accumulated set (i.e., hiding information about the set). In the first category, we have: (strong) one-wayness, collision resistance, one-way domain, and undeniability. In the second category, we have: indistinguishability, zero-knowledge, and obliviousness. It's worth noting that the properties in the first category are computational, while in the second category, they are decisional. Also, there is no security property that protects the accumulated value, perhaps because the latter is mostly computed publicly.

Note 14. Properties that protect the accumulated set define privacy security for accumulators schemes. As already observed in [26,42,43], when formulating a notion of privacy for cryptographic accumulators the fact that the accumulation value computation must be randomized becomes evident.

Comparison Between Properties of the Second Category. The notion of zero-knowledge differs from the privacy notion *indistinguishability* of [26], by protecting not only the originally accumulated set but also all subsequent updates. In fact, [30] formally proved in Sect. 3.3 the following theorem that states that for cryptographic accumulators, zero-knowledge is a strictly stronger property than indistinguishability.

Theorem 3. *Every zero-knowledge dynamic universal accumulator is indistinguishable under the definition of [26], while the opposite is not always true.*

While being really similar at first glance, zero-knowledge and obliviousness are actually different: in the former auxiliary information aux is not given while it is in the latter. It seems then that obliviousness is stronger than zero-knowledge. However, obliviousness requires some particular requirements in the accumulator's algorithms. Thus it cannot be applied to all schemes. Plus taking into account the above discussion, we decided not to include this property in our comparison.

Relations Between Other Properties. First, as the adversary is given more and more flexibility, it is easy to see that the theorem below holds, while the opposite is not true.

Theorem 4. *Every accumulator satisfying strong one-wayness satisfies one-wayness; every collision resistant accumulator satisfies strong one-wayness; every one-way domain accumulator is collision resistant.*

Due to lack of space, we furnish the proof that every collision resistance accumulator satisfies strong one-wayness. The rest of the proof can easily be derived.

Proof. We prove the contrapositive: we suppose that there exists an adversary $\mathcal{B}$ that breaks the strong one-wayness property, and we build an adversary $\mathcal{A}$ that breaks the collision resistance property, using $\mathcal{B}$. Let $\mathcal{C}$ be the challenger of the collision resistance security game. $\mathcal{C}$ run $\mathsf{Gen}(\lambda)$ to get $\mathfrak{K} = (\mathsf{sk}_{\mathsf{acc}}, \mathsf{pk}_{\mathsf{acc}})$ and sends $\mathsf{pk}_{\mathsf{acc}}$ to $\mathcal{A}$, who sends it to $\mathcal{B}$. $\mathcal{A}$ then chooses a set $\mathcal{X}$ and queries the oracle $\mathcal{O}^E$ to get $\mathsf{acc}_\mathcal{X}$. Then, she sends $\mathcal{X}, \mathsf{acc}_\mathcal{X}$ to $\mathcal{B}$. The latter returns an element $x' \notin \mathcal{X}$ and a membership witness wit' such that $\mathsf{Verify}(\mathsf{pk}_{\mathsf{acc}}, \mathsf{acc}_\mathcal{X}, \mathsf{Proof}, 0) = 1$, where $\mathsf{Proof} = \mathsf{CompProof}(\mathfrak{K}, \mathsf{acc}_\mathcal{X}, \mathsf{aux}, \mathsf{wit}', x', 0) = 1$ with non negligible probability. Therefore, $\mathcal{A}$ outputs $(\mathcal{X}, x', \mathsf{wit}')$ and wins the collision resistance security game with non negligible advantage.

For undeniability, the following lemma has been proven in Appendix C.1 of [26]

Lemma 3. *Every undeniable universal accumulator is collision-resistant.*

As mentioned in [38], a black-box reduction in the other direction is impossible. In particular, [17] provides a collision-resistant universal accumulator and exhibit an example to show that their scheme is not undeniable. This proves the following lemma.

Lemma 4. *Not every collision resistant scheme is undeniable.*

It remains to make the link between undeniability and one-way domain. At first, we focus on the scheme based on sorted hash tree given in [17]. This one is proven to be universal and collision resistant, and as state before it is not undeniable. It can moreover be used for domain that is in the span of a one-way function. Hence, one-way domain does not imply undeniability. Therefore, we can establish the following lemma that is proven using the above counterexample.

Lemma 5. *Not every one-way domain accumulator is undeniable.*

For the opposite, we do not succeed in proving that this is true or false, and we leave it as an open problem. In Fig. 1, we summarize all the above properties and their relation, based on related work, but also on our new results. In the figure an arrow means "implies", a crossed out arrow means "does not imply" and a dash arrow means "not proven". Notice that as there is no relation between *obliviousness* and other properties we do not include the former in the figure.

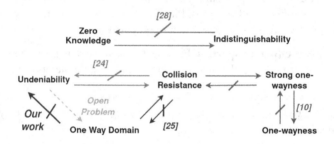

Fig. 1. Relations between security properties of accumulators.

4   New Security Property

In a centralized cryptocurrency system, the accumulator represents spent transaction outputs, enabling users to verify specific transactions through a publicly generated membership witness. Until recently, there was no accumulator scheme offering both private evaluation and public evaluation. Consequently, the scheme depended on a signature scheme to ensure the accuracy of the accumulator in representing approved transactions. Bridging this gap, Barthoulot *et al.* [12] introduced the first accumulator scheme with private evaluation and public witness generation. However, utilizing their scheme in the described scenario lacks a mechanism (distinct from the signature) to safeguard the accumulator. Our contribution addresses this security concern by introducing a novel property, making it challenging to "forge" a privately computed accumulator that passes verification with a legitimate witness. Implementing an accumulator with this property eliminates the need for a signature, simplifying the overall system.

Definition 5. *Unforgeability of private evaluation (UPE). A static non-universal accumulator scheme with private evaluation and public generation is said to satisfy* unforgeability of private evaluation *if for all PPT adversaries $\mathcal{A}$ there is a negligible function $\epsilon(.)$ such that, for any y chosen randomly in $\mathcal{X}^*$:*

$$\Pr \begin{bmatrix} (\text{sk}_{\text{acc}}, \text{pk}_{\text{acc}}) \leftarrow \text{Gen}(\lambda), (\mathcal{X}^*, \text{acc}^*) \leftarrow \mathcal{A}(\text{pk}_{\text{acc}}); \\ (\text{acc}_{\mathcal{X}^*}, \text{aux}) \leftarrow \text{Eval}(\text{sk}_{\text{acc}}, \mathcal{X}^*), y \leftarrow \mathcal{X}^*; \\ \text{wit}_y \leftarrow \text{WitCreate}(\text{pk}_{\text{acc}}, \mathcal{X}^*, \text{acc}_{\mathcal{X}^*}, \text{aux}, y) \\ \text{Proof} \leftarrow \text{CompProof}(\text{pk}_{\text{acc}}, \text{acc}_{\mathcal{X}^*}, \text{aux}, \text{wit}_y, y) : \\ \text{Verify}(\text{pk}_{\text{acc}}, \text{acc}^*, \text{Proof}) = 1 \end{bmatrix} \leq \epsilon(\lambda),$$

In other words, the adversary cannot convincingly demonstrate that they honestly computed an accumulator for the chosen set $\mathcal{X}^*$. Therefore, the proof must be rejected for any $y \in \mathcal{X}^*$ (except with negligible probability), which is why y is randomly selected in the definition.

Note 15. This definition, which aims to address a gap in accumulator security, might also be useful for advancing a study presented at CFail 2023 [13] where the authors attempt to establish a connection between a primitive known as *locally verifiable aggregate signatures* and asymmetric accumulators. The authors fail to prove this connection, partly due to the absence of a security property for an accumulator that can be considered analogous to the unforgeability of signature schemes.

In the following we prove that [12] accumulator satisfies our new security property. Before to present [12]'s scheme, we recall informally some notation and definition. First, for any group element g and any vectors $\boldsymbol{v} = (v_1, \cdots, v_l)$, $\boldsymbol{u} = (u_1, \cdots, u_l)$, we denote by $g^{\boldsymbol{v}}$ the vector $(g^{v_1}, \cdots, g^{v_l})$ and define $e(g^{\boldsymbol{v}}, g^{\boldsymbol{u}}) := \prod_{i=1}^{l} e(g^{v_i}, g^{u_i}) = e(g, g)^{\boldsymbol{v} \cdot \boldsymbol{u}}$. Let $\mathbb{B} = (\boldsymbol{b}_1, \cdots, \boldsymbol{b}_n)$ and $\mathbb{B}^* = (\boldsymbol{b}_1^*, \cdots, \boldsymbol{b}_n^*)$ be two basis of $\mathbb{Z}_p^n$ (p prime, n fixed dimension). The two basis are **dual orthonormal**, meaning that $\boldsymbol{b}_i \cdot \boldsymbol{b}_j^* = 0$ (mod p) whenever $i \neq j$, and $\boldsymbol{b}_i \cdot \boldsymbol{b}_i^* = \psi$ (mod p) for all i, where ψ is a uniformly random element of $\mathbb{Z}_p^*$. A tuple $(\mathbb{B}, \mathbb{B}, \psi)$, called **Dual pairing vector spaces** (DPVS) [23,47], is generated by the algorithm $\text{Dual}(\mathbb{Z}_p^n)$. We now briefly present [12]'s scheme, which is bounded by $q \in \mathbb{N}$:

- The secret key is $\text{sk}_{\text{acc}} = (s, \mathbb{D}, \mathbb{D}^*)$, where $(\mathbb{D}, \mathbb{D}^*) \leftarrow \text{Dual}(\mathbb{Z}_p^2)$, $\psi \in \mathbb{Z}_p$ is the random such that $d_1 \cdot d_1^* = d_2 \cdot d_2^* = \psi$, and s is a random element of $\mathbb{Z}_p^*$. The public key is $\text{pk}_{\text{acc}} = \left(\Gamma, g_1^{d_2}, g_1^{d_2 s}, \cdots, g_1^{d_2 s^q}, g_2^{d_1^*}, g_2^{d_2^*}, g_2^{d_2^* s}, \cdots, g_2^{d_2^* s^q} \right)$, where $\Gamma = (p, \mathbb{G}_1, \mathbb{G}_2, \mathbb{G}_T, e, g_1, \frac{g}{2})$ is an asymmetric bilinear group.
- For a set $\mathcal{X}$, its accumulator is $\text{acc}_{\mathcal{X}} = g_1^{d_1 \sum_{i=0}^{q} a_i s^i} \in \mathbb{G}_1^2$, where $\{a_i\}_{i=0,\cdots,q}$ are the coefficients of the polynomial $\text{Ch}_{\mathcal{X}}[Z] = \prod_{x \in \mathcal{X}}(Z + x)$.
- For an element y, its witness is $\text{wit}_y = g_2^{d_2^* \sum_{i=0}^{q} b_i s^i}$, where $\{b_i\}_{i=0,\cdots,q}$ are the coefficients of the polynomial $\text{Ch}_{\mathcal{X} \setminus \{y\}}[Z] = \prod_{x \in \mathcal{X} \setminus \{y\}}(x + Z)$.
- The verification is done by checking if $e(\text{acc}_{\mathcal{X}}, g_2^{d_1^*}) = e(g_1^{d_2(y+s)}, \text{wit}_y)$.

To prove that the scheme satisfies this new property, we introduce the following assumption, that can be reduced to CDH, as we prove in the extended version of our work [14]. This assumption is the first *computational* assumption for dual pairing vector spaces, and therefore might be of independent interest for future works.

Definition 6. *Fixed argument dual pairing vector spaces inversion assumption(FA-DPVS-I). Let $\Gamma = (p, \mathbb{G}_1, \mathbb{G}_2, \mathbb{G}_T, e, g_1, g_2)$ be an asymmetric bilinear pairing group and $(\mathbb{D}^*, \mathbb{D}) \leftarrow \mathsf{Dual}(\mathbb{Z}_p^2)$ be two dual orthonormal bases. The assumption states that given $(\Gamma, g_1^{d_2}, g_2^{d_1^*}, g_2^{d_2^*})$ it is hard to compute $g_1^{d_1}$.*

Theorem 5. *If the fixed argument dual pairing vector spaces inversion assumption holds, then [12]'s accumulator satisfies unforgeability of private evaluation.*

Proof. We prove the contrapositive. Let $\mathcal{B}$ be an adversary that breaks [12]'s scheme UPE security with non negligible advantage. We build $\mathcal{A}$ an adversary that uses $\mathcal{B}$ to break FA-DPVS-I assumption. $\mathcal{A}$ is given $(\Gamma, g_1^{d_2}, g_2^{d_1^*}, g_2^{d_2^*})$. She chooses $s \leftarrow \mathbb{Z}_p$, creates $\mathsf{pk}_{\mathsf{acc}}$ and sends it to $\mathcal{B}$. $\mathcal{B}$ answer to $\mathcal{A}$ with a tuple of message-forged accumulator $(\mathcal{X}^*, \mathsf{acc}^*)$. $\mathcal{A}$ knows that for any $y \in \mathcal{X}^*$, $e(\mathsf{acc}^*, g_2^{d_1^*}) = e(g_1^{d_2(y+s)}, \mathsf{wit}_y)$ and that $e(g_1^{d_2(y+s)}, \mathsf{wit}_y) = e(g_1, g_2)^{\psi \sum_{i=1}^q a_i s^i}$. Thus $e(\mathsf{acc}^*, g_2^{d_1^*}) = e(g_1, g_2)^{\psi \sum_{i=1}^q a_i s^i}$. Thanks to the knowledge of $\mathcal{X}^*$ and s, $\mathcal{A}$ can recover $\{a_i\}_{i=0}^q$, computes $(\sum_{i=0}^q a_i s^i)^{-1}$ and obtains that $e((\mathsf{acc}^*)^{(\sum_{i=0}^q a_i s^i)^{-1}}, g_2^{d_1^*}) = e(g_1, g_2)^{\psi}$. $\mathcal{A}$ outputs $(\mathsf{acc}^*)^{(\sum_{i=0}^q a_i s^i)^{-1}}$ as her answer and wins the game with an advantage equal to $\mathcal{B}$'s advantage, therefore with non-negligible advantage.

5   Delegatable Proofs

In this section we focus on a property introduced in 2010 by Acar and Nguyen [2]: *delegatable* non-membership proofs. Our aim is to understand what is necessary to obtain delegatable proofs. Before to do this, we briefly recall some applications of accumulators to highlight the interest of the delegatable property.

Accumulators' Applications. As already mentioned in the introduction, originally accumulators served purposes such as timestamping and membership testing [15]. Their applications expanded to include fail-stop signatures [11], membership revocation in group signatures [19], anonymous credentials (delegatable) [2], and e-cash [5] along others. This list is not exhaustive; detailed applications are covered in surveys such as [50]. An intriguing observation is that, while cryptographic accumulators aim to maintain the size of cryptographic objects as constant, they are infrequently incorporated into encryption schemes. Works like [3,29,56] explore this avenue. [3,29] propose broadcast encryption schemes using cryptographic accumulators (based on RSA) for managing users' secret keys. Wang and Chow [56] introduce an identity-based broadcast encryption scheme relying on a simplified form of accumulators. They leverage the compactness of accumulator outputs for scheme efficiency but do not consider other accumulator functionalities. Some research incorporates accumulators to add revocation functionality to existing encryption schemes. For instance, [32] adds revocation to Lewko and Waters' hierarchical identity-based encryption scheme [33]. Notably, [12] proposes a scheme using cryptographic accumulators for both key management and encryption, making it the only known scheme utilizing accumulators for encryption. They employ dually computable accumulators to construct attribute-based encryption schemes, albeit with a larger public key size, paving the way for future works in building encryption schemes from accumulators.

Applications of Delegatable Proofs. Delegatable (non-)membership proofs, initially designed for anonymous credentials, find utility in access control systems and permission delegation in distributed environments. As accumulators gain traction in encryption schemes, a promising avenue involves crafting a re-encryption proxy from an accumulator. By integrating delegation into an accumulator-based encryption scheme, the potential for establishing a re-encryption proxy arises. Also, accumulators hold significance in blockchain and digital cash. Introducing delegatable proofs can significantly enhance the efficiency of both systems while preserving privacy. Our goal is to discover a generic method for obtaining accumulators with this property. Focusing solely on delegatable non-membership proofs, we simplify the discussion for clarity, noting that the insights presented apply equally to delegatable membership proofs. We begin by formally define an accumulator scheme with delegatable non-membership proofs.

Definition 7. *Delegatable non-membership proofs* [2]. *A universal accumulator* (Gen, Eval, WitCreate, CompProof, Verify) *allows delegatable non-membership proofs if it additionally provides the following algorithms.*

- Dele($\mathsf{pk}_{\mathsf{acc}}, y$): *the delegation algorithm takes as input the public key* $\mathsf{pk}_{\mathsf{acc}}$ *and an element* y. *It outputs a delegating key* Del_y.
- Vali($\mathsf{pk}_{\mathsf{acc}}, \mathsf{Del}_y$): *the validation algorithm takes as input the public key* $\mathsf{pk}_{\mathsf{acc}}$ *and a delegating key* Del_y. *If* Del_y *is valid it returns 1, otherwise it returns 0.*
- Rede($\mathsf{pk}_{\mathsf{acc}}, \mathsf{Del}_y$): *the re-delegation algorithm takes as input the public key* $\mathsf{pk}_{\mathsf{acc}}$ *and a delegating key* Del_y. *If* $\mathsf{Vali}(\mathsf{pk}_{\mathsf{acc}}, \mathsf{Del}_y) = 1$, *the algorithm returns an other delegating key* Del'_x, *otherwise it outputs* $\bot$.
- CompNMProof($\mathsf{pk}_{\mathsf{acc}}, \mathsf{Del}_y, \mathcal{X}, \mathsf{acc}_{\mathcal{X}}$): *the proof computation algorithm takes as input the public key* $\mathsf{pk}_{\mathsf{acc}}$, *a delegating key* Del_y, *a set* $\mathcal{X}$ *and the associated accumulated value* $\mathsf{acc}_{\mathcal{X}}$. *It returns a non-membership proof.*

These algorithms verify, for every PPT adversaries $\mathcal{A}, \mathcal{A}_1, \mathcal{A}_2$:

- *Delegability*: it states that a proof computed using a delegation key is indistinguishable from a proof computed using a witness if the following is negligible

$$\left| \Pr \left[\begin{array}{c} \mathfrak{K} = (\mathsf{sk}_{\mathsf{acc}}, \mathsf{pk}_{\mathsf{acc}}) \leftarrow \mathsf{Gen}(\lambda); (y, \mathcal{X}) \leftarrow \mathcal{A}_1(\mathsf{pk}_{\mathsf{acc}}); \\ (\mathsf{acc}_{\mathcal{X}}, \mathsf{aux}) \leftarrow \mathsf{Eval}(\mathsf{pk}_{\mathsf{acc}}, \mathcal{X}); \\ \mathsf{wit}_y \leftarrow \mathsf{WitCreate}(\mathsf{pk}_{\mathsf{acc}}, \mathcal{X}, \mathsf{acc}_{\mathcal{X}}, \mathsf{aux}, y, \mathsf{Type} = 1); \\ \mathsf{Proof}_0 \leftarrow \mathsf{CompProof}(\mathsf{pk}_{\mathsf{acc}}, \mathsf{acc}_{\mathcal{X}}, \mathsf{aux}, \mathsf{wit}_y, y, \mathsf{Type} = 1); \\ \mathsf{Del}_y \leftarrow \mathsf{Dele}(\mathsf{pk}_{\mathsf{acc}}, y); \\ \mathsf{Proof}_1 \leftarrow \mathsf{CompNMProof}(\mathsf{pk}_{\mathsf{acc}}, \mathsf{Del}_y, \mathcal{X}, \mathsf{acc}_{\mathcal{X}}); \\ b \leftarrow \{0,1\}; b' \leftarrow \mathcal{A}_2(\mathsf{acc}_{\mathcal{X}}, \mathsf{wit}_y, \mathsf{Del}_y, \mathsf{Proof}_b) : b = b' \end{array} \right] - \frac{1}{2} \right|$$

- *Unlinkability*: this property states that a delegation key for y_0 is indistinguishable from a delegation key for y_1 if the following is negligible

$$\left| \Pr \left[\begin{array}{c} \mathfrak{K} = (\mathsf{sk}_{acc}, \mathsf{pk}_{acc}) \leftarrow \mathsf{Gen}(\lambda); (y_0, y_1) \leftarrow \mathcal{D}; \mathsf{Del}_y \leftarrow \mathsf{Dele}(\mathsf{pk}_{acc}, y_0); \\ b \leftarrow \{0,1\}; \mathsf{Del}_{y_b} \leftarrow \mathsf{Dele}(\mathsf{pk}_{acc}, y_b); b' \leftarrow \mathcal{A}(\mathsf{pk}_{acc}, \mathsf{Del}_y, \mathsf{Del}_{y_b}) : b = b' \end{array} \right] - \frac{1}{2} \right|$$

- *Redelegability*: this property states that a delegation key output by the algorithm Rede is indistinguishable from a delegation key output by the algorithm Dele if the following is negligible

$$\left| \Pr \left[\begin{array}{c} \mathfrak{K} = (\mathsf{sk}_{\mathsf{acc}}, \mathsf{pk}_{\mathsf{acc}}) \leftarrow \mathsf{Gen}(\lambda); y \leftarrow \mathcal{A}_1(\mathsf{pk}_{\mathsf{acc}}); \mathsf{Del}_y \leftarrow \mathsf{Dele}(\mathsf{pk}_{\mathsf{acc}}, y); \\ \mathsf{Del}_y^0 \leftarrow \mathsf{Dele}(\mathsf{pk}_{\mathsf{acc}}, y); \mathsf{Del}_y^1 \leftarrow \mathsf{Rede}(\mathsf{pk}_{\mathsf{acc}}, \mathsf{Del}_y); b \leftarrow \{0,1\}; \\ b' \leftarrow \mathcal{A}_2(\mathsf{pk}_{\mathsf{acc}}, \mathsf{Del}_y, \mathsf{Del}_y^b) : b = b' \end{array} \right] - \frac{1}{2} \right|$$

- *Verifiability*: this property states that a delegation key generated honestly will always pass the Vali algorithm while this is not the case for a not honestly computed delegation key, if the following are negligible

$$\left| \Pr \left[\begin{array}{c} \mathfrak{K} = (\mathsf{sk}_{\mathsf{acc}}, \mathsf{pk}_{\mathsf{acc}}) \leftarrow \mathsf{Gen}(\lambda); x \leftarrow \mathcal{A}(\mathsf{pk}_{\mathsf{acc}}); \mathsf{Del}_y \leftarrow \mathsf{Dele}(\mathsf{pk}_{\mathsf{acc}}, y) : \\ \mathsf{Vali}(\mathsf{pk}_{\mathsf{acc}}, \mathsf{Del}_x) = 1 \text{ if } y \in \mathcal{D} \end{array} \right] - 1 \right|$$

$$\left| \Pr \left[\begin{array}{c} (\mathsf{sk}_{\mathsf{acc}}, \mathsf{pk}_{\mathsf{acc}}) \leftarrow \mathsf{Gen}(\lambda); \mathsf{Del}' \leftarrow \mathcal{A}(\mathsf{pk}_{\mathsf{acc}}) : \mathsf{Vali}(\mathsf{pk}_{\mathsf{acc}}, \mathsf{Del}') = 0 \\ \text{if } \mathsf{Del}' \notin \left\{ \mathsf{Del} \, \middle| \, \mathsf{Del} \leftarrow \mathsf{Dele}(\mathsf{pk}_{\mathsf{acc}}, y'); y' \in \mathcal{D} \right\} \end{array} \right] - 1 \right|,$$

where the condition $\mathsf{Del}' \notin \left\{ \mathsf{Del} \middle| \mathsf{Del} \leftarrow \mathsf{Dele}(\mathsf{pk}_{\mathsf{acc}}, y'); y' \in \mathcal{D} \right\}$ means that the delegation key Del' does not correspond to a delegation key correctly computed, for any element y' of the domain $\mathcal{D}$.

How to Obtain Delegatable Proofs? To the best of our knowledge, only one accumulator provides delegatable non-membership proofs: [2]. The key idea proposed by Acar and Nguyen is to use a specific type of proof system: one that has *homomorphic proofs*, a concept that they introduced. Informally, a proof system is said to be homomorphic if it is associated with a law, denoted $+_\Pi$, such that the result of $+_\Pi((\mathsf{Sta}_1, \mathsf{Wit}_1, \mathsf{Proof}_1), (\mathsf{Sta}_1, \mathsf{Wit}_2, \mathsf{Proof}_2))$, denoted $(\mathsf{Sta}, \mathsf{Wit}, \mathsf{Proof})$, is a valid tuple composed of a proof Proof computed from the statement Sta and witness Wit. Therefore, if the accumulator can be expressed as a linear combination of public elements, then a delegating key will correspond to a set of proofs (one per public element). Constructing the proof associated with the statement corresponding to the accumulator is done by computing the correct operation on the proofs.

Efficiency and Aggregation (Batching). As described, a delegation key is a set of proofs. Therefore its size is dependent on the number of basis elements in the public key, which might be high. A solution to improve the efficiency of the scheme is to use a proof system with *aggregation* techniques (as done by Acar and Nguyen): the delegation key is not a set of proofs, but an aggregation (or any batch) of the proofs, *i.e.* one proof. In the following, we suppose that our non-membership proof system also has batching techniques, represented by the algorithm Batch that batches proofs, an algorithm BatchVerif that verifies a batched proof, knowing the associated set of statements, and a extracting algorithm Extract that extract from the batched proof all the proofs. Let us now see formally that all properties of a delegatable accumulator can be achieved using the underlying proof system properties.

Delegatable Non-membership Proofs and Proof Systems. First, we define the proof system properties that we will need: *witness indistinguishability* and *randomizable*.

Definition 8. *Witness indistinguishability* [1,31]. *A proof system is said to satisfy witness indistinguishability if for any malicious verifier* $\mathcal{V}$, *the following is negligible:*

$$\Pr\left[\begin{array}{l} \mathsf{Para} \leftarrow \mathsf{Setup}(\lambda, \mathcal{R}), (\mathsf{Sta}, \mathsf{Wit}_0, \mathsf{Wit}_1) \leftarrow \mathcal{V}(\mathsf{Para}), b \leftarrow \{0,1\}, \\ \mathsf{Proof}_b \leftarrow \mathsf{Prove}(\mathsf{Para}, \mathsf{Sta}, \mathsf{Wit}_b), b' \leftarrow \mathcal{V}(\mathsf{Proof}_b): b' = b \end{array}\right].$$

Definition 9. *Randomizable proof system* [1]. *A proof system is said to be randomizable if has another PPT algorithm* RandProof *that takes as input a tuple* (Para, Sta, Proof) *of setup parameters* Para, *statement* Sta *and proof* Proof *and returns another valid proof* Proof$'$, *which is indistinguishable from a proof produced by* Prove.

Let us rewrite the additional algorithms Dele, Rede, Vali, CompProof required to obtain an accumulator with delegatable non-membership proofs to highlight the non-membership proof system (Setup, Prove, Verif). Doing so, we can see that the properties of *witness indistinguishability* and *randomizable* of the proof system guarantees *unlinkability* and *redelegability*, while *Verifiability* comes directly from the proof system completeness and soundness. Notice that the proof system parameters Para are included in $\mathsf{pk}_{\mathsf{acc}}$, and that there exists an algorithm CompWit that takes as input public parameters Para, statement Sta and an element y, and returns a witness Wit_y for y.

- Dele($\mathsf{pk}_{\mathsf{acc}}, y$): the algorithm extracts the public parameters Para from the accumulator public key $\mathsf{pk}_{\mathsf{acc}}$, and from Para it extracts the basis elements that forms a set of statement $\{\mathsf{Sta}_l\}_l$. For each l it runs CompWit(Para, Sta_l, y) to get Wit_l and then computes Prove(Para, $\mathsf{Sta}_l, \mathsf{Wit}_l$) to get Proof_l. It runs Batch(Para, $\{\mathsf{Sta}_l, \mathsf{Proof}_l\}_l$) to get Proof and outputs $\mathsf{Del}_y = \mathsf{Proof}$.
- Vali($\mathsf{pk}_{\mathsf{acc}}, \mathsf{Del}_y$): the algorithm runs the batch verification algorithm BatchVerif on public parameters Para, statement $\{\mathsf{Sta}_l\}_l$ and the batched proof Del_y.
- Rede($\mathsf{pk}_{\mathsf{acc}}, \mathsf{Del}_y$): if Vali($\mathsf{pk}_{\mathsf{acc}}, \mathsf{Del}_y$) = 1, the algorithm runs the randomization algorithm RandProof on public parameters Para, statement $\{\mathsf{Sta}_l\}$ and proof Proof to get a randomized proof Proof$'$.
- CompProof($\mathsf{pk}_{\mathsf{acc}}, \mathsf{Del}_y, \mathcal{X}, \mathsf{acc}_{\mathcal{X}}$): from Para, $\mathcal{X}$ and $\mathsf{acc}_{\mathcal{X}}$ the algorithms finds the linear relation between $\mathsf{acc}_{\mathcal{X}}$ and the basis elements contained in Para. Then, it first extracts the proofs Proof_l of Del_y, then it uses homomorphic property of the proof system to obtain Proof_y, and finally it uses the randomization algorithm RandProof(Para, $\mathsf{acc}_{\mathcal{X}}, \mathsf{Proof}_y$) to get a randomized proof Proof'_y that it outputs.

Lemma 6. *Verifiability is satisfied thanks to the completeness and soundness of the non-membership proof system.*

Proof. First, let us see that the first condition is satisfied if the proof system scheme satisfies completness. Let $y \in \mathcal{D}$ and $\{\mathsf{Sta}_l\}_l$ be the basis elements. Then Dele computes honestly $\left\{\mathsf{Wit}_y^l\right\}_l$, from CompWit, $\{\mathsf{Proof}_l\}_l$, and Proof from Batch. Then, from completeness, we have that the probability that BatchVerif returns 1 is equal to 1. Thus, as Vali runs BatchVerif, we have the first condition. Then, it is easy to see that if the second condition does not hold, that means that the underlying proof system does not satisfy soundness. Indeed, if there is an adversary that can creates a fake delegation key that passes the verification algorithm, we can create an adversary to win the soundness game, using the adversary against verifiability's second condition.

Lemma 7. *Redelagability is satisfied thanks to the randomizable property of the non-membership proof system.*

Proof. Let us see that if there is an adversary, let us say $\mathcal{B}$, that breaks the redelagability property, then we can build an adversary, denoted $\mathcal{A}$, that breaks the randomizable property of the proof system. First, $\mathcal{A}$ is given Para from the challenger, and she simulates the accumulator challenger by computing $\mathsf{pk}_{\mathsf{acc}}$, that she sends to $\mathcal{B}$. The latter chooses y that she sends to $\mathcal{A}$. $\mathcal{A}$ then creates the witnesses $\left\{\mathsf{Wit}_y^l\right\}_l$ that she sends to the challenger, along with $\{\mathsf{Sta}_l\}_l$. The challenger computes $\{\mathsf{Proof}_l\}$, then runs Batch to get Proof. She picks $b \in \{0,1\}$: if $b = 0$, she sends $\mathsf{Proof}_0 = \mathsf{Proof}$ to $\mathcal{A}$, otherwise she runs the randomization algorithm RandProof to get $\mathsf{Proof}' = \mathsf{Proof}_1$ that she sends to $\mathcal{A}$. The latter also computes $\widetilde{\mathsf{Proof}}$ from Batch and $\{\mathsf{Proof}_l\}_l$, and she sends Proof_b, $\widetilde{\mathsf{Proof}}$ to $\mathcal{B}$. $\mathcal{B}$ can distinguish a proof computed by Dele from a proof computed by Rede, therefore she wins the game with non-negligible advantage, and so does $\mathcal{A}$ by outputting $\mathcal{B}$'s answer.

Lemma 8. *Unlinkability is satisfied thanks to the witness indistinguishability property of the non-membership proof system.*

Proof. Let us see that if there is an adversary, let us say $\mathcal{B}$, that breaks the unlinkability property, then we can build an adversary, denoted $\mathcal{A}$, that breaks the witness indistinguishability property of the proof system. First, $\mathcal{A}$ is given Para from the challenger, and she simulates the accumulator challenger by computing $\mathsf{pk}_{\mathsf{acc}}$, that she sends to $\mathcal{B}$. The latter chooses y_0, y_1 that she sends to $\mathcal{A}$. $\mathcal{A}$ then creates the witnesses $\left\{\mathsf{Wit}_{y_0}^l, \mathsf{Wit}_{y_1}^l\right\}_l$ that she sends to the challenger, along with $\{\mathsf{Sta}_l\}_l$. The challenger picks $b \in \{0,1\}$ and computes $\{\mathsf{Proof}_l\}$ from $\left\{\mathsf{Wit}_{y_b}^l\right\}_l$, then she runs Batch to get Proof, that is sent to $\mathcal{A}$. The latter then computes a proof Proof_0 for y_0 and she sends to $\mathcal{B}$ $(\mathsf{Proof}, \mathsf{Proof}_0)$. $\mathcal{B}$ can distinguish a proof computed for y_0 from a proof computed by for y_1, therefore she wins the game with non-negligible advantage, and so does $\mathcal{A}$ by outputting $\mathcal{B}$'s answer.

Note 16. In [1], they proved that their accumulator satisfies unlinkability as they used a composable ZK proof system. Actually, only witness indistinguishability is required.

How to Obtain Delegability? The witness indistinguishability and randomizable property of proof systems are not enough to obtain an accumulator with delegatable non-membership proof as *delegability* cannot be proven. To solve this issue, [2] uses a primitive they introduced: homomorphic proofs.

Definition 10. Homomorphic proofs [2]. *Let* (Setup, Prove, Verif) *be a proof system for a relation R and* Para $\leftarrow$ Setup(λ). *Consider a subset Π of all* (Sta, Wit, Proof) *such that* $(\mathsf{Para}, \mathsf{Sta}, \mathsf{Wit}) \in R$ *and* $\mathsf{Verif}(\mathsf{Para}, \mathsf{Sta}, \mathsf{Proof}) = 1$, *and an operation* $+_\Pi : \Pi \times \Pi \to \Pi$. Π *is a set of homomorphic proofs if* $(\Pi, +_\Pi)$ *satisfies* **closure**, **associativity** *and* **commutativity**. *Consider an* $I_\Pi = (\mathsf{Sta}_0, \mathsf{Wit}_0, \mathsf{Proof}_0) \in \Pi$. Π *is a set of strongly homomorphic proofs if* $(\Pi, +_\Pi, I_\Pi)$ *forms an Abelian group where* I_Π *is the identity element.*

Lemma 9. *Delegability is satisfied thanks to the homomorphic proofs and the randomizable property of the non-membership proof system.*

Proof. Thanks to the homomorphic property, the proof output by CompNMProof is a valid proof for statement $\mathsf{Sta} = (\mathsf{acc}_\chi, \mathsf{aux})$. Plus, as CompNMProof is using RandProof to randomize the computed proof, the proof is indistinguishable from a proof computed using the proof system Prove algorithm, for statement $\mathsf{Sta} = (\mathsf{acc}_\chi, \mathsf{aux})$.

Conclusion. To obtain an accumulator scheme that has delegatable proofs, the used proof systems must: **i)** satisfy witness indistinguishability, **ii)** be randomizable, **iii)** have homomorphic proofs, and **iv)** support batching techniques. The last two points are the most complicated to obtain. Indeed, currently (as far as we know) there is only one proof system proven to have homomorphic proofs: Groth Sahai proofs. However, this holds only if some conditions on parameters Para, statements Sta and witnesses Wit are satisfied, such as the fact that witnesses and statements must have some constant parts. Quite the same goes for batching techniques: Groth-Sahai proofs support batching on some conditions only. Taking all that into account it seems that not all accumulators can be added delegation property and thus providing a generic construction is not possible.

Acknowledgement. The authors would like to thank anonymous reviewers for their helpful discussions and valuable comments. This work is supported in part by the Banque Publique d'Investissement under the VisioConfiance project and the French ANR SANGRIA project (ANR-21-CE39-0006).

References

1. Acar, T., Nguyen, L.: Revocation for delegatable anonymous credentials. Technical Repost MSR-TR-2010-170, Microsoft Research (2010)
2. Acar, T., Nguyen, L.: Revocation for delegatable anonymous credentials. In: Catalano, D., Fazio, N., Gennaro, R., Nicolosi, A. (eds.) PKC 2011. LNCS, vol. 6571, pp. 423–440. Springer, Heidelberg (2011). https://doi.org/10.1007/978-3-642-19379-8_26
3. Asano, T.: A revocation scheme with minimal storage at receivers. In: Zheng, Y. (ed.) ASIACRYPT 2002. LNCS, vol. 2501, pp. 433–450. Springer, Heidelberg (2002). https://doi.org/10.1007/3-540-36178-2_27
4. Au, M.H., Tsang, P.P., Susilo, W., Mu, Y.: Dynamic universal accumulators for DDH groups and their application to attribute-based anonymous credential systems. In: Fischlin, M. (ed.) CT-RSA 2009. LNCS, vol. 5473, pp. 295–308. Springer, Heidelberg (2009). https://doi.org/10.1007/978-3-642-00862-7_20
5. Au, M.H., Wu, Q., Susilo, W., Mu, Y.: Compact E-cash from bounded accumulator. In: Abe, M. (ed.) CT-RSA 2007. LNCS, vol. 4377, pp. 178–195. Springer, Heidelberg (2006). https://doi.org/10.1007/11967668_12

6. Ayebie, E.B., Souidi, E.M.: New code-based cryptographic accumulator and fully dynamic group signature. DCC **90**(12), 2861–2891 (2022). https://doi.org/10.1007/s10623-022-01007-5

7. Baldimtsi, F., et al.: Accumulators with applications to anonymity-preserving revocation. Cryptology ePrint Archive, Paper 2017/043 (2017). https://eprint.iacr.org/2017/043

8. Baldimtsi, F., et al.: Accumulators with applications to anonymity-preserving revocation, pp. 301–315 (2017). https://doi.org/10.1109/EuroSP.2017.13

9. Badimtsi, F., Canetti, R., Yakoubov, S.: Universally composable accumulators. In: Jarecki, S. (ed.) CT-RSA 2020. LNCS, vol. 12006, pp. 638–666. Springer, Cham (2020). https://doi.org/10.1007/978-3-030-40186-3_27

10. Baldimtsi, F., Karantaidou, I., Raghuraman, S.: Oblivious accumulators. In: Tang, Q., Teague, V. (eds.) PKC 2024. LNCS, vol. 14602, pp. 99–131. Springer, Cham (2024). https://doi.org/10.1007/978-3-031-57722-2_4

11. Barić, N., Pfitzmann, B.: Collision-free accumulators and fail-stop signature schemes without trees. In: Fumy, W. (ed.) EUROCRYPT 1997. LNCS, vol. 1233, pp. 480–494. Springer, Heidelberg (1997). https://doi.org/10.1007/3-540-69053-0_33

12. Barthoulot, A., Blazy, O., Canard, S.: Dually computable cryptographic accumulators and their application to attribute based encryption. Cryptology ePrint Archive, Paper 2023/1277 (2023). https://eprint.iacr.org/2023/1277

13. Barthoulot, A., Blazy, O., Canard, S.: Locally verifiable signatures and cryptographic accumulators: different names, same thing? (2023)

14. Barthoulot, A., Blazy, O., Canard, S.: Cryptographic accumulators: new definitions, enhanced security, and delegatable proofs. Cryptology ePrint Archive, Paper 2024/657 (2024). https://eprint.iacr.org/2024/657

15. Benaloh, J., de Mare, M.: One-way accumulators: a decentralized alternative to digital signatures. In: Helleseth, T. (ed.) EUROCRYPT 1993. LNCS, vol. 765, pp. 274–285. Springer, Heidelberg (1994). https://doi.org/10.1007/3-540-48285-7_24

16. Boneh, D., Bünz, B., Fisch, B.: Batching techniques for accumulators with applications to IOPs and stateless blockchains. In: Boldyreva, A., Micciancio, D. (eds.) CRYPTO 2019. LNCS, vol. 11692, pp. 561–586. Springer, Cham (2019). https://doi.org/10.1007/978-3-030-26948-7_20

17. Buldas, A., Laud, P., Lipmaa, H.: Eliminating counterevidence with applications to accountable certificate management. J. Comput. Secur. **10**, 273–296 (2002). https://doi.org/10.3233/JCS-2002-10304

18. Camenisch, J., Kohlweiss, M., Soriente, C.: An accumulator based on bilinear maps and efficient revocation for anonymous credentials. In: Jarecki, S., Tsudik, G. (eds.) PKC 2009. LNCS, vol. 5443, pp. 481–500. Springer, Heidelberg (2009). https://doi.org/10.1007/978-3-642-00468-1_27

19. Camenisch, J., Lysyanskaya, A.: Dynamic accumulators and application to efficient revocation of anonymous credentials. In: Yung, M. (ed.) CRYPTO 2002. LNCS, vol. 2442, pp. 61–76. Springer, Heidelberg (2002). https://doi.org/10.1007/3-540-45708-9_5

20. Campanelli, M., Fiore, D., Han, S., Kim, J., Kolonelos, D., Oh, H.: Succinct zero-knowledge batch proofs for set accumulators. In: Yin, H., Stavrou, A., Cremers, C., Shi, E. (eds.) ACM CCS 2022, pp. 455–469. ACM Press (2022). https://doi.org/10.1145/3548606.3560677

21. Canard, S., Gouget, A.: Multiple denominations in E-cash with compact transaction data. In: Sion, R. (ed.) FC 2010. LNCS, vol. 6052, pp. 82–97. Springer, Heidelberg (2010). https://doi.org/10.1007/978-3-642-14577-3_9

22. Catalano, D., Fiore, D.: Vector commitments and their applications. In: Kurosawa, K., Hanaoka, G. (eds.) PKC 2013. LNCS, vol. 7778, pp. 55–72. Springer, Heidelberg (2013). https://doi.org/10.1007/978-3-642-36362-7_5

23. Chen, J., Lim, H.W., Ling, S., Wang, H., Wee, H.: Shorter IBE and signatures via asymmetric pairings. In: Abdalla, M., Lange, T. (eds.) Pairing 2012. LNCS, vol. 7708, pp. 122–140. Springer, Heidelberg (2013). https://doi.org/10.1007/978-3-642-36334-4_8
24. Couteau, G., Lipmaa, H., Parisella, R., Ødegaard, A.T.: Efficient NIZKs for algebraic sets. In: Tibouchi, M., Wang, H. (eds.) ASIACRYPT 2021. LNCS, vol. 13092, pp. 128–158. Springer, Cham (2021). https://doi.org/10.1007/978-3-030-92078-4_5
25. Damgard, I., Triandopoulos, N.: Supporting non-membership proofs with bilinear-map accumulators. Cryptology ePrint Archive, Report 2008/538 (2008). http://eprint.iacr.org/2008/538
26. Derler, D., Hanser, C., Slamanig, D.: Revisiting cryptographic accumulators, additional properties and relations to other primitives. In: Nyberg, K. (ed.) CT-RSA 2015. LNCS, vol. 9048, pp. 127–144. Springer, Cham (2015). https://doi.org/10.1007/978-3-319-16715-2_7
27. Dodis, Y., Kiayias, A., Nicolosi, A., Shoup, V.: Anonymous identification in *ad hoc* groups. In: Cachin, C., Camenisch, J.L. (eds.) EUROCRYPT 2004. LNCS, vol. 3027, pp. 609–626. Springer, Heidelberg (2004). https://doi.org/10.1007/978-3-540-24676-3_36
28. Fazio, N., Nicolosi, A.: Cryptographic accumulators: definitions, constructions and applications (2002)
29. Gentry, C., Ramzan, Z.: RSA accumulator based broadcast encryption. In: Zhang, K., Zheng, Y. (eds.) ISC 2004. LNCS, vol. 3225, pp. 73–86. Springer, Heidelberg (2004). https://doi.org/10.1007/978-3-540-30144-8_7
30. Ghosh, E., Ohrimenko, O., Papadopoulos, D., Tamassia, R., Triandopoulos, N.: Zero-knowledge accumulators and set algebra. In: Cheon, J.H., Takagi, T. (eds.) ASIACRYPT 2016. LNCS, vol. 10032, pp. 67–100. Springer, Heidelberg (2016). https://doi.org/10.1007/978-3-662-53890-6_3
31. Groth, J.: Short pairing-based non-interactive zero-knowledge arguments. In: Abe, M. (ed.) ASIACRYPT 2010. LNCS, vol. 6477, pp. 321–340. Springer, Heidelberg (2010). https://doi.org/10.1007/978-3-642-17373-8_19
32. Jia, H., Chen, Y., Lan, J., Huang, K., Wang, J.: Efficient revocable hierarchical identity-based encryption using cryptographic accumulators. Int. J. Inf. Secur. (2018)
33. Lewko, A.B., Waters, B.: Unbounded HIBE and attribute-based encryption. In: Paterson, K.G. (ed.) EUROCRYPT 2011. LNCS, vol. 6632, pp. 547–567. Springer, Heidelberg (May 2011). https://doi.org/10.1007/978-3-642-20465-4_30
34. Li, F., Hu, Y., Zhang, C.: An identity-based signcryption scheme for multi-domain ad hoc networks. In: Katz, J., Yung, M. (eds.) ACNS 2007. LNCS, vol. 4521, pp. 373–384. Springer, Heidelberg (2007). https://doi.org/10.1007/978-3-540-72738-5_24
35. Li, J., Li, N., Xue, R.: Universal accumulators with efficient nonmembership proofs. In: Katz, J., Yung, M. (eds.) ACNS 2007. LNCS, vol. 4521, pp. 253–269. Springer, Heidelberg (2007). https://doi.org/10.1007/978-3-540-72738-5_17
36. Libert, B., Ling, S., Nguyen, K., Wang, H.: Zero-knowledge arguments for lattice-based accumulators: logarithmic-size ring signatures and group signatures without trapdoors. In: Fischlin, M., Coron, J.-S. (eds.) EUROCRYPT 2016. LNCS, vol. 9666, pp. 1–31. Springer, Heidelberg (2016). https://doi.org/10.1007/978-3-662-49896-5_1
37. Libert, B., Ramanna, S.C., Yung, M.: Functional commitment schemes: from polynomial commitments to pairing-based accumulators from simple assumptions. In: Chatzigiannakis, I., Mitzenmacher, M., Rabani, Y., Sangiorgi, D. (eds.) ICALP 2016. LIPIcs, vol. 55, pp. 30:1–30:14. Schloss Dagstuhl (Jul 2016). https://doi.org/10.4230/LIPIcs.ICALP.2016.30
38. Lipmaa, H.: Secure accumulators from Euclidean rings without trusted setup. In: Bao, F., Samarati, P., Zhou, J. (eds.) ACNS 2012. LNCS, vol. 7341, pp. 224–240. Springer, Heidelberg (2012). https://doi.org/10.1007/978-3-642-31284-7_14

39. Fauzi, P., Lipmaa, H., Zhang, B.: Efficient non-interactive zero knowledge arguments for set operations. In: Christin, N., Safavi-Naini, R. (eds.) FC 2014. LNCS, vol. 8437, pp. 216–233. Springer, Heidelberg (2014). https://doi.org/10.1007/978-3-662-45472-5_14
40. Lipmaa, H., Parisella, R.: Set (non-)membership NIZKs from determinantal accumulators. Cryptology ePrint Archive, Paper 2022/1570 (2022). https://eprint.iacr.org/2022/1570
41. Jhanwar, M.P., Safavi-Naini, R.: Compact accumulator using lattices. In: Chakraborty, R.S., Schwabe, P., Solworth, J. (eds.) SPACE 2015. LNCS, vol. 9354, pp. 347–358. Springer, Cham (2015). https://doi.org/10.1007/978-3-319-24126-5_20
42. de Meer, H., Liedel, M., Pohls, H.C., Posegga, J.: Indistinguishability of one-way accumulators. Technical report MIP-1210, Faculty of Computer Science and Mathematics (FIM), University of Passau (2012)
43. de Meer, H., Pöhls, H.C., Posegga, J., Samelin, K.: Redactable signature schemes for trees with signer-controlled non-leaf-redactions. In: Obaidat, M.S., Filipe, J. (eds.) ICETE 2012. CCIS, vol. 455, pp. 155–171. Springer, Heidelberg (2014). https://doi.org/10.1007/978-3-662-44791-8_10
44. Nguyen, K., Tang, H., Wang, H., Zeng, N.: New code-based privacy-preserving cryptographic constructions. In: Galbraith, S.D., Moriai, S. (eds.) ASIACRYPT 2019, Part II. LNCS, vol. 11922, pp. 25–55. Springer, Cham (2019). https://doi.org/10.1007/978-3-030-34621-8_2
45. Nguyen, L.: Accumulators from bilinear pairings and applications. In: Menezes, A. (ed.) CT-RSA 2005. LNCS, vol. 3376, pp. 275–292. Springer, Heidelberg (2005). https://doi.org/10.1007/978-3-540-30574-3_19
46. Nguyen, L.: Accumulators from bilinear pairings and applications. In: Menezes, A. (ed.) CT-RSA 2005. LNCS, vol. 3376, pp. 275–292. Springer, Heidelberg (2005). https://doi.org/10.1007/978-3-540-30574-3_19
47. Okamoto, T., Takashima, K.: Hierarchical predicate encryption for inner-products. In: Matsui, M. (ed.) ASIACRYPT 2009. LNCS, vol. 5912, pp. 214–231. Springer, Heidelberg (2009). https://doi.org/10.1007/978-3-642-10366-7_13
48. Papamanthou, C., Shi, E., Tamassia, R., Yi, K.: Streaming authenticated data structures. In: Johansson, T., Nguyen, P.Q. (eds.) EUROCRYPT 2013. LNCS, vol. 7881, pp. 353–370. Springer, Heidelberg (2013). https://doi.org/10.1007/978-3-642-38348-9_22
49. Papamanthou, C., Tamassia, R., Triandopoulos, N.: Optimal verification of operations on dynamic sets. In: Rogaway, P. (ed.) CRYPTO 2011. LNCS, vol. 6841, pp. 91–110. Springer, Heidelberg (2011). https://doi.org/10.1007/978-3-642-22792-9_6
50. Ren, Y., Liu, X., Wu, Q., Wang, L., Zhang, W.: Cryptographic accumulator and its application: a survey. Secur. Commun. Netw. **2022**, 1–13 (2022). https://doi.org/10.1155/2022/5429195
51. Reyzin, L., Yakoubov, S.: Efficient asynchronous accumulators for distributed PKI. In: Zikas, V., De Prisco, R. (eds.) SCN 2016. LNCS, vol. 9841, pp. 292–309. Springer, Cham (2016). https://doi.org/10.1007/978-3-319-44618-9_16
52. Reyzin, L., Yakoubov, S.: Efficient asynchronous accumulators for distributed PKI. In: Zikas, V., De Prisco, R. (eds.) SCN 2016. LNCS, vol. 9841, pp. 292–309. Springer, Cham (2016). https://doi.org/10.1007/978-3-319-44618-9_16
53. Tomescu, A., Bhupatiraju, V., Papadopoulos, D., Papamanthou, C., Triandopoulos, N., Devadas, S.: Transparency logs via append-only authenticated dictionaries. In: Cavallaro, L., Kinder, J., Wang, X., Katz, J. (eds.) ACM CCS 2019, pp. 1299–1316. ACM Press (2019). https://doi.org/10.1145/3319535.3345652
54. Tsudik, G., Xu, S.: Accumulating composites and improved group signing. In: Laih, C.-S. (ed.) ASIACRYPT 2003. LNCS, vol. 2894, pp. 269–286. Springer, Heidelberg (2003). https://doi.org/10.1007/978-3-540-40061-5_16

55. Wang, P., Wang, H., Pieprzyk, J.: A new dynamic accumulator for batch updates. In: Qing, S., Imai, H., Wang, G. (eds.) ICICS 2007. LNCS, vol. 4861, pp. 98–112. Springer, Heidelberg (2007). https://doi.org/10.1007/978-3-540-77048-0_8
56. Wang, X., Chow, S.S.M.: Cross-domain access control encryption: arbitrary-policy, constant-size, efficient. In: 2021 IEEE Symposium on Security and Privacy, pp. 748–761. IEEE Computer Society Press (2021). https://doi.org/10.1109/SP40001.2021.00023

Advanced Primitives (II)

Efficient Oblivious Transfer for One-Sided Active Adaptive Adversaries

Isheeta Nargis[(✉)]

University of Calgary, Calgary, AB, Canada
isheeta@gmail.com

Abstract. Nargis designed an oblivious transfer protocol secure against erasure-free one-sided active adaptive adversaries (Nargis, AFRICACRYPT 2017). Her protocol uses a two-party lossy threshold public key encryption scheme that is secure in the same setting. We design a new two-party lossy threshold public key encryption scheme secure against erasure-free one-sided active adaptive adversaries. Using this new encryption scheme as a tool, we modify the oblivious protocol of Nargis. The new string OT protocol for string of length linear in the security parameter asymptotically improves the communication complexity, the number of public key encryption operations and the number of exponentiation operations by a factor of the security parameter over the string oblivious transfer protocol of Nargis. The new encryption scheme is of independent interest. It can be used as a tool in other two-party computation protocols for adaptive adversaries.

Keywords: Oblivious Transfer · One-Sided Adaptive Adversary · Active Adversary · Lossy Encryption · Threshold Encryption · Public Key Encryption · Homomorphic Encryption

1 Introduction

In secure multiparty computation (MPC) problem, a group of parties, who do not trust one another, compute a function of their inputs in such a way that the computed output is correct and it is not possible to learn more about the inputs of honest parties than what can be deduced from the output of the computation. MPC is a very strong primitive in cryptography since almost all cryptographic problems can be solved, in principle, by a general secure MPC protocol.

Oblivious transfer (OT) is a fundamental primitive of cryptography. OT is a protocol between two parties – the sender S and the receiver R. In a bit OT, the input of S is an ordered pair of bits $\{x_0, x_1\}$, and the input of R is a choice bit σ. The goal is that R learns only x_σ without learning $x_{1-\sigma}$, and S remains oblivious to which bit was requested. OT is 'complete' for secure multiparty computation in the sense that if an implementation of OT is given, then it is possible to securely evaluate any polynomial time computable function, without any additional primitive.

S. Vaudenay and C. Petit (Eds.): AFRICACRYPT 2024, LNCS 14861, pp. 123–148, 2024.
https://doi.org/10.1007/978-3-031-64381-1_6

Let s denote the security parameter. In a string OT, the input of S is $(\overline{b_0}, \overline{b_1}) = (\{b_{0,1}, b_{0,2}, \ldots, b_{0,\ell}\}, \{b_{1,1}, b_{1,2}, \ldots, b_{1,\ell}\})$, ℓ is a fixed integer and each $b_{i,j} \in \{0,1\}$. R has input $\sigma \in \{0,1\}$. The output of R is $\overline{b_\sigma} = \{b_{\sigma,1}, b_{\sigma,2}, \ldots, b_{\sigma,\ell}\}$, and the output of S is an empty string. String OT for string length ℓ linear in the security parameter s is of utmost importance since string OT of this length and other variants of string OT of this length (e.g. cut-and-choose OT, committed OT) are widely used in many two-party computation (2PC) protocols. In many such protocols, OT constitute a significant portion of the overall computation and communication. For this reason, improving the efficiency of string OT protocols results in a significant efficiency improvement in the 2PC protocols that use string OT protocols.

In *passive adversary model*, the corrupted parties try to learn the inputs and outputs of the honest parties but still follow the protocol. In *active adversary model*, the corrupted parties may behave in any possible way, including the violation of the protocol. Active adversary model portrays the real world better. In *static adversary model*, the adversary fixes the set of parties to corrupt before the protocol starts, and this set remains fixed throughout the execution of the protocol. In *adaptive adversary model*, the adversary may corrupt a party at any time of the protocol, and even after the protocol has finished its execution. Adaptive adversary model captures the real-world scenario better than the static adversary model. *Adaptive adversary model with erasure* assumes that parties can erase some of its local data and randomness. *Erasure-free adaptive adversary model* assumes that the adversary can see all history of a party when it corrupts that party. Assuming erasure is unrealistic as complete erasure is sometimes impossible to achieve. Moreover, erasure is a property that cannot be verified by another party. For these reasons, erasure-free adaptive adversary model is more realistic. In the common reference string (CRS) model, it is assumed that all parties have access to a common string that is selected from some specified distribution. CRS model is a trusted setup phase.

Efficiency of protocols are measured by some metrics. One *round* is a sequence of steps of the protocol such that each party sends one message to each other party in that sequence. The *round complexity* is the number of rounds needed for executing the protocol. The *communication complexity* is the total communication (in bits) among the parties during the execution of the protocol. Many protocols use public key encryption (PKE) scheme as a tool. Usually the PKE operations constitute the main bottleneck in the time consumed by a protocol. For this reason, the number of PKE operations performed by each party gives a good measure of the computational complexity of protocols. The number of exponentiation operations performed by each party is another performance metric of protocols since the exponentiation operations take a big amount of time.

"Opening a ciphertext" means supplying the plaintext and randomness used during the generation of that ciphertext. In a traditional encryption scheme, encryption is binding; meaning that a given ciphertext can be opened to only the original plaintext with which it was created. In a *lossy PKE scheme*, there are two modes of operation – injective mode and lossy mode. In the *injective mode*, the encryption operation is binding. In the *lossy mode*, if the private key is known, then a ciphertext can be opened to any plaintext of choice.

In a *threshold PKE scheme*, the public key is known to all but the private key is shared among the parties. The parties can encrypt alone but the participation of all parties is necessary for decrypting any ciphertext. Parties decrypt a ciphertext using a threshold decryption protocol. A distributed key generation protocol (DKG) is a protocol by which the parties can generate the public key and private key shares of the parties without using a trusted dealer.

In *one-sided adaptive adversary model* for 2PC, it is assumed that the adversary is adaptive and it can corrupt at most one party [10]. This is a relaxation from the standard adaptive adversary model or the *fully adaptive adversary* for 2PC, where the adversary can corrupt both parties. This relaxed model is used to achieve more efficient protocols. Garay et al. [7] designed the most efficient OT protocol secure against erasure-free active fully adaptive adversaries. For string OT for string length ℓ, their protocol requires $O(\ell)$ PKE operations in the worst case. Here, ℓ is a polynomial of s. Hazay and Patra [10] designed an OT protocol for erasure-free one-sided active adaptive adversary model. For string OT for string length ℓ, their protocol requires a constant number of PKE operations in the expected case. So, relaxing the notion of security has resulted in a protocol requiring significantly smaller number of PKE operations, in the expected case. Both of the OT protocol of [7] and the OT protocol of [10] work in the CRS model and achieve universally composable security. The bit OT protocol of Hazay and Patra [10] requires $O(s^2)$ communication complexity, $O(s)$ PKE operations and $O(s)$ exponentiation operations in the worst case. The string OT protocol of [10] requires $O(s^2)$ communication complexity, $O(s)$ PKE operations and $O(s)$ exponentiation operations in the worst case.

Nargis [13] designed an OT protocol secure against erasure-free one-sided active adaptive adversaries. Her protocol is secure according to the simulation-based security definition of Canetti [2], which satisfies the sequential composition theorem. Nargis [13] designed a lossy threshold two-party PKE scheme based on the decisional Diffie-Hellman (DDH) assumption that is used as a tool in her OT protocol. She designed a two-party DKG protocol for the lossy threshold PKE scheme she designed. Her OT protocol uses this DKG protocol. Her bit OT protocol requires $O(s)$ communication complexity, a constant number of PKE operations and a constant number of exponentiation operations in the worst case. That means, her bit OT protocol asymptotically improved the communication complexity, the number of PKE operations and the number of exponentiation operations by a factor of s over the bit OT protocol of [10]. Her string OT protocol for string length linear in s improved the communication complexity, the number of PKE operations and the number of exponentiation operations by constant factors over the string OT protocol of [10].

Motivated by the extensive use of string OT in 2PC protocols, one important research question is whether it is possible to design an OT protocol that can improve the efficiency of the string OT protocol of [13].

Our Contribution. We answer the above research question in the affirmative by designing a string OT protocol by modifying the OT protocol of [13] in the following way.

We design a new two-party lossy threshold PKE scheme secure against erasure-free one-sided active adaptive adversaries. The new PKE scheme is based on the decisional composite residuosity assumption (DCRA). This encryption scheme is of independent interest. It can be used as a tool in other 2PC protocols.

The OT protocol of [13] uses a two-party lossy threshold PKE scheme that is secure against erasure-free one-sided active adaptive adversaries, additive homomorphic, blindable and has an efficient *Opener* algorithm. The OT protocol of [13] uses the lossy threshold PKE scheme based on the DDH assumption of [13]. It is possible to use other PKE scheme that has the same properties mentioned above in that OT protocol.

We modify the OT protocol of [13] by using the new lossy threshold PKE scheme instead of the lossy threshold PKE scheme of [13]. The lossy threshold PKE scheme of [13] which is based on the DDH assumption encrypts a single bit. The new lossy threshold PKE scheme based on the DCRA assumption encrypts an s-bit number. For this reason, the modified OT protocol asymptotically improves the efficiency parameters over the OT protocol of [13] for string OT of string length linear in s.

The DKG protocol of the lossy threshold two-party PKE scheme based on the DDH assumption of [13] is efficient, it has $O(s)$ communication complexity. Each party needs to perform a constant number of exponentiation operations in that DKG protocol. The new lossy threshold PKE scheme is designed with the objective of improving the efficiency of the OT protocol of [13]. For threshold Paillier encryption scheme, there exists two-party threshold DKG protocol secure against active static adversaries [9] but that DKG protocol is computationally quite complex and takes a significant amount of computations and communication. It is possible to design a DKG protocol for the new lossy threshold PKE scheme but the DKG protocol will be computationally and communication-wise very expensive. If we include that DKG protocol in the OT protocol, then the resulting OT protocol will not be efficient. For this reason, in the new OT protocol, parties do not generate the key shares using a DKG protocol. In stead, in a trusted setup phase, a trusted dealer generates the key shares and distributes the key shares to the parties before the computation starts. Using a trusted setup phase where a trusted dealer generates the key shares and distributes the key shares to parties is quite common in many other MPC protocols that use threshold PKE scheme as a tool. The OT protocol of [13] does not need a trusted setup phase. This is an important difference between the OT protocol of [13] and the new OT protocol.

The new string OT protocol for string of length linear in s asymptotically improves the communication complexity, the number of PKE operations and the number of exponentiation operations by a factor of s over the string OT protocol of [13].

Table 1 compares the efficiency of the new bit OT protocol with related works. All efficiency parameters of the protocols are calculated including the zero-knowledge proofs used in the protocols. The new bit OT protocol has asymptotically similar communication complexity, the number of PKE operations and the number of exponentiation operations as the bit OT protocol of [13].

Table 1. Efficiency Comparison of bit OT Protocols.

Protocol	Garay et al. [7]	Hazay and Patra [10]	Nargis [13]	This work
Adversary Model	Erasure-Free Active Fully Adaptive	Erasure-Free One-Sided Active Adaptive	Erasure-Free One-sided Active Adaptive	Erasure-Free One-Sided Active Adaptive
Trusted Setup Phase	Yes	Yes	No	Yes
Communication Cost	$O(s^2)$	$O(s^2)$	$O(s)$	$O(s)$
Public Key Encryption	$O(s)$	$O(s)$	$O(1)$	$O(1)$
Exponentiation	$O(s)$	$O(s)$	$O(1)$	$O(1)$
Round	$O(1)$	$O(1)$	$O(1)$	$O(1)$

Table 2 compares the efficiency of the new string OT protocol for string of length ℓ where ℓ is linear in s with related works. The new string OT protocol asymptotically improves the communication complexity, the number of PKE operations and the number of exponentiation operations by a factor of s^2 over the most efficient string OT protocol secure against erasure-free fully adaptive adversaries (the protocol of [7]). Here, the relaxation of security from fully adaptive to one-sided adaptive adversary results in $O(s^2)$ efficiency improvement which is quite significant. The new string OT protocol asymptotically improves the communication complexity, the number of PKE operations and the number of exponentiation operations by a factor of s over the most efficient string OT protocols secure against erasure-free one-sided active adaptive adversaries (the protocol of [10] and the protocol of [13]).

If the DKG protocol of the OT protocol of [13] is replaced by a trusted setup where a trusted party generates the key shares and distributes the key shares to the parties, then the resulting string OT protocol for string length ℓ has communication cost $(34\ell s + 21s + 13)$ and each party needs to perform $(2\ell + 2)$ PKE operations and $(56\ell+12)$ exponentiation operations. For string OT of string length $\ell = cs$, the resulting protocol has communication cost $34\ell s + 65s + 25 = 34cs \cdot s + 65s + 25 = 34cs^2 + 21s + 13 \in O(s^2)$. In that protocol, each party performs $2\ell+2 = 2cs+2 \in O(s)$ PKE operations and $56\ell+12 = 56cs+12 \in O(s)$ exponentiation operations. The bit OT protocol of [13] where the DKG protocol is replaced by a trusted setup has communication cost $34s+21s+13 = 55s+13 \in O(s)$. In that protocol, each party performs $2s + 2 \in O(s)$ PKE operations and $56s + 12 \in O(s)$ exponentiation operations. That means, the asymptotic efficiency parameters of the OT protocol of [13] remains the same when the DKG protocol is replaced by a trusted setup. The new string OT protocol for string length linear in s asymptotically improves the communication cost, the

Table 2. Efficiency Comparison of String OT Protocol for String of length ℓ where ℓ is linear in the security parameter s.

Protocol	Garay et al. [7]	Hazay and Patra [10]	Nargis [13]	This work
Adversary Model	Erasure-Free Active Fully Adaptive	Erasure-Free One-Sided Active Adaptive	Erasure-Free One-Sided Active Adaptive	Erasure-Free One-Sided Active Adaptive
Trusted Setup Phase	Yes	Yes	No	Yes
Communication Cost	$O(s^3)$	$O(s^2)$	$O(s^2)$	$O(s)$
Public Key Encryption	$O(s^2)$	$O(s)$	$O(s)$	$O(1)$
Exponentiation	$O(s^2)$	$O(s)$	$O(s)$	$O(1)$
Round	$O(1)$	$O(1)$	$O(1)$	$O(1)$

number of PKE operations and the number of exponentiation operations by a factor of s over the modified string OT protocol of [13] where the DKG protocol is replaced by a trusted setup.

2   Background

Notation. Let $\mathbb{Z}_q = \{0, 1, \ldots, q-1\}$ where q is a prime. Let $\mathbb{Z}_q^* = \{1, 2, \ldots, q-1\}$. For all elements a and $b \neq 1$ in group $\mathbb{G}$, the discrete logarithm of a in base b is denoted by $\log_b(a)$. For a set R, let $r \xleftarrow{\$} R$ denote that r is selected uniformly at random from R. Let A be a probabilistic polynomial-time algorithm. Let $coins(A)$ denote the distribution of the internal randomness of A. $y \leftarrow A(x)$ means that y is computed by running A on input x and randomness r where $r \xleftarrow{\$} coins(A)$. Let $E_{pk}(m, r)$ denote the result of encryption of plaintext m using encryption key pk and randomness r. Let $D_{sk}(c)$ denote the result of decryption of ciphertext c using decryption key sk. Let $Com_\mu(a, r)$ denote the commitment of secret a using commitment key μ and randomness r.

The Decisional Composite Residuosity Assumption (DCRA). Let $N = pq$ be a product of two large primes p and q. Let $\phi(N)$ denote the Euler's totient function, that is, $\phi(N) = (p-1)(q-1)$.

Definition 1 ([16]). *A number z is said to be a N-th residue modulo N^2, if there exists a number $y \in \mathbb{Z}_{N^2}^*$ such that $z = y^N \bmod N^2$.*

Definition 2 ([16]). *The problem of deciding N-th residuosity is defined to be the problem of distinguishing N-th residues from the non-N-th residues.*

Definition 3 ([16]). *The decisional composite residuosity assumption (DCRA) states that there exists no polynomial time algorithm for deciding N-th residuosity.*

Trapdoor Commitment Scheme. A *trapdoor commitment scheme* is a commitment scheme such that during the key generation a trapdoor is generated along with the commitment key. With the trapdoor, one can efficiently compute a randomness to open a given commitment to any value of choice. Without the trapdoor, the binding property of the commitment scheme holds. Pedersen [17] designed a trapdoor commitment scheme based on the DDH assumption. In Pedersen's commitment scheme, the commitment key is $\mu = g^\delta$, and δ is the trapdoor.

Zero-Knowledge Proofs and Σ-Protocols. For definition of zero-knowledge proofs, see [8]. For definition of Σ-protocol and non-erasure Σ-protocol, see [4, 15].

Additive Homomorphic PKE Scheme. In an *additive homomorphic PKE scheme*, it is possible to efficiently compute an encryption c of $(m_1 + m_2)$ from ciphertexts c_1 and c_2 encrypting plaintexts m_1 and m_2, respectively. This is called *homomorphic addition* and denoted by $c = c_1 +_h m_2$. In an additive homomorphic PKE scheme, it is also possible to efficiently compute an encryption c_2 of $(m_1 \times m_2)$ from an encryption c_1 of m_1 and the plaintext m_2. This is called *homomorphic multiplication by constant* and denoted by $c_2 = c_1 \times_h m_2$.

Randomizable or Blindable PKE Scheme. In a *randomizable or blindable PKE scheme*, there exists a probabilistic polynomial-time algorithm *Blind*, which, on input public key pk and an encryption c of plaintext m, produces another encryption c_1 of plaintext m such that c_1 is distributed identically to $E_{pk}(m, r)$ where $r \xleftarrow{\$} Coins(E)$.

Definition 4 ([1]). *A **lossy PKE scheme** is a tuple (G, E, D) of probabilistic polynomial time algorithms such that keys generated by $G(1^s, 1)$ and $G(1^s, 0)$ are called injective keys and lossy keys, respectively. The algorithms must satisfy the following properties.*

1 **Correctness on Injective Keys:** *If $(pk_I, sk_I) \leftarrow G(1^s, 1)$, then, for all plaintexts m,*
$$D_{sk}(E_{pk}(m, r)) = m.$$

2 **Indistinguishability of Keys:** *The lossy public keys are computationally indistinguishable from the injective public keys.*

3 **Lossiness on Lossy Keys:** *If $(pk_L, sk_L) \leftarrow G(1^s, 0)$, then, for any pair (m_0, m_1) of distinct plaintexts, $E_{pk_L}(m_0, r_0)$ and $E_{pk_L}(m_1, r_1)$ are statistically indistinguishable.*

4 **Openability:** *If $(pk_L, sk_L) \leftarrow G(1^s, 0)$ and $r_0 \xleftarrow{\$} Coins(E)$, then, for all m_0, m_1, with overwhelming probability, there exists $r_1 \in Coins(E)$ such that $E_{pk_L}(m_0, r_0) = E_{pk_L}(m_1, r_1)$. That is, there exists a (possibly inefficient) algorithm Opener that can open a lossy ciphertext to any arbitrary plaintext with all but negligible probability.*

The semantic security of a lossy PKE scheme is implied by definition [1].

Security Model. The security of the new protocols are proved following the simulation based security definition by Canetti [2].

3   New Security Definitions for Lossy Threshold Public Key Encryption Schemes

3.1   Threshold Public Key Encryption Scheme Secure Against Adaptive Adversaries

There are two types of functionalities – non-reactive functionalities and reactive functionalities. In a *standard functionality or non-reactive functionality*, each party has a single input and a single output. The output of each party is a possibly randomized function of the inputs of all the parties. This is also called secure function evaluation (SFE) which is a widely used term. In a *reactive functionality*, parties perform some computations for multiple iterations. There exists a global state that is updated in each iteration. The global state may not be known by any individual party. It is shared among the parties. Initially, the global state is an empty state. In each iteration, each party receives its input for that iteration and parties compute the outputs of that iteration based on their inputs in that iteration and the global state in that iteration, then parties update the global state for the next iteration based on their inputs in that iteration and the global state in that iteration.

In this section, we present a new definition for threshold PKE schemes secure against adaptive adversaries. In this definition, the threshold PKE scheme is treated as a reactive functionality. In this reactive functionality, there are two phases – the key generation phase and the decryption phase. In the key generation phase, a trusted dealer generates the key and distributes the key shares to the parties. In the decryption phase, parties together perform threshold decryption protocol to decrypt a ciphertext.

A threshold PKE scheme secure against adaptive adversaries is a PKE scheme that has a key generation algorithm to generate public key and secret key shares, an encryption algorithm, a threshold decryption protocol whose security are defined considering the reactive nature of the encryption scheme and which satisfies threshold semantic security defined in such a way that the adaptive nature of the adversaries is completely taken care of. In *private threshold decryption protocol*, parties together perform a threshold decryption in such a way that a single party receives the output of threshold decryption. Since the functionality is reactive, the security of threshold decryption protocol is defined in a different way than an MPC protocol for non-reactive functionalities. The difference is in the input that is supplied to the simulator in their security definition. These simulators are given a list of simulated outputs in the key generation phase and the trapdoor of the commitment key as additional inputs, which are not present in the security definition of MPC protocols for non-reactive functionalities. This simulated list of outputs have to be computationally indistinguishable from the list of outputs generated in a real execution of the key generation algorithm. The security definition of a threshold decryption protocol secure against adaptive adversaries is presented below.

Definition 5. *The ideal functionality $\mathcal{F}_{DEC}$ for the threshold decryption protocol is defined in the following way. The common inputs are the public key*

pk, the ciphertext c, the set of verification keys $\{vk, vk_1, \ldots, vk_n\}$, and the commitment key ck. The private input of each party P_i is its secret key share sk_i. If $c = E_{pk}(m, r)$, then the output is m. Otherwise, the output is $\bot$, denoting decryption failure. Let x_i denote the input of P_i for $\mathcal{F}_{DEC}$. Let $SIM_{IN} = \{pk, \{vk, vk_1, \ldots, vk_n\}, ck, tr, \{sk_1, \ldots, sk_n\}, c, m\}$ where $\{\{vk, vk_1, \ldots, vk_n\}, ck, \{sk_1, \ldots, sk_n\}\}$ are the simulated values of these parameters, tr is the trapdoor of the commitment key ck, c is the input ciphertext, and m is the output plaintext. Let the input vector be $\overline{x} = \{x_1, \ldots, x_n\}$. Let z be the input of the environment $\mathcal{Z}$. Let $\mathcal{F}_{KG}$ denote the ideal functionality for the key generation algorithm of a threshold PKE scheme. Let $\mathcal{F}_{ZK}^R$ denote the ideal functionality for the zero-knowledge proof.

Protocol Π_{DEC} is said to **securely compute $\mathcal{F}_{DEC}$ in the presence of erasure-free t-limited adaptive adversaries**, if, for each probabilistic polynomial-time erasure-free t-limited adaptive adversary $\mathcal{A}$ and each environment $\mathcal{Z}$, there exists a probabilistic polynomial-time simulator $\mathcal{S}_{DEC}$, that has input SIM_{IN}, and that produces an output such that the following two distribution ensembles are computationally indistinguishable for any balanced vector $\overline{x}$, where the random inputs of the adversary, the environment and the parties are selected uniformly at random from the corresponding domains:

- The global output after parties $P_1, \ldots, P_n$ performing an evaluation of $\mathcal{F}_{DEC}$ on input vector $\overline{x}$ in the ideal world of adaptive adversary model in the presence of the simulator $\mathcal{S}_{DEC}$ (or the ideal world adversary) and environment $\mathcal{Z}$.
- The global output after parties $P_1, \ldots, P_n$ performing an execution of Protocol Π_{DEC} on input vector $\overline{x}$ in the $(\mathcal{F}_{KG}, \mathcal{F}_{ZK}^R)$-hybrid world in the presence of adversary $\mathcal{A}$ and environment $\mathcal{Z}$.

The security of a private threshold decryption protocol secure against adaptive adversaries is defined similar to the security definition of a threshold decryption protocol.

For defining the threshold semantic security, the new definition uses a new game called **GA** where the adaptive nature of the adversary is completely taken care of. This game GA is created by modifying the game of the threshold semantic security in the definition of Fouque et al. [6], as follows: In between each pair of steps in the game for static adversaries, there is an additional step where the adversary can corrupt parties in an adaptive way. The threshold semantic security definition of a threshold PKE scheme is presented below.

Definition 6. Let $\mathcal{A}$ denote an erasure-free t-limited adaptive adversary in the $(\mathcal{F}_{KG}, \mathcal{F}_{ZK}^R)$-hybrid world, and $\mathcal{Z}$ denote an environment. Let Π_{DEC} be the threshold decryption protocol of the threshold PKE scheme. There exists a probabilistic polynomial-time simulator $\mathcal{S}_{DEC}$ for Protocol Π_{DEC} for adversary $\mathcal{A}$ and environment $\mathcal{Z}$ such that the following conditions hold.

Consider the following game GA between a challenger and adversary $\mathcal{A}$.

GA1 – The Corruption Query. $\mathcal{A}$ may corrupt one or more parties until the total number of corrupted parties exceeds t. If $\mathcal{A}$ corrupts P_i, then $\mathcal{A}$ learns the history of P_i. If $\mathcal{A}$ is an active adaptive adversary, then P_i may violate the protocol and follows the instruction of $\mathcal{A}$.

GA2 – The Key Generation. The challenger executes algorithm KG, and broadcasts the public outputs of KG. For each corrupted party P_i, the challenger sends the secret output of P_i from KG, to $\mathcal{A}$.

GA3. $\mathcal{A}$ repeats step GA3 as many times it wishes.

Let u denote the number of iterations of step GA3 by $\mathcal{A}$. For convenience, the variables in the v-th iteration of step GA3 are denoted using (v) as a superscript in the original notation. For each $v \in \{1, \ldots, u\}$, in the v-th iteration of step GA3, $\mathcal{A}$ performs the following two steps.

GA3(1) – The Corruption Query. This step is similar to step GA1.

GA3(2) – The Decryption Query. $\mathcal{A}$ selects a plaintext $m^{(v)} \in M_{pk}$, a randomness $r^{(v)} \in Coins(E)$, and computes $c^{(v)} = E_{pk}\left(m^{(v)}, r^{(v)}\right)$.

Then, $\mathcal{A}$ sends $c^{(v)}$ to the challenger. Let $x_i^{\left(c^{(v)}\right)}$ denote the input of P_i for $\mathcal{F}_{DEC}$ for ciphertext $c^{(v)}$. Let $z^{(v)}$ denote the internal history of $\mathcal{A}$ at the start of the v-th iteration of step GA3.

GA4. $\mathcal{A}$ selects two plaintexts sm_0 and sm_1 from M_{pk}, and sends (sm_0, sm_1) to the challenger. The challenger selects $b \xleftarrow{\$} \{0,1\}$, and sends an encryption c of sm_b, to $\mathcal{A}$.

GA5. $\mathcal{A}$ repeats step GA3 as many times as it wishes. $\mathcal{A}$ is not allowed to use the plaintext sm_0 or sm_1 as the chosen plaintext in step GA3(2).

GA6. $\mathcal{A}$ outputs a guess bit b_1.

A threshold PKE scheme is said to be **semantically secure against erasure-free t-limited adaptive adversaries** if, for any probabilistic polynomial time erasure-free t-limited adaptive adversary $\mathcal{A}$ and any given environment $\mathcal{Z}$, the following two conditions hold:

1. $b = b_1$ with probability only negligibly greater than $\frac{1}{2}$, and
2. There exists a probabilistic polynomial-time simulator $\mathcal{S}_{DEC}$ such that, for each $v \in \{1, \ldots, u\}$, in the v-th iteration of step GA3, the following two distribution ensembles are computationally indistinguishable, where party P_i has input $x_i^{\left(c^{(v)}\right)}$, $\mathcal{Z}$ has input $z^{(v)}$, the input vector is $\left\{x_1^{\left(c^{(v)}\right)}, \ldots, x_n^{\left(c^{(v)}\right)}\right\}$, s is the security parameter, and the random inputs of the adversary, the environment and the parties are selected uniformly at random from the corresponding domains:

   - The global output after parties $P_1, \ldots, P_n$ performing an evaluation of $\mathcal{F}_{DEC}$ on input $\left\{x_1^{\left(c^{(v)}\right)}, \ldots, x_n^{\left(c^{(v)}\right)}\right\}$ in the ideal world of adaptive adversary model in the presence of the simulator $\mathcal{S}_{DEC}$ (or the ideal world adversary) and environment $\mathcal{Z}$.
   - The global output after parties $P_1, \ldots, P_n$ performing an execution of Protocol Π_{DEC} on input $\left\{x_1^{\left(c^{(v)}\right)}, \ldots, x_n^{\left(c^{(v)}\right)}\right\}$ in the $(\mathcal{F}_{KG}, \mathcal{F}_{ZK}^R)$-hybrid world in the presence of adversary $\mathcal{A}$ and environment $\mathcal{Z}$.

In step GA3 of game GA, the adversary views the decryption shares and the validity proofs of all parties for the encryption of the plaintext chosen by the adversary. This step is used to ensure that seeing all the decryption shares and the validity proofs do not give the adversary any advantage in guessing the plaintext from the ciphertext. In other words, the existence of this step in the game implies that that even after seeing all these information which are not available in a non-threshold PKE scheme, the adversary cannot distinguish between the ciphertexts of two different plaintexts. The new definition of threshold PKE scheme secure against adaptive adversaries is presented below.

Definition 7. *A **threshold PKE scheme secure against erasure-free t-limited adaptive adversaries** for the multiparty model without honest majority (meaning that where the adversary may corrupt up to $t < n$ parties) for the set of parties $P = \{P_1, \ldots, P_n\}$, and security parameter s, is a 5-tuple $(K, KG, E, \Pi_{DEC}, \Pi_{PDEC})$ possessing the following properties.*

Key Generation: *The key generation algorithm KG takes input (1^s) where s is the security parameter. The public outputs of KG are a public key pk, and a list $\{vk, vk_1, \ldots, vk_n\}$ of verification keys. The secret output of P_i from KG is its secret key sk_i. A trusted dealer executes algorithm KG, then broadcasts the public key and the list of verification keys, and sends the secret key sk_i to P_i, for each $i \in \{1, \ldots, n\}$.*

Encryption: *The encryption algorithm E takes as input a public key pk, a plaintext m, and a randomness r, and outputs a ciphertext c.*

Threshold Decryption Protocol: *There exists a threshold decryption protocol Π_{DEC} that securely computes $\mathcal{F}_{DEC}$ in the presence of erasure-free t-limited adaptive adversaries, according to Definition 5. In Protocol Π_{DEC}, each party P_i uses validity proof through which P_i can convince P_j that P_i performed its calculation in Π_{PDEC} correctly, without disclosing its secret key. The verification keys are used in the validity proofs.*

Threshold Semantic Security: *The encryption scheme is semantically secure in the presence of erasure-free t-limited adaptive adversaries according to Definition 6.*

3.2   Lossy Threshold Public Key Encryption Scheme

Simply stated, a lossy threshold PKE scheme is the combination of a lossy PKE scheme and a threshold PKE scheme.

Definition 8. *A **lossy threshold PKE scheme secure against erasure-free t-limited active adaptive adversaries** is a threshold PKE scheme (K, KG, E, Π_{DEC}) according to Definition 7, with the following modifications.*

Key Generation: *The input of the key generation algorithm KG is $(1^s, mode)$. Here, s is the security parameter, and $mode \in \{0, 1\}$ denotes the mode of the key generated, for a lossy PKE scheme (Definition 4).*

Lossy Encryption Properties: *The encryption scheme is a lossy PKE scheme according to Definition 4.*

Next, a special case of this new definition – a two-party lossy threshold PKE scheme secure against adaptive adversaries is presented.

Definition 9. *A **lossy threshold two-party PKE scheme secure against erasure-free one-sided active adaptive adversaries** is a lossy threshold PKE scheme according to Definition 8 such that the number of parties $n = 2$, and the threshold $t = 1$.*

4   A New Two-Party Lossy Threshold Homomorphic Public Key Encryption Scheme

In this section, we present a new two-party lossy threshold homomorphic PKE scheme $ELTAP = (K, KG, \Pi_{DKG}, E, \Pi_{DEC})$. $ELTAP$ is based on the DCRA assumption. All protocols of $ELTAP$ work in the CRS model.

Lysyanskaya and Peikert [12] designed a threshold Paillier PKE scheme secure against adaptive adversaries. Hemenway et al. designed a lossy PKE scheme from Paillier encryption scheme ([11], Appendix C.1). $ELTAP$ is created by adding the lossy properties to the threshold Paillier PKE scheme of [12], following the ideas similar to the lossy PKE scheme of [11]. $ELTAP$ uses a zero-knowledge proof for proving the equality of discrete logarithm. Let R_{EQ} be the relation denoting equality of discrete logarithm. Here, the common input is (x_1, x_2, y_1, y_2), and P knows a witness $w \in \mathbb{Z}_{n\lambda}$ such that $x_1 = (y_1)^w \bmod N^2$, and $x_2 = (y_2)^w \bmod N^2$. Let QR_{N^2} denote the group of squares modulo N^2. For this relation it must hold that x_1, y_1, x_2, y_2 all are elements of the group QR_{N^2}, and y_2 is a generator of QR_{N^2}. Note that λ is unknown to all parties. Then, R_{EQ} is defined as $R_{EQ} = \Big\{ \big((x_1, x_2, y_1, y_2), w\big) : x_1 \equiv (y_1)^w \bmod N^2, x_2 \equiv$ $(y_2)^w \bmod N^2 \Big\}$.

Key Generation. The key generation algorithm KG is presented below.

Algorithm KG.

– **Inputs:** Security parameter s, and $mode \in \{0, 1\}$. Here, $mode = 1$ denotes injective mode, and $mode = 0$ denotes lossy mode.

Outputs:

– **Public Outputs:** The public key pk, the set of verification keys $\{vk, vk_1, vk_2\}$, and a commitment key ck.
– **Secret Output of P_i:** Secret key share sk_i.

1. Select two $\frac{s}{2}$ bit primes p, q such that $p = 2p' + 1, q = 2q' + 1$, where p', q' are also primes, $N = pq$, and $gcd(N, \phi(N)) = 1$.

2. Set $\lambda = 2p'q'$. Select $\beta \xleftarrow{\$} \mathbb{Z}_N^*$.
3. Select $sk_1 \xleftarrow{\$} \mathbb{Z}_{N\lambda}$. Set $sk_2 \in \mathbb{Z}_{N\lambda}$ such that $sk_1 + sk_2 = \beta\lambda \bmod N\lambda$.
4. Select $(a, b) \xleftarrow{\$} \mathbb{Z}_N^*$. Set $g = (1 + N)^a \cdot b^N \bmod N^2$. Set $\theta = a\beta\lambda \bmod N$.
5. Select $ck \xleftarrow{\$} \mathbb{Z}_p$.
6. Select $r_q \xleftarrow{\$} \mathbb{Z}_N^*$. Set $Q = g^{mode} \cdot (r_q)^N \bmod N^2$.
7. Set $pk = (N, g, \theta, Q)$.
8. Choose a random square v from $\mathbb{Z}_{N^2}^*$. Set $vk = v$. For each $i \in \{1, 2\}$, set
$vk_i = (vk)^{(sk_i)}$.
9. For each $i \in \{1, 2\}$, send $(pk, \{vk, vk_1, vk_2\}, ck, sk_i)$ to P_i as its output.

The first five steps of Algorithm KG are the steps of the key generation algorithm of the threshold Paillier PKE scheme of [12]. Here, $\lambda(N)$ denote the Carmichael's function taken on N, that is, $\lambda(N) = lcm(p - 1)(q - 1)$. Then, Algorithm KG computes an encryption Q of plaintext $mode$ with randomness $r_q \xleftarrow{\$} \mathbb{Z}_N^*$ using the Paillier [16] encryption under public key (N, g), that is, $Q = g^{mode} \cdot (r_q)^N \bmod N^2$. Then, it sets the public key of the new encryption scheme to $pk = (N, g, \theta, Q)$. Note that N is chosen such that $gcd(N, \phi(N)) = 1$. Setting N in this way ensures that the function $f(a, b) = (1 + a)^N \cdot b^N \bmod N^2$ is a bijection from $\mathbb{Z}_N \times \mathbb{Z}_N^*$ to $\mathbb{Z}_{N^2}^*$. Let QR_{N^2} denote the cyclic group of squares modulo N^2. Then, $vk \xleftarrow{\$} QR_{N^2}$. By the Chinese remainder theorem, QR_{N^2} is isomorphic to $QR_{p^2} \times QR_{q^2}$ where the mapping from QR_{N^2} to $QR_{p^2} \times QR_{q^2}$ is given by $v \mapsto (v_{p^2}, v_{q^2}) = (v \bmod p^2, v \bmod q^2)$. QR_{p^2} and QR_{q^2} are cyclic group of order pp' and qq', respectively. Since pp' and qq' are relatively prime, QR_{N^2} is cyclic and its order is $pp'qq'$. Number of generators of QR_{N^2} is $\phi(pqp'q') = (p-1)(q-1)(p'-1)(q'-1) = (2p'+1-1)(2q'+1-1)(p'-1)(q'-1) = 4p'q'(p'-1)(q'-1)$. Then, the probability of a uniformly selected vk from QR_{N^2} to be a generator of QR_{N^2} is

$$
\begin{aligned}
\frac{\phi(pqp'q')}{|QR_{N^2}|} &= \frac{4p'q'(p'-1)(q'-1)}{pqp'q'} = \frac{4p'q'(p'q'-p'-q'+1)}{p'q'(2p'+1)(2q'+1)} \\
&= \frac{4p'q'-4p'-4q'+4}{4p'q'+2p'+2q'+1} = 1 - \frac{6p'+6q'-3}{(2p'+1)(2q'+1)} \\
&= 1 - \frac{6p'+6q'-3}{N} = 1 - O\left(N^{-\frac{1}{2}}\right).
\end{aligned}
$$

Then, the probability that a uniformly selected vk from QR_{N^2} is not a generator of QR_{N^2} is negligible in the security parameter s.

Encryption. The encryption algorithm E, on input public key $pk = (N, g, \theta, Q)$, plaintext $m \in \mathbb{Z}_N$, and randomness $r \in \mathbb{Z}_N^*$, returns $c = Q^m \cdot r^N \bmod N^2$. Since N is the product of two $\frac{s}{2}$-bit primes, N can be represented using s bits. A ciphertext $c \in \mathbb{Z}_{N^2}^*$, so the size of a ciphertext is $2s$ bits.

Threshold Decryption Protocol. The threshold decryption protocol Π_{DEC} of $ELTAP$ is the same as the threshold decryption protocol of threshold Paillier

PKE scheme of [12]. L is a function whose domain is the set $S_N = \{u < N : u \bmod N = 1\}$. The function L is defined as $L(u) = \frac{u-1}{N}$. Protocol Π_{DEC} is presented below.

Protocol Π_{DEC}.

1. P_1 sends $ds_1 = c^{sk_1} \bmod N^2$.
2. P_1 proves that $\log_{c^2}\left((ds_1)^2\right) = \log_{vk}(vk_1)$, using a zero-knowledge proof for relation R_{EQ}. If P_1 fails, then P_2 aborts.
3. P_2 sends $ds_2 = c^{sk_2} \bmod N^2$.
4. P_2 proves that $\log_{c^2}\left((ds_2)^2\right) = \log_{vk}(vk_2)$, using a zero-knowledge proof for relation R_{EQ}. If P_2 fails, then P_1 aborts.
5. $m = \frac{L(ds_1 ds_2)}{\theta}$.

The verification key vk_i of P_i was set to $(vk)^{sk_i}$ in Algorithm KG. Each party P_i proves that it correctly computed its decryption share by using a zero-knowledge proof for R_{EQ} that is secure against erasure-free adaptive adversaries. Damgård et al. [5] designed a Σ-protocol for relation R_{EQ}. The zero-knowledge proofs in Π_{DEC} are obtained by converting the non-erasure Σ-protocol for R_{EQ} using the conversion method of Damgård [3]. The proof for R_{EQ} for $ELTAP$ requires that all the common inputs are elements of the group QR_{N^2}. For this reason, the prover P_i has to prove that $\log_{c^2}\left((ds_i)^2\right) = \log_{vk}(vk_i)$. If the computation of ds_i is correctly performed, then this relation holds.

Private Threshold Decryption to One Party P_j. The private threshold decryption protocol Π_{PDEC} is presented below.

Protocol Π_{PDEC}.

1. P_{3-j} sends $ds_{3-j} = c^{sk_{3-j}} \bmod N^2$.
2. P_{3-j} proves that $\log_{c^2}\left((ds_{3-j})^2\right) = \log_{vk}(vk_{3-j})$, using a zero-knowledge proof for relation R_{EQ}. If P_{3-j} fails, then P_j aborts.
3. P_j computes $ds_j = c^{(sk_j)} \bmod N^2$. P_j outputs $m = \frac{L(ds_1 ds_2)}{\theta}$.

Additive Homomorphic Properties and Blindability. Let $c_1 = E_{pk}(m_1, r_1)$ and $c_2 = E_{pk}(m_2, r_2)$ be two ciphertexts. Homomorphic addition of c_1 and c_2 is done by computing $c = c_1 \cdot c_2 \bmod N^2$. Homomorphic multiplication of a ciphertext c_1 by a plaintext m_2 is done by computing $c_2 = (c_1)^{m_2} \bmod N^2$. The *Blind* algorithm, on input ciphertext $c_1 = E_{pk}(m_1, r_1)$ works as follows: It selects $r \xleftarrow{\$} \mathbb{Z}_N^*$, then returns $c_3 = c_1 \cdot (r)^N \bmod N^2$.

The following theorem describes the efficiency of Protocol Π_{DEC} and Protocol Π_{PDEC}.

Theorem 1. *The number of rounds of Protocol Π_{DEC} and Protocol Π_{PDEC} is constant. The communication complexity of Protocol Π_{DEC} and Protocol Π_{PDEC} is $O(s)$ bits. The number of exponentiation operations performed by each party in Protocol Π_{DEC} and Protocol Π_{PDEC} is constant.*

The proof of this theorem is available in [14].

4.1 Security of the New Encryption Scheme

A one-sided adaptive adversary corrupts at most one party out of two parties in a 2PC protocol. That means, an erasure-free one-sided active adaptive adversary for a 2PC protocol is the same as an erasure-free t-limited active adaptive adversary where number of parties $n = 2$, and the threshold $t = 1$.

Lemma 1. *If the DCRA assumption holds, then ELTAP is a lossy PKE scheme. It has an efficient (polynomial-time) Opener algorithm.*

Proof. The lossy encryption properties for *ELTAP* are proved below.

Correctness of Decryption in the Injective Mode. Suppose that both parties are honest, pk is an injective key and $c = E_{pk}(m, r)$. In the injective mode, the parameter $mode = 1$. Then, $c = E_{pk}(m, r) = Q^m \cdot r^N = \left(g^{mode} \cdot (r_q)^N \right)^m \cdot$
$r^N = g^{m \cdot mode} \cdot \left(r \cdot (r_q)^m \right)^N = g^{m \cdot 1} \cdot \left(r \cdot (r_q)^m \right)^N = g^m \cdot \left(r \cdot (r_q)^m \right)^N \bmod N^2$.
Since both parties are honest, they compute ds_1 and ds_2 correctly. Note that $ds_1 \cdot ds_2 = c^{sk_1} \cdot c^{sk_2} = c^{sk_1 + sk_2} = c^{\beta\lambda}$. Since the calculation is done modulo N^2, $(r_q)^m \cdot r \in \mathbb{Z}^*_{N^2}$. By Carmichael's Theorem [16], $\left((r_q)^m \cdot r \right)^{N\lambda} = 1 \bmod N^2$.
Then, $c^{\beta\lambda} = \left(g^m \cdot \left(r \cdot (r_q)^m \right)^N \right)^{\beta\lambda} = g^{m\beta\lambda} \cdot \left(r \cdot (r_q)^m \right)^{N\beta\lambda} = g^{m\beta\lambda} \cdot 1^\beta = g^{m\beta\lambda} =$
$\left((1 + N)^a b^N \right)^{m\beta\lambda} = (1 + N)^{am\beta\lambda} \cdot b^{Nm\beta\lambda} \bmod N^2$. Since $b \in \mathbb{Z}^*_N$, so $b \in \mathbb{Z}^*_{N^2}$. By
Carmichael's Theorem, $b^{N\lambda} = 1 \bmod N^2$. Then, $c^{\beta\lambda} = (1 + N)^{am\beta\lambda} \cdot b^{Nm\beta\lambda} =$
$(1 + N)^{am\beta\lambda} \cdot 1^{m\beta} = (1 + N)^{am\beta\lambda} \bmod N^2$. By the binomial theorem, $(1 +$
$N)^{am\beta\lambda} = \sum_{k=0}^{am\beta\lambda} \cdot \binom{am\beta\lambda}{k} N^k = 1 + am\beta\lambda \cdot N + \binom{am\beta\lambda}{2} \cdot N^2 + \binom{am\beta\lambda}{3} \cdot N^3 + \ldots +$
$N^{am\beta\lambda}$. Then, $(1 + N)^{am\beta\lambda} \bmod N^2 = (1 + am\beta\lambda \cdot N + \binom{am\beta\lambda}{2} N^2 + \binom{am\beta\lambda}{3} N^3 +$
$\ldots + N^{am\beta\lambda}) \bmod N^2 = 1 + am\beta\lambda N$. Parties compute $\frac{L(ds_1 \cdot ds_2)}{\theta} = \frac{L(c^{\beta\lambda})}{a\beta\lambda} =$
$\frac{L(1 + am\beta\lambda N)}{a\beta\lambda} = \frac{am\beta\lambda}{a\beta\lambda} = m$.

Indistinguishability of Keys. The public key $pk = (g, N, \theta, Q)$. Q is computed by performing Pailler [16] encryption of plaintext $mode$ with randomness r_q under public key (N, g). By semantic security of Paillier encryption scheme, the value of Q for a lossy public key and the value of Q for an injective public key are computationally indistinguishable. Then, a lossy public key is computationally indistinguishable from an injective public key.

Lossiness on Lossy Keys. Let pk_L be a lossy public key. Then, $pk_L = (g, N, \theta, Q) = \left(g, N, \theta, g^{mode} \cdot (r_q)^N \bmod N^2 \right) = \left(g, N, \theta, g^0 \cdot (r_q)^N \bmod N^2 \right) = \left(g, N, \theta, (r_q)^N \bmod N^2 \right)$. Then, $E_{PK_L}(m, r) = Q^m \cdot r^N \bmod N^2 = \left((r_q)^N \right)^m \cdot$
$r^N \bmod N^2 = \left(r \cdot (r_q)^m \right)^N \bmod N^2$. Then, c is an encryption of zero in the Paillier [16] PKE scheme. Since $r_q \xleftarrow{\$} \mathbb{Z}^*_N$, c is uniformly distributed in the set of Paillier ciphertexts encrypting zero. Then, for any pair m_0, m_1 of distinct plaintexts, $E_{pk_L}(m_0, r_0)$ and $E_{pk_L}(m_1, r_1)$ are identically distributed.

Efficient *Opener* Algorithm. Let (pk_L, sk_L) be a lossy key pair. Then, $pk_L = (g, N, \theta, Q) = \left(g, N, \theta, (r_q)^N \bmod N^2 \right)$, and $sk_L = (\beta\lambda, r_q)$. Let $c =$

$E_{pk_L}(m, r) = ((r_q)^m \cdot r)^N \bmod N^2$ be the input ciphertext. The inputs of the *Opener* algorithm are the public key pk_L, the secret key sk_L, the ciphertext c, the original plaintext m, the original randomness r, and a new plaintext $m_2 \in \mathbb{Z}_N$ with which the caller wants the ciphertext c to be opened. The output is a randomness $r_2 \in \mathbb{Z}_N^*$ such that $E_{pk}(m_2, r_2) = c$. At first, the *Opener* algorithm computes $r_1 = r \cdot (r_q)^m$. Note that $c = (r_1)^N \bmod N^2$. Since g is an N-th residue in $\mathbb{Z}_{N^2}$, $g = (g_0)^N \bmod N^2$ where $g_0 \in \mathbb{Z}_N$. Note that $gcd(N, \phi(N)) = 1$. Then, the *Opener* algorithm computes $g_0 = (g \bmod N)^{\frac{1}{N}} \bmod N$, using the factorization of N. It then computes $\kappa = N^{-1} \bmod \phi(N)$. Now, the *Opener* algorithm has to find randomness r_2 such that $c = r_1{}^N = g^{m_2} \cdot ((r_q)^{m_2} \cdot r_2)^N = (g_0)^{m_2 N} \cdot (r_q)^{m_2 \cdot N} \cdot (r_2)^N \bmod N^2$. *Opener* algorithm computes $r_2 = r_1 \cdot (g_0 \cdot r_q)^{-m_2} \bmod N$.

Single inconsistent party (SIP) technique is a technique for proving security against adaptive adversaries. In this technique, at the start of simulation, the simulator generates the identity of the single inconsistent party (SIP) uniformly at random from the set of participating parties. The simulator is constructed in such a way that the following property is satisfied for any party P_i except the SIP: the view of P_i in the simulation is computationally indistinguishable from the view of P_i in the real world. It is guaranteed that the view of the adversary is independent from the choice of the SIP. During the simulation, if the adversary corrupts the SIP, then the simulator rewinds to the start of simulation, generates a new SIP uniformly at random from the set of parties, and proceeds again.

Lemma 2. *Provided that the DCRA assumption holds and trapdoor commitment scheme exists, Protocol Π_{DEC} securely computes $\mathcal{F}_{DEC}$ in the presence of erasure-free t-limited active adaptive adversaries for $n = 2$ and $t = 1$.*

Proof. This lemma is proved using the SIP technique. Its security is proved in the $\mathcal{F}_{ZK}^R$-hybrid world. Let $\mathcal{A}$ be an erasure-free one-sided active adaptive adversary in the hybrid world and let $\mathcal{Z}$ be the environment. A simulator $\mathcal{S}_{DEC}$ is created for adversary $\mathcal{A}$ and environment $\mathcal{Z}$. The inputs of the simulator $\mathcal{S}_{DEC}$ is $SIM_{IN} = \{pk, \{vk, vk_1, vk_2\}, ck, tr, \{sk_1, sk_2\}, c, m\}$ where $\{\{vk, vk_1, vk_2\}, ck, \{sk_1, sk_2\}\}$ are the simulated values of these parameters, tr is the trapdoor of the commitment key ck, c is the input ciphertext, and m is the output plaintext. If Protocol Π_{DEC} is invoked from another protocol, then the identity I of the SIP is also supplied as part of the input SIM_{IN} of $\mathcal{S}_{DEC}$. Otherwise, at start, $\mathcal{S}_{DEC}$ selects the index I of the SIP as $I \overset{\$}{\leftarrow} \{1, 2\}$. If $\mathcal{A}$ corrupts P_I at any step, then the simulator rewinds to the start of simulation, generates another $I \overset{\$}{\leftarrow} \{1, 2\}$, and proceeds again. A one-sided adaptive adversary corrupts at most one party out of two parties, so the probability of P_I being corrupted is at most $\frac{1}{2}$. That means the expected number of rewinding the simulator is two, and the simulator runs in expected polynomial time.

There are two possible cases, as described below separately.

Case 1: $I = P_1$.

$\mathcal{S}_{DEC}$ performs the steps of Protocol Π_{DEC} honestly on behalf of the honest party or the honest parties, with the following exceptions. In step 1, $\mathcal{S}_{DEC}$

computes $ds_2 = c^{sk_2} \bmod N^2, \widehat{ds}_1 = (1 + m\theta N)c^{-sk_2} \bmod N^2$. $\mathcal{S}_{DEC}$ supplies $\widehat{ds}_1$ as the message from P_1. Since $I = P_1$, $\mathcal{A}$ does not corrupt P_1 and does not learn sk_1. Then, ds_1 and $\widehat{ds}_1$ are computationally indistinguishable. In step 2, if P_2 is corrupted, then $\mathcal{S}_{DEC}$ sends 1 on behalf of $\mathcal{F}_{ZK}^R$ to $\mathcal{A}$. If P_2 is honest, then $\mathcal{S}_{DEC}$ performs steps 3 honestly on behalf of P_2. In the proof of Theorem 4, in the case where $I = P_1$, it will be proved that the distribution of sk_2 in the two worlds are statistically indistinguishable. Since the distribution of sk_2 in the two worlds are statistically indistinguishable, the distribution of ds_2 in the two worlds are statistically indistinguishable. If P_2 is corrupted, then $\mathcal{S}_{DEC}$ receives the input and witness from $\mathcal{A}$ in step 4. If the condition for the relation does not hold, $\mathcal{S}_{DEC}$ sends 0 to $\mathcal{A}$ and halts. In this case, the honest P_1 halts in the hybrid world. In the simulation, in step 5, if P_2 is honest, then P_2 computes $\frac{L(\widehat{ds}_1 ds_2)}{\theta} = \frac{L((1+m\theta N)c^{-sk_2}c^{sk_2})}{\theta} = \frac{L(1+m\theta N)}{\theta} = \frac{m\theta}{\theta} = m$. In the real world, honest P_2 receives the given output m. If $\mathcal{A}$ corrupts P_2 after any step of Protocol Π_{DEC}, then $\mathcal{S}_{DEC}$ corrupts P_2 in the ideal world. Then, $\mathcal{A}$ sees that $ds_2 = c^{sk_2} \bmod N^2$, so everything is consistent for P_2.

Case 2: $I = P_2$.

$\mathcal{S}_{DEC}$ performs the steps of Protocol Π_{DEC} honestly on behalf of the honest party or the honest parties, with the following exceptions. If P_1 is honest, then $\mathcal{S}_{DEC}$ performs steps 1 honestly on behalf of P_1. Proof argument is similar to the proof argument of step 3 in case 1. In step 2, if P_1 is corrupted, then $\mathcal{S}_{DEC}$ receives the input and witness from $\mathcal{A}$. If the condition for the relation does not hold, $\mathcal{S}_{DEC}$ sends 0 to $\mathcal{A}$ and halts. In step 3, $\mathcal{S}_{DEC}$ computes $ds_1 = c^{(sk_1)} \bmod N^2, \widehat{ds}_2 = (1+m\theta N)c^{-sk_1} \bmod N^2$. $\mathcal{S}_{DEC}$ supplies $\widehat{ds}_2$ as the message from P_2. Proof argument is similar to step 1 in case 1. In step 4, if P_1 is corrupted, then $\mathcal{S}_{DEC}$ sends 1 on behalf of $\mathcal{F}_{ZK}^R$ to $\mathcal{A}$. Proof argument for step 5 is similar to step 5 in case 1. If $\mathcal{A}$ corrupts P_1 after any step of Protocol Π_{DEC}, then $\mathcal{S}_{DEC}$ corrupts P_1 in the ideal world. Then, $\mathcal{A}$ sees that $ds_1 = c^{sk_1} \bmod N^2$, so everything is consistent for P_1.

Corollary 1. *Provided that the DCRA assumption holds and trapdoor commitment scheme exists, Protocol Π_{PDEC} securely computes $\mathcal{F}_{PDEC}$ in the presence of erasure-free t-limited active adaptive adversaries for $n = 2$ and $t = 1$.*

Lemma 3. *Provided that the DCRA assumption holds and trapdoor commitment scheme exists, ELTAP is semantically secure against erasure-free t-limited active adaptive adversaries for $n = 2$ and $t = 1$.*

Proof. ELTAP is created by adding the threshold properties to the non-threshold lossy Paillier PKE scheme of [11]. Hemenway et al. [11] proved the lossy encryption properties of their encryption scheme. Since any lossy PKE scheme is semantically secure [1], the lossy PKE scheme of [11] is semantically secure.

The threshold semantic security of ELTAP is proved by reduction, following the idea in [6]. Assume that there exists a probabilistic polynomial-time t-limited active adaptive adversary $\mathcal{A}_1$ that can break the semantic security of $ELTAP$. We then describe how to construct a probabilistic polynomial-time t-limited active adaptive adversary $\mathcal{A}_2$, using $\mathcal{A}_1$, that can break the semantic security of the non-threshold lossy PKE scheme of [11]. As the lossy PKE scheme of [11] is semantically secure, a contradiction is reached. In this way, it will demonstrate that $ELTAP$ is also semantically secure. To convert $\mathcal{A}_1$ to $\mathcal{A}_2$, it is necessary to simulate the extra information that are not available in the non-threshold lossy PKE scheme of [11]. The inputs of the simulator are the public key $pk = (N, g_1, Q)$ of the non-threshold lossy Paillier PKE scheme of [11], the mode parameter $mode$, and the identity I of the SIP.

In step GA1, if $\mathcal{A}_1$ corrupts a party P_j, then $\mathcal{A}_2$ corrupts P_j and receives the history of P_j from $\mathcal{Z}$. In step GA2, $\mathcal{A}_2$ simulates the key generation, mainly following the simulation strategy of the threshold Paillier PKE scheme of Lysyanskaya and Peikert ([12], Sect. 5.2). $\mathcal{A}_2$ selects $x, y, \hat{\theta}, \alpha \xleftarrow{\$} \mathbb{Z}_N^*$. Then, $\mathcal{A}_2$ sets $\hat{g} = (g_1)^x \cdot y^N \bmod N^2$. $\mathcal{A}_2$ sets $pk = (N, \hat{g}, \hat{\theta}, Q)$. Let $\mathcal{B}_\tau \subset \mathbb{Z}_{N^2}^*$ denote the set of elements of order $n\tau$. Let $\mathcal{B} = \bigcup_{\tau=1}^{\lambda} \mathcal{B}_\tau$. In the real execution, $a, b \xleftarrow{\$} \mathbb{Z}_N^*$, and $g = (1+N)^a \cdot b^N \bmod N^2$. The order of g in $\mathbb{Z}_{N^2}^*$ is $N\chi$ where χ is the order of b. Since $a, b \xleftarrow{\$} \mathbb{Z}_N^*$, it holds that $g \xleftarrow{\$} \mathcal{B}$. Recall that (N, g_1, Q) is a public key of the lossy Paillier PKE scheme of [11]. Then, (N, g_1) is a public key of Paillier PKE scheme [16], and $g_1 \xleftarrow{\$} \mathcal{B}$. Since $x, y \xleftarrow{\$} \mathbb{Z}_N^*, g_1 \xleftarrow{\$} \mathcal{B}$, and $\hat{g} = (g_1)^x \cdot y^N \bmod N^2$, it holds that $\hat{g} \xleftarrow{\$} \mathcal{B}$. Then, the distribution of g and $\hat{g}$ are identical. In the real execution, $a, \beta \xleftarrow{\$} \mathbb{Z}_N^*, \lambda = 2p'q'$, and $\theta = a\beta\lambda \bmod N$. Then, $\theta \xleftarrow{\$} \mathbb{Z}_N^*$. In the simulation, $\hat{\theta} \xleftarrow{\$} \mathbb{Z}_N^*$. Then, the distribution of θ and $\hat{\theta}$ are identical. For each $i \in \{1, 2\}$, $\mathcal{A}_2$ selects $\widehat{sk}_i \xleftarrow{\$} [0, \ldots, \lfloor N^2/2 \rfloor - 1]$. In the real execution, for each $i \in \{1, 2\}$, $sk_i \xleftarrow{\$} \mathbb{Z}_{N\lambda}$. Let $\mathcal{X}_1$ denote a random variable from range $[0, \ldots, \lfloor N^2/2 \rfloor - 1]$. Let $\mathcal{X}_2$ denote a random variable from range $\{0, \ldots, N\lambda - 1\}$. The statistical distance between $\mathcal{X}_1$ and $\mathcal{X}_2$ is

$$\frac{1}{2} \sum_a |Prob(\mathcal{X}_1 = a) - Prob(\mathcal{X}_2 = a)|$$

$$= \frac{1}{2} \sum_{a \in \{0, \ldots, N\lambda - 1\}} |Prob(\mathcal{X}_1 = a) - Prob(\mathcal{X}_2 = a)|$$

$$+ \frac{1}{2} \sum_{a \in \{N\lambda, \ldots, N^2/2\}} |Prob(\mathcal{X}_1 = a) - Prob(\mathcal{X}_2 = a)|$$

$$= \frac{1}{2} \sum_{a \in \{0, \ldots, N\lambda - 1\}} \left| \frac{1}{\frac{N^2}{2}} - \frac{1}{N\lambda} \right| + \frac{1}{2} \sum_{a \in \{N\lambda, \ldots, N^2/2\}} \left| \frac{1}{\frac{N^2}{2}} - 0 \right|$$

$$= \frac{1}{2} \cdot N\lambda \cdot \left| \frac{2\lambda - N}{N^2 \lambda} \right| + \frac{1}{2} \cdot \left(\frac{N^2}{2} - N\lambda + 1 \right) \cdot \frac{1}{\frac{N^2}{2}}$$

$$= \frac{1}{2N} |(2 \cdot 2p'q' - (2p' + 1)(2q' + 1))| + \frac{1}{N^2} \cdot \left(\frac{N^2}{2} - N\lambda + 1 \right)$$

$$= \frac{1}{2N} |(4p'q' - 4p'q' - 2p' - 2q' - 1)| + \frac{1}{N^2} \cdot \left(\frac{N^2}{2} - N\lambda + 1 \right)$$

$$= \frac{1}{2N} (2p' + 2q' + 1) + \frac{1}{N^2} \cdot \left(\frac{N^2}{2} - N\lambda + 1 \right).$$

Note that $(2p' + 2q' + 1) \in O(N^{\frac{1}{2}})$, and $\frac{N^2}{2} - N\lambda = N\left(\frac{N}{2} - \lambda\right) = N\left(\frac{(2p'+1)(2q'+1)}{2} - 2p'q'\right) = N\left(2p'q' + p' + q' + \frac{1}{2} - 2p'q'\right) = N\left(p' + q' + \frac{1}{2}\right) \in N \cdot O\left(N^{\frac{1}{2}}\right) \in O\left(N^{\frac{3}{2}}\right)$. Then,

$$\frac{1}{2} \sum_a |Prob(\mathcal{X}_1 = a) - Prob(\mathcal{X}_2 = a)|$$

$$= \frac{1}{2N} (2p' + 2q' + 1) + \frac{1}{N^2} \cdot \left(\frac{N^2}{2} - N\lambda + 1 \right)$$

$$\in \frac{1}{2N} \cdot O\left(N^{\frac{1}{2}}\right) + \frac{1}{N^2} \cdot O\left(N^{\frac{3}{2}}\right)$$

$$\in O\left(N^{-\frac{1}{2}}\right).$$

The statistical distance between $\mathcal{X}_1$ and $\mathcal{X}_2$ is negligible in s. That means, if P_i is corrupted, then the distribution of the secret key share sk_i in the two worlds are statistically indistinguishable. $\mathcal{A}_2$ selects $\alpha \xleftarrow{\$} \mathbb{Z}_N^*$, and sets $\widehat{vk} = g^{(2\alpha)}$. $\mathcal{A}_2$ sets $\widehat{vk}_{3-I} = \widehat{vk}^{(sk_{3-I})}$. Then, $\mathcal{A}_2$ sets $\widehat{vk}_I = (1 + 2\alpha\theta N)\widehat{vk}^{-sk_{3-I}} \mod N^2$. In the real execution, $vk \xleftarrow{\$} QR_{N^2}^*$. $\mathcal{A}_2$ selects $\alpha \xleftarrow{\$} \mathbb{Z}_N^*$ and sets $\widehat{vk} = g^{2\alpha}$. Then, $\widehat{vk} \xleftarrow{\$} QR_{N^2}^*$. In the real execution, for each $i \in \{1,2\}$, $vk_i = vk^{(sk_i)}$. Since I is the SIP, the adversary does not corrupt I. Since the distribution of sk_{3-I} in the two worlds are statistically indistinguishable, the distribution of vk_{3-I} in the two worlds are statistically indistinguishable. In the simulation, it must be maintained that $\prod_{i\in\{1,2\}} \widehat{vk}_i = \prod_{i\in\{1,2\}} (\widehat{vk})^{(sk_i)} = (\widehat{vk})^{\beta\lambda} \mod N^2$, and $\beta \xleftarrow{\$} \mathbb{Z}_{N^2}$. $\mathcal{A}_2$ does not know β, but it selects the verification keys in such a way that $\prod_{i\in\{1,2\}} \widehat{vk}_i = (\widehat{vk})^{\beta\lambda} = (1 + 2\alpha\theta N) \mod N^2$, by selecting $\theta \xleftarrow{\$} \mathbb{Z}_N$, so that $\beta \xleftarrow{\$} \mathbb{Z}_{N^2}$. $\mathcal{A}_2$ selects $tr \xleftarrow{\$} \mathbb{Z}_p$, and sets $\widehat{ck} = g^{tr}$. $\mathcal{A}_2$ stores tr as the trapdoor for the commitment key. Since $tr \xleftarrow{\$} \mathbb{Z}_p$ and $\widehat{ck} = g^{tr}$, so $\widehat{ck} \xleftarrow{\$} \mathbb{Z}_p$. Then, the distribution of ck and $\widehat{ck}$ is identical.

For each $v \in \{1, \ldots, u\}$, $\mathcal{A}_2$ simulates the v-th iteration of step GA3 in the following way.

GA3(1): Corruption Query. $\mathcal{A}_2$ simulates this step similar to step $GA1$.

GA3(2): Decryption Query. $\mathcal{A}_1$ selects a message $m^{(v)} \in M_{pk}$, and sends $m^{(v)}$ to $\mathcal{A}_2$. $\mathcal{A}_2$ selects $r^{(v)} \xleftarrow{\$} \mathbb{Z}_N^*$, and computes $c^{(v)} = Q^{(m^{(v)})} \cdot \left(r^{(v)}\right)^N \mod N^2$. Then, $c^{(v)}$ is a valid encryption of $m^{(v)}$. Then, $\mathcal{A}_2$ simulates the steps of Protocol Π_{DEC} using the steps the simulator $\mathcal{S}_{DEC}$ uses in the proof of

Lemma 2. The proof arguments are similar. By Lemma 2, the second condition of threshold semantic security in Definition 6 is satisfied.

In step GA4, $\mathcal{A}_1$ chooses two plaintexts $sm_0, sm_1 \in M_{pk}$, and sends them to $\mathcal{A}_2$. $\mathcal{A}_2$ sends (sm_0, sm_1) to the challenger of the non-threshold lossy Paillier PKE scheme of [11]. Then, the challenger of the lossy Paillier PKE scheme of [11] selects $b \xleftarrow{\$} \{0,1\}$, computes an encryption c of sm_b, and returns c to $\mathcal{A}_2$. $\mathcal{A}_2$ sends c to $\mathcal{A}_1$. $\mathcal{A}_2$ simulates step GA5 is similar to step GA3. The proof argument is similar to step GA3. In step GA6, $\mathcal{A}_1$ returns a guess b_1. $\mathcal{A}_2$ returns b_1. Since the non-threshold lossy PKE scheme of [11] is semantically secure, it holds that $b = b_1$ with probability negligibly greater than $\frac{1}{2}$. That means, the first condition stated in Definition 6 is satisfied.

Lemma 4. *Provided that the DCRA assumption holds and trapdoor commitment scheme exists, ELTAP is a threshold PKE scheme secure against erasure-free t-limited active adaptive adversaries for $n = 2$ and $t = 1$.*

Proof. ELTAP has a key generation algorithm (Algorithm KG) satisfying the property given in Definition 7. It has an encryption algorithm E satisfying the property given in Definition 7. By Lemma 2, Protocol Π_{DEC} securely computes $\mathcal{F}_{DEC}$ in the presence of erasure-free t-limited active adaptive adversaries for $n = 2$ and $t = 1$ By Lemma 3, ELTAP is semantically secure against erasure-free t-limited active adaptive adversaries for $n = 2$ and $t = 1$ Then, ELTAP is a threshold PKE scheme secure against erasure-free t-limited active adaptive adversaries for $n = 2$ and $t = 1$.

Theorem 2. *Provided that the DCRA assumption holds and trapdoor commitment scheme exists, ELTAP is a two-party lossy threshold PKE scheme secure against erasure-free one-sided active adaptive adversaries, according to Definition 9.*

Proof. By Lemma 1, ELTAP satisfies the lossy PKE scheme properties. By Lemma 4, ELTAP is a two-party threshold PKE scheme secure against erasure-free t-limited active adaptive adversaries for $n = 2$ and $t = 1$. The key generation algorithm has input $(1^s, mode)$ where s is the security parameter and $mode$ is the mode parameter of the lossy PKE scheme of Definition 4. Then, ELTAP is a lossy threshold PKE scheme secure against erasure-free t-limited active adaptive adversaries for $n = 2$ and $t = 1$. Then, ELTAP is a two-party lossy threshold PKE scheme secure against erasure-free one-sided active adaptive adversaries.

5 Non-erasure Σ-Protocols for the New Encryption Scheme

In this section, we describe the non-erasure Σ-protocols for ELTAP used in the new OT Protocol.

Σ-Protocol for Equality of Discrete Logarithm. Damgård et al. [5] designed a Σ-protocol for R_{EQ}.

Σ-Protocol for Proving that a Given Ciphertext Encrypts Zero. In $ELTAP$, the encryption of a plaintext $m = 0$ using randomness w is $c = Q^m \cdot w^N \bmod N^2 = Q^0 \cdot w^N \bmod N^2 = w^N \bmod N^2$. The common input of relation R_{ZERO} is $c \in \mathbb{Z}_{N^2}$. The prover P knows a witness $w \in \mathbb{Z}_N^*$. So, R_{ZERO} is defined as follows: $R_{ZERO} = \{(c, w) : c \equiv w^N \bmod N^2\}$. Damgård et al. [5] designed a Σ-protocol for R_{ZERO}.

Σ-Protocol for Proving That One of Two Given Ciphertexts Encrypts Zero. Let $R_{OR\text{-}ZERO}$ be the relation that one of two given ciphertexts (generated in the injective mode of the lossy threshold PKE scheme) encrypts zero, without disclosing which one. The Σ-Protocol for $R_{OR\text{-}ZERO}$ is created by the OR-composition [4] of two Σ-protocols for R_{ZERO}.

Σ-Protocol for Proving that a Given Ciphertext Encrypts One. In $ELTAP$, the encryption of a plaintext $m = 1$ using randomness w is $c = Q^m \cdot w^N \bmod N^2 = Q^1 \cdot w^N \bmod N^2 = Q \cdot w^N \bmod N^2$. Then, it holds that $\frac{c}{Q} = w^N \bmod N^2$. That means, proving the relation R_{ONE} on common input Q is the same as proving the relation R_{ZERO} on common input $\frac{c}{Q}$. The witness w of prover is the same in both relations. The common input of relation R_{ONE} is $c \in \mathbb{Z}_{N^2}$. The prover P knows a witness $w \in \mathbb{Z}_{N^2}^*$. So, R_{ONE} is defined as follows: $R_{ONE} = \left\{(c, w) : \frac{c}{Q} \equiv w^N \bmod N^2\right\}$.

Σ-Protocol for Proving That One of Two Given Ciphertexts Encrypts One. Let $R_{OR\text{-}ONE}$ be the relation that one of two given ciphertexts (generated in the injective mode of the lossy threshold PKE scheme) encrypts one, without disclosing which one. The Σ-Protocol for $R_{OR\text{-}ONE}$ is created by the OR-composition [4] of two Σ-protocols for relation R_{ONE}.

Σ-Protocol for Proof of Correct Multiplication. The prover P performs the homomorphic multiplication in the following way in the OT protocol. At first, P selects randomness $\tau_2 \in \mathbb{Z}_{N^2}^*$, and computes $c_2 = E_{pk}(m_2, \tau_2)$. Then, P computes $c_3 = m_2 \times_h c_1$. Then, P computes $c_4 = Blind(pk, c_3)$, using randomness τ_4. The common input for relation R_{MULT} is a triple (c_1, c_2, c_4) of ciphertexts such that c_1 encrypts plaintext m_1, c_2 encrypts plaintext m_2, and c_4 encrypts a plaintext that is the product of m_1 and m_2. P proves to V that P obtained c_4 by correctly performing homomorphic multiplication of c_1 by m_2. The common input of R_{MULT} is $(c_1, c_2, c_4) \in \mathbb{Z}_{N^2} \times \mathbb{Z}_{N^2} \times \mathbb{Z}_{N^2}$. The witness w for relation R_{MULT} consists of the known plaintext m_2, the randomness τ_2 used in the computation of ciphertext c_2 and the randomness τ_4 used in the $Blind$ function. The relation R_{MULT} is defined as follows:
$R_{MULT} = \{((c_1, c_2, c_4), (m_2, \tau_2, \tau_4)) : Q^{m_1}(\tau_1)^N \bmod N^2, Q^{m_2}(\tau_2)^N \bmod N^2, (c_1)^{m_2}(\tau_4)^N \bmod N^2\}$.
A new Σ-protocol $\Pi_{\Sigma MULT}$ for relation R_{MULT} for $ELTAP$ is presented below.

Σ-Protocol $\Pi_{\Sigma MULT}$ for Relation R_{MULT} for $ELTAP$.

- **System Parameter:** $pk = (N, g, \theta, Q)$: the public key of $ELTAP$.
- **Inputs:**
  - **Common Input:** $(c_1, c_2, c_4) \in \mathbb{Z}_{N^2} \times \mathbb{Z}_{N^2} \times \mathbb{Z}_{N^2}$.
  - **Witness of** P: $(m_2, \tau_2, \tau_4) \in \mathbb{Z}_{N^2}^* \times \mathbb{Z}_{N^2}^* \times \mathbb{Z}_{N^2}^*$.

1. P chooses $r_1 \xleftarrow{\$} \mathbb{Z}_N$ and $r_2, r_3 \xleftarrow{\$} \mathbb{Z}_{N^2}$. P computes $a_1 = (c_1)^{r_1} \cdot (r_2)^N \mod N^2$, and $a_2 = Q^{r_1} \cdot (r_3)^N \mod N^2$. P sends $a = (a_1, a_2)$.
2. V chooses a challenge $e \xleftarrow{\$} \{0,1\}^{s-1}$ and sends it.
3. P computes $z_1 = r_1 + em_2 \mod N$, $z_2 = r_3(\tau_2)^e \cdot Q^t \mod N^2$, and $z_3 = r_2(c_1)^t \cdot (\tau_4)^e \mod N^2$ where t is defined by $r_1 + em_2 = z_1 + tN$. P sends $z = (z_1, z_2, z_3)$. V accepts if and only if $Q^{z_1} z_2{}^N = a_2 \cdot (c_2)^e \mod N^2$, and $(c_1)^{z_1} \cdot (z_3)^N = a_1 \cdot (c_4)^e \mod N^2$.

The security proof of $\Pi_{\Sigma MULT}$ is available in [14].

6   The New Oblivious Transfer Protocol

In this section, we present the new OT protocol. It is designed by modifying the OT protocol of [13] by using the new lossy threshold PKE scheme $ELTAP$. The new OT protocol uses a trusted setup phase where a trusted dealer generates the key shares and distributes the key shares to the parties. The zero-knowledge proofs used in the new OT protocol are converted from the non-erasure Σ-protocols for the corresponding relations, using Damgård's conversion method [3]. The new OT protocol Π_{OT} is presented in Fig. 1.

In step 2, R sends an ordered pair (c_0, c_1) of ciphertexts such that c_σ encrypts one and $c_{1-\sigma}$ encrypts zero. If a corrupted R could set both c_0 and c_1 to encryptions of one, then R could learn both x_0 and x_1 later. To prevent this type of cheating by R, the zero-knowledge proof of step 3 is added. In step 4, R gives a zero-knowledge proof for relation $R_{OR\text{-}ONE}$, proving that at least one of c_0 and c_1 encrypts one. If this proof was not added, then an adversary may send both c_0 and c_1 to encryptions of zero on behalf of a corrupted R, and as a result, R will not obtain its output. But such an event cannot happen in the ideal world. Then, the adversary can distinguish between the ideal world and the real world. Adding this zero-knowledge proof also prevents the situation that a corrupted R sends encryption of values other than zero or one. In step 6, for each $i \in \{0,1\}$, S computes d_i by performing homomorphic multiplication of c_i by b_i, and then computes v_i by applying the $Blind$ algorithm on d_i. Then, S sends (v_0, v_1). Note that R knows the ciphertext c_i for each $i \in \{0,1\}$. The $Blind$ algorithm is applied so that new randomness is added to the result d_i. Then, it holds that R cannot learn the constant b_i after seeing the ciphertext v_i. A corrupted S may supply incorrect result of this calculation so that R does not get the correct output. To prevent this type of cheating, the zero-knowledge proof of step 6 is added. The reason for S sending the encryptions u_0 and u_1 of its inputs b_0 and b_1 to R in step 5 is that a ciphertext encrypting the plaintext

---

Protocol Π_{OT}.

- **Common Reference String:** $\mu \xleftarrow{\$} \mathbb{Z}_{p_1}$. Here, p_1 is a prime such that $p_1 = 2q_1 + 1$, q_1 is an s-bit prime.
- **Input of** $S : (b_0, b_1) \in \{0, 1\}^2$.
- **Input of** $R : \sigma \in \{0, 1\}$.
- **Output of** $S :$ An Empty String.
- **Output of** $R : b_\sigma$.

1. A trusted dealer generates an injective key pair using $\mathcal{F}_{KG}$ on input $(1^s, 1)$. In the key generation, S and R acts as party P_1 and P_2, respectively. The trusted dealer sends $\{pk, \{vk, vk_1, vk_2\}, ck, sk_1\}$ to S and $\{pk, \{vk, vk_1, vk_2\}, ck, sk_2\}$ to R.

2. R generates an ordered pair of ciphertexts (c_0, c_1) such that c_σ encrypts one and $c_{1-\sigma}$ encrypts zero.
   R sends (c_0, c_1).

3. R proves that at least one of c_0 and c_1 encrypts zero, by using a zero-knowledge proof for relation $R_{OR-ZERO}$.
   If R fails, then S aborts.

4. R proves that at least one of c_0 and c_1 encrypts one, by using a zero-knowledge proof for relation R_{OR-ONE}.
   If R fails, then S aborts.

5. For each $i \in \{0, 1\}$, S selects $r_i \xleftarrow{\$} Coins(E)$, and computes $u_i = E_{pk}(b_i, r_i)$.
   S sends (u_0, u_1).

6. For each $i \in \{0, 1\}$, S computes $d_i = b_i \times_h c_i$, $v_i = Blind(pk, d_i)$.
   S sends (v_0, v_1).

7. For each $i \in \{0, 1\}$, S proves that it computed v_i correctly, by using a zero-knowledge proof for relation R_{MULT}.
   If S fails in any of these proofs, then R aborts.

8. For each $i \in \{0, 1\}$, S and R uses $\mathcal{F}_{PDEC}$ for performing private threshold decryption of v_i to R.
   Let w_0 and w_1 be the result of the decryption of v_0 and v_1, respectively.

9. R outputs w_σ.

Note: The common reference string μ is used as the commitment key in the zero-knowledge proofs.

Fig. 1. The New OT Protocol Π_{OT}.

with which the homomorphic multiplication is performed is part of the common input of the Σ-protocol for the relation R_{MULT} for $ELTAP$.

Protocol Π_{OT} works in the $\left(\mathcal{F}_{KG}, \mathcal{F}_{PDEC}, \mathcal{F}_{ZK}^R \right)$-hybrid world. The following theorem describes the security of Protocol Π_{OT}.

Theorem 3. *Assume that zero-knowledge proofs secure against erasure-free adaptive adversaries and trapdoor commitment scheme exist. Assume that there exists a two-party lossy threshold PKE scheme which is secure against erasure-free one-sided active adaptive adversaries, is additive homomorphic, is blindable, and has an efficient (polynomial-time) Opener algorithm. Then, Protocol Π_{OT} is a bit OT protocol secure under sequential composition in the presence of* *erasure-free one-sided active adaptive adversaries in the* $\left(\mathcal{F}_{KG}, \mathcal{F}_{PDEC}, \mathcal{F}_{ZK}^R\right)$-*hybrid world, in the CRS model.*

Proof of this theorem is available in [13].

6.1   Extension to String OT

If $\ell = s$, then Protocol Π_{OT} can be extended to a string OT protocol as follows. $ELTAP$ can encrypt an s-bit number. Then, for each $i \in \{0,1\}$, $\bar{b}_i$ can be encrypted using a single encryption operation using $ELTAP$. In step 5, for each $i \in \{0,1\}$, S selects $r_i \overset{\$}{\leftarrow} Coins(E)$, and sends $u_i = E_{pk}(\bar{b}_i, r_i)$. S sends the set $\{u_i\}_{i \in \{0,1\}}$. In step 6, for each $i \in \{0,1\}$, S computes $d_i = \bar{b}_i \times_h c_i$, and sends $v_i = Blind(pk, d_i)$. In step 7, for each $i \in \{0,1\}$, S performs a proof of correct multiplication for v_i. In step 8, for each $i \in \{0,1\}$, S and R jointly perform private threshold decryption of v_i to R. Let $\overline{w_i}$ denote the result that R obtains from the decryption of v_i. In step 9, R outputs $\overline{w_i}$.

If ℓ is a polynomial of s, then Protocol Π_{OT} can be extended similar to the case where $\ell = s$, by encrypting each s-bit blocks of the input of S by using a single encryption operation using $ELTAP$. The homomorphic multiplication and the decryption are done on each of the s-bit blocks. Note that the homomorphic multiplication is done with ciphertexts encrypting the value of one and zero only, so the result of the homomorphic multiplication can be encrypted using a single ciphertext.

6.2   Efficiency

$ELTAP$ encrypts an s-bit number. For encrypting s-bit numbers, the key has to be generated in such a way that N can be represented using $(s+2)$ bits. A ciphertext of this scheme is an element of $\mathbb{Z}_{N^2}$. Then, the size of a ciphertext is $2(s+2) = (2s+4)$ bits.

Theorem 4. *The communication complexity of Protocol Π_{OT} for bit OT is $O(s)$ bits. The number of rounds of this protocol is constant. The number of PKE operations performed by each party in this protocol is constant. The number of exponentiation operations performed by each party in this protocol is constant.*

Theorem 5. *Let ℓ be linear in security parameter s, that is, $\ell = cs$ where c is a constant. The communication complexity of the extension of Protocol Π_{OT} for string of length ℓ is $O(s)$ bits. The number of rounds of this protocol is constant. The number of PKE operations performed by each party in this protocol is constant. The number of exponentiation operations performed by each party in this protocol is constant.*

Proofs of Theorem 4 and Theorem 5 are available in [14].

7   Future Work

One future research work is to design an efficient 2PC protocol for one-sided active adaptive adversary model, using the new efficient string OT protocol. Another research direction is to design efficient OT protocol for the fully adaptive adversary model.

References

1. Bellare, M., Hofheinz, D., Yilek, S.: Possibility and impossibility results for encryption and commitment secure under selective opening. In: Joux, A. (ed.) EUROCRYPT 2009. LNCS, vol. 5479, pp. 1–35. Springer, Heidelberg (2009). https://doi.org/10.1007/978-3-642-01001-9_1
2. Canetti, R.: Security and composition of multiparty cryptographic protocols. J. Cryptol. **13**, 143–202 (2000). https://doi.org/10.1007/s001459910006
3. Damgård, I.: Efficient concurrent zero-knowledge in the auxiliary string model. In: Preneel, B. (ed.) EUROCRYPT 2000. LNCS, vol. 1807, pp. 418–430. Springer, Heidelberg (2000). https://doi.org/10.1007/3-540-45539-6_30
4. Damgård, I.: On Σ-Protocols (2010). https://cs.au.dk/~ivan/Sigma.pdf
5. Damgård, I., Jurik, M., Nielsen, J.B.: A generalization of Paillier's public-key system with applications to electronic voting. Int. J. Inf. Secur. **9**, 371–385 (2010). https://doi.org/10.1007/s10207-010-0119-9
6. Fouque, P.-A., Poupard, G., Stern, J.: Sharing decryption in the context of voting or lotteries. In: Frankel, Y. (ed.) FC 2000. LNCS, vol. 1962, pp. 90–104. Springer, Heidelberg (2001). https://doi.org/10.1007/3-540-45472-1_7
7. Garay, J.A., Wichs, D., Zhou, H.-S.: Somewhat non-committing encryption and efficient adaptively secure oblivious transfer. In: Halevi, S. (ed.) CRYPTO 2009. LNCS, vol. 5677, pp. 505–523. Springer, Heidelberg (2009). https://doi.org/10.1007/978-3-642-03356-8_30
8. Goldreich, O.: Foundations of Cryptography, vol. 1. Cambridge University Press, Cambridge (2006)
9. Hazay, C., Mikkelsen, G.L., Rabin, T., Toft, T.: Efficient RSA key generation and threshold Paillier in the two-party setting. In: Dunkelman, O. (ed.) CT-RSA 2012. LNCS, vol. 7178, pp. 313–331. Springer, Heidelberg (2012). https://doi.org/10.1007/978-3-642-27954-6_20
10. Hazay, C., Patra, A.: One-sided adaptively secure two-party computation. In: Lindell, Y. (ed.) TCC 2014. LNCS, vol. 8349, pp. 368–393. Springer, Heidelberg (2014). https://doi.org/10.1007/978-3-642-54242-8_16
11. Hemenway, B., Libert, B., Ostrovsky, R., Vergnaud, D.: Lossy encryption: constructions from general assumptions and efficient selective opening chosen ciphertext security. Cryptology ePrint Archive, Report 2009/088 (2009). https://eprint.iacr.org/2009/088
12. Lysyanskaya, A., Peikert, C.: Adaptive security in the threshold setting: from cryptosystems to signature schemes. In: Boyd, C. (ed.) ASIACRYPT 2001. LNCS, vol. 2248, pp. 331–350. Springer, Heidelberg (2001). https://doi.org/10.1007/3-540-45682-1_20
13. Nargis, I.: Efficient oblivious transfer from lossy threshold homomorphic encryption. In: Joye, M., Nitaj, A. (eds.) AFRICACRYPT 2017. LNCS, vol. 10239, pp. 165–183. Springer, Cham (2017). https://doi.org/10.1007/978-3-319-57339-7_10

14. Nargis, I.: Efficient multiparty computation from lossy threshold encryption. Ph.D. thesis, University of Calgary (2019). https://prism.ucalgary.ca/items/adf498e9-d4fc-439a-be2e-49470bcbb574
15. Nielsen, J.B.: On protocol security in the cryptographic model. Ph.D. thesis, University of Aarhus (2003). https://www.brics.dk/DS/03/8/BRICS-DS-03-8.pdf
16. Paillier, P.: Public-key cryptosystems based on composite degree residuosity classes. In: Stern, J. (ed.) EUROCRYPT 1999. LNCS, vol. 1592, pp. 223–238. Springer, Heidelberg (1999). https://doi.org/10.1007/3-540-48910-X_16
17. Pedersen, T.P.: Non-interactive and information-theoretic secure verifiable secret sharing. In: Feigenbaum, J. (ed.) CRYPTO 1991. LNCS, vol. 576, pp. 129–140. Springer, Heidelberg (1992). https://doi.org/10.1007/3-540-46766-1_9

Reducing Garbled Circuit Size While Preserving Circuit Gate Privacy

Yongge Wang[1]([⊠])[iD] and Qutaibah M. Malluhi[2,3][iD]

[1] Department of SIS, UNC Charlotte, Charlotte, NC 28223, USA
yongge.wang@uncc.edu
[2] Department of Computer Science and Engineering, Qatar University, Doha, Qatar
qmalluhi@qu.edu.qa
[3] KINDI Center for Computing Research, Qatar University, Doha, Qatar

Abstract. This paper investigates efficient and confidential circuit garbling techniques. The primary contribution of this research is the introduction of GPGRR2 (Gate Privacy preserving Garbled Row Reduction), a technique aimed at constructing garbled circuits using at most two ciphertexts per garbled gate while ensuring gate privacy preservation. When compared to the state-of-the-art gate-privacy-preserving garbling scheme GRR3, GPGRR2 shows a remarkable reduction in the size of garbled circuits by at least 33%. Another significant achievement is the development of a linear garbling scheme for odd gates, enabling the garbling of a single gate to one ciphertext. Furthermore, leveraging the GPGRR2 scheme facilitates a substantial decrease in the number of ciphertexts in non-universal-circuit based PFE protocols by a factor of 25%.

Keywords: garbled circuit · privacy preserving garbled circuit · secure function evaluation · private function evaluation

1 Introduction

Yao [18] introduced the garbled circuit concept which allows computing a function f on an input x without leaking any information about the input x or individual circuit gate functionality used for the computation of $f(x)$. Since then, garbled circuit based protocols have been used in numerous places and it has become one of the fundamental components of secure multi-party computation (SMC), secure function evaluation (SFE), and private function evaluation (PFE) protocols. In a PFE protocol, one participant P_1 holds a circuit C and a private input x_1 and every other participant P_i ($i \geq 2$) holds a private input x_i. The PFE protocol's goal is that a subset (or all) of the participants learns the circuit output $C(x_1, \cdots, x_n)$ but nothing beyond this. In particular, the participant P_i ($i \geq 2$) should not learn anything else except the size of C and, optionally, the output. Note that a PFE protocol is different from standard SMC/SFE protocols where the circuit C is publicly known to all participants in SMC/SFE protocols.

This work was supported by the Qatar National Research Fund (Member of the Qatar Foundation) under Grant NPRP X-063-1-014.
An earlier version of this paper appeared as a technical report in [17].

Bellare et al. [3] provides a rigorous definition of circuit garbling schemes and analyzed garbling scheme security from aspects of privacy, obliviousness, and authenticity. Specifically, Bellare et al. [3] pointed out that garbling schemes that are secure for Φ_{circ} (that is, it does not conceal the circuit) is sufficient for the design of SFE/SMC protocols. However, for a PFE protocol, one needs a garbling scheme that is secure for Φ_{size} (that is, it only leaks the circuit size). Though Yao's circuit garbling scheme is only secure for Φ_{topo} (that is, it only reveals the circuit topology) and not secure for Φ_{size}, one can use universal circuit to convert a Φ_{topo}-secure garbling scheme to a Φ_{size}-secure garbling scheme (see, e.g., Bellare et al. [3]).

We first review Yao's garbled circuit construction using Beaver, Micali, and Rogaway's point-permute (or called external index) technique [2]. Note that the external index technique makes it possible to design garbled circuits without using CPA-secure encryption schemes. Unless stated otherwise, throughout the paper we will use lower case letters u, v, w, x, y, z etc. to denote wires within a circuit and use $b_u, b_v, b_w, b_x, b_y, b_z \in \{0, 1\}$ as variables to denote the values on the wires u, v, w, x, y, z respectively. For a given number t that is dependent on the security parameter κ, the circuit owner assigns two random values $k_x^0, k_x^1 \in \{0, 1\}^t$ to each wire x corresponding to 0 and 1 values of the wire. The circuit owner chooses a secret random permutation π_x over $\{0, 1\}$ for each wire x. The garbled values for the wire x consist of $k_x^0 \| \pi_x(0)$ and $k_x^1 \| \pi_x(1)$ where $\pi_x(b)$ is considered as an external index for k_x^b. It is easily observed that for any $b \in \{0, 1\}$, we have $b = \pi_x(b) \oplus \pi_x(0)$. For a gate $z = g(x, y)$, the garbled gate $\tilde{g}$ consists of four ciphertexts that are ordered using the external index $\pi_x(b_x) \| \pi_y(b_y)$. For example, if we assume that $\pi_x(0) = \pi_y(0) = 1$ and $\pi_x(1) = \pi_y(1) = 0$, then the garbled gate $\tilde{g}$ is described using the following four ciphertexts.

$$
\begin{aligned}
\pi_x(1) \| \pi_y(1) &: (k_z^{g(1,1)} \| \pi_z(g(1,1))) \oplus H_g(k_x^1 \circ k_y^1) \\
\pi_x(1) \| \pi_y(0) &: (k_z^{g(1,0)} \| \pi_z(g(1,0))) \oplus H_g(k_x^1 \circ k_y^0) \\
\pi_x(0) \| \pi_y(1) &: (k_z^{g(0,1)} \| \pi_z(g(0,1))) \oplus H_g(k_x^0 \circ k_y^1) \\
\pi_x(0) \| \pi_y(0) &: (k_z^{g(0,0)} \| \pi_z(g(0,0))) \oplus H_g(k_x^0 \circ k_y^0)
\end{aligned}
\tag{1}
$$

where H_g is a gate g specific pseudorandom function (e.g., a secure hash function or an encryption scheme) whose output length is $|k_z^b| + 1$ and $\circ$ is an operator. For example, one may define $k_1 \circ k_2 = k_1 \| k_2$ or $k_1 \circ k_2 = k_1 \oplus k_2$ or $k_1 \circ k_2 = k_1 + k_2 \mod 2^t$ etc. For most applications, we take a pseudorandom function H (e.g., a cryptographic hash function) and define $H_g(\cdot) = H(\text{gID}, \cdot)$ where gID is an identity string for the gate g. At the start of the protocol, the circuit owner provides the evaluator with a garbled version $\tilde{g}$ for each gate g of the circuit. During the evaluation process, the circuit owner provides garbled input values to the evaluator and the evaluator evaluates the garbled circuits gate by gate. As an example, if the input is $(x, y) = (1, 0)$, then the circuit owner sends garbled values $k_x^1 \| \pi_x(1) = k_x^1 \| 0$ and $k_y^0 \| \pi_y(0) = k_y^0 \| 1$ to the evaluator. Since the external index bit value $\pi_x(1) \| \pi_y(0) = 01$, the evaluator uses the corresponding second ciphertext to recover the garbled value $k_z^{g(1,0)} \| \pi_z(g(1,0))$ for the output wire z, which corresponds to the output $g(1, 0)$.

Several efforts have been made to reduce the garbled circuit size. Kolesnikov and Schneider [9] observed that if there is a circuit-wide global offset value $\Delta \in \{0, 1\}^t$ such that garbled values for each wire x within the circuit satisfy the invariance property

$k_x^1 = k_x^0 \oplus \Delta$, then the XOR gate could be garbled for free since we have $k_x^{b_x} \oplus k_y^{b_y} = k_x^0 \oplus k_y^0 \oplus \left((b_x \oplus b_y) \cdot \Delta\right)$ where $1 \cdot \Delta = \Delta$ and $0 \cdot \Delta = 0^t$.

Naor, Pinkas, and Sumner [12] observed that one can choose a randomly fixed pair $(b_x, b_y) \in \{0, 1\}^2$ and let

$$k_z^{g(b_x, b_y)} \| \pi(g(b_x, b_y)) = H_g(k_x^{b_x} \circ k_y^{b_y}).$$

Then the corresponding ciphertext for the row $(\pi(b_x), \pi(b_y))$ is a zero string and one does not need to store it. In other words, one can reduce the number of ciphertexts from 4 to 3 for each garbled gate. In this paper, we will refer this approach as GRR3.

Pinkas et al. [14] used polynomial interpolation to reduce each gate to two ciphertexts. However, Pinkas et al's technique is not compatible with the free-XOR technique. Recently, Zahur, Rosulek, and Evans [19] introduced the state-of-the-art half-gates technique to design free-XOR compatible garbling schemes so that each AND/OR gate could be represented using two ciphertexts.

The aforementioned free-XOR, GRR2, and half-gates garbling schemes reduce garbled circuit sizes by leaking the number and locations of XOR gates within circuits. This kind of side information leakage is acceptable for SFE (secure function evaluation) though it may be unacceptable for other applications. For example, these techniques cannot be used to improve the efficiency of non-universal circuit based PFE protocols in Katz and Malka [6] and Mohassel and Sadeghian [11]. In this paper, we investigate the possibility of reducing garbled circuit size without leaking any further information beyond circuit topology. Specifically, we design garbled circuits with at most two ciphertexts for each garbled gate such that the only leaked information is the circuit topology. We then apply our techniques to PFE protocols in Katz and Malka [6] and Mohassel and Sadeghian [11] to reduce the number of ciphertexts by a factor of 25%.

It has been an interesting and challenging question to study the lower bounds of garbled circuit sizes. Zahur, Rosulek, and Evans [19] proved that any "linear" garbling scheme garbles an AND gate to at least two ciphertexts. However, the statement of their lower bound theorem is inaccurate. In this paper, we present a linear (over integers) garbling scheme that garbles an AND gate to one ciphertext. By examining the proofs in [19], it is clear that their proof is based on linear operations in the finite field $\mathbb{F}_{2^l}$. Thus one should bear in mind that the result in [19] only applies to the finite field $\mathbb{F}_{2^l}$.

We conclude this section with the introduction of some notations. We use κ to denote the security parameter, $p(\cdot)$ to denote a function p that takes one input, and $p(\cdot, \cdot)$ to denote a function p that takes two inputs. A function f is said to be negligible in an input parameter κ if for all $d > 0$, there exists K such that for all $\kappa > K$, $f(\kappa) < \kappa^{-d}$. For convenience, we write $f(\kappa) = \mathrm{negl}(\kappa)$. Two ensembles, $X = \{X_\kappa\}_{\kappa \in N}$ and $Y = \{Y_\kappa\}_{\kappa \in N}$, are said to be computationally indistinguishable (written as $X \overset{c}{\sim} Y$ or $X \overset{c}{=} Y$) if for all probabilistic polynomial-time algorithm D, we have

$$|Pr[D(X_\kappa, 1^\kappa) = 1] - Pr[D(Y_\kappa, 1^\kappa) = 1]| = \mathrm{negl}(\kappa).$$

Throughout the paper, we use probabilistic experiments and denote their outputs using random variables. For example, $\mathrm{Exp}_{E,A}^{\mathrm{real}}(1^\kappa)$ represents the output of the real experiment for scheme E with adversary A on security parameter κ.

The structure of this paper is as follows. Section 2 reviews security definition for garbling schemes. Section 3 reviews GRR2 techniques. Section 4 presents our linear interpolation based garbled circuit construction techniques where each garbled gate uses two ciphertexts. Section 5 provides an optimization of GPGRR2 and shows that one can linearly garble an AND gate with one ciphertext. Section 6 uses linear interpolation garbling schemes to reduce the size of garbled circuits for PFE protocols in various adversary security models. Section 7 presents a revised circuit garbling scheme GRRcirc that is only secure for input privacy (it reveals the number and positions of XOR gates).

2   Circuit Garbling Schemes and Their Security

In this section, we briefly review the formal definition of circuit garbling schemes formalized by Bellare, Hoang, and Rogaway [3].

Definition 1. *Let $C = \{C_n\}_{n \in N}$ be a family of circuits such that C_n is a set of boolean circuits that take n-bit inputs. A garbling scheme for C is a tuple of probabilistic polynomial time algorithms* GS = (Gb, Enc, Eval, Dec) *with the following properties*

- $(\tilde{C}, \mathsf{sk}, \mathsf{dk}) = \mathsf{GS.Gb}(1^\kappa, C)$ *outputs a garbled circuit $\tilde{C}$, a secret key* sk, *and a decoding key* dk *for circuits $C \in C_n$ on the security parameter input κ.*
- $c = \mathsf{GS.Enc}(\mathsf{sk}, x)$ *outputs an encoding c for an input $x \in \{0, 1\}^*$.*
- $\tilde{y} = \mathsf{GS.Eval}(\tilde{C}, c)$ *outputs a garbled value $\tilde{y}$.*
- $y = \mathsf{GS.Dec}(\mathsf{dk}, \tilde{y})$ *outputs a circuit output.*

The garbling scheme GS *is* correct *if we have*

$$Pr[\mathsf{GS.Dec}(\mathsf{dk}, \mathsf{GS.Eval}(\tilde{C}, \mathsf{GS.Enc}(\mathsf{sk}, x))) \neq C(x)|\mathsf{GS}] = \mathsf{negl}(\kappa).$$

The garbling scheme GS *is* efficient *if the size of $\tilde{C}$ is bounded by a polynomial and the run-time of $c = \mathsf{GS.Enc}(\mathsf{sk}, x)$ is also bounded by a polynomial.*

The security of garbling schemes is defined in terms of input and circuit privacy in the literature. For a garbled circuit, some side-information such as the number of inputs, outputs, gates, and the topology of the circuit C (that is, the connection of gates but not gate types) and other information is leaked inherently. We denote such kind of side information as $\Phi(C)$. Thus a security definition of garbling schemes should capture the intuition that the adversary learns no information except $\Phi(C)$ and the output given one evaluation of the garbled circuit. The following definition requires that for any circuit or input chosen by the adversary, one can simulate the garbled circuit and the encoding based on the computation result and $\Phi(C)$ in polynomial time. In the definition, the variable α represents any state that the adversary A may want to give to the algorithm D.

Definition 2. *(Privacy for garbling schemes) A garbling scheme* GS *for a family of circuits C is said to be* input and circuit private *if there exists a probabilistic polynomial* *time simulator* Sim$_{GS}$ *such that for all probabilistic polynomial time adversaries A and algorithms D and all large κ, we have*

$$\left| Pr[D(\alpha, x, C, \tilde{C}, c) = 1 | \text{REAL}] - Pr[D(\alpha, x, C, \tilde{C}_{\text{sim}}, \tilde{c}) = 1 | \text{SIM}] \right| = \text{negl}(\kappa)$$

where REAL *is the following event*

$$(x, C, \alpha) = A(1^\kappa); (\tilde{C}, \text{sk}, \text{dk}) = \text{GS.Gb}(1^\kappa, C); c = \text{GS.Enc}(\text{sk}, x);$$
$$C(x) = \text{GS.Dec}(\text{dk}, \text{GS.Eval}(\tilde{C}, c))$$

and SIM *is the following event*

$$(x, C, \alpha) = A(1^\kappa); \quad (\tilde{C}_{\text{sim}}, \tilde{c}) = \text{Sim}_{GS}(1^\kappa, C(x), \Phi(C), 1^{|C|}, 1^{|x|}).$$

The authors of [3] considered the following three kinds of commonly used side-information functions.

1. $\Phi_{\text{size}}(C) = (n, m, q)$ where n, m, q are the number of inputs, outputs, and gates of the circuit C respectively.
2. $\Phi_{\text{topo}}(C) = C_{\text{topo}}$ where a topological circuit C_{topo} is like the conventional circuit C except that the functionality of the gates is unspecified.
3. $\Phi_{\text{circ}}(C) = C$ where the side information is the circuit itself. That is, the entire circuit C is revealed.

It is pointed out in Bellare et al. [3, Sections 3.8] that, for both indistinguishability-based security notion and simulation-based security notion, each Φ_{topo}-secure garbling scheme GS$_{\text{topo}}$ can be converted to a Φ_{size}-secure garbling scheme GS$_{\text{size}}$ using universal circuits. GS$_{\text{size}}$ and oblivious transfers can then be used to design secure PFE protocols. If the security notion is based on simulation, then one can use Φ_{circ}-secure garbling schemes, universal circuits, and oblivious transfers to design secure PFE protocols. However, no proof has been presented to show whether one can use Φ_{circ}-secure garbling schemes, universal circuits, and oblivious transfers to design secure PFE protocols using the indistinguishability-based security notion[1].

We conclude this section by pointing out a circuit complexity result which shows the important information leakage by identifying the number (or locations) of XOR gates within a topological circuit C_{topo}. Let AC^i denote the family of polynomial size circuits of depth $O(\log^i n)$ with unlimited-fanin AND and OR gates (NOT gates are only allowed at inputs). Let NC^i denote the family of polynomial size circuits of depth $O(\log^i n)$ with bounded-fanin AND and OR gates. It is a folklore that

$$\text{NC}^i \subseteq \text{AC}^i \subseteq \text{NC}^{i+1}.$$

Let $f_{\text{parity}}(x_1, \cdots, x_n) = x_1 \oplus x_1 \oplus \cdots \oplus x_n$ be the parity function. It is well known that $f_{\text{parity}} \in \text{NC}^1$. Ajtai et al. [1] and Furst et al. [5] showed that $f_{\text{parity}} \notin \text{AC}^0$. That is, $f_{\text{parity}} \in \text{NC}^1 \setminus \text{AC}^0$.

---

[1] The authors would like to thank Dr. Viet Tung Hoang for several valuable discussions on this question and other results in [3].

Let C_{parity} be a randomly selected polynomial size circuit of constant depth with unlimited-fanin XOR gates that computes f_{parity}. Note that there are many such kind of circuits. Let $f_{\text{ac}_0} \in \text{AC}^0$ and $C_{f_{\text{ac}_0}}$ be a circuit that computes f_{ac_0} such that $C_{f_{\text{ac}_0},\text{topo}} = C_{\text{parity},\text{topo}}$. That is, the topological circuits of $C_{f_{\text{ac}_0}}$ and C_{parity} are identical.

Assume that a circuit owner randomly selects C_{parity} or $C_{f_{\text{ac}_0}}$ to garble. Given Φ_{topo}-secure garbled circuits for C_{parity} or $C_{f_{\text{ac}_0}}$, the evaluator cannot tell whether the evaluated function is in AC^0 or not. On the other hand, if the evaluator receives Φ_{circ}-secure garbled circuits for C_{parity} or $C_{f_{\text{ac}_0}}$, it can distinguish whether the evaluated function is in AC^0.

3   Pinkas et al.'s Garbled Row Reduction GRR2

We first review Pinkas et al's Garbled Row Reduction GRR2 [14]. Let t be the length in terms of number of bits of wire lables. That is, we have $t = |k_x^b|$ for all wires x and $b = 0, 1$. Wire labels k_x^b and integers $0, 1, 2, 3, \cdots$ can be interpreted as elements of the finite field $\mathbb{F}_{2^t}$. A binary gate is said to be odd if its truth table has an odd number of '1' entries (e.g. an AND or OR gate), otherwise it is called an even gate (e.g., an XOR gate). Using polynomial interpolation, Pinkas et al. showed that each gate could be represented by only two ciphertexts. Specifically, for an odd gate g (e.g., an AND or OR gate), assume that the first three ciphertexts C_1, C_2, C_3 encrypt the same wire label $k_z^b \| \pi_z(b)$ via $C_i = (k_z^b \| \pi_z(b)) \oplus (K_i \| M_i)$ (for $i = 1, 2, 3$) and the fourth ciphertext C_4 encrypts the wire label $k_z^{1-b} \| \pi_z(1-b)$ via $C_4 = (k_z^{1-b} \| \pi_z(1-b)) \oplus (K_4 \| M_4)$ where $b, M_i \in \{0, 1\}$ for $i = 1, 2, 3, 4$. Let $P(X)$ be a degree two polynomial over $\mathbb{F}_{2^t}$ passing through points $(1, K_1), (2, K_2)$, and $(3, K_3)$. Let $Q(X)$ be another degree two polynomial over $\mathbb{F}_{2^t}$ passing through points $(5, P(5)), (6, P(6))$, and $(4, K_4)$. Then by setting $k_z^b = P(0)$ and $k_z^{1-b} = Q(0)$, one can replace the garbled table with $\langle P(5), P(6), c_1, c_2, c_3, c_4 \rangle$ where $P(5)$ and $P(6)$ are elements from $\mathbb{F}_{2^t}$ and c_1, c_2, c_3, c_4 are bits encrypting the external index bits. That is, $\pi_z(g(b_x, b_y)) = c_i \oplus M_i$ for $i = 2\pi_x(b_x) + \pi_y(b_y) + 1$. The total size of the garbled gate is $2t + 4$ bits. Interpolating the polynomial passing through points $(5; P(5)), (6; P(6))$, and $(i; K_i)$ for $i = 1, 2, 3, 4$ will produce either polynomial $P(X)$ or $Q(X)$, which can be evaluated at $X = 0$ to get the appropriate value k_z^b or k_z^{1-b}.

For an even gate g (e.g., an XOR or NXOR gate), assume that ciphertexts C_{i_1}, C_{i_2} encrypt the wire label $k_z^0 \| \pi_z(0)$ via $C_{i_j} = (k_z^0 \| \pi_z(0)) \oplus (K_{i_j} \| M_{i_j})$ (for $j = 1, 2$) and the ciphertexts C_{i_3}, C_{i_4} encrypt the wire label $k_z^1 \| \pi_z(1)$ via $C_{i_j} = (k_z^1 \| \pi_z(1)) \oplus (K_{i_j} \| M_{i_j})$ (for $j = 3, 4$) where $M_{i_j} \in \{0, 1\}$ for $i_j = 1, 2, 3, 4$. Let $P(X)$ be a linear polynomial over $\mathbb{F}_{2^t}$ passing through points (i_1, K_{i_1}) and (i_2, K_{i_2}). Let $Q(X)$ be another linear polynomial over $\mathbb{F}_{2^t}$ passing through points (i_3, K_{i_3}) and (i_4, K_{i_4}). Define $k_z^0 = P(0)$ and $k_z^1 = Q(0)$. If $\pi_z(0) = 0$ then the garbled gate is represented as $\langle P(5), Q(5), c_1, c_2, c_3, c_4 \rangle$. Otherwise, $\pi_z(1) = 0$ and the garbled gate is represented as $\langle Q(5), P(5), c_1, c_2, c_3, c_4 \rangle$. In the garbled gate, $P(5)$ and $Q(5)$ are elements from $\mathbb{F}_{2^t}$ and c_1, c_2, c_3, c_4 are bits encrypting the external index bits. That is, $\pi_z(g(b_x, b_y)) = c_i \oplus M_i$ for $i = 2\pi_x(b_x) + \pi_y(b_y) + 1$. The total size of the garbled gate is $2t + 4$ bits. The evaluator receives the garbled gate in the format of $\langle Y_1, Y_2, c_1, c_2, c_3, c_4 \rangle$. At the time of evaluation, the evaluator first calculates the value $\pi_z(b_z)$ using the ingoing wire labels. If $\pi_z(b_z) = 0$, then it interpolates the linear polynomial passing through points $(5; Y_1)$ and $(i; K_i)$ for $i = 1, 2, 3, 4$ which will produce either polynomial $P(X)$ or $Q(X)$, which can be evaluated at $X = 0$ to get the appropriate value $k_z^{b_z}$. If $\pi_z(b_z) = 1$, then it interpolates the linear polynomial passing through points $(5; Y_2)$ and $(i; K_i)$ for $i = 1, 2, 3, 4$ to obtain the appropriate value $k_z^{b_z}$.

The ciphertexts for odd gates and even gates have different format with GRR2 techniques. Thus GGR2 garbled circuits are not secure for Φ_{topo}. It is easy to check that in the GRR2 garbling scheme, the number of ciphertexts for an even gate could be reduced to one ciphertext by using the GRR3 approach.

3.1   Zahur, Rosulek, and Evans's Half-Gates

Zahur, Rosulek, and Evans [19] proposes a free-XOR compatible half-gates garbling scheme so that each odd gate is garbled to two ciphertexts and each even gate is free. In the half-gates technique, the circuit owner first chooses a circuit-wide global offset value Δ. The circuit is garbled in such a way that garbled values for each wire x within the circuit satisfy the invariance property $k_x^1 = k_x^0 \oplus \Delta$. Thus an even gate could be garbled for free. Assume that $z = g(x, y)$ is the odd gate "$x \wedge y$". Then it can be written as $(x \wedge r) \oplus (x \wedge (r \oplus y))$ where r is a random bit. Zahur, Rosulek, and Evans [19] recommends the use of $r = \pi_y(0)$. Let $r_x = \pi_x(0)$ and $r_y = \pi_y(0)$. Let $r\Delta$ denote the zero string for $r = 0$ and denote the string Δ for $r = 1$. Then the two gates $(x \wedge r)$ and $(x \wedge (r \oplus y))$ are garbled separately. The XOR of the output of these two gates is free.

- For the first gate $u = (x \wedge r)$, we can choose a random value k_u^0 and garble it using two ciphertexts "$H(k_x^0) \oplus k_u^0$" and "$H(k_x^1) \oplus (k_u^0 \oplus r\Delta)$". By using the standard garbled row reduction technique GGR3, the gate "$x \wedge r$" could be garbled using one ciphertext $H(k_x^0) \oplus H(k_x^1) \oplus r_y\Delta$
- For the second gate $v = (x \wedge (r \oplus y))$, the evaluator knows the value of "$r \oplus y$" since we have $r \oplus b_y = \pi_y(0) \oplus b_y = \pi_y(b_y)$. First choose a random value k_v^0. If "$r \oplus y = 0$" then "$v = 0$". In this case, the ciphertext should decrypt to k_v^0. If "$r \oplus y = 1$" then "$v = x$". In this case, it suffices for the evaluator to decrypt the ciphertext to $k_v^0 \oplus k_x^0$ since the evaluator could get the actual output label as $k_v^0 \oplus k_x^0 \oplus k_x^{b_x}$ where $k_x^{b_x}$ is the received value on wire x. By using the standard row reduction technique GGR3, the gate $v = (x \wedge (r \oplus y))$ could be garbled using one ciphertext $H(k_y^0) \oplus H(k_y^1) \oplus k_x^0$.

In the summary, the AND gate $z = x \wedge y$ is garbled into two ciphertexts:

$$H(k_x^0) \oplus H(k_x^1) \oplus r_y\Delta; \quad H(k_y^0) \oplus H(k_y^1) \oplus k_x^0$$

and the OR gate $z = x \vee y$ is garbled into two ciphertexts:

$$H(k_x^0) \oplus H(k_x^1) \oplus (1 - r_y)\Delta; \quad H(k_y^0) \oplus H(k_y^1) \oplus k_x^1$$

The garbled labels for the output wire z is

$$k_z^0 = H(k_x^{r_x}) \oplus g(r_x, r_y)\Delta \oplus H(k_y^{r_y}); \quad k_z^1 = H(k_x^{r_x}) \oplus g(r_x, r_y)\Delta \oplus H(k_y^{r_y}) \oplus \Delta$$

Evaluation of a Garbled Gate. The evaluator receives the garbled values $k_x^{b_x}$, $k_y^{b_y}$ and learns the value of $b_y \oplus r_y$ from the external index bits. Based on the external index values, the evaluator first calculates $k_1 = H(k_x^{r_x}) \oplus g(r_x, r_y)\Delta$ from the first ciphertext. Secondly, If $b_y \oplus r_y = 0$, then the evaluator calculates $k_2 = H(k_y^{b_y})$. Otherwise, if $b_y \oplus r_y = 1$, then the evaluator calculates $k_2 = H(k_y^{1-b_y}) \oplus k_x^0 \oplus k_x^{b_x}$ from the second ciphertext and $k_x^{b_x}$. Finally let $k_z^{g(b_x,b_y)} = k_1 \oplus k_2$.

As an example to show that the above evaluation process works, we assume that g is an AND gate and assume that $r = 0$. For the input $x = 0, y = 1$, we get $k_1 = H(k_x^0)$ and $k_2 = H(k_y^0) \oplus k_x^0 \oplus k_x^0 = H(k_y^0)$. Thus $k_z^0 = H(k_x^0) \oplus H(k_y^0)$. For the input $x = 1, y = 1$, we get $k_1 = H(k_x^0) \oplus r\Delta = H(k_x^0)$ and $k_2 = H(k_y^0) \oplus k_x^0 \oplus k_x^1 = H(k_y^0) \oplus \Delta$. Thus $k_z^1 = H(k_x^0) \oplus H(k_y^0) \oplus \Delta$.

4 Garbled Gate Size Reduction Using Linear Interpolation

4.1 Gate Privacy Preserving Garbled Row Reduction GPGRR2

As we mentioned in the preceding section, Pinkas et al's GRR2 garbling scheme [14] leaks the number and positions of even/odd gate types. For example, an evaluator evaluates a garbled odd gate using degree two polynomial interpolation and evaluates a garbled even gate using linear interpolation. The free-XOR techniques proposed by Kolesnikov and Schneider [9] leaks the number and positions of XOR gates and the half-gates techniques by Zahur, Rosulek, and Evans [19] leaks the number and positions of XOR gates also. In this section, we propose a gate privacy preserving garbled row reduction GPGRR2 technique to garble circuits with security for Φ_{topo}. Our garbling scheme GPGRR2 does not require the external index bits. For reason of convenience, the following construction still includes the external index bits.

First select two parameters t and τ based on the security requirements. It is recommended to select τ such that $10 \le \tau < t$. Each ciphertext will be of length $t + 1$ bits. In order to garble a circuit C, the circuit owner first chooses a circuit-wide global offset value $\Delta \in \{0, 1\}^t$ uniformly at random. Furthermore, let H be a pseudo-random function with $(t + \tau + 1)$-bits output. The circuit C will be garbled in such a way that for all wires x, the garbled values $k_x^0\|\pi_x(0)$ and $k_x^1\|\pi_x(1)$ for the wire x satisfy the following invariance property:

$$k_x^1 = k_x^0 + \Delta \mod 2^t \tag{2}$$

In the following, we formally describe the process of garbling a gate $z = g(x, y)$ in a circuit C. Let $k_x^0\|\pi_x(0)$, $k_x^1\|\pi_x(1)$, $k_y^0\|\pi_y(0)$, and $k_y^1\|\pi_y(1)$ be the garbled input wire values for the wires x and y respectively. Let $k_z^0\|\pi_z(0)$, $k_z^1\|\pi_z(1)$ be the garbled output wire values for the output wire $z = g(x, y)$ that will be defined. Define the operator $\circ$ as the integer addition modulo 2^t. Then we have

$$\begin{aligned} k_x^0 \circ k_y^0 &= k_x^0 + k_y^0 = \bar{x}_1 \mod 2^t \\ k_x^0 \circ k_y^1 &= k_x^1 \circ k_y^0 = k_x^0 + k_y^0 + \Delta = \bar{x}_1 + \Delta \mod 2^t \\ k_x^1 \circ k_y^1 &= k_x^0 + k_y^0 + 2\Delta = \bar{x}_1 + 2\Delta \mod 2^t \end{aligned} \tag{3}$$

for some $\bar{x}_1 \in \{0, 1\}^t$. For these garbled input wire values, we have

$$
\begin{aligned}
K_{00}\|M_{00}\|N_{00} &= H_g(k_x^0 \circ k_y^0) = H_g(\bar{x}_1 \quad \mod 2^t) \\
K_{01}\|M_{01}\|N_{01} &= H_g(k_x^0 \circ k_y^1) = H_g(\bar{x}_1 + \Delta \quad \mod 2^t) \\
K_{10}\|M_{10}\|N_{10} &= H_g(k_x^1 \circ k_y^0) = H_g(\bar{x}_1 + \Delta \quad \mod 2^t) \\
K_{11}\|M_{11}\|N_{11} &= H_g(k_x^1 \circ k_y^1) = H_g(\bar{x}_1 + 2\Delta \quad \mod 2^t)
\end{aligned} \tag{4}
$$

where $M_{00}, M_{01}, M_{10}, M_{11} \in \{0, 1\}$ and $N_{00}, N_{01}, N_{10}, N_{11} \in \{0, 1\}^\tau$. It follows that

$$
K_{01}\|M_{01}\|N_{01} = K_{10}\|M_{10}\|N_{10}.
$$

In case that there exist two values in

$$
N_{00}, \ N_{10}, \text{ and } N_{11} \tag{5}
$$

that are identical, re-start the garbling process and choose different garbled input wire values for the wires x and y. We distinguish the following two cases depending on whether g is an even gate or an odd gate.

Garbling an Odd Gate g. We begin by assuming that g represents an OR gate. Let $P(X)$ denote a linear polynomial over $\mathbb{F}_{2^t}$ that passes through two given points:

$$
(N_{10}, K_{10}) \text{ and } (N_{11}, K_{11}).
$$

We define k_z^1 as $P(0)$ and k_z^0 as $k_z^1 - \Delta \mod 2^t$, where k_z^0, k_z^1, and Δ are interpreted as integers modulo 2^t. Similarly, let $Q(X)$ be another linear polynomial over $\mathbb{F}_{2^t}$ passing through

$$
(0, k_z^0) \text{ and } (N_{00}, K_{00}).
$$

It's important to note that $P(X)$ is interpolated based on situations where the output of the OR gate is 1, while $Q(X)$ corresponds to situations where the output is 0. Let X_z be a solution of the equation $P(X) = Q(X)$ over $\mathbb{F}_{2^t}$. Then, the garbled table for gate g is represented as $\langle X_z, P(X_z), c_1, c_2, c_3, c_4 \rangle = \langle X_z, Q(X_z), c_1, c_2, c_3, c_4 \rangle$, where X_z and $P(X_z)$ are elements from $\mathbb{F}_{2^t}$ and c_1, c_2, c_3, c_4 are bits encrypting the external index bits. In other words, $\pi_z(g(b_x, b_y)) = c_i \oplus M_i$ for $i = 2\pi_x(b_x) + \pi_y(b_y) + 1$. The total size of the garbled gate is $2t + 4$ bits. Excluding the external index bits, the size is $2t$ bits.

For an AND gate, start by selecting a linear polynomial, denoted as $P(X)$, that passes through the points (N_{10}, K_{10}) and (N_{00}, K_{00}). Define k_z^0 as $P(0)$ and k_z^1 as $k_z^0 + \Delta \mod 2^t$. Next, construct another linear polynomial, denoted as $Q(X)$, passing through the points $(0, k_z^1)$ and (N_{11}, K_{11}). Essentially, $P(X)$ is interpolated based on when the output of the AND gate is 0, while $Q(X)$ is interpolated for an output of 1. The subsequent steps remain unchanged.

Alternatively, for the gate g, one can employ $\langle P(2^\tau), Q(2^\tau), c_1, c_2, c_3, c_4 \rangle$ as the garbled table, rather than using the solution point X_z for the equation $P(X) = Q(X)$. In this scenario, the external index bit determines whether $P(2^\tau)$ or $Q(2^\tau)$ is used for linear interpolation during evaluation.

Garbling an Even Gate g. Without loss of generality, let's assume g is an XOR gate. For an NXOR gate, we can handle it similarly by swapping k_z^0 and k_z^1. Consider $P(X)$ as a linear polynomial over $\mathbb{F}_{2^t}$ passing through points

$$
(N_{00}, K_{00}) \text{ and } (N_{11}, K_{11}).
$$

Set $k_z^0 = P(0)$ and $k_z^1 = k_z^0 + \Delta \mod 2^t$, interpreting k_z^0, k_z^1, and Δ as integers modulo 2^t. Similarly, let $Q(X)$ be a linear polynomial over $\mathbb{F}_{2^t}$ passing through points

$$(0, k_z^1) \text{ and } (N_{10}, K_{10}).$$

$P(X)$ is interpolated for the situation when the XOR gate's output is 0, and $Q(X)$ for the output being 1. Find X_z, a solution of $P(X) = Q(X)$ over $\mathbb{F}_{2^t}$. The garbled table for gate g becomes $\langle X_z, P(X_z), c_1, c_2, c_3, c_4 \rangle$, where X_z and $P(X_z)$ are elements from $\mathbb{F}_{2^t}$, and c_1, c_2, c_3, c_4 are bits encrypting the external index bits. In other words, $\pi_z(g(b_x, b_y)) = c_i \oplus M_i$ for $i = 2\pi_x(b_x) + \pi_y(b_y) + 1$. The total size of the garbled gate is $2t + 4$ bits. Excluding external index bits, it's $2t$ bits. Similarly, we can use $\langle P(2^\tau), Q(2^\tau), c_1, c_2, c_3, c_4 \rangle$ as the garbled table for gate g, using external index bit information to determine whether $P(2^\tau)$ or $Q(2^\tau)$ should be used for linear interpolation during evaluation.

Evaluation of a Garbled Circuit. For a garbled gate $\tilde{g} = \langle X_z, P(X_z), c_1, c_2, c_3, c_4 \rangle$, where the evaluator is uncertain whether it's an even or odd gate, the evaluator receives encoded values $k_x^{b_x} \| \pi(b_x)$ and $k_y^{b_y} \| \pi(b_y)$ on wires x and y. The initial step involves computing

$$K \| M \| N = H_g(k_x^{b_x} + k_y^{b_y} \mod 2^t).$$

Then, utilizing a linear polynomial $R(X)$ over $\mathbb{F}_{2^t}$ passing through points (N, K) and $(X_z, P(X_z))$, the evaluator determines $k_z^{g(b_x, b_y)} = R(0)$. The output wire's external index bit is determined by $\pi_z(g(b_x, b_y)) = c_{2\pi_x(b_x) + \pi_y(b_y) + 1} \oplus M$.

This evaluation process entails a cryptographic hash function operation and a linear polynomial interpolation. For the interpolation, the evaluator must find a and b in $\mathbb{F}_{2^t}$ such that $aN_i + b = K_i$ and $aX_z + b = P(X_z)$, i.e., $a = (N_i - X_z)^{-1}(K_i - P(X_z))$ over $\mathbb{F}_{2^t}$. In summary, the primary costs for the evaluator are one cryptographic hash function operation and one field element inverse operation over $\mathbb{F}_{2^t}$.

In the above garbling scheme, an additional parameter τ is used. For larger circuits, one should choose a larger τ though for smaller circuits, one can use a smaller τ. The value of τ does not have impact on the garbling scheme security. However, it has impact on the efficiency of the garbling process. If the value of τ is too small, then the probability for two values in (5) to be identical is high and one has to re-start the garbling process more frequently. On the other hand, for large enough τ, the probability for two values in (5) to be identical is very small and one does not need to restart the garbling process at all. It is also noted that the value of τ has no impact on the garbled circuit size.

4.2 Provable Security of GPGRR2 for Φ_{topo}

In Sect. 4.1, we proposed a Gate Privacy preserving Garbled Row Reduction technique GPGRR2 such that each garbled gate contains two ciphertexts and a four-bits ciphertext. The four-bits ciphertext is optional and could be ignored since we do not use it for the scheme GPGRR2. For both odd gates and even gates, the two ciphertexts are the coordinates of a point in a two dimensional space over $\mathbb{F}_{2^t}$. Thus the evaluator cannot distinguish the type of a garbled gate. The remaining part of the security proof is similar to that of the garbling scheme Garble1 security for Φ_{topo} by Bellare, Hoang, and Rogaway [3]. The proof of Garble1 security in [3] is based on the observation that, given a pair of garbled values of the input wires, the evaluator can compute one garbled output value, but cannot distinguish the other garbled output value from random. This is true for GPGRR2 since the other garbled value is defined using a linear interpolation with a value which is unknown to the evaluator (indeed, the evaluator cannot distinguish that unknown value from random). The details are omitted here.

5   Optimized GPGRR2 and Lower Bounds

GPGRR2 is secure for Φ_{topo} and has comparable efficiency with other GRR techniques that are only secure for Φ_{circ}. For example, Pinkas et al's Garbled Row Reduction GRR2 [14] converts each odd gate to two ciphertexts and each even gate to one ciphertext. Pinkas et al's GRR2 technique requires the evaluator to carry out a degree two polynomial interpolation while GPGRR2 only requires a linear interpolation.

Zahur, Rosulek, and Evans [19] proved that "every ideally secure linear garbling scheme for AND gates must have two ciphertexts for each garbled gate". Zahur, Rosulek, and Evans's proof is based on linear operations in the finite field $\mathbb{F}_{2^t}$. In this section, we show that if we use linear operations over integers (instead of linear operations over $\mathbb{F}_{2^t}$), we can design a secure linear garbling scheme that garbles an AND/OR gate to only one ciphertext. This technique is further used to optimize the garbling scheme GPGRR2. In an ideal case, the optimized garbling scheme GPGRR2 may generate garbled circuits of $1.5n$ ciphertexts for circuits of n gates. That is, the garbled circuit is around $1.5nt$ bits. But the reader should be reminded that generally this ideal size is not achievable. Indeed, the problem of finding an optimized garbled circuit for a given circuit is **NP**-complete following a similar proof as that in FleXOR [8].

The garbling scheme GPGRR2 in Sect. 4.1 used a circuit-wide global offset value Δ though it is not necessary to have this offset value Δ to be global. In order for the construction in Sect. 4.1 to work, it suffices to have the following invariance property

$$k_x^0 + k_y^1 = k_x^1 + k_y^0 \quad \mod 2^t \tag{6}$$

for all gates $z = g(x, y)$ with garbled input wire values $k_x^0 \| \pi_x(0)$, $k_x^1 \| \pi_x(1)$, $k_y^0 \| \pi_y(0)$, and $k_y^1 \| \pi_y(1)$ respectively. Based on this observation, the garbling scheme GPGRR2 could be optimized using the following principle: for each gate g with two input wires x and y, if x is the output wire of a gate g_1 and y is the output wire of a gate g_2, then we can construct a garbled gate for g_1 with one ciphertext and a garbled gate for g_2 with two ciphertexts. The gates g_1 and g_2 are constructed in such a way that the Eq. (6) is satisfied.

As an example of optimized garbling scheme GPGRR2, we construct a Φ_{topo}-secure garbled circuit of 4-ciphertexts for the 3-gate circuit "$(x_1 \land x_2) \lor (x_3 \land x_4)$". Let g_1 be the gate $x_5 = (x_1 \land x_2)$, g_2 be the gate $x_6 = (x_3 \land x_4)$, and g_3 be the gate $x_7 = (x_5 \lor x_6)$ respectively. Assume that the invariance property (6) is satisfied for garbled input wire labels for gates g_1 and g_2. That is, (6) is satisfied by replacing x, y with x_1, x_2 (or with x_3, x_4) respectively. Similar to the original GPGRR2 garbling scheme, we define the operator $\circ$ as the integer addition modulo 2^t.

Garbling the Gate g_1: "$x_5 = (x_1 \wedge x_2)$". Let $k_{x_1}^0 \| \pi_{x_1}(0)$, $k_{x_1}^1 \| \pi_{x_1}(1)$, $k_{x_2}^0 \| \pi_{x_2}(0)$, and $k_{x_2}^1 \| \pi_{x_2}(1)$ be the garbled input wire values for the wires x_1 and x_2 respectively. For $i_1, i_2 \in \{0, 1\}$, let

$$K_{i_1 i_2} \| M_{i_1 i_2} \| N_{i_1 i_2} = H_{g_1}(k_{x_1}^{i_1} \circ k_{x_2}^{i_2}).$$

By the invariance property (6), we have

$$k_{x_1}^0 \circ k_{x_2}^1 = k_{x_1}^1 \circ k_{x_2}^0 \quad \mod 2^t$$

This implies that $K_{01} \| M_{01} \| N_{01} = K_{10} \| M_{10} \| N_{10}$. In case that there are two values from N_{00}, N_{01}, and N_{11} that are identical, re-start the garbling process to choose different garbled input wire values for the wires x_1 and x_2.

Let $P(X)$ be a linear polynomial over $\mathbb{F}_{2^t}$ passing through the two points (N_{00}, K_{00}) and (N_{01}, K_{01}). Let $Q(X)$ be a linear polynomial over $\mathbb{F}_{2^t}$ passing through the two points (N_{11}, K_{11}) and $(2^\tau, P(2^\tau))$. Set $k_{x_5}^0 = P(0)$ and $k_{x_5}^1 = Q(0)$. Then the garbled table for the gate g_1 is $\langle P(2^\tau), c_1, c_2, c_3, c_4 \rangle$ where $P(2^\tau)$ is an element from $\mathbb{F}_{2^t}$ and c_1, c_2, c_3, c_4 are bits encrypting the external index bits. That is, $\pi_{x_5}(g(b_{x_1}, b_{x_2})) = c_i \oplus M_i$ for $i = 2\pi_{x_1}(b_{x_1}) + \pi_{x_2}(b_{x_2}) + 1$. The total size of the garbled gate is $t + 4$ bits.

Garbling the Gate g_2: "$x_6 = (x_3 \wedge x_4)$". Let $k_{x_3}^0 \| \pi_{x_3}(0)$, $k_{x_3}^1 \| \pi_{x_3}(1)$, $k_{x_4}^0 \| \pi_{x_4}(0)$, and $k_{x_4}^1 \| \pi_{x_4}(1)$ be the garbled input wire values for the wires x_3 and x_4 respectively. For $i_1, i_2 \in \{0, 1\}$, let

$$K_{i_1 i_2} \| M_{i_1 i_2} \| N_{i_1 i_2} = H_{g_1}(k_{x_3}^{i_1} \circ k_{x_4}^{i_2}).$$

By the invariance property (6), we have

$$k_{x_3}^0 \circ k_{x_4}^1 = k_{x_3}^1 \circ k_{x_4}^0 \quad \mod 2^t$$

This implies that $K_{01} \| M_{01} \| N_{01} = K_{10} \| M_{10} \| N_{10}$. In case that there are two values from N_{00}, N_{01}, and N_{11} that are identical, re-start the garbling process to choose different garbled input wire values for the wires x_3 and x_4.

Let $P(X)$ be a linear polynomial over $\mathbb{F}_{2^t}$ passing through the two points (N_{00}, K_{00}) and (N_{01}, K_{01}). Set $k_{x_6}^0 = P(0)$ and

$$k_{x_6}^1 = k_{x_6}^0 + k_{x_5}^1 - k_{x_5}^0 \quad \mod 2^t \tag{7}$$

where we interpret $k_{x_5}^0, k_{x_5}^1, k_{x_6}^0$, and $k_{x_6}^1$ as integers modulo 2^t. Note that the Eq. (7) guarantees that the invariance (6) is satisfied for the gate g_3 with input wires x_5, x_6. Let $Q(X)$ be a linear polynomial over $\mathbb{F}_{2^t}$ passing through the two points $(0, k_{x_6}^1)$ and (N_{11}, K_{11}). Let X_z, be a solution of the equation $P(X) = Q(X)$ over $\mathbb{F}_{2^t}$. Then the garbled table for the gate g is $\langle X_z, P(X_z), c_1, c_2, c_3, c_4 \rangle$ where X_z and $P(X_z)$ are elements from $\mathbb{F}_{2^t}$ and c_1, c_2, c_3, c_4 are bits encrypting the external index bits. That is, $\pi_{x_6}(g(b_{x_3}, b_{x_4})) = c_i \oplus M_i$ for $i = 2\pi_{x_2}(b_{x_2}) + \pi_{x_4}(b_{x_4}) + 1$. The total size of the garbled gate is $2t + 4$ bits.

Garbling the Gate g_3: "$x_7 = (x_5 \vee x_6)$". By the Eq. (7), the invariance (6) is satisfied for the gate g_3 with input wires x_5, x_6. Thus the garbling process for the gate g_1 could be used to construct a garbled gate $\tilde{g}_3$ with one ciphertext and 4 bits. That is, the total size of the garbled gate $\tilde{g}_3$ is $t + 4$ bits. The details are omitted here.

As a summary, the garbled circuit for the 3-gate circuit "$(x_1 \wedge x_2) \vee (x_3 \wedge x_4)$" contains four ciphertexts (one for g_1, two for g_2, and one for g_3) and twelve bits. The total size of the garbled circuit is $4t + 12$ bits. Note that for such kind of 3-gate circuit, the best reported garbled circuit size in the literature is $6t + 12$ bits. The proof of security for the optimized GPGRR2 remains the same as that for GPGRR2 and the details are omitted here.

6   Reducing Ciphertext Size in Private Function Evaluations

In a two party PFE protocol, participant P_1 has a string x, participant P_2 has a function f and the outcome of the protocol is that P_2 learns $f(x)$ and nothing about x (beyond its length), while P_1 learns nothing about f (beyond side information we are willing to leak, such as the number of gates in the circuit f). Similarly, the outcome of the two party PFE protocol could be that P_1 learns $f(x)$ and nothing about f, while P_2 learns nothing about x. For the general case that P_2 has a private input x_2 himself, one can include the value of x_2 in the circuit computing f itself.

Traditionally, there are two approaches to design PFE protocols: using universal circuits and using homomorphic encryption. Universal circuit based PFE protocols introduce extra overhead and result in more complicated implementations. For the class of size n circuits, Valiant's universal circuit [16] is of size $19n \log n$ with depth $O(n)$ and Kolesnikov and Schneider's universal circuit [10] is of size $1.5n \log^2 n$ though it has smaller universal circuits for circuit sizes less than 5000. Kiss and Schneider [7] further reduced Valiant's bound by constructing universal circuit where the number of AND gates is bounded by $5n \log n$ and where the number of total gates is bounded by $20n \log n$. Though Kiss and Schneider [7] showed that it is practical to implement PFE using Valiant's size-optimized universal circuits, they claimed that "*universal circuits are not the most efficient solution to perform PFE*". Specifically, SFE protocol implementation for functions with billions of gates has been reported in the literature though the best reported universal circuit based PFE protocol implementation [7] is for simulated circuits of 300,000 gates, which results in a universal circuit of at most $245, 627, 140$ gates (and at most $61,406,785$ AND gates).

6.1   PFE in Semi-honest Security Model

Katz and Malka [6] and Mohassel and Sadeghian [11] proposed efficient constant-round Yao's garbled circuit based PFE protocols with communication/computational complexity linear in the size of the circuit computing f. The PFE protocols in [6] and [11] require that each circuit gate contain four ciphertexts. In the following, we use our GPGGR2 techniques to reduce the number of each garbled gate's ciphertexts to three in these PFE protocols. Thus we have a 25% reduction in the garbled circuit size for these PFE protocols. Note that free-XOR, GGR2, and half-gates could not be used to reduce the ciphertext numbers in these PFE protocols. The garble row reduction technique GGR3 cannot be used to reduce the ciphertext numbers in these PFE protocols either since the wire label values are obliviously chosen by both parties.

Katz and Malka [6] introduced one PFE protocol with provable security in the semi-honest security model with the assumption of semantic security for homomorphic encryption schemes and linear-related key security for symmetric encryption schemes. They also introduced a more efficient variant PFE protocol with provable security in the random oracle model. The second protocol is roughly twice as efficient as the first one. The authors of [6] mentioned that the random oracle requirement for the second protocol may not be necessary and its security without random oracle may be proved if further assumptions on the symmetric-key encryption scheme is made. In the following, we reduce the number of ciphertexts in the second PFE protocol [6] (with security in random oracle) by a factor of 25%. The same reduction could be made for the PFE protocols in Mohassel and Sadeghian [11].

PFE protocols in [6,11] use a singly homomorphic public-key encryption scheme sHE(Gen, Enc, Dec) such as the additive homomorphic Paillier encryption scheme [13]. In the following, we will give the protocol description in sufficient details without a formal definition. For a formal definition, the readers are referred to [6]. In our discussion, we assume that P_2 learns the output $f(x)$. The protocol can be modified to let P_1 learn the output straightforwardly. Let C_f be a circuit that computes P_2's function f and that C_f contains only NAND gates. Assume that C_f have n gates and it take l-bit inputs. In a high level, the PFE protocol proceeds as follows.

1. Given the pair (n, l), P_1 generates a sequence of n gates.
2. P_2 obliviously connects these gates to form a circuit C_f using a singly homomorphic encryption scheme.
3. P_1 produces a garbled circuit corresponding to the circuit C_f by garbling the n gates independently (which are connected obliviously).
4. P_1 gives an encoded version of the input x to P_2 and P_2 evaluates the garbled circuit to obtain the circuit output $C_f(x) = f(x)$.

Now we describe an instantiation of the above PFE protocol with reduced number of ciphertexts for each garbled gate. Let the outgoing wires set $\text{OW} = \{\text{ow}_1, \cdots, \text{ow}_l, \cdots, \text{ow}_{l+n}\}$ be the union of the set of l input wires and the n output wires for all gates in the circuit C_f. Let the incoming wires set $\text{IW} = \{\text{iw}_1, \cdots, \text{iw}_{2n}\}$ be the set of input wires to each gate of the circuit. The topology of the circuit C_f can be described by a mapping $\pi_C : \{1, \cdots, |\text{OW}|\} \rightarrow \{1, \cdots, |\text{IW}|\}$. Though each internal gate has only a single outgoing wire, it can have arbitrary fan-out. This is handled by mapping an outgoing wire $\text{ow}_i \in \text{OW}$ to multiple incoming wires in IW. The full protocol semiPFE is described in Fig. 1.

Correctness. In step (5) of the protocol semiPFE, if the linear polynomial $T_i(X) = P_i(X)$, then the equation (9) shows that $k_{l+i} = k_{l+i}^0 + \Delta$. Otherwise $T_i(X) = Q_i(X)$ and the equation (9) shows that $k_{l+i} = k_{l+i}^0$. This shows the correctness of the protocol.

Security. The security for PFE protocols can be defined in the semi-honest adversary model and in the malicious adversary model. In the semi-honest model, we assume that both participants follow the protocol honestly but both of them may be curious and try to learn some additional information from their protocol view. Let $\text{view}_i(1^\kappa, x, C_f)$ $(i = 1, 2)$ be the view of the participant P_i during the PFE protocol execution when P_1 holds input x and P_2 holds $C_f \in C$, where C is a class of circuits. The protocol is called

1. P_1 generates a private and public key pair $(\mathsf{sk}, \mathsf{pk})$ for an additive homomorphic encryption scheme such as Paillier scheme and chooses a circuit-wide global offset value $\Delta \in \mathbb{F}_{2^t}$. P_1 chooses $l + n$ outgoing-wire keys $k_i^0 \in \mathbb{F}_{2^t}$ and sets $k_i^1 = k_i^0 + \Delta$ for $1 \le i \le l + n$. P_1 sends $\mathsf{pk}, \mathsf{Enc}_{\mathsf{pk}}(k_1^0), \cdots, \mathsf{Enc}_{\mathsf{pk}}(k_{l+n}^0)$ to P_2.
2. For each gate i with incoming wires $\mathsf{ow}_j, \mathsf{ow}_k$, P_2 chooses random $a_i, a_i' \in \mathbb{F}_{2^t}$ and re-randomize the encrypted wire labels for gate i as

$$\mathsf{encG}_i = \left(\mathsf{Enc}_{\mathsf{pk}}(k_j^0 + a_i), \mathsf{Enc}_{\mathsf{pk}}(k_k^0 + a_i'), \mathsf{Enc}_{\mathsf{pk}}(k_{l+i}^0) \right).$$

   P_2 sends $\mathsf{encG}_1, \cdots, \mathsf{encG}_n$ to P_1.
3. For each $i = 1, \cdots, n$, P_1 decrypts encG_i to obtain the keys $(L_i^0, R_i^0, k_{l+i}^0)$ where $L_i^0 = k_j^0 + a_i$ and $R_i^0 = k_k^0 + a_i'$. P_1 defines $L_i^1 = L_i^0 + \Delta$, $R_i^1 = R_i^0 + \Delta$, and prepares the garbled version of the i-th gate as follows. Let H_i be a gate i specific hash function with $(t + \tau)$-bit outputs and let

$$\begin{aligned} K_{00} \| N_{00} &= H_i(L_i^0 + R_i^0 \quad \mathrm{mod}\ 2^t) \\ K_{01} \| N_{01} &= H_i(L_i^0 + R_i^0 + \Delta \quad \mathrm{mod}\ 2^t) \\ K_{10} \| N_{10} &= H_i(L_i^0 + R_i^0 + \Delta \quad \mathrm{mod}\ 2^t) \\ K_{11} \| N_{11} &= H_i(L_i^0 + R_i^0 + 2\Delta \quad \mathrm{mod}\ 2^t) \end{aligned} \tag{8}$$

   where $K_{00}, K_{01}, K_{10}, K_{11} \in \mathbb{F}_{2^t}$ and $N_{00}, N_{01}, N_{10}, N_{11} \in \mathbb{F}_{2^\tau}$.

   (a) Let $P_i(X)$ be a linear polynomial passing through the points: (N_{00}, K_{00}) and (N_{01}, K_{01}).
   (b) Set $\gamma_i^0 = P_i(0) - \Delta \ \mathrm{mod}\ 2^t$ and let $Q_i(X)$ be a linear polynomial passing through the points: $(0, \gamma_i^0)$ and (N_{11}, K_{11}).
   (c) Let $X_{i,0}$ be a solution of the equation $P_i(X) = Q_i(X)$.
   (d) The garbled version of the i-th gate is $\mathsf{GG}_i = \langle X_{i,0}, P_i(X_{i,0}), k_{l+i}^0 - \gamma_i^0 \rangle$.
4. P_1 sends $\mathsf{GG}_1, \cdots, \mathsf{GG}_n$ to P_2. In addition, for the input $x = x_1 \cdots x_l$ that P_1 holds, P_1 sends $k_1^{x_1}, \cdots, k_l^{x_l}$ to P_2.
5. Now P_2 has the keys $k_1^{x_1}, \cdots, k_l^{x_l}$ for the outgoing wire $i \in \{1, \cdots, l\}$. For each gate i that P_2 has both incoming wire key labels, P_2 computes the i-gate outgoing wire key label k_{l+i} as follows: Assume that the i-th gate have incoming wires $\mathsf{ow}_j, \mathsf{ow}_k$ and P_2 have already determined keys k_j, k_k for outgoing wires $\mathsf{ow}_j, \mathsf{ow}_k$. P_2 computes keys $L_i = k_j + a_i$ and $R_i = k_k + a_i'$ for the left and right incoming wires to gate i respectively. P_2 computes

$$K_i \| N_i = H_i(R_i + L_i \quad \mathrm{mod}\ 2^t).$$

   Let $T_i(X)$ be a linear polynomial passing through the following two points: (N_i, M_i) and $(X_{i,0}, P_i(X_{i,0}))$. P_2 sets the outgoing wire keys

$$k_{l+i} = T_i(0) + k_{l+i}^0 - \gamma_i^0 = k_{l+i}^0 + T_i(0) - P_i(0) + \Delta \quad \mathrm{mod}\ 2^t. \tag{9}$$

   Once P_2 has determined key k_{l+n}, it can use an oblivious transfer protocol with P_1 to learn the circuit output $f(x)$.

Fig. 1. Protocol $\mathsf{semiPFE}$

a secure C-PFE protocol if there exist probabilistic polynomial time simulators S_1 and S_2 such that for all probabilistic polynomial time algorithm D, we have

$$\left| Pr[D(S_1(1^\kappa, x)) = 1] - Pr[D(\text{view}_1(1^\kappa, x, C_f)) = 1] \right| = \text{negl}(\kappa)$$

and

$$\left| Pr[D(S_2(1^\kappa, C_f, C_f(x))) = 1] - Pr[D(\text{view}_2(1^\kappa, x, C_f)) = 1] \right| = \text{negl}(\kappa)$$

The provable security in the above semi-honest adversary model for our protocol semiPFE follows from the proof in Katz and Malka [6] by observing the following fact: given a pair of key values of the incoming wires of a gate, P_2 can compute one key values for the outgoing wire, but cannot distinguish the other key values for the outgoing wire from random. This is true for the protocol semiPFE since the other key values for the outgoing wire is defined using a linear interpolation with a value which is unknown to P_2. The details are omitted here.

Mohassel and Sadeghian [11] proposed a framework for designing PFE protocols by considering circuit topology privacy and secure evaluation of circuit gates independently. Specifically, they reduce the task of the circuit topology hiding (CTH) to oblivious evaluation of a mapping that encodes the topology of the circuit and they design a private gate evaluation (PGE) sub-protocol. Mohassel and Sadeghian then showed how to naturally combine CTH and PGE to obtain an efficient and secure PFE. The CTH functionality is implemented by an efficient oblivious evaluation of the mapping π_C using generalized switching networks and oblivious transfers. The PGE functionality is a PFE protocol for a single gate circuit where P_2 provides the gate's functionality and P_1 provides the input to the gate. The PGE functionality is based on Yao's garbled circuit and our above linear interpolation approach in the protocol semiPFE could be used in the same way to improve the PGE efficiency by a factor of 25%. The details are omitted here.

6.2   PFE Protocols Against Malicious Participants

Section 6.1 presents an efficient protocol semiPFE against semi-honest adversaries. This protocol is insecure against active adversaries. For example, in step (2) of the protocol semiPFE, P_2 may generate the wires encG_i in a malicious way to learn P_1's private input x. Specifically, assume that $\text{ow}_1, \cdots, \text{ow}_l$ are the circuit input wires. For each gate i, P_2 can choose random $a_i, a_i' \in \mathbb{F}_{2^l}$ and re-randomize the encrypted wire labels for gate i as

$$\text{encG}_i = (\text{Enc}_{\text{pk}}(\lambda(j, l)k_j^0 + a_i), \text{Enc}_{\text{pk}}(\lambda(j, l)k_k^0 + a_i'), \text{Enc}_{\text{pk}}(k_{l+i}^0))$$

where

$$\lambda(j, l) = \begin{cases} 0 & \text{if } j < l \\ 1 & \text{if } j \geq l \end{cases}$$

P_2 sends $\text{encG}_1, \cdots, \text{encG}_n$ to P_1. With this revision of the encG_i, P_2 may learn the last bit x_l of P_1's private input $x = x_1 \cdots x_l$. Assume that P_1 provide the wire labels $k_1^{x_1}, \cdots, k_l^{x_l}$ for the private input x. By the construction of encG_i, P_2 can evaluate the garbled circuit to obtain $f(0, \cdots, 0, x_l)$. By comparing whether $f(0, \cdots, 0, x_l) = f(0, \cdots, 0, 0)$ or $f(0, \cdots, 0, x_l) = f(0, \cdots, 0, 1)$, P_2 may learn the value of x_l.

Zero-knowledge proofs could be used to make the protocol semiPFE secure against active malicious participants. However, performance of the resulting protocol could not compete with PFE protocols based on SFE with universal circuits in the malicious adversary model.

Security definition for PFE protocols against malicious adversaries uses the real protocol execution to simulate an ideal world protocol execution by a trusted party (see, e.g., Canetti [4]). In the real-world execution, protocol participants jointly run the protocol and the adversary $\mathcal{A}$ is allowed to corrupt a participant. Let $\mathcal{A}_i$ $(i = 1, 2)$ be the probabilistic polynomial time adversary that corrupts the participant P_i. In the ideal world evaluation, all participants submit their inputs to a trusted party who will evaluate the entire protocol himself and there is a simulator $\mathcal{S}_i$ for the subset of participants controlled by the adversary $\mathcal{A}_i$ in the real world evaluation. Intuitively, a protocol is called a secure C-PFE protocol if there exist simulators such that the real world protocol evaluation simulates the ideal world protocol evaluation. This intuition is formally captured by requiring that the following two distributions are computationally indistinguishable.

– The honest participants' outputs and the adversary $\mathcal{A}$'s view in the real-world execution.
– The honest participants' outputs and the simulator S's view in the ideal-world execution.

Real-World Execution. In the real world execution, let $\mathsf{out}_1, \mathsf{out}_2$ denote the output of P_1 and P_2 respectively. For each individual adversary $\mathcal{A}_i$ $(i = 1, 2)$, there are two candidate views that we should consider. As an example, for the adversary $\mathcal{A}_1$, we need to consider the following two scenarios.

– If P_2 is honest, then we need to consider $\mathsf{view}_{\mathcal{A}_1,1} = \mathsf{view}_{\mathcal{A}_1} \cup \mathsf{out}_2$.
– If P_2 is dishonest, then we need to consider $\mathsf{view}_{\mathcal{A}_1,0} = \mathsf{view}_{\mathcal{A}_1}$.

Ideal-World Execution. In the ideal world execution, P_1 sends x to the trusted party and P_2 sends C_f to the trusted party if they are honest. For a dishonest participant, she sends either what she holds or a random string (it could be in the correct syntax format of a legal protocol message) to the trusted party. The trusted party computes $C_f(x)$ and sends it to P_2. We use $\mathsf{out}_1, \mathsf{out}_2$ to denote the output sent to P_1 and P_2 respectively by the trusted party and use $\mathcal{S}_1, \mathcal{S}_1$ to denote the simulators for $\mathcal{A}_1$ and $\mathcal{A}_2$ respectively. For each individual adversary, we need to construct a simulator S (that is, $\mathcal{S}_1$ or $\mathcal{S}_2$). But for this single simulator S, we need to consider two candidate views derived from the other adversary who may control the other participants. As an example, for the adversary $\mathcal{A}_1$, we need to consider the following two potential views.

– If P_2 is honest, then we need to consider $\mathsf{view}_{S_1,1} = \mathsf{view}_{S_1} \cup \mathsf{out}_2$.
– If P_2 is dishonest, then we need to consider $\mathsf{view}_{S_1,0} = \mathsf{view}_{S_1}$.

Definition 3. *A two party protocol Π is called a* secure C-PFE protocol *if there are probabilistic polynomial time simulators S_1 and S_2 such that the following four pairs* *of probabilistic distributions are computationally indistinguishable over the security parameter κ.*

$$\text{views}_{S_1,0}(1^\kappa, x, C_f) \overset{c}{\sim} \text{view}_{\mathcal{A}_1,0}(1^\kappa, x, C_f)$$
$$\text{views}_{S_1,1}(1^\kappa, x, C_f) \overset{c}{\sim} \text{view}_{\mathcal{A}_1,1}(1^\kappa, x, C_f)$$
$$\text{views}_{S_2,0}(1^\kappa, x, C_f) \overset{c}{\sim} \text{view}_{\mathcal{A}_2,0}(1^\kappa, x, C_f)$$
$$\text{views}_{S_2,1}(1^\kappa, x, C_f) \overset{c}{\sim} \text{view}_{\mathcal{A}_2,1}(1^\kappa, x, C_f).$$

In the above list, the views are dependent on the security parameter κ which is omitted.

Katz and Malka [6] proposed a revision of their PFE protocol to achieve security against a malicious participant P_1. Specifically, they revised their protocol by requiring P_1 to prove to P_2 the following facts (in the following, we use our protocol semiPFE instead of their original protocols):

- The public key pk communicated in Step 1 of semiPFE was generated using the specified key generation algorithm sHE.Gen.
- The ciphertexts $\text{Enc}_{\text{pk}}(k_1^0), \cdots, \text{Enc}_{\text{pk}}(k_{l+n}^0)$ communicated in Step 1 of semiPFE are well-formed ciphertexts using the public key pk.
- The garbled circuits in Step 3 are constructed correctly.
- The inputs are encoded correctly in Step 4.

A similar proof as in [6] could be used to show that

$$\text{views}_{S_1,1}(1^\kappa, x, C_f) \overset{c}{\sim} \text{view}_{\mathcal{A}_1,1}(1^\kappa, x, C_f)$$
$$\text{views}_{S_1,0}(1^\kappa, x, C_f) \overset{c}{\sim} \text{view}_{\mathcal{A}_1,0}(1^\kappa, x, C_f)$$

for our protocol semiPFE. In the same way, if we require P_2 to prove to P_1 the knowledge of $a_i, a_i' \in \mathbb{F}_{2^l}$ $(i = 1, \cdots, n)$ for the ciphertexts

$$\text{encG}_i = \left(\text{Enc}_{\text{pk}}(k_j^0 + a_i), \text{Enc}_{\text{pk}}(k_k^0 + a_i'), \text{Enc}_{\text{pk}}(k_{l+i}^0) \right)$$

communicated in Step 2 and that the circuit encoded using $\text{encG}_1, \cdots, \text{encG}_{n+l}$ belongs to C, then we can show that

$$\text{views}_{S_2,1}(1^\kappa, x, C_f) \overset{c}{\sim} \text{view}_{\mathcal{A}_2,1}(1^\kappa, x, C_f)$$
$$\text{views}_{S_2,0}(1^\kappa, x, C_f) \overset{c}{\sim} \text{view}_{\mathcal{A}_2,0}(1^\kappa, x, C_f).$$

6.3 Circuit Private PFE Protocols with Malicious P_1

The discussion in the preceding section shows that the protocol semiPFE could be revised to be secure against malicious participants using zero-knowledge proofs. Zero-knowledge proofs are normally expensive and the resulting protocols may not outperform universal circuit based PFE protocols. In certain practical applications, we may want to protect the circuit privacy from a malicious participant P_1 and assume that P_2 is semi-honest. For this kind of scenarios, it is not necessary for the participant P_1 to prove to P_2 that the garbled circuits in Step 3 are constructed correctly. Since it will not help P_1 to learn any information of P_2's circuit C_f by constructing incorrect garbled circuits in Step 3 of semiPFE. Similarly, P_1 does not need to prove to P_2 that the inputs are encoded correctly in Step 4. In the following paragraphs, we sketch the construction of a more efficient protocol privPFE that leaks zero information about the circuit C_f to a malicious P_1.

Though other singly homomorphic encryption schemes could be used, we use Paillier's encryption scheme to simplify the discussion. In Paillier's scheme, the public key $\mathrm{pk} = (n, g)$ consists of two integers where $n = pq$ divides the order of $g \in \mathbb{Z}_{n^2}^*$ and p, q are two prime numbers. The private key $\mathrm{sk} = (\lambda, \mu)$ is a pair of integers where $\lambda = \mathrm{lcm}(p - 1, q - 1)$ and $\mu = \left(\frac{(g^\lambda \bmod n^2) - 1}{n} \right)^{-1} \bmod n$. A message m is encrypted to $c = \mathrm{Enc}_{\mathrm{pk}}(m) = g^m \cdot r^n \bmod n^2$ for a randomly selected $r \in \mathbb{Z}_n^*$. A ciphertext c is decrypted to the message $m = \mathrm{Dec}_{\mathrm{sk}}(c) = \frac{\mu((c^\lambda \bmod n^2) - 1)}{n} \bmod n$.

In the protocol semiPFE, the only message that P_2 sends to P_1 is the oblivious gates encG_i ($i = 1, \cdots, n$). P_1 will not learn any information about the circuit C_f if P_1 cannot correlate the ciphertext $\mathrm{Enc}_{\mathrm{pk}}(k_j^0 + a_i)$ to the ciphertext $\mathrm{Enc}_{\mathrm{pk}}(k_j^0)$. This is guaranteed

---

1. P_1 generates a private and public key pair $(\mathrm{sk}, \mathrm{pk})$ for Paillier's encryption scheme where $\mathrm{sk} = (\lambda, \mu)$, $\mathrm{pk} = (n, g)$, and $n = pq$.
2. P_1 chooses two circuit-wide global offset values $\Delta, \Gamma \in \mathbb{F}_{2^t}$. P_1 chooses $l + n$ outgoing-wire keys $k_i^0 \in \mathbb{F}_{2^t}$ and sets $k_i^1 = k_i^0 + \Delta$ for $1 \leq i \leq l + n$. P_1 sends $\mathrm{pk}, \mathrm{Enc}_{\mathrm{pk}}(k_1^0), \cdots, \mathrm{Enc}_{\mathrm{pk}}(k_{l+n}^0)$ to P_2.
3. P_2 verifies that $g \in \mathbb{Z}_{n^2}^*$ and $\mathrm{Enc}_{\mathrm{pk}}(k_i^0) \in \mathbb{Z}_{n^2}^*$ for $i = 1, \cdots, n + l$.
4. For each gate i with incoming wires $\mathrm{ow}_j, \mathrm{ow}_k$, P_2 chooses random $a_i, a_i' \in \mathbb{F}_{2^t}$ and re-randomize the encrypted wire labels for gate i as

$$\mathrm{encG}_i = \left(\mathrm{Enc}_{\mathrm{pk}}(k_j^0 + a_i), \mathrm{Enc}_{\mathrm{pk}}(k_k^0 + a_i'), \mathrm{Enc}_{\mathrm{pk}}(k_{l+i}^0) \right).$$

   P_2 sends $\mathrm{encG}_1, \cdots, \mathrm{encG}_n$ to P_1.
5. For each $i = 1, \cdots, n$, P_1 decrypts encG_i to obtain the keys $(L_i^0, R_i^0, k_{l+i}^0)$ where $L_i^0 = k_j^0 + a_i$ and $R_i^0 = k_k^0 + a_i'$. P_1 defines $L_i^1 = L_i^0 + \Delta$, $R_i^1 = R_i^0 + \Delta$, and prepares the garbled version of the i-th gate as follows. Let H_i be a gate i specific hash function with $(t + \tau)$-bit outputs and let

$$\begin{aligned}
K_{00} \| N_{00} &= H_i(\Gamma + L_i^0 + R_i^0 \quad \bmod 2^t) \\
K_{01} \| N_{01} &= H_i(\Gamma + L_i^0 + R_i^0 + \Delta \quad \bmod 2^t) \\
K_{10} \| N_{10} &= H_i(\Gamma + L_i^0 + R_i^0 + \Delta \quad \bmod 2^t) \\
K_{11} \| N_{11} &= H_i(\Gamma + L_i^0 + R_i^0 + 2\Delta \quad \bmod 2^t)
\end{aligned} \tag{10}$$

   where $K_{00}, K_{01}, K_{10}, K_{11} \in \mathbb{F}_{2^t}$ and $N_{00}, N_{01}, N_{10}, N_{11} \in \mathbb{F}_{2^\tau}$. Set the garbled version of the i-th gate as $\mathrm{GG}_i = \langle X_{i,0}, P_i(X_{i,0}), k_{l+i}^0 - \gamma_i^0 + \Gamma \rangle$ where $\langle X_{i,0}, P_i(X_{i,0}), k_{l+i}^0 - \gamma_i^0 \rangle$ is constructed in the same way as Step 5 of the protocol semiPFE.
6. P_1 sends $\mathrm{GG}_1, \cdots, \mathrm{GG}_n$ to P_2. In addition, for the input $x = x_1 \cdots x_l$ that P_1 holds, P_1 sends $\Gamma + k_1^{x_1}, \cdots, \Gamma + k_l^{x_l}$ to P_2.
7. The process for P_2 to evaluate the garbled circuit to obtain $C_f(x)$ remains the same as the Step 5 of the protocol semiPFE.

Fig. 2. Protocol privPFE

by the semantic security of the homomorphic encryption scheme. In other words, if P_1 can prove to P_2 that the public key is generated using the specified key generation algorithm then the circuit privacy is guaranteed. However, if Paillier's scheme is used then zero knowledge proof is necessary. It is sufficient for P_2 to check that the condition $g \in \mathbb{Z}_{n^2}^*$ holds for the public key (n, g) generated by P_1 where we assume that P_2 will not leak any information about the circuit C_f on purpose. Specifically, the new protocol privPFE is described in Fig. 2.

Correctness. The correctness of the protocol privPFE can be verified straightforwardly in the same way as that for the protocol semiPFE.

Privacy. In the following, we sketch a proof of privacy for the protocol privPFE against malicious P_1. First we show that a dishonest P_1 will learn nothing about the circuit C_f except the circuit size unless P_2 leaks certain information about C_f on purpose. As we have mentioned in the preceding paragraphs, the only information that P_2 sends to P_1 is the set of oblivious gates

$$\text{encG}_i = \left(\text{Enc}_{\text{pk}}(k_j^0 + a_i), \text{Enc}_{\text{pk}}(k_k^0 + a_i'), \text{Enc}_{\text{pk}}(k_{l+i}^0) \right)$$

for $i = 1, \cdots, n$. In Step 3, P_2 verifies that $g \in \mathbb{Z}_{n^2}^*$ and $\text{Enc}_{\text{pk}}(k_i^0) \in \mathbb{Z}_{n^2}^*$ for $i = 1, \cdots, n + l$. Thus if a_i, a_i' are chosen uniformly at random, then $\text{Enc}_{\text{pk}}(k_j^0 + a_i), \text{Enc}_{\text{pk}}(k_k^0 + a_i')$ are values distributed uniformly at random over $\mathbb{Z}_{n^2}^*$ and are independent of the values $\text{Enc}_{\text{pk}}(k_j^0)$ and $\text{Enc}_{\text{pk}}(k_k^0)$. In a summary, unless P_2 chooses a_i, a_i' nonuniformly, P_1 learns no information about the circuit C_f except the circuit size. Note that the privacy of C_f is preserved unconditionally. Secondly, a semi-honest participant P_2 learns nothing about the private input x except the final output $f(x)$. The proof is similar to the proofs in [6] and the details are omitted. This completes the proof of privacy.

6.4   Secure PFE Protocols Against Two Malicious Participants

In order to protect the privacy of P_1's input x against a malicious P_2 in the protocol privPFE, P_2 needs to prove to P_1 that the circuit defined by the oblivious gates $\text{encG}_1, \cdots, \text{encG}_{n+l}$ belongs to the specified circuit class C. Otherwise, the circuit corresponding to these oblivious gates could be a simple circuit such as $\neg(x_1 \wedge x_1)$ which leaks information about the input value $x = x_1 \cdots x_l$ from the output $C_f(x)$. In other words, the protocol privPFE is not secure against malicious participant P_2.

For PFE protocols with circuit owner P_2 learning the final output $C_f(x)$, it seems to be inherently necessary to have participant P_2 to prove to P_1 that the circuit defined by the oblivious gates $\text{encG}_1, \cdots, \text{encG}_{n+l}$ belongs to the specified circuit class C. Otherwise, the protocol could not be secure against a malicious participant P_2. For applications where only the participant P_1 needs to learn the final output $C_f(x)$, the protocol privPFE is also secure against both malicious P_1 and malicious P_2. Let us revise the protocol privPFE to a new protocol secPFE as in Fig. 3.

The correctness of the protocol secPFE is straightforward. For the security proof, we distinguish two cases. In the first case we assume that P_1 is malicious. In this case the proof is identical to the privacy proof for the protocol privPFE since the only extra information that P_2 delivers to P_1 is the final output key label k_{n+l}^0 or $k_{n+l}^0 + \Delta$ which

> The protocol proceeds as in privPFE. In the last step, instead of P_2 obliviously learning exactly one of the key labels k^0_{n+l} and $k^0_{n+l} + \Delta$, P_2 handles the garbled circuit evaluation output to P_1. Note that the garbled circuit evaluation output is either k^0_{n+l} or $k^0_{n+l} + \Delta$.

Fig. 3. Protocol secPFE

leaks no information about the circuit topology. In other words, a malicious P_1 learns no information about the circuit C_f. In the second case, we assume that P_2 is malicious. In this case, let $ow_1, \cdots, ow_l$ be the l input wires. Assume that the ith gate

$$encG_i = \left(Enc_{pk}(k^0_j + a_i), Enc_{pk}(k^0_k + a'_i), Enc_{pk}(k^0_{l+i}) \right)$$

contains one or two input wires. Note that P_1 garbles this ith gate using ingoing key labels $(\Gamma + k^0_j + a_i, \Gamma + k^0_j + a_i + \Delta)$ and $(\Gamma + k^0_k + a_k, \Gamma + k^0_k + a_k + \Delta)$ respectively. Without loss of generality, we may assume that $j \leq l$ (that is, ow_j is an input wire). For the input wire ow_j, P_1 provides the input key label $\Gamma + k^{x_j}_j = \Gamma + k^0_j + x_j\Delta$ to P_2 corresponding to the input bit x_j. We can distinguish the following two cases:

- P_2 knows the value of $k^0_j + a_i$. In this case, unless Paillier's encryption scheme is not semantically secure, P_2 does not follow the protocol by choosing a random a_i to generate the ciphertext $Enc_{pk}(k^0_j + a_i)$. Instead, P_2 chooses a value $c_i = k^0_j + a_i$ and let $Enc_{pk}(k^0_j + a_i) = Enc_{pk}(c_i)$. In this case, P_2 can not distinguish a_i from a random value. Thus P_2 can not distinguish $\Gamma + k^0_j + a_i + x_j\Delta$ from a random value. Consequently, P_2 cannot go ahead to evaluate the ith garbled gate.
- P_2 does not know the value of $k^0_j + a_i$. In this case, P_2 may or may not follow the protocol. In either case, P_2 can not distinguish k^0_j from a random value. If P_2 followed the protocol and selected a known value a_i, then P_2 can compute the key value $\Gamma + k^0_j + a_i + x_j\Delta$ and continue the garbled gate evaluation. If P_2 has not followed the protocol and selected $k^0_j + a_i$ in a way that she does not know the value of a_i, then P_2 can not compute the key value $\Gamma + k^0_j + a_i + x_j\Delta$ and cannot continue the garbled gate evaluation.

With above discussion, a similar proof for garbled circuit security as in [3,6] could be used to show that a malicious participant P_2 learns no information about the input x in case that the Paillier's encryption scheme is semantically secure and the hash functions used in the protocol can be considered as random oracles. The details of the proof are omitted.

7   Circuit Garbling Scheme GRRcirc

The half-gates technique garbles each odd gates to two ciphertexts and even gates are free. However, the evaluator needs to carry out two cryptographic hash (or encryption) operations for each odd gate. In our GPGRR2 scheme, the evaluator needs to carry out one cryptographic hash (or encryption) operation and one multiplicative inverse operation in the finite field $\mathbb{F}_{2^t}$. In case that one needs a Φ_{circ}-secure garbling scheme and prefers multiplicative inverse operations than cryptographic hash (or encryption) operations, one may revise the scheme GPGRR2 by adding additional conversion processes (either free or with one additional ciphertexts) to obtain a free-XOR compatible GRRcirc scheme.

As a high level description, the conversion process is as follows. For each odd gate, if an output wire z is going to even gates, then we can let the output wire z to satisfy the condition "$k_z^1 = k_z^0 \oplus \Delta$" instead of "$k_z^1 = k_z^0 + \Delta \mod 2^t$". For each odd gate, if one or two input wires x satisfy "$k_x^1 = k_x^0 \oplus \Delta$" instead of "$k_z^1 = k_z^0 + \Delta \mod 2^t$", we can add a conversion ciphertext to translate the condition "$k_x^1 = k_x^0 \oplus \Delta$" to the condition "$k_z^1 = k_z^0 + \Delta \mod 2^t$". Furthermore, we use the GPGRR2 optimization technique to reduce two ciphertexts to one ciphertext for as many odd gates as possible. After the above revision, all even gates are free and each odd gate has one, two, or three ciphertexts. Specifically, the garbling scheme GRRcirc proceeds as follows.

1. For each odd gate such that all input wire labels satisfy the invariance property (6) and the output wire is only used by odd gates, garble the gate using the scheme GPGRR2. That is, let the garbled output wire labels satisfy the property $k_z^1 = k_z^0 + \Delta$ mod 2^t. This garbled gate contains two ciphertexts.
2. For each odd gate such that at least one input wire label does not satisfy the invariance property (6) and the output is only used by odd gates, garble the gate using the GRR3 with three ciphertexts.
3. For each odd gate with all fanout wires z going to even gates, depending on whether the input wires satisfy the invariance property (6) or not, revise either the above step 1 or the above step 2 to garble the gate so that the output wire has garbled wire labels k_z^0 and $k_z^1 = k_z^0 \oplus \Delta$. This garbled gate contains two or three ciphertexts.
4. For each odd gate with fanout wires going to both odd and even gates, garble it with three ciphertexts so that the output wire has garbled wire labels k_z^0 and $k_z^1 = k_z^0 \oplus \Delta$ for even gates and has garbled wire labels k_z^0 and $k_z^1 = k_z^0 + \Delta \mod 2^t$ for odd gates. Our experiments have not found such kind of gates for the commonly used circuits that we will discuss later.
5. For each odd gate, use the following process to reduce the number of ciphertexts to one if possible. In the following process, a gate g_1 is called a sibling gate of g_2 if there exists a gate g_3 such that the two input wires of g_3 are the output wires of g_1 and g_2 respectively.
   (a) Mark all even gates as "FINAL".
   (b) If all gates are marked either as "1-Cipher" or as "FINAL". Then the process is over. Otherwise, choose a random odd gate g that is not marked as "1-Cipher" or "FINAL". Let $S = \{g\}$.
   (c) If there exists a gate $g' \notin S$, g' is a sibling of some gate in S, and g' is marked as "1-Cipher" or "FINAL", mark all gates in S as "FINAL" and go to Step (5b).
   (d) If there exists a gate $g' \notin S$, g' is a sibling of some gate in S, and g' is neither marked as "1-Cipher" nor marked as "FINAL", let $S = S \cup \{g'\}$ and go to Step (5c).
   (e) If there is no gate $g' \notin S$ such that g' is a sibling of some gate in S, use the optimized GPGRR2 technique to garble g using one ciphertext and all other

gates in S using two ciphertexts appropriately. It is noted that if the garbled gate g contains three ciphertexts originally, then we can only reduce the number of ciphertexts to two instead of one. Mark g as "1-Cipher" and all other gates in S as "FINAL". Go to Step (5b).

6. Each even gate is for free. That is, no ciphertext is required.

We used the above process to compare the proposed garbling scheme GRRcirc against other garbling schemes from the literature. Since it is optional to use the external index bits in GRRcirc, we do not include the external index bits for GRRcirc garbling scheme in the following comparison. Specifically, we compare the garbled circuit sizes for the following circuits that are available from [15]: AES (Key Expanded), DES (Key Expanded), MD5, SHA-1, SHA-256. Note that the circuits for these functions [15] contains AND, XOR, and INV gates. For our comparison, we integrated the INV gates into the AND/XOR gates to obtain OR and NXOR gates. Thus we will only consider circuits with AND/OR/XOR/NXOR gates. We will use t to denote the size of wire labels (e.g., we may take $t = 80$). For the garbling schemes, we compare Yao's classical scheme [18], point-permute [2], GRR3 [12], GRR2 [14], free XOR+GRR3 [9], FleXOR [8], and half-gates [19]. For the FleXOR garbling scheme [8], we used the data for the best performance "safe ordering heuristics" reported in Fig. 9 of [8]. For each garbling scheme in Table 1, we have two rows of values for each circuit. The top row contains the number of ciphertexts of the garbled circuits and the bottom row contains the size of the garbled circuits when $t = 80$.

The comparison results in Table 1 show that, GRRcirc has comparable performance with FleXOR. However, it has large garbled circuit size compared with half-gates techniques. As we have mentioned in the previous sections, one may choose to use GRRcirc

Table 1. Garbled Circuit Size Comparison

	AES (KE)	DES (KE)	MD5	SHA-1	SHA-256
# AND/OR [15]	5440	18175	29084	37300	90825
# XOR/NXOR [15]	20325	1351	14150	24166	42029
# Total gates	25765	19526	43234	61466	132854
classical [18]	103060t	78104t	172936t	245864t	531416t
	0.98MB	0.74MB	1.65MB	2.34MB	5.07MB
point-permute [2]	103060(t+1)t	78104(t+1)	172936(t+1)	245864(t+1)	531416(t+1)
	1MB	0.75MB	1.67MB	2.37MB	5.13MB
GGR3 [12]	77295(t+1)	58578(t+1)	129702(t+1)	184398(t+1)	398562(t+1)
	0.75MB	0.57MB	1.25MB	1.78MB	3.85MB
GGR2 [14]	51530(t+1)	39052(t+1)	86468(t+1)	122932(t+1)	265708(t+1)
	0.50MB	0.38MB	0.83MB	1.19MB	2.57MB
free XOR+GRR3 [9]	16320(t+1)	54525(t+1)	87252(t+1)	111900(t+1)	272475(t+1)
	0.16MB	0.53MB	0.84MB	1.08MB	2.63MB
FleXOR [8]	18550(t+1)	36904(t+1)	N/A	85438(t+1)	207253(t+1)
	0.18MB	0.36MB	N/A	0.82MB	2MB
half-gates [19]	10880(t+1)	36350(t+1)	58168(t+1)	74600(t+1)	181650(t+1)
	0.11MB	**0.35MB**	**0.56MB**	**0.72MB**	**1.75MB**
GRRcirc	16640t	37198t	75584t	97080t	225498t
	0.16MB	**0.35MB**	**0.72MB**	**0.92MB**	**2.15MB**

instead of half-gates if one prefers field multiplicative inverse operations than crypto-graphic hash (or encryption) operations since for half-gates garbled circuits, each odd gate evaluation requires two cryptographic hash (or encryption) operations while for GRRcirc garbled circuits, each odd gate evaluation requires one cryptographic hash (or encryption) operation and one field multiplicative inverse operation.

8 Conclusion

Using a linear interpolation method, we proposed a circuit garbling scheme to garble each circuit gate to at most two ciphertexts with gate functionality privacy. We also proposed an optimization process to garble a circuit in such a way that some gates only contain one ciphertext. It would be interesting to investigate the lower bound for garbled circuit size. We also applied our garbling schemes to constant round PFE protocols and proposed a more efficient PFE protocol that is secure against malicious participant P_1 if P_2 learns the final output and is secure against two malicious participants P_1/P_2 if only P_1 learns the final output.

References

1. Ajtai, M., Komlós, J., Szemerédi, E.: An $o(n \log n)$ sorting network. In: Proceedings of the Fifteenth Annual ACM Symposium on Theory of Computing, pp. 1–9. ACM (1983)
2. Beaver, D., Micali, S., Rogaway, P.: The round complexity of secure protocols. In: Proceedings of the 22nd ACM STOC, pp. 503–513. ACM (1990)
3. Bellare, M., Hoang, V., Rogaway, P.: Foundations of garbled circuits. In: Proceedings of the 2012 ACM CCS, pp. 784–796. ACM (2012)
4. Canetti, R.: Universally composable security: a new paradigm for cryptographic protocols. In: IEEE Proceedings of the FOCS, pp. 136–145. IEEE (2001)
5. Furst, M., Saxe, J.B., Sipser, M.: Parity, circuits, and the polynomial-time hierarchy. Math. Syst. Theory **17**(1), 13–27 (1984)
6. Katz, J., Malka, L.: Constant-round private function evaluation with linear complexity. In: Lee, D.H., Wang, X. (eds.) ASIACRYPT 2011. LNCS, vol. 7073, pp. 556–571. Springer, Heidelberg (2011). https://doi.org/10.1007/978-3-642-25385-0_30
7. Kiss, Á., Schneider, T.: Valiant's universal circuit is practical. In: Fischlin, M., Coron, J.-S. (eds.) EUROCRYPT 2016. LNCS, vol. 9665, pp. 699–728. Springer, Heidelberg (2016). https://doi.org/10.1007/978-3-662-49890-3_27
8. Kolesnikov, V., Mohassel, P., Rosulek, M.: FleXOR: flexible garbling for XOR gates that beats free-XOR. In: Garay, J.A., Gennaro, R. (eds.) CRYPTO 2014. LNCS, vol. 8617, pp. 440–457. Springer, Heidelberg (2014). https://doi.org/10.1007/978-3-662-44381-1_25
9. Kolesnikov, V., Schneider, T.: Improved garbled circuit: free XOR gates and applications. In: Aceto, L., Damgård, I., Goldberg, L.A., Halldórsson, M.M., Ingólfsdóttir, A., Walukiewicz, I. (eds.) ICALP 2008. LNCS, vol. 5126, pp. 486–498. Springer, Heidelberg (2008). https://doi.org/10.1007/978-3-540-70583-3_40
10. Kolesnikov, V., Schneider, T.: A practical universal circuit construction and secure evaluation of private functions. In: Tsudik, G. (ed.) FC 2008. LNCS, vol. 5143, pp. 83–97. Springer, Heidelberg (2008). https://doi.org/10.1007/978-3-540-85230-8_7

11. Mohassel, P., Sadeghian, S.: How to hide circuits in MPC an efficient framework for private function evaluation. In: Johansson, T., Nguyen, P.Q. (eds.) EUROCRYPT 2013. LNCS, vol. 7881, pp. 557–574. Springer, Heidelberg (2013). https://doi.org/10.1007/978-3-642-38348-9_33

12. Naor, M., Pinkas, B., Sumner, R.: Privacy preserving auctions and mechanism design. In: Proceedings of the 1st ACM Conference on Electronic Commerce, pp. 129–139. ACM (1999)

13. Paillier, P.: Public-key cryptosystems based on composite degree residuosity classes. In: Stern, J. (ed.) EUROCRYPT 1999. LNCS, vol. 1592, pp. 223–238. Springer, Heidelberg (1999). https://doi.org/10.1007/3-540-48910-x_16

14. Pinkas, B., Schneider, T., Smart, N.P., Williams, S.C.: Secure two-party computation is practical. In: Matsui, M. (ed.) ASIACRYPT 2009. LNCS, vol. 5912, pp. 250–267. Springer, Heidelberg (2009). https://doi.org/10.1007/978-3-642-10366-7_15

15. Smart, N.P., Tillich, S.: Circuits of basic functions suitable for MPC and FHE. http://www.cs.bris.ac.uk/Research/CryptographySecurity/MPC/

16. Valiant, L.: Universal circuits. In: Proceedings of the 8th ACM STOC, pp. 196–203. ACM (1976)

17. Wang, Y., Malluhi, Q.M.: Reducing Garbled Circuit Size While Preserving Circuit Gate Privacy. Cryptology ePrint Archive, Paper 2017/041 (2017). https://eprint.iacr.org/2017/041

18. Yao, A.: How to generate and exchange secrets. In: Proceedings 27th IEEE FOCS, pp. 162–167. IEEE (1986)

19. Zahur, S., Rosulek, M., Evans, D.: Two halves make a whole. In: Oswald, E., Fischlin, M. (eds.) EUROCRYPT 2015. LNCS, vol. 9057, pp. 220–250. Springer, Heidelberg (2015). https://doi.org/10.1007/978-3-662-46803-6_8

iUC-Secure Distributed File Transfer from Standard Attribute-Based Encryption

Pascal Lafourcade[1]($\boxtimes$)(iD), Gael Marcadet[1]($\boxtimes$)(iD), and Léo Robert[2]($\boxtimes$)(iD)

[1] Université Clermont-Auvergne, CNRS, Clermont-Auvergne-INP, LIMOS,
Clermont-Ferrand, France
`pascal.lafourcade@uca.fr, gael.marcadet@limos.fr`
[2] MIS, Université de Picardie Jules Verne, Amiens, France
`leo.robert@u-picardie.fr`

Abstract. Attribute-Based Encryption (ABE) stands as a cryptographic cornerstone, enabling access control to messages based on user attributes. The security definition of standard ABE is shown to be impossible in Universal Composability (UC) against an *active* adversary. To overcome this issue, existing formal UC security definitions of ABE rely on additional properties for ABE, necessary to prove security against an active adversary, excluding standard ABE by definition. In light of the composability feature offered by UC and the absence of ideal functionality tailored for standard ABE, we propose the two following contributions: (1) We construct the first ideal functionality $\mathcal{F}_{ABE}$ for ABE which, under reasonable hypothesis against static corruption, can be realized using an IND-CCA2-secure ABE scheme; and (2) our $\mathcal{F}_{ABE}$ leads us to propose a protocol solving a simple yet highly practical, world-scaled company-focused problem: efficient file transfer. The proposed construction provides data integrity, sender authentication, attribute-based file access, featured with *constant* data size transferred between users. This is achieved by relying on two efficient building blocks: ABE and signature, which are layered atop of the hash-based distributed storage system IPFS. Our protocol, strengthened by a formal security definition and analysis under the Universally Composable (UC) framework called iUC, is proved to realize our problem-oriented authenticated attribute-based file transfer ideal functionality. Finally, we implement our proposal with a proof-of-concept written in Rust, and show it is practical and efficient.

Keywords: Universal Composability · Attribute-Based Encryption · Authenticated Attribute-based File Transfer

1 Introduction

Attribute-based encryption (ABE) is a fine-grained access encryption scheme in which a user securely shares a message to a group of users once, every user of

S. Vaudenay and C. Petit (Eds.): AFRICACRYPT 2024, LNCS 14861, pp. 174–198, 2024.
https://doi.org/10.1007/978-3-031-64381-1_8

this group being able to recover the encrypted message while every other users out of this group does not. Briefly, the formal definition of the aforementioned "group" is realized by associating to each user an attribute x and by adding an access policy y to the ciphertext, the decryption procedure failing if the attribute x does not satisfy the access policy y. ABE has received lot of attention over the years to construct interesting primitive [4,16]. From a security standpoint, similarly to standard encryption schemes where indistinguishability holds only if the decryption key has not been corrupted, in ABE the indistinguishability for a ciphertext ψ holds only if the adversary does not have access to an attribute that can decrypt ψ. In game-based security, this is prevented by adding a winning condition preventing the adversary to decrypt the challenge ciphertext. Sadly, this mitigation cannot be transposed directly to the Universally Composable (UC) paradigm. Indeed in UC, traditional ideal functionalities for encryption aim to replace *all* plaintexts whose indistinguishability can be ensured by leakages. This is not suitable against *active* attribute corruption in which the adversary asks for the key-material associated to an attribute of its choice at *any time*. This issue has already been noticed by [19] in a closely related field of Role-Based Access Control (RBAC), where a user grants an access to some resources based on attributes. Security against *active* attribute corruption has already been achieved, for example by Camenisch *et al.* [7] using ABE equipped of an interactive decryption procedure between the user owning a ciphertext and a trusted third-party, owning decryption key for users. On one hand security against active adversary is achieved, but on the other hand, protocols using standard ABE have to integrate a more complex ABE primitive to fit in UC. This replacement is not always desirable, in particular for protocols whose efficiency is critical and may prefer standard ABE, even at the cost of a restricted security setting.

Contribution. We consider *standard* ABE to propose the first ideal functionality $\mathcal{F}_{\mathsf{ABE}}$ secure in the *static* attribute corruption setting. The protocol execution is divided into two distinct phases. The first phase, corresponding to a setup phase, consists for the adversary to instantiate any parties of its choice, with the possibility to corrupt them. During the second phase, the adversary is still allowed to instantiate parties but corruption of parties asking for decryption keys is no longer accepted. Then, assuming this constraint and an IND-CCA2-secure ABE scheme[1], we prove that our real protocol $\mathcal{P}_{\mathsf{ABE}}$ securely realize $\mathcal{F}_{\mathsf{ABE}}$. To increase usability, we have written $\mathcal{F}_{\mathsf{ABE}}$ and $\mathcal{P}_{\mathsf{ABE}}$ using the iUC framework, having the particularity to rely on the same formalism to express ideal, real and hybrid protocols. Based on the IITM model [17], this framework has been designed to be user-friendly, a welcomed feature to limit the complexity of reading and writing UC protocols.

To motivate the usability of our ideal functionality $\mathcal{F}_{\mathsf{ABE}}$, already strengthened by the easy-to-use iUC framework, we put it in practice to solve the file transfer problem in a large-scaled company. In particular, we construct a protocol

---

[1] An IND-CCA2-secure scheme can be efficiently derived from any IND-CPA-secure scheme via the Fujisaki-Okamoto transform [13].

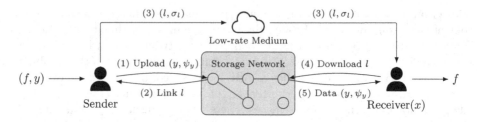

Fig. 1. Representation of our system where a sender shares a file f to a receiver.

allowing a user to share a document, let say, to all users working in a department. Attribute-based encryption is interesting in this setting, but confidentiality is not the only desired property. To increase confidence in our file transfer system, we add sender authentication and also integrity guarantee of the shared files. In addition to all these security properties, we dedicate our system to be particularly efficient in the case of large transferred files. Our study leads to the real protocol $\mathcal{P}_{\mathsf{AAFT}}$ a file transfer system ensuring the following three properties: (i) integrity of the transferred files, (ii) attribute-based file access, and (iii) explicit authentication of the sender. Our construction has the particularity to be constructed atop of a *distributed storage network*, a system composed of many servers whose general behavior is similar to a graph. A neat feature, compared to the single-server setting, is that it faces communication delay and workload issues. Inter-Planetary File System (IPFS) is an hash-based distributed storage system in which a server maintains a list of link-file pair (l, f) where l is the link of the file f, computed with a cryptographic hash function h as $l \leftarrow h(f)$. Later on, given the link, the server easily recovers and returns the file. We give an overview of our protocol in Fig. 1, acting between a sender and a receiver. The sender obtains as an input a (potentially large) file f as well as some access policy y, and sends the file to every receiver having an attribute x satisfying y. As depicted in Fig. 1, during step (1), the sender computes an encryption of f denoted ψ_y using attribute-based encryption where y is the access policy, and sends the couple (y, ψ_y) on a storage server of its choice. At step (2), the storage server responds with a link l computed as the hash of (y, ψ_y). At step (3), the sender computes σ_l the signature of l and sends the tuple (l, σ_l) through a limited communication medium, restricted to transmit data having length independent of the message. When the receiver obtains the link l and the associated signature σ_l, it obtains a proof of integrity and authenticates the sender simultaneously. At step (4) and (5), the receiver downloads the couple (y, ψ_y) using the link l, decrypts the result and checks authenticity of l using σ_l. This protocol is proved to securely realize our Authenticated Attribute-based File Transfer ideal functionality $\mathcal{F}_{\mathsf{AAFT}}$, but also to be highly-practical, confirmed by our proof-of-concept fully-written in Rust and available at [2], sending up to 450 megabytes of data in 474 ms.

Related Work. As explained above, the state-of-the-art for ABE in UC already proposes ideal functionality, but always equipped of an additional property or having a different design to guarantee security against active adversary. Abe and Ambrona [3] introduced an ideal functionality for ABE where the key generation is replaced by a blind key generation procedure including a non-interactive zero-knowledge proof. To obtain active security, Camenisch *et al.* [7] proposes to rely on a trusted third party owning the decryption key of users. To decrypt a ciphertext, the ABE protocol is equipped of an interactive decryption procedure with the third party, which is not able to identify which ciphertext is being decrypted. These two works need an ABE scheme having either a blind key generation or interactive decryption procedure, excluding every standard efficient attribute-based encryption schemes such that [4]. To the best of our knowledge, there is no ideal functionality tailored for standard ABE.

We stress that our hybrid protocol $\mathcal{P}_{\mathsf{AAFT}}$, putting into application our ideal functionality $\mathcal{F}_{\mathsf{ABE}}$, constitutes a novel improvement in distributed file-transfer literature. Distributed file-transfer system has been introduced many years ago by Garay *et al.* [14], proposing a system based on a verifiable secret sharing, ensuring both confidentiality by distributing shares among the storage servers, as done in the more recent system called SAFE [6] with critical security and performance improvements. Due to the nature of secret sharing, confidentiality is only ensured with several storage servers and need to reconstruct the file. In contrast, by the confidentiality ensured by ABE, our system is still secure even with a (possibly corrupted) single storage server. Role-Based Access Control (RBAC) systems, a closely related topic, allows (or restricts) users to access some resources based on owned attribute. When a user accesses some content, it has first to be authenticated by an access-granting server. This is the case for the SESAME protocol [20], a RBAC based itself on Kerberos. The work of Freudenthal *et al.* [12], proposes to check the access permission of users with multiple trust authorities (*e.g.,* a public key infrastructure). The role-based access for distributed storage system is presented in [15]. They proposed a fix for the Object Store Devices specification [1] where unrestricted delegation is possible, in which confidentiality cannot be ensured. The proposed solution, elegantly modifies the original protocol by adding secure channels and signature, to enforce role-based access to the files, without modifying the specification. All of these papers differ from our contribution by the introduction of authorities in charge of granting an access to some content. Our work requires trusted authorities to handle public keys and to provide decryption keys, but are involved only during the initialisation, no authorization is required hereinafter. Introduced by Rizwan Ashgar *et al.* [5], ESPOON is a protocol working as RBAC but in outsourced environment with untrusted entities. Integrity is not ensured, whereas our work ensures the integrity and confidentiality of data in addition to sender authentication. The work of [10] proposes a solution between RBAC and a storage system. They formally defined a new security definition of RBAC, in the spirit of encryption indistinguishability. The adversary is asked to guess an encrypted message, and is assumed to have a full-control on a file system where the encrypted message is stored. It can also corrupt any user of its choice. To achieve the proposed definition, a new protocol is introduced relying on attribute-based encryption, as done hereinafter. Our work adds more features: we ensure data integrity and data authentication (thanks to hash-based distributed storage and signatures, respectively) in addition to data confidentiality brought by the attribute-based encryption. Universal Composability (UC) has already been applied on the RBAC, initiated by Halevi *et al.* [15] proposing a UC model which requires at every communication a secure channel between the two parties, even if the entity is corrupted (but in this case, the secret key might be leaked), a standard assumption in UC. In our work, we have chosen to not consider any particular property on communication channels for two reasons. First, secrecy is not always possible for example with anonymous protocols, or even desirable for example when transferred data can be read in clear by the adversary. Second, authenticity is traditionally achieved using digital signature, that can also be used to sign messages in other protocols. Introducing an ideal functionality for digital signature is hence more appropriate. Even if it does not constitute an issue, their UC model is built on the original UC model of Canetti [9] in which session identifier prevents communication between sessions. In comparison, our protocol is proven under the iUC framework, where every entity is allowed to communicate with the others without restriction, a useful property for example with signature whose signing key are used in practice across multiple protocols.

Outline. In Sect. 2, we briefly introduce all the necessary notions and terminology to understand our modelisation. In Sect. 3, we present our ideal functionality $\mathcal{F}_{\mathsf{ABE}}$ and real protocol $\mathcal{P}_{\mathsf{ABE}}$ along the proof of realization. In Sect. 4, we present the application of $\mathcal{F}_{\mathsf{ABE}}$ on the authenticated attribute-based file transfer with our ideal functionality $\mathcal{F}_{\mathsf{AAFT}}$ along our hybrid protocol $\mathcal{P}_{\mathsf{AAFT}}$ and our proof-of-concept.

2   On iUC Framework

We provide an overview of the iUC framework. We refer interested readers looking for more details at the original paper [8]. A party pid involved in a protocol is traditionally equipped with session identifier sid, and acts in the protocol following a code specification called a role, and denoted role. The combination of the party identifier, the session identifier and the role constitutes the triplet (pid, sid, role) and is called an *entity*. The existing role is specific to the designed protocol; for example a signature protocol consists of a role `signer` to sign messages and a role `verifier` to verify signed messages. The notion of entity is at the heart of the iUC framework, sharing similarities with object-oriented programming. In iUC, a *machine* denoted M_{role} implementing a role role corresponds to a class, both equipped with internal state used to store data. In a real protocol, a machine manages a single entity *i.e.*, represents a single party running in a single protocol execution. Yet, notice that a machine can be naturally extended to manage arbitrary number of entities, having different roles as well, the internal state being now used to share data across entities. For example, a signature ideal functionality benefits from this feature by adding authenticated messages in the internal state. In iUC, a machine, just like a class, can be instantiated several times, an instantiation being called an *instance*. Two important observations are to be made: First, the notion of entities and machines is sufficient to handle both real and ideal protocols. Second, a machine is not required to only handle entities sharing the same sid but any entities, a particularly useful property to handle cross-protocols party such as certificate authority.

The iUC framework provides algorithms to describe behavior of instances *e.g.*, the number of accepted entities, the corruption model, the instance and entity initialization, and more. When an entity (pid, sid, role) is contacted for the first time, the identity is submitted to every instances implementing the role role, until one instance accepts the entity, decided by the CheckID algorithm. If the instance does not have any accepted entity yet, it executes the Initialization algorithm to initialize its internal state. Once initialized, an entity executes the Main block containing the code to be executed by *honest* entities. Each role is associated with either a *public* or a *private* visibility. A public role is accessible to the environment, whereas a private role is limited to entities inside the protocol. An entity accepts requests coming from the environment via the input-output interface I/O, but also requests coming from the adversary via the network interface NET, possibly modelling interactions of an ideal functionality with the simulator. When needed, an entity may also accepts requests from more specific entities. The current running entity $(\mathsf{pid}_{\mathsf{cur}}, \mathsf{sid}_{\mathsf{cur}}, \mathsf{role}_{\mathsf{cur}})$ is denoted $\mathsf{entity}_{\mathsf{cur}}$. An higher-protocol calling entity $(\mathsf{pid}_{\mathsf{call}}, \mathsf{sid}_{\mathsf{call}}, \mathsf{role}_{\mathsf{call}})$ is denoted $\mathsf{entity}_{\mathsf{call}}$. An instance has access to the set of managed entities that has been corrupted, denoted by CorruptionSet. An entity has to be considered if a subroutine has been corrupted, the corruption of an entity being verified by the corr algorithm returning true if the entity provided as an input has been corrupted, false otherwise. By $\mathsf{alg}^{(p)}$ we denote the execution of an algorithm alg whose the execution time is bounded by the polynomial p.

3 Standard Attribute-Based Encryption Realization

Attribute-based Encryption, ABE for short, allows to broadcast a message to all users, whose only users having the read access with respect to an *access policy* associated to the message are able to read the message. We say that a user has a read access when it is associated to some *attribute*, say x, respecting the policy of the message, say y. In the paper, this statement is represented by $x \in y$. Briefly, an ABE scheme is defined by the tuple (Setup, Enc, KeyGen, Dec). The Setup algorithm takes as an input the unary representation of the security parameter λ and it outputs a master key pair (msk, mpk). The encryption algorithm Enc expects as an input the master public key mpk, the access policy y and a message m, and it outputs the ciphertext ψ_y. To decrypt a message, one may previously asks to the authority owning the master key pair a decryption key denoted sk_x associated to some attribute x. This decryption key generation is handled by the KeyGen algorithm taking as input the master secret key msk as well as the attribute x and outputs the decryption key sk_x. This decryption key sk_x along a ciphertext ψ_x are provided to the decryption algorithm Dec, returning either the underlying plaintext m if and only if $x \in y$, or $\bot$ otherwise. An ABE scheme is said *correct* if for every master key pair $(msk, mpk) \leftarrow \mathsf{Setup}(1^\lambda)$, every ciphertext $\psi_y \leftarrow \mathsf{Enc}(mpk, y, m)$ for any message m and access policy y, every decryption key $\mathsf{sk}_x \leftarrow \mathsf{KeyGen}(msk, x)$ for any attribute x with $x \in y$, we have $\Pr\left[\mathsf{Dec}(\mathsf{sk}_x, \psi_y) = m\right] = 1 - \epsilon$ for some negligible probability ϵ. In this work, we require an IND-CCA2-secure ABE which informally states that it must be infeasible to tell if a ciphertext ψ_y encrypts either the message m_0 or m_1 as long as no corrupted user has a secret key sk_x allowing to decrypt ψ_y. The security experiment is presented in Fig. 2.

$\mathsf{Exp}_{\mathcal{A}}^{\text{IND-CCA2}}(\lambda)$	**Oracle** $\mathsf{OKeyGen}(msk, \mathcal{X}, y^*; x)$
$\mathcal{X} \leftarrow \emptyset$	**if** $x \in y^*$: **return** $\bot$
$(msk, mpk) \leftarrow \mathsf{Setup}(1^\lambda)$	$\mathcal{X} \leftarrow \mathcal{X} \cup \{x\}$
$\mathcal{O} \leftarrow \{\mathsf{OKeyGen}(msk, \mathcal{X}, \bot; \cdot), \mathsf{ODec}(msk, \bot; \cdot, \cdot)\}$	$\mathsf{sk}_x \leftarrow \mathsf{KeyGen}(msk, x)$
$(y^*, m_0, m_1), \mathsf{state} \leftarrow \mathcal{A}_1^{\mathcal{O}}(mpk)$	**return** sk_x
$b \leftarrow\!\!\$\ \{0, 1\}$	**Oracle** $\mathsf{ODec}(msk, \psi_{y^*}; \psi_y, x)$
$\psi_{y^*} \leftarrow \mathsf{Enc}(mpk, y^*, m_b)$	**if** $\psi_{y^*} = \psi_y$: **return** $\bot$
$\mathcal{O}' \leftarrow \{\mathsf{OKeyGen}(msk, \mathcal{X}, y^*; \cdot), \mathsf{ODec}(msk, \psi_{y^*}; \cdot, \cdot)\}$	$\mathsf{sk}_x \leftarrow \mathsf{KeyGen}(msk, x)$
$b' \leftarrow \mathcal{A}_2^{\mathcal{O}'}(\psi_{y^*}, \mathsf{state})$	$m \leftarrow \mathsf{Dec}(\mathsf{sk}_x, \psi_y)$
return $b = b' \land (\nexists x \in \mathcal{X} : x \in y^*)$	**return** m

Fig. 2. Experiment of the IND-CCA2 security for a ABE scheme.

Description of $\mathcal{F}_{\mathsf{ABE}}$ and $\mathcal{P}_{\mathsf{ABE}}$. The ideal functionality $\mathcal{F}_{\mathsf{ABE}}$, presented in Fig. 3, proposes an instance managing several encryptors and decryptors as well as a *single* setup entity designated by the setup role. This setup entity, as its name suggests, deals with the setup algorithm and hence owns the master key pair, which has to remain private. Observe that using hierarchical session identifier property of iUC, an entity in $\mathcal{F}_{\mathsf{ABE}}$ and $\mathcal{P}_{\mathsf{ABE}}$ is supposed to have a session identifier sid the form $(\mathsf{pid}', \mathsf{sid}')$ with pid' the party identifier of the setup entity.

Recall that when encrypting a message, the set of corrupted attributes is required to be static *i.e.*, the environment is not allowed to dynamically obtain decryption key, otherwise is able to trivial distinguish by looking for ciphertext encrypting a leakage, so being impossible to prove secure as shown in [19]. Many scenarios are possible to obtain static corruption of attributes. We have chosen to divide the time in two distinct phases separated by a time $T \in \mathbb{N}$. During the first phase, when $t \leq T$, the environment is allowed to instantiate entities, corrupt them, but also to instantiate decryptors with attributes (thus to obtain decryption keys by corrupting decryptors as well). During the second phase, when $t > T$, the environment is no more allowed to obtain a decryption key of its choice. This modelisation is not unique, one may change hypothesis but is still required to prevent dynamic corruption of decryption keys and attributes.

The encryptor handles Encrypt requests used to encrypt a message. The security of the ABE ideal functionality states that for a given a master public key mpk, a message m and an access policy y, *if mpk is the valid master public key and if there is no corrupted attribute x such that $x \in y$,* then it must be infeasible to distinguish the real message m encrypted in the real protocol and the encryption of the leakage $L(\lambda, m)$ where L is the length-preserving deterministic leakage function. Note that this leakage function is given as a protocol parameter, and can be instantiated by an higher-protocol. A winning adversary against the indistinguishability property of the ABE scheme can be used to construct an distinguisher against the $\mathcal{P}_{ABE}$ and $\mathcal{F}_{ABE}$. In case where the ciphertext encrypts a leakage, the ciphertext and the associated message are stored in the internal state of the instance, later used for the decryption. A ciphertext decryption request handled by entities having the decryptor role expects as an input a ciphertext ψ_y. The procedure is only executed when the decryptor entity has been registered to have a decryption key sk_x. In case where the received ciphertext is stored in the internal state, along the associated plaintext then the plaintext is directly returned as a response. If the ciphertext is not stored in the internal state, therefore the ciphertext has been computed outside of the ideal functionality and hence no security can be proven. So we decrypt ψ_y using the provided decryption algorithm Dec and returns the output as the plaintext response. Our real attribute-based encryption protocol $\mathcal{P}_{ABE}$, presented in Fig. 4, follows the specification of $\mathcal{F}_{ABE}$, hence we omit the full description.

Lemma 1. *Assuming the existence of a perfectly-correct and IND-CCA2-secure attribute-based encryption $\Pi = (\mathsf{Setup}, \mathsf{Enc}, \mathsf{KeyGen}, \mathsf{Dec})$, then $\mathcal{P}_{ABE} \leq \mathcal{F}_{ABE}$.*

Proof. Suppose a perfectly-correct IND-CCA2-secure attribute-based encryption Π. We start by giving the description of our simulator $\mathcal{S}$, used with our ideal functionality $\mathcal{F}_{ABE}$ in order to show that $\mathcal{P}_{ABE} \leq \mathcal{F}_{ABE}$. The simulator $\mathcal{S}$ starts the simulation by generating a new master key pair $(msk, mpk) \leftarrow \Pi.\mathsf{Setup}(1^\lambda)$, and it sends the initialization request $(mpk, \Pi.\mathsf{Enc}, \Pi.\mathsf{Dec})$ to $\mathcal{F}_{ABE}$. When a request of the form $(\mathtt{InitReceiver}, x)$ is sent from $\mathcal{F}_{ABE}$ to $\mathcal{S}$, an honest decryptor is initialized and hence the simulator generates the decryption key $\mathsf{sk}_x \leftarrow \Pi.\mathsf{KeyGen}(msk, x)$ and responds with sk_x. A notification of the form $(\mathtt{Registered}, x, b)$ is then received from the ideal functionality. If the bit b equals 1, then $\mathcal{S}$ registers than this decryptor has claimed the attribute x, otherwise it ignores the notification. Recall that we place ourself under the static corruption in which the adversary is allowed to corrupt only an entity directly after its initialization and only at this point of the entity lifetime. In details, the static corruption is initiated by the entity, asking to the environment $\mathcal{E}$ its initial corruption status. We now specify the behavior of our simulator acting differently depending on the current time $t \in \mathbb{N}$ with respect to the time $T \in \mathbb{N}$:

Ideal functionality $\mathcal{F}_{ABE} = (\text{setup}, \text{encryptor}, \text{decryptor})$:

Participating roles: setup, encryptor, decryptor
Corruption model: static corruption
Protocol parameters:
- A polynomial $p \in \mathbb{Z}[x]$ used to bound the runtime execution of provided algorithms.
- A deterministic length-preserving leakage function L used to compute leakages.
- A time $T \in \mathbb{N}$ delimiting phase in which decryption keys are provided, from the phase where encryption and decryption are operated. We denote by $t \in \mathbb{N}$ the current time.

$M_{\text{setup,encryptor,decryptor}}$:

Implemented role(s): setup, encryptor, decryptor
Internal state:
- msgList $\subset \{0,1\}^* \times \{0,1\}^* \times \{0,1\}^*$ {*Set of encrypted messages*
- keys $\subset (\{0,1\}^*)^3 \mapsto \{0,1\}^* \times \{0,1\}^*$
- $(mpk, \text{Enc}, \text{Dec}) \in (\{0,1\}^* \cup \bot)^3 = (\bot, \bot, \bot)$
- pidsetup $\in \{0,1\}^* \cup \{\bot\} = \bot$
- corrAttr $\subseteq \{0,1\}^* = \emptyset$

CheckID(pid, sid, role): Check that sid $= (pid', sid')$, then accept every entity with the same SID, otherwise reject.

Corruption behavior:

- **AllowCorruption(pid, sid, role)**: Returns false if role = setup or role = decryptor and $T < t$, otherwise returns true.

Initialization:
  send responsively InitABE **to** NET
  wait for (Init, (mpk', Enc, Dec))
  $(mpk, \text{Enc}, \text{Dec}) \leftarrow mpk', Enc, Dec$
  parse sid_{cur} **as** (pid, sid)
  pidsetup $\leftarrow$ pid

Main:
  recv (InitAttr, x) **from** I/O **to** (_, _, decryptor) **s.t.** keys[entity$_{\text{call}}$] $\neq \bot$:
    send responsively (InitReceiver, x) **to** NET
    wait for (Init, sk$_x$)
    for $(m, y, \psi_y) \in$ msgList:
      $m' \leftarrow \text{Dec}^{(p)}(\text{sk}_x, \psi_y)$
      if $(x \in y \wedge m' \neq L(\lambda, m)) \vee (x \notin y \wedge m' \neq \bot)$:
        send (Registered, x, 0) **to** NET   {*Decryption correctness failure*
    keys[entity$_{\text{call}}$] $\leftarrow (x, \text{sk}_x)$
    send (Registered, x, 1) **to** NET

  recv (CorrAttr, x) **from** NET **s.t.** $t \leq T$:
    add x **to** corrAttr

  recv PubKey? **from** _ **to** (pidsetup, _, setup) :
    reply (PubKey, mpk)

  recv (Encrypt, y, m, mpk') **from** I/O **to** (_, _, encryptor) **s.t.** $T < t$:
    if $mpk \neq mpk' \vee \exists x \in$ corrAttr **s.t.** $x \in y$:
      $\psi_y \leftarrow \text{Enc}^{(p)}(mpk', y, m)$
      reply (Ciphertext, ψ_y)
    $m' \leftarrow L(\lambda, m)$
    $\psi_y \leftarrow \text{Enc}^{(p)}(mpk, y, m')$
    for $(\_, (x, \text{sk}_x)) \in$ keys:
      if $(x \in y \wedge \text{Dec}^{(p)}(\text{sk}_x, \psi_y) \neq m') \vee (x \notin y \wedge \text{Dec}^{(p)}(\text{sk}_x, \psi_y) \neq \bot)$:
        reply (Ciphertext, $\bot$)   {*Encrytion correctness failure*
    add (m, y, ψ_y) **to** msgList
    reply (Ciphertext, ψ_y)

  recv (Decrypt, ψ_y) **from** I/O **to** (_, _, decryptor) **s.t.** $T < t \wedge$ keys[entity$_{\text{cur}}$] $\neq \bot$:
    $(x, \text{sk}_x) \leftarrow$ keys[entity$_{\text{cur}}$]
    if $\nexists(\_, \_, \psi_y) \in$ msgList: **reply** (Plaintext, $\text{Dec}^{(p)}(\text{sk}_x, \psi_y)$)
    if $\exists m, m'$ **s.t.** $(m, \_, \psi_y), (m', \_, \psi_y) \in$ msgList $\wedge m \neq m'$: **reply** (Plaintext, $\bot$)
    get (m, y, ψ_y) **from** msgList
    if $x \notin y$: **reply** (Plaintext, $\bot$)   {*Incompatible policy-access*
    reply (Plaintext, m)

Fig. 3. Description of our ideal functionality $\mathcal{F}_{ABE}$.

Protocol $\mathcal{P}_{\mathsf{ABE}} = (\texttt{setup}, \texttt{encryptor}, \texttt{decryptor})$:

Participating roles: setup, encryptor, decryptor
Corruption model: static corruption
Protocol parameters:
  – An IND-CCA2 attribute-based encryption scheme $\Pi = (\mathsf{Setup}, \mathsf{KeyGen}, \mathsf{Enc}, \mathsf{Dec})$
  – A time $T \in \mathbb{N}$ from which corruption and decryption keys are not allowed. We denote by $t \in \mathbb{N}$ the current time.

$M_{\texttt{setup}}$:

Implemented role(s): setup
Internal state:
  – $mpk \in \{0,1\}^* \cup \{\bot\} = \bot$
  – $msk \in \{0,1\}^* \cup \{\bot\} = \bot$
  – $\mathsf{pidsetup} \in \{0,1\}^* \cup \{\bot\} = \bot$
  – $\mathsf{keys} : (\{0,1\}^*)^3 \to \{0,1\}^*$

CheckID(pid, sid, role): Check that $\mathsf{sid} = (\mathsf{pid}', \mathsf{sid}')$. Accept a single entity.
Corruption behavior:

  – **AllowCorruption**(pid, sid, role): return false
Initialization:
  $(msk, mpk) \leftarrow \mathsf{Setup}(1^\lambda)$
  parse $\mathsf{sid_{cur}}$ **as** $(\mathsf{pid}, \mathsf{sid})$
  $\mathsf{pidsetup} \leftarrow \mathsf{pid}$
Main:
  recv PubKey? **from** _ **to** (pidsetup, _, setup) :
    reply (PubKey, mpk)

  recv (Register, x) **from** (_, _, decryptor) **to** (pidsetup, _, setup) :
    if keys[entity$_{\mathsf{call}}$] $\neq \bot$: **reply** (Registered, $\bot$)
    $\mathsf{sk}_x \leftarrow \mathsf{KeyGen}(msk, x)$
    keys[entity$_{\mathsf{call}}$] $\leftarrow \mathsf{sk}_x$
    reply (Registered, sk_x)

$M_{\texttt{encryptor}}$:

Implemented role(s): encryptor
CheckID(pid, sid, role): Check that $\mathsf{sid} = (\mathsf{pid}', \mathsf{sid}')$. Accept a single entity.
Corruption behavior:

  – **AllowAdvMessage**(pid, sid, role, pid$_{\mathsf{recv}}$, sid$_{\mathsf{recv}}$, role$_{\mathsf{recv}}$, m): Check that (pid = pid$_{\mathsf{recv}}$). Otherwise, returns role$_{\mathsf{recv}} \neq$ setup or m does not start with Register.
Main:
  recv (Encrypt, y, m, mpk) **from** I/O **s.t.** $T < t$:
    $\psi_y \leftarrow \mathsf{Enc}(mpk, y, m)$
    reply (Ciphertext, ψ_y)

$M_{\texttt{decryptor}}$:

Implemented role(s): decryptor
Internal state: $(x, \mathsf{sk}_x) \in \{0,1\}^* \times \{0,1\}^* = (\bot, \bot)$ {*Decryption key*
CheckID(pid, sid, role): Check that $\mathsf{sid} = (\mathsf{pid}', \mathsf{sid}')$. Accept a single entity.
Corruption behavior:

  – **AllowAdvMessage**(pid, sid, role, pid$_{\mathsf{recv}}$, sid$_{\mathsf{recv}}$, role$_{\mathsf{recv}}$, m): If role$_{\mathsf{recv}} =$ setup and m starts with Register and $T < t$, outputs false. Otherwise, outputs pid = pid$_{\mathsf{recv}}$.
Main:
  recv (InitAttr, x) **from** I/O **s.t.** $\mathsf{sk}_x = \bot$:
    parse $\mathsf{sid_{cur}}$ **as** $(\mathsf{pid}, \mathsf{sid})$
    send (Register, x) **to** (pid, sid$_{\mathsf{cur}}$, setup)
    wait for (Registered, sk'_x)
    if $\mathsf{sk}'_x \neq \bot$: $\mathsf{sk}_x \leftarrow \mathsf{sk}'_x$

  recv (Decrypt, ψ_y) **from** I/O **s.t.** $T < t \wedge \mathsf{sk}_x \neq \bot$:
    $m \leftarrow \mathsf{Dec}(\mathsf{sk}_x, \psi_y)$
    reply (Plaintext, m)

Fig. 4. Description of the protocol $\mathcal{P}_{\mathsf{ABE}}$.

- Case $t \leq T$: In case where the adversary corrupts (directly after the initialization) a decryptor and asks in the decryptor's name to obtain a decryption key to the setup entity using a request of the form (Register, x) in the simulated real protocol, then the simulator executes honestly the decryption key generation code, but also notifies the ideal functionality of the corruption of x with the CorrAttr request.
- Case $T < t$: By construction of our real protocol, every Register requests are blocked and hence no more decryption key is provided to the environment.

Since we assume static corruption, every corruption request sent by the environment to initialized entities is blocked by the simulator, preventing dynamic corruption (under which no security can be proven). To be more clear, we suppose without loss of security that $\mathcal{E}$ always use the valid master public encryption key to an encryptor, since it does not provide any advantage for $\mathcal{E}$ to break the security of Π.

Hybrid 0. This hybrid corresponds to the execution of the ideal protocol $\mathcal{S}|\mathcal{F}_{\mathsf{ABE}}$ with the environment $\mathcal{E}$.

Hybrid 1. In this hybrid, we replace $\mathcal{S}|\mathcal{F}_{\mathsf{ABE}}$ with $\mathcal{S}'|\mathcal{F}_{\mathsf{Fwd}}$ where $\mathcal{S}'$ simulating $\mathcal{S}|\mathcal{F}_{\mathsf{ABE}}$ and where $\mathcal{F}_{\mathsf{Fwd}}$ is a forwarding IITM, transferring every request from $\mathcal{S}'$ to $\mathcal{E}$ and $\mathcal{E}$ to $\mathcal{S}'$. Requests coming from the network interface of $\mathcal{S}'$ are directly transferred to $\mathcal{S}$. Since we do not have perform any modification, we have perfect indistinguishability: $\Pr\left[(\mathcal{E}|\mathcal{S}|\mathcal{F}_{\mathsf{ABE}})(1^\lambda) \to 1\right] = \Pr\left[(\mathcal{E}|\mathcal{S}'|\mathcal{F}_{\mathsf{Fwd}})(1^\lambda) \to 1\right]$. For more clarity, we index all the simulators by the hybrid's index, hence $\mathcal{S}'$ is referred as $\mathcal{S}'_1$.

Hybrid 2. Observe that by the perfect correctness of the attribute-based encryption, the correctness issues occurring during both the register procedure (ensuring valid generation of decryption keys) and during encryption cannot occurs. Hence in this hybrid, we modify $\mathcal{S}'_1$ to construct $\mathcal{S}'_2$ in which we remove these correctness validation procedures in this hybrid without impacting the view of $\mathcal{E}$. Hence, $\Pr\left[(\mathcal{E}|\mathcal{S}'_1|\mathcal{F}_{\mathsf{Fwd}})(1^\lambda) \to 1\right] = \Pr\left[(\mathcal{E}|\mathcal{S}'_2|\mathcal{F}_{\mathsf{Fwd}})(1^\lambda) \to 1\right]$.

Hybrid i for $i \in [2, n+2]$. In this hybrid, we focus on the i-th encryption request sent to the simulator $\mathcal{S}'_i$. In this hybrid, we replace the encryption of the leakage $L(\lambda, m_i)$ by the encryption of the message m_i. Suppose that $\mathcal{E}$ is able to distinguish with a non-negligible probability between $(\mathcal{E}|\mathcal{S}'_i|\mathcal{F}_{\mathsf{Fwd}})(1^\lambda)$ and $(\mathcal{E}|\mathcal{S}'_{i-1}|\mathcal{F}_{\mathsf{Fwd}})(1^\lambda)$. We construct an adversary $\mathcal{A} = (\mathcal{A}_1, \mathcal{A}_2)$ against the security of Π, simulating $\mathcal{E}$ and whose the role is create a perfect simulation of $\mathcal{S}'_i|\mathcal{F}_{\mathsf{Fwd}}$ without having access to the master secret key msk owned by the challenger of the IND-CCA2 game. In details, $\mathcal{A}_1$ is running *before* obtaining the challenge ciphertext, and $\mathcal{A}_2$ continues the run of the simulation of $\mathcal{E}$ *after* that the challenge ciphertext was obtained. The adversary $\mathcal{A}_1$ obtains as the input the encryption key mpk, and has access to the key generation oracle OKeyGen and the decryption oracle ODec. The adversary $\mathcal{A}_1$ works as follows:

- When receiving a PubKey? request, it responds (PubKey, mpk).
- When receiving a InitAttr request, it simulates a Register request with the same provided parameters, described below.

- When $\mathcal{E}$ sends a key generation request of the form $(\mathtt{Register}, x)$ from a decryptor entity: If there is no record $(\mathtt{entity}, \_, \_)$ yet, then it calls the OKeyGen oracle to generate a secret decryption key sk_x associated to the provided attribute x, it registers $(\mathtt{entity}, \mathsf{sk}_x, x)$ and returns sk_x. Otherwise, it returns an error.
- When $\mathcal{E}$ sends a request of the form $(\mathtt{Encrypt}, mpk, y_j, m_j)$ for some $j < i$, then $\mathcal{A}_1$ computes $\psi_j \leftarrow \mathsf{Enc}(mpk, y_j, m_j)$ and responds with $(\mathtt{Ciphertext}, \psi_j)$. When $j = i$, then $\mathcal{A}_1$ computes the leakage $\bar{m}_j \leftarrow L(\lambda, m_j)$ where L is a length-preserving leakage function, and encodes its all internal state in the $\mathtt{state}$ variable, and sends to the challenger the challenge response $((y_j, m_j, \bar{m}_j), \mathtt{state})$.
- When $\mathcal{E}$ sends a decryption request of the form $(\mathtt{Dec}, \psi_j)$ from entity for $j < i$, it checks that the entity has already asked for decryption key sk_x by checking if there is a record $(\mathtt{entity}, \mathsf{sk}_x, x)$. If there is no match, aborts with $(\mathtt{Plaintext}, \bot)$. Otherwise, computes $m_j \leftarrow \Pi.\mathsf{Dec}(\mathsf{sk}_x, \psi_j)$ and returns $(\mathtt{Plaintext}, m_j)$.

We now describe our second adversary $\mathcal{A}_2$ taking as an input the challenge ciphertext ψ_i and the state $\mathtt{state}$ constructed by $\mathcal{A}_1$ used to continue the simulation of $\mathcal{E}$. The adversary $\mathcal{A}_2$ works as follows:

- The adversary $\mathcal{A}_2$ begins its simulation by sending the ciphertext ψ_i to $\mathcal{E}$, that is supposed to encrypt either m_i or $\bar{m}_i$. Observe that when m_i is encrypted, then $\mathcal{A}$ is simulating $(\mathcal{E}|\mathcal{S}_i')$ or $(\mathcal{E}|\mathcal{S}_{i-1}')$ otherwise.
- The InitAttr and Register requests are the same as defined for $\mathcal{A}_1$.
- When $\mathcal{E}$ sends a request of the form $(\mathtt{Encrypt}, mpk, y_j, m_j)$ for some $j > i$, then it computes $\psi_j \leftarrow \mathsf{Enc}(mpk, y_j, L(\lambda, m_j))$ and records (ψ_j, y, m) and finally responds with $(\mathtt{Ciphertext}, \psi_j)$.
- When $\mathcal{E}$ sends a decryption request of the form $(\mathtt{Dec}, \psi_j)$ from entity for $j > i$: If there is no record $(\mathtt{entity}, \mathsf{sk}_x, x)$ or no record (ψ_j, y, m_j) then it responds with a failure. The case where there is several records for the same ciphertext is not considered since prevented by the attribute-based encryption scheme Π. If $x \in y$, then it responds with $(\mathtt{Plaintext}, m)$, otherwise it responds with $(\mathtt{Plaintext}, \bot)$.
- When $\mathcal{E}$ stops the simulation, $\mathcal{A}_2$ outputs 1 if $\mathcal{E}$ outputs 1. Otherwise, $\mathcal{A}_2$ outputs 0.

It is clear that our adversary $\mathcal{A}$ is polynomial-time. Since $\mathcal{E}$ is universally bounded, hence $\mathcal{A}$ constitutes a valid adversary for our IND-CCA2 experiment. Hence, we have:

$$
\begin{aligned}
\mathsf{Adv}_{\mathcal{A}, \Pi}^{\text{IND-CCA2}} &= \left| \frac{1}{2} \cdot \Pr\left[b' = 0 | b = 0\right] + \frac{1}{2} \cdot \Pr\left[b' = 1 | b = 1\right] - \frac{1}{2} \right| \\
&= \left| \frac{1}{2} \cdot (\Pr\left[b' = 0 | b = 0\right] - \Pr\left[b' = 1 | b = 0\right]) \right| \\
&= \frac{1}{2} \cdot \left| \Pr\left[(\mathcal{E}|\mathcal{S}_i' | \mathcal{F}_{\mathsf{Fwd}})(\lambda) \to 1\right] - \Pr\left[(\mathcal{E}|\mathcal{S}_{i-1}' | \mathcal{F}_{\mathsf{Fwd}})(\lambda) \to 0\right] \right|
\end{aligned}
$$

Therefore, we conclude on the indistinguishability between $\mathcal{E}|\mathcal{S}_2'|\mathcal{F}_{\mathsf{Fwd}}$ and $\mathcal{E}|\mathcal{S}_{n+2}'|\mathcal{F}_{\mathsf{Fwd}}$ by:

$$\left| \Pr\left[(\mathcal{E}|\mathcal{S}_2'|\mathcal{F}_{\mathsf{Fwd}})(\lambda) \to 1 \right] - \Pr\left[(\mathcal{E}|\mathcal{S}_{n+2}'|\mathcal{F}_{\mathsf{Fwd}})(\lambda) \to 0 \right] \right|$$

$$\leq n \cdot \sum_{i=3}^{n+2} \left| \Pr\left[(\mathcal{E}|\mathcal{S}_i'|\mathcal{F}_{\mathsf{Fwd}})(\lambda) \to 1 \right] - \Pr\left[(\mathcal{E}|\mathcal{S}_{i-1}'|\mathcal{F}_{\mathsf{Fwd}})(\lambda) \to 0 \right] \right|$$

$$\leq 2n \cdot \mathsf{Adv}_{\mathcal{A}, \Pi}^{\mathrm{IND\text{-}CCA2}}$$

Hybrid $n + 3$. Observe that at this point, every ciphertext is encrypting the real message. Hence, instead of performing a plaintext recovery from the internal state of our simulator, our modified simulator $\mathcal{S}_{n+3}'$ ignores the ciphertext register and directly performs the decryption. As a consequence, we do not perform the attribute validation check $x \in y$, that we remove from the (simulated) ideal functionality $\mathcal{F}_{\mathsf{ABE}}$. By correctness of the attribute-based encryption, we have $\Pr\left[(\mathcal{E}|\mathcal{S}_{n+2}'|\mathcal{F}_{\mathsf{Fwd}})(1^\lambda) \to 1 \right] = \Pr\left[(\mathcal{E}|\mathcal{S}_{n+3}'|\mathcal{F}_{\mathsf{Fwd}})(1^\lambda) \to 1 \right]$.

Hybrid $n + 4$. This hybrid works exactly as the previous hybrid except that we do not share the master public key in the simulated $\mathcal{F}_{\mathsf{ABE}}$. Instead, the simulated $\mathcal{F}_{\mathsf{ABE}}$ asks the simulator $\mathcal{S}_{n+4}'$ to obtain the master public key and is returned back to the environment. Since the master public key initially stored in the simulated $\mathcal{F}_{\mathsf{ABE}}$ is already the master public key generated by the simulator, then the view of $\mathcal{E}$ is not changed. Similarly, the encryption and the decryption procedures done in the simulated ideal functionality $\mathcal{F}_{\mathsf{ABE}}$ are delegated to the simulators, forwarding for instance the request $(\mathbf{Encrypt}, y, m, mpk)$ to the same encryptor in the simulated $\mathcal{P}_{\mathsf{ABE}}$. We follow the same approach for decryption requests. The response produced by the encryptor or the decryptor in the simulated protocol $\mathcal{P}_{\mathsf{ABE}}$ is returned back to the simulated ideal functionality $\mathcal{F}_{\mathsf{ABE}}$, forwarding the response to the environment $\mathcal{E}$. Finally, since the simulated $\mathcal{F}_{\mathsf{ABE}}$ does note use its internal state anymore, we remove it. Observe that all these modifications does not affect the view of $\mathcal{E}$ since the simulated ideal functionality $\mathcal{F}_{\mathsf{ABE}}$ was not performing any check or internal state access. Hence, we have $\Pr\left[(\mathcal{E}|\mathcal{S}_{n+3}'|\mathcal{F}_{\mathsf{Fwd}})(1^\lambda) \to 1 \right] = \Pr\left[(\mathcal{E}|\mathcal{S}_{n+4}'|\mathcal{F}_{\mathsf{Fwd}})(1^\lambda) \to 1 \right]$.

At this point, our simulator $\mathcal{S}_{n+4}'$ constitutes the most interesting part of the protocol, encrypting, decrypting and generating keys for entities, without performing any attribute validation (as done in our original $\mathcal{F}_{\mathsf{ABE}}$ *i.e.*, $x \in y$), and does not consider any internal state between the simulated entities. In other words, $\mathcal{S}_{n+4}'$ is our real protocol $\mathcal{P}_{\mathsf{ABE}}$. Even more, the simulated ideal functionality $\mathcal{F}_{\mathsf{ABE}}$ is now limited to forward the machine. As result, our simulator $\mathcal{S}_{n+4}'$ is now connected to the environment via the intermediate of two forwards machines. By removing these two forward machines $\mathcal{F}_{\mathsf{Fwd}}$ from $\mathcal{S}'|\mathcal{F}_{\mathsf{Fwd}}|\mathcal{F}_{\mathsf{Fwd}}$ and connect every wires from the environment via the $\mathtt{I/O}$ interface directly to $\mathcal{S}_{n+4}'$, all these modifications being structural, we are ensured to have a perfect indistinguishability. Since all parties are simulated by $\mathcal{F}_{\mathsf{ABE}}$ and each party follows the instruction of the real protocol $\mathcal{P}_{\mathsf{ABE}}$ without having access to any shared register between entities, we have $(\mathcal{E}|\mathcal{S}_{n+4}') = (\mathcal{E}|\mathcal{P}_{\mathsf{ABE}})$. By our hybrid argument, we have shown that $(\mathsf{Enc}|\mathcal{S}|\mathcal{F}_{\mathsf{ABE}}) \equiv (\mathsf{Enc}|\mathcal{P}_{\mathsf{ABE}})$, thus $\mathcal{P}_{\mathsf{ABE}} \le \mathcal{F}_{\mathsf{ABE}}$. Since the protocol is environmentally bounded and complete, then the Lemma 1 holds.

4   Authenticated Attribute-Based File Transfer

4.1   Description of Our Ideal Functionality $\mathcal{F}_{\mathsf{AAFT}}$

Our authenticated attribute-based file transfer ideal functionality $\mathcal{F}_{\mathsf{AAFT}}$ depicted in Fig. 5, has been designed to allow an higher-protocol to easily rely on authenticated attribute-based file transfer. Each entity managed by the instance of $\mathcal{F}_{\mathsf{AAFT}}$ is associated to one of two following roles: A role sender representing an entity sending a file and a role receiver receiving a file. The ideal functionality maintains three distinct internal states attr, sentFiles and receivedFiles used

Ideal functionality $\mathcal{F}_{\mathsf{AAFT}} = (\mathbf{sender}, \mathbf{receiver})$:

Participating roles: sender, receiver
Corruption model: static corruption
Protocol parameters:
 – A time $T \in \mathbb{N}$ delimiting phase in which file sending is not accessible. We denote by $t \in \mathbb{N}$ the current time.

$M_{\mathbf{sender},\mathbf{receiver}}$:

CheckID(pid, sid, role): Accept all entities with the same SID.
Corruption behavior:
 – **AllowCorruption**(pid, sid, role): Returns role $\neq$ decryptor or $t < T$.
Internal state:
 – attr $\subseteq (\{0,1\}^*)^3 \times \{0,1\}^* \times \{0,1\} = \emptyset$
 – sentFiles $\subseteq (\{0,1\}^*)^3 \times \{0,1\}^* \times \{0,1\}^* \times \{0,1\}^* = \emptyset$
 – receivedFiles $\subseteq (\{0,1\}^*)^3 \times \{0,1\}^* = \emptyset$
Main:
   recv (InitAttr, x) from I/O to ($\_, \_$, receiver) s.t. $\nexists$(entity$_{\mathbf{cur}}, \cdot, \cdot$) $\in$ attr :
     add (entity$_{\mathbf{cur}}, x, 0$) to attr
     send (Registered, x) to NET

   recv (CorrAttr, $receiver, x$) from NET s.t. $t \le T$:
     get $(receiver, x, b)$ from attr
     $b \leftarrow 1$

   recv (Send, f, y) from I/O to ($\_, \_$, sender) s.t. $T < t$:
     $r \leftarrow\!\!\$\ \{0,1\}^\lambda$
     add (entity$_{\mathbf{cur}}, y, r, f$) to sentFiles
     if $\exists\ (\cdot, x, 1)$ s.t. $x \in y$:
       send (SendCorrupted, y, r, f) to NET
     else:
       send (SendHonest, $y, r, |f|$) to NET

   recv (Receive, $y, r, sender$) from NET to ($\_, \_$, receiver) :
     if $\nexists\ (sender, \cdot, r, \cdot) \in$ sentFiles:
       send responsively (WaitFile, $y, r, sender$) to NET
       wait for (ProvideFile, b, f)
       if $b = 1$:
         add (entity$_{\mathbf{cur}}, f$) to receivedFiles
     else:
       get $(sender, y, r, f)$ from sentFiles
       if attr[entity$_{\mathbf{cur}}$] $\in y$:
         add (entity$_{\mathbf{cur}}, f$)

   recv Collect from I/O to ($\_, \_$, receiver) :
     reply $\mathcal{F} = \{f : (\text{entity}_{\mathbf{cur}}, f) \in \text{receivedFiles}\}$

Fig. 5. Description of our ideal functionality $\mathcal{F}_{\mathsf{AAFT}}$.

respectively to remember inputted and corrupted attributes, to authenticate files sent by honest senders and finally to store valid received files, eventually shared with the environment via the Collect request.

A sender handles only Send requests coming from the I/O interface, expecting as a parameter the input data file f as well as the access policy y. A short tag r is uniformly sampled from $\{0,1\}^\lambda$ and stored along the file f and the access policy y into the sentFiles internal states, shared between all entities (sharing the same session identifier). This set consists of all authenticated files. To send the file, the ideal functionality shares the file to the simulator $\mathcal{S}$ using one of two manner depending on the corruption of attributes: If the environment has an attribute $x \in y$ then confidentiality of the file f cannot be ensured, hence shared with $\mathcal{S}$. On the other hand, the environment does not have an attribute $x \in y$, hence the file is not shared with the simulator $\mathcal{S}$. It models confidentiality in the sense that it remains safely in the ideal functionality, following the standard encryption in UC such that [18] producing ciphertext encrypting a leakage instead of the real plaintext. In contrast with the Send request handling requests from the higher-protocol, the file reception modelled by the Receive request is received from the NET interface $i.e.$, from the simulator. This is motivated by the real-life mail system in which the server receives files from the network, awaiting the user to connect in order to collect messages. It is up to the simulator to correctly simulates the protocol and notifies the ideal functionality if a receiver receives a file. Observe that the code for Receive ensures, in case of honest sender, authentication and file access depending on the attribute x owned by the current receiver by checking if $x \in y$. If the sender is corrupted, then authentication and file access is delegated to the simulator.

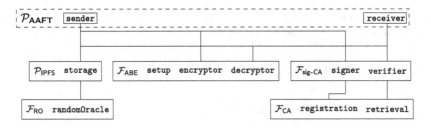

Fig. 6. Graphical representation of our protocol $\mathcal{P}_{\mathsf{AAFT}}$. The random oracle ideal functionality $\mathcal{F}_{\mathsf{RO}}$ comes from [18], whereas the ideal functionalities for digital signature $\mathcal{F}_{\mathsf{sig\text{-}CA}}$ and certificate authority $\mathcal{F}_{\mathsf{CA}}$ comes from [8].

Observe that the Send and CorrAttr functions are accessible only if the current time $t \in \mathbb{N}$ is strictly greater than a constant time $T \in \mathbb{N}$ defined as a parameter of the protocol, a crucial restriction to include the ABE ideal functionality in our hybrid protocol. This restriction leads us to seperate the time in two distinct phases. During the first phase, we allow the environment to instantiate any entities but also to *statically corrupt* any entity of its choice, including receivers and hence to obtain attributes. During the second phase, we prevent the environment to corrupt a receiver, and allow the environment to send a file.

4.2 Our Hybrid Protocol $\mathcal{P}_{\mathsf{AAFT}}$

Depicted in Fig. 6, our hybrid protocol $\mathcal{P}_{\mathsf{AAFT}}$ is proved to realize our ideal functionality $\mathcal{F}_{\mathsf{AAFT}}$. It relies on several subroutines to model respectively a certificate

Ideal functionality $\mathcal{F}_{\mathsf{CA}} = (\texttt{registration}, \texttt{retrieval})$:

Participating roles: registration, retrieval
Corruption model: incorruptible

$M_{\texttt{registration,retrieval}}$:

Implemented role(s): {registration, retrieval}
Internal state:
- keys : $(\{0,1\}^*)^2 \to \{0,1\}^* \cup \{\bot\}$

CheckID(pid, sid, role): Accept all entities.
Main:
　recv (RegisterKey, key) from I/O to ($\_$, $\_$, registration) :
　　if keys[pid$_{\mathsf{call}}$, sid$_{\mathsf{call}}$] $\neq \bot$:
　　　reply (RegisteredKey, false)
　　else:
　　　keys[pid$_{\mathsf{call}}$, sid$_{\mathsf{call}}$] $\leftarrow key$
　　　reply (RegisteredKey, true)
　recv (RetrieveKey, (pid, sid)) from $\_$ to ($\_$, $\_$, retrieval) :
　　reply (RetrievedKey, keys[pid, sid])

Ideal functionality $\mathcal{F}_{\mathsf{RO}} = (\texttt{randomOracle})$:

Participating roles: randomOracle
Corruption model: incorruptible

$M_{\texttt{randomOracle}}$:

Implemented role(s): randomOracle
Internal state:
- H $\subseteq \{0,1\}^* \times \{0,1\}^\lambda = \emptyset$

CheckID(pid, sid, role): Accept all entities.
Main:
　recv (Hash, m) from $\_$:
　　if $\exists (m, h) \in$ H:
　　　reply (Hashed, h)
　　else:
　　　$h \leftarrow\!\!{}_\$ \{0,1\}^\lambda$
　　　add (m, h) to H
　　　reply (Hashed, h)

Fig. 7. Ideal functionalities $\mathcal{F}_{\mathsf{CA}}$ [8] and $\mathcal{F}_{\mathsf{RO}}$ [18].

authority, the random oracle, digital signatures, but also IPFS being part of our contribution. We first present all these subroutines before to introduce our hybrid protocol $\mathcal{P}_{\mathsf{AAFT}}$.

Description of $\mathcal{F}_{\mathsf{CA}}$. The Certificate Authority (CA) allows to register public keys and certifying that a given public key corresponds to some user. The modelisation of $\mathcal{F}_{\mathsf{CA}}$ presented in Fig. 7 is taken from [8], consisting of two roles `registration` and `retrieval`, permitting respectively to register key and to retrieve a public key pk associated to the pair (pid, sid). Since the ideal functionality is self-explained, we omit its description, and only notice that the instance of $\mathcal{F}_{\mathsf{CA}}$ cannot be corrupted by the adversary and manages all entities, meaning that there is a single instance.

Description of $\mathcal{F}_{\mathsf{RO}}$. The ideal functionality $\mathcal{F}_{\mathsf{RO}}$ introduced in [18] and presented in Fig. 7 exposes a single role `randomOracle`. This straightforward ideal functionality handles `Hash` requests given an arbitrary-sized bitstring m, associates a λ-sized random bitstring h. In particular, if m was never queried before, then $\mathcal{F}_{\mathsf{RO}}$ generates a random bitstring h, stores the couple (m, h) and returns h. Otherwise (m has already been queried), and thus $\mathcal{F}_{\mathsf{RO}}$ returns the h associated to m. Similarly to $\mathcal{F}_{\mathsf{CA}}$, we assume that the ideal functionality $\mathcal{F}_{\mathsf{RO}}$ manages all entities, meaning that there is a single instance of $\mathcal{F}_{\mathsf{RO}}$ in the protocol.

Protocol $\mathcal{P}_{\mathsf{IPFS}} = (\texttt{storage})$:

Participating roles: storage
Corruption model: dynamic corruption without erasure

$M_{\texttt{storage}}$:

Subroutines: $\mathcal{F}_{\mathsf{RO}}$: `randomOracle`
Implemented role(s): storage
Internal state:
  – files : $\{0,1\}^* \to \{0,1\}^* = \emptyset$ {*Stored files*
CheckID(pid, sid, role): Accept a single entity.
Main:
   recv (Upload, f) from _____ :
      send (Hash, f) to $(\overline{\mathsf{pid}}_{\mathbf{cur}}, \mathsf{sid}_{\mathbf{cur}}, \mathcal{F}_{\mathsf{RO}} : \texttt{randomOracle})$
      wait for (Hashed, l)
      files[l] $\leftarrow f$
      reply (Uploaded, l)

   recv Links from _____ :
      reply $\{l : \forall l \mapsto f \in \mathsf{files}\}$

   recv (Download, l) from _____ :
      reply (Downloaded, files[l])

Fig. 8. Protocol $\mathcal{P}_{\mathsf{IPFS}}$ for a storage server in the IPFS network.

Description of $\mathcal{P}_{\mathsf{IPFS}}$. An IPFS network consists of connected servers, maintaining an internal state associating to a file f a link l where l is the hash of f computed using the cryptographic hash function. IPFS plays a central role in the efficiency of our construction by allowing a potentially large data to be transferred over a distributed storage network. We have modelled a single storage server in iUC as a real protocol denoted $\mathcal{P}_{\mathsf{IPFS}}$ and depicted in Fig. 8. A storage server having the role storage, relies on the random oracle $\mathcal{F}_{\mathsf{RO}}$ used to hash files. It is equipped of the three following functions: Upload used to store files, Links returning all saved links, and Download which given a link l returns

---

Ideal functionality $\mathcal{F}_{\mathsf{sig\text{-}CA}} = (\mathsf{signer}, \mathsf{verifier})$:

Participating roles: signer, verifier
Corruption model: static corruption
Protocol parameters:
- A polynomial $p \in \mathbb{Z}[x]$ used to bound the runtime execution of provided algorithms.

$M_{\mathsf{signer,verifier}}$:

Implemented role(s): signer, verifier
Subroutines: $\mathcal{F}_{\mathsf{CA}}$: registration
Internal state:
- $(\mathsf{Sign}, \mathsf{Verif}, \mathsf{pk}, \mathsf{sk}) \in (\{0,1\}^* \cup \{\bot\})^4 = (\bot, \bot, \bot, \bot)$
- $\mathsf{pidowner} \in \{0,1\}^* \cup \{\bot\} = \bot$
- $\mathsf{msgList} \subseteq \{0,1\}^* = \emptyset$
- $\mathsf{KeysGenerated} \in \{\mathsf{ready}, \bot\} = \bot$

CheckID(pid, sid, role): Check that sid has a $(\mathsf{pid}', \mathsf{sid}')$ format. If the check fails, return false, otherwise accept all entities with the same SID.

Corruption behavior:
- **LeakedData(pid, sid, role):** If called while (pid, sid, role) determines its initial corruption status, use the default behavior of **LeakedData**. That is, output the initially received message and the sender of that message. Otherwise, if role = signer and pid = pidowner, return KeysGenerated. In all other cases, return $\bot$.
- **AllowAdvMessage(pid, sid, role, pid$_{\mathsf{recv}}$, sid$_{\mathsf{recv}}$, role$_{\mathsf{recv}}$, m):** Check that (pid = pid$_{\mathsf{recv}}$). If role$_{\mathsf{recv}}$ = $\mathcal{F}_{\mathsf{CA}}$: registration, also check that role = signer and sid = (pid, sid'). If all checks succeed, output true, otherwise output false.

Initialization:
  send responsively InitMe **to** NET
  wait for (Init, $(Sign, Verif, pk, sk)$)
  $(\mathsf{Sign}, \mathsf{Verif}, \mathsf{pk}, \mathsf{sk}) \leftarrow (Sign, Verif, pk, sk)$
  parse sid$_{\mathsf{cur}}$ **as** (pid, sid)
  pidowner $\leftarrow$ pid

Main:
  recv InitSign **from** I/O **to** (pidowner, _, signer) :
    send (RegisterKey, pk) **to** (pid$_{\mathsf{cur}}$, ϵ, $\mathcal{F}_{\mathsf{CA}}$: registration)
    wait for (RegisterKey, _)
    KeysGenerated $\leftarrow$ true
    reply (InitSign, 1)

  recv (Sign, m) **from** I/O **to** (pidowner, _, signer) **s.t.** KeysGenerated = true :
    $\sigma_m \leftarrow \mathsf{Sign}^{(p)}(m, \mathsf{sk})$
    $b \leftarrow \mathsf{Verif}^{(p)}(m, \sigma_m, \mathsf{pk})$
    if $\sigma_m = \bot \vee b \neq 1$:
      reply (Signature, $\bot$)
    else:
      add m to msgList
      reply (Signature, σ_m)

  recv (Verify, m, σ_m, pk) **from** I/O **to** (_, _, verifier) :
    $b \leftarrow \mathsf{Verif}^{(p)}(m, \sigma_m, pk)$
    if $pk = \mathsf{pk} \wedge b = 1 \wedge m \notin \mathsf{msgList} \wedge (\mathsf{pidowner}, \mathsf{sid}_{\mathsf{cur}}, \mathsf{signer}) \notin$ CorruptionSet:
      reply (VerResult, false)   *{Prevents the signature forgeries*
    reply (VerResult, b)

Fig. 9. Description of the ideal functionality $\mathcal{F}_{\mathsf{sig\text{-}CA}}$ [8].

the file f associated with l. A storage server is not intended to provide more than the efficiency in our construction. Hence it can be dynamically corrupted without erasure *i.e.*, corruption occurs at any time, leaving the full control of the corrupted server to the adversary, all its internal state being leaked.

Description of $\mathcal{F}_{\text{sig-CA}}$. The ideal functionality for digital signature, introduced in [8] and recalled in Fig. 9, is composed of the two roles **signer** and **verifier**, allowing respectively to create a signature of a given message and to verify a signature. During the instance initialization, the party identifier pid' of the signer is obtained from the session identifier having the form $\text{sid} = (\text{pid}', \text{sid}')$. Before providing any signature, the signer expects from the higher protocol an initialization request allowing the signer to register the verification key pk to the certificate authority, modelled via the $\mathcal{F}_{\text{CA}}$ ideal functionality. After this initialization step, the signer is allowed to sign any message. Note that before returning the signature, the signer stores the signed message m in a set of authenticated messages

Protocol $\mathcal{P}_{\text{AAFT}} = (\textsf{sender}, \textsf{receiver})$:

Participating roles: sender, receiver
Subroutines: $\mathcal{F}_{\text{ABE}}, \mathcal{F}_{\text{sig-CA}}, \mathcal{F}_{\text{CA}}$: retrieval, $\mathcal{F}_{\text{RO}}, \mathcal{P}_{\text{IPFS}}$
Corruption model: static corruption
Protocol parameters:
- The party identifier pidsetup, identifying the entity of the ABE scheme handling the master keys.
- A time $T \in \mathbb{N}$ delimiting phase in which decryption keys are provided, from the phase where encryption and decryption are operated. We denote by $t \in \mathbb{N}$ the current time.

$M_{\textsf{sender}}$:

Implemented role(s): sender
CheckID(pid, sid, role): Accept a single entity.
Internal state:
  - $mpk \in \{0,1\}^* \cup \{\bot\} = \bot$
Corruption behavior:
  - **DetermineCorrStatus**(pid, sid, role): return corr(pid, (pid, ϵ), signer) or corr(pid, (pidsetup, sid), encryptor).
  - **AllowAdvMessage**(pid, sid, role, pid_{recv}, sid_{recv}, $\text{role}_{\text{recv}}$, m): Check that (pid = pid_{recv}).
Initialization:
  send PubKey? to (pidsetup, (pidsetup, sid_{cur}), $\mathcal{F}_{\text{ABE}}$: setup)
  wait for mpk'
  $mpk \leftarrow mpk'$
  send InitSign to $(\text{pid}_{\text{cur}}, (\text{pid}_{\text{cur}}, \epsilon)), \mathcal{F}_{\text{sig-CA}}$: signer)
  wait for _
Main:
  recv (Send, y, f) from I/O s.t. $T < t$:
    send responsively Storage? to NET
    wait for (Storage, $storage$)
    send (Encrypt, y, f, mpk) to $(\text{pid}_{\text{cur}}, \text{sid}_{\text{cur}}, \mathcal{F}_{\text{ABE}}$: encryptor)
    wait for (Ciphertext, ψ_y)
    send (Upload, (y, ψ_y)) to $storage$
    wait for _
    send (Hash, (y, ψ_y)) to $(\text{pid}_{\text{cur}}, \text{sid}_{\text{cur}}, \mathcal{F}_{\text{RO}}$: randomOracle)
    wait for (Hashed, l)
    send (Sign, l) to $(\text{pid}_{\text{cur}}, (\text{pid}_{\text{cur}}, \epsilon), \mathcal{F}_{\text{sig-CA}}$: signer)
    wait for (Signature, σ_l)
    send (Sent, l, σ_l) to NET

Fig. 10. Description of our protocol $\mathcal{P}_{\text{AAFT}}$ (Part 1)

managed by the instance, used later for the signature verification. To verify a signature, an entity having the verifier role expects as an input a message m, a signature σ_m and a public verification key pk. The security of a digital signature is modelled by the ideal functionality by always rejecting every valid signature σ_m coming from an uncorrupted signer whose the message m does not belong to the set of authenticated messages, and whose the provided verification key pk is the valid one (*i.e.*, the public verification key provided by the adversary in the ideal functionality).

$$M_{\text{receiver}}:$$

Implemented role(s): receiver
Internal state:
  − initiated $\in \{0, 1\} = 0$
  − files $\subseteq \{0, 1\}^* = \emptyset$
CheckID(pid, sid, role): Check that sid $=$ (pid′, sid′). Accept a single entity.
Corruption behavior:
  − **AllowCorruption**(pid, sid, role): Returns $t < T$.
  − **DetermineCorrStatus**(pid, sid, role): return corr(pid, (pidsetup, sid), decryptor).
  − **AllowAdvMessage**(pid, sid, role, pid_{recv}, sid_{recv}, $\text{role}_{\text{recv}}$, m): Check that (pid $=$ pid_{recv}).
Main:
  recv (InitAttr, x) **from** I/O **s.t.** initiated $= 0$:
    initiated $\leftarrow 1$
    send (InitAttr, x) **to** (pid_{cur}, sid_{cur}, $\mathcal{P}_{\text{ABE}}$: decryptor)

  recv (Receive, *sender*, *storage*, l, σ_l) **from** NET **s.t.** $T < t \wedge$ initiated $= 1$:
    parse *storage* **as** (_, _, $\mathcal{P}_{\text{IPFS}}$: storage), *sender* **as** (pid, _, sender)
    send (Download, l) **to** *storage*
    wait for (Downloaded, (y, ψ_y))
    send (RetreiveKey, (pid, ϵ)) **to** (pid_{cur}, sid_{cur}, $\mathcal{F}_{\text{CA}}$: retrieval)
    wait for (RetreivedKey, pk)
    send (Verify, l, σ_l, pk) **to** (pid_{cur}, (pid, ϵ), $\mathcal{F}_{\text{sig-CA}}$: verifier)
    wait for (VerResult, b)
    send (Hash, (y, ψ_y)) **to** (pid_{cur}, sid_{cur}, randomOracle)
    wait for (Hashed, l')
    send (Decrypt, ψ_y) **to** (pid_{cur}, (pidsetup, sid_{cur}), $\mathcal{F}_{\text{ABE}}$: decryptor)
    wait for (Plaintext, f)
    if $l = l' \wedge b = 1 \wedge f \neq \perp$: **add** f to files

  recv Collect **from** I/O :
    reply files

Fig. 11. Description of our protocol $\mathcal{P}_{\text{AAFT}}$ (Part 2)

Description of Our Hybrid Protocol $\mathcal{P}_{\text{AAFT}}$. We are now ready to introduce $\mathcal{P}_{\text{AAFT}}$ our hybrid file transfer protocol based on a hash-based distributed storage system in Fig. 10 and Fig. 11. Since our protocol is self-explained, we only highlight the overall behavior. During the reception of a file f along an access policy y, an honest sender encrypts f using the ideal functionality $\mathcal{F}_{\text{ABE}}$ to obtain the ciphertext ψ_y. This ciphertext is hashed to obtain the link l and is sent to the storage (chosen by environment $\mathcal{E}$). After having obtained the signature σ_l for l, the sender shares the link l along the signature σ_l with the environment $\mathcal{E}$. When receiving a link l, a signature σ_l and two identities respectively for the storage and the sender, an honest receiver checks the validity of the signature with respect to the signer and the link and decrypts the ciphertext ψ_y, previously obtained from the designated storage server.

Theorem 1. *Assuming ideal functionalities for certificate authority $\mathcal{F}_{CA}$, digital signature $\mathcal{F}_{sig\text{-}CA}$, random oracle $\mathcal{F}_{RO}$ and attribute-based encryption $\mathcal{F}_{ABE}$ and the IPFS protocol $\mathcal{P}_{IPFS}$, then $(\text{sender}, \text{receiver}|\mathcal{F}_{RO}, \mathcal{F}_{ABE}, \mathcal{F}_{sig\text{-}CA}, \mathcal{F}_{CA}, \mathcal{P}_{IPFS})$ realizes $\mathcal{F}_{AAFT}$.*

Proof. We start this proof by giving a description of our simulator $\mathcal{S}$, used with the ideal functionality $\mathcal{F}_{AAFT}$ to show that $\mathcal{P}_{AAFT} \leq \mathcal{S}|\mathcal{F}_{AAFT}$. In a nutshell, $\mathcal{S}$ runs a simulation of the real protocol and handles request coming from both the environment and the ideal functionality. During the simulation, without loss of security and functionality, we require the leakage function $L(\lambda, m)$ used by the ideal functionality $\mathcal{F}_{ABE}$ to return a zero-string $0^{|m|}$. We now provide the description of $\mathcal{S}$:

- When receiving a notification request of the form $(\texttt{Registered}, x)$ from the ideal functionality (simulating a receiver), attesting the access to some attribute x. In such case, inputs the same receiver in the simulated real protocol with $(\texttt{InitAttr}, x)$.
- When receiving a corruption request from the environment to corrupt the entity entity defined by the triplet (pid, sid, role). If the current time $t < T$, then it accepts the corruption request. Otherwise, ignore the corruption request. Each time a corruption request leads to the corruption either of a sender or a receiver, the simulator notifies the ideal functionality as well, leading to a synchronization of senders and receivers corruption between the simulated real protocol and the ideal functionality. In case where the entity in charge of handling the master secret keys receives a decryption key, assuming $t < T$, then the decryption key sk_x is computed and sent back to the corrupted decryptor. Observe that by construction, a corrupted decryptor equals a corrupted receiver. The simulator $\mathcal{S}$ notifies the ideal functionality that the environment is allowed to decrypt any ciphertext associated with a policy access y whose $x \in y$ by sending the request $(\texttt{CorrAttr}, x)$ to $\mathcal{F}_{AAFT}$.
- When receiving a request of the form $(\texttt{SendHonest}, y, r, |f|)$ or the request of the form $(\texttt{SendCorrupted}, y, r, f)$ from the initial functionality, the simulator inputs the simulated sender of $\mathcal{P}_{AAFT}$ with the access policy y and the real file f in the case of $\texttt{SendCorrupted}$, or the zero-string $0^{|f|}$ of the case of $\texttt{SendHonest}$. In addition, in case of $\texttt{SendHonest}$, the simulator records the pair (r, ψ_y) where ψ_y is the ciphertext obtained via the simulated $\texttt{encryptor}$ from the ideal functionality $\mathcal{F}_{ABE}$. This record is used later to provide the random r to the ideal functionality $\mathcal{F}_{AAFT}$.
- When receiving a request of the form $(\texttt{Receiver}, sender, storage, l, \sigma_l)$ from the environment $\mathcal{E}$ via the network interface, then it inputs the simulated real receiver, running all sanity checks including decryption, signature verification and link validation. Let ψ_y be the ciphertext obtained during the execution of the simulated receiver in $\mathcal{P}_{AAFT}$. If all checks success, then if the simulator recovers the pair (r, ψ_y) and sends $(\texttt{Receive}, y, r, sender)$ to the

ideal functionality $\mathcal{F}_{\mathsf{AAFT}}$, and no response is expected later. Otherwise, there is no records (r, ψ_y) and hence it sends $(\texttt{Receive}, y, \bot, sender)$ to the ideal functionality. By construction, the ideal functionality $\mathcal{F}_{\mathsf{AAFT}}$ responds with a responsive request $(\texttt{WaitFile}, y, r, sender)$ where r equals $\bot$. At this point, the ideal functionality expects a file f to register. Since there is no records by the simulator but the decryptor file f being authenticated, the simulator responds to this responsive request with $(\texttt{ProvideFile}, 1, f)$.

It is clear that our simulator $\mathcal{S}$ is polynomial-time. We are now ready to initiate our sequence of hybrids, where our first hybrid consists of the $(\mathcal{S}|\mathcal{F}_{\mathsf{AAFT}})$ ideal protocol, and our last hybrid is our hybrid protocol $\mathcal{P}_{\mathsf{AAFT}}$:

Hybrid 0. This hybrid is the execution of the ideal protocol $(\mathcal{S}|\mathcal{F}_{\mathsf{AAFT}})$ with the environment $\mathcal{E}$, connected respectively to the NET interface of $\mathcal{S}$ and to the I/O interface of $\mathcal{F}_{\mathsf{AAFT}}$, with $\mathcal{S}$ being connected to the NET interface of $\mathcal{F}_{\mathsf{AAFT}}$.

Hybrid 1. This hybrid works as the previous hybrid, except that we now execute the protocol $(\mathcal{S}'|\mathcal{F}_{\mathsf{Fwd}})$ where $\mathcal{S}'$ runs the simulated ideal protocol $(\mathcal{S}|\mathcal{F}_{\mathsf{AAFT}})$ and where $\mathcal{F}_{\mathsf{Fwd}}$ simply forwards every request from the environment $\mathcal{E}$ to $\mathcal{S}'$ and conversely. Since this modification is only structural without any modification on the ideal protocol behavior, then we have a perfect indistinguishability between these two hybrids. In the following, for a better clarity, we index each simulator $\mathcal{S}'$ with the current hybrid index, hence: $\Pr\left[(\mathcal{E}|\mathcal{S}_1'|\mathcal{F}_{\mathsf{Fwd}})(1^\lambda) \to 1\right] = \Pr\left[(\mathcal{E}|\mathcal{S}|\mathcal{F}_{\mathsf{AAFT}})(1^\lambda) \to 1\right]$.

Hybrid 2. This hybrid works as the previous hybrid, except that we introduce a new simulator $\mathcal{S}_2'$ consisting of $\mathcal{S}_1'$ where we delegate the all attribution verification both during the Send and Receive requests to the simulator $\mathcal{S}$. First, let focus on the Send part of the ideal functionality $\mathcal{F}_{\mathsf{AAFT}}$, currently simulated by our simulator $\mathcal{S}_2'$. We rewrite the code of Send to remove the random r as well as the corrupted attribute condition, all of these lines being replaced only by a request of the form $(\texttt{Send}, y, f)$. The code still stores files being sent by an honest sender, but omits the random r *i.e.,* it records a tuple of the form $(sender, y, f)$. The file reception request in the ideal functionality $\mathcal{F}_{\mathsf{AAFT}}$, handling requests of the form $(\texttt{Receive}, y, r, sender)$, now handles requests of the form $(\texttt{Receive}, y, f, sender)$. The condition verifying of there is no tuple of the form $(sender, \cdot, r, \cdot)$ is still performed but with the tuple of the form $(sender, \cdot, f)$. The random r is replaced by $\bot$ in the code which is executed when the condition is checked. The executed code when the condition fails, including the attribute verification $(x \in y)$, is replaced by the insertion of the file f to the received file register. The simulator, on its side, does not register the pair (r, ψ_y) anymore.

Observe that all these modifications are hidden to the environment, and we claim that the view of the environment remains unchanged. This can be easily deduced since the at this point, the ideal functionality does not perform the attribute verification by itself but rather delegate this task to the ideal functionality $\mathcal{F}_{\mathsf{ABE}}$, which is secure and correct by design. However, compared to the previous hybrid, the received file is now always f instead of the zero-string. In case where the environment does not have a valid decryption key to decrypt ψ_y, it encrypts the leakage $L(\lambda, f)$ in this hybrid, instead of

$L(\lambda, 0^{|f|})$ in the previous one. Thanks to our specification of L, always out-putting a zero-string, both of these leakages are the same. Therefore, by construction of the ideal functionality $\mathcal{F}_{\mathsf{ABE}}$ and by the leakage function L, the environment cannot distinguish, otherwise breaking the security of $\mathcal{F}_{\mathsf{ABE}}$. Hence, $\Pr\left[(\mathcal{E}|\mathcal{S}'_2|\mathcal{F}_{\mathsf{Fwd}})(1^\lambda) \to 1\right] = \Pr\left[(\mathcal{E}|\mathcal{S}'_1|\mathcal{F}_{\mathsf{Fwd}})(1^\lambda) \to 1\right]$.

Hybrid 3. At this point, the (simulated) ideal functionality $\mathcal{F}_{\mathsf{AAFT}}$ still maintain a set of sent files, essentially used to provide authentication of the files for honest senders. An honest receiver, on its side, verifies that a received file f belongs to the set of sent files (with respect to the provided sender) and responds to the simulator via the network interface if the file is not found. Observe that in this case, the simulator already activates the (honest) receiver with a request Receive if and only if the provided signature σ_l authenticates the link l, which corresponds to the hash of the ABE ciphertext ψ_y. Hence, by construction, authentication of the file with respect to the provided sender is already ensured by the signature ideal functionality $\mathcal{F}_{\mathsf{sig-CA}}$. Hence, the condition in the ideal functionality $\mathcal{F}_{\mathsf{AAFT}}$ is no more necessary and all the code handling Receive requests is now limited to add the received file f (added in the previous hybrid) to the set of received files. This constitutes our new simulator $\mathcal{S}'_3$. Since the authentication in the ideal functionality $\mathcal{F}_{\mathsf{sig-CA}}$ is correct and secure by definition, this modification does not impact the view of the environment $\mathcal{E}$ and hence $\Pr\left[(\mathcal{E}|\mathcal{S}'_3|\mathcal{F}_{\mathsf{Fwd}})(1^\lambda) \to 1\right] = \Pr\left[(\mathcal{E}|\mathcal{S}'_2|\mathcal{F}_{\mathsf{Fwd}})(1^\lambda) \to 1\right]$.

Hybrid 4. This hybrid works as the previous hybrid, except that we remove the attribute state attr that are not used anymore in this hybrid. Additionally, we replace the internal state receivedFiles by a local internal state specific to each receiver. This last modification clearly does not affect the view of the environment $\mathcal{E}$. Hence, we have $\Pr\left[(\mathcal{E}|\mathcal{S}'_4|\mathcal{F}_{\mathsf{Fwd}})(1^\lambda) \to 1\right] = \Pr\left[(\mathcal{E}|\mathcal{S}'_3|\mathcal{F}_{\mathsf{Fwd}})(1^\lambda) \to 1\right]$.

Observe that in our last hybrid, the ideal functionality $\mathcal{F}_{\mathsf{AAFT}}$ simulated in our last simulator $\mathcal{S}'_4$ never rely on internal state and essentially constitutes a forward machine between the simulated hybrid protocol and the I/O interface where the environment is connected. As a result, we claim that $\Pr\left[(\mathcal{E}|\mathcal{S}'_4|\mathcal{F}_{\mathsf{Fwd}})(1^\lambda) \to 1\right] = \Pr\left[(\mathcal{E}|\mathcal{P}_{\mathsf{AAFT}})(1^\lambda) \to 1\right]$. Hence, we have $\mathcal{P}_{\mathsf{AAFT}} \leq \mathcal{F}_{\mathsf{AAFT}}$.

4.3   Implementation of $\mathcal{P}_{\mathsf{AAFT}}$

Our open-source proof-of-concept written in Rust confirms the practicality of our protocol [2]. We have chosen the Schnorr signature over the curve25519 curve as our EUF-CMA digital signature. Since our cryptographic hash function handles potentially large files, we have chosen to construct a parallelized Merkle-tree-based hash function using the standard SHA-256 cryptographic hash function as the underlying building block. To construct our IND-CCA2-secure ABE, we have applied the Fujisaki-Okamoto transform [13] on the Agrawal-Chase IND-CPA Ciphertext-Policy ABE scheme [4]. We have used AES-256-CTR as the secret-key encryption within the transform. Benchmarks have been performed on an Ubuntu, embedding a 64 bits Intel Core i5-6500 processor cadenced at 3.20GHz including four cores, and embedding 16Gb of memory.

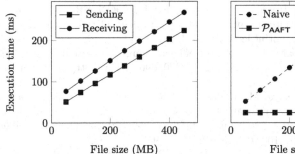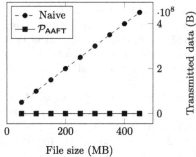

Fig. 12. Evaluation of the sending and receiving execution time (left) and the exchanged data size between users (right).

In Fig. 12 is depicted the execution time of the sending and receiving procedures depending on the input file size. We directly observe that both procedures are mlinear. For a 450 megabytes file the sending procedure requires approximately 216 milliseconds, whereas the file receiving procedure expects 258 milliseconds. The difference between the sending and reception is explained by the Fujisaki-Okamoto transform, executing during the reception the encryption algorithm, used to reject malformed ciphertext. In Fig. 12, we compare the amount of data sent by a sender to a receiver through the low-rate medium between the *naive* corresponding to the situation where the encrypted file is directly sent to the receiver (for example with OpenPGP [11]), and the approach motivated in the $\mathcal{P}_{\mathsf{AAFT}}$ protocol. Compared to the naive approach, our solution provides a *constant* amount of transferred data of 96 bytes corresponding to the link (*i.e.,* the hash of the encrypted file) and the signature σ_l. This constant communication size is explained by the encrypted file being sent over the distributed storage network instead of being directly transferred, still with the guarantee to have confidentiality and integrity of the file but also authentication of the sender.

Acknowledgement. We thank the anonymous referees for their useful suggestions and remarks. This work was partially supported by the DataLake-For-Nuclear (D4N) project funded by the BPI institute.

References

1. Object storage devices (2004). http://webstore.ansi.org/standards/incits/ansiincit s4002004
2. Daft: Proof-of-concept (2024). https://anonymous.4open.science/r/DAFT/
3. Abe, M., Ambrona, M.: Blind key-generation attribute-based encryption for general predicates. Des. Codes Crypt. **90**, 08 (2022)
4. Agrawal, S., Chase, M.: FAME: fast attribute-based message encryption. In: Thuraisingham, B., Evans, D., Malkin, T., Xu, D. (eds.) Proceedings of the 2017 ACM SIGSAC Conference on Computer and Communications Security, CCS 2017, Dallas, TX, USA, 30 October–03 November 2017, pp. 665–682. ACM (2017)

5. Asghar, M.R., Ion, M., Russello, G., Crispo, B.: ESPOON ERBAC: enforcing security policies in outsourced environments. Cryptology ePrint Archive, Paper 2013/587 (2013). https://eprint.iacr.org/2013/587

6. Buchmann, J., et al.: Safe: a secure and efficient long-term distributed storage system. Cryptology ePrint Archive, Paper 2020/690 (2020). https://eprint.iacr.org/2020/690

7. Camenisch, J., Dubovitskaya, M., Enderlein, R.R., Neven, G.: Oblivious transfer with hidden access control from attribute-based encryption. In: Visconti, I., De Prisco, R. (eds.) SCN 2012. LNCS, vol. 7485, pp. 559–579. Springer, Heidelberg (2012). https://doi.org/10.1007/978-3-642-32928-9_31

8. Camenisch, J., Krenn, S., Küsters, R., Rausch, D.: iUC: flexible universal composability made simple. In: Galbraith, S.D., Moriai, S. (eds.) ASIACRYPT 2019. LNCS, vol. 11923, pp. 191–221. Springer, Cham (2019). https://doi.org/10.1007/978-3-030-34618-8_7

9. Canetti, R.: Universally composable security: a new paradigm for cryptographic protocols. In: 42nd Annual Symposium on Foundations of Computer Science, FOCS 2001, Las Vegas, Nevada, USA, 14–17 October 2001, pp. 136–145. IEEE Computer Society (2001)

10. Ferrara, A.L., Fuchsbauer, G., Warinschi, B.: Cryptographically enforced RBAC. Cryptology ePrint Archive, Paper 2013/492 (2013). https://eprint.iacr.org/2013/492

11. Finney, H., Donnerhacke, L., Callas, J., Thayer, R.L., Shaw, D.: OpenPGP Message Format. RFC 4880, November 2007

12. Freudenthal, E., Pesin, T., Port, L., Keenan, E., Karamcheti, V.: dRBAC: distributed role-based access control for dynamic coalition environments. In: Proceedings 22nd International Conference on Distributed Computing Systems, pp. 411–420 (2002)

13. Fujisaki, E., Okamoto, T.: Secure integration of asymmetric and symmetric encryption schemes. J. Cryptol. **26**(1), 80–101 (2013)

14. Garay, J.A., Gennaro, R., Jutla, C., Rabin, T.: Secure distributed storage and retrieval. Cryptology ePrint Archive, Paper 1998/025 (1998). https://eprint.iacr.org/1998/025

15. Halevi, S., Karger, P.A., Naor, D.: Enforcing confinement in distributed storage and a cryptographic model for access control. IACR Cryptology ePrint Archive, p. 169 (2005)

16. Hohenberger, S., Lu, G., Waters, B., Wu, D.J.: Registered attribute-based encryption. In: Hazay, C., Stam, M. (eds.) EUROCRYPT 2023. LNCS, vol. 14006, pp. 511–542. Springer, Cham (2023). https://doi.org/10.1007/978-3-031-30620-4_17

17. Küsters, R., Tuengerthal, M., Rausch, D.: The IITM model: a simple and expressive model for universal composability. J. Cryptol. **33**(4), 1461–1584 (2020)

18. Küsters, R., Tuengerthal, M., Rausch, D.: Joint state composition theorems for public-key encryption and digital signature functionalities with local computation. J. Cryptol. **33**(4), 1585–1658 (2020)

19. Liu, B., Warinschi, B.: Universally composable cryptographic role-based access control. Cryptology ePrint Archive, Paper 2016/902 (2016). https://eprint.iacr.org/2016/902

20. Vandenwauver, M., Govaerts, R., Vandewalle, J.: Role based access control in distributed systems. In: Katsikas, S. (ed.) Communications and Multimedia Security. IAICT, pp. 169–177. Springer, Boston, MA (1997). https://doi.org/10.1007/978-0-387-35256-5_13

Post-quantum Cryptography (I)

On the Generalizations of the Rank Metric over Finite Chain Rings

Hermann Tchatchiem Kamche[1] and Hervé Talé Kalachi[2,3]([✉])

[1] Centre for Cybersecurity and Mathematical Cryptology,
The University of Bamenda, Bamenda, Cameroon
[2] National Advanced School of Engineering of Yaoundé,
University of Yaounde I, Yaoundé, Cameroon
hervekalachi@gmail.com
[3] LITIS UR 4108, 76000 Rouen, France

Abstract. The rank metric over finite fields has received a lot of attention these last decades. Several works propose generalizations of this metric to finite rings, each one using a particular notion of module theory. The first work that generalizes the rank metric to finite rings defines a new metric over finite principal ideal rings by replacing the notion of dimension of vector spaces by the minimum number of generators of modules. A second work also defines a new metric over Galois rings by using the notion of cardinal of modules, while another idea is to use the length of modules as a generalization of the dimension. In this paper, we study these three generalizations of the rank metric from fields to finite chain rings. We show that the generalizations using the length and the cardinal of modules are decoding equivalent, and give connections between the minimum distances and the packing radii of the three metrics. These links make it possible to show that up to the packing radii, the generalization using the minimum number of generators of modules corrects more errors than the metric using the length and the one defined by the cardinal of modules. Finally, we show that the use of linear codes with the metric based on the minimum number of generators in a McEliece type encryption scheme results in a cryptosystem with smaller public key sizes.

Keywords: Cryptography · Finite chain ring · Minimum distance · Packing radius · Rank metric

1 Introduction

Error-correcting codes were introduced by Claude Shannon in 1948 [37]. At the origin, this theory aims at combating (detecting and/or correcting) errors created by noise during data transmission or data storage. The idea is then to transform messages into codewords that will be subject to errors during the transmission in a noisy channel and then exploit the properties of the encoder to detect and/or correct introduced errors. Nowadays, error correcting codes are also used

S. Vaudenay and C. Petit (Eds.): AFRICACRYPT 2024, LNCS 14861, pp. 201–221, 2024.
https://doi.org/10.1007/978-3-031-64381-1_9

in cryptography where an important branch of public key cryptography called code-based cryptography is developing [5, 32, 38].

The general principle in code-based cryptography [28, 32] is for the receiver to choose a linear secret code and subject it to a series of transformations to then obtain a new linear code that will be published. Without the knowledge of the applied transformations, the public code is assumed to be indistinguishable from a random linear code, and in this case, decoding a noisy word of the public code is a difficult algorithmic problem. The public key is usually the code obtained after transformation together with a parameter t depending mainly on the *packing radius*[1] of the secret code. Thus, the encryption consists in choosing a codeword **c** (considered here as the plain text) and generating the cipher text **y** as an arbitrary element in the ball of radius t centred on **c**. This is where the notion of distance comes in, and will play a non-negligible role in the security of the encryption system. Indeed, a natural brute force attack would consist in going through all the elements of the ball with radius t centred on **y** to look for the unique codeword. The complexity of such an attack mainly depends on the cardinal of the underlined ball, and this cardinal is intrinsically linked to the distance used.

Several distances are used in code-based cryptography. The Hamming distance is the oldest one, and is at the basis of the McEliece cryptosystem [28]. Another well known distance is the rank metric, used in code-based cryptography for the first time in 1991 by Gabidulin, Paramonov and Tretjakov [14]. This last proposal has known several moments of rebound with successions of attacks and reparations (see [5] for a brief overview). Despite everything, rank-metric based cryptography knows a strong attraction today, especially in the field of post-quantum cryptography where a NIST competition [31] is underway, a competition in which we have noted a strong participation of numerous rank-metric based candidates. It is important to remark that the main advantage of the rank metric over the Hamming metric is the quantity of words in the balls in the rank metric compared to the Hamming metric. So despite the fact that all the rank based candidates are now out of the NIST competition, rank based cryptography is still a nice alternative to traditional Hamming metric code-based cryptography, and the NIST believes research in that direction should continue [1].

The rank metric is classically defined over finite fields and is given by the dimension of some vector spaces. This last decade has seen the appearance of various generalizations of the rank metric to finite rings. The first work that generalizes the rank metric to finite rings is [24], where the authors defined a new metric over finite principal ideal rings by replacing the notion of dimension of vector spaces by the minimum number of generators of modules. Epelde and Rúa [11] also defined a new metric over Galois rings by using the notion of cardinal of modules to generalize the notion of dimension of vector spaces. Another notion

---

[1] In the theory of error-correcting codes, the *packing radius* of a code, also called *error correction capability*, can be defined as the largest value of t for which the balls of radius t centred on distinct codewords are all pairwise disjoint.

that generalizes the dimension is the length of modules. This notion was used in [17] to generalize the subspace distance [25], but can also be used to generalize the rank metric over finite rings.

It is important to underline that any change of metric leads to possible changes of packing radii, density of the balls and several other important parameters. Therefore, while all these metrics can be used to decode noisy codewords, it is an interesting study to compare them in terms of packing radii, quantities of elements in balls for each metric. These comparisons are of interest in coding theory and specially in code-based cryptography. Another aspect when dealing with two distances is the notion of *decoding equivalence* defined in [9]. This notion is quite significant, since running a minimum distance decoder with two distances that are decoding equivalent will always output the same codeword in case of uniqueness.

In this paper, we study the above three distances generalizing the rank distance from fields to finite chain rings. We show that the generalizations using the length and the cardinal of modules are decoding equivalents, and give connections between the minimum distances and the packing radii of the three metrics. These links make it possible to show that up to the packing radii, the generalization using the minimum number of generators of modules corrects more errors than those using the length and the cardinal of modules. Finally, we use these results to show that the use of the metric based on the minimum number of generators in code-based cryptography, particularly with linear codes in a McEliece/Niederreiter settings, results in a cryptosystem with smaller public key sizes.

The rest of the paper is organized as follows. We start by some preliminary results on distances over finite sets in Sect. 2, where we show that there are connections between minimum distances and packing radii of a code with two distances that are decoding equivalent and translation invariant. Then, our main results is presented in Sect. 3, followed by its cryptographic consequences in Sect. 4, and we finish by a conclusion of the work and some perspectives in Sect. 5.

2 Preliminaries

Throughout the paper, $\mathbb{F}_q$ will denote the finite field with q elements. Unless otherwise stated, $\mathcal{V}$ will denote a finite set and any subset $\mathcal{C}$ of $\mathcal{V}$ will be called "a code". The cardinal of $\mathcal{V}$ is denoted by $|\mathcal{V}|$. We will also use the following notion of distance, very useful in the theory of error correcting codes.

2.1 Distance Function

The notion of distance, that can be found in [8], can be defined as follows:

Definition 1 (Distance). *For a given set $\mathcal{V}$, a function $d : \mathcal{V} \times \mathcal{V} \longrightarrow \mathbb{R}$ is a **distance** if the following properties are satisfied for all $\mathbf{x}, \mathbf{y} \in \mathcal{V}$:*

(i) $d(\mathbf{x}, \mathbf{y}) \geqslant 0$;
(ii) $d(\mathbf{x}, \mathbf{x}) = 0$;
(iii) $d(\mathbf{x}, \mathbf{y}) = d(\mathbf{y}, \mathbf{x})$.

It is well known that a distance $d : V \times V \longrightarrow \mathbb{R}$ which satisfies the following additional conditions (iv) and (v) is called a **metric**:

(iv) For all $\mathbf{x}, \mathbf{y} \in V$, if $d(\mathbf{x}, \mathbf{y}) = 0$ then $\mathbf{x} = \mathbf{y}$;
(v) For all $\mathbf{x}, \mathbf{y}, \mathbf{z} \in V$, $d(\mathbf{x}, \mathbf{z}) \leqslant d(\mathbf{x}, \mathbf{y}) + d(\mathbf{y}, \mathbf{z})$.

Several distances are commonly used in coding theory. In the following example, we enumerate some distances that are related to this work and that are also known to be metrics.

Example 1. 1. The Hamming distance [18] between $\mathbf{x} = (x_1, \ldots, x_n) \in \mathbb{F}_q^n$ and $\mathbf{y} = (y_1, \ldots, y_n) \in \mathbb{F}_q^n$ is the number of positions where $\mathbf{x}$ and $\mathbf{y}$ differ, that is to say,
$$d_H(\mathbf{x}, \mathbf{y}) = |\{i : x_i \neq y_i\}|.$$

2. The subspace distance [25] between two subspaces F and G of $\mathbb{F}_q^n$ is defined by
$$d_S(F, G) = \dim(F) + \dim(G) - 2\dim(F \cap G).$$

3. The rank distance [7, 13] between two matrices $\mathbf{A}$ and $\mathbf{B}$ with the same size and entries from a field $\mathbb{F}_q$, is the rank of their difference, that is to say,
$$d_R(\mathbf{A}, \mathbf{B}) = \operatorname{rank}(\mathbf{A} - \mathbf{B}).$$

4. The rank distance can also be defined on vectors with coefficients in a Galois extension $\mathbb{F}_{q^m}$ of $\mathbb{F}_q$ as follows, given $\mathbf{a} = (a_1, \ldots, a_n) \in \mathbb{F}_{q^m}^n$ and $\mathbf{b} = (b_1, \ldots, b_n) \in \mathbb{F}_{q^m}^n$, the rank distance $d_R'(\mathbf{a}, \mathbf{b})$ between $\mathbf{a}$ and $\mathbf{b}$ is the dimension of the $\mathbb{F}_q$–subspace of $\mathbb{F}_{q^m}$ generated by $a_1 - b_1, \ldots, a_n - b_n$, that is to say,
$$d_R'(\mathbf{a}, \mathbf{b}) = \dim\langle a_1 - b_1, \ldots, a_n - b_n\rangle_{\mathbb{F}_q}.$$

There is a well-known link between d_R and d_R'. Indeed, using a $\mathbb{F}_q$–basis of $\mathbb{F}_{q^m}$, the vectors $\mathbf{a}$ and $\mathbf{b}$ from $\mathbb{F}_{q^m}^n$ can be respectively decomposed as $m \times n$ matrices $\mathbf{A}$ and $\mathbf{B}$ with entries in $\mathbb{F}_q$. Then, we have
$$d_R'(\mathbf{a}, \mathbf{b}) = d_R(\mathbf{A}, \mathbf{B}).$$

When a codeword $\mathbf{c} \in \mathcal{C}$ passes via a noisy channel, it is quite well known that on arrival, a potentially different word $\mathbf{y} \in V$ is received. Given a distance d on V, and assuming that $\mathbf{c}$ is the closest codeword to $\mathbf{y}$, the receiver who searches for the transmitted codeword then faces the following problem known as the "General Decoding Problem".

Definition 2 (General decoding problem). *Let V be a set and $\mathcal{C}$ a subset of V. The **general decoding problem** for the code $\mathcal{C}$ with the distance d on V is, given a word $\mathbf{y} \in V$, to find a codeword $\hat{\mathbf{x}}$ in $\operatorname{argmin}\{d(\mathbf{x}, \mathbf{y}) : \mathbf{x} \in \mathcal{C}\}$.[2]*

---

[2] $\operatorname{argmin}\{d(\mathbf{x}, \mathbf{y}) : \mathbf{x} \in \mathcal{C}\} = \{\mathbf{x}_0 \in \mathcal{C} : d(\mathbf{x}_0, \mathbf{y}) \leqslant d(\mathbf{x}, \mathbf{y}), \forall \mathbf{x} \in \mathcal{C}\}$.

The general decoding problem is known to be NP-Hard for several metrics, and is thus intensively used in cryptography [28,29,36]. A current research trend today consists in defining new distances and then study the hardness of the corresponding general decoding problems [11,20,21,34,39]. In the sequel, any algorithm that solves the above general decoding problem will be called a **minimum distance decoder**. It can be noted that executing a minimum distance decoder numerous times on the same problem can result in different solutions, and this is not always good news in practice, specially in cryptography. In what follows, we define the notion of packing radius that provides a condition to have at most one solution to the decoding problem.

2.2 Packing Radius and Minimum Distance

As in [6], we will use the distance set to define the packing radius.

Definition 3. *Let $\mathcal{V}$ be a set, d a distance on $\mathcal{V}$, $\mathcal{C}$ a subset of $\mathcal{V}$ and r a real number.*

(i) *The **ball** of radius r centred at $\mathbf{x} \in \mathcal{V}$ with the distance d, denoted by $B_d(\mathbf{x}, r)$, is the set*

$$B_d(\mathbf{x}, r) = \{\mathbf{y} \in \mathcal{V} : d(\mathbf{x}, \mathbf{y}) \leqslant r\}.$$

(ii) *The **distance set** of $\mathcal{V}$ with the distance d, denoted by $D_d(\mathcal{V})$, is the set of distances between pairs of elements of $\mathcal{V}$, that is,*

$$D_d(\mathcal{V}) = \{d(\mathbf{x}, \mathbf{y}) : \mathbf{x}, \mathbf{y} \in \mathcal{V}\}.$$

(iii) *The **minimum distance** of $\mathcal{C}$ with the distance d, denoted by $d(\mathcal{C})$, is the number*

$$d(\mathcal{C}) = \min\{d(\mathbf{x}, \mathbf{y}) : \mathbf{x}, \mathbf{y} \in \mathcal{C}, \mathbf{x} \neq \mathbf{y}\}.$$

If $\mathcal{C}$ has only one element, then we set $d(\mathcal{C}) = 0$.

(iv) *The **packing radius** of $\mathcal{C}$ with the distance d, denoted by $R_d(\mathcal{C})$, is the greatest r in $D_d(\mathcal{V})$ such that $B_d(\mathbf{x}, r) \cap B_d(\mathbf{y}, r) = \emptyset$, for any $\mathbf{x}, \mathbf{y} \in \mathcal{C}$ with $\mathbf{x} \neq \mathbf{y}$, that is to say,*

$$R_d(\mathcal{C}) = \max\{r \in D_d(\mathcal{V}) : B_d(\mathbf{x}, r) \cap B_d(\mathbf{y}, r) = \emptyset, \forall \mathbf{x}, \mathbf{y} \in \mathcal{C}, \mathbf{x} \neq \mathbf{y}\}.$$

The packing radius is also called the error correction capability because if the distance between the transmitted codeword $\mathbf{x} \in \mathcal{C}$ and the received word $\mathbf{y} \in \mathcal{V}$ is smaller or equal to the packing radius, then $\mathbf{x}$ is the unique element in the set $\operatorname{argmin}\{d(\mathbf{a}, \mathbf{y}) : \mathbf{a} \in \mathcal{C}\}$. Thus, a minimum distance decoder returns $\mathbf{x}$. As stated in [10], if d is a metric and $D_d(\mathcal{V}) \subset \mathbb{N}$, then

$$\lfloor (d(\mathcal{C}) - 1)/2 \rfloor \leqslant R_d(\mathcal{C}) \leqslant d(\mathcal{C}) - 1.$$

The following proposition extends this result to the general case.

Proposition 1. *Let $\mathcal{V}$ be a set, d a metric on $\mathcal{V}$ and $\mathcal{C}$ a subset of $\mathcal{V}$. Then, we have*

$$\alpha \leqslant R_d(\mathcal{C}) \leqslant \beta$$

where $\alpha = \max\{r \in D_d(\mathcal{V}): \ 2r < d(\mathcal{C})\}$ and $\beta = \max\{r \in D_d(\mathcal{V}) : r < d(\mathcal{C})\}$.

Proof. Suppose that there are $\mathbf{x}$ and $\mathbf{y}$ in $\mathcal{C}$ such that $\mathbf{x} \neq \mathbf{y}$ and $B_d(\mathbf{x}, \alpha) \cap B_d(\mathbf{y}, \alpha) \neq \emptyset$. Let $\mathbf{z} \in B_d(\mathbf{x}, \alpha) \cap B_d(\mathbf{y}, \alpha)$. Then $d(\mathbf{x}, \mathbf{y}) \leqslant d(\mathbf{x}, \mathbf{z}) + d(\mathbf{z}, \mathbf{y}) \leqslant 2\alpha < d(\mathcal{C})$, which is impossible since $d(\mathcal{C})$ is the minimum distance of $\mathcal{C}$. Thus $\alpha \leqslant R_d(\mathcal{C})$. Let $\mathbf{x}$ and $\mathbf{y}$ in $\mathcal{C}$ such that $d(\mathcal{C}) = d(\mathbf{x}, \mathbf{y})$. Then $\mathbf{x} \in B_d(\mathbf{x}, d(\mathcal{C})) \cap B_d(\mathbf{y}, d(\mathcal{C}))$. Therefore, $R_d(\mathcal{C}) < d(\mathcal{C})$. Consequently, $R_d(\mathcal{C}) \leqslant \beta$. $\qquad\square$

By Proposition 1 the minimum distance can be used to give lower and upper bounds of the packing radius. The above lower bound is reached for certain metrics like Hamming metric and rank metric. For the upper bound, it can also be reached in some cases, as specified in [33, Theorem 5].

Given a code $\mathcal{C}$ and two metrics d_1 and d_2 to choose from, one might be tempted to choose the metric with a greater packing radius. But in practice, one would also like to compare the balls $B_{d_1}(\mathbf{y}, R_{d_1}(\mathcal{C}))$ and $B_{d_2}(\mathbf{y}, R_{d_2}(\mathcal{C}))$ for every $\mathbf{y}$ in $\mathcal{V}$. This comparison is very important for instance in code-based cryptography, where the encryption process generally considers a codeword $\mathbf{c} \in \mathcal{C}$ as a plaintext, and takes as ciphertext a random element $\mathbf{y}$ from $B_d(\mathbf{c}, R_d(\mathcal{C}))$ for a given metric d. A brute force attack is then to browse the set $B_d(\mathbf{y}, R_d(\mathcal{C}))$, looking for the unique codeword. In the following, we give some examples of comparisons.

Example 2. In this example, d_H is the Hamming distance and d'_R is the rank distance as defined in Example 1.

(i) Let us consider the repetition code $\mathcal{C} = \{(x, x, x), x \in \mathbb{F}_{q^m}\}$. For the Hamming distance, we have $d_H(\mathcal{C}) = 3$, $R_{d_H}(\mathcal{C}) = 1$ and $|B_{d_H}(\mathbf{y}, R_{d_H}(\mathcal{C}))| = 3(q^m - 1) + 1$, for all $\mathbf{y}$ in $\mathbb{F}_{q^m}^3$. For the rank distance, $d'_R(\mathcal{C}) = 1$, $R_{d'_R}(\mathcal{C}) = 0$ and $|B_{d'_R}(\mathbf{y}, R_{d'_R}(\mathcal{C}))| = 1$, for all $\mathbf{y}$ in $\mathbb{F}_{q^m}^3$.

(ii) Assume that $m \geqslant 3$. Let a_1, a_2, a_3 in $\mathbb{F}_{q^m}$ which are $\mathbb{F}_q$−linearly independent. The code $\mathcal{C} = \{(xa_1, xa_2, xa_3), \ x \in \mathbb{F}_{q^m}\}$ is a Gabidulin code [13]. Thus, for the Hamming distance we have $d_H(\mathcal{C}) = 3$, $R_{d_H}(\mathcal{C}) = 1$ and $|B_{d_H}(\mathbf{y}, R_{d_H}(\mathcal{C}))| = 3(q^m - 1) + 1$, for all $\mathbf{y}$ in $\mathbb{F}_{q^m}^3$. For the rank distance, $d'_R(\mathcal{C}) = 3$, $R_{d'_R}(\mathcal{C}) = 1$ and $|B_{d'_R}(\mathbf{y}, R_{d'_R}(\mathcal{C}))| = (q^m - 1)(q^2 + q + 1) + 1$, for all $\mathbf{y}$ in $\mathbb{F}_{q^m}$.

Example 2 shows that in general $|B_{d_H}(\mathbf{y}, R_{d_H}(\mathcal{C}))|$ and $|B_{d'_R}(\mathbf{y}, R_{d'_R}(\mathcal{C}))|$ are different. We will see in the next section that this happens because d'_R and d_H are not decoding equivalent.

2.3   Decoding Equivalent Distances

As in [9, Definition 3] we give the following:

Definition 4. *Two distances d_1 and d_2 on a set $\mathcal{V}$ are **decoding equivalent** if they define the same minimum distance decoder, that is, for any subset $\mathcal{C}$ of $\mathcal{V}$ and any $\mathbf{y}$ in $\mathcal{V}$,*

$$\mathrm{argmin}\{d_1(\mathbf{x}, \mathbf{y}) : \mathbf{x} \in \mathcal{C}\} = \mathrm{argmin}\{d_2(\mathbf{x}, \mathbf{y}) : \mathbf{x} \in \mathcal{C}\}.$$

According to [9, Proposition 1] we have the following:

Proposition 2. *Let d_1 and d_2 be two distances on a set $\mathcal{V}$. Then, d_1 and d_2 are decoding equivalent if and only if for every $\mathbf{x}, \mathbf{x}', \mathbf{y}$ in $\mathcal{V}$,*

$$d_1(\mathbf{x}, \mathbf{y}) \leqslant d_1(\mathbf{x}', \mathbf{y}) \Longleftrightarrow d_2(\mathbf{x}, \mathbf{y}) \leqslant d_2(\mathbf{x}', \mathbf{y}).$$

Recall that if $\mathcal{V}$ is a commutative group, then a distance d on $\mathcal{V}$ is said to be **translation invariant** if for all $\mathbf{x}, \mathbf{y}, \mathbf{z}$ in $\mathcal{V}$, $d(\mathbf{x} + \mathbf{z}, \mathbf{y} + \mathbf{z}) = d(\mathbf{x}, \mathbf{y})$. Similar to [9, Corollary 1] we have the following:

Lemma 1. *Let $\mathcal{V}$ be a commutative group. Let d_1 and d_2 be two distances on $\mathcal{V}$ which are decoding equivalent and translation invariant. Given $\mathbf{y}_0$ in $\mathcal{V}$, set $r_1 = d_1(\mathbf{0}, \mathbf{y}_0)$ and $r_2 = d_2(\mathbf{0}, \mathbf{y}_0)$. Then, for all $\mathbf{x}$ in $\mathcal{V}$, $B_{d_1}(\mathbf{x}, r_1) = B_{d_2}(\mathbf{x}, r_2)$.*

Proof. Let $\mathbf{y} \in \mathcal{V}$. Then, $\mathbf{y} \in B_{d_1}(\mathbf{x}, r_1) \Longleftrightarrow d_1(\mathbf{x}, \mathbf{y}) \leqslant d_1(\mathbf{0}, \mathbf{y}_0) \Longleftrightarrow d_1(\mathbf{0}, \mathbf{y} - \mathbf{x}) \leqslant d_1(\mathbf{0}, \mathbf{y}_0) \Longleftrightarrow d_2(\mathbf{0}, \mathbf{y} - \mathbf{x}) \leqslant d_2(\mathbf{0}, \mathbf{y}_0) \Longleftrightarrow \mathbf{y} \in B_{d_2}(\mathbf{x}, r_2)$. □

The following theorem gives the link between the minimum distances and the packing radii for two distances that are decoding equivalent.

Theorem 1. *Let $\mathcal{V}$ be a commutative group, $\mathcal{C}$ a subset of $\mathcal{V}$, d_1 and d_2 be two distances on $\mathcal{V}$ that are decoding equivalent and translation invariant.*

(a) Given $\mathbf{x}_0 \in \mathcal{C}$, $d_1(\mathcal{C}) = d_1(\mathbf{0}, \mathbf{x}_0) \Longleftrightarrow d_2(\mathcal{C}) = d_2(\mathbf{0}, \mathbf{x}_0)$.
(b) Given $\mathbf{y}_0 \in \mathcal{V}$, $R_{d_1}(\mathcal{C}) = d_1(\mathbf{0}, \mathbf{y}_0) \Longleftrightarrow R_{d_2}(\mathcal{C}) = d_2(\mathbf{0}, \mathbf{y}_0)$.

Proof. (a) Let $\mathbf{x} \in \mathcal{C}$. Then, by Proposition 2, $d_1(\mathbf{0}, \mathbf{x}_0) \leqslant d_1(\mathbf{0}, \mathbf{x})$ if and only if $d_2(\mathbf{0}, \mathbf{x}_0) \leqslant d_2(\mathbf{0}, \mathbf{x})$. Thus, the result follows.

(b) Assume that $R_{d_1}(\mathcal{C}) = d_1(\mathbf{0}, \mathbf{y}_0)$. Let $\mathbf{x}, \mathbf{x}'$ be two elements of $\mathcal{C}$ and, set $r_1 = d_1(\mathbf{0}, \mathbf{y}_0)$ and $r_2 = d_2(\mathbf{0}, \mathbf{y}_0)$. By Lemma 1, $B_{d_1}(\mathbf{x}, r_1) \cap B_{d_1}(\mathbf{x}', r_1) = B_{d_2}(\mathbf{x}, r_2) \cap B_{d_2}(\mathbf{x}', r_2)$. By the definition of $R_{d_1}(\mathcal{C})$, $B_{d_1}(\mathbf{x}, r_1) \cap B_{d_1}(\mathbf{x}', r_1) = \emptyset$. Thus, $B_{d_2}(\mathbf{x}, r_2) \cap B_{d_2}(\mathbf{x}', r_2) = \emptyset$ and then $d_2(\mathbf{0}, \mathbf{y}_0) \leqslant R_{d_2}(\mathcal{C})$. Let $\mathbf{y}'_0 \in \mathcal{V}$ such that $R_{d_2}(\mathcal{C}) = d_2(\mathbf{0}, \mathbf{y}'_0)$. Set $r'_1 = d_1(\mathbf{0}, \mathbf{y}'_0)$ and $r'_2 = d_2(\mathbf{0}, \mathbf{y}'_0)$. Then $B_{d_2}(\mathbf{x}, r'_2) \cap B_{d_2}(\mathbf{x}', r'_2) = \emptyset$ and $B_{d_1}(\mathbf{x}, r'_1) \cap B_{d_1}(\mathbf{x}', r'_1) = B_{d_2}(\mathbf{x}, r'_2) \cap B_{d_2}(\mathbf{x}', r'_2) = \emptyset$. Hence, $r'_1 \leqslant R_{d_1}(\mathcal{C})$, implying that $d_1(\mathbf{0}, \mathbf{y}'_0) \leqslant d_1(\mathbf{0}, \mathbf{y}_0)$. Consequently, $d_2(\mathbf{0}, \mathbf{y}'_0) \leqslant d_2(\mathbf{0}, \mathbf{y}_0)$, that is to say $R_{d_2}(\mathcal{C}) \leqslant d_2(\mathbf{0}, \mathbf{y}_0)$. Therefore, $R_{d_2}(\mathcal{C}) = d_2(\mathbf{0}, \mathbf{y}_0)$. □

The above theorem shows that for two distances d_1 and d_2 that are decoding equivalent and translation invariant, one can easily deduce the minimum distance $d_1(\mathcal{C})$ and the packing radius $R_{d_1}(\mathcal{C})$ of a code $\mathcal{C}$ from the knowledge of $d_2(\mathcal{C})$ and $R_{d_2}(\mathcal{C})$. A natural consequence of Theorem 1 and Lemma 1 is the following.

Corollary 1. *Let $\mathcal{V}$ be a commutative group, d_1 and d_2 be two distances on $\mathcal{V}$ that are decoding equivalent and translation invariant. Given a subset C of $\mathcal{V}$, we have,*

$$B_{d_1}(\mathbf{0}, R_{d_1}(C)) = B_{d_2}(\mathbf{0}, R_{d_2}(C))$$

We will also need the following corollary.

Corollary 2. *Let $\mathcal{V}$ be a commutative group. Let d_1 and d_2 be two distances on $\mathcal{V}$ that are translation invariant. If $d_2 = \alpha d_1$ with $\alpha \in \mathbb{R}$, then $d_2(C) = \alpha d_1(C)$ and $R_{d_2}(C) = \alpha R_{d_1}(C)$.*

We see from the above that, when going from one distance to another, some notions must be taken into account, namely for a code, its minimum distance, its packing radius, the cardinal of the balls with some specific radius. In what follows, we propose to study these notions for several distances that have emerged over the last decade. As they are all related to the rank metric and also defined over finite chain rings, we use "rank metrics over finite chain rings" as their global name.

3   Packing Radius and Minimum Distance of Rank-Metric Codes over Finite Chain Rings

In the following, R is a finite commutative chain ring[3] with maximal ideal $\mathfrak{m}$, residue field $\mathbb{F}_q = R/\mathfrak{m}$, π is a generator of $\mathfrak{m}$, and ν the nilpotency index of π, i.e., the smallest positive integer such that $\pi^\nu = 0$. Let m be a non-zero positive integer and S a Galois extension of R of degree m, that is to say, $S = R[X]/(h)$, where $h \in R[X]$ is a monic polynomial of degree m such that its projection into $\mathbb{F}_q[X]$ is irreducible and (h) denotes the ideal of $R[X]$ generated by h. By [27], S is also a finite commutative chain ring, with maximal ideal $\mathfrak{m}S$ and residue field $\mathbb{F}_{q^m}$.

Example 3. Let $R = \mathbb{Z}_4$, the ring of integers modulo 4. It is a finite chain ring for which the maximal ideal is $2\mathbb{Z}_4$ and the residue field is $\mathbb{F}_2 = \mathbb{Z}_4/2\mathbb{Z}_4$. The generator of the maximal ideal is 2 and its nilpotency index is 2 because $2^2 = 0$ in $\mathbb{Z}_4$. Let

$$h(X) = X^6 + 2X^5 + X^4 + X^3 + 3X + 1 \in R[X],$$

then the projection of $h(X)$ into $\mathbb{F}_2[X]$ is $\overline{h}(X) = X^6 + X^4 + X^3 + X + 1$ which is irreducible in $\mathbb{F}_2[X]$. Thus, $S = R[X]/(h(X))$ is a Galois extension of R of dimension 6. By setting $a = X + (h(X))$, $\{1, a, a^2, a^3, a^4, a^5\}$ is a basis of S as an R−module.

As we have seen in the beginning of the previous section, the rank metric over finite fields can be defined by the notion of dimension of a vector space. However, when it comes to rings, the notion of module replaces that of a vector space. In the following, we recall some notions that have been used over finite rings to generalize the rank metric from finite fields to finite rings.

---

[3] For more details on chain rings, we refer the readers to [27,30].

Definition 5. *Let M be a finitely generated $R-$module.*

(i) *The minimum among the cardinals of the generator families of M is denoted by $\mu_R(M)$.*

(ii) *The length of M, denoted by $\lambda_R(M)$, is the length of a longest chain of its submodules.*

(iii) *The logarithm function in base $|R|$ of $|M|$ is denoted by $\mathrm{logcard}_R(M)$, that is to say, $\mathrm{logcard}_R(M) = log_{|R|}(|M|)$.*

Some properties of $\mu_R(M)$ and $\lambda_R(M)$ can be found in [26]. The minimum among the cardinals of the generator families was used in [24] to generalize the rank metric over finite principal ideal rings. In [17], the length of a module was used to define the submodule distance over finite rings and very recently, the cardinal of a module was used in [11] to generalize the rank metric over Galois rings. The following proposition shows how to calculate them on finite chain rings.

Proposition 3. *Given a finitely generated $R-$module M, there exists an integer s such that,*

(a) *M is isomorphic to the product ring $\pi^{\alpha_1} R \times \cdots \times \pi^{\alpha_s} R$ where $\alpha_1, \ldots, \alpha_s$ are integers satisfying $0 \leqslant \alpha_1 \leqslant \cdots \leqslant \alpha_s < \nu$.*

(b) *$\mu_R(M) = s$.*

(c) *$\lambda_R(M) = \sum_{1 \leqslant i \leqslant s}(\nu - \alpha_i)$.*

(d) *$\mathrm{logcard}_R(M) = \lambda_R(M)/\nu$.*

Proof. (a) is due to [19, Theorem 2.2], while (b) is a direct consequence of [26, Corollary 2.4] and [19, Theorem 2.2]. A detailed proof of (c) can be found in [17]. The idea is that we have $\lambda_R(M) = \sum_{1 \leqslant s \leqslant s} \lambda_R(\pi^{\alpha_i} R) = \sum_{1 \leqslant i \leqslant s}(\nu - \alpha_i)$. For the proof of (d), one can remark that $|M| = |\pi^{\alpha_1} R| \times \cdots \times |\pi^s R| = q^{\nu-\alpha_s} \times \cdots \times q^{\nu-\alpha_s}$. As $|R| = q^\nu$, then $log_{|R|}(|M|) = \lambda_R(M)/\nu$. $\qquad\square$

A direct consequence of Proposition 3 is the following:

Corollary 3. *Let M be a finitely generated $R-$module. Then,*

$$\mathrm{logcard}_R(M) \leqslant \mu_R(M) \leqslant \lambda_R(M) \leqslant \nu\mu_R(M).$$

In Example 1 we have seen the well known definition of the rank metric on vectors with components in a finite field. In the following, we will do the same by using the Galois extension S of R to define the generalizations of rank metric on vectors with entries in S.

Notation 1. *Let $\mathbf{u} = (u_1, \ldots, u_n) \in S^n$, $\mathbf{a} \in S^n$, and $\mathbf{b} \in S^n$.*

(i) *The support of $\mathbf{u}$, denoted by $\mathrm{supp}(\mathbf{u})$, is the $R-$submodule of S generated by $u_1, \ldots, u_n$, that is,*

$$\mathrm{supp}(\mathbf{u}) = <u_1, \ldots, u_n>_R.$$

(ii) *The distance between* **a** *and* **b**, *defined by the minimum among the cardinals of the generator families of* supp(**a** − **b**) *is:*

$$d_g(\mathbf{a}, \mathbf{b}) = \mu_R(\text{supp}(\mathbf{a} - \mathbf{b})).$$

(iii) *The distance between* **a** *and* **b** *defined by the length of* supp(**a** − **b**) *is:*

$$d_l(\mathbf{a}, \mathbf{b}) = \lambda_R(\text{supp}(\mathbf{a} - \mathbf{b})).$$

(iv) *The distance between* **a** *and* **b** *defined by the logarithm of the cardinal of* supp(**a** − **b**) *is:*

$$d_c(\mathbf{a}, \mathbf{b}) = \log_{|R|}(|\text{supp}(\mathbf{a} - \mathbf{b})|).$$

According to [11, 24] and [17, Lemma 2.6] d_g, d_c and d_l are metrics. By Proposition 3, we have $d_l = \nu d_c$ and thus d_c and d_l are decoding equivalent. But d_g and d_c are not decoding equivalent in general. Recall that the metric d_g was used in [24] to extend the theory of rank-metric codes to finite principal ideal rings, and the metric d_c was used in [11] to extend the same theory to Galois rings, which are specific cases of finite chain rings. The following theorem gives a link between the minimum distances and the packing radii of codes in these three metrics.

Theorem 2. *Let* $\mathcal{C}$ *be an* R−*submodule of* S^n. *Then,*

(a) $d_g(\mathcal{C}) = d_l(\mathcal{C}) = \nu \, d_c(\mathcal{C})$;
(b) $R_{d_g}(\mathcal{C}) = \lfloor (d_g(\mathcal{C}) - 1)/2 \rfloor$;
(c) $R_{d_l}(\mathcal{C}) = \lfloor (d_l(\mathcal{C}) - 1)/2 \rfloor$;
(d) $R_{d_c}(\mathcal{C}) = \lfloor (\nu \, d_c(\mathcal{C}) - 1)/2 \rfloor / \nu$.

Proof. Set $d = d_g(\mathcal{C})$. Let **c** in $\mathcal{C}$ such that $d_g(\mathbf{c}, \mathbf{0}) = d$. Then, by [24, Proposition 3.2] there are $b_1, \ldots, b_d \in S$ that are R−linearly independent, and $\alpha_1, \ldots, \alpha_d$ in $\mathbb{N}$ such that supp(**c**) = $<\pi^{\alpha_1} b_1, \ldots, \pi^{\alpha_d} b_d>$. We claim that $\alpha_1 = \cdots = \alpha_d$. Indeed, assume that $\alpha_i > \alpha_j$ for some i and j belonging to $\{1, \ldots, d\}$. Then, $\pi^{\nu - \alpha_j} \mathbf{c} \in \mathcal{C}$ and $0 < d_g(\pi^{\nu - \alpha_j} \mathbf{c}, \mathbf{0}) < d$ which contradicts the fact that $d = d_g(\mathcal{C})$. By setting $\mathbf{c}' = \pi^{\nu - 1 - \alpha_1} \mathbf{c}$, supp(**c**′) = $<\pi^{\nu - 1} b_1, \ldots, \pi^{\nu - 1} b_d>$ and $d_g(\mathbf{c}', \mathbf{0}) = d_l(\mathbf{c}', \mathbf{0}) = d$.
  (a) By Corollary 3, $d_g(\mathcal{C}) \leqslant d_l(\mathcal{C})$. Since $d_l(\mathbf{c}', \mathbf{0}) = d$, then $d_g(\mathcal{C}) = d_l(\mathcal{C})$.
  (b–c) Set $t = \lfloor (d_g(\mathcal{C}) - 1)/2 \rfloor$. By the triangle inequalities of the metrics d_g and d_l, we have $t \leqslant R_{d_g}(\mathcal{C})$ and $t \leqslant R_{d_l}(\mathcal{C})$, since $d_g(\mathcal{C}) = d_l(\mathcal{C})$. As supp(**c**′) = $<\pi^{\nu - 1} b_1, \ldots, \pi^{\nu - 1} b_d>$, there exists **A** in $R^{d \times n}$ such that $\mathbf{c}' = (\pi^{\nu - 1} b_1, \ldots, \pi^{\nu - 1} b_d)\mathbf{A}$. Set $t' = t + 1$ and $\mathbf{y} = (\pi^{\nu - 1} b_1, \ldots, \pi^{\nu - 1} b_{t'}, 0, \ldots, 0)\mathbf{A}$. Since $0 \leqslant d - t' \leqslant t'$, $\mathbf{y} \in B_{d_g}(\mathbf{0}, t') \cap B_{d_g}(\mathbf{c}', t')$ and $\mathbf{y} \in B_{d_l}(\mathbf{0}, t') \cap B_{d_l}(\mathbf{c}', t')$. Consequently, $R_{d_g}(\mathcal{C}) < t'$ and $R_{d_l}(\mathcal{C}) < t'$. As $R_{d_g}(\mathcal{C})$ and $R_{d_l}(\mathcal{C})$ are positive integers, then $R_{d_g}(\mathcal{C}) = R_{d_l}(\mathcal{C}) = t$.
  (d) The relation $R_{d_c}(\mathcal{C}) = \lfloor (\nu \, d_c(\mathcal{C}) - 1)/2 \rfloor / \nu$ is a direct consequence of Proposition 3 and Corollary 2. □

By Theorem 2, $R_{d_c}(\mathcal{C}) \leqslant R_{d_l}(\mathcal{C}) = R_{d_g}(\mathcal{C})$. It will then be interesting to compare the number of errors that a given linear code can correct with each of the three metrics up to the packing radii.

Corollary 4. *Let $\mathcal{C}$ be an $R-$submodule of S^n. Then,*

$$B_{d_c}(\mathbf{0}, R_{d_c}(\mathcal{C})) = B_{d_l}(\mathbf{0}, R_{d_l}(\mathcal{C})) \subset B_{d_g}(\mathbf{0}, R_{d_g}(\mathcal{C})).$$

Proof. Since d_c and d_l are decoding equivalent, then by Corollary 1, we have $B_{d_c}(\mathbf{0}, R_{d_c}(\mathcal{C})) = B_{d_l}(\mathbf{0}, R_{d_l}(\mathcal{C}))$. For $\mathbf{x} \in B_{d_l}(\mathbf{0}, R_{d_l}(\mathcal{C}))$ we have $d_l(\mathbf{x}, \mathbf{0}) \leqslant R_{d_l}(\mathcal{C})$ and by Corollary 3, $d_g(\mathbf{x}, \mathbf{0}) \leqslant d_l(\mathbf{x}, \mathbf{0})$. Using Theorem 2, we then have $R_{d_l}(\mathcal{C}) = R_{d_g}(\mathcal{C})$ and finally, $\mathbf{x} \in B_{d_g}(\mathbf{0}, R_{d_g}(\mathcal{C}))$. □

The first information given by Corollary 4 is that, up to the error correction capacity, the general decoding problems with the metrics d_l and d_c reduce to the same problem with the metric d_g because $B_{d_c}(\mathbf{0}, R_{d_c}(\mathcal{C}))$ is contained in $B_{d_g}(\mathbf{0}, R_{d_g}(\mathcal{C}))$. Thus, up to the error correction capability, the combinatorial and algebraic attacks described in [21,22] for the metric d_g can be applied to the metrics d_c and d_l. Another information given by Corollary 4 is that a linear code can correct, up to the error correction capacity, more errors with the metric d_g than errors with the metrics d_l and d_c. For example, the decoding algorithm of Gabidulin codes with the metric d_g given in [24,35] corrects more errors than the decoding algorithm of the same code with the metric d_c given [11]. The following example is given for illustration.

Example 4. Consider the extension S of $R = \mathbb{Z}_4$ given in Example 3. Let $\mathcal{C}$ be the Gabidulin code generated by $\mathbf{u}_1 = (1, a, a^2, a^3, a^4, a^5)$ and $\mathbf{u}_2 = (1, a^2, a^4, a^6, a^8, a^{10})$. By [24, Theorem 3.24], $d_g(\mathcal{C}) = 5$. By Theorem 2 or by [11, Theorem 4], $d_c(\mathcal{C}) = 5/2$. So, the error correction capacity of $\mathcal{C}$ with the metric d_g is $R_{d_g}(\mathcal{C}) = 2$ and the error correction capacity of $\mathcal{C}$ with the metric d_c is $R_{d_c}(\mathcal{C}) = 1$. There is a one-to-one correspondence between S^6 and the set of matrices of size 6×6 over R. Thus, according to Proposition 3 and [12, Theorem 2], the number of errors that $\mathcal{C}$ can correct up to $R_{d_g}(\mathcal{C})$ with the metric d_g is $|B_{d_g}(\mathbf{0}, 2)\backslash\{\mathbf{0}\}| = 2674147519575$ and the number of errors that $\mathcal{C}$ can correct up to $R_{d_c}(\mathcal{C})$ with the metric d_c is $|B_{d_c}(\mathbf{0}, 1)\backslash\{\mathbf{0}\}| = 10675287$, (See Example 5 in the appendix for more details).

Note that the above comparison was also made in [11], but in a biased manner since they did not take into account the packing radii, and resulted on a wrong conclusion stating that the metric d_c is more suitable for code-based cryptography compared to the metric d_g. In what follows, we show that this statement was incorrect.

4   Cryptographic Consequences

The foundation of code-based cryptography is the decoding problem for a random linear code [3]. Known in the context of rank metric codes as the Rank Decoding Problem, it is generally studied in a context of codes over finites fields. However, it was recently shown in [21] that the rank decoding problem over finite principal ideal rings is at least as hard as the rank decoding problem over finite fields. Furthermore, moving from finite fields to finite rings allows avoiding some algebraic attacks recently proposed on rank-based cryptosystems over finite fields [21]. So, there is clearly a possible gain in using rank-metric codes over finite rings. Nevertheless, if we limit ourselves for example to the case of finite chain rings, there are several possible generalizations of the rank metric as seen above, and the question here is to discuss which one is the most advantageous. In this section, we exploit the previous results on the packing radii of codes in the metrics d_g, d_c and d_l to show that the metric d_g is more suitable for code-based cryptography.

4.1 General Idea of Code-Based Cryptosystems

Here, we describe a canonical cryptosystem that can work with each of the metrics d_l, d_c and d_g.

Key Generation. Let $\mathcal{C}_d$ be a linear code in the metric d, with parity check matrix $\mathbf{H}$, packing radius $t_d = R_d(\mathcal{C})$ and decoding algorithm $\Gamma(\mathcal{C}_d)$. We assume that there exists a reversible transformation f so that applying f to $\mathbf{H}$ results in a parity check matrix $f(\mathbf{H})$ looking like a random matrix or a parity check matrix of a random linear code. The public key is then $\mathsf{pk} = (\mathbf{H}_{\mathrm{pub}}, t_d)$ with $\mathbf{H}_{\mathrm{pub}} = f(\mathbf{H})$, while the secret is the decoding algorithm $\Gamma(\mathcal{C}_d)$. As examples, $\mathcal{C}_d$ can be a Gabidulin code [11,24] or a Low Rank Parity Check (LRPC) code [23]. In the case of LRPC codes, f operates a series of row transformations on $\mathbf{H}$ [15], that is to say, $f(\mathbf{H}) = \mathbf{QH}$ where $\mathbf{Q}$ is an invertible matrix with entries in the Galois extension S of R.

Encryption. The encryption algorithm takes as input an error vector $\mathbf{e}$ with $d(\mathbf{e}, \mathbf{0}) \leqslant t_d$ and output it syndrome $\mathbf{s} = \mathbf{e}\mathbf{H}_{\mathrm{pub}}^{\top}$.

Decryption. The decryption process uses the decoding algorithm $\Gamma(\mathcal{C}_d)$ and, possibly, the reverse of the transformation f to output $\mathbf{e}$.

4.2 Comparison of Security Levels

In view of the different relations established between d_l, d_g and d_c, it is clear that the security levels of the above scheme will vary from a metric to another one. First, let us recall that, under the assumption that the public matrix $\mathbf{H}_{\mathrm{pub}}$ is indistinguishable from a random matrix, an attacker intercepting $\mathbf{s}$ and in possession of $\mathbf{H}_{\mathrm{pub}}$ should solve the following syndrome decoding problem associated to the metric d.

Definition 6 (Syndrome Decoding Problem). *Let $\mathbf{H} \in S^{(n-k)\times n}$, $\mathbf{s}$ an element of S^{n-k} and $t_d \in \mathbb{N}^*$. The* Syndrome Decoding Problem *is to find $\mathbf{e}$ in S^n such that*

$$\mathbf{s} = \mathbf{e}\mathbf{H}^{\top} \tag{1}$$

with $d(\mathbf{e}, \mathbf{0}) \leqslant t_d$.

One can remark that for all the above metrics, the above problem is easy to solve once we know the support of $\mathbf{e}$. So the best known technique for solving the above problem is to first find a support of $\mathbf{e}$ or a submodule containing it via a process called "Error Support Attack".

Error Support Attack. For all the above metrics, the Error Support Attack [16,21] will consist in choosing a free R–submodule F of S which contains the support supp($\mathbf{e}$) of $\mathbf{e}$ and then solve a system of linear equations to recover $\mathbf{e}$. Indeed, let F be a free R–submodule of S of rank u such that supp($\mathbf{e}$) $\subset F$ and consider $\mathbf{f} = (f_1, \ldots, f_u)$ be a vector with entries forming a basis of F. Let $\mathbf{X}$ be the $u \times n$ matrix with entries in R such that

$$\mathbf{e} = \mathbf{fX}. \tag{2}$$

Then, solving system (1) is equivalent to solve the system

$$\mathbf{s} = \mathbf{fXH}^\top. \tag{3}$$

Thus, the Error Support Attack [16,21] is to:

i) Choose a free R–submodule F of S of rank $u = \lfloor (n-k)m/n \rfloor$ with a basis $\{f_1, \ldots, f_u\}$.
ii) Solve the system of linear equations (3) with unknown $\mathbf{X}$.
iii) If Eq. (3) has a solution, then recover $\mathbf{e}$ using (2).

The success of the Error Support Attack depends on whether the free submodule F contains supp($\mathbf{e}$) or not. Thus, similar to the proof of [21, Theorem 5.4.], an average complexity of the Error Support Attack is

$$\mathcal{O}\left(m\left(n-k\right)u^2 n^2/p_d\right)$$

where p_d is the probability that supp($\mathbf{e}$) $\subset F$, $\mathbf{e}$ being an element of S^n such that $d(\mathbf{e}, \mathbf{0}) = r \leqslant t_d$.

Note that the distances d_c and d_l are decoding equivalent. Thus, we will only evaluate the average complexities of the Error Support Attack for the metrics d_g and d_l. Remember that given a linear code $\mathcal{C}$, $R_{d_g}(\mathcal{C})$ is equal to $R_{d_l}(\mathcal{C})$ and $B_{d_l}(\mathbf{0}, R_{d_l}(\mathcal{C})) \subset B_{d_g}(\mathbf{0}, R_{d_g}(\mathcal{C}))$. As a consequence, up to the error correction capabilities, any algorithm that solves the Syndrome Decoding Problem with the metric d_g also solves the Syndrome Decoding Problem with the metric d_l. In what follows, we work in the case $t_d = R_{d_l}(\mathcal{C}) = R_{d_g}(\mathcal{C})$.

Average Complexity for the Metric d_g. In [21, Remark 5.5.], it was proven that if $\mathbf{e}$ is an element of S^n such that $d_g(\mathbf{e}, \mathbf{0}) = r$, then the inverse of the probability p_{d_g} is given by $1/p_{d_g} \approx q^{\nu r(m-u)}$. Thus, when $\mathbf{e}$ is an element of S^n such that $d_g(\mathbf{e}, \mathbf{0}) = r$, an average complexity of the Error Support Attack is

$$\mathcal{O}\left(m\left(n-k\right)u^2 n^2 q^{\nu r(m-u)}\right). \tag{4}$$

Average Complexity for the Metric d_l. In Appendix B we proved as in [21] that for an element $\mathbf{e}$ of S^n such that $d_l(\mathbf{e}, \mathbf{0}) = r$, the inverse of the probability

p_{d_l} that supp($\mathbf{e}$) is contained in a free module F of rank u is given by $1/p_{d_l} \approx q^{r(m-u)}$. Thus, an average complexity of the Error Support Attack for the metric d_l is

$$\mathcal{O}\left(m\left(n-k\right)u^2n^2q^{r(m-u)}\right). \tag{5}$$

Comparison of the Two Complexities. The average complexities (4) and (5) show that the Error Support Attack is $q^{(\nu-1)r(m-u)}$ more powerful on the Syndrome Decoding Problem with the metric d_l compared to the same problem with the metric d_g. Note that for $\nu = 1$, R is a field and $d_g = d_l$. When $\nu > 1$, (4) is greater than (5). These observations were confirmed by our simulations, see Table 1 for illustration. The SageMath code used for our simulations is available at https://github.com/hervekalachi/Ring_Rank_Metrics. In Table 1, $Cost_{d_g}$ and $Cost_{d_l}$ correspond to the log in base 2 of the average complexities of the Error Support Attack on the Syndrome Decoding Problem with the metrics d_g and d_l respectively.

Table 1. Average Complexities of the Error Support Attack for $m = n = 32$, $k = 16$, $r = 4$.

q	2	2	2	2	4	4
ν	1	2	3	4	1	2
$Cost_{d_l}$	91	91	91	91	155	155
$Cost_{d_g}$	91	155	219	283	155	283

It is important to highlight the fact that the Error Support Attack (also known as combinatorial attack [21]) used here to evaluate and compare the security levels of the system with the different metrics d_g and d_l, is the best algorithm known until now for solving the rank syndrome decoding problem over finite rings. A problem that remains open is that of exploiting the ring structure to propose a better algorithm for solving the rank decoding problem over finite rings.

Comparison of Public Key Sizes. In Table 2, we suggest some parameters for our system with the metric d_g, resulting in security levels of 128 and 256 bits, and then provide the corresponding public key sizes. We also do the same with the metric d_l and, it appears as one can see in Table 2 that for the fixed security levels, the public key sizes with the metric d_l is approximately 5 to 10 times bigger than the public key sizes of the system with the metric d_g. In our simulations, we noticed that the more we increase the security level, the greater the gap between the public key sizes.

We can also notice that the public key sizes of our encryption scheme with the metric d_g are around 100 times smaller than the key sizes of classic McEliece [4], and 2 to 5 times smaller than LowMS [2].

Table 2. Key sizes comparison with the two metrics

Metrics	m	n	k	r	q	ν	Public Key sizes	Security Levels
d_g	34	34	17	3	2	2	2.4 KB	128
	38	40	20	3	2	4	7.6 KB	256
d_l	58	58	24	4	2	2	11.8 KB	128
	80	87	40	6	2	4	75.2 KB	256

5   Conclusion

In this work, we have studied three different ways to generalize the rank metric from finite fields to finite chain rings. One is using the minimum number of generators of modules d_g, another one is on the length of modules d_l, and the final one is based on the cardinal of modules d_c. It comes out that d_l and d_c are decoding equivalents, and connections between the minimum distances and the packing radii of codes in the three metrics are given. These connections make it possible to show that the general decoding problems bounded by the packing radii with the metrics d_c and d_l reduces to the same problem with the metric d_g. We have also proposed a McEliece/Niederreiter type cryptosystem that can be used with codes in the metrics d_l, d_c or d_g and showed that this encryption scheme with the metric d_g results in public key sizes at least 5 to 10 times smaller than the public key sizes of the system with the other metrics.

However, we underline the fact that the distances d_c, d_l, d_g can also be defined over finite commutative rings and, in that case, d_c and d_l will not be decoding equivalent in general. It will therefore be interesting to study the properties of these three distances when the ring R is not a finite chain ring. For some codes, it is possible to uniquely decode beyond error-correcting capability. This is the case for example with interleaved Gabidulin codes defined in [24] over finite principal ideal rings, and low-rank parity check codes defined in [23] over finite rings. For these codes, it will also be of interest to study and compare the probability of uniqueness decoding beyond the error correction capacity for these three metrics.

Acknowledgments. The first author acknowledges the Swiss Government Excellence for the financial support under grant ESKAS No. 2022.0689. The second author acknowledges the UNESCO-TWAS and the German Federal Ministry of Education and Research (BMBF) for the financial support under the SG-NAPI grant number 4500454079.

Disclosure of Interests. The authors have no competing interests to declare that are relevant to the content of this article.

A   Appendix

In this appendix, we use the work of [12] to give a method to find $|B_{d_g}(\mathbf{0}, r)|$, $|B_{d_l}(\mathbf{0}, r)|$, and $|B_{d_c}(\mathbf{0}, r)|$. Recall that $d_l = \nu d_c$, thus $B_{d_c}(\mathbf{0}, r) = B_{d_l}(\mathbf{0}, \nu r)$. By

Proposition 3, a module M over R can be decomposed as

$$M \cong \pi^{\alpha_1} R \times \cdots \times \pi^{\alpha_s} R.$$

This isomorphism can be expressed as

$$M \cong \underbrace{\pi^0 R \times \cdots \times \pi^0 R}_{k_0} \times \cdots \times \underbrace{\pi^{\nu-1} R \times \cdots \times \pi^{\nu-1} R}_{k_{\nu-1}}$$

where

$$k_i = |\{j \in \{1, \ldots, s\} : \alpha_j = i\}|, \text{ for } i = 0, \ldots, \nu - 1.$$

The ν−tuple $(k_0, \ldots, k_{\nu-1})$ is called the **type** of M and as in [12] the **shape**[4] of M is $(\beta_1, \ldots, \beta_\nu)$ where

$$\beta_1 = k_0 \text{ and } \beta_{i+1} = \beta_i + k_i, \text{ for } i = 1, \ldots, \nu - 1. \tag{6}$$

The type and the shape of a module can be extended to matrices, so if $\mathbf{A}$ is a matrix of size $m \times n$ with entries in R, then the type of $\mathbf{A}$ and the shape of $\mathbf{A}$ are respectively the type and the shape of the R−module generated by the column vectors of $\mathbf{A}$. the relationship between the shape of a matrix and its Smith normal form was given in [12].

Over finite fields with q elements, the number of k−dimensional subspaces in an n−dimensional vector space is given by the Gaussian binomial coefficient:

$$\begin{bmatrix} n \\ k \end{bmatrix}_q := \prod_{i=0}^{k-1} \frac{q^n - q^i}{q^k - q^i}$$

and the number of matrices of size $m \times n$ of rank k is

$$\prod_{i=0}^{k-1} \frac{(q^n - q^i)(q^m - q^i)}{q^k - q^i}.$$

These results were extended over finite chain rings using the shape. By [12] the number of R−submodules of R^n of shape $(\beta_1, \ldots, \beta_\nu)$ is

$$\prod_{i=1}^{\nu} q^{\beta_{i-1}(n-\beta_i)} \begin{bmatrix} n - \beta_{i-1} \\ \beta_i - \beta_{i-1} \end{bmatrix}_q \tag{7}$$

and by [12, Theorem 2] the number of matrices of size $m \times n$ with entries in R of shape $(\beta_1, \ldots, \beta_\nu)$ is

$$q^{\nu m k} \prod_{j=0}^{k-1} (1 - q^{j-m}) \prod_{i=1}^{\nu} q^{\beta_{i-1}(n-\beta_i)} \begin{bmatrix} n - \beta_{i-1} \\ \beta_i - \beta_{i-1} \end{bmatrix}_q \tag{8}$$

---

[4] Note that the definition of the shape in this paper corresponds to the conjugation of the shape in descending order defined in [19,21].

where $\beta_0 := 0$.

As S is a free R-module of rank m, there exists a one-to-one correspondence between S^n and the set $R^{m \times n}$ of matrices of size $m \times n$ with entries in R. Thus, the number of $\mathbf{a}$ in S^n such that the shape of supp($\mathbf{a}$) is $(\beta_1, \ldots, \beta_\nu)$ is equal to the number of $\mathbf{A}$ in $R^{m \times n}$ of shape $(\beta_1, \ldots, \beta_\nu)$. Thus, we can use (8) to find $|B_{d_g}(\mathbf{0}, r)|$ and $|B_{d_l}(\mathbf{0}, r)|$.

Calculation of $|B_{d_g}(\mathbf{0}, r)|$. According to Proposition 3,

$$\mathbf{a} \in B_{d_g}(\mathbf{0}, r) \iff \mu_R(\text{supp}(\mathbf{a})) \leqslant r \iff \sum_{0 \leqslant i \leqslant \nu - 1} k_i \leqslant r$$

where $(k_0, \ldots, k_{\nu-1})$ is the type of supp($\mathbf{a}$). Thus, to calculate $|B_{d_g}(\mathbf{0}, r)|$, the following steps can be used:

1. Find the set K of all types $(k_0, \ldots, k_{\nu-1})$ such that $\sum_{1 \leqslant i \leqslant \nu - 1} k_i \leqslant r$;
2. Construct the set B of all the shapes $(\beta_1, \ldots, \beta_\nu)$ associated to each type $(k_0, \ldots, k_{\nu-1})$ in K using (6);
3. Sum the number of matrices of shape $(\beta_1, \ldots, \beta_\nu)$ for $(\beta_1, \ldots, \beta_\nu)$ in B using (8).

Calculation of $|B_{d_l}(\mathbf{0}, r)|$. According to Proposition 3,

$$\mathbf{a} \in B_{d_l}(\mathbf{0}, r) \iff \lambda_R(\text{supp}(\mathbf{a})) \leqslant r \iff \sum_{0 \leqslant i \leqslant \nu - 1} (\nu - i) k_i \leqslant r$$

where $(k_0, \ldots, k_{\nu-1})$ is the type of supp($\mathbf{a}$). Thus, to calculate $|B_{d_l}(\mathbf{0}, r)|$, the following steps can be used:

1. Find the set K of all types $(k_0, \ldots, k_{\nu-1})$ such that $\sum_{0 \leqslant i \leqslant \nu - 1} (\nu - i) k_i \leqslant r$;
2. Construct the set B of all shapes $(\beta_1, \ldots, \beta_\nu)$ associated to each type $(k_0, \ldots, k_{\nu-1})$ in K using (6);
3. Sum the number of matrices of shape $(\beta_1, \ldots, \beta_\nu)$ for $(\beta_1, \ldots, \beta_\nu)$ in B using (8).

Example 5. Here we give more details on the calculation of $|B_{d_g}(\mathbf{0}, 2)|$ and $|B_{d_l}(\mathbf{0}, 2)|$ of Example 4. Recall that in this case, $q = 2$, $\nu = 2$, $m = n = 6$ and $r = 2$.

(i) The calculation of $|B_{d_g}(\mathbf{0}, 2)|$.

The set of types (k_0, k_1) such that $k_0 + k_1 \leqslant 2$ is

$$K = \{(0,0), (0,1), (1,0), (1,1), (0,2), (2,0)\}.$$

The set of associated shapes is $B = \{(0,0), (0,1), (1,1), (1,2), (0,2), (2,2)\}$.

For each (β_1, β_2) in B we calculate the number of matrices of shape (β_1, β_2) and sum them.

Thus, $|B_{d_g}(\mathbf{0}, 2)| = 2674147519576$.

(ii) Computing $|B_{d_l}(\mathbf{0}, 2)|$

Shapes	Number of matrices
$(0,0)$	1
$(0,1)$	3969
$(1,1)$	8128512
$(1,2)$	7811500032
$(0,2)$	2542806
$(2,2)$	2666325344256
Total	2674147519576

The set of type (k_0, k_1) such that $2k_0 + k_1 \leqslant 2$ is $K = \{(0,0), (0,1), (1,0), (0,2)\}$.

The set of associated shape is $B = \{(0,0), (0,1), (1,1), (0,2)\}$.

For each (β_1, β_2) in B we calculate the number of matrices of shape (β_1, β_2) and sum them.

Shapes	Number of matrices
$(0,0)$	1
$(0,1)$	3969
$(1,1)$	8128512
$(0,2)$	2542806
Total	10675288

Thus, $|B_{d_l}(\mathbf{0}, 2)| = 10675288$.

B   Appendix

In this appendix, we prove as in [21, Remark 5.5.] that, if $\mathbf{e}$ is an element of S^n such that $d_l(\mathbf{e}, \mathbf{0}) = r$, then the inverse of the probability p_{d_l} that $\mathrm{supp}(\mathbf{e})$ is contained in a free module F of rank u is given by $1/p_l \approx q^{r(m-u)}$. Recall that $d_l(\mathbf{e}, \mathbf{0}) = r$ if and only if $\lambda_R(\mathrm{supp}(\mathbf{e})) = r$. Using the same notations as in Proposition 3 and in (6) we have

$$\lambda_R(M) = \sum_{1 \leqslant i \leqslant s} (\nu - \alpha_i) = \sum_{0 \leqslant i \leqslant \nu - 1} (\nu - i)k_i = \sum_{1 \leqslant i \leqslant \nu} \beta_i.$$

Hence, if M is a module of shape $(\beta_1, \ldots, \beta_\nu)$, then $\lambda_R(M) = r$ if and only if $\sum_{1 \leqslant i \leqslant \nu} \beta_i = r$. Thus, according to (7) the number of R-submodule M of length $\lambda_R(M) = r$ contained in a free module F of rank u is

$$\Psi(q, \nu, r, u) := \sum_{\substack{0 = \beta_0 \leqslant \beta_1 \leqslant \cdots \leqslant \beta_\nu \\ \beta_1 + \cdots + \beta_\nu = r}} \prod_{i=1}^{\nu} q^{\beta_{i-1}(u - \beta_i)} \begin{bmatrix} u - \beta_{i-1} \\ \beta_i - \beta_{i-1} \end{bmatrix}_q. \qquad (9)$$

Recall that from [25], we have

$$q^{k(n-k)} \leqslant \begin{bmatrix} n \\ k \end{bmatrix}_q \leqslant 4q^{k(n-k)}.$$

Thus,

$$q^{\sum_{i=1}^{\nu} \beta_i(u-\beta_i)} \leqslant \prod_{i=1}^{\nu} q^{\beta_{i-1}(u-\beta_i)} \begin{bmatrix} u - \beta_{i-1} \\ \beta_i - \beta_{i-1} \end{bmatrix}_q \leqslant 4^{\nu} q^{\sum_{i=1}^{\nu} \beta_i(u-\beta_i)}. \qquad (10)$$

Using the fact that $0 \leqslant \beta_1 \leqslant \cdots \leqslant \beta_\nu$ and $\beta_1 + \cdots + \beta_\nu = r$, we obtain, $\sum_{i=1}^{\nu} \beta_i(u - \beta_i) \leqslant \beta_\nu(u - r) \leqslant r(u - r)$, since the optimal value of β_ν is r. Thus (10) is upper bounded by $4^{\nu} q^{r(u-r)}$. Hence, an upper bound of (9) is $4^{\nu} \binom{r+\nu-1}{\nu-1} q^{r(u-r)}$ where $\binom{r+\nu-1}{\nu-1}$ is a binomial coefficient which is equal to the number of ν−tuple $(\beta_1, \ldots, \beta_\nu)$ such that $\beta_1 + \cdots + \beta_\nu = r$.

Among the ν−tuples $(\beta_1, \ldots, \beta_\nu)$ such that $\beta_1 + \cdots + \beta_\nu = r$, one has the ν−tuple $(0, \ldots, 0, r)$. Thus, (10) implies that (9) is lower bounded by $q^{r(u-r)}$. Therefore,

$$q^{r(u-r)} \leqslant \Psi(q, \nu, r, u) \leqslant 4^{\nu} \binom{r + \nu - 1}{\nu - 1} q^{r(u-r)}. \qquad (11)$$

The probability p_{d_l} that supp($\mathbf{e}$) of length r is contained in a free module F of rank u is equal to the number of submodules of S of length r in a free submodule of S of rank u divided by the number of submodules of S of length r, that is to say,

$$p_{d_l} = \Psi(q, \nu, r, u)/\Psi(q, \nu, r, m).$$

Using (11), we obtain $p_{d_l} \approx q^{r(u-r)}/q^{r(m-r)} = q^{r(u-m)}$. So,

$$1/p_{d_l} \approx q^{r(m-u)}.$$

References

1. Alagic, G., et al.: Status report on the second round of the NIST post-quantum cryptography standardization process. US Department of Commerce, NIST 2 (2020)
2. Aragon, N., Dyseryn, V., Gaborit, P., Loidreau, P., Renner, J., Wachter-Zeh, A.: LowMS: a new rank metric code-based KEM without ideal structure. Des. Codes Crypt. **92**(4), 1075–1093 (2024)
3. Berlekamp, E., McEliece, R., van Tilborg, H.: On the inherent intractability of certain coding problems. IEEE Trans. Inform. Theory **24**(3), 384–386 (1978)
4. Bernstein, D.J., et al.: Classic McEliece: conservative code-based cryptography (2019). https://classic.mceliece.org. Second round submission to the NIST post-quantum cryptography call
5. Bucerzan, D., Dragoi, V., Kalachi, H.T.: Evolution of the McEliece public key encryption scheme. In: Farshim, P., Simion, E. (eds.) SecITC 2017. LNCS, vol. 10543, pp. 129–149. Springer, Cham (2017). https://doi.org/10.1007/978-3-319-69284-5_10

6. Campello, A., Jorge, G.C., Strapasson, J.E., Costa, S.I.: Perfect codes in the lp metric. Eur. J. Comb. **53**, 72–85 (2016)
7. Delsarte, P.: Bilinear forms over a finite field, with applications to coding theory. J. Comb. Theory, Ser. A **25**(3), 226–241 (1978)
8. Deza, E., Deza, M.M., Deza, M.M., Deza, E.: Encyclopedia of Distances. Springer, Cham (2009)
9. D'Oliveira, R.G., Firer, M.: Channel metrization. Eur. J. Comb. **80**, 107–119 (2019)
10. D'Oliveira, R.G.L., Firer, M.: The packing radius of a code and partitioning problems: the case for poset metrics on finite vector spaces. Discret. Math. **338**(12), 2143–2167 (2015)
11. Epelde, M., Rúa, I.F.: Cardinal rank metric codes over Galois rings. Finite Fields Appl. **77**, 101946 (2022)
12. Feng, C., Nóbrega, R.W., Kschischang, F.R., Silva, D.: Communication over finite-chain-ring matrix channels. IEEE Trans. Inf. Theory **60**(10), 5899–5917 (2014)
13. Gabidulin, È.M.: Theory of codes with maximum rank distance. Problemy Peredachi Informatsii **21**(1), 3–16 (1985)
14. Gabidulin, E.M., Paramonov, A.V., Tretjakov, O.V.: Ideals over a non-commutative ring and their application in cryptology. In: Davies, D.W. (ed.) EUROCRYPT 1991. LNCS, vol. 547, pp. 482–489. Springer, Heidelberg (1991). https://doi.org/10.1007/3-540-46416-6_41
15. Gaborit, P., Murat, G., Ruatta, O., Zémor, G.: Low rank parity check codes and their application to cryptography. In: Proceedings of the Workshop on Coding and Cryptography, WCC 2013, Bergen, Norway (2013). www.selmer.uib.no/WCC2013/pdfs/Gaborit.pdf
16. Gaborit, P., Ruatta, O., Schrek, J.: On the complexity of the rank syndrome decoding problem. IEEE Trans. Inf. Theory **62**(2), 1006–1019 (2016). https://doi.org/10.1109/TIT.2015.2511786
17. Gorla, E., Ravagnani, A.: An algebraic framework for end-to-end physical-layer network coding. IEEE Trans. Inf. Theory **64**(6), 4480–4495 (2017)
18. Hamming, R.W.: Error detecting and error correcting codes. Bell Syst. Tech. J. **29**(2), 147–160 (1950)
19. Honold, T., Landjev, I.: Linear codes over finite chain rings. Electron. J. Comb. **7**, R11–R11 (2000)
20. Horlemann, A.L.: Code-based cryptography with the subspace metric. In: SIAM Conference on Applied Geometry (2021)
21. Kalachi, H.T., Kamche, H.T.: On the rank decoding problem over finite principal ideal rings. Adv. Math. Commun. (2023). https://doi.org/10.3934/amc.2023003
22. Kamche, H.T., Kalachi, H.T.: Solving systems of algebraic equations over finite commutative rings and applications. In: Applicable Algebra in Engineering, Communication and Computing, pp. 1–29 (2024)
23. Kamche, H.T., Kalachi, H.T., Djomou, F.R.K., Fouotsa, E.: Low-rank parity-check codes over finite commutative rings. In: Applicable Algebra in Engineering, Communication and Computing, pp. 1–27 (2024)
24. Kamche, H.T., Mouaha, C.: Rank-metric codes over finite principal ideal rings and applications. IEEE Trans. Inf. Theory **65**(12), 7718–7735 (2019)
25. Koetter, R., Kschischang, F.R.: Coding for errors and erasures in random network coding. IEEE Trans. Inf. Theory **54**(8), 3579–3591 (2008)
26. Kunz, E.: Introduction to Commutative Algebra and Algebraic Geometry. Springer, Cham (1985)
27. McDonald, B.R.: Finite Rings with Identity, vol. 28. Marcel Dekker Incorporated (1974)

28. McEliece, R.J.: A Public-Key System Based on Algebraic Coding Theory, pp. 114–116. Jet Propulsion Lab (1978). dSN Progress Report 44
29. Melchor, C.A., et al.: Rollo–rank-ouroboros, lake & locker. Round-2 submission to the NIST PQC project (2019)
30. Nechaev, A.A.: Finite rings with applications. Handb. Algebra **5**, 213–320 (2008)
31. NIST: Post-quantum cryptography standardization (2017). https://csrc.nist.gov/Projects/Post-Quantum-Cryptography/Post-Quantum-Cryptography-Standardization
32. Overbeck, R., Sendrier, N.: Code-based cryptography. In: Bernstein, D.J., Buchmann, J., Dahmen, E. (eds.) Post-Quantum Cryptography, pp. 95–145. Springer, Heidelberg (2009). https://doi.org/10.1007/978-3-540-88702-7_4
33. Panek, L., Firer, M., Alves, M.M.S.: Classification of Niederreiter-Rosenbloom-Tsfasman block codes. IEEE Trans. Inf. Theory **56**(10), 5207–5216 (2010)
34. Puchinger, S., Renner, J., Rosenkilde, J.: Generic decoding in the sum-rank metric. IEEE Trans. Inf. Theory **68**(8), 5075–5097 (2022)
35. Puchinger, S., Renner, J., Wachter-Zeh, A., Zumbrägel, J.: Efficient decoding of Gabidulin codes over Galois rings. In: 2021 IEEE International Symposium on Information Theory (ISIT), pp. 25–30. IEEE (2021)
36. Ritterhoff, S., et al.: FuLeeca: a Lee-based signature scheme. In: Esser, A., Santini, P. (eds.) CBCrypto 2023. LNCS, vol. 14311, pp. 56–83. Springer, Cham (2023). https://doi.org/10.1007/978-3-031-46495-9_4
37. Shannon, C.E.: A mathematical theory of communication. Bell Syst. Tech. J. **27**(4), 623–656 (1948)
38. Weger, V., Gassner, N., Rosenthal, J.: A survey on code-based cryptography. In: Coding Theory and Applications V, Applications of Coding Theory in Quantum Computing and Cryptography. Springer, Cham (2022)
39. Weger, V., Khathuria, K., Horlemann, A.L., Battaglioni, M., Santini, P., Persichetti, E.: On the hardness of the Lee syndrome decoding problem. Adv. Math. Commun. **18**(1), 233–266 (2024)

Polynomial-Time Key-Recovery Attack on the NIST Specification of PROV

River Moreira Ferreira$^{(\boxtimes)}$ and Ludovic Perret

Sorbonne Université, CNRS, LIP6, 75005 Paris, France
{river.moreira-ferreira,ludovic.perret}@lip6.fr

Abstract. In this paper, we present an efficient attack against PROV, a recent variant of the popular Unbalanced Oil and Vinegar (UOV) multivariate signature scheme, that has been submitted to the ongoing NIST standardization process for additional post-quantum signature schemes. A notable feature of PROV is its proof of security, namely, existential unforgeability under a chosen-message attack (EUF-CMA), assuming the hardness of solving the system formed by the public-key non-linear equations. We present a polynomial-time key-recovery attack against the first specification of PROV (v1.0). To do so, we remark that a small fraction of the PROV secret-key is leaked during the signature process. Adapting and extending previous works on basic UOV, we show that the entire secret-key can be then recovered from such a small fraction in polynomial-time. This leads to an efficient attack against PROV that we validated in practice. For all the security parameters suggested by the authors of PROV, our attack recovers the secret-key in at most 8 seconds. We conclude the paper by discussing the apparent mismatch between such a practical attack and the theoretical security claimed by PROV designers. Our attack is not structural but exploits that the current specification of PROV differs from the required security model. A simple countermeasure makes PROV immune against our attack and led the designers to update the specification of PROV (v1.1).

Keywords: Post-quantum · NIST PQC · Cryptanalysis · Key-Recovery

1 Introduction

In 2022, the National Institute of Standards and Technology (NIST) selected the first post-quantum cryptographic standards after five years of competition. In particular, three digital signature schemes (DSS) relying either on structured lattices (Dilithium [16] and Falcon [13]) or hash functions (SPHINCS+ [10]) have been selected for standardization. NIST also decided to start a new standardization process for additional post-quantum DSS to increase the diversity of hardness assumptions. From a practical point of view, the new call was especially targeting schemes with *"short signature"* and *"fast verification"* [1].

© The Author(s), under exclusive license to Springer Nature Switzerland AG 2024
S. Vaudenay and C. Petit (Eds.): AFRICACRYPT 2024, LNCS 14861, pp. 222–235, 2024.
https://doi.org/10.1007/978-3-031-64381-1_10

Such practical features are typical of multivariate schemes. As such, UOV [11] appears today as the most appealing candidate such that round-1 candidates of the new NIST standardization process [1] includes about 8 UOV-based DSS[1]. A promising candidate among these UOV-variants is the PRovable Unbalanced Oil and Vinegar (PROV) that includes a strong security argument with an EUF-CMA security proof under the hardness assumption of solving PROV public-key multivariate equations. Until now, no security weakness has been reported against PROV.

1.1   Organization of the Paper and Main Results

We organize the paper as follows. In Sect. 2, we introduce the necessary notations, mathematical objects, and the security framework used in PROV. In Sect. 3, we recall the PROV signature scheme as defined in the NIST-specification v1.0 [6]. Also, we extend the new Kipnis-Shamir attack on UOV of [14] to PROV, which recovers the secret-key in polynomial-time for small parameters. Section 4 describes our attack: Sects. 4.1 and 4.2 details a polynomial-time key-recovery attack against PROV specification v1.0 (Theorem 1). To do so, we exploit the fact that a small fraction of the secret-key is leaked during the signature generation. Then, we extend to the specific characteristics of PROV results from [2,14] on UOV demonstrating that the entire secret-key can be then recovered from this small leakage. The attack has a polynomial-time complexity and is also very efficient in practice. In Sect. 4.3, we present experimental results and show that the secret key can be recovered in a few seconds for all security levels (Table 2). Section 4.4 discusses a simple tweak that prevents this attack and reestablishes the validity of the security model used in [6]. The vulnerability was reported to the designers of PROV who then updated the specification (v1.1, [7]) with this countermeasure.

2   Preliminaries

2.1   Notations

Let q be a prime or a prime power (for PROV, $q = 2^8$). We denote by bold lowercase (resp. capital) letter any column vector $\mathbf{v} \in \mathbb{F}_q^n$ of size n in $\mathbb{F}_q$ or respectively any matrix $\mathbf{M} \in \mathbb{F}_q^{n \times m}$ of size $n \times m$ in $\mathbb{F}_q$. In particular, let $\mathbf{0}_n$ be the zero column vector of size n in $\mathbb{F}_q$, $\mathbf{0}_{n \times m}$ be the zero matrix of size $n \times m$ in $\mathbb{F}_q$ and $\mathbf{1}_n$ be the n-by-n identity matrix in $\mathbb{F}_q$. For a set of vector $\mathbf{b} = (\mathbf{b}_1, \ldots, \mathbf{b}_m) \in (\mathbb{F}_q^n)^m$, we denote by $\mathsf{span}(\mathbf{b}) \subset \mathbb{F}_q^n$ the linear span of $\mathbf{b}$. Also, we express the kernel of a matrix $\mathbf{M} \in \mathbb{F}_q^{n \times m}$ or a linear map f respectively by $\mathsf{Ker}(\mathbf{M})$ and $\mathsf{Ker}(f)$. For the complexity analysis, we consider ω the exponent of matrix multiplication where $2 \leq \omega \leq 3$.

The function Upper takes as input a square matrix $\mathbf{A} = \{a_{i,j}\}_{1 \leq i,j \leq n}$ and outputs an upper triangular matrix $\mathsf{Upper}(\mathbf{A}) = \{b_{i,j}\}_{1 \leq i,j \leq n}$ such that $b_{i,j} = a_{i,j} + a_{j,i}$ if $i < j$, $b_{i,j} = a_{i,j}$ if $i = j$ or $b_{i,j} = 0$ otherwise. We refer by the symbol

---

[1] https://csrc.nist.gov/Projects/pqc-dig-sig/round-1-additional-signatures.

|| either the concatenation of two bit-strings or the horizontal concatenation of two matrices depending on the context. Let $\emptyset$ be the empty set, i.e. the set with no element.

Let $\mathbb{F}_q[x_1, \ldots, x_n]$ be the ring of multivariate polynomials in n variables with coefficients over $\mathbb{F}_q$. In this work, every quadratic polynomial $p \in \mathbb{F}_q[x_1, \ldots, x_n]$ will be homogeneous, i.e. $p(\lambda(x_1, \ldots, x_n)) = \lambda^2 p(x_1, \ldots, x_n)$, for all $\lambda \in \mathbb{F}_q^*$. The polar form $p^* : \mathbb{F}_q^n \times \mathbb{F}_q^n \to \mathbb{F}_q$ of a homogeneous quadratic polynomial $p \in \mathbb{F}_q[x_1, \ldots, x_n]$ is a bi-linear and symmetric function defined as $p^*(\mathbf{x}, \mathbf{y}) := p(\mathbf{x} + \mathbf{y}) - p(\mathbf{x}) - p(\mathbf{y})$ for all $\mathbf{x}, \mathbf{y} \in \mathbb{F}_q^n$. Any homogeneous quadratic polynomial $p \in \mathbb{F}_q[x_1, \ldots, x_n]$ can be uniquely represented as $p(\mathbf{x}) = \mathbf{x}^\mathsf{T} \mathbf{Q} \mathbf{x}$, where $\mathbf{Q} \in \mathbb{F}_q^{n \times n}$ is an upper triangular matrix, and the corresponding polar form as $p^*(\mathbf{x}, \mathbf{y}) = \mathbf{x}^\mathsf{T}(\mathbf{Q} + \mathbf{Q}^\mathsf{T})\mathbf{y}$ with $\mathbf{x}, \mathbf{y} \in \mathbb{F}_q^n$. A multivariate quadratic map $\mathcal{P} : \mathbb{F}_q^n \to \mathbb{F}_q^m$ is defined by a set of multivariate quadratic polynomials $(p_1, \ldots, p_m) \in \mathbb{F}_q[x_1, \ldots, x_n]^m$.

2.2 Security Framework of PROV

Here, we recall the definition of a Weak Preimage-Sampleable Function (WPSF) used in the security analysis of PROV [6].

Definition 1 (WPSF [6]). *A WPSF* **T** *consists of four probabilistic polynomial-time algorithms:*

- **Gen**: *this algorithm takes as input a security parameter 1^λ and outputs a function* $\mathbf{F} : \mathcal{X} \to \mathcal{Y}$ *with a trapdoor* **I**;
- **F**: *this algorithm takes as input a value $x \in \mathcal{X}$ and deterministically outputs* $\mathbf{F}(x)$;
- $\mathbf{I} = (\mathbf{I}^1, \mathbf{I}^2)$: *the algorithm* $\mathbf{I}^1$ *takes no input and outputs a value $z \in \mathcal{Z}$; the algorithm* $\mathbf{I}^2$ *takes as input $z \in \mathcal{Z}$, $y \in \mathcal{Y}$, and outputs $x \in \mathcal{X}$ such that* $\mathbf{F}(x) = y$, *or outputs $\perp$ if it failed;*
- **SampDom**: *this algorithm takes as input a function* $\mathbf{F} : \mathcal{X} \to \mathcal{Y}$ *and outputs a value $x \in \mathcal{X}$.*

The Preimage Sampling (PS) security of a WPSF is defined as:

Definition 2 (PS security [6]). *Let T be a WPSF. The advantage of an adversary $\mathcal{A}$ against the PS security of* **T** *is defined as:*

$$\mathbf{Adv}_{\mathbf{T}}^{PS}(\mathcal{A}) = \left| \Pr\left[PS_0^{\mathcal{A}} = 1 \right] - \Pr\left[PS_1^{\mathcal{A}} = 1 \right] \right|$$

where PS_0 and PS_1 are the security games defined in Fig. 1.

PS_b	Sample_0	Sample_1
$(\mathbf{F}, \mathbf{I}) \leftarrow \mathbf{Gen}(1^\lambda)$	$z_i \leftarrow \mathbf{I}^1()$	$x_i \leftarrow \mathbf{SampDom}(\mathbf{F})$
$b^* \leftarrow \mathcal{A}^{\text{Sample}_b}(\mathbf{F})$	**repeat**	**Return** x_i
Return b^*	$\quad y_i \xleftarrow{\$} \mathcal{Y}$	
	$\quad x_i \leftarrow \mathbf{I}^2(z_i, y_i)$	
	until $x_i \neq \perp$ **Return** x_i	

Fig. 1. PS security games.

3   Description of PROV

PRovable Unbalanced Oil and Vinegar (PROV) is a new signature scheme [6] submitted to the recent NIST standardization process for additional post-quantum signature schemes [1]. As several multivariate schemes submitted to this standardization process, PROV is a variant of the Unbalanced Oil and Vinegar (UOV) multivariate signature scheme [11].

PROV uses the the recent definition of UOV introduced by W. Beullens in [5] in combination with an efficient variant of the so-called salt-UOV [15], a provably secure variant of UOV. In [5], the traditional UOV trapdoor [11] is rephrased as the vanishing subspace of a multivariate quadratic map.

Definition 3. *Let $\mathcal{P} : \mathbb{F}_q^n \to \mathbb{F}_q^m$ be a multivariate quadratic map and $\mathbf{O} \subset \mathbb{F}_q^n$ be a linear subspace. We shall say that $\mathbf{O}$ is a vanishing subspace of $\mathcal{P}$ if:*

$$\forall \mathbf{o} \in \mathbf{O}, \ \mathcal{P}(\mathbf{o}) = \mathbf{0}_m.$$

From a high-level point of view, the public-key in PROV is given by the multivariate quadratic map $\mathcal{P} : \mathbb{F}_q^n \to \mathbb{F}_q^m$ and the corresponding secret-key is a vanishing subspace $\mathbf{O} \subset \mathbb{F}_q^n$ of dimension $m + \delta$ with $\delta \geq 1$. The main specificity of PROV is related to the parameter δ that allows a more efficient reduction than salt-UOV [15]. From now on, we set $v = n - m - \delta$.

3.1   Key-Generation in PROV

In order to generate a PROV key pair (Definition 3) $(\mathcal{P}, \mathbf{O})$ with $\mathcal{P} : \mathbb{F}_q^n \to \mathbb{F}_q^m$ and a vanishing subspace $\mathbf{O} \subset \mathbb{F}_q^n$ of dimension $m + \delta$ with $\delta \geq 1$, [6] suggests to first generate a random basis of $\mathbf{O}$ in systematic form, i.e. namely a basis of the form:

$$(\mathbf{O}^\mathsf{T} \ \mathbf{1}_{m+\delta}) \in \mathbb{F}_q^{(m+\delta) \times n}, \text{ with } \mathbf{O} \in \mathbb{F}_q^{v \times (m+\delta)}. \tag{1}$$

Then, the components $p_1, \ldots, p_m \in \mathbb{F}_q[x_1, \ldots, x_n]$ of $\mathcal{P} : \mathbb{F}_q^n \to \mathbb{F}_q^m$ are constructed as follows:

$$p_i(\mathbf{x}) = \mathbf{x}^\mathsf{T} \mathbf{P}_i \mathbf{x}, \quad \mathbf{P}_i = \begin{pmatrix} \mathbf{P}_i^{(1)} & \mathbf{P}_i^{(2)} \\ \mathbf{0}_{(m+\delta) \times v} & \mathbf{P}_i^{(3)} \end{pmatrix} \in \mathbb{F}_q^{n \times n}, \ \forall i, \ 1 \leq i \leq m, \tag{2}$$

with $\mathbf{x} = (x_1, \ldots, x_n) \in \mathbb{F}_q^n, \mathbf{P}_i^{(1)} \in \mathbb{F}_q^{v \times v}$ be an upper triangular matrix, $\mathbf{P}_i^{(2)} \in \mathbb{F}_q^{v \times (m+\delta)}$ be a matrix and $\mathbf{P}_i^{(3)} = \mathsf{Upper}\left(-\mathbf{O}^\mathsf{T}\mathbf{P}_i^{(1)}\mathbf{O} - \mathbf{O}^\mathsf{T}\mathbf{P}_i^{(2)}\right) \in \mathbb{F}_q^{(m+\delta) \times (m+\delta)}$ The linear subspace $\mathbf{O}$ generated as in (1) is a vanishing subspace of the map defined by the polynomials (2).

3.2 Signature Verification and Generation

The PROV signature for a message $\mathsf{msg} \in \{0,1\}^*$ is given by a vector $\mathbf{s} \in \mathbb{F}_q^n$ and a fixed-length bit string $\mathsf{salt} \in \{0,1\}^{\mathsf{len_{salt}}}$ such that

$$\mathcal{P}(\mathbf{s}) = \mathcal{H}(\mathsf{msg}\|\mathsf{salt}),$$

where $\mathcal{H} : \{0,1\}^* \to \mathbb{F}_q^m$ is a hash function[2].

The PROV trapdoor is based on the result below, demonstrating that the knowledge of the vanishing subspace allows one to compute a valid signature by solving a linear system.

Lemma 1. *Let* $\mathbf{O} \in \mathbb{F}_q^{v \times (m+\delta)}$, $\mathcal{P} : \mathbb{F}_q^n \to \mathbb{F}_q^m$ *be represented with matrices* $(\mathbf{P}_1, \ldots, \mathbf{P}_m) \in (\mathbb{F}_q^{n \times n})^m$ *as defined in* (2), $\bar{\mathbf{v}} = \begin{pmatrix} \mathbf{v} \\ \mathbf{0}_{m+\delta} \end{pmatrix}, \bar{\mathbf{o}} = \begin{pmatrix} \mathbf{O} \\ \mathbf{1}_{m+\delta} \end{pmatrix} \mathbf{o} \in \mathbb{F}_q^n$, *with* $\mathbf{v} \in \mathbb{F}_q^v$ *and* $\mathbf{o} \in \mathbb{F}_q^{(m+\delta)}$. *For all* $\mathbf{h} = (h_1, \ldots, h_m) \in \mathbb{F}_q^m$, *it holds that:*

$$\mathcal{P}(\bar{\mathbf{v}} + \bar{\mathbf{o}}) = \mathbf{h} \quad \Longleftrightarrow \quad \mathbf{v}^\mathsf{T}\mathbf{S}_i\mathbf{o} = h_i - \mathbf{v}^\mathsf{T}\mathbf{P}_i^{(1)}\mathbf{v}, \ \forall i, \ 1 \le i \le m,$$

with $\mathbf{S}_i = (\mathbf{P}_i^{(1)} + \mathbf{P}_i^{(1)\mathsf{T}})\mathbf{O} + \mathbf{P}_i^{(2)} \in \mathbb{F}_q^{v \times (m+\delta)}$.

In order to generate a signature of $\mathsf{msg} \in \{0,1\}^*$, the signer generates a random pair $(\mathbf{v}, \mathsf{salt}) \in \mathbb{F}_q^v \times \{0,1\}^{\mathsf{len_{salt}}}$ and solves the corresponding linear system of Lemma 1 with $\mathbf{h} = \mathcal{H}(\mathsf{msg}\|\mathsf{salt}) \in \mathbb{F}_q^m$. If the linear system has no solution, then the signer samples a new $\mathsf{salt} \in \{0,1\}^{\mathsf{len_{salt}}}$ and solves the new system. The process is repeated until a solution exists. Finally, he recovers the signature $\mathbf{s} = \bar{\mathbf{v}} + \bar{\mathbf{o}} \in \mathbb{F}_q^n$, with $\bar{\mathbf{v}}, \bar{\mathbf{o}} \in \mathbb{F}_q^n$ as in Lemma 1. We detail the PROV signature generation in Algorithm 1.

Remark 1. Note that the vector $\bar{\mathbf{o}}$ belongs in the secret vanishing subspace $\mathbf{O}$ of the public key.

Given a matrix $\mathbf{A} \in \mathbb{F}_q^{m \times n}$, and vector $\mathbf{b} \in \mathbb{F}_q^m$, the algorithm LinSolve outputs the set of all solutions $\mathbf{x} \in \mathbb{F}_q^n$ of the linear system $\mathbf{Ax} = \mathbf{b}$.

---

[2] Precisely, in [6], they generate $\mathbf{h}$ as $\mathcal{H}(4\|\mathsf{hpk}\|\mathsf{msg}\|\mathsf{salt})$ where hpk is a hash of the public key and a secret seed. We omit this detail to simplify the presentation.

3.3 Security of PROV

An appealing feature of PROV lies in its security proof where existential forgery under chosen message attacks (EUF-CMA) can be reduced to the problem of inverting the public-key polynomials defined as follows:

Definition 4 (UOV⁻ problem). *Let $\boldsymbol{p} = (p_1, \ldots, p_m) \in \mathbb{F}_q[x_1, \ldots, x_n]^m$ be quadratic polynomials corresponding to a PROV public-key and $\boldsymbol{d} = (d_1, \ldots, d_m) \in \mathbb{F}_q^m$. The UOV⁻ problem asks to find a solution to the non-linear system of equations:*

$$p_1 - d_1 = 0, \ldots, p_m - d_m = 0.$$

As discussed in [6], the best approaches known for solving the UOV⁻ problem are generic techniques for solving non-linear equations and then exponential in the classical and quantum settings [3,4,8,9].

Algorithm 1: PROV Signing

Data: The secret key $\mathbf{O} \in \mathbb{F}_q^{v \times (m+\delta)}$, the public key $(\mathbf{P}_1, \ldots, \mathbf{P}_m) \in (\mathbb{F}_q^{n \times n})^m$ and a message msg $\in \{0,1\}^*$.
Result: The signature $(\mathbf{s}, \text{salt}) \in \mathbb{F}_q^n \times \{0,1\}^{\text{len}_{\text{salt}}}$ of message msg.

1   $\mathbf{v} \xleftarrow{\$} \mathbb{F}_q^v$
2   $\mathcal{S} \leftarrow \emptyset$
3   **while** $\mathcal{S} = \emptyset$ **do**
4   salt $\xleftarrow{\$} \{0,1\}^{\text{len}_{\text{salt}}}$
5      $(h_1, \ldots, h_m) \leftarrow \mathcal{H}(\text{msg}\|\text{salt})$
6   **for** i *from* 1 *to* m **do**
7         $\mathbf{a}_i \leftarrow \mathbf{v}^\mathsf{T}((\mathbf{P}_i^{(1)} + \mathbf{P}_i^{(1)\mathsf{T}})\mathbf{O} + \mathbf{P}_i^{(2)})$
8         $b_i = h_i - \mathbf{v}^\mathsf{T}\mathbf{P}_i^{(1)}\mathbf{v}$
9   **end**
10     $\mathbf{A} := (\mathbf{a}_1^\mathsf{T}\|\ldots\|\mathbf{a}_m^\mathsf{T})^\mathsf{T}$
11     $\mathbf{b} := (b_1\|\ldots\|b_m)^\mathsf{T}$
12     $\mathcal{S} \leftarrow \text{LinSolve}(\mathbf{A}, \mathbf{b})$
13 **end**
14 $\mathbf{o} \xleftarrow{\$} \mathcal{S}$
15 $\mathbf{s} \leftarrow \begin{pmatrix} \mathbf{v} \\ \mathbf{0}_{m+\delta} \end{pmatrix} + \begin{pmatrix} \mathbf{O} \\ \mathbf{1}_{m+\delta} \end{pmatrix} \mathbf{o}$
16 **Return** $(\mathbf{s}, \text{salt})$

3.4 Kipnis-Shamir Attack When $n \leq 2m$ and $\delta \geq 1$

In [12], Kipnis and Shamir introduced a polynomial-time key-recovery attack on Oil and Vinegar signature scheme (when $n = 2m$ and $\delta = 0$). This attack has been improved in [14] when $n \leq 2m$ and $\delta = 0$. Here, we extend this attack to PROV when $n \leq 2m$ and $\delta \geq 1$. First, let recall a special property of the polar form of a PROV key pair.

Lemma 2 ([14]). *Let $\mathcal{P} : \mathbb{F}_q^n \to \mathbb{F}_q^m$ be a multivariate quadratic map, $\mathbf{O} \subset \mathbb{F}_q^n$ be a vanishing subspace of $\mathcal{P}$ and $\mathcal{P}^* : \mathbb{F}_q^n \times \mathbb{F}_q^n \to \mathbb{F}_q^m$ be the polar form of $\mathcal{P}$. Then, for all $(\mathbf{o}_1, \mathbf{o}_2) \in \mathbf{O}^2$, we have $\mathcal{P}^*(\mathbf{o}_1, \mathbf{o}_2) = \mathcal{P}^*(\mathbf{o}_2, \mathbf{o}_1) = \mathbf{0}_m$.*

This characteristic restricts the rank of the matrices representing the polar form for large dimensional vanishing subspace.

Corollary 1. *Let $p \in \mathbb{F}_q[x_1, \ldots, x_n]$ be a homogeneous polynomial represented as $p(\mathbf{x}) = \mathbf{x}^\mathsf{T} \mathbf{P} \mathbf{x}$ with $\mathbf{P} \in \mathbb{F}_q^{n \times n}$ and $\mathbf{x} \in \mathbb{F}_q^n$, $O \subset \mathbb{F}_q^n$ be a vanishing subspace of p with $\dim(O) = m + \delta$. Then, the rank of the matrix $\mathbf{P}' = (\mathbf{P} + \mathbf{P}^\mathsf{T}) \in \mathbb{F}_q^{n \times n}$ is at most $2n - 2(m + \delta)$.*

This proof combines ideas of [14] but is provided for the sake of correctness and completeness.

Proof. Let $\mathbf{B}_1 \in \mathbb{F}_q^{n \times (m+\delta)}$ be a basis of O and $\hat{\mathbf{B}} \in \mathbb{F}_q^{n \times n}$ be a basis of $\mathbb{F}_q^n$ such that $\hat{\mathbf{B}} = (\mathbf{B}_1 \| \mathbf{B}_2)$ with $\mathbf{B}_2 \in \mathbb{F}_q^{n \times v}$. By Lemma 2, we obtain $\mathbf{B}_1^\mathsf{T} \mathbf{P}' \mathbf{B}_1 = \mathbf{0}_{m+\delta}$. Therefore, the matrix $\mathbf{P}'$ in the basis $\hat{\mathbf{B}}$ has the following form

$$\hat{\mathbf{B}}^\mathsf{T} \mathbf{P}' \hat{\mathbf{B}} = \begin{pmatrix} \mathbf{0}_{(m+\delta) \times (m+\delta)} & \mathbf{C}_1 \\ \mathbf{C}_2 & \mathbf{C}_3 \end{pmatrix}$$

with $\mathbf{C}_1 \in \mathbb{F}_q^{(m+\delta) \times v}$, $\mathbf{C}_2 \in \mathbb{F}_q^{v \times (m+\delta)}$ and $\mathbf{C}_3 \in \mathbb{F}_q^{v \times v}$. Then, the rank of the matrix $\hat{\mathbf{B}}^\mathsf{T} \mathbf{P}' \hat{\mathbf{B}}$ is at most $2n - 2(m+\delta)$ because of the block of zero of size $m+\delta$ in the top left. Since the rank of a matrix is invariant by change of basis, this proves the rank of $\mathbf{P}'$ is at most $2n - 2(m + \delta)$. □

In [14], the author exploits this rank defect to recover a basis of the vanishing subspace by computing the kernel of the matrices $\mathbf{P}'_i \in \mathbb{F}_q^{n \times n}$ representing the polar form based on the assumption that $\mathsf{Ker}(\mathbf{P}'_i) \subset O$ with high probability for key pair obtained with PROV key-generation. In the next lemma, we precise the condition underlying this assumption.

Lemma 3. *Let $p \in \mathbb{F}_q[x_1, \ldots, x_n]$ be a homogeneous polynomial represented as $p(\mathbf{x}) = \mathbf{x}^\mathsf{T} \mathbf{P} \mathbf{x}$ with $\mathbf{P} \in \mathbb{F}_q^{n \times n}$, $O \subset \mathbb{F}_q^n$ be a vanishing subspace of p with $\dim(O) = m + \delta$ and $p^* : \mathbb{F}_q^n \times \mathbb{F}_q^n \to \mathbb{F}_q$ be the polar form of p. If there exist no subspace $V \subset \mathbb{F}_q^n$ with dimension $m + \delta + r$ for any $1 \leq r \leq n - m - \delta$ where for all pairs $(\mathbf{v}_1, \mathbf{v}_2) \in V$, $p^*(\mathbf{v}_1, \mathbf{v}_2) = 0$ then $\mathsf{Ker}(\mathbf{P}') \subset O$ where $\mathbf{P}' = \mathbf{P} + \mathbf{P}^\mathsf{T}$.*

Proof. Let assume $\mathsf{Ker}(\mathbf{P}') \not\subset O$. Therefore, there exists a vector $\mathbf{x} \in \mathsf{Ker}(\mathbf{P}')$ such that $\mathbf{x} \notin O$. Since O is a vector space in a finite field and $\mathbf{x} \notin O$, then we have $\mathsf{span}(\mathbf{x}) \not\subset O$ and $\dim(\mathsf{span}(\mathbf{x})) = 1$. Consider the vector space V defined by the closure of $\mathsf{span}(\mathbf{x})$ and O under the addition and the scalar multiplication. The linear subspace V is of dimension $m + \delta + 1$ because $\mathbf{x} \notin O$. Also, let two vectors $\mathbf{v}_1$ and $\mathbf{v}_2$ of V that can be expressed as $\mathbf{v}_1 = \mathbf{o}_1 + \mathbf{x}_1$ and $\mathbf{v}_2 = \mathbf{o}_2 + \mathbf{x}_2$ with $\mathbf{o}_1, \mathbf{o}_2 \in O$ and $\mathbf{x}_1, \mathbf{x}_2 \in \mathsf{span}(\mathbf{x})$. If we evaluate the polar p^* on $\mathbf{v}_1$ and $\mathbf{v}_2$, we obtain

$$p^*(\mathbf{v}_1, \mathbf{v}_2) = \mathbf{o}_1^\mathsf{T} \mathbf{P}' \mathbf{o}_2 + \mathbf{x}_1^\mathsf{T} \mathbf{P}' \mathbf{o}_2 + \mathbf{o}_1^\mathsf{T} \mathbf{P}' \mathbf{x}_2 + \mathbf{x}_1^\mathsf{T} \mathbf{P}' \mathbf{x}_2.$$

By Lemma 2, we deduce $\mathbf{o}_1^\mathsf{T} \mathbf{P}' \mathbf{o}_2 = 0$. Also, the matrix $\mathbf{P}'$ is symmetric, therefore $\mathsf{Ker}(\mathbf{P}') = \mathsf{Ker}(\mathbf{P}'^\mathsf{T})$. This implies $\mathbf{x}_1^\mathsf{T} \mathbf{P}' = \mathbf{0}_n^\mathsf{T}$ and $\mathbf{P}' \mathbf{x}_2 = \mathbf{0}_n$ because $\mathsf{span}(\mathbf{x}) \subset$

Ker($\mathbf{P}'$). We conclude $p^*(\mathbf{v}_1, \mathbf{v}_2) = 0$ for any vector $\mathbf{v}_1$ and $\mathbf{v}_2$ of V. This proves by contradiction that Ker($\mathbf{P}'$) $\subset \boldsymbol{O}$ because V is of dimension strictly larger than $\boldsymbol{O}$. $\qquad\square$

Now, we extend the polynomial-time key-recovery attack of [14] to PROV where $n \leq 2m$ and $\delta \geq 1$.

Lemma 4 (Kipnis-Shamir attack – Kernel Approach). *Let* $\mathcal{P} : \mathbb{F}_q^n \to \mathbb{F}_q^m$ *be a* PROV *public-key,* $\boldsymbol{O} \subset \mathbb{F}_q^n$ *be the vanishing subspace of* $\mathcal{P}$ *with* $\dim(\boldsymbol{O}) = m + \delta$ *and* $\delta \geq 1$ *obtained with* PROV *key-generation (Subsect. 3.1). Then, there exists an algorithm that recovers a basis* $\mathbf{B} \in \mathbb{F}_q^{n \times (m+\delta)}$ *of* $\boldsymbol{O}$ *in time* $O(mn^\omega)$ *with high probability when* $n \leq 2m$.

Proof. Let $(\mathbf{P}_1, \ldots, \mathbf{P}_m) \in (\mathbb{F}_q^{n \times n})^m$ be the matrices representing the PROV public-key $\mathcal{P}$. By Corollary 1, we deduce the rank of the matrix $\mathbf{P}_i + \mathbf{P}_i^\mathsf{T}$ is at most $2n - 2(m + \delta)$ for $1 \leq i \leq m$. Since we clearly have $-2m \leq -n$, it follows that $2n - 2m - 2\delta \leq n - 2\delta$. Also, we know $-2\delta \leq -2$, therefore we obtain $2n - 2m - 2\delta \leq n - 2$. This implies the kernel of $\mathbf{P}_i + \mathbf{P}_i^\mathsf{T}$ is at least of dimension 2 because $\mathsf{rank}(\mathbf{P}_i + \mathbf{P}_i^\mathsf{T}) \leq n - 2$ for $1 \leq i \leq m$. We assume the condition of Lemma 3 is satisfied with high probability, therefore we have Ker($\mathbf{P}_i + \mathbf{P}_i^\mathsf{T}$) $\subset \boldsymbol{O}$ for $1 \leq i \leq m$. Since the m kernels of the polar form are at least of dimension 2 and $m + \delta \leq 2m$, an adversary recovers a basis of $\boldsymbol{O}$ with high probability by computing the m random kernels for key pair obtained with PROV key generation. Finally, computing these kernels takes time $O(mn^\omega)$. This concludes the proof. $\qquad\square$

4   Polynomial-Time Attack Against PROV Specification

4.1   Overview

Our attack relies on the fact that the (vinegar) vector $\mathbf{v} \in \mathbb{F}_q^v$ is leaked and constant in the PROV specification v1.0 [6]. More precisely, the designers described a probabilistic signature generation, similar to Algorithm 1, only for "*ease of exposition*". In practice, they deterministically generate $\mathbf{v}$ as $\mathcal{H}(3\|\mathsf{msg})$ where $\mathcal{H}$ is the hash function SHAKE256. We emphasize that the reference implementation generates the vinegar vector $\mathbf{v} \in \mathbb{F}_q^v$ similarly.

The vinegar vector (and the corresponding signature) leaks information about the secret-key, precisely it reveals one vector in the secret linear subspace $\boldsymbol{O} \subset \mathbb{F}_q^n$. Recently, [2] demonstrated an efficient attack allowing recovery of the entire secret-key from such a vector. Soon after in [14], it was proposed an even more efficient polynomial-time key-recovery attack on UOV using elementary linear algebra. In the next part, we adapt this key-recovery attack on PROV.

4.2 Description of the Attack

First, we explain why the PROV specification leaks one vector in the secret linear subspace.

Let $(\mathbf{v}, \mathbf{s}) \in \mathbb{F}_q^v \times \mathbb{F}_q^n$ be a pair of a vinegar vector and a signature[3] for the message msg $\in \{0,1\}^*$ and the PROV key pair $(\mathcal{P}, \mathbf{O})$ with $\mathcal{P} : \mathbb{F}_q^n \to \mathbb{F}_q^m$ and $\mathbf{O} \subset \mathbb{F}_q^n$. We recall that $\mathbf{s} = \bar{\mathbf{v}} + \bar{\mathbf{o}}$ where $\bar{\mathbf{v}}^\mathsf{T} = (\mathbf{v}^\mathsf{T} \| \mathbf{0}_{m+\delta}^\mathsf{T}) \in \mathbb{F}_q^n$ and $\bar{\mathbf{o}} \in \mathbb{F}_q^n$. As discussed above, the pair $(\mathbf{v}, \mathbf{s})$ is public. Therefore, any adversary can compute a vector in the secret linear subspace $\bar{\mathbf{o}} = \mathbf{s} - \bar{\mathbf{v}} \in \mathbf{O}$ (see Remark 1).

In the following, we focus on the key-recovery attack assuming the knowledge of one non-zero vector in the linear subspace. Also, we assume that $n \leq 3m$ (this statement holds for concrete parameters proposed in the PROV submission, see Table 1) and that the rank of the matrices $\mathbf{P}_1 + \mathbf{P}_1^\mathsf{T}, \ldots, \mathbf{P}_m + \mathbf{P}_m^\mathsf{T}$ defined as in (2) is n. Now, we present an adaption of the attack from [14] to the PROV case (see Remark 2).

Lemma 5. *Let $\mathcal{P} : \mathbb{F}_q^n \to \mathbb{F}_q^m$ be a PROV public-key, $\mathbf{O} \subset \mathbb{F}_q^n$ be the vanishing subspace of $\mathcal{P}$ where $\mathcal{P}$ are represented with matrices $\mathbf{P}_1, \ldots, \mathbf{P}_m \in \mathbb{F}_q^{n \times n}$ defined as in (2). Let $\mathbf{o} \in \mathbf{O} \setminus \{\mathbf{0}\}$ and $J_{\mathbf{o}}(\mathbf{z}) = (\mathbf{o}^\mathsf{T}(\mathbf{P}_1 + \mathbf{P}_1^\mathsf{T})\mathbf{z}, \ldots, \mathbf{o}^\mathsf{T}(\mathbf{P}_m + \mathbf{P}_m^\mathsf{T})\mathbf{z})$ with $\mathbf{z} = (z_1, \ldots, z_n)$ a vector of variables. Then, the subspace $\mathsf{Ker}(J_{\mathbf{o}})$ is a $(n-m)$-dimensional subspace with high probability and always satisfies*

$$\mathbf{O} \subset \mathsf{Ker}(J_{\mathbf{o}}).$$

Proof. Let $\mathcal{P}^* : \mathbb{F}_q^n \times \mathbb{F}_q^n \to \mathbb{F}_q^m$ be the polar form of $\mathcal{P}$ with components $p_1^*, \ldots, p_m^*$ where $p_i^*(\mathbf{y}, \mathbf{z}) = \mathbf{y}^\mathsf{T}(\mathbf{P}_i + \mathbf{P}_i^\mathsf{T})\mathbf{z}$ for all $1 \leq i \leq m$. By Lemma 2, for all $\mathbf{x} \in \mathbf{O}$.

$$p_i^*(\mathbf{o}, \mathbf{x}) = 0, \forall 1 \leq i \leq m.$$

This implies that the kernel of the linear application $p_{i,\mathbf{o}}^*(\mathbf{z}) = \mathbf{o}^\mathsf{T}(\mathbf{P}_i + \mathbf{P}_i^\mathsf{T})\mathbf{z}$ contains $\mathbf{O}$. By hypothesis, all the matrices $\mathbf{P}_1 + \mathbf{P}_1^\mathsf{T}, \ldots, \mathbf{P}_m + \mathbf{P}_m^\mathsf{T}$ are of rank n and $\mathbf{o} \neq \mathbf{0}_n$, therefore $p_{i,\mathbf{o}}^*(\mathbf{z})$ is non-zero. Since the linear map is non-zero, its kernel is a hyperplane. We have shown that $\mathbf{O} \subset \mathsf{Ker}(p_{i,\mathbf{o}}^*)$, for all $1 \leq i \leq m$. Therefore, we obtain:

$$\mathbf{O} \subset \bigcap_{1 \leq i \leq m} \mathsf{Ker}(p_{i,\mathbf{o}}^*) = \mathsf{Ker}(J_{\mathbf{o}})$$

Also, the hyperplanes are non-parallel, because we have $\mathbf{O} \subset \mathsf{Ker}(p_{i,\mathbf{o}}^*)$ for all $1 \leq i \leq m$. Finally, the hyperplanes (i.e. the vectors $\mathbf{o}^\mathsf{T}(\mathbf{P}_1 + \mathbf{P}_1^\mathsf{T}), \ldots, \mathbf{o}^\mathsf{T}(\mathbf{P}_m + \mathbf{P}_m^\mathsf{T}) \in \mathbb{F}_q^{1 \times n})$ are linearly independent with high probability for key pair obtained with PROV key-generation.[4] Therefore, the intersection of the m hyperplanes has dimension $n - m$. This concludes the proof.   □

---

[3] The salt is irrelevant for the attack, therefore we ignore it.

[4] We verify in practice that this statement holds true.

Remark 2. In [14], the authors consider finite fields of odd characteristics and exploit the bijective relation $p = 2^{-1}p^*$ between any quadratic homogeneous polynomial $p \in \mathbb{F}_q[x_1, \ldots, x_n]$ and its polar form $p^* : \mathbb{F}_q^n \times \mathbb{F}_q^n \to \mathbb{F}_q$. Therefore, any homogeneous quadratic polynomial $p \in \mathbb{F}_q[x_1, \ldots, x_n]$ can be represented with a symmetric matrix $\mathbf{M} \in \mathbb{F}_q^{n \times n}$ such that $p(\mathbf{x}) = \mathbf{x}^\mathsf{T}\mathbf{M}\mathbf{x}$. However, a polynomial $p(\mathbf{x}) = \mathbf{x}^\mathsf{T}\mathbf{M}\mathbf{x}$ with a symmetric matrix $\mathbf{M}$ is either linear or zero in a finite field of characteristic two (as with PROV). In other words, the bijective relation does not hold for finite fields of characteristic two (as discussed in [14,17]). Therefore, we need to slightly adapt the approach from [14] by considering the polar form of the public-key and not by exploiting a symmetric representation of the public-key as in [14].

The next step is then essentially similar to [14, Theorem 7], namely we restrict the public-key polynomials on $\mathsf{Ker}(J_o)$ and obtain new polynomial with fewer variables and the same secret vanishing subspace O. The secret-key can be recovered in polynomial-time from these new polynomials.

Theorem 1. *Let* $\mathcal{P} : \mathbb{F}_q^n \to \mathbb{F}_q^m$ *be a* PROV *public-key,* $O \subset \mathbb{F}_q^n$ *be the vanishing subspace of* $\mathcal{P}$ *with* $\dim(O) = m+\delta$ *where* $\delta \geq 1$ *and* $\mathcal{P}$ *be represented by matrices* $(\mathbf{P}_1, \ldots, \mathbf{P}_m) \in (\mathbb{F}_q^{n \times n})^m$ *defined as in* (2). *Then, there exists an adversary* $\mathcal{A}$ *taking as input* $((\mathbf{P}_1, \ldots, \mathbf{P}_m), \mathbf{o}) \in (\mathbb{F}_q^{n \times n})^m \times O \setminus \{0\}$ *that outputs a basis of* O *in polynomial-time with high probability.*

The proof is similar to [14] but again provided for the sake of correctness and completeness.

Proof. Let $J_o(\mathbf{z}) = (\mathbf{o}^\mathsf{T}(\mathbf{P}_1 + \mathbf{P}_1^\mathsf{T})\mathbf{z}, \ldots, \mathbf{o}^\mathsf{T}(\mathbf{P}_m + \mathbf{P}_m^\mathsf{T})\mathbf{z})$ with $\mathbf{z} = (z_1, \ldots, z_n)$ a vector of variables. By Lemma 5, $O \subset \mathsf{Ker}(J_o)$ for which a basis $\mathbf{B} \in \mathbb{F}_q^{n \times (n-m)}$ can be computed in $O(n^\omega)$, with $2 \leq \omega \leq 3$ the matrix multiplication exponent. Then, we restrict the public-key polynomials to $\mathsf{Ker}(J_o)$. This yields:

$$\mathbf{P}_{i,\mathsf{Ker}(J_o)} = \mathbf{B}^\mathsf{T}\mathbf{P}_i\mathbf{B}, \ \forall i, \ 1 \leq i \leq m.$$

The restricted public-key $\mathcal{P}_{\mathsf{Ker}(J_o)} : \mathbb{F}_q^{(n-m)} \to \mathbb{F}_q^m$ can be computed in polynomial-time $O(mn^\omega)$ and be represented with matrices $\mathbf{P}_{1,\mathsf{Ker}(J_o)}, \ldots, \mathbf{P}_{m,\mathsf{Ker}(J_o)} \in \mathbb{F}_q^{(n-m) \times (n-m)}$ is a PROV public key with parameters $(q, n - m, m, \delta)$ because $O \subset \mathsf{Ker}(J_o)$. Let $\bar{O} \subset \mathbb{F}_q^{n-m}$ be the vanishing subspace of $\mathcal{P}_{\mathsf{Ker}(J_o)}$ with $\dim(\bar{O}) = m + \delta$. With our assumption $n \leq 3m$, we obtain $n - m \leq 2m$. The attack described in Lemma 4 recovers a basis $\mathbf{C} \in \mathbb{F}_q^{(n-m) \times (m+\delta)}$ of the secret subspace $\bar{O}$ in time $O(mn^\omega)$. Then, for all i with $1 \leq i \leq m$, we have

$$(\mathbf{BC})^\mathsf{T}\mathbf{P}_i\mathbf{BC} = \mathbf{C}^\mathsf{T}(\mathbf{B}^\mathsf{T}\mathbf{P}_i\mathbf{B})\mathbf{C} = \mathbf{C}^\mathsf{T}\mathbf{P}_{i,\mathsf{Ker}(J_o)}\mathbf{C} = \mathbf{0}_{(m+\delta) \times (m+\delta)}.$$

Namely, the matrix $\mathbf{BC} \in \mathbb{F}_q^{n \times (m+\delta)}$ is a basis of O. Multiplying these matrices takes time $O(n^\omega)$ and concludes the proof that the secret-key can be recovered in $O(mn^\omega)$. $\qquad\square$

Remark 3. Our attack recovers the secret-key in polynomial-time with only one signature. However, an adversary can directly recover the secret-key with multiple signatures because we can view the PROV signature generation as an oracle of vectors in O. Precisely, an adversary would recover uniformly distributed vectors in O for signature requests on uniformly distributed messages (because the linear systems will be uniformly distributed, see Remark 1 of [6]). Therefore, an equivalent secret-key (i.e. $m + \delta$ linearly independent vectors of O) can be recovered in a small amount of signature requests.

4.3 Experimental Results

In this part, we show that our attack is not only efficient from a theoretical point of view but also very practical. To do so, we implemented the attack (Theorem 1) in Sagemath[5] [18] (taking as reference the code used in [14]) with the parameters of PROV suggested in [6] (Table 1). The non-zero vector of the vanishing subspace of the public key is generated with an oracle since such vector is leaked in PROV specification (Subsect. 4.2).

Table 1. Parameter sets of the PROV signature scheme.

Variant	λ	q	n	m	δ	v
PROV-I	128	256	136	46	8	82
PROV-III	192	256	200	70	8	122
PROV-V	256	256	264	96	8	160

We estimate the performance of the implementation on a single thread of a laptop with an Intel CPU i7-1365U at 5.2 GHz and with 32 GB of RAM. In Table 2, we report the experimental results obtained. To summarize, we recover the secret-key of PROV in a few seconds for every security level.

Table 2. Key-recovery attack of PROV.

Variant	PROV-I	PROV-III	PROV-V
Time	$1.78.s$	$4.72.s$	$7.93s$

4.4 Countermeasure

Before presenting the countermeasure, we briefly recall the security model used PROV. One idea of the proof is to model the PROV signature scheme as a weak preimage-sampleable function (WPSF) (Definition 1), denoted $\mathbf{T}_{\text{PROV}}$, such as:

---

[5] Our implementation is available at https://github.com/River-Moreira-Ferreira/prov-attack.

- The algorithm $(\mathsf{pk}, \mathsf{sk}) \leftarrow \mathbf{Gen}$ is the PROV key-generation;
- The algorithm $\mathbf{F}$ evaluates the PROV public-key;
- The algorithm $\mathbf{SampDom}$ uniformly generates a value in $\mathbb{F}_q^n$;
- The pair of algorithms $\mathbf{I} = (\mathbf{I}^1, \mathbf{I}^2)$ are defined as follows:
  - The algorithm $\mathbf{I}^1$ outputs a uniformly distributed vector $\mathbf{v} \in \mathbb{F}_q^v$;
  - The algorithm $\mathbf{I}^2$ takes as input $(\mathsf{pk}, \mathsf{sk}, \mathbf{v}, \mathbf{y})$ with $\mathbf{v} \in \mathbb{F}_q^v$ and $\mathbf{y} \in \mathbb{F}_q^m$, performs one iteration of the while loop in the signature generation (see Algorithm 1) for the given vector $\mathbf{v}$ and outputs a PROV signature $\mathbf{s} \in \mathbb{F}_q^n$ for $\mathbf{h} = \mathbf{y}$ or $\perp$ if the iteration failed.

One can remark that the model assumes, in particular, that the vinegar vector should be uniform and kept secret to the adversary in PS security of $\mathbf{T}_{\mathsf{PROV}}$ (see Definition 2). Precisely, in the PS_0 game, the adversary has access to the oracle Sample_0 (both described in Fig. 1). The oracle Sample_0 keeps secret the value $z_i \leftarrow \mathbf{I}^1$ used for $\mathbf{I}^2$ from the adversary $\mathcal{A}$. Also, the algorithm $\mathbf{I}^1$ uniformly generates the vector $z_i \in \mathbb{F}_q^v$ for $\mathbf{T}_{\mathsf{PROV}}$.

The specification of PROV v.1.0 differs from this model as the vinegar vector, which corresponds to a value $z_i \in \mathbb{F}_q^v$, is leaked during signature generation and constant.

The countermeasure appears evident when knowing this flaw in the security model: the vinegar vector should be uniformly generated and kept secret. This tweak will prevent an adversary from recovering easily a vector in the secret linear subspace with the previous strategy and makes PROV immune against our polynomial-time key-recovery attack.

For example, we can suggest generating the vector $\mathbf{v}$ as $\mathcal{H}(3\|\mathsf{s}_{\mathsf{sk}}\|\mathsf{msg})$ where s_{sk} is the secret seed uniformly generated during the key-generation (this was the strategy followed by others UOV candidates to the ongoing NIST standardization process). We will obtain a deterministic signature generation, as desired in the PROV specification.

Finally, we have reported this vulnerability to the designers of PROV and they updated the specification (v1.1, [7]) with such countermeasure.

Acknowledgement. We thank Pierre Pébereau, who helped us with some technical details of his attack and implementation [14]. Before publishing this work, we informed the authors of PROV that confirmed the flaw and released quickly a new specification (v.1.1). We would like to thank them for the constructive discussions. The second author would like to thank Google which partially supported this work thanks to a gift dedicated to post-quantum research. Also, we acknowledge the financial support of the French *Ministère des Armées - Agence de l'innovation de défense* on this research. Finally, the authors thanks the financial support on this research by QuanTEdu-France project (ANR-22-CMAS-0001) as part of France 2030.

References

1. NIST. Call for Additional Digital Signature Schemes for the Post-Quantum Cryptography Standardization Process
2. Aulbach, T., Campos, F., Krämer, J., Samardjiska, S., Stöttinger, M.: Separating oil and vinegar with a single trace side-channel assisted Kipnis-Shamir attack on UOV. IACR Trans. Cryptogr. Hardw. Embed. Syst. **2023**(3), 221–245 (2023)
3. Bettale, L., Faugère, J.-C., Perret, L.: Hybrid approach for solving multivariate systems over finite fields. J. Math. Cryptol. **3**(3), 177–197 (2009)
4. Bettale, L., Faugere, J.C., Perret, L.: Solving polynomial systems over finite fields: improved analysis of the hybrid approach. In: van der Hoeven, J., van Hoeij, M (eds.), International Symposium on Symbolic and Algebraic Computation, ISSAC'12, Grenoble, France - 22–25 July 2012, pp. 67–74. ACM (2012)
5. Beullens, W.: Improved cryptanalysis of UOV and rainbow. In: Canteaut, A., Standaert, F.-X. (eds.) EUROCRYPT 2021. LNCS, vol. 12696, pp. 348–373. Springer, Cham (2021). https://doi.org/10.1007/978-3-030-77870-5_13
6. Cogliati, B., et al.: PROV: provable unbalanced oil and vinegar specification v1.0, 06 January 2023
7. Cogliati, B., et al.: PROV: provable unbalanced oil and vinegar specification v1.1, 19 February 2024
8. Esser, A., Verbel, J.A., Zweydinger, F., Bellini, E.: Ttcryptographicestimators: a software library for cryptographic hardness estimation. IACR Cryptol. ePrint Arch., p. 589 (2023)
9. Faugere, J.C., Horan, K., Kahrobaei, D., Kaplan, M., Kashefi, E., Perret, L.: Fast quantum algorithm for solving multivariate quadratic equations. Cryptology ePrint Archive, Paper 2017/1236, 2017. https://eprint.iacr.org/2017/1236
10. Hülsing, A., et al.: SPHINCS$^+$. Technical report, National Institute of Standards and Technology, 2022. https://csrc.nist.gov/Projects/post-quantum-cryptography/selected-algorithms-2022
11. Kipnis, A., Patarin, J., Goubin, L.: Unbalanced oil and vinegar signature schemes. In: Stern, J. (ed.) EUROCRYPT 1999. LNCS, vol. 1592, pp. 206–222. Springer, Heidelberg (1999). https://doi.org/10.1007/3-540-48910-X_15
12. Kipnis, A., Shamir, A.: Cryptanalysis of the oil and vinegar signature scheme. In: Krawczyk, H. (eds.) Advances in Cryptology – CRYPTO '98. CRYPTO 1998. LNCS, vol. 1462, pp. 257–266. Springer, Berlin, Heidelberg (1998). https://doi.org/10.1007/BFb0055733
13. Prest, T., et al.: FALCON. Technical report, National Institute of Standards and Technology, 2022. https://csrc.nist.gov/Projects/post-quantum-cryptography/selected-algorithms-2022
14. Pébereau, P.: One vector to rule them all: key recovery from one vector in UOV schemes. Cryptology ePrint Archive, Paper 2023/1131, 2023. https://eprint.iacr.org/2023/1131
15. Sakumoto, K., Shirai, T., Hiwatari, H.: On provable security of UOV and HFE signature schemes against chosen-message attack. In: Yang, B.-Y. (ed.) PQCrypto 2011. LNCS, vol. 7071, pp. 68–82. Springer, Heidelberg (2011). https://doi.org/10.1007/978-3-642-25405-5_5

16. Schwabe, P., et al.: CRYSTALS-KYBER. Technical report, National Institute of Standards and Technology, 2022. https://csrc.nist.gov/Projects/post-quantum-cryptography/selected-algorithms-2022
17. Serre, J.-P.: A Course in Arithmetic, volume 7 of Graduate Texts in Mathematics. Springer, New York, NY (1973). https://doi.org/10.1007/978-1-4684-9884-4
18. The Sage Developers. SageMath, the Sage Mathematics Software System (Version 9.5) (2022). https://www.sagemath.org

Post-quantum Cryptography (II)

QCCA Security of Fujisaki-Okamoto Transformation in the Quantum Random Oracle Model

Xu Liu[1,2] and Mingqiang Wang[1,2(✉)]

[1] School of Mathematics, Shandong University, Jinan, China
liuxu17@mail.sdu.edu.cn, wangmingqiang@sdu.edu.cn
[2] Key Laboratory of Cryptologic Technology and Information Security, Ministry of Education, Shandong University, Jinan, China

Abstract. We analyze the IND-qCCA security of Fujisaki-Okamoto transformation in the QROM. Liu and Wang (PKC 2021) proved it for the implicit rejection variant at the cost of an additional hash; Ge, Shan and Xue (CRYPTO 2023) proved it for the explicit rejection variant if the underlying PKE satisfies γ-spreadness. In this work, we remove the additional hash for the implicit rejection FO. Besides, we show an example of PKE that is secure but is not γ-spread. And we remove the γ-spreadness requirement for the explicit rejection FO, however, at the cost of an additional hash.

Keywords: Fujisaki-Okamoto transformation · Quantum chosen ciphertext security · Quantum random oracle model

1 Introduction

Key encapsulation mechanism (KEM) aims to send a random key between two parties securely. It is widely used in hybrid encryption and authenticated key exchange (AKE) and others. Indistinguishability under chosen ciphertext attacks (IND-CCA) is the security notion for KEM that we desired usually. To achieve it, many transformations are proposed which bring weakly secure, such as one-wayness under chosen plaintext attacks (OW-CPA) or indistinguishability under chosen plaintext attacks (IND-CPA), PKEs into IND-CCA secure KEMs. The Fujisaki-Okamoto (FO) transformation [9,10] is the most famous one.

The security of FO has been analyzed in many works. Hofheinz, Hövelmanns and Kiltz [13] analyzed FO-like transformations in a modular way, decomposing it into two transformations named T and U. The transformation U has four variants, $U^{\not\perp}$, $U_m^{\not\perp}$, $U^\perp$ and $U_m^\perp$, corresponding to $FO^{\not\perp}$, $FO_m^{\not\perp}$, $FO^\perp$ and $FO_m^\perp$. They gave concrete results of these transformations in the random oracle model (ROM) [4], showing that FO can transform an IND-CPA secure PKE into an IND-CCA secure KEM tightly in the ROM.

S. Vaudenay and C. Petit (Eds.): AFRICACRYPT 2024, LNCS 14861, pp. 239–259, 2024.
https://doi.org/10.1007/978-3-031-64381-1_11

However, the threat of quantum computation [12,24] requires us to analyze cryptosystems in the presence of a quantum adversary. Specially, for constructions analyzed in the ROM, Boneh et al. [6] argued that quantum random oracle model (QROM) should be used instead of ROM. Adversaries are allowed to make quantum queries to the random oracle in the QROM. Besides, Boneh and Zhandry [7] introduced the IND-qCCA security notion for encryption schemes, where adversaries can make quantum queries to the decryption oracle. Their goal is to construct classical systems that remain secure even when implemented on a quantum computer, thereby potentially giving the attacker the ability to issue quantum queries. Following it, Xagawa and Yamakawa [26] considered the IND-qCCA security for KEM, where adversaries can make quantum queries to the decapsulation oracle.

For the IND-CCA security of FO-like transformations in the QROM, several works [5,8,14,15,17–20] are devoted to its analysis. The core tool used in these analysis is the One-Way to Hiding (O2H) Lemma [25] and its variants [2,5,14,20]. In addition, Saito, Xagawa and Yamakawa [23] introduced a new security notion named disjoint simulatability (DS). They also gave a transformation named SXY (essentially $U_m^{\not\perp}$) which can tightly turn DS secure PKEs into IND-CCA secure KEMs. Furthermore, they find it can be easily extended to the stronger IND-qCCA security tightly also [26].

However, above results suffer from the square-root advantage loss due to the O2H lemma. Kuchta et al. [20] deal with it using a novel O2H variant named Measure-Rewind-Measure One-Way to Hiding (MRM-O2H) Lemma. And they gave a security proof for FO from IND-CPA security to IND-CCA security without the square-root advantage loss for the first time. Using their MRM-O2H lemma, Liu and Wang [21] gave a tighter result for the transformation KC, making the transformation SXY ∘ KC ∘ T achieved IND-qCCA security from IND-CPA security without quadratic security loss in the QROM. Recently, Ge, Shan and Xue [11] analyzed the explicit rejection variant of FO ($FO_m^{\perp}$). The analysis of explicit rejection variant is more complex than the implicit rejection variant ($FO_m^{\not\perp}$). Specifically, they used the compressed oracle technique [27], online-extractable RO-simulator [8] and the MRM-O2H lemma, proving the IND-qCCA security of $FO_m^{\perp}$ without quadratic security loss in the QROM, if underlying PKEs satisfy γ-spreadness.

Now there are two questions raised. As we can see, the transformation SXY∘ KC ∘ T actually is the combination of $FO_m^{\not\perp}$ and KC, i.e., $FO_m^{\not\perp}$ ∘KC. Bindel et al. gave the result that $U^{\perp}$'s security implies $U^{\not\perp}$'s security [5, Theorem 3]. Liu and Wang's result for SXY ∘ KC ∘ T [21] is similar with Ge, Shan and Xue's result for $FO_m^{\perp}$ [11] except for the γ-spreadness requirement. So the first question is, *can we get similar result for standard $FO_m^{\not\perp}$ without KC?* On the other hand, γ-spreadness essentially means that the ciphertext should be distributed relatively evenly, its entropy must be sufficiently large. It seems that common PKEs might satisfy this requirement. But we will show in Sect. 5 that there exists secure PKE that does not have this property, although the PKE is artificially constructed.[1] Besides, [5, Theorem 4] says that $U^{\not\perp}$'s security implies $U^{\perp} \circ KC$'s security under certain conditions. Then the second question is, *can we get similar result for* $FO_m^{\perp} \circ KC$ *without* γ*-spreadness requirement at the cost of additional* KC?

Our Contributions. In this paper, we give concrete proofs for both $FO_m^{\not\perp}$ and $FO_m^{\perp} \circ KC$, showing that they can transform IND-CPA secure PKEs into IND-qCCA secure KEMs without quadratic security loss and any other requirements in the QROM. A comparison table is given in Table 1.

Table 1. Comparison of KEM transformations from IND-CPA secure PKEs in the QROM. The "Security bound" column shows the dependence of the approximate upper bound on attacker's advantage $\mathsf{Adv}(\mathcal{A})$ against the KEM in terms of the attacker advantage ϵ against the underlying PKE, and $\mathcal{A}$'s total query depth d to quantum random oracles.

Transformation	Underlying security	Achievedsecurity	Security bound	Otherrequirements
$FO^{\not\perp}$ [20]	IND-CPA	IND-CCA	$d^2\epsilon$	T[PKE, G] is η-injective.
$FO_m^{\not\perp} \circ KC$ [21]	IND-CPA	IND-qCCA	$d^2\epsilon$	-
$FO_m^{\not\perp}$ [This work]	IND-CPA	IND-qCCA	$d^2\epsilon$	-
$FO_m^{\perp}$ [11]	IND-CPA	IND-qCCA	$d^2\epsilon$	PKE is γ-spread.
$FO_m^{\perp} \circ KC$ [This work]	IND-CPA	IND-qCCA	$d^2\epsilon$	-

The proof of these two transformations does not need new techniques. Liu and Wang's proof [21] use DS as intermediate security, inducing additional KC. In this work, we reduce to OW-CPA security directly as in Kuchta et al.'s proof [20] by using the MRM-O2H lemma. We only need to change the last game in Liu and Wang's proof. The overall proof framework of the explicit rejection variant is similar with the implicit rejection variant due to additional KC. Specially, we use the analysis method in [18,26] to deal with the simulation of the decapsulation oracle.

At the end, we construct a PKE that is secure but is not γ-spread, indicating that we should choose underlying PKEs carefully for transformations requiring γ-spreadness.

2   Preliminaries

We present symbol notations and some lemmas in this section. The definitions and security notions for PKE and KEM are given in Appendix A.

---

[1] As mentioned by the reviewer, the property used in some proofs of explicit rejection FO is weaker than the γ-spreadness. And the PKE constructed in Sect. 5 might still satisfy this property, therefore it might not be a separation example.

2.1 Notation

For a finite set S, $|S|$ denotes the cardinality of S, and we denote the sampling of a uniformly random element x from S by $x \xleftarrow{\$} S$. By $[\![B]\!]$ we denote the bit that is 1 if the Boolean statement B is true, and otherwise 0.

We denote deterministic computation of an algorithm A on input x by $y := \mathsf{A}(x)$. We denote algorithms with access to an oracle O by A^O. Unless stated otherwise, we assume all our algorithms to be probabilistic and denote the computation by $y \leftarrow \mathsf{A}(x)$. We also use the notation $y := \mathsf{A}(x; r)$ to make the randomness r explicit. By $\mathsf{Time}(\mathsf{A})$ we denote the running time of A.

Some algorithms such as Gen need a security parameter $\lambda \in \mathbb{N}$ as input. However, we usually omit it for simplicity. We say a function is *negligible* in λ if $f(\lambda) = \lambda^{-\omega(1)}$. PPT stands for probabilistic polynomial time.

2.2 Quantum Computation

We refer to [22] for basic of quantum computation. In this subsection we mainly present several useful lemmas.

Quantum Random Oracle Model. Following [3,6], we review a quantum oracle O as a mapping

$$|x\rangle|y\rangle \to |x\rangle|y \oplus O(x)\rangle,$$

where $O : \{0,1\}^n \to \{0,1\}^m, x \in \{0,1\}^n$ and $y \in \{0,1\}^m$. Roughly speaking, the quantum random oracle model (QROM) is an idealized model where a hash function is modeled as a publicly and quantumly accessible random oracle, while adversaries are only given classical oracle access in the classical random oracle model (ROM).

Lemma 1 ([23, **Lemma 2.2**]). *Let l be an integer. Let $\mathsf{H} : \{0,1\}^l \times X \to Y$ and $\mathsf{H}' : X \to Y$ be two independent random oracles. If an unbounded time quantum adversary $\mathcal{A}$ makes a query to H at most q_{H} times, then we have*

$$\left| \Pr[1 \leftarrow \mathcal{A}^{\mathsf{H},\mathsf{H}(s,\cdot)} | s \leftarrow \{0,1\}^l] - \Pr[1 \leftarrow \mathcal{A}^{\mathsf{H},\mathsf{H}'}] \right| \leq 2q_{\mathsf{H}} \cdot 2^{-l/2},$$

where all oracle accesses of $\mathcal{A}$ can be quantum.

Lemma 2 (Generic Distinguishing Problem with Bounded Probabilities [1,15,16]). *Let X be a finite set, and let $\lambda \in [0,1]$. $\mathsf{F}_1 : X \to \{0,1\}$ is the following function: For each $x \in X$, $\mathsf{F}_1(x) = 1$ with probability λ_x ($\lambda_x \leq \lambda$), and $\mathsf{F}_1(x) = 0$ else. F_2 is the constant zero function. Then, for any algorithm A issuing at most q quantum queries to F_1 or F_2, $| \Pr[1 \leftarrow \mathsf{A}^{\mathsf{F}_1}] - \Pr[1 \leftarrow \mathsf{A}^{\mathsf{F}_2}]| \leq 8q^2\lambda$.*

Lemma 3 (Measure-Rewind-Measure One-Way to Hiding [20, Lemma 3.3]). *Let $G, H : X \to Y$ be random functions, z be a random value, and $S \subseteq X$ be a random set such that $G(x) = H(x)$ for every $x \notin S$. The tuple (G, H, S, z) may have arbitrary joint distribution. Furthermore, let $\mathcal{A}^O$ be a quantum oracle* *algorithm which queries oracle O with query depth d. Then we can construct an algorithm $\mathcal{D}^{G,H}(z)$ such that $\mathsf{Time}(\mathcal{D}^{G,H}) \approx 2 \cdot \mathsf{Time}(\mathcal{A}^O)$ and*

$$\mathsf{Adv}(\mathcal{A}^O) \leq 4d \cdot \mathsf{Adv}(\mathcal{D}^{G,H}).$$

Here $\mathsf{Adv}(\mathcal{A}^O) := |P_{\mathsf{left}} - P_{\mathsf{right}}|$ *with*

$$P_{\mathsf{left}} := \Pr_{H,z}[1 \leftarrow \mathcal{A}^H(z)], \quad P_{\mathsf{right}} := \Pr_{G,z}[1 \leftarrow \mathcal{A}^G(z)],$$

and

$$\mathsf{Adv}(\mathcal{D}^{G,H}) := \Pr_{G,H,S,z}[T \cap S \neq \varnothing | T \leftarrow \mathcal{D}^{G,H}(z)].$$

3   Security of $\mathsf{FO}_m^{\not\perp}$ in the QROM

In this section, we mainly prove the IND-qCCA security of $\mathsf{U}_m^{\not\perp}$ in the QROM. Then combining with the result of T [5, Theorem 1], we show that $\mathsf{FO}_m^{\not\perp}$ can transform IND-CPA secure PKEs into IND-qCCA secure KEMs in the QROM without other requirements, the security loss is d^2 approximately, where d is adversary's query depth to the random oracles.

Transformation T. To a public-key encryption scheme $\mathsf{PKE}_0 = (\mathsf{Gen}_0, \mathsf{Enc}_0, \mathsf{Dec}_0)$ with message space $\mathcal{M}$ and randomness space $\mathcal{R}$, and a hash function $G : \mathcal{M} \to \mathcal{R}$, we associate $\mathsf{PKE} := \mathsf{T}[\mathsf{PKE}_0, G]$. The algorithms of $\mathsf{PKE} = (\mathsf{Gen}, \mathsf{Enc}, \mathsf{Dec})$ are defined in Fig. 1.

$\underline{\mathsf{Gen}}$	$\underline{\mathsf{Enc}(pk, m)}$	$\underline{\mathsf{Dec}(sk, c)}$
$(pk, sk) \leftarrow \mathsf{Gen}_0$	$c := \mathsf{Enc}_0(pk, m; G(m))$	$m' := \mathsf{Dec}_0(sk, c)$
return (pk, sk)	**return** c	**return** m'

Fig. 1. $\mathsf{PKE} = (\mathsf{Gen}, \mathsf{Enc}, \mathsf{Dec}) := \mathsf{T}[\mathsf{PKE}_0, G]$.

Transformation $\mathsf{U}_m^{\not\perp}$. To a deterministic public-key encryption scheme $\mathsf{PKE} = (\mathsf{Gen}, \mathsf{Enc}, \mathsf{Dec})$ with message space $\mathcal{M}$ and ciphertext space $\mathcal{C}$, and two hash functions $H : \mathcal{M} \to \mathcal{K}$, $H_1 : \{0,1\}^l \times \mathcal{C} \to \mathcal{K}$, we associate $\mathsf{KEM} := \mathsf{U}_m^{\not\perp}[\mathsf{PKE}, H, H_1]$. The algorithms of $\mathsf{KEM} = (\mathsf{Gene}, \mathsf{Enca}, \mathsf{Deca})$ are defined in Fig. 2.

$\underline{\mathsf{Gene}}$	$\underline{\mathsf{Enca}(pk)}$	$\underline{\mathsf{Deca}((sk, s), c)}$
$(pk, sk) \leftarrow \mathsf{Gen}$	$m \xleftarrow{\$} \mathcal{M}$	$m' := \mathsf{Dec}(sk, c)$
$s \xleftarrow{\$} \{0,1\}^l$	$c := \mathsf{Enc}(pk, m)$	**if** $m' = \perp$ **or** $\mathsf{Enc}(pk, m') \neq c$
return $(pk, (sk, s))$	$k := \mathsf{H}(m)$	**return** $k' := \mathsf{H}_1(s, c)$
	return (c, k)	**else return** $k' := \mathsf{H}(m')$

Fig. 2. $\mathsf{KEM} = (\mathsf{Gene}, \mathsf{Enca}, \mathsf{Deca}) := \mathsf{U}_m^{\not\perp}[\mathsf{PKE}, H, H_1]$.

Theorem 1 (IND-qCCA Security of $\mathsf{U}_m^{\not\perp}$ in the QROM). *Let* PKE *be a dPKE transformed from* PKE_0 *by* T, *i.e.,* $\mathsf{PKE} := \mathsf{T}[\mathsf{PKE}_0, \mathsf{G}]$. PKE_0 *is a δ-correct rPKE with message space* $\mathcal{M}$, *ciphertext space* $\mathcal{C}$ *and randomness space* $\mathcal{R}$. *Let* $\mathsf{G} : \mathcal{M} \to \mathcal{R}$, $\mathsf{H} : \mathcal{M} \to \mathcal{K}$, $\mathsf{H}_1 : \{0,1\}^l \times \mathcal{C} \to \mathcal{K}$ *be hash functions modeled as quantum random oracles. Then for any adversary $\mathcal{A}$ against the* IND-qCCA *security of* $\mathsf{KEM} := \mathsf{U}_m^{\not\perp}[\mathsf{PKE}, \mathsf{H}, \mathsf{H}_1]$ *issuing* $q_\mathsf{G}, q_\mathsf{H}, q_{\mathsf{H}_1}$ *and* q_Deca *quantum queries to* $\mathsf{G}, \mathsf{H}, \mathsf{H}_1$ *and the decapsulation oracle* Deca *with depth* $d_\mathsf{G}, d_\mathsf{H}, d_{\mathsf{H}_1}$ *and* d_Deca, *there exists an adversary $\mathcal{B}$ against the* OW-CPA *security of* PKE *such that*

$$\mathsf{Adv}_{\mathsf{KEM},\mathcal{A}}^{\mathsf{IND\text{-}qCCA}} \leq 4d_\mathsf{H} \cdot \mathsf{Adv}_{\mathsf{PKE},\mathcal{B}}^{\mathsf{OW\text{-}CPA}} + (16q_\mathsf{G}'^2 + 16q_\mathsf{G}''^2 + 8d_\mathsf{H} + 2)\delta + 4q_{\mathsf{H}_1} \cdot 2^{-l/2}$$

and $\mathsf{Time}(\mathcal{B}) \approx 2 \cdot \mathsf{Time}(\mathcal{A})$, *where* $q_\mathsf{G}' = q_\mathsf{G} + q_\mathsf{Deca} + 1, q_\mathsf{G}'' = q_\mathsf{G} + q_\mathsf{H} + 1$.

Proof. Our game-based proof is essentially the same as the proof of [21, Theorem 3], except that in the last game we reduce to OW-CPA directly as in the proof of [20, Theorem 4.6]. The IND-qCCA games are given in Fig. 3. We note that the adversary is allowed to query quantum states to the decapsulation oracle.

GAME G_0: This is the original game, IND-qCCA$_{\mathsf{KEM}}^{\mathcal{A}}$.

We have

$$\mathsf{Adv}_{\mathsf{KEM},\mathcal{A}}^{\mathsf{IND\text{-}qCCA}} = 2|\Pr[G_0 \Rightarrow 1] - 1/2|$$

by the definition.

GAME G_1: This game is the same as G_1 except that $\mathsf{H}_1(s, c)$ in the decapsulation oracle is replaced with $\mathsf{H}_q(c)$ where $\mathsf{H}_q : \mathcal{C} \to \mathcal{K}$ is another random oracle. We remark that $\mathcal{A}$ is not given direct access to H_q.

We have

$$|\Pr[G_1 \Rightarrow 1] - \Pr[G_0 \Rightarrow 1]| \leq 2q_{\mathsf{H}_1} \cdot 2^{-l/2}.$$

This is obvious from Lemma 1.

Let G' be a random function such that $\mathsf{G}'(m)$ is sampled according to the uniform distribution over $\mathcal{R}_{(pk,sk),m}^{good} := \{r \in \mathcal{R} | \mathsf{Dec}_0(sk, \mathsf{Enc}_0(pk, m; r)) = m\}$. Let $\Omega_{\mathsf{G}'}$ be the set of all functions G'. Define $\delta_{(pk,sk),m} = \frac{|\mathcal{R} \backslash \mathcal{R}_{(pk,sk),m}^{good}|}{|\mathcal{R}|}$ as the fraction of bad randomness and $\delta_{(pk,sk)} = \max_{m \in \mathcal{M}} \delta_{(pk,sk),m}$. With this notation $\delta = \mathrm{E}[\delta_{(pk,sk)}]$, where the expectation is taken over $(pk, sk) \leftarrow \mathsf{Gen}_0$.

GAME G_2: This game is the same as G_1 except that we replace G by G' that uniformly samples from "good" randomness at random, i.e., $\mathsf{G}' \xleftarrow{\$} \Omega_{\mathsf{G}'}$.

GAME IND-qCCA$_{\mathsf{KEM}}^{\mathcal{A}}$	$\mathsf{H}(m)$
$(pk, sk) \leftarrow \mathsf{Gen}$	**return** $\overline{\mathsf{H}}(m)$ //$G_0 - G_2$
$s \xleftarrow{\$} \{0,1\}^l$ //G_0	**if** $m = m^*$ **and** $b = 0$ //G_6
$\mathsf{G} \xleftarrow{\$} \Omega_\mathsf{G}$ //$G_0 - G_1, G_5 - G_6$	$\quad$**return** r //G_6
$\mathsf{G} \xleftarrow{\$} \Omega_{\mathsf{G}'}$ //$G_2 - G_4$	**return** $\mathsf{H}_q(\mathsf{Enc}(pk, m))$ //$G_3 - G_6$
$\overline{\mathsf{H}} \xleftarrow{\$} \Omega_\mathsf{H}$ //$G_0 - G_2$	
$\mathsf{H}_q \xleftarrow{\$} \Omega_{\mathsf{H}_q}$ //$G_3 - G_6$	$\mathsf{Deca}(c)$
$\mathsf{H}_1 \xleftarrow{\$} \Omega_{\mathsf{H}_1}$	**if** $c = c^*$
$b \xleftarrow{\$} \{0,1\}$	$\quad$**return** $\perp$
$m^* \xleftarrow{\$} \mathcal{M}$	$m' := \mathsf{Dec}(sk, c)$ //$G_0 - G_3$
$c^* := \mathsf{Enc}(pk, m^*)$	**if** $m' = \perp$ **or** $\mathsf{Enc}(pk, m') \neq c$ //$G_0 - G_3$
$\quad = \mathsf{Enc}_0(pk, m^*; \mathsf{G}(m^*))$	$\quad$**return** $\mathsf{H}_1(s, c)$ //G_0
$r \xleftarrow{\$} \mathcal{R}$	$\quad$**return** $\mathsf{H}_q(c)$ //$G_1 - G_3$
$k_0^* := \mathsf{H}(m^*)$	**else return** $\mathsf{H}(m')$ //$G_0 - G_3$
$k_1^* := r$	**return** $\mathsf{H}_q(c)$ //$G_4 - G_6$
$b' \leftarrow \mathcal{A}^{\mathsf{G}, \mathsf{H}_1, \mathsf{H}, \mathsf{Deca}}(pk, c^*, k_b^*)$	
return $[\![b' = b]\!]$	

Fig. 3. IND-qCCA Games $G_0 - G_6$ for the proof of Theorem 1.

Following the same analysis as in the proof of [17, Theorem 1], we can show that the distinguishing problem between G_1 and G_2 is essentially the distinguishing problem between G and G', which can be converted into a distinguishing problem between F_1 and F_2, where F_1 is a function such that $\mathsf{F}_1(m)$ is sampled according to Bernoulli distribution $B_{\delta_{(pk,sk),m}}$, i.e., $\Pr[\mathsf{F}_1(m) = 1] = \delta_{(pk,sk),m}$ and $\Pr[\mathsf{F}_1(m) = 0] = 1 - \delta_{(pk,sk),m}$, and F_2 is a constant function that always outputs 0 for any input. Thus, conditioned on a fixed (pk, sk) we obtain by Lemma 2, $|\Pr[G_2 \Rightarrow 1|(pk, sk)] - \Pr[G_1 \Rightarrow 1|(pk, sk)]| \leq 8q_\mathsf{G}'^2 \delta_{(pk,sk)}$, where $q_\mathsf{G}' = q_\mathsf{G} + q_{\mathsf{Deca}} + 1$. By averaging over $(pk, sk) \leftarrow \mathsf{Gen}_0$ we finally obtain

$$|\Pr[G_2 \Rightarrow 1] - \Pr[G_1 \Rightarrow 1]| \leq 8q_\mathsf{G}'^2 \mathrm{E}[\delta_{(pk,sk)}] = 8q_\mathsf{G}'^2 \delta.$$

GAME G_3: This game is the same as G_2 except that the random oracle $\mathsf{H}(\cdot)$ is simulated by $\mathsf{H}_q(\mathsf{Enc}(pk, \cdot))$. We remark that the decapsulation oracle and generation of k_0^* also use $\mathsf{H}_q(\mathsf{Enc}(pk, \cdot))$ as $\mathsf{H}(\cdot)$.

Here we define an event:

$$\mathsf{Bad} := [\exists m \in \mathcal{M}, \mathcal{R}_{(pk,sk),m}^{good} = \varnothing | (pk, sk) \leftarrow \mathsf{Gen}_0].$$

Then by the definition, we have

$$
\begin{aligned}
&\Pr[\mathsf{Bad}] \\
&= \Pr[\exists m \in \mathcal{M}, \mathcal{R}^{good}_{(pk,sk),m} = \varnothing \mid (pk, sk) \leftarrow \mathsf{Gen}_0] \\
&= \Pr[\exists m \in \mathcal{M}, \delta_{(pk,sk),m} = 1 \mid (pk, sk) \leftarrow \mathsf{Gen}_0] \\
&= \Pr[\delta_{(pk,sk)} = 1 \mid (pk, sk) \leftarrow \mathsf{Gen}_0] \\
&\leq \mathrm{E}[\delta_{(pk,sk)}] \\
&= \delta.
\end{aligned}
$$

From the definition of G', if Bad doesn't happen, any message can be decrypted correctly for the PKE, i.e., $\mathsf{Dec}(sk, \mathsf{Enc}(pk, m)) = m$ for all $m \in \mathcal{M}$. Therefore, $\mathsf{Enc}(pk, \cdot)$ is injective. And if $\mathsf{H}_q(\cdot)$ is a random function, then $\mathsf{H}_q(\mathsf{Enc}(pk, \cdot))$ is also a random function.

Besides, we say that a ciphertext c is valid if we have $\mathsf{Enc}(pk, \mathsf{Dec}(sk, c)) = c$ and invalid otherwise. We remark that H_q is used only for decrypting an invalid ciphertext c as $\mathsf{H}_q(c)$ in G_2. This means that a value of $\mathsf{H}_q(c)$ for a valid c is not used at all in G_2. On the other hand, any output of $\mathsf{Enc}(pk, \cdot)$ is valid if Bad doesn't happen.

Remarking that access to H_q is not given to $\mathcal{A}$, it causes no difference from the view of $\mathcal{A}$ if we replace $\mathsf{H}(\cdot)$ with $\mathsf{H}_q(\mathsf{Enc}(pk, \cdot))$.

Thus we have

$$
\Pr[G_3 \Rightarrow 1 \mid \overline{\mathsf{Bad}}] = \Pr[G_2 \Rightarrow 1 \mid \overline{\mathsf{Bad}}].
$$

GAME G_4: This game is the same as G_3 except that the decapsulation oracle always returns $\mathsf{H}_q(c)$ as long as $c \neq c^*$.

Since we set $\mathsf{H}(\cdot) := \mathsf{H}_q(\mathsf{Enc}(pk, \cdot))$, for any valid c and $m' := \mathsf{Dec}(sk, c)$, we have $\mathsf{H}(m') = \mathsf{H}_q(\mathsf{Enc}(pk, m')) = \mathsf{H}_q(c)$. Therefore, responses of the decapsulation oracle are unchanged. We have

$$
\Pr[G_4 \Rightarrow 1] = \Pr[G_3 \Rightarrow 1].
$$

GAME G_5: This game is the same as G_4 except that we switch G' back to the ideal random oracle G.

In the same way above, we have

$$
|\Pr[G_5 \Rightarrow 1] - \Pr[G_4 \Rightarrow 1]| \leq 8 q''^2_{\mathsf{G}} \delta,
$$

where $q''_{\mathsf{G}} = q_{\mathsf{G}} + q_{\mathsf{H}} + 1$.

GAME G_6: This game is the same as G_5 except that in the case $b = 0$ we reprogram $\mathsf{H}(m^*)$ to the random value r. Now, we have $k_0^* = k_1^* = r$.

It is obvious that the change is purely conceptual and does not change the joint distribution of the view of $\mathcal{A}$. Thus

$$
\Pr[G_6 \Rightarrow 1] = \Pr[G_5 \Rightarrow 1].
$$

In game G_6, the distribution of the input $z = (pk, c^*, k_b^* = r)$ to $\mathcal{A}$ is independent of b, and the random oracle queried to H by $\mathcal{A}$ and the simulator is either H if $b = 1$ (where $H(m) = H_q(\text{Enc}(pk, m))$) or H' if $b = 0$ (where $H'(m) = H(m)$ for $m \neq m^*$). The simulation in game G_6 runs in time $\approx \text{Time}(\mathcal{A})$. Therefore, the algorithm $\mathcal{A}$ together with the simulator in game G_6 constitutes an O2H distinguisher algorithm for distinguishing oracle H from H' with run-time $\approx \text{Time}(\mathcal{A})$. That is,

$$2|\Pr[G_6 \Rightarrow 1] - 1/2| = |\Pr[1 \leftarrow \mathcal{A}|b = 1] - \Pr[1 \leftarrow \mathcal{A}|b = 0]|$$
$$= |\Pr[1 \leftarrow \mathcal{A}^{\mathsf{H}}] - \Pr[1 \leftarrow \mathcal{A}^{\mathsf{H}'}]|.$$

Applying Lemma 3, we can construct algorithm $\mathcal{D}$, with run-time $\approx 2 \cdot \text{Time}(\mathcal{A})$ and making oracle calls to H and H', such that

$$|\Pr[1 \leftarrow \mathcal{A}^{\mathsf{H}}] - \Pr[1 \leftarrow \mathcal{A}^{\mathsf{H}'}]| \leq 4d_{\mathsf{H}} \cdot \Pr[T \cap \{m^*\} \neq \varnothing | T \leftarrow \mathcal{D}^{\mathsf{H},\mathsf{H}'}(z)].$$

Using $\mathcal{D}$, we can construct an adversary $\mathcal{B}$ against the OW-CPA security of PKE. The OW-CPA game for PKE and the construction of $\mathcal{B}$ is given in Fig. 4. The adversary $\mathcal{B}$ invoke $\mathcal{D}$ using its input (pk, c^*) and oracle G by simulating $\mathcal{D}$'s input (pk, c^*, r) and all oracles $(\mathsf{G}, \mathsf{H}_1, \mathsf{H}, \mathsf{H}', \mathsf{Deca})$. When $\mathcal{D}$ returns its output set T, $\mathcal{B}$ tests each $m \in T$ to check whether $m \in S_{c^*}$, i.e., whether $\text{Enc}(pk, m) = c^*$, and returns any such m if found. Note that $\text{Time}(\mathcal{B}) \approx \text{Time}(\mathcal{D})$. We can see that if $S_c^* = \{m^*\}$, the adversary $\mathcal{B}$ can simulate $\mathcal{D}$'s environment perfectly. Further, adversary $\mathcal{B}$ succeeds (i.e., outputs m^*) if $T \cap S_{c^*} \neq \varnothing$. Then using [21, Lemma 4], $\Pr[S_{c^*} \neq \{m^*\}]$ is bounded by 2δ. Thus we have

$$\Pr[T \cap \{m^*\} \neq \varnothing | T \leftarrow \mathcal{D}^{\mathsf{H},\mathsf{H}'}(z)] \leq \text{Adv}_{\text{PKE},\mathcal{B}}^{\text{OW-CPA}} + 2\delta.$$

GAME OW-CPA$_{\text{PKE}}^{\mathcal{B}}$	$\mathcal{B}^{\mathsf{G}}(pk, c^*)$	$\mathsf{H}(m)$
$(pk, sk) \leftarrow \text{Gen}$	$H_1 \xleftarrow{\$} \Omega_{H_1}$	**return** $H_q(\text{Enc}(pk, m))$
$G \xleftarrow{\$} \Omega_{\mathsf{G}}$	$H_q \xleftarrow{\$} \Omega_{H_q}$	
$m^* \xleftarrow{\$} \mathcal{M}$	$S_{c^*} := \{m \in \mathcal{M} | \text{Enc}(pk, m) = c^*\}$	$\mathsf{H}'(m)$
$c^* := \text{Enc}(pk, m^*)$	$r \xleftarrow{\$} \mathcal{R}$	**if** $m \in S_{c^*}$
$\quad = \text{Enc}_0(pk, m^*; \mathsf{G}(m^*))$	$T \leftarrow \mathcal{D}^{\mathsf{G},\mathsf{H}_1,\mathsf{H},\mathsf{H}',\text{Deca}}(pk, c^*, r)$	$\quad$ **return** r
$m' \leftarrow \mathcal{B}^{\mathsf{G}}(pk, c^*)$	**if** $T \cap S_{c^*} \neq \varnothing$	**else return** $\mathsf{H}(m)$
return $[\![m' = m^*]\!]$	$\quad$ **return** any element$\in T \cap S_{c^*}$	
	else return $\bot$	$\text{Deca}(c)$
		if $c = c^*$
		$\quad$ **return** $\bot$
		else return $H_q(c)$

Fig. 4. Game OW-CPA$_{\text{PKE}}^{\mathcal{B}}$ for the proof of Theorem 1.

Summing up the differences of $\Pr[G_i \Rightarrow 1]$ over all games, we get

$$\mathsf{Adv}_{\mathsf{KEM},\mathcal{A}}^{\mathsf{IND\text{-}qCCA}} = 2|\Pr[G_0 \Rightarrow 1] - 1/2|$$
$$\leq 16(q_G'^2 + q_G''^2)\delta + 4q_{\mathsf{H}_1} \cdot 2^{-l/2} + 2\delta + 4d_{\mathsf{H}} \cdot (\mathsf{Adv}_{\mathsf{PKE},\mathcal{B}}^{\mathsf{OW\text{-}CPA}} + 2\delta)$$
$$= 4d_{\mathsf{H}} \cdot \mathsf{Adv}_{\mathsf{PKE},\mathcal{B}}^{\mathsf{OW\text{-}CPA}} + (16q_G'^2 + 16q_G''^2 + 8d_{\mathsf{H}} + 2)\delta + 4q_{\mathsf{H}_1} \cdot 2^{-l/2}.$$

$\square$

The following Lemma 4 about T shows that T can transform IND-CPA secure rPKEs into OW-CPA secure dPKEs, the security loss is d approximately, where d is adversary's query depth to the random oracle.

Lemma 4 (Security of T in the QROM [5, Theorem 1]). *Let PKE_0 be a rPKE with messages space $\mathcal{M}$ and random space $\mathcal{R}$. Let $\mathsf{G} : \mathcal{M} \to \mathcal{R}$ be a hash function modeled as a quantum random oracle. Then for any adversary $\mathcal{A}$ against the OW-CPA security of $\mathsf{PKE} := \mathsf{T}[\mathsf{PKE}_0, \mathsf{G}]$ issuing q_G quantum queries to G with depth d_G, there exists an adversary $\mathcal{B}$ against the IND-CPA security of PKE_0 such that*

$$\mathsf{Adv}_{\mathsf{PKE},\mathcal{A}}^{\mathsf{OW\text{-}CPA}} \leq (d_G + 2) \cdot \left(\mathsf{Adv}_{\mathsf{PKE}_0,\mathcal{B}}^{\mathsf{IND\text{-}CPA}} + \frac{8(q_G + 1)}{|\mathcal{M}|} \right)$$

and $\mathsf{Time}(\mathcal{B}) \approx \mathsf{Time}(\mathcal{A})$.

Combining above Theorem 1 with Lemma 4, we obtain the following result of $\mathsf{FO}_m^{\perp}$.

Corollary 1 (IND-qCCA Security of $\mathsf{FO}_m^{\perp}$ in the QROM). *Let PKE_0 be a δ-correct rPKE with message space $\mathcal{M}$, ciphertext space $\mathcal{C}$ and randomness space $\mathcal{R}$. Let $\mathsf{G} : \mathcal{M} \to \mathcal{R}$, $\mathsf{H} : \mathcal{M} \to \mathcal{K}$, $\mathsf{H}_1 : \{0,1\}^l \times \mathcal{C} \to \mathcal{K}$ be hash functions modeled as quantum random oracles. Then for any adversary $\mathcal{A}$ against the IND-qCCA security of $\mathsf{KEM} := \mathsf{FO}_m^{\perp}[\mathsf{PKE}_0, \mathsf{G}, \mathsf{H}, \mathsf{H}_1]$ issuing $q_G, q_H, q_{\mathsf{H}_1}$ and q_{Deca} quantum queries to $\mathsf{G}, \mathsf{H}, \mathsf{H}_1$ and the decapsulation oracle Deca with depth $d_G, d_H, d_{\mathsf{H}_1}$ and d_{Deca}, there exists an adversary $\mathcal{B}$ against the IND-CPA security of PKE_0 such that*

$$\mathsf{Adv}_{\mathsf{KEM},\mathcal{A}}^{\mathsf{IND\text{-}qCCA}} \leq 4d_{\mathsf{H}}(d_G^* + 2) \cdot \left(\mathsf{Adv}_{\mathsf{PKE}_0,\mathcal{B}}^{\mathsf{IND\text{-}CPA}} + \frac{8(q_G^* + 1)}{|\mathcal{M}|} \right)$$
$$+ (16q_G'^2 + 16q_G''^2 + 8d_{\mathsf{H}} + 2)\delta + 4q_{\mathsf{H}_1} \cdot 2^{-l/2}$$

and $\mathsf{Time}(\mathcal{B}) \approx 2 \cdot \mathsf{Time}(\mathcal{A})$, *where* $d_G^* = 2(d_G + d_H + 1)$, $q_G^* = 2(q_G + q_H + n_p)$, $q_G' = q_G + q_{\mathsf{Deca}} + 1$, $q_G'' = q_G + q_H + 1$, n_p *is the number of $\mathcal{A}$'s parallel queries to H.*

4   Security of $\mathsf{FO}_m^{\perp} \circ \mathsf{KC}$ in the QROM

In this section, we mainly prove the IND-qCCA security of $\mathsf{U}_m^{\perp} \circ \mathsf{KC}$ in the QROM. Then combining with the result of T [5, Theorem 1], we show that $\mathsf{FO}_m^{\perp} \circ \mathsf{KC}$ can transform IND-CPA secure PKEs into IND-qCCA secure KEMs in the QROM without other requirements, the security loss is d^2 approximately, where d is adversary's query depth to the random oracles.

Transformation $U_m^\perp \circ KC$. To a deterministic public-key encryption scheme PKE = (Gen, Enc, Dec) with message space $\mathcal{M}$ and ciphertext space $\mathcal{C}$, and two hash functions H : $\mathcal{M} \to \mathcal{K}$, $H_1 : \mathcal{M} \to \{0,1\}^n$, we associate KEM := $U_m^\perp \circ KC^2$ [PKE, H, H_1]. The algorithms of KEM = (Gene, Enca, Deca) are defined in Fig. 5.

Gene	Enca(pk)	Deca($sk, (c_1, c_2)$)
$(pk, sk) \leftarrow$ Gen	$m \xleftarrow{\$} \mathcal{M}$	$m' := \text{Dec}(sk, c_1)$
return (pk, sk)	$c_1 := \text{Enc}(pk, m)$	**if** $m' = \perp$ **or** $(\text{Enc}(pk, m'), H_1(m')) \neq (c_1, c_2)$
	$c_2 := H_1(m)$	**return** $k' := \perp$
	$k := H(m)$	**else return** $k' := H(m')$
	return $((c_1, c_2), k)$	

Fig. 5. KEM = (Gene, Enca, Deca) := $U_m^\perp \circ KC[PKE, H, H_1]$.

Theorem 2 (IND-qCCA Security of $U_m^\perp \circ KC$ in the QROM). *Let PKE be a dPKE transformed from PKE_0 by T, i.e., PKE := $T[PKE_0, G]$. PKE_0 is a δ-correct rPKE with message space $\mathcal{M}$, ciphertext space $\mathcal{C}$ and randomness space $\mathcal{R}$. Let G : $\mathcal{M} \to \mathcal{R}$, H : $\mathcal{M} \to \mathcal{K}$, $H_1 : \mathcal{M} \to \{0,1\}^n$ be hash functions modeled as quantum random oracles. Then for any adversary $\mathcal{A}$ against the IND-qCCA security of KEM := $U_m^\perp \circ KC[PKE, H, H_1]$ issuing q_G, q_H, q_{H_1} and q_{Deca} quantum queries to G, H, H_1 and the decapsulation oracle Deca with depth d_G, d_H, d_{H_1} and d_{Deca}, there exists an adversary $\mathcal{B}$ against the OW-CPA security of PKE such that*

$$\text{Adv}_{KEM,\mathcal{A}}^{IND\text{-}qCCA} \leq 4d_H \cdot \text{Adv}_{PKE,\mathcal{B}}^{OW\text{-}CPA} + (16q_G'^2 + 16q_G''^2 + 8d_H + 2)\delta + 16q_{Deca}^2 \cdot 2^{-n}$$

and $\text{Time}(\mathcal{B}) \approx 2 \cdot \text{Time}(\mathcal{A})$, *where* $q_G' = q_G + q_{Deca} + 1, q_G'' = q_G + q_H + q_{H_1} + 1$.

Proof. Our game-based proof is essentially the same as the proof of above Theorem 1, except that we simulate the decapsulation oracle as in the proof of [26, Theorem 5.1]. The IND-qCCA games are given in Fig. 6. We note that the adversary is allowed to query quantum states to the decapsulation oracle.

GAME G_0: This is the original game, IND-qCCA$_{KEM}^{\mathcal{A}}$. We have

$$\text{Adv}_{KEM,\mathcal{A}}^{IND\text{-}qCCA} = 2|\Pr[G_0 \Rightarrow 1] - 1/2|$$

by the definition.

---

[2] In some papers [13,18], $U_m^\perp \circ KC$ ($FO_m^\perp \circ KC$) also refers to $QU_m^\perp$ or $HU_m^\perp$ ($QFO_m^\perp$ or $HFO_m^\perp$).

GAME IND-qCCA$_{\mathsf{KEM}}^{\mathcal{A}}$	$\mathsf{H}_1(m)$
$(pk, sk) \leftarrow \mathsf{Gen}$	$\mathbf{return}\ \overline{\mathsf{H}_1}(m)\quad //G_0 - G_1$
$\mathsf{G} \xleftarrow{\$} \Omega_\mathsf{G}\quad //G_0, G_5 - G_6$	$\mathbf{return}\ \mathsf{H}_q'(\mathsf{Enc}(pk, m))\quad //G_2 - G_6$
$\mathsf{G} \xleftarrow{\$} \Omega_{\mathsf{G}'}\quad //G_1 - G_4$	
$\overline{\mathsf{H}_1} \xleftarrow{\$} \Omega_{\mathsf{H}_1}\quad //G_0 - G_1$	$\mathsf{H}(m)$
$\mathsf{H}_q' \xleftarrow{\$} \Omega_{\mathsf{H}_q'}\quad //G_2 - G_6$	$\mathbf{return}\ \overline{\mathsf{H}}(m)\quad //G_0 - G_1$
$\overline{\mathsf{H}} \xleftarrow{\$} \Omega_\mathsf{H}\quad //G_0 - G_1$	$\mathbf{if}\ m = m^*\ \mathbf{and}\ b = 0\quad //G_6$
$\mathsf{H}_q \xleftarrow{\$} \Omega_{\mathsf{H}_q}\quad //G_2 - G_6$	$\quad\mathbf{return}\ r\quad //G_6$
$b \xleftarrow{\$} \{0, 1\}$	$\mathbf{return}\ \mathsf{H}_q(\mathsf{Enc}(pk, m))\quad //G_2 - G_6$
$m^* \xleftarrow{\$} \mathcal{M}$	
$c_1^* := \mathsf{Enc}(pk, m^*)$	$\underline{\mathsf{Deca}(c_1, c_2)}$
$\quad = \mathsf{Enc}_0(pk, m^*; \mathsf{G}(m^*))$	$\mathbf{if}\ (c_1, c_2) = (c_1^*, c_2^*)$
$c_2^* := \mathsf{H}_1(m^*)$	$\quad\mathbf{return}\ \bot$
$r \xleftarrow{\$} \mathcal{R}$	$m' := \mathsf{Dec}(sk, c_1)\quad //G_0 - G_3$
$k_0^* := \mathsf{H}(m^*)$	$\mathbf{if}\ (\mathsf{Enc}(pk, m'), \mathsf{H}_1(m')) = (c_1, c_2)\quad //G_0 - G_2$
$k_1^* := r$	$\quad\mathbf{return}\ \mathsf{H}(m')\quad //G_0 - G_2$
$b' \leftarrow \mathcal{A}^{\mathsf{G},\mathsf{H}_1,\mathsf{H},\mathsf{Deca}}(pk, (c_1^*, c_2^*), k_b^*)$	$\mathbf{if}\ (\mathsf{Enc}(pk, m'), \mathsf{H}_q'(c_1)) = (c_1, c_2)\quad //G_3$
$\mathbf{return}\ [\![b' = b]\!]$	$\mathbf{if}\ \mathsf{H}_q'(c_1) = c_2\quad //G_4 - G_6$
	$\quad\mathbf{return}\ \mathsf{H}_q(c_1)\quad //G_3 - G_6$
	$\mathbf{else\ return}\ \bot\quad //G_0 - G_6$

Fig. 6. IND-qCCA Games $G_0 - G_6$ for the proof of Theorem 2.

Let G' be a random function such that $\mathsf{G}'(m)$ is sampled according to the uniform distribution over $\mathcal{R}_{(pk,sk),m}^{good} := \{r \in \mathcal{R} | \mathsf{Dec}_0(sk, \mathsf{Enc}_0(pk, m; r)) = m\}$. Let $\Omega_{\mathsf{G}'}$ be the set of all functions G'.

GAME G_1: This game is the same as G_0 except that we replace G by G' that uniformly samples from "good" randomness at random, i.e., $\mathsf{G}' \xleftarrow{\$} \Omega_{\mathsf{G}'}$.

It is a same change as in the proof of Theorem 1, we also have

$$|\Pr[G_1 \Rightarrow 1] - \Pr[G_0 \Rightarrow 1]| \le 8q_\mathsf{G}'^2 \delta,$$

where $q_\mathsf{G}' = q_\mathsf{G} + q_{\mathsf{Deca}} + 1$.

GAME G_2: This game is the same as G_1 except that the random oracle $\mathsf{H}(\cdot)$ and $\mathsf{H}_1(\cdot)$ are simulated by $\mathsf{H}_q(\mathsf{Enc}(pk, \cdot))$ and $\mathsf{H}_q'(\mathsf{Enc}(pk, \cdot))$ respectively, where $\mathsf{H}_q : \mathcal{C} \to \mathcal{K}$ and $\mathsf{H}_q' : \mathcal{C} \to \{0, 1\}^n$ are other random oracles. With this change, c_2^* can be replaced by $\mathsf{H}_q'(c_1^*)$. We remark that $\mathcal{A}$ is not given direct access to H_q and H_q'.

Let Bad be the same event as defined in the proof of Theorem 1:

$$\mathsf{Bad} := [\exists m \in \mathcal{M}, \mathcal{R}_{(pk,sk),m}^{good} = \varnothing | (pk, sk) \leftarrow \mathsf{Gen}_0].$$

Then following the same analysis, we have $\Pr[\mathsf{Bad}] \le \delta$. If Bad doesn't happen, any message can be decrypted correctly for the PKE, i.e.,

$\mathsf{Dec}(sk, \mathsf{Enc}(pk, m)) = m$ for all $m \in \mathcal{M}$. Therefore, $\mathsf{Enc}(pk, \cdot)$ is injective. And if $\mathsf{H}_q(\cdot), \mathsf{H}'_q(\cdot)$ are random functions, then $\mathsf{H}_q(\mathsf{Enc}(pk, \cdot)), \mathsf{H}'_q(\mathsf{Enc}(pk, \cdot))$ are also random functions. Remarking that access to H_q and H'_q are not given to $\mathcal{A}$, it causes no difference from the view of $\mathcal{A}$ if we replace $\mathsf{H}(\cdot)$ and $\mathsf{H}_1(\cdot)$ with $\mathsf{H}_q(\mathsf{Enc}(pk, \cdot))$ and $\mathsf{H}'_q(\mathsf{Enc}(pk, \cdot))$.

Thus we have

$$\Pr[G_2 \Rightarrow 1 | \overline{\mathsf{Bad}}] = \Pr[G_1 \Rightarrow 1 | \overline{\mathsf{Bad}}].$$

GAME G_3: This game is the same as G_2 except that the decapsulation oracle returns $\mathsf{H}_q(c_1)$ if $(\mathsf{Enc}(pk, m'), \mathsf{H}'_q(c_1)) = (c_1, c_2)$, instead of returning $\mathsf{H}(m')$ if $(\mathsf{Enc}(pk, m'), \mathsf{H}_1(m')) = (c_1, c_2)$.

This change is just conceptual. Suppose that $\mathsf{Enc}(pk, m') = c_1$, we have that $\mathsf{H}(m') = \mathsf{H}_q(\mathsf{Enc}(pk, m')) = \mathsf{H}_q(c_1), \mathsf{H}_1(m') = \mathsf{H}'_q(\mathsf{Enc}(pk, m')) = \mathsf{H}'_q(c_1)$. Thus, we have

$$\Pr[G_3 \Rightarrow 1] = \Pr[G_2 \Rightarrow 1].$$

GAME G_4: This game is the same as G_3 except that the decapsulation oracle returns $\mathsf{H}_q(c_1)$ if $\mathsf{H}'_q(c_1) = c_2$. That is, the decapsulation oracle do not use sk and the re-encryption check any more.

Using similar method as in above game G_1, we can conclude that any adversary that are affected by this change can be used to deal with the generic distinguishing problem. The detailed reduction algorithm is given below.

Firstly, we define a function $\mathsf{F}_1 : \mathcal{C} \times \{0,1\}^n \to \{0,1\}$. For each $c_1 \in \mathcal{C}$, choose h_{c_1} uniformly at random from $\{0,1\}^n$. Then $\mathsf{F}_1(c_1, h)$ is set to 1 if $h = h_{c_1}$ or 0 otherwise. For each (c_1, h) we have $\Pr[\mathsf{F}_1(c_1, h) = 1] = 2^{-n}$.

Now, the reduction algorithm $\mathcal{R}$ is given a function $f : \mathcal{C} \times \{0,1\}^n \to \{0,1\}$, which is above function F_1 or the zero function F_2. $\mathcal{R}$ then play the IND-qCCA game just the same as game G_3 except for the decapsulation oracle. $\mathcal{R}$ simulate $\mathsf{Deca}(c_1, c_2)$ as follows:

- compute $m' := \mathsf{Dec}(sk, c_1)$.
- if $(c_1, c_2) = (c_1^*, c_2^*)$, return $\perp$.
- if $\mathsf{Enc}(pk, m') = c_1$ and $\mathsf{H}'_q(c_1) = c_2$, return $\mathsf{H}_q(c_1)$.
- if $\mathsf{Enc}(pk, m') = c_1$ and $\mathsf{H}'_q(c_1) \neq c_2$, return $\perp$.
- if $\mathsf{Enc}(pk, m') \neq c_1$ and $f(c_1, c_2) = 1$, return $\mathsf{H}_q(c_1)$.
- if $\mathsf{Enc}(pk, m') \neq c_1$ and $f(c_1, c_2) = 0$, return $\perp$.

Notice that the adversary cannot access to H'_q directly, $\mathsf{H}'_q(c_1)$ is a random value from the view of the adversary if $c_1 \notin \mathsf{Enc}(pk, \mathcal{M})$. Because G' only samples from "good" randomness, in the case of $\mathsf{Enc}(pk, m') \neq c_1$, we have $c_1 \notin \mathsf{Enc}(pk, \mathcal{M})$ and $\Pr[\mathsf{H}'_q(c_1) = c_2] = 2^{-n}$.

We can see that $\mathcal{R}$ perfectly simulate game G_3 if it is given F_2 and perfectly simulate game G_4 if it is given F_1. Thus, according to Lemma 2, we have

$$|\Pr[G_4 \Rightarrow 1] - \Pr[G_3 \Rightarrow 1]| = |\Pr[1 \leftarrow \mathcal{R}^{\mathsf{F}_1}] - \Pr[1 \leftarrow \mathcal{R}^{\mathsf{F}_2}]| \leq 8q_{\mathsf{Deca}}^2 \cdot 2^{-n}.$$

GAME G_5: This game is the same as G_4 except that we switch G' back to the ideal random oracle G.

In the same way above, we have

$$|\Pr[G_5 \Rightarrow 1] - \Pr[G_4 \Rightarrow 1]| \le 8q_G''^2\delta,$$

where $q_G'' = q_G + q_H + q_{H_1} + 1$.

GAME G_6: This game is the same as G_5 except that in the case $b = 0$ we reprogram $H(m^*)$ to the random value r. Now, we have $k_0^* = k_1^* = r$.

It is obvious that the change is purely conceptual and does not change the joint distribution of the view of $\mathcal{A}$. Thus

$$\Pr[G_6 \Rightarrow 1] = \Pr[G_5 \Rightarrow 1].$$

In game G_6, the distribution of the input $z = (pk, (c_1^*, c_2^*), k_b^* = r)$ to $\mathcal{A}$ is independent of b, and the random oracle queried to H by $\mathcal{A}$ and the simulator is either H if $b = 1$ (where $H(m) = H_q(\mathsf{Enc}(pk, m))$) or H' if $b = 0$ (where $H'(m) = H(m)$ for $m \ne m^*$). The simulation in game G_6 runs in time $\approx \mathsf{Time}(\mathcal{A})$. Therefore, the algorithm $\mathcal{A}$ together with the simulator in game G_6 constitutes an O2H distinguisher algorithm for distinguishing oracle H from H' with run-time $\approx \mathsf{Time}(\mathcal{A})$. That is,

$$2|\Pr[G_6 \Rightarrow 1] - 1/2| = |\Pr[1 \leftarrow \mathcal{A}|b = 1] - \Pr[1 \leftarrow \mathcal{A}|b = 0]|$$
$$= |\Pr[1 \leftarrow \mathcal{A}^H] - \Pr[1 \leftarrow \mathcal{A}^{H'}]|.$$

Applying Lemma 3, we can construct algorithm $\mathcal{D}$, with run-time $\approx 2 \cdot \mathsf{Time}(\mathcal{A})$ and making oracle calls to H and H', such that

$$|\Pr[1 \leftarrow \mathcal{A}^H] - \Pr[1 \leftarrow \mathcal{A}^{H'}]| \le 4d_H \cdot \Pr[T \cap \{m^*\} \ne \varnothing | T \leftarrow \mathcal{D}^{H,H'}(z)].$$

Using $\mathcal{D}$, we can construct an adversary $\mathcal{B}$ against the OW-CPA security of PKE. The OW-CPA game for PKE and the construction of $\mathcal{B}$ is given in Fig. 7. The adversary $\mathcal{B}$ invoke $\mathcal{D}$ using its input (pk, c^*) and oracle G by simulating $\mathcal{D}$'s input $(pk, (c^*, H_q'(c^*)), r)$ and all oracles $(G, H_1, H, H', \mathsf{Deca})$. When $\mathcal{D}$ returns its output set T, $\mathcal{B}$ tests each $m \in T$ to check whether $m \in S_{c^*}$, i.e., whether $\mathsf{Enc}(pk, m) = c^*$, and returns any such m if found. Note that $\mathsf{Time}(\mathcal{B}) \approx \mathsf{Time}(\mathcal{D})$. We can see that if $S_{c^*} = \{m^*\}$, the adversary $\mathcal{B}$ can simulate $\mathcal{D}$'s environment perfectly. Further, adversary $\mathcal{B}$ succeeds (i.e., outputs m^*) if $T \cap S_{c^*} \ne \varnothing$. Then using [21, Lemma 4], $\Pr[S_{c^*} \ne \{m^*\}]$ is bounded by 2δ. Thus we have

$$\Pr[T \cap \{m^*\} \ne \varnothing | T \leftarrow \mathcal{D}^{H,H'}(z)] \le \mathsf{Adv}_{\mathsf{PKE},\mathcal{B}}^{\mathsf{OW\text{-}CPA}} + 2\delta.$$

Summing up the differences of $\Pr[G_i \Rightarrow 1]$ over all games, we get

$$\mathsf{Adv}_{\mathsf{KEM},\mathcal{A}}^{\mathsf{IND\text{-}qCCA}} = 2|\Pr[G_0 \Rightarrow 1] - 1/2|$$
$$\le (16q_G'^2 + 16q_G''^2)\delta + 16q_{\mathsf{Deca}}^2 \cdot 2^{-n} + 2\delta + 4d_H \cdot (\mathsf{Adv}_{\mathsf{PKE},\mathcal{B}}^{\mathsf{OW\text{-}CPA}} + 2\delta)$$
$$= 4d_H \cdot \mathsf{Adv}_{\mathsf{PKE},\mathcal{B}}^{\mathsf{OW\text{-}CPA}} + (16q_G'^2 + 16q_G''^2 + 8d_H + 2)\delta + 16q_{\mathsf{Deca}}^2 \cdot 2^{-n}.$$

$\square$

GAME OW-CPA$_{PKE}^{B}$	$B^G(pk, c^*)$	$H_1(m)$
$(pk, sk) \leftarrow$ Gen	$H_q' \xleftarrow{\$} \Omega_{H_q'}$	return $H_q'(\text{Enc}(pk, m))$
$G \xleftarrow{\$} \Omega_G$	$H_q \xleftarrow{\$} \Omega_{H_q}$	
$m^* \xleftarrow{\$} \mathcal{M}$	$S_{c^*} := \{m \in \mathcal{M} \mid \text{Enc}(pk, m) = c^*\}$	$H(m)$
$c^* := \text{Enc}(pk, m^*)$	$c_2^* := H_q'(c^*)$	return $H_q(\text{Enc}(pk, m))$
$\quad = \text{Enc}_0(pk, m^*; G(m^*))$	$r \xleftarrow{\$} \mathcal{R}$	
$m' \leftarrow B^G(pk, c^*)$	$T \leftarrow \mathcal{D}^{G, H_1, H, H', \text{Deca}}(pk, (c^*, c_2^*), r)$	$H'(m)$
return $[\![m' = m^*]\!]$	if $T \cap S_{c^*} \neq \varnothing$	if $m \in S_{c^*}$
	$\quad$ return any element $\in T \cap S_{c^*}$	$\quad$ return r
	else return $\bot$	else return $H(m)$
		$\text{Deca}(c_1, c_2)$
		if $(c_1, c_2) = (c_1^*, c_2^*)$ or $H_q'(c_1) \neq c_2$
		$\quad$ return $\bot$
		else return $H_q(c_1)$

Fig. 7. Game OW-CPA$_{PKE}^{B}$ for the proof of Theorem 2.

Combining above Theorem 2 with Lemma 4, we obtain the following result of $FO_m^\perp \circ KC$.

Corollary 2 (IND-qCCA Security of $FO_m^\perp \circ KC$ in the QROM). *Let* PKE_0 *be a δ-correct rPKE with message space $\mathcal{M}$, ciphertext space $\mathcal{C}$ and randomness space $\mathcal{R}$. Let $G: \mathcal{M} \rightarrow \mathcal{R}$, $H: \mathcal{M} \rightarrow \mathcal{K}$, $H_1: \mathcal{M} \rightarrow \{0, 1\}^n$ be hash functions modeled as quantum random oracles. Then for any adversary $\mathcal{A}$ against the IND-qCCA security of $KEM := FO_m^\perp \circ KC[PKE_0, G, H, H_1]$ issuing q_G, q_H, q_{H_1} and q_{Deca} quantum queries to G, H, H_1 and the decapsulation oracle Deca with depth d_G, d_H, d_{H_1} and d_{Deca}, there exists an adversary $\mathcal{B}$ against the IND-CPA security of PKE_0 such that*

$$\text{Adv}_{KEM, \mathcal{A}}^{\text{IND-qCCA}} \leq 4d_H(d_G^* + 2) \cdot \left(\text{Adv}_{PKE_0, \mathcal{B}}^{\text{IND-CPA}} + \frac{8(q_G^* + 1)}{|\mathcal{M}|} \right)$$
$$+ (16q_G'^2 + 16q_G''^2 + 8d_H + 2)\delta + 16q_{\text{Deca}}^2 \cdot 2^{-n}$$

and $\text{Time}(\mathcal{B}) \approx 2 \cdot \text{Time}(\mathcal{A})$, *where* $d_G^* = 2(d_G + d_H + d_{H_1} + 1)$, $q_G^* = 2(q_G + q_H + q_{H_1} + n_p)$, $q_G' = q_G + q_{\text{Deca}} + 1$, $q_G'' = q_G + q_H + q_{H_1} + 1$, n_p *is the number of $\mathcal{A}$'s parallel queries to* H.

5 Not All Secure PKE is γ-Spread

The ciphertext of a semantically secure PKE should be designed to "look" as random as possible. It seems that γ-spreadness might be satisfied accordingly. However, it is not the case. We can construct a PKE that there almost always exist messages that its corresponding ciphertexts are determined while no efficient algorithms can find these messages, which implies that the PKE is not γ-spread but might be secure. The idea is simple, we partly derandomized a secure PKE only at points where $H(m) = 0$ such that a search problem is embedded.

Theorem 3. *Let* PKE *be a PKE that satisfies* IND-CPA *security, δ-correctness and weak γ-spreadness with message space $\mathcal{M}$. Let* $G : \mathcal{M} \to \mathcal{R}, H : \mathcal{M} \to \{0,1\}^n$ *be hash functions modeled as quantum random oracles. Then there exists a PKE that satisfies* IND-CPA *security and δ'-correctness, but 0-spreadness.*

Proof. We construct PKE′ based on PKE. PKE′ is essentially the same as PKE except that it additionally check whether $H(m) = 0$ at first, and if so, return $Enc(pk, m; G(m))$, otherwise return $Enc(pk, m)$.

We first show that PKE′ keeps IND-CPA secure. The IND-CPA game for PKE′ against adversary $\mathcal{A} = (\mathcal{A}_1, \mathcal{A}_2)$ is given in Fig. 8.

We consider the following event Find that $\mathcal{A}_1$ returns H's preimage of 0:

$$\text{Find} := [H(m_0) = 0 \vee H(m_1) = 0 | \{m_0^*, m_1^*, st\} \leftarrow \mathcal{A}_1^{G,H}(pk)].$$

If $\mathcal{A}_1$ makes at most q_H queries to H, it is well known that $\Pr[\text{Find}]$ is bounded by $O(q_H^2/2^n)$.

In the case that Find does not happen, $Enc'(pk, m_b^*) = Enc(pk, m_b^*)$. The game in Fig. 8 can be seen as the IND-CPA game for PKE, i.e.,

$$\Pr[\text{IND-CPA}_{\text{PKE}'}^{\mathcal{A}} \Rightarrow 1 | \overline{\text{Find}}] = \Pr[\text{IND-CPA}_{\text{PKE}}^{\mathcal{A}} \Rightarrow 1 | \overline{\text{Find}}].$$

GAME IND-CPA$_{\text{PKE}'}^{\mathcal{A}}$

$(pk, sk) \leftarrow$ Gen
$G \xleftarrow{\$} \Omega_G$
$H \xleftarrow{\$} \Omega_H$
$b \xleftarrow{\$} \{0,1\}$
$\{m_0^*, m_1^*, st\} \leftarrow \mathcal{A}_1^{G,H}(pk)$
$c^* \leftarrow Enc'(pk, m_b^*)$
$b' \leftarrow \mathcal{A}_2^{G,H}(pk, c^*, st)$
return $[\![b' = b]\!]$

Fig. 8. Game IND-CPA$_{\text{PKE}'}^{\mathcal{A}}$ for the proof of Theorem 3.

Thus, we have

$$\begin{aligned}
\text{Adv}_{\text{PKE}',\mathcal{A}}^{\text{IND-CPA}} &= 2|\Pr[\text{IND-CPA}_{\text{PKE}'}^{\mathcal{A}} \Rightarrow 1] - 1/2| \\
&\leq 2|\Pr[\text{IND-CPA}_{\text{PKE}}^{\mathcal{A}} \Rightarrow 1] - 1/2| + 2\Pr[\text{Find}] \\
&= \text{Adv}_{\text{PKE},\mathcal{A}}^{\text{IND-CPA}} + O(q_H^2/2^n).
\end{aligned}$$

For the correctness, we use the correctness notion relative to random oracles [13]. Let q_G be the number of $\mathcal{A}$'s queries to G. By [13, Lemma 4.3], it is easy to see that $\delta \leq \delta' \leq 8(q_G + 1)^2\delta$ as PKE′ is only partly derandomized and it would be closer to δ.

At last, for any m satisfied $\mathsf{H}(m) = 0$ (such m exists with probability closer to 1 as long as $|\mathcal{M}|$ is larger enough than 2^n), $c := \mathsf{Enc}(pk, m; \mathsf{G}(m))$, we have $\Pr[\mathsf{Enc}'(pk, m) = c] = 1$, which implies that PKE' is 0-spread.

$\square$

Remark 1. The theorem still holds for other security, such as IND-CCA, IND-qCCA, OW-CPA, etc.

Acknowledgments. We thank the anonymous reviewers for their comments and suggestions. The authors are supported by the National Key Research and Development Program of China (No. 2021YFA1000600) and Key Research and Development Program of Shandong province (No. 2022CXGC020101).

A   Definitions and Security Notions

A.1   Public-Key Encryption

Definition 1 (PKE). *A* (randomized) *public-key encryption scheme ((r)PKE) is defined over a message space $\mathcal{M}$, a ciphertext space $\mathcal{C}$, a public key space $\mathcal{PK}$ and a secret key space $\mathcal{SK}$. It consists of a triple of algorithms $\mathsf{PKE} = (\mathsf{Gen}, \mathsf{Enc}, \mathsf{Dec})$ defined as follows.*

- $\mathsf{Gen} \rightarrow (pk, sk)$ *is a randomized algorithm that returns a public key $pk \in \mathcal{PK}$ and a secret key $sk \in \mathcal{SK}$.*
- $\mathsf{Enc}(pk, m) \rightarrow c$ *is a randomized algorithm that takes as input a public key pk and a message $m \in \mathcal{M}$, and outputs a ciphertext $c \in \mathcal{C}$. If necessary, we make the used randomness of Enc explicit by writing $c := \mathsf{Enc}(pk, m; r)$, where $r \xleftarrow{\$} \mathcal{R}$ and $\mathcal{R}$ is the randomness space.*
- $\mathsf{Dec}(sk, c) \rightarrow m/\perp$ *is a deterministic algorithm that takes as input a secret key $sk \in \mathcal{SK}$ and a ciphertext $c \in \mathcal{C}$ and returns either a message $m \in \mathcal{M}$ or a failure symbol $\perp \notin \mathcal{M}$.*

A deterministic public-key encryption scheme (dPKE) is defined the same way, except that Enc is a deterministic algorithm.

Definition 2 (Correctness [13]). *A public-key encryption scheme PKE is δ-correct if*

$$\mathop{\mathrm{E}}_{(pk,sk) \leftarrow \mathsf{Gen}} \left[\max_{m \in \mathcal{M}} \Pr[\mathsf{Dec}(sk, c) \neq m | c \leftarrow \mathsf{Enc}(pk, m)] \right] \leq \delta.$$

We say the PKE is perfectly correct if $\delta = 0$.

Definition 3 (Spreadness [9,10]). *A public-key encryption scheme PKE is γ-spread if*

$$-\log \max_{m \in \mathcal{M}, c \in \mathcal{C}, pk \in \mathcal{PK}} \Pr[c = \mathsf{Enc}(pk, m)] \geq \gamma.$$

Definition 4 (Weak Spreadness [8]). *A public-key encryption scheme* PKE *is weakly γ-spread if*

$$-\log \mathop{E}_{(pk,sk)\leftarrow\text{Gen}} \left[\max_{m\in\mathcal{M},c\in\mathcal{C}} \Pr[c=\text{Enc}(pk,m)] \right] \geq \gamma.$$

Let PKE = (Gen, Enc, Dec) be a public-key encryption scheme with message space $\mathcal{M}$. We now define three security notions for it. We say the PKE is GOAL-ATK secure if $\text{Adv}_{\text{PKE},\mathcal{A}}^{\text{GOAL-ATK}}$ is negligible for any PPT adversary $\mathcal{A}$.

Definition 5 (OW-CPA). *The One-Wayness under Chosen Plaintext Attacks* (OW-CPA) *game for* PKE *is defined in Fig. 9, and the* OW-CPA *advantage of an adversary $\mathcal{A}$ against* PKE *is defined as* $\text{Adv}_{\text{PKE},\mathcal{A}}^{\text{OW-CPA}} := \Pr[\text{OW-CPA}_{\text{PKE}}^{\mathcal{A}} \Rightarrow 1]$.

Definition 6 (IND-CPA). *The Indistinguishability under Chosen Plaintext Attacks* (IND-CPA) *game for* PKE *is defined in Fig. 9, and the* IND-CPA *advantage of an adversary $\mathcal{A} = (\mathcal{A}_1, \mathcal{A}_2)$ against* PKE *is defined as* $\text{Adv}_{\text{PKE},\mathcal{A}}^{\text{IND-CPA}} := 2|\Pr[\text{IND-CPA}_{\text{PKE}}^{\mathcal{A}} \Rightarrow 1] - 1/2|$.

Definition 7 (IND-qCCA [7]). *The Indistinguishability under quantum Chosen Ciphertext Attacks* (IND-qCCA) *game for* PKE *is defined in Fig. 10, and the* IND-qCCA *advantage of an adversary $\mathcal{A} = (\mathcal{A}_1, \mathcal{A}_2)$ against* PKE *is defined as* $\text{Adv}_{\text{PKE},\mathcal{A}}^{\text{IND-qCCA}} := 2|\Pr[\text{IND-qCCA}_{\text{PKE}}^{\mathcal{A}} \Rightarrow 1] - 1/2|$.

GAME OW-CPA$_{\text{PKE}}^{\mathcal{A}}$	**GAME** IND-CPA$_{\text{PKE}}^{\mathcal{A}}$
$(pk,sk) \leftarrow$ Gen	$(pk,sk) \leftarrow$ Gen
$m^* \xleftarrow{\$} \mathcal{M}$	$b \xleftarrow{\$} \{0,1\}$
$c^* \leftarrow \text{Enc}(pk,m^*)$	$(m_0^*,m_1^*,st) \leftarrow \mathcal{A}_1(pk)$
$m' \leftarrow \mathcal{A}(pk,c^*)$	$c^* \leftarrow \text{Enc}(pk,m_b^*)$
return $[\![m'=m^*]\!]$	$b' \leftarrow \mathcal{A}_2(pk,c^*,st)$
	return $[\![b'=b]\!]$

Fig. 9. Games OW-CPA and IND-CPA for PKE.

GAME IND-qCCA$_{\text{PKE}}^{\mathcal{A}}$	$\text{Dec}_a(\sum_{c,m} \psi_{c,m} |c,m\rangle)$
$(pk,sk) \leftarrow$ Gen	**return** $\sum_{c,m} \psi_{c,m} |c, m \oplus f_a(c)\rangle$
$b \xleftarrow{\$} \{0,1\}$	
$(m_0^*,m_1^*,st) \leftarrow \mathcal{A}_1^{\text{Dec}\perp}(pk)$	$f_a(c)$
$c^* \leftarrow \text{Enc}(pk,m_b^*)$	**if** $c=a$
$b' \leftarrow \mathcal{A}_2^{\text{Dec}_{c^*}}(pk,c^*,st)$	**return** $m':=\perp$
return $[\![b'=b]\!]$	**else return** $m':=\text{Dec}(sk,c)$

Fig. 10. Game IND-qCCA for PKE.

A.2   Key Encapsulation Mechanism

Definition 8 (KEM). *A key encapsulation mechanism (KEM) is defined over a key space* $\mathcal{K}$, *a ciphertext space* $\mathcal{C}$, *a public key space* $\mathcal{PK}$ *and a secret key space* $\mathcal{SK}$. *It consists of a triple of algorithms* KEM = (Gene, Enca, Deca) *defined as follows.*

- Gene $\to (pk, sk)$ *is a randomized algorithm that returns a public key* $pk \in \mathcal{PK}$ *and a secret key* $sk \in \mathcal{SK}$.
- Enca$(pk) \to (c, k)$ *is a randomized algorithm that takes as input a public key* pk *and outputs a ciphertext* $c \in \mathcal{C}$ *as well as a key* $k \in \mathcal{K}$.
- Deca$(sk, c) \to k/\perp$ *is a deterministic algorithm that takes as input a secret key* $sk \in \mathcal{SK}$ *and a ciphertext* $c \in \mathcal{C}$ *and returns either a key* $k \in \mathcal{K}$ *or a failure symbol* $\perp \notin \mathcal{K}$.

Let KEM = (Gene, Enca, Deca) be a key encapsulation mechanism with key space $\mathcal{K}$. Following the definition of IND-qCCA for PKE, the KEM version for it can be defined similarly. We say the KEM is IND-qCCA secure if $\mathsf{Adv}_{\mathsf{KEM},\mathcal{A}}^{\mathsf{IND\text{-}qCCA}}$ is negligible for any PPT adversary $\mathcal{A}$.

Definition 9 (IND-qCCA [26]). *The* IND-qCCA *game for* KEM *is defined in Fig. 11, and the* IND-qCCA *advantage of an adversary* $\mathcal{A}$ *against* KEM *is defined as* $\mathsf{Adv}_{\mathsf{KEM},\mathcal{A}}^{\mathsf{IND\text{-}qCCA}} := 2|\Pr[\mathsf{IND\text{-}qCCA}_{\mathsf{KEM}}^{\mathcal{A}} \Rightarrow 1] - 1/2|$.

GAME IND-qCCA$_{\mathsf{KEM}}^{\mathcal{A}}$	Deca$_a(\sum_{c,k} \psi_{c,k}\,|c,k\rangle)$
$(pk, sk) \leftarrow$ Gene	**return** $\sum_{c,k} \psi_{c,k}\,|c, k \oplus f_a(c)\rangle$
$b \xleftarrow{\$} \{0,1\}$	
$(c^*, k_0^*) \leftarrow$ Enca(pk)	$f_a(c)$
$k_1^* \xleftarrow{\$} \mathcal{K}$	**if** $c = a$
$b' \leftarrow \mathcal{A}^{\mathsf{Deca}_{c^*}}(pk, c^*, k_b^*)$	**return** $k' := \perp$
return $[\![b' = b]\!]$	**else return** $k' :=$ Deca(sk, c)

Fig. 11. Game IND-qCCA for KEM.

References

1. Ambainis, A., Rosmanis, A., Unruh, D.: Quantum attacks on classical proof systems: the hardness of quantum rewinding. In: 2014 IEEE 55th Annual Symposium on Foundations of Computer Science. pp. 474–483, October 2014. https://doi.org/10.1109/FOCS.2014.57
2. Ambainis, A., Hamburg, M., Unruh, D.: Quantum security proofs using semiclassical oracles. In: Boldyreva, A., Micciancio, D. (eds.) CRYPTO 2019. LNCS, vol. 11693, pp. 269–295. Springer, Cham (2019). https://doi.org/10.1007/978-3-030-26951-7_10

3. Beals, R., Buhrman, H., Cleve, R., Mosca, M., de Wolf, R.: Quantum lower bounds by polynomials. J. ACM **48**(4), 778–797 (2001). https://doi.org/10.1145/502090.502097

4. Bellare, M., Rogaway, P.: Random oracles are practical: a paradigm for designing efficient protocols. In: Proceedings of the 1st ACM Conference on Computer and Communications Security, pp. 62–73. CCS '93, Association for Computing Machinery, New York, NY, USA (1993). https://doi.org/10.1145/168588.168596

5. Bindel, N., Hamburg, M., Hövelmanns, K., Hülsing, A., Persichetti, E.: Tighter proofs of CCA security in the quantum random oracle model. In: Hofheinz, D., Rosen, A. (eds.) TCC 2019. LNCS, vol. 11892, pp. 61–90. Springer, Cham (2019). https://doi.org/10.1007/978-3-030-36033-7_3

6. Boneh, D., Dagdelen, Ö., Fischlin, M., Lehmann, A., Schaffner, C., Zhandry, M.: Random oracles in a quantum world. In: Lee, D.H., Wang, X. (eds.) ASIACRYPT 2011. LNCS, vol. 7073, pp. 41–69. Springer, Heidelberg (2011). https://doi.org/10.1007/978-3-642-25385-0_3

7. Boneh, D., Zhandry, M.: Secure signatures and chosen ciphertext security in a quantum computing world. In: Canetti, R., Garay, J.A. (eds.) CRYPTO 2013. LNCS, vol. 8043, pp. 361–379. Springer, Heidelberg (2013). https://doi.org/10.1007/978-3-642-40084-1_21

8. Don, J., Fehr, S., Majenz, C., Schaffner, C.: Online-extractability in the quantum random-oracle model. In: Dunkelman, O., Dziembowski, S. (eds.) Advances in Cryptology – EUROCRYPT 2022. EUROCRYPT 2022. LNCS, vol. 13277, pp. 677–706. Springer, Cham (2022). https://doi.org/10.1007/978-3-031-07082-2_24

9. Fujisaki, E., Okamoto, T.: Secure integration of asymmetric and symmetric encryption schemes. In: Wiener, M. (ed.) CRYPTO 1999. LNCS, vol. 1666, pp. 537–554. Springer, Heidelberg (1999). https://doi.org/10.1007/3-540-48405-1_34

10. Fujisaki, E., Okamoto, T.: Secure integration of asymmetric and symmetric encryption schemes. J. Cryptol. **26**(1), 80–101 (2013). https://doi.org/10.1007/s00145-011-9114-1

11. Ge, J., Shan, T., Xue, R.: Tighter QCCA-secure key encapsulation mechanism with explicit rejection in the quantum random oracle model. In: Handschuh, H., Lysyanskaya, A. (eds.) Advances in Cryptology – CRYPTO 2023. CRYPTO 2023. LNCS, vol. 14085, pp. 292–324. Springer, Cham (2023). https://doi.org/10.1007/978-3-031-38554-4_10

12. Grover, L.K.: A fast quantum mechanical algorithm for database search. In: Proceedings of the Twenty-Eighth Annual ACM Symposium on Theory of Computing, pp. 212–219. STOC '96, Association for Computing Machinery, New York, NY, USA (1996). https://doi.org/10.1145/237814.237866

13. Hofheinz, D., Hövelmanns, K., Kiltz, E.: A modular analysis of the Fujisaki-Okamoto transformation. In: Kalai, Y., Reyzin, L. (eds.) TCC 2017. LNCS, vol. 10677, pp. 341–371. Springer, Cham (2017). https://doi.org/10.1007/978-3-319-70500-2_12

14. Hövelmanns, K., Hülsing, A., Majenz, C.: Failing gracefully: decryption failures and the Fujisaki-Okamoto transform. In: Agrawal, S., Lin, D. (eds.) Advances in Cryptology – ASIACRYPT 2022. ASIACRYPT 2022. LNCS, vol. 13794, pp. 414–443. Springer, Cham (2022). https://doi.org/10.1007/978-3-031-22972-5_15

15. Hövelmanns, K., Kiltz, E., Schäge, S., Unruh, D.: Generic authenticated key exchange in the quantum random oracle model. In: Kiayias, A., Kohlweiss, M., Wallden, P., Zikas, V. (eds.) PKC 2020. LNCS, vol. 12111, pp. 389–422. Springer, Cham (2020). https://doi.org/10.1007/978-3-030-45388-6_14

16. Hülsing, A., Rijneveld, J., Song, F.: Mitigating multi-target attacks in hash-based signatures. In: Cheng, C.-M., Chung, K.-M., Persiano, G., Yang, B.-Y. (eds.) PKC 2016. LNCS, vol. 9614, pp. 387–416. Springer, Heidelberg (2016). https://doi.org/10.1007/978-3-662-49384-7_15

17. Jiang, H., Zhang, Z., Chen, L., Wang, H., Ma, Z.: IND-CCA-secure key encapsulation mechanism in the quantum random oracle model, revisited. In: Shacham, H., Boldyreva, A. (eds.) CRYPTO 2018. LNCS, vol. 10993, pp. 96–125. Springer, Cham (2018). https://doi.org/10.1007/978-3-319-96878-0_4

18. Jiang, H., Zhang, Z., Ma, Z.: Key encapsulation mechanism with explicit rejection in the quantum random oracle model. In: Lin, D., Sako, K. (eds.) PKC 2019. LNCS, vol. 11443, pp. 618–645. Springer, Cham (2019). https://doi.org/10.1007/978-3-030-17259-6_21

19. Jiang, H., Zhang, Z., Ma, Z.: Tighter security proofs for generic key encapsulation mechanism in the quantum random oracle model. In: Ding, J., Steinwandt, R. (eds.) PQCrypto 2019. LNCS, vol. 11505, pp. 227–248. Springer, Cham (2019). https://doi.org/10.1007/978-3-030-25510-7_13

20. Kuchta, V., Sakzad, A., Stehlé, D., Steinfeld, R., Sun, S.-F.: Measure-Rewind-Measure: tighter quantum random oracle model proofs for one-way to hiding and CCA security. In: Canteaut, A., Ishai, Y. (eds.) EUROCRYPT 2020. LNCS, vol. 12107, pp. 703–728. Springer, Cham (2020). https://doi.org/10.1007/978-3-030-45727-3_24

21. Liu, X., Wang, M.: QCCA-secure generic key encapsulation mechanism with tighter security in the quantum random oracle model. In: Garay, J.A. (ed.) PKC 2021. LNCS, vol. 12710, pp. 3–26. Springer, Cham (2021). https://doi.org/10.1007/978-3-030-75245-3_1

22. Nielsen, M.A., Chuang, I.L.: Quantum Computation and Quantum Information: 10th Anniversary Edition, 10th edn. Cambridge University Press, USA (2011)

23. Saito, T., Xagawa, K., Yamakawa, T.: Tightly-secure key-encapsulation mechanism in the quantum random oracle model. In: Nielsen, J.B., Rijmen, V. (eds.) EUROCRYPT 2018. LNCS, vol. 10822, pp. 520–551. Springer, Cham (2018). https://doi.org/10.1007/978-3-319-78372-7_17

24. Shor, P.W.: Polynomial-time algorithms for prime factorization and discrete logarithms on a quantum computer. SIAM J. Comput. 26(5), 1484–1509 (1997). https://doi.org/10.1137/S0097539795293172

25. Unruh, D.: Revocable quantum timed-release encryption. In: Nguyen, P.Q., Oswald, E. (eds.) EUROCRYPT 2014. LNCS, vol. 8441, pp. 129–146. Springer, Heidelberg (2014). https://doi.org/10.1007/978-3-642-55220-5_8

26. Xagawa, K., Yamakawa, T.: (Tightly) QCCA-secure key-encapsulation mechanism in the quantum random oracle model. In: Ding, J., Steinwandt, R. (eds.) PQCrypto 2019. LNCS, vol. 11505, pp. 249–268. Springer, Cham (2019). https://doi.org/10.1007/978-3-030-25510-7_14

27. Zhandry, M.: How to record quantum queries, and applications to quantum indifferentiability. In: Boldyreva, A., Micciancio, D. (eds.) CRYPTO 2019. LNCS, vol. 11693, pp. 239–268. Springer, Cham (2019). https://doi.org/10.1007/978-3-030-26951-7_9

Side-Channel Analysis of Arithmetic Encodings for Post-Quantum Cryptography: Cautionary Notes with Application to Kyber

Duyên Pay$^{(\boxtimes)}$ and François-Xavier Standaert

UCLouvain, ICTEAM, Crypto Group, Louvain-la-Neuve, Belgium
`thl.pay@uclouvaln.be`

Abstract. The unprotected implementations of `Kyber` and `Dilithium` have recently been shown to offer a variety of side-channel attack paths. These attacks have in turn triggered the investigation of secure and efficient masked implementations. In this paper, we observe that the design and evaluation of such masked implementations come with new challenges, due to the manipulation of small and non-uniform secrets that is common in post-quantum encryption algorithms, which may hinder their good understanding. On the one hand, we show that using the Signal-to-Noise Ratio (SNR) per share to select Points-of-Interest (POIs) in leakage traces, as it is common in symmetric cryptography, can lead to confusing outcomes where leakage samples that correspond to the manipulation of another share than the targeted one are detected. On the other hand, we show that the arithmetic encoding of small and non-uniform secrets leads to representation-dependencies so that summing or subtracting shares leads to different amounts of information leakage. We apply these observations to `Kyber` and show that they essentially vanish when increasing the number of shares. Incidentally, we also discuss the attack strategies to recover small and non-uniform secrets with side-channel attacks efficiently. We hope these observations can help implementers and evaluators to better interpret their security claims.

1 Introduction

The implementation of post-quantum cryptographic algorithms with security guarantees against side-channel attacks is known to be challenging. Focusing on recently selected standards, powerful attacks against `Crystals-Kyber` [56] have been put forward in an already long sequence of works, for example including [47,51,53,59,60,62], which then motivated the investigations of protected implementations [2,9,10,14]; similar efforts exist for `Crystals-Dilithium` [38], both on the attack side [7,37,43,52] and on the protection side [1,15,46].

The main countermeasure used in these protected implementations is masking [13,27]. It allows building on a broad literature primarily developed for symmetric cryptography, which clarified the theoretical guarantees that masking

S. Vaudenay and C. Petit (Eds.): AFRICACRYPT 2024, LNCS 14861, pp. 260–281, 2024.
https://doi.org/10.1007/978-3-031-64381-1_12

offers [20,21,33,50] and the various challenges for these guarantees to be observed in practice [3,16,23,42,48]. Yet, and despite conceptual similarity, masking post-quantum cryptographic algorithms also comes with specificities. One of them, already covered in the aforementioned references, is the requirement to mix Boolean encodings and prime encodings. Negatively, this implies expensive conversion algorithms, a topic that was itself the focus of a long sequence of works (e.g., see [17,26] for early results and [6,8,18,19] for more recent ones). Positively, arithmetic masking in prime fields has recently been shown to offer a better tolerance to low-noise leakages, due to its reduced "algebraic compatibility" with the typical (linear) leakage models observed in practice [45].

In this paper, we are concerned with another difference, namely the fact that post-quantum algorithms require the manipulation of small and non-uniform secrets. Despite looking innocuous at first sight (e.g., it does not affect the security order of the countermeasure), this implies that a number of convenient intuitions that hold when masking symmetric algorithms like the AES do not apply to post-quantum algorithms, which we summarize in two cautionary notes.

The first observation relates to the selection of Points-of-Interest (POIs) in the leakage traces, which is an important step toward mounting powerful profiled attacks [22,25]. The Signal-to-Noise ratio is among the most popular tools for this purpose [39], since it allows spotting all the (bijectively connected) POIs that can be characterized with a single template. However, we show that the natural approach of estimating the SNR per share of a masked implementation can lead to confusion in the case of a small non-uniform secret. Namely, if such a small secret is shared in two pieces, it inevitably implies that the leakage of the shares is (mathematically) correlated. As a result, the SNR estimated for the first share will also lead to detect samples that depend on the second share, which may degrade the quality of the templates built for each share.

The second observation relates to the increased representation-dependency of post-quantum arithmetic encodings compared to Boolean masking. In the case of Boolean masking which is most frequently used in symmetric cryptography, there is a single way to write the additive encoding. But for arithmetic encodings, one can choose to sum or subtract shares, which creates a representation-dependency of the leakage informativeness computed with the mutual information [58]. This representation-dependency is then amplified by the small size of the secret, which implies that only selected distributions can be observed by the adversary.

As part of our investigations we also discuss the (e.g., maximum likelihood and maximum a posteriori) attack strategies that can be used to efficiently recover small and non-uniform secrets with profiled side-channel attacks.

We illustrate these notes using both simulated leakages and actual measurements, show that they hold for Simple Power Analysis (SPA) and Differential Power Analysis (DPA), and discuss their application to Kyber.[1] We also relativise their impact by showing that they essentially vanish when the number of shares used in the encodings increases. Overall, we nevertheless believe these

---

[1] In the SPA case, the leakage informativeness depends on the few inputs that the adversary can observe, so the representation-dependency is less unique [41].

observations are important to highlight the specificities of post-quantum arithmetic encodings. They have a direct impact on first-order masking that remains popular due to the reduced overheads it leads to. For example, [31,34] are specialized to first-order and [5,9,24] are only evaluated for first-order. They also convey the message that post-quantum cryptography comes with side-channel evaluation challenges that differ from the ones observed in symmetric cryptography.

2   Background

2.1   Kyber Algebraic Structure

Kyber is an IND-CCA2-secure key-encapsulation mechanism that allows the establishing of a shared secret key between two communicating parties. Its security is based on the hardness of solving the Learning-With-Errors problem in Module lattices (MLWE problem). In short, the MLWE problem is to distinguish between the uniform samples $(\mathbf{a}_i, b_i)$ from $R_q^k \times R_q$ and samples $(\mathbf{a}_i, b_i)$, where $\mathbf{a}_i$ is uniformly distributed from R_q^k and $b_i = \mathbf{a}_i^T \mathbf{s} + e_i$, and where the secret $\mathbf{s}$ and the noise e_i follow special distributions. The polynomial ring is defined to be $R_q = \mathbb{Z}_q[X]/(X^n + 1)$ consisting of polynomials of the form

$$f = f_0 + f_1 X + \cdots + f_n X^n, \tag{1}$$

where $f_i \in \mathbb{Z}_q$ for all j. The noise polynomials in Kyber are sampled from the Centered Binomial Distribution (CBD). The CBD is parameterized by an integer $\eta \in \{2, 3\}$. To sample a polynomial e, from CBD (B_η) requires to sample each of its coefficients e_j independently from B_η, with B_η defined as

$$(a_1, a_2, \ldots, a_\eta, b_1, b_2, \ldots, b_\eta) \xleftarrow{\$} \{0, 1\}^{2\eta},$$
$$e_j = \sum_{i=1}^{\eta} (a_i - b_i). \tag{2}$$

Kyber comes with different sets of parameters, which depend on the target security level (see Table 1 in [56]). For the sake of simplicity, we fixed the parameters in this note to Kyber512, where $n = 256, q = 3329, \eta = 2$, and $k = 1$.

Notations. For the rest of the note we use, calligraphic letters (e.g., $\mathcal{X}$) for sets, capital letters (e.g., X) for random variables, small letters (e.g., x) for realizations of the random variable. Bold capital and bold small letters (e.g., $\mathbf{X}$, $\mathbf{x}$) further denote random vectors and their realizations, respectively

We use the notation $X \xleftarrow{\$} \mathcal{X}$ for X being sampled uniformly at random from the set $\mathcal{X}$ and $X \leftarrow B_\eta$ if it follows the CBD distribution with parameter η. Due to our choice of parameters, the set of secrets is fixed to

$$\mathcal{S} = \{0, 1, -1, 2, -2\}, \tag{3}$$

of which the corresponding prior distribution is given by

$$\mathsf{p}_\mathcal{S} = [0.375, 0.25, 0.25, 0.0625, 0.0625]. \tag{4}$$

2.2 Boolean and Arithmetic Masking

In a dth-order masked implementation, each intermediate variable is split into $d+1$ shares, leading to so-called encodings that we define next [50].

Definition 1 (d-share encoding). *Let $\mathcal{X}$ be a set in a group $(\mathcal{G}, *)$ where $*$ is some group operation, and let d be a positive integer. The d-share encoding of $X \in \mathcal{X}$ is a mapping*

$$\mathsf{Enc}_d^{\mathsf{g},*} : \mathcal{X} \to \mathcal{G}^d :$$
$$X \mapsto (X_1, \ldots, X_d)$$

such that $(X_i)_{i=1}^{d-1} \xleftarrow{\$} \mathcal{G}$, $X = \mathsf{g}(X_1, X_2, \ldots, X_d)$ and g acts on X_i through $*$.

In this definition, the g function dictates how shares are combined at the beginning (resp., unmasked at the end) of a sensitive operation. For example, in a symmetric cipher like the AES Rijndael, where the underlying group is $\mathbb{Z}_{2^8}$, the Boolean additive 2-share encoding is defined as

$$\mathsf{Enc}_d^{\mathsf{g},\oplus}(X) = (X_1, X_2),$$

where $X_1 \xleftarrow{\$} \mathbb{Z}_{2^8}$ and $X = \mathsf{g}(X_1, X_2) = X_1 \oplus X_2$ (i.e., $X_2 = X \oplus X_1$).

The arithmetic 2-share encoding in an additive group $(\mathcal{G}, +)$ can be defined similarly as $\mathsf{Enc}_d^{g_i,+}(X) = (X_1, X_2)$, with as only difference that it can be expressed in two different ways, with

$$X = \mathsf{g}_1(X_1, X_2) = X_1 + X_2 \qquad \text{or} \qquad X = \mathsf{g}_2(X_1, X_2) = X_2 - X_1.$$

For the rest of the note, we focus on such additive masking, omit the group operation on the superscript, and use the simplified notations

$$\mathsf{Enc}_d^{\mathsf{sum}} \text{ for } g(X_1, X_2, \ldots, X_d) = \sum_{i=1}^{d} X_i, \qquad \text{i.e., } X_d^{\mathsf{sum}} = X - \sum_{i=1}^{d-1} X_i,$$

$$\mathsf{Enc}_d^{\mathsf{diff}} \text{ for } g(X_1, X_2, \ldots, X_d) = X_d - \sum_{i=1}^{d-1} X_i, \qquad \text{i.e., } X_d^{\mathsf{diff}} = X + \sum_{i=1}^{d-1} X_i.$$

Lastly, the noise polynomials in Kyber consist of $n = 256$ coefficients that are independently sampled from B_η and are masked independently. Without losing generality, we consider the masking of one coefficient of such polynomials.

2.3 POI Detection with the SNR

Side-channel attacks exploit leakage traces $\mathbf{L} = \{\mathbf{l}_i\}_{i=1}^{q}$ that correspond to data $X = \{x_i\}_{i=1}^{q}$. Each trace may contain hundreds of thousands of samples, i.e., $\mathbf{l} = \{l_t\}_{t=0}^{N}$ with large N values, where only a few of them are actually informative for the attack in the sense that they directly depend on the target variable X. As a result, selecting such POIs usually comes as a preliminary step in side-channel attacks. A popular statistical tool for this purpose is the side-channel SNR [40]. Assuming standard modeling of the leakage traces such that every sample is the sum of a deterministic $\delta_t(x)$ part and a noise part n_t [55], namely

$$l_t^x = \delta_t(x) + n_t, \tag{5}$$

the side-channel SNR can be directly estimated as

$$\mathrm{SNR}_t = \frac{\hat{\mathrm{var}}_x[\hat{\mathrm{E}}[l_t^x]]}{\hat{\mathrm{E}}_x[\hat{\mathrm{var}}[l_t^x]]}. \tag{6}$$

Next, the adversary can work on a subtrace made of samples with sufficient SNR rather than working on the full trace, leading to better efficiency.

2.4   Profiled Attacks

From profiling samples $(\mathbf{L}, X)$, a profiled distinguisher estimates a model of the conditional Probability Mass Function (PMF) $\hat{\mathrm{p}}(x|\mathbf{l})$, from which a maximum a posteriori attack can be launched, with the most likely secret chosen as

$$x^* = \arg\max_{x \in \mathcal{X}} \hat{\mathrm{p}}(x|\mathbf{l}).$$

In the following, we estimate such a model using Fisher's Linear Discriminant Analysis (LDA), which can be viewed as an improvement of Chari et all.'s seminal template attacks [13,57]. We then exploit the information extracted from individual shares using a Soft-Analytical Side-channel Attack (SASCA), which allows us to efficiently recover information on the target secret [29,61]. We will denote such a combination as LDAxSASCA for the rest of the note.

Linear Discriminant Analysis. The task of modeling $\hat{\mathrm{p}}(x|\mathbf{l})$ is well-known to suffer the *curse of dimensionality* [36]. So to further reduce the number of dimensions after POI selection, LDA projects the original data to a subspace of lower dimension which maximizes the inter-class variance and minimizes the intra-class variance. LDA is known to be optimal in terms of minimizing the Bayes error for binary classification under normality and homoscedasticity assumptions [30]. The LDA directions $\mathbf{w}$ are the solution of the maximization problem of the objective $\frac{\mathbf{w}^T \mathbf{S}_B \mathbf{w}}{\mathbf{w}^T \mathbf{S}_W \mathbf{w}}$, where $\mathbf{S}_B$ and $\mathbf{S}_W$ are the inter-class scatter and intra-class scatter matrices, respectively. They can be estimated as

$$\hat{\mathbf{S}}_B = \sum_{c=1}^{n_c} N_c (\hat{\boldsymbol{\mu}}_c - \hat{\boldsymbol{\mu}})(\hat{\boldsymbol{\mu}}_c - \hat{\boldsymbol{\mu}})^T,$$

$$\hat{\mathbf{S}}_W = \sum_{c=1}^{n_c} \sum_{i=1}^{N} (\mathbf{l}_i^c - \hat{\boldsymbol{\mu}}_c)(\mathbf{l}_i^c - \hat{\boldsymbol{\mu}}_c)^T,$$

where $\hat{\boldsymbol{\mu}}_c = \frac{1}{N_c}\sum_{i=1}^{N_c} \mathbf{l}_i^c$ is the empirical mean of the traces corresponding to x in class c, and, $\hat{\boldsymbol{\mu}} = \frac{1}{N}\sum_{c=1}^{n_c} \hat{\boldsymbol{\mu}}_c N_c$ is the total mean of all classes.

Finding $\mathbf{w}$ is usually reduced to the problem of finding the eigenvectors of the matrix $\hat{\mathbf{S}}_W^{-1}\hat{\mathbf{S}}_B$ and several eigenvectors that correspond to the highest eigenvalues are composed into a projection matrix $\mathbf{W}$. The original data is then transformed to lower dimension space (i.e., $\mathbf{l}_{lda} = \mathbf{W}\mathbf{l}$). The leakage traces after LDA projection are finally used to model the leakage Probability Density Function (PDF) as multivariate Gaussian templates, leading to the conditional PDF

$$\hat{f}(\mathbf{l}|x) = \frac{1}{\sqrt{(2\pi)^k \det \hat{\boldsymbol{\Sigma}}}} \exp\left(-\frac{1}{2}(\mathbf{l} - \hat{\boldsymbol{\nu}}_c)^T \hat{\boldsymbol{\Sigma}}^{-1}(\mathbf{l} - \hat{\boldsymbol{\nu}}_c)\right), \qquad (7)$$

where $\hat{\boldsymbol{\nu}}_c$ is the empirical mean of the projected traces corresponding to x in class c and the covariance matrix $\hat{\boldsymbol{\Sigma}}$ (also estimated from projected traces) is pooled from the covariance matrices of all classes $\hat{\boldsymbol{\Sigma}}_c$ as

$$\hat{\boldsymbol{\Sigma}} = \frac{1}{N}\sum_{c=1}^{n_c} N_c \hat{\boldsymbol{\Sigma}}_c.$$

Soft-Analytical Side-Channel Attacks. SASCAs were introduced in [61] and have recently gained popularity in analyzing masked implementations of symmetric ciphers [12], to perform single-trace attacks against Keccak implementations [35] or to target the Number Theoretic Transform (NTT) used in lattice-based cryptosystems [49]. In general, a SASCA combines a description of a leaking implementation thanks to a factor graph with a decoding, for example using the Belief Propagation (BP) algorithm. While initially introduced as a way to exploit the deeper leakage samples of block cipher implementations (i.e., where the intermediate computations depend on too many key bits to be targeted via a divide-and-conquer approach), it also turns out to be very handy to analyze the leakage of masked implementations at limited computational cost [28].

Precisely, in the context of this paper, we want to estimate the leakage PDF $\hat{f}(\mathbf{l}|s)$ of a d-share encoding $\mathsf{Enc}_d(S) = (X_1,\ldots,X_d)$, which corresponds to the following (Gaussian) mixture distribution

$$\hat{f}(\mathbf{l}|s) = \sum_{x_1,\ldots,x_{d-1}\in\mathbb{Z}_Q} \hat{f}(\mathbf{l}|x_1)\cdot\hat{f}(\mathbf{l}|x_2)\cdot\ldots\cdot\hat{f}(\mathbf{l}|x_d)\cdot\mathsf{p}(x_1)\cdot\mathsf{p}(x_2)\cdot\ldots\cdot\mathsf{p}(x_{d-1}),$$

without exhaustively summing over all the shares. The latter can be done efficiently by using Proposition 1 in [44] and computing

$$\hat{f}(\mathbf{l}|s) = \hat{f}(\mathbf{l}|x_1) \circ \hat{f}(\mathbf{l}|x_2) \circ \ldots \hat{f}(\mathbf{l}|x_d), \qquad (8)$$

where $\circ$ denotes the convolution operation. Performing these convolutions can be seen as a SASCA on a tree-like graph, and the BP algorithm is known to provide an exact solution in this case. We use the optimized library SCALib for this purpose, adjusted to fit with the special distribution of the secret.[2] Based on the obtained PDF, we finally compute the PMF $\hat{\mathsf{p}}(s|\mathbf{l})$ thanks to Bayes.

2.5 Evaluation Metrics

We will use information theoretic metrics (namely, the mutual & perceived information) in order to assess security against DPA (since they provide a tight quantification of such attacks' data complexities) and security metrics (namely the guessing entropy) in order to assess security against SPA.

Mutual Information and Perceived Information. Information theoretic metrics are common tools to evaluate the worst-case security against DPA [58]. The most popular such metric is the Mutual Information (MI), defined as

$$\mathrm{MI}(S;\mathbf{L}) = \mathrm{H}(S) + \sum_{s\in\mathcal{S}} \mathsf{p}(s) \int_{\mathbf{l}\in\mathcal{L}^d} \mathsf{f}(\mathbf{l}|s) \cdot \log_2 \mathsf{p}(s|\mathbf{l}).$$

The MI value can be used to bound the minimum number of measurements N_a that an adversary must obtain in order to recover X via DPA [4]. In practice, the MI is usually estimated by sampling to avoid the intractable cost of the integration when the dimension of $\mathbf{L}$ grows as

$$\widehat{\mathrm{MI}}(S;\mathbf{L}) = \mathrm{H}(S) + \sum_{s\in\mathcal{S}} \mathsf{p}(s) \sum_{i=1}^{N_s} \frac{1}{N_s} \cdot \log_2 \mathsf{p}(s|\mathbf{l}^s(i)), \tag{9}$$

where $\mathbf{l}^s(i)$ and N_s are ith leakage trace generated with the secret $S = s$ and the total number of traces corresponds to this secret, respectively. This estimation is known to converge to the correct MI value as N_s grows [11].

The MI can however only be computed in case the adversary has access to the true leakage distribution. In concrete settings, this leakage distribution is usually unknown, leading to the need to estimate either the model $\hat{\mathsf{p}}(.|.)$ or the metric. The Perceived Information (PI) captures the first approach and allows evaluating the amount of information that can be extracted from an estimated model, possibly biased by estimation or assumption errors [54]. It can be computed by sampling as

$$\widehat{\mathrm{PI}}(S;\mathbf{L}) = \mathrm{H}(S) + \sum_{s\in\mathcal{S}} \mathsf{p}(s) \sum_{i=1}^{N_s} \frac{1}{N_s} \cdot \log_2 \hat{\mathsf{p}}(s|\mathbf{l}^s(i)). \tag{10}$$

The sampling process to estimate $\widehat{\mathrm{PI}}(S;\mathbf{L})$ needs to be carried out on a separate set than used to estimate $\hat{\mathsf{p}}(.|.)$, to ensure it is unbiased. It is shown in [11] that the PI upper bounds the MI, and the equality holds if the model is perfect.

---

[2] https://scalib.readthedocs.io/en/stable/.

Guessing Entropy. While information theoretic metrics offer an efficient way to predict the data complexity of side-channel attacks, they ignore their time complexity and therefore, are usually paired with security metrics that give a more direct view of an implementation's concrete security level. A popular option for this purpose is to estimate the Guessing Entropy (GE), which measures the average amount of keys an adversary must enumerate to perform a side-channel key recovery. Typically, after performing an attack, the adversary has a guess vector $\mathbf{g} = [g_1, \ldots, g_{|\mathcal{S}|}]$, where target secret candidates g_i's are sorted by decreasing likelihood. Then GE of such the attack is

$$\widehat{\mathbf{GE}} = \hat{\mathop{\mathrm{E}}_{\text{attacks}}}[i|g_i \text{ is the correct key}]. \tag{11}$$

In the context of SPA, one can directly estimate such a metric (without information theoretic ones), since the attack complexity is fixed by the context.

3   Leakage Simulation and Real Measurement Setup

We illustrate our cautionary notes with both simulations and actual measurements. The first ones aim to enable easier interpretation, since they correspond to a more controlled environment where the leakage function is known. The second ones aim to confirm the practical relevance of our observations.

3.1   Simulated Leakages

The secrets are generated from the set of Eq. 3 and follow the distribution of Eq. 4. The leakages for d-share encodings are generated as follows:

1. First, generate $\mathsf{Enc}_d(S)$ where the first $d-1$ shares are drawn uniformly at random from $\mathbb{Z}_q$, and the last share X_d is computed to ensure correctness.
2. Next, the leakage of each share L_i is computed with the Hamming Weight (HW) model and additive Gaussian noise: $L_i = \mathrm{HW}(X_i) + B_i$, where $B_i \leftarrow \mathcal{N}(0, \sigma^2)$. As a result, the share's leakage PDF has the form

$$\mathsf{f}(l_i|x_i) = \frac{1}{\sigma\sqrt{2\pi}}\, e^{-\frac{1}{2}\left(\frac{l_i - \mathrm{HW}(x_i)}{\sigma}\right)^2}. \tag{12}$$

3. Finally, the leakage vector corresponding to the processing of S, $\mathbf{L}$ is the concatenation of the shares' leakages, i.e., $\mathbf{L} = [L_1, \ldots, L_d]$.

Integrating such leakage into Eq. 6, the SNR for each share can be computed as a function of the noise variance σ^2, i.e., $\mathrm{SNR} = \frac{2.67}{\sigma^2} \approx \frac{11/4}{\sigma^2}$, where 11 is the number of bits used to represent the moduli and $11/4$ is the variance of the Hamming weights corresponding to random 11-bit values (and the $\approx$ sign reflects the fact that shares are uniform in $\mathbb{Z}_q$ for q prime rather than $\mathbb{Z}_{2^{11}}$).

3.2 Measurement Setup

We measured an implementation similar to the public one from [10], running on an ARM Cortex-M4 STM32F415. This implementation uses $\mathsf{Enc}_2^{\mathrm{sum}}$ and we tweaked it in order to produce traces for $\mathsf{Enc}_2^{\mathrm{diff}}$ as well. The noise coefficients are generated following Eq. 2 with $\{a_i, b_i\}$ produced by the AES128.

The MCU was mounted on the CW308 UFO board, with an external 8 MHz crystal oscillator to fix the system clock. The leakages were measured with the CT1 current probe and the signal was sampled by a PicoScope 5244D at 500 MSamples/s with 12-bit resolution with no signal pre-processing nor averaging. We collected two million traces for each target and focused our analysis on the encoding loaded before the execution of the NTT in Kyber's re-encryption.

3.3 Evaluation Methodology

Based on the previous background, our evaluations (both with simulated leakages and actual measurements) are based on the following steps:

1. Divide the dataset into a profiling dataset and an attack dataset.
2. **On measurements** Use the SNR in order to select POIs (i.e., pick the points with highest SNR for evaluation). Then estimate (for the POIs) the leakage PDF given the shares $\hat{\mathsf{f}}(\mathsf{l}|x_i)$ for each share using LDA.
   In simulations Compute $\mathsf{f}(\mathsf{l}|x_i)$ directly as given by Eq. 12.
3. Estimate the secret PDF $\hat{\mathsf{f}}(\mathsf{l}|s)$ from the shares PDF using SASCA.
4. Compute the MI/PI/GE using the secret PDF on the attack dataset.

4 Cautionary Note on POI Detection

As mentioned in the introduction, the SNR is a popular tool for selecting POIs in leakage traces. In this section, we show that its application to the shares of an arithmetic encoding can create confusion when the encoded value is small. For this purpose, we first report the SNR computed from the measurements of Sect. 3.2 for the two shares of an arithmetic encoding in Fig. 1a, where the first share is manipulated around time sample 100 and the second share is manipulated around time sample 275. One can see that the POIs suggested by the SNR are not perfectly isolated: the SNR computed for the first (resp., second) share can pop up at the position of the second (resp., first) share. Such *ghost peaks* give the incorrect impression that there is useful information about a share beyond the points in time where it is manipulated. As a result, blindly applying this POI selection can disturb the performances of a profiled attack.

One important remark in this respect is that since conditioned on the secret, the shares are not independent, it also implies that wrongly selecting POIs for the first share (resp., second share) in the time samples corresponding to the second share (resp., first share) does not only increase the profiling data (and time) complexity, as would be expected if they were independent [36]. We report the

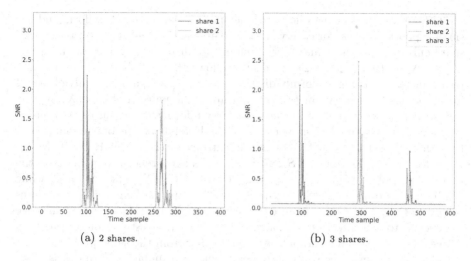

(a) 2 shares.

(b) 3 shares.

Fig. 1. Shares' SNR of an arithmetic encoding.

PI estimated from the LDAxSASCA profiled with a blind application of the SNR-based POI detection vs. an informed one where we only keep the samples that match the actual manipulation of the shares in Fig. 2b. It shows that the ghost peaks perturb the model persistently, as reflected by a negative PI when incorrect POIs are used.[3] This is because errors are not averaged by using more profiling data in this case, which is in contrast with the selection of non-informative points that do not correspond to any of the shares.

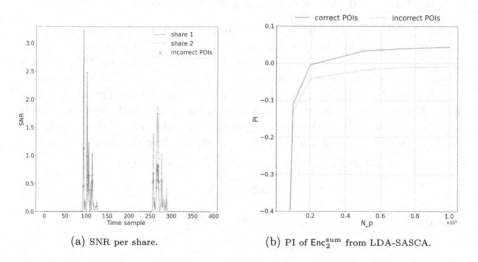

(a) SNR per share.

(b) PI of Enc_2^{sum} from LDA-SASCA.

Fig. 2. Impact of wrong POI selection on LDAxSASCA: 2-share case.

---

[3] Here, the model is computed with a non-uniform prior. A similar observation holds with uniform prior. We discuss the impact of these priors in Sect. 6.4.

These ghost peaks exist due to the fact that the secret is not uniform and has small support. That is, for each value of the first share (e.g., $X_1 = 0$), the second share only takes some values corresponding to all possible values of the secret S (i.e., $X_2 \in \{0, 1, -1, 2, -2\}$), and also follows the secret's distribution. As a result, instead of being uniformly distributed over $\mathbb{Z}_q \times \mathbb{Z}_q$ as classically observed for encodings used in symmetric cryptography, the pairs of shares (X_1, X_2) lie in a specific/restricted set and therefore carry information about each other.

More precisely, in the 2-share case, the conditional entropy of one share given the other, $H(X_1|X_2)$, exactly equals the entropy of the secret $H(S)$. This fact holds for all distributions of S and is an unchanged relationship between the two shares' values. Combined with the fact that $H(X_1|X_2)$ spreads on $\mathbb{Z}_q$ while $H(S)$ spreads only on S where $|S| \ll q$, each share mathematically correlates with the other. This explains our observations of Fig. 1a and shows that they are not specific to one detection tool: any tool relying on the estimation of statistical moment (e.g., Pearson's correlation) would suffer from the same problem.

This phenomenon however disappears when the number of shares is more than two, as illustrated in Fig. 1b, which we will explain based on an example. Say we consider the pair (X_1, X_3). Since the secret's distribution is now *absorbed* by the uniform distribution of X_2, the pair (X_1, X_3) is uniform over $\mathbb{Z}_q \times \mathbb{Z}_q$ and the correlation between them vanishes. As a result, the SNR per share rightfully spots leakage samples that correspond to the shares' manipulation only.

Based on this first cautionary note, and when considering a 2-share case, our following experiments will therefore all be based on an informed POI selection, where we manually isolate POIs that correspond to the target share.

5   Interlude on Attack Strategies

A natural next step after identifying POIs is to perform a profiled attack. In the case of Kyber, we can for example target the encoding manipulated just before the NTT computation in the re-encryption step with an SPA (since it is an ephemeral secret), and therefore estimate the resulting guessing entropy.

Yet, since the secret we target is then non-uniform, the maximum likelihood and maximum a posteriori attack strategies are not equivalent anymore. This is again in contrast with the situation in symmetric cryptography, where the target secrets always have a uniform prior. We next detail these different strategies.

The Maximum Likelihood (ML) approach selects the secret as

$$\tilde{s} = \underset{s}{\text{argmax}}\ f(l|s),$$

while the Maximum A Posteriori (MAP) approach selects it as:

$$\tilde{s} = \underset{s}{\text{argmax}}\ p(s|l),$$

$$= \underset{s}{\text{argmax}}\ \frac{f(l|s) \cdot p(s)}{\sum_{s^*} f(l|s^*) \cdot p(s^*)},$$

$$= \underset{s}{\text{argmax}}\ f(l|s) \cdot p(s).$$

When extended to multi-trace leakage vectors **l** it directly gives

$$\tilde{s} = \underset{s}{\operatorname{argmax}} \prod_{i=1}^{N_a} \mathsf{f}(\mathbf{l}(i)|s),$$

in the ML case, while the generalization of the MAP given in [32, 58] is

$$\tilde{s} = \underset{s}{\operatorname{argmax}} \; \mathsf{p}(s) \cdot \prod_{i=1}^{N_a} \mathsf{f}(\mathbf{l}(i)|s).$$

Those strategies can be equivalently written in logarithmic form as:

$$\tilde{s} = \underset{s}{\operatorname{argmax}} \sum_{i=1}^{N_a} \log \mathsf{f}(\mathbf{l}(i)|s) \qquad \text{(ML)} \qquad (13)$$

$$\tilde{s} = \underset{s}{\operatorname{argmax}} \left[\sum_{i=1}^{N_a} \log \mathsf{f}(\mathbf{l}(i)|s) + \log \mathsf{p}(s) \right] \qquad \text{(MAP)}, \qquad (14)$$

where N_a denotes the total number of attack traces. As a result, the two approaches are equivalent when there is a uniform prior on s and differ otherwise Interestingly, the latter happens in our Kyber case study. Furthermore, the arithmetic encoding we target enables SPA with repetition. That is, the adversary can repeatedly observe the leakage of this encoding for the same (stable) secret s. We analyzed the efficiency of these different strategies with the simulated leakages of Sect. 3.1. The guessing entropy of attacks exploiting 1, 10, 50, and 100 repetitions in function of the shares' SNR is given in Figs. 3 and 4 for the sum and diff. encodings (and 500, 1000, 2000, 10000, 20000 repetitions in Figs. 5 and 6), leading to the following observations.

Firstly, when the prior information of the secret is available, MAP consistently performs better for every noise level. More precisely, both the ML and MAP approaches allow accumulating information from multiple traces. Yet, whenever the distinguisher encounters an non-informative leakage (e.g., when $\mathsf{f}(\mathbf{l}(i)|\cdot)$ is equal for correct and incorrect secrets), ML guesses the secret at random while MAP bases its guess on the prior distribution. Hence, for low number of repetitions, MAP leads to better results, as shown in Figs. 3 and 4.

Secondly, MAP is essentially ML one-time-weighted by the prior. Thus, both converge towards the same value and correctly guess the secret when the model is sound with enough data, as shown for high SNRs in Figs. 5 and 6.

Additionally, we observe that the guessing entropy of Fig. 4 sometimes saturates, which is due to the distributions of some secret values that remain hard to distinguish and will be discussed in the next section.

6   Cautionary Note on Representation-Dependency

In this section, we investigate the dependency of arithmetic encodings protecting small and non-uniform secrets to their representation (i.e., whether they

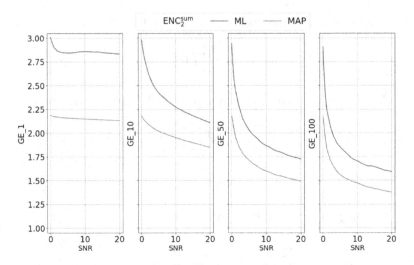

Fig. 3. GE of simulated attacks against the sum encoding with different strategies.

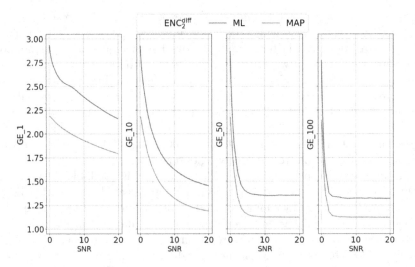

Fig. 4. GE of simulated attacks against the diff. encoding with different strategies.

sum or subtract shares). As already mentioned, a natural application of such encodings is before the NTT in Kyber's re-encryption step, where a SPA with repetition is possible. More precisely, the previous section already hinted towards this representation-dependency and we now aim to discuss it more in depth. For this purpose, we will start with an intuitive discussion based on PDF plots in Sect. 6.1, follow with a simulated analysis that puts forward this dependency and how it vanishes with a larger number of shares in Sect. 6.2, confirm these findings with experiments in Sect. 6.3 and discuss their extension to DPA for completeness (since not motivated by a concrete case study) in Sect. 6.4.

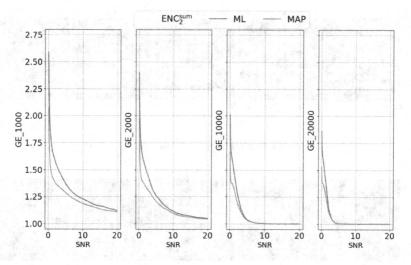

Fig. 5. GE of simulated attacks against the sum encoding with more averaging.

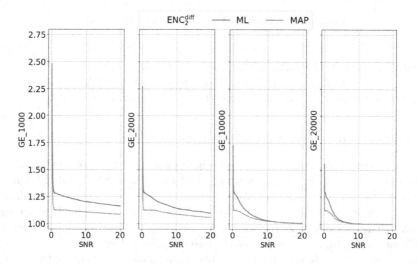

Fig. 6. GE of simulated attacks against the diff encoding with more averaging.

6.1 PDF Plots for the Two Encodings

The plots corresponding to the mixture PDF of the two (sum and diff.) encodings in the noisy Hamming weight leakage model are given in Figs. 7 and 8.

They lead to two main observations. First, we see that the diff. encoding seems more informative than the sum one. This is because the distributions in Fig. 8 are (visually) more separated than the ones in Fig. 7. Second, we also see that some distributions are very hard to distinguish in the diff. encoding case (e.g., those of $s = 1,2$ or $s = -1,-2$). This suggests that the diff. encoding will lead

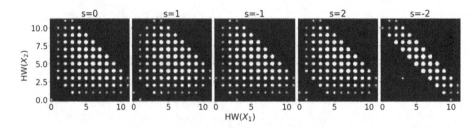

Fig. 7. Bivariate PDF $f(l|s)$ for the sum encoding.

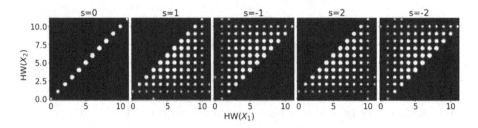

Fig. 8. Bivariate PDF $f(l|s)$ for the diff. encoding.

to easier attacks in the DPA setting and (on average) in the SPA setting, but some of these keys may remain hard to distinguish in the SPA setting (which is what we observed with the saturation effect in the previous section).

6.2 Simulated Leakages

Moving to a more quantitative analysis, Fig. 9 shows the evolution of the guessing entropy for the two encodings, in function of the shares' SNR and the number of shares, for an increasing number of repetitions (when moving from left to right). It confirms the previous intuition that the diff. encoding leads to stronger attacks than the sum one (in similar conditions). It also highlights that the gap between the informativeness of the two encodings decreases when the noise and the number of shares increases. This is presumably explained by the fact that when combining more (noisy) shares, the mixture PDFs tend to be more uniform, which therefore flattens patterns that may appear with a low number of shares. Note that the reduction of this gap is combined with the reduction of informativeness caused by lower SNR and larger number of shares. It will be easier to observed in the information theoretic plots of Sect. 6.4.

6.3 Actual Measurements

Figure 10 provides the guessing entropy in function of the number traces used to profile the leakage model (N_p) of the two encodings, for two shares and the noise level provided by our actual measurements (again for increasing the number

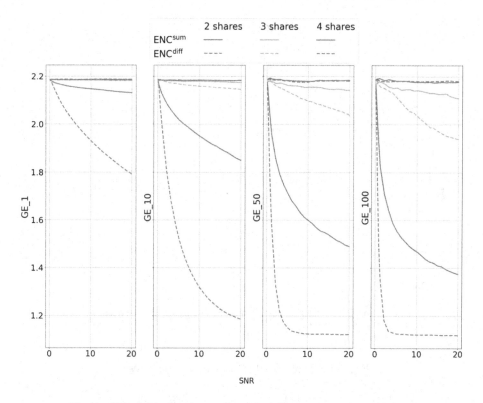

Fig. 9. GE of simulated attacks with different numbers of shares.

of repetitions in the attack). It confirms that the conclusions obtained with simulated leakages are also matched for our software implementation setting.

6.4   From SPA to DPA

Eventually, and for completeness, we provide results similar to those of the previous section but replacing the guessing entropy (i.e., a security metric that captures SPA) by the MI/PI (i.e., information theoretic metrics that efficiently capture DPA) in Fig. 11. The mutual information is used for simulated leakages, the perceived information is used for actual measurements. Our conclusions are again essentially similar (exhibiting even simpler patterns). Namely, the gap between the two encodings is clear and vanishes with more shares. As in Sect. 4, we used a non-uniform prior to estimate the MI and PI. Results with a uniform prior lead to the same conclusions. The study of how such information theoretic metrics can be formally connected to the different attack strategies outlined in Sect. 5 is an interesting scope for further investigations.

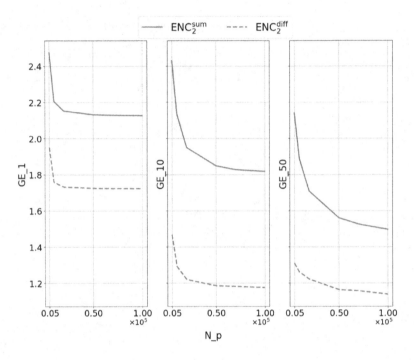

Fig. 10. GE of actual attacks with two shares.

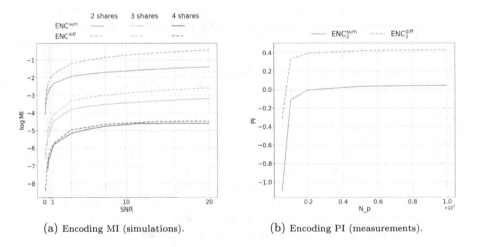

(a) Encoding MI (simulations).   (b) Encoding PI (measurements).

Fig. 11. MI and PI of simulated and actual attacks

7 Conclusions

This note highlights some new challenges that the design and evaluation of post-quantum cryptographic implementations against side-channel attacks may lead to. For example, confusion in the detection of POIs, need of different attack strategies and representation-dependencies in arithmetic encodings. It suggests that some of the (now standard) tools and intuitions that emerged from the study of symmetric cryptographic implementations cannot be straightforwardly extended to the post-quantum context without caution. The main reason of this gap is the manipulation of small and non-uniform secrets. While it raises no fundamental impossibilities (i.e., standard attacks can be mounted and standard countermeasures are still effective), it nevertheless requires slight adaptations for existing tools to be used in this case. We hope the notes in this paper can help implementers and evaluators to gain a good understanding of the physical security provided by masked implementations of post-quantum algorithms.

Acknowledgments. François-Xavier Standaert is a senior research associate of the Belgian Fund for Scientific Research (FNRS-F.R.S.). This work has been funded in part by the Walloon Region through the project CyberExcellence (convention number 2110186) and by the ERC Advanced Grant 101096871 (BRIDGE). Views and opinions expressed are those of the authors only and do not necessarily reflect those of the European Union or the ERC. Neither the European Union nor the granting authority can be held responsible for them.

References

1. Azouaoui, M., et al.: Protecting dilithium against leakage revisited sensitivity analysis and improved implementations. IACR Trans. Cryptogr. Hardw. Embed. Syst. **2023**(4), 58–79 (2023)
2. Azouaoui, M., Bronchain, O., Hoffmann, C., Kuzovkova, Y., Schneider, T., Standaert, F.-X.: Systematic study of decryption and re-encryption leakage: the case of Kyber. In: Balasch, J., O'Flynn, C. (eds.) COSADE 2022. LNCS, vol. 13211, pp. 236–256. Springer, Cham (2022). https://doi.org/10.1007/978-3-030-99766-3_11
3. Balasch, J., Gierlichs, B., Grosso, V., Reparaz, O., Standaert, F.-X.: On the cost of lazy engineering for masked software implementations. In: Joye, M., Moradi, A. (eds.) CARDIS 2014. LNCS, vol. 8968, pp. 64–81. Springer, Cham (2015). https://doi.org/10.1007/978-3-319-16763-3_5
4. Béguinot, J., et al.: Removing the field size loss from Duc et al.'s conjectured bound for masked encodings. In: Kavun, E.B., Pehl, M. (eds.) Constructive Side-Channel Analysis and Secure Design. COSADE 2023. LNCS, vol. 13979, pp. 86–104. Springer, Cham (2023). https://doi.org/10.1007/978-3-031-29497-6_5
5. Beirendonck, M.V., D'anvers, J.P., Karmakar, A., Balasch, J., Verbauwhede, I.: A side-channel-resistant implementation of SABER. ACM J. Emerg. Technol. Comput. Syst. **17**(2), 10:1–10:26 (2021)
6. Van Beirendonck, M., D'Anvers, J.-P., Verbauwhede, I.: Analysis and comparison of table-based arithmetic to Boolean masking. IACR Trans. Cryptogr. Hardw. Embed. Syst. **2021**(3), 275–297 (2021)
7. Berzati, A., Viera, A.C., Chartouny, M., Madec, S., Vergnaud, D., Vigilant, D.: Exploiting intermediate value leakage in dilithium: a template-based approach. IACR Trans. Cryptogr. Hardw. Embed. Syst. **2023**(4), 188–210 (2023)
8. Bettale, L., Coron, J.-S., Zeitoun, R.: Improved high-order conversion from Boolean to arithmetic masking. IACR Trans. Cryptogr. Hardw. Embed. Syst. **2018**(2), 22–45 (2018)

9. Bos, J.W., Gourjon, M., Renes, J., Schneider, T., van Vredendaal, C.: Masking Kyber: first- and higher-order implementations. IACR Trans. Cryptogr. Hardw. Embed. Syst. **2021**(4), 173–214 (2021)

10. Bronchain, O., Cassiers, G.: Bitslicing arithmetic/Boolean masking conversions for fun and profit with application to lattice-based KEMs. IACR Trans. Cryptogr. Hardw. Embed. Syst. **2022**(4), 553–588 (2022)

11. Bronchain, O., Hendrickx, J.M., Massart, C., Olshevsky, A., Standaert, F.-X.: Leakage certification revisited: bounding model errors in side-channel security evaluations. In: Boldyreva, A., Micciancio, D. (eds.) CRYPTO 2019. LNCS, vol. 11692, pp. 713–737. Springer, Cham (2019). https://doi.org/10.1007/978-3-030-26948-7_25

12. Bronchain, O., Standaert, F.-X.: Breaking masked implementations with many shares on 32-bit software platforms or when the security order does not matter. IACR Trans. Cryptogr. Hardw. Embed. Syst. **2021**(3), 202–234 (2021)

13. Chari, S., Jutla, C.S., Rao, J.R., Rohatgi, P.: Towards sound approaches to counteract power-analysis attacks. In: Wiener, M. (ed.) CRYPTO 1999. LNCS, vol. 1666, pp. 398–412. Springer, Heidelberg (1999). https://doi.org/10.1007/3-540-48405-1_26

14. Coron, J.-S., Gérard, F., Montoya, S., Zeitoun, R.: High-order polynomial comparison and masking lattice-based encryption. IACR Trans. Cryptogr. Hardw. Embed. Syst. **2023**(1), 153–192 (2023)

15. Coron, J.-S., Gérard, F., Trannoy, M., Zeitoun, R.: Improved gadgets for the high-order masking of dilithium. IACR Trans. Cryptogr. Hardw. Embed. Syst. **2023**(4), 110–145 (2023)

16. Coron, J.-S., Giraud, C., Prouff, E., Renner, S., Rivain, M., Vadnala, P.K.: Conversion of security proofs from one leakage model to another: a new issue. In: Schindler, W., Huss, S.A. (eds.) COSADE 2012. LNCS, vol. 7275, pp. 69–81. Springer, Heidelberg (2012). https://doi.org/10.1007/978-3-642-29912-4_6

17. Coron, J.-S., Goubin, L.: On Boolean and arithmetic masking against differential power analysis. In: Koç, Ç.K., Paar, C. (eds.) CHES 2000. LNCS, vol. 1965, pp. 231–237. Springer, Heidelberg (2000). https://doi.org/10.1007/3-540-44499-8_18

18. Coron, J.-S., Großschädl, J., Tibouchi, M., Vadnala, P.K.: Conversion from arithmetic to Boolean masking with logarithmic complexity. In: Leander, G. (ed.) FSE 2015. LNCS, vol. 9054, pp. 130–149. Springer, Heidelberg (2015). https://doi.org/10.1007/978-3-662-48116-5_7

19. D'Anvers, J.P.: One-hot conversion: towards faster table-based A2B conversion. In: Hazay, C., Stam, M. (eds.) Advances in Cryptology – EUROCRYPT 2023. EUROCRYPT 2023. LNCS, vol. 14007, pp. 628–657. Springer, Cham (2023). https://doi.org/10.1007/978-3-031-30634-1_21

20. Duc, A., Dziembowski, S., Faust, S.: Unifying leakage models: from probing attacks to noisy leakage. In: Nguyen, P.Q., Oswald, E. (eds.) EUROCRYPT 2014. LNCS, vol. 8441, pp. 423–440. Springer, Heidelberg (2014). https://doi.org/10.1007/978-3-642-55220-5_24

21. Duc, A., Faust, S., Standaert, F.-X.: Making masking security proofs concrete. In: Oswald, E., Fischlin, M. (eds.) EUROCRYPT 2015. LNCS, vol. 9056, pp. 401–429. Springer, Heidelberg (2015). https://doi.org/10.1007/978-3-662-46800-5_16

22. Durvaux, F., Standaert, F.-X.: From improved leakage detection to the detection of points of interests in leakage traces. In: Fischlin, M., Coron, J.-S. (eds.) EUROCRYPT 2016. LNCS, vol. 9665, pp. 240–262. Springer, Heidelberg (2016). https://doi.org/10.1007/978-3-662-49890-3_10

23. Faust, S., Grosso, V., Pozo, S.M.D., Paglialonga, C., Standaert, F.-X.: Composable masking schemes in the presence of physical defaults & the robust probing model. IACR Trans. Cryptogr. Hardw. Embed. Syst. **2018**(3), 89–120 (2018)

24. Fritzmann, T., et al.: Masked accelerators and instruction set extensions for post-quantum cryptography. IACR Trans. Cryptogr. Hardw. Embed. Syst. **2022**(1), 414–460 (2022)

25. Gierlichs, B., Lemke-Rust, K., Paar, C.: Templates vs. stochastic methods. In: Goubin, L., Matsui, M. (eds.) CHES 2006. LNCS, vol. 4249, pp. 15–29. Springer, Heidelberg (2006). https://doi.org/10.1007/11894063_2

26. Goubin, L.: A sound method for switching between Boolean and arithmetic masking. In: Koç, Ç.K., Naccache, D., Paar, C. (eds.) CHES 2001. LNCS, vol. 2162, pp. 3–15. Springer, Heidelberg (2001). https://doi.org/10.1007/3-540-44709-1_2

27. Goubin, L., Patarin, J.: DES and differential power analysis the duplication method. In: Koç, Ç.K., Paar, C. (eds.) CHES 1999. LNCS, vol. 1717, pp. 158–172. Springer, Heidelberg (1999). https://doi.org/10.1007/3-540-48059-5_15

28. Grosso, V., Standaert, F.-X.: Masking proofs are tight and how to exploit it in security evaluations. In: Nielsen, J.B., Rijmen, V. (eds.) EUROCRYPT 2018. LNCS, vol. 10821, pp. 385–412. Springer, Cham (2018). https://doi.org/10.1007/978-3-319-78375-8_13

29. Guo, Q., Grosso, V., Standaert, F.-X., Bronchain, O.: Modeling soft analytical side-channel attacks from a coding theory viewpoint. IACR Trans. Cryptogr. Hardw. Embed. Syst. **2020**(4), 209–238 (2020)

30. Hamsici, O.C., Martínez, A.M.: Bayes optimality in linear discriminant analysis. IEEE Trans. Pattern Anal. Mach. Intell. **30**(4), 647–657 (2008)

31. Heinz, D., Kannwischer, M.J., Land, G., Pöppelmann, T., Schwabe, P., Sprenkels, A.: First-order masked kyber on ARM cortex-m4. IACR Cryptol. ePrint Arch., p. 58, 2022

32. Heuser, A., Rioul, O., Guilley, S.: Good is not good enough. In: Batina, L., Robshaw, M. (eds.) CHES 2014. LNCS, vol. 8731, pp. 55–74. Springer, Heidelberg (2014). https://doi.org/10.1007/978-3-662-44709-3_4

33. Ishai, Y., Sahai, A., Wagner, D.: Private circuits: securing hardware against probing attacks. In: Boneh, D. (ed.) CRYPTO 2003. LNCS, vol. 2729, pp. 463–481. Springer, Heidelberg (2003). https://doi.org/10.1007/978-3-540-45146-4_27

34. Kamucheka, T., Nelson, A., Andrews, D., Huang, M.: A masked pure-hardware implementation of kyber cryptographic algorithm. In: FPT, p. 1. IEEE (2022)

35. Kannwischer, M.J., Pessl, P., Primas, R.: Single-trace attacks on keccak. IACR Trans. Cryptogr. Hardw. Embed. Syst. **2020**(3), 243–268 (2020)

36. Lerman, L., Poussier, R., Markowitch, O., Standaert, F.-X.: Template attacks versus machine learning revisited and the curse of dimensionality in side-channel analysis: extended version. J. Cryptogr. Eng. **8**(4), 301–313 (2018)

37. Liu, Y., Zhou, Y., Sun, S., Wang, T., Zhang, R., Ming, J.: On the security of lattice-based Fiat-Shamir signatures in the presence of randomness leakage. IEEE Trans. Inf. Forensics Secur. **16**, 1868–1879 (2021)

38. Lyubashevsky, V., et al.: Crystals-dilithium algorithm specifications and supporting documentation. NIST Post-Quantum Cryptography Standard, 2022

39. Mangard, S.: Hardware countermeasures against DPA – a statistical analysis of their effectiveness. In: Okamoto, T. (ed.) CT-RSA 2004. LNCS, vol. 2964, pp. 222–235. Springer, Heidelberg (2004). https://doi.org/10.1007/978-3-540-24660-2_18

40. Mangard, S., Oswald, E., Popp, T.: Power Analysis Attacks - Revealing the Secrets of Smart Cards. Springer, New York (2007). https://doi.org/10.1007/978-0-387-38162-6
41. Mangard, S., Oswald, E., Standaert, F.-X.: One for all - all for one: unifying standard differential power analysis attacks. IET Inf. Secur. **5**(2), 100–110 (2011)
42. Mangard, S., Popp, T., Gammel, B.M.: Side-channel leakage of masked CMOS gates. In: Menezes, A. (ed.) CT-RSA 2005. LNCS, vol. 3376, pp. 351–365. Springer, Heidelberg (2005). https://doi.org/10.1007/978-3-540-30574-3_24
43. Marzougui, S., Ulitzsch, V., Tibouchi, M., Seifert, J.-P.: Profiling side-channel attacks on dilithium: a small bit-fiddling leak breaks it all. IACR Cryptol. ePrint Arch., p. 106, 2022
44. Masure, L., Cristiani, V., Lecomte, M., Standaert, F.-X.: Don't learn what you already know scheme-aware modeling for profiling side-channel analysis against masking. IACR Trans. Cryptogr. Hardw. Embed. Syst. **2023**(1), 32–59 (2023)
45. Masure, L., Méaux, P., Moos, T., Standaert, F.X.: Effective and efficient masking with low noise using small-mersenne-prime ciphers. In: Hazay, C., Stam, M. (eds.) Advances in Cryptology – EUROCRYPT 2023. EUROCRYPT 2023. LNCS, vol. 14007, pp. 596–627. Springer, Cham (2023). https://doi.org/10.1007/978-3-031-30634-1_20
46. Migliore, V., Gérard, B., Tibouchi, M., Fouque, P.-A.: Masking dilithium. In: Deng, R.H., Gauthier-Umaña, V., Ochoa, M., Yung, M. (eds.) ACNS 2019. LNCS, vol. 11464, pp. 344–362. Springer, Cham (2019). https://doi.org/10.1007/978-3-030-21568-2_17
47. Ngo, K., Dubrova, E., Guo, Q., Johansson, T.: A side-channel attack on a masked IND-CCA secure saber KEM implementation. IACR Trans. Cryptogr. Hardw. Embed. Syst. **2021**(4), 676–707 (2021)
48. Nikova, S., Rijmen, V., Schläffer, M.: Secure hardware implementation of nonlinear functions in the presence of glitches. J. Cryptol. **24**(2), 292–321 (2011)
49. Primas, R., Pessl, P., Mangard, S.: Single-trace side-channel attacks on masked lattice-based encryption. In: Fischer, W., Homma, N. (eds.) CHES 2017. LNCS, vol. 10529, pp. 513–533. Springer, Cham (2017). https://doi.org/10.1007/978-3-319-66787-4_25
50. Prouff, E., Rivain, M.: Masking against side-channel attacks: a formal security proof. In: Johansson, T., Nguyen, P.Q. (eds.) Advances in Cryptology – EUROCRYPT 2013. EUROCRYPT 2013. LNCS, vol. 7881, pp. 142–159. Springer, Berlin, Heidelberg (2013). https://doi.org/10.1007/978-3-642-38348-9_9
51. Rajendran, G., Ravi, P., D'Anvers, J.-P., Bhasin, S., Chattopadhyay, A.: Pushing the limits of generic side-channel attacks on LWE-based KEMs - parallel PC oracle attacks on kyber KEM and beyond. IACR Trans. Cryptogr. Hardw. Embed. Syst. **2023**(2), 418–446 (2023)
52. Ravi, P., Jhanwar, M.P., Howe, J., Chattopadhyay, A., Bhasin, S.: Side-channel assisted existential forgery attack on dilithium - a NIST PQC candidate. IACR Cryptol. ePrint Arch., p. 821, 2018
53. Ravi, P., Roy, S.S., Chattopadhyay, A., Bhasin, S.: Generic side-channel attacks on CCA-secure lattice-based PKE and KEMs. IACR Trans. Cryptogr. Hardw. Embed. Syst. **2020**(3), 307–335 (2020)
54. Renauld, M., Standaert, F.-X., Veyrat-Charvillon, N., Kamel, D., Flandre, D.: A formal study of power variability issues and side-channel attacks for nanoscale devices. In: Paterson, K.G. (ed.) EUROCRYPT 2011. LNCS, vol. 6632, pp. 109–128. Springer, Heidelberg (2011). https://doi.org/10.1007/978-3-642-20465-4_8

55. Schindler, W., Lemke, K., Paar, C.: A stochastic model for differential side channel cryptanalysis. In: Rao, J.R., Sunar, B. (eds.) CHES 2005. LNCS, vol. 3659, pp. 30–46. Springer, Heidelberg (2005). https://doi.org/10.1007/11545262_3
56. Schwabe, P., et al.: Crystals-kyber algorithm specifications and supporting documentation. NIST Post-Quantum Cryptography Standard (2022)
57. Standaert, F.-X., Archambeau, C.: Using subspace-based template attacks to compare and combine power and electromagnetic information leakages. In: Oswald, E., Rohatgi, P. (eds.) CHES 2008. LNCS, vol. 5154, pp. 411–425. Springer, Heidelberg (2008). https://doi.org/10.1007/978-3-540-85053-3_26
58. Standaert, F.-X., Malkin, T.G., Yung, M.: A unified framework for the analysis of side-channel key recovery attacks. In: Joux, A. (ed.) EUROCRYPT 2009. LNCS, vol. 5479, pp. 443–461. Springer, Heidelberg (2009). https://doi.org/10.1007/978-3-642-01001-9_26
59. Tanaka, Y., Ueno, R., Xagawa, K., Ito, A., Takahashi, J., Homma, N.: Multiple-valued plaintext-checking side-channel attacks on post-quantum KEMs. IACR Trans. Cryptogr. Hardw. Embed. Syst. **2023**(3), 473–503 (2023)
60. Ueno, R., Xagawa, K., Tanaka, Y., Ito, A., Takahashi, J., Homma, N.: Curse of re-encryption: a generic power/EM analysis on post-quantum KEMs. IACR Trans. Cryptogr. Hardw. Embed. Syst. **2022**(1), 296–322 (2022)
61. Veyrat-Charvillon, N., Gérard, B., Standaert, F.-X.: Soft analytical side-channel attacks. In: Sarkar, P., Iwata, T. (eds.) ASIACRYPT 2014. LNCS, vol. 8873, pp. 282–296. Springer, Heidelberg (2014). https://doi.org/10.1007/978-3-662-45611-8_15
62. Xu, Z., Pemberton, O., Roy, S.S., Oswald, D., Yao, W., Zheng, Z.: Magnifying side-channel leakage of lattice-based cryptosystems with chosen ciphertexts: the case study of kyber. IEEE Trans. Comput. **71**(9), 2163–2176 (2022)

Elliptic Curve Cryptography and RSA

Special TNFS-Secure Pairings on Ordinary Genus 2 Hyperelliptic Curves

Mónica P. Arenas[1], Georgios Fotiadis[1,2]([✉]), and Elisavet Konstantinou[3]

[1] SnT, University of Luxembourg, Esch-sur-Alzette, Luxembourg
{monica.arenas,georgios.fotiadis}@uni.lu
[2] =nil; Foundation, Limassol, Cyprus
gfotiadis@nil.foundation
[3] Department of Information and Communication Systems Engineering, University of the Aegean, Samos, Greece
ekonstantinou@aegean.gr

Abstract. Pairings on genus 2 hyperelliptic curves are believed to be far less efficient compared to elliptic curve ones. The main reason is the structure of their Jacobian which leads to slower doubling and addition operations. However, genus 2 curves have attractive features that, when properly exploited, can counter the computationally expensive Jacobian operations. One of these features is that they admit twists of higher degrees than elliptic curves, allowing to map Jacobian operations to smaller extension fields. In this paper, we apply generalizations of elliptic curve constructions based on the Cocks–Pinch and Brezing–Weng methods to derive instances of efficient genus 2 pairings, focusing on curves with embedding degrees 8, 16, and 24 that admit degree 8 twists. We present a theoretical comparison with their elliptic curve counterparts, based on the number of prime field multiplications. Our examples target 128- and 192-bit security, considering the progress of STNFS attacks on the DLP in extension fields of composite degree. We propose the first STNFS-secure genus 2 pairings at 128-bit security, as well as more promising candidates for 192-bit security compared to previous works. Finally, we present a proof-of-concept implementation in SageMath that can serve as a baseline for future benchmarks and efficient implementations.

Keywords: Jacobian · Pairing · Hyperelliptic curve · Genus 2 · STNFS

1 Introduction

Pairings were introduced in 1940 by André Weil and their first application was the Menezes–Okamoto–Vanstone (MOV) attack [4, 43]. The MOV attack exploits the properties of the *Weil pairing* to reduce the complexity of the discrete logarithm problem (DLP) in a supersingular elliptic curve to the DLP in a

S. Vaudenay and C. Petit (Eds.): AFRICACRYPT 2024, LNCS 14861, pp. 285–310, 2024.
https://doi.org/10.1007/978-3-031-64381-1_13

finite field where subexponential attacks are known. In 1994, Frey and Rück [28] showed that an analogous reduction is also possible for ordinary (hyper)elliptic curves, using a variant of the Weil pairing called the *Tate pairing*. However, in early 2000 it was shown that pairings can also be used for building secure cryptosystems [9,10,38], triggering a research area known as *pairing-based cryptography*. Since then, numerous research papers on pairings have been published and pairing applications have been developed in the market, such as ZCash [11] in blockchains, or the Direct Anonymous Attestation (DAA) [13,15] in TPMs.

Given three cyclic groups $\mathbb{G}_1, \mathbb{G}_2$ (*source groups*) and $\mathbb{G}_T$ (*target group*) of the same prime order r, a *pairing* is a bilinear, non-degenerate, efficiently computable map $e : \mathbb{G}_1 \times \mathbb{G}_2 \mapsto \mathbb{G}_T$, which is called *symmetric* if $\mathbb{G}_1 = \mathbb{G}_2$ and *asymmetric* otherwise [8]. The core security requirement is that the DLP is intractable in the three *pairing groups* $\mathbb{G}_1, \mathbb{G}_2, \mathbb{G}_T$. Secure and efficient implementations suggest that the source groups are r-order subgroups of ordinary elliptic curves, defined over a prime field $\mathbb{F}_p$ and the target group is an r-order subgroup of an extension field $\mathbb{F}_{p^k}$, for some small *embedding degree* $k > 0$. The complexity of the DLP in the source groups is $O(\sqrt{r})$, due to Pollard's rho algorithm, while in the target group, it depends on whether p is *special* (it is derived from the evaluation of a polynomial) or not, and on whether k is prime or composite. For elliptic curves, p is usually special and k is composite. In this case, the Special Tower Number Field Sieve (STNFS) algorithm of Kim and Barbulescu [41] has a significant impact on the security of pairings forcing the size of the target group to be considerably larger than before. Several constructions of STNFS-secure pairing-friendly elliptic curves appear in [5,21,22,31–33].

Over the past years, there has been a debate on whether pairings on higher-dimensional Jacobians, especially in dimension 2, can offer any advantages in terms of security and/or efficiency, compared to elliptic curves. For pairings on ordinary 2-dimensional Jacobians, the source groups $\mathbb{G}_1, \mathbb{G}_2$ are r-order subgroups of the Jacobian $J_{\mathcal{C}}$ of a genus 2 curve $\mathcal{C}$ defined over a prime field $\mathbb{F}_p$, with DLP complexity $O(\sqrt{r})$ due to Pollard's rho algorithm. The target group is also an r-order subgroup of $\mathbb{F}_{p^k}$, hence the STNFS attack is applicable for composite k. In terms of efficiency, the operations in 2-dimensional Jacobians are performed with Cantor's algorithm [14], which is by far more expensive compared to elliptic curve operations. However, significant improvements can be achieved with alternative representations of Jacobian elements, as in [18].

Methods for constructing pairing-friendly, ordinary 2-dimensional Jacobians are studied in [16,24,26,27,34,39,40,42]. However, these examples are not considering the improved STNFS attacks, as they were published before [41]. In [20], recommendations for 2-dimensional Jacobians based on the asymptotic complexity of the STNFS algorithm were presented. An example for embedding degree 16 is presented in [36] aiming at a security level of 192-bits. In particular, a first hint by Ishii et al. [37, Table 1] shows that, in terms of efficiency, it is around five times slower compared to the elliptic curve case, for primes p of the same size. In addition, and to the best of our knowledge, there is currently no example of an efficient pairing on an ordinary 2-dimensional Jacobian for 128-bit security.

Contribution. This paper aims to construct pairings on ordinary 2-dimensional Jacobians, which are secure with respect to the STNFS attack [41] and are competitive to elliptic curve pairings. We use the extensions of the Cocks–Pinch and Brezing–Weng elliptic curve methods to higher genus [16] in order to construct pairing-friendly genus 2 curves with embedding degrees 8, 16, and 24. The advantage of these curves is that they admit degree 8 twists allowing to map costly operations in $\mathbb{F}_{p^k}$ to a smaller field $\mathbb{F}_{p^{k/8}}$, while for elliptic curves, quartic twists apply for $k = 8, 16$ and sextic twists for $k = 24$. We show that the use of degree 8 twists enables a significant speedup in the pairing computation and, at the same time, we deploy well-known optimization techniques used in elliptic curves for further improvements. We present the first STNFS-secure example of a pairing on a genus 2 curve with $k = 8$ (CP8-544) targeting 128-bit security. Our theoretical analysis shows that our genus 2 pairing is 87% competitive with the best elliptic curve example with embedding degree 8 [32], based on the number of $\mathbb{F}_p$-multiplications for a prime p of the same size. For 192-bit security, we introduce pairing instances on genus 2 curves with embedding degrees 16 and 24. In both cases, we applied the state-of-the-art STNFS DLP complexity simulator of Guillevic and Singh [33] to estimate the security level of the target group. Our theoretical analysis shows that our pairings improve on the previous examples of Ishii [36] and Ishii et al. [37], both in terms of efficiency and security. In addition, we compare our results with the latest developments of elliptic curve pairings for $k = 16, 24$ reported in [19]. We also present a proof-of-concept implementation of our proposed genus 2 pairings in SageMath [2], which can serve as a baseline for future optimized implementations of genus 2 pairings.

Outline. We present in Sect. 2 the background related to pairing-friendly genus 2 curves and Jacobians. In Sect. 3 we present the methods for constructing pairing-friendly Jacobians and our concrete examples that lead to efficient genus 2 pairings. In Sect. 4 we apply specific pairing types to our Jacobians and give a theoretical analysis of their cost, as well as a comparison with their elliptic curve analogs. We conclude this work in Sect. 5.

2 Preliminaries

2.1 Pairing-Friendly Genus 2 Curves

In this paper, we assume that $\mathcal{C}$ is an ordinary hyperelliptic curve of genus 2 defined over a prime field $\mathbb{F}_p$, represented by the equation $\mathcal{C} : y^2 = F(x)$, where $F \in \mathbb{F}_p[x]$ is monic, square-free, with $\deg(F) = 5$. A hyperelliptic curve of this form has only one *point at infinity*, denoted by ∞. For any finite extension $\mathbb{F}_{p^k} \subseteq \overline{\mathbb{F}}_p$ of the base field, we denote by $\mathcal{C}(\mathbb{F}_{p^k})$ the set of points with coordinates in $\mathbb{F}_{p^k}$ that satisfy the curve equation, including the point at infinity. Unlike elliptic curves, $\mathcal{C}(\mathbb{F}_{p^k})$ is not a group and hence it cannot be used to instantiate DLP-based protocols. In hyperelliptic curve cryptography we use the *Jacobian*

J_C of the curve C and denote by $J_C(\mathbb{F}_{p^k})$ the Jacobian of C with elements in $\mathbb{F}_{p^k}$, which is an additive group[1].

The elements of $J_C(\mathbb{F}_{p^k})$ are called *reduced $\mathbb{F}_{p^k}$-rational divisors* and they are usually written in *Mumford representation*. For $P_i = (x_i, y_i) \in C(\mathbb{F}_{p^k})$ with $i = 1, 2$, an element $D \in J_C(\mathbb{F}_{p^k})$ in Mumford representation is written as $D = [u(x), v(x)]$ where $u, v \in \mathbb{F}_{p^k}[x]$, are such that: (1) $u(x) = (x - x_1)(x - x_2)$, (2) $u(x)$ divides $F(x) - v(x)^2$, (3) $\deg(v) < \deg(u) \le 2$ and (4) $v(x_i) = y_i$, for $i = 1, 2$. This results in three types of elements, namely *general elements* where $\deg(u) = 2$, *special elements* where $\deg(u) = 1$ (also known as *degenerate divisors*) and the *identity element* $0_{J_C} = [1, 0] \in J_C(\mathbb{F}_{p^k})$. The process of adding two reduced divisors in $J_C(\mathbb{F}_{p^k})$ given in Mumford representation, is described by Cantor's algorithm [14] (see also Algorithm 1 in [29]).

Let $\#J_C(\mathbb{F}_p) = hr$, where r is a large prime and h is the *cofactor*. We define the *r-torsion group* $J_C[r]$ of J_C as the group $J_C[r] = \{D \in J_C(\overline{\mathbb{F}}_p) : [r]D = 0\}$. Let $\mathbb{F}_{p^k} \subseteq \overline{\mathbb{F}}_p$ be a finite extension of the base field. We denote by π the pth *Frobenius endomorphism*, with *characteristic polynomial of Frobenius*:

$$\chi(t) = \prod_{i=1}^{4} (t - \sigma_i(\pi)) = t^4 + a_1 t^3 + a_2 t^2 + a_1 p t + p^2, \tag{1}$$

where $\chi(t) \in \mathbb{Z}[t]$ and σ_i are the embeddings from $\mathbb{Q}(\pi)$ to $\mathbb{C}$. Furthermore, π is a *p-Weil number*, meaning that $|\sigma_i(\pi)| = \sqrt{p}$, for all $i = 1, 2, 3, 4$. The order of the Jacobian and the characteristic polynomial of Frobenius endomorphism satisfy $\#J_C(\mathbb{F}_p) = \chi(1) \approx p^2$. We also say that a Jacobian (and the corresponding curve C) is *ordinary* if the middle coefficient of the characteristic polynomial χ is coprime to p and it is called *simple* if it is not isogenous over $\mathbb{F}_p$ to a product of elliptic curves. The latter is equivalent to χ being irreducible over $\mathbb{Z}[t]$. In addition, J_C is *absolutely simple*, if it remains simple over $\overline{\mathbb{F}}_p$.

For the rest of this paper, we will focus on ordinary Jacobians (and hence ordinary hyperelliptic curves) over a prime field $\mathbb{F}_p$. In this case, the number field $K = \mathbb{Q}(\pi)$ is a *CM-field*[2], with $[K : \mathbb{Q}] = \deg(\chi) = 4$. Then the order of the Jacobian over $\mathbb{F}_p$ satisfies: $\#J_C(\mathbb{F}_p) = \chi(1) = \text{Norm}_{K/\mathbb{Q}}(\pi - 1)$ (see [44,45] for more information on abelian varieties).

Pairing-friendly hyperelliptic curves [26] have *embedding degree* $k \in \mathbb{Z}_{>0}$, which is the smallest positive integer, such that the r-torsion group $J_C[r]$ contains all $\mathbb{F}_{p^k}$-rational divisors. Freeman et al. give the necessary conditions for 2-dimensional abelian variety to have embedding degree k [26, Proposition 2.1.3]. More concretely, if:

$$\#J_C(\mathbb{F}_p) = \chi(1) = \text{Norm}_{K/\mathbb{Q}}(\pi - 1) \equiv 0 \bmod r \quad \text{and} \quad \Phi_k(\pi\overline{\pi}) \equiv 0 \bmod r, \tag{2}$$

where $\Phi_k(x)$ is the kth-cyclotomic polynomial, $K = \mathbb{Q}(\pi)$ and r is a prime such that $\gcd(r, p) = 1$, then J_C has embedding degree k with respect to r.

---

[1] In particular, it is an instance of an abelian variety of dimension 2.
[2] An imaginary quadratic extension of a totally real field.

2.2   Pairing Types on Genus 2 Curves

We will work with the Ate_i and twisted Ate pairings for the genus 2 pairings, as they support a short Miller loop. The Ate_i pairing was introduced by Zhao et al. [47] for elliptic curves and extended by Zhang [46] for genus 2 curves. It is also known as the *generalized Ate pairing* in that it is defined in the same way as the Ate pairing [30] with a Miller loop of length $\log_2(s)$, where $s \equiv p^i \bmod r$, for some $i = 1, \ldots, k-1$, such that $\log_2(s)$ is minimum:

$$e_{Ate_i} : \mathbb{G}_2 \times \mathbb{G}_1 \longrightarrow \mu_r \quad \text{s.t.} \quad (D_2, D_1) \longmapsto f_{s,D_2}(D_1)^{\frac{p^k-1}{r}}.$$

As stated in [3], the Ate_i pairing also applies for $s = p^i$, with no final exponentiation needed, but in this case the length of the Miller loop is $i \log_2(p)$.

The genus 2 twisted Ate pairing is introduced by Zhang [46] and can be computed on curves that admit high-degree twists. Let $\mathcal{C}$ be a hyperelliptic curve, $\mathcal{C}^t$ a twist of $\mathcal{C}$ of degree $\delta > 0$ and $r \mid \#J_{\mathcal{C}}(\mathbb{F}_p)$. Set $m = \gcd(k, \delta)$ and $e = k/m$. There exists an isomorphism $[\cdot] : \mu_\delta \longrightarrow \mathrm{Aut}(\mathcal{C})$, with $\xi \longmapsto [\xi]$, where ξ is the automorphism defined by the twist. Then for $\mathbb{G}_2$ we have:

$$\mathbb{G}_2 = J_{\mathcal{C}}(\mathbb{F}_{p^k})[r] \cap \ker(\pi - [p]) = J_{\mathcal{C}}(\mathbb{F}_{p^k})[r] \cap \ker([\xi]\pi^e - [1])$$

and we can define a bilinear, non-degenerate pairing

$$e_{Ate}^{twist} : \mathbb{G}_1 \times \mathbb{G}_2 \longrightarrow \mu_r \quad \text{s.t.} \quad (D_1, D_2) \longmapsto f_{p^e, D_1}(D_2)^{\frac{p^k-1}{r}}.$$

2.3   Previous Work on Genus 2 Pairings

Elliptic curves are Jacobians of dimension 1. There are two basic strategies for constructing pairing-friendly elliptic curves; the Cocks–Pinch [25] (and its polynomial version, the Brezing–Weng method [12]) and the Dupont–Enge–Morain (DEM) [17] methods. Freeman et al. [26] generalized the Cocks–Pinch method for higher-dimensional Jacobians. Various construction methods have followed Freeman et al.'s Cocks–Pinch analogue [16,27,34,40]. An alternative way to construct pairing-friendly Jacobians is to apply the Cocks–Pinch method on a polynomial representation, (*polynomial family*), of the Jacobian parameters (p, r, π). This idea was introduced by Freeman [24] and it is known as the generalized Brezing–Weng method since it was inspired by the Brezing-Weng method for elliptic curves [12]. We can generate the actual Jacobian parameters by evaluating these polynomials at some $u \in \mathbb{Z}$ (called the *seed*), such that p and r are both primes of desired size. Additional instances of the generalized Brezing-Weng method can be found in [16,20,39]. In this paper we will focus on the construction methods of [16,39,40] (see Sect. 3).

3   Constructing Pairing-Friendly Genus 2 Curves

We describe the methods in [16] for generating pairing-friendly Jacobians of dimension 2 and present our proposed examples for embedding degrees 8, 16, and 24. Recall from Sect. 2.2 that in order to construct such Jacobians J_C with order $\#J_C(\mathbb{F}_p) = hr$, it suffices to determine a quartic CM-field $K = \mathbb{Q}(\pi)$, such that System (2) has solutions modulo r, for some fixed r.

3.1   Cocks–Pinch Genus 2 Curves

Given k, Dryło's Cocks–Pinch variant [16] fixes a Frobenius endomorphism $\pi = \zeta_s \pi_0$, where ζ_s is a primitive s^{th}-root of unity, with $s \mid k$ and $\pi_0 \in \mathbb{Q}(\sqrt{-d})$, for some square-free integer $d > 0$. Such choices of π enable quartic CM-fields $K = \mathbb{Q}(\zeta_s, \sqrt{-d})$, when $\varphi(s) = 4$ and $\sqrt{-d} \in \mathbb{Q}(\zeta_s)$, or $\varphi(s) = 2$ and $\sqrt{-d} \notin \mathbb{Q}(\zeta_s)$. Jacobians with $\pi = \zeta_s \pi_0$ correspond to curves with equations $C : y^2 = x^5 + ax^3 + bx$ and $C : y^2 = x^6 + ax^3 + b$ [27] and they are isogenous over some extension of $\mathbb{F}_p$ to a power of an elliptic curve, hence they are simple.

More concretely, the key idea is to fix $\pi = \zeta_s \pi_0$, where $\pi_0 = x + y\sqrt{-d}$ and search for a prime r such that the system:

$$\chi(1) = \text{Norm}_{K/\mathbb{Q}}(\zeta_s(x + y\sqrt{-d}) - 1) \equiv \Phi_k(x^2 + dy^2) \equiv 0 \bmod r \qquad (3)$$

has solutions $(x_0, y_0) \in \mathbb{F}_r^2$ and in addition $\Phi_k(u) \equiv 0 \bmod r$, for some primitive k^{th}-root of unity $u \in \mathbb{Z}$. By [16, Lemma 6], such solutions are of the form:

$$(x_0, y_0) = \left(\frac{\zeta_s^{-1} + \zeta_s \zeta_k}{2}, \pm \frac{\zeta_s^{-1} - \zeta_s \zeta_k}{2\sqrt{-d}} \right) \qquad (4)$$

when $\sqrt{-d} \notin \mathbb{Q}(\zeta_s)$, while for $\sqrt{-d} \in \mathbb{Q}(\zeta_s)$, one of these pairs is a solution for System (3). In order to fix the base field prime p, we take small lifts $l_x, l_y \in \mathbb{Z}$ of the solution (x_0, y_0), such that $p = (l_x r + x_0)^2 + d(l_y r + y_0)^2$ is prime.

Dryło's Cocks–Pinch algorithm is given in Appendix A.1 (see Algorithm 2). According to Guillevic et al. [32], for Cocks–Pinch elliptic curves, the base field prime is not special and hence the STNFS variants do not apply. In their paper, they present examples with embedding degrees 5, 6, 7, and 8, that are secure against any type of NFS variant. We introduce an analogous example of a genus 2 curve with $k = 8$ that is generated via the Cocks–Pinch method.

Curve 1 (Genus 2 Cocks–Pinch with $k = 8$). Let $k = s = 8$ and set u, r as in [32]. That is $u = \texttt{0xffc00020ffffffc}$, which is a primitive 8th root of unity modulo r, where:

$r = \texttt{0xff0060739e18d7594a978b0ab6ae4ce3dbfd52a9d00197603fffdf00000}$
$\texttt{00101}$

and $\log_2(r) = 256$. We set $d = 2$ so that $K = \mathbb{Q}(\zeta_8, \sqrt{-2})$. Then $\sqrt{-2} = \zeta_8(\zeta_4 + 1)$ in $\mathbb{F}_r$ (hence $\sqrt{-2} \in \mathbb{Q}(\zeta_8)$). We choose $\zeta_k = u$ and $\zeta_s = u^5 \bmod r$ and substitute into Eq. (4) to obtain:

$x_0 = \texttt{0x7fa0182f67431e596adfdc83eb3fe4757900039bfffffffd8}$

$y_0 = \texttt{0x3fc0181ce78635d69275eeda614d2265ac6f42ec69a058128c8ff985c00}$
$\texttt{0002d}$

We take $l_x = \texttt{0xa031}$ and $l_y = 1$, producing $\pi = \zeta_8 \left[l_x r + x_0 + (l_y r + y_0)\sqrt{-2} \right] \in$ K and the prime $p = \pi\overline{\pi} = (l_x r + x_0)^2 + 2(l_y r + y_0)^2 = x^2 + 2y^2$. The lifts l_x, l_y are chosen in this way to improve the performance of the final exponentiation (see Sect. 4). Note that $p \equiv 1 \bmod 8$ and $\log_2(p) = 544$, thus the extension field $\mathbb{F}_{p^k}$ has size 4352-bits and the Jacobian has $\rho = 4.25$, while the hyperelliptic curve equation is $\mathcal{C} : y^2 = x^5 + 3x$. By [46], $\mathcal{C}$ admits twists of degree 8, which we exploit in Sect. 4 in order to speed up the pairing computation. Furthermore, the characteristic polynomial of Frobenius is defined as:

$$\chi(t) = t^4 + 4yt^3 + 8y^2 t^2 + 4ypt + p^2 \in \mathbb{Z}[t],$$

which is irreducible over $\mathbb{Z}[t]$ and thus, the order of the Jacobian $J_\mathcal{C}$ over $\mathbb{F}_p$ can be obtained by substituting $t = 1$ in the polynomial $\chi(t)$. Note that since $\gcd(8y^2, p) = 1$, the Jacobian $J_\mathcal{C}$ is ordinary. For the security in the target group, since the prime p is constructed in the same way as Guillevic et al. [32], we expect that the security level in $\mathbb{F}_{p^8}$ is the same as the elliptic curve Cocks–Pinch example, namely 131-bits. We refer to this genus 2 curve as CP8-544. $\qquad\square$

3.2 Brezing–Weng Genus 2 Curves

Algorithm 2 can be generalized using polynomials to represent the Jacobian parameters. This parametric representation is known as *polynomial family* of pairing-friendly Jacobians. This idea was introduced by Brezing and Weng in [12] for elliptic curves and the benefit is the lower ρ-values compared to Cocks–Pinch analogs. The extension of the Brezing–Weng method to higher dimensional Jacobians is due to Freeman [24]. We concentrate on a particular instance of Freeman's generalized Brezing–Weng algorithm that was presented by Dryło [16] and it is specific to quartic CM-fields $K = \mathbb{Q}(\pi)$, where $\pi = \zeta_s(x + y\sqrt{-d})$.

Given $k > 0$, let $K = \mathbb{Q}(\zeta_s, \sqrt{-d})$ be a quartic CM-field, for some positive $s \mid k$ and square-free integer $d > 0$. We define the *Frobenius polynomial* as:

$$\pi(x) = \zeta_s \left(X(x) + Y(x)\sqrt{-d} \right), \tag{5}$$

where $X(x), Y(x) \in \mathbb{Q}[x]$. In order to use such polynomial representation for π, we need to determine a number field L that contains the quartic CM-field K and the primitive k^{th}-roots of unity and then define a polynomial $r(x) \in \mathbb{Q}[x]$ such that $L \cong \mathbb{Q}[x]/\langle r(x)\rangle$ and $r(x)$ *represents primes*[3]. The construction of L ensures that the elements ζ_k, ζ_s and $\sqrt{-d}$ have polynomial representatives $w(x), v(x)$ and $z(x)$ respectively, modulo $r(x)$. Then substituting $\pi(x)$ in System (3) we get:

$$\text{Norm}_{K/\mathbb{Q}}(\zeta_s(X(x) + Y(x)\sqrt{-d}) - 1) \equiv \Phi_k(X(x)^2 + dY(x)^2) \equiv 0 \bmod r(x). \tag{6}$$

We note that if $w(x)$ is a primitive k^{th}-root of unity in $\mathbb{Q}[x]/\langle r(x)\rangle$, then so is $w(x)^i$, for every $i = 1, \ldots, k$, such that $\gcd(i, k) = 1$.

---

[3] A polynomial represents primes if it is non-constant, irreducible, with positive leading coefficient, producing also integer values.

The common strategy is to fix L as the lth cyclotomic field $\mathbb{Q}(\zeta_l)$, for some $l > 0$, such that $l = \text{lcm}(s, k, m)$, where $m > 0$ is the smallest integer, such that $\sqrt{-d} \in \mathbb{Q}(\zeta_m)$. Therefore, $L = \mathbb{Q}(\zeta_k, \zeta_s, \zeta_m) = \mathbb{Q}(\zeta_l)$ and choosing $r(x) = \Phi_l(x)$ we obtain $L \cong \mathbb{Q}[x]/\langle r(x) \rangle$. We refer to such families as *cyclotomic families*. Alternatively, we can choose $r(x)$ as any irreducible polynomial that represents primes (*non-cyclotomic* families). Either way, the solutions of System (6) in $\mathbb{Q}[x]/\langle r(x) \rangle$ are given by:

$$(X_0(x), Y_0(x)) = \left(\frac{v(x)^{-1} + v(x)w(x)}{2}, \pm \frac{v(x)^{-1} - v(x)w(x)}{2z(x)} \right). \qquad (7)$$

Then the polynomial $p(x)$ is defined as $p(x) = X_0(x)^2 + dY_0(x)^2$. Dryło's Brezing–Weng algorithm is given in Appendix A.2 (see Algorithm 3).

In the case of polynomial families, we redefine the ρ-value as the ratio $\rho = 2 \deg(p) / \deg(r)$ [24]. In general, the Brezing–Weng method produces polynomial families with $\rho < 4$. However, in some instances, it might be beneficial to construct families with $\rho \geq 4$. This can be done by lifting the polynomials $X_0(x), Y_0(x)$ by some lifts $l_x(x)$ and $l_y(x)$. This is, $X(x) = l_x(x)r(x) + X_0(x)$ and $Y(x) = l_y(x)r(x) + Y(x)$, where in this case the field polynomial $p(x) = X(x)^2 + dY(x)^2$. The idea of allowing larger ρ-values for a polynomial family was first introduced in [22] for elliptic curves. Note also that the characteristic polynomial of Frobenius has a parametric representation of the form:

$$\chi(x, t) = t^4 + a_1(x)t^3 + a_2(x)t^2 + a_1(x)p(x)t + p(x)^2 \in \mathbb{Z}[x, t],$$

and the order of the Jacobian in polynomial form is $\#J_\mathcal{C}(\mathbb{F}_p)(x) = \chi(x, 1)$.

Below we present the examples of Brezing–Weng families of 2-dimensional Jacobians that we have considered in our analysis.

Family 1 (Kawazoe–Takahashi family for $k = 16$). Let $l = k = 16$, $s = 8$ and $d = 2$. We define the polynomial $r(x) = \Phi_{16}(x)$. We set $w(x) = x^5$, $v(x) = x^2$ and $z(x) = x^2(x^4 + 1) \mapsto \sqrt{-2}$ in $L = \mathbb{Q}(\zeta_{16}) = \mathbb{Q}[x]/\langle r(x) \rangle$. Substituting into Eq. (5) we obtain the Frobenius polynomial:

$$\pi(x) = \zeta_8 \left(X(x) + Y(x)\sqrt{-2} \right) = \zeta_8 \left(\frac{x^7 - x^6}{2} - \frac{x^5 + x^4 + x + 1}{4}\sqrt{-2} \right).$$

This results in the field polynomial $p(x) = \pi(x)\overline{\pi}(x)$, which is irreducible and integer valued for every $x \equiv 1 \mod 2$. In addition, the characteristic polynomial of Frobenius in $\mathbb{Z}[x, t]$ is represented by:

$$\chi(x, t) = t^4 + 4Y(x)t^3 + 8Y(x)^2t^2 + 4Y(x)p(x)t + p(x)^2.$$

The pair $[\pi, r]$ represents a family of pairing-friendly Jacobians with $k = 16$ and $\rho = 3.5$, known as Kawazoe–Takahashi family, initially presented in [40].   □

Family 2 (Arenas–Fotiadis–Konstantinou family for $k = 16$). We use the same setting as in Family 1, namely $l = k = 16$, $s = 8$, $d = 2$ and $r(x) = \Phi_{16}(x)$.

We take $w(x) = x^5$, $v(x) = x^2$, only now we take the lifts $l_x(x) = 1$ and $l_y(x) = 0$, where we obtain the Frobenius polynomial:

$$\pi(x) = \zeta_8 \left(\frac{2x^8 + x^7 - x^6 + 2}{2} - \frac{x^5 + x^4 + x + 1}{4} \sqrt{-2} \right).$$

This results in the field polynomial $p(x) = \pi(x)\overline{\pi}(x)$, which is irreducible and integer valued for every $x \equiv 1 \bmod 2$. The characteristic polynomial of Frobenius in $\mathbb{Z}[x,t]$ is computed using the same formula as in Family 1. Thus, the pair $[\pi, r]$ represents a complete family of pairing-friendly Jacobians with embedding degree 16 with $\rho = 4$. We refer to this family as AFK16. $\qquad\square$

Family 3 (Arenas–Fotiadis–Konstantinou family for $k = 24$). We set $l = k = 24$, $s = 4$, $d = 2$ and $r(x) = \Phi_{24}(x)$. We take $w(x) = x^7 - x^3$, $v(x) = x^6$ and $z(x) = x(x^4 - x^2 + 1) \mapsto \sqrt{-2}$ in $L = \mathbb{Q}(\zeta_{24}) = \mathbb{Q}[x]/\langle r(x) \rangle$. Substituting into Eq. (5) we obtain the Frobenius polynomial:

$$\pi(x) = \zeta_4 \left(-\frac{x^6 + x^5}{2} + \frac{x^5 - x^4 - x^3 + x^2 - x + 1}{4} \sqrt{-2} \right).$$

This results in the field polynomial $p(x) = \pi(x)\overline{\pi}(x)$, which is irreducible and integer valued for every $x \equiv 1 \bmod 2$. The characteristic polynomial of Frobenius in $\mathbb{Z}[x,t]$ is computed using the same formula:

$$\chi(x,t) = t^4 + 2 \left(X(x)^2 - 2Y(x)^2 \right) t^2 + p(x)^2.$$

The pair $[\pi, r]$ represents a family of pairing-friendly Jacobians with $k = 24$ and $\rho = 3$. We refer to this family as AFK24. $\qquad\square$

In [16], Dryło introduced a family for $k = 12$ that is analogous to the Barreto–Naehrig (BN) family [7] of elliptic curves. In the case of elliptic curve pairings, the Barreto–Lynn–Scott (BLS) [6] and Fotiadis–Konstantinou (FK) [22,23] pairing-friendly elliptic curve families lead to the fastest pairing implementations for 128-bit security[4]. We present their genus 2 analogues in Appendix A.2. We point out that genus 2 curves with Jacobians of embedding degree 12 have, under certain conditions, twists of degree 6, hence it is possible to improve computations. However, we do not report specific examples for these cases, since they are not expected to be competitive to the elliptic curve case. This is mainly because both BLS and FM curves admit twists of degree 6 as well and since the addition and doubling process is more expensive in the genus 2 case, the total cost of the pairing should be significantly larger in the genus 2 case.

3.3   Evaluating a Polynomial Family

In Table 1 we report the genus 2 curves that we considered in our analysis for embedding degrees 8, 16, and 24 along with their identifying parameters and

---

[4] See e.g. https://members.loria.fr/AGuillevic/pairing-friendly-curves/.

the seeds we used to instantiate the polynomial families. The curve CP8-544 refers to Curve 1 i.e., the Cocks–Pinch curve with $k = 8$. On the other hand, KT16 curves refer to genus 2 curves derived from the Kawazoe–Takahashi family of curves 1. AFK16 and AFK24 curves are derived from the evaluation of the Arenas–Fotiadis–Konstantinou polynomial families 2 and 3 respectively. The curves are grouped in terms of the security level that they provide. CP8-544 and KT16-447 are targeting 128-bit security, while KT16-671, KT16-685, AFK16-767, AFK24-575 and AFK24-576 are aiming at 192-bit security.

Table 1. Instantiation of pairing-friendly genus 2 curves of the form $\mathcal{C} : y^2 = x^5 + ax$.

k	Curve name	Seed u	a	$\log_2(p)$ (bits)	$\log_2(r)$ (bits)	ρ	$\log_2(p^k)$ (bits)	Sec. Lev. in $\mathbb{F}^*_{p^k}$ (bits)
128-bit security								
8	CP8-544	–	3	544	256	4.2500	4352	131
16	KT16-447	$2^{32} + 2^{14} + 2^1 + 1$	7	447	256	3.4922	7152	157
192-bit security								
16	KT16-671 [36]	$2^{48} + 2^{40} + 2^{30} + 2^{16} + 2^1 + 1$	7	671	384	3.4948	10736	178
	KT16-685 [37]	$2^{49} + 2^{33} + 2^8 + 2^1 + 1$	11	685	392	3.4949	10960	180
	AFK16-767	$2^{48} - 2^{44} - 2^{32} - 2^{15} - 1$	13	767	383	4.0052	12272	197
24	AFK24-575	$2^{48} + 2^{32} + 1$	7	575	385	2.9870	13800	196
	AFK24-576	$2^{48} + 2^{44} + 2^6 + 2^4 + 2^3 + 1$	2	576	385	2.9922	13824	196

The third column in Table 1 reports the seeds used to instantiate Families 1, 2 and 3. For CP8-544, no seed is reported since this curve is derived from the Cocks–Pinch method which does not rely on polynomial evaluations. In our search for suitable seeds, we opt for the ones that have the smallest possible (NAF) Hamming weight, which affects the performance of the genus 2 pairing as it determines the number of divisor additions in the Miller loop (see Sect. 4). In all examples, the equation of the genus 2 curve has the special form $\mathcal{C}/\mathbb{F}_p$: $y^2 = x^5 + ax$, for some $a \in \mathbb{F}_p$ reported in the fourth column. Further, we give the sizes of the primes p and r obtained by evaluating the corresponding polynomials at u, as well as the size of the extension field $\mathbb{F}_{p^k}$.

The extension field size is crucial as it determines the security level in $\mathbb{F}^*_{p^k}$ concerning the STNFS attacks. For all curves derived from polynomial evaluations, we estimated the security level in $\mathbb{F}^*_{p^k}$ using the STNFS simulator developed by Guillevic and Singh [33]. We note that in [36], Ishii presented an instance of the KT16 Family 1 for 192-security. Using the Guillevic–Singh simulator, we find that the curve KT16-671 offers a security level of 178-bit in $\mathbb{F}^*_{p^{16}}$, which falls short of 192-bit security. In addition, the curve KT16-685 given by Ishii et al. [37] provides a security level of 180-bits in in $\mathbb{F}^*_{p^{16}}$. On the other hand, our curves AFK16-767, AFK24-575, and AFK24-576 offer a security level above 192-bit, while our curves CP8-544 and KT16-447, both offer a security level over 128-bit as intended.

4   Efficient Pairings on Selected Jacobians

The computation of a pairing on a Jacobian of dimension 2 is split into two parts; the Miller loop and the final exponentiation. We study how to apply optimal pairings on the curves presented in Sect. 3, considering different optimization strategies for both parts. In Table 2 we quote the relevant operations required to analyze the cost of the Miller loop and the final exponentiation.

Table 2. Notation of operations in finite field extension $\mathbb{F}_{p^i}$ for $1 \leq i \leq k$.

Operation	Description	Operation	Description
$\mathbf{m}_i$	Multiplication in $\mathbb{F}_{p^i}$	$\mathbf{f}_i$	Frobenius exp. by p^i in $\mathbb{F}_{p^k}$
$\mathbf{s}_i$	Squaring in $\mathbb{F}_{p^i}$	$\mathbf{s}_i^{\mathrm{cyclo}}$	Cyclotomic squaring in $\mathbb{F}_{p^i}$
$\mathbf{i}_i$	Inversion in $\mathbb{F}_{p^i}$	$\mathbf{e}_u$	Exponentiation by u in $\mathbb{F}_{p^k}$
$\mathbf{cm}_i$	$a \times b$, where $a \in \mathbb{F}_p$, $b \in \mathbb{F}_{p^i}$		

4.1   Genus 2 Miller Algorithm

Miller's algorithm for the genus 2 case is presented in Algorithm 1. The positive integer S in the input determines the number of iterations in the Miller loop. Algorithm 1 is designed to include the case where S is in NAF representation, inspired by [32, Algorithm 3]. In particular, we write $S = \sum_{i=0}^{n} b_i 2^i = (b_n, b_{n-1}, \ldots, b_1, b_0)_{2\text{-NAF}}$, with $b_i \in \{0, \pm 1\}$ and we write $\mathrm{hw}_{\mathrm{NAF}}(S)$ to denote the NAF Hamming weight of S and $\mathrm{hw}(S)$ for the usual Hamming weight.

For the first input divisor $D_1 \in J_C(\mathbb{F}_p)[r]$ in Algorithm 1, we use the representation of Fan et al.'s [18] projective coordinate system. More concretely, recall that the Mumford representation is $D_1 = [u_1(x), v_1(x)]$, where

$$u_1(x) = (x - x_1)(x - x_2) = x^2 + U_{11}x + U_{10} \quad \text{and} \quad v_1(x) = V_{11}x + V_{10},$$

such that $v_1(x_i) = y_i$ and $P_i = (x_i, y_i) \in \mathcal{C}(\mathbb{F}_p)$, for $i = 1, 2$. Then, we write $D_1 = [U_{11}, U_{10}, V_{11}, V_{10}, Z_1, Z_2, z_1, z_2]$, where $z_1 = Z_1^2$ and $z_2 = Z_2^2$.

The second input divisor $D_2 \in J_C(\mathbb{F}_{p^k})$ can be either represented as a degenerate divisor or as a general divisor, where the first case results in more efficient computations. In particular, we distinguish the following two cases for D_2:

Case 1. D_2 is a degenerate divisor. That is $D_2 = [x - x_Q, y_Q]$ for some point $Q = (x_Q, y_Q) \in \mathcal{C}(\mathbb{F}_{p^k})$.

Case 2. D_2 is a general divisor. That is $D_2 = [u_2(x), v_2(x)]$ in Mumford representation, where $u_2(x) = x^2 + U_{21}x + U_{20}$ and $v_2(x) = V_{21}x + V_{20}$.

In this paper, we apply the twisted Ate pairing $(e_{\mathrm{Ate}}^{\mathrm{twist}}(D_1, D_2))$ and the Ate_i pairing $(e_{\mathrm{Ate}_i}(D_2, D_1))$. In the second case, the order of the divisors is reversed.

Algorithm 1: MILLERLOOP(S, D_1, D_2)

Input: $D_1 \in J_C(\mathbb{F}_p)[r]$, $D_2 \in J_C(\mathbb{F}_{p^k})$ and $S = (b_n, b_{n-1}, \ldots, b_1, b_0)_2$.
Output: Miller function $f_{S,D_1}(D_2)$.

1 $(f_n, f_d) \leftarrow (1, 1), T \leftarrow D_1$
2 **for** $i \leftarrow \lfloor \log_2(S) \rfloor - 1$ downto 0 **do**
3 $\quad (\lambda_n, \lambda_d) \leftarrow c_{T,T}(D_2)$ // DOUBLELINE
4 $\quad (\mu_n, \mu_d) \leftarrow u_3(D_2)$ // VERTICALLINE
5 $\quad T \leftarrow [2]T$ // DBL
6 $\quad (f_n, f_d) \leftarrow (f_n^2 \lambda_n \mu_d, f_d^2 \lambda_d \mu_n)$ // UPDATEDBL
7 $\quad$ **if** $b_i = \pm 1$ **then**
8 $\quad\quad (\lambda_n, \lambda_d) \leftarrow c_{T,[b_i]D_1}(D_2)$ // ADDLINE
9 $\quad\quad (\mu_n, \mu_d) \leftarrow u_3(D_2)$ // VERTICALLINE
10 $\quad\quad T \leftarrow T \oplus [b_i]D_1$ // ADD
11 $\quad\quad (f_n, f_d) \leftarrow (f_n \lambda_n \mu_d, f_d \lambda_d \mu_n)$ // UPDATEADD

12 **if** $S < 0$ **then**
13 $\quad (f_n, f_d) \leftarrow (f_d, f_n)$

14 **return** (f_n / f_d)

This means that $D_2 \in J_C(\mathbb{F}_{p^k}[r])$ is represented in the Fan et al. [18] coordinate system and $D_1 \in J_C(\mathbb{F}_p)$ is a degenerate (*case 1*) or a general (*case 2*) divisor.

In all examples of this paper, k is divisible by 8 and $p \equiv 1 \mod 8$. Then the genus 2 curve $C : y^2 = x^5 + ax$ has a degree $\delta = 8$ twist with equation $C^t : y^2 = x^5 + a\lambda x$, defined by the isomorphism $\phi_t : C \longrightarrow C^t$, such that $(x, y) \longmapsto (\lambda^{1/4}x, \lambda^{5/8}y)$, where λ in not an lth power residue in $\mathbb{F}_p$ for $l \in \{1, 2, 4, 8\}$ [18]. Then, the second input divisor in Miller's algorithm is taken as an element $D_2 \in J_{C^t}(\mathbb{F}_{p^{k/\delta}})$ i.e., in the Jacobian of the degree 8 twist C^t of C.

The computation of the Miller function is composed of the doubling step (DBLSTEP) and addition step (ADDSTEP). In each iteration of DBLSTEP the four operations DOUBLELINE, VERTICALLINE, DBL and UPDATEDBL (steps 3 to 6) are executed, while in ADDSTEP the ADDLINE, VERTICALLINE, ADD and UPDATEADD are performed (steps 8 to 11).

In the DBL function, the divisor $[2]T$ is computed, while the ADD function computes the divisor $T \oplus [b]D_1$. In both functions, the rational function $G_{T,D}$ is also computed as $G_{T,D}(x, y) = c_{T,D}(x, y)/u_3(x)$, where:

$$c_{T,D}(x, y) = y - l(x) = \frac{l'y - (l_3 x^3 + l_2 x^2 + l_1 x + l_0)}{l'} = \frac{\lambda_n}{\lambda_d}. \tag{8}$$

and the denominator $u_3(x)$ is defined as:

$$u_3(x) = \frac{z_{31} x^2 + U_{31} x + U_{30}}{z_{31}} = \frac{\mu_n}{\mu_d}, \tag{9}$$

where $D = [2]T$ in DBLSTEP, $D = T \oplus [b]D_1$ in ADDSTEP. We refer to [18] for the definition of l_3, l_2, l_1, l_0, l' in Eq. (8), the variables U_{31}, U_{30}, z_{31} in Eq. (9), as well as the formulas for DBL and ADD.

The two functions DOUBLELINE and ADDLINE evaluate the rational function $c_{T,D}(D_2)$ in the DBLSTEP and ADDSTEP respectively. In addition, the function VERTICALLINE evaluates the rational function $u_3(D_2)$. The evaluation of these rational functions depends on whether the divisor D_2 is a degenerate or a general divisor. By UPDATEDBL and UPDATEADD we denote the update of the Miller function components (f_n, f_d) in the DBLSTEP and ADDSTEP respectively.

Remark 1. For the evaluation of the rational functions $c_{T,D}$ and u_3, Algorithm 1 outputs the values (λ_n, λ_d) and (μ_n, μ_d), where λ_d, μ_d refer to the denominators $\lambda_d = l'$ and $\mu_d = z_{31}$ of Eqs. (8) and (9). As reported in [32], this is in order to avoid the inversions λ_n/λ_d and μ_n/μ_d in each iteration, saving also the inversions $c_{T,T}(D_2)/u_3(D_2)$ and $c_{T,[b_i]D_1}(D_2)/u_3(D_2)$. Instead, we only perform one inversion and one multiplication in $\mathbb{F}_{p^k}$ in the end to compute the Miller function $f = f_n/f_d$. In the case where the denominators λ_d, μ_d and $u_3(D_2)$ lie in a subfield of $\mathbb{F}_{p^k}$, which happens when using twists, these values are mapped to 1 in the final exponentiation and hence they can be omitted from computations.

Remark 2. The divisor $D_1 \in J_{\mathcal{C}}(\mathbb{F}_p)$ is initialized with $Z_1 = Z_2 = 1$ and hence $D_1 = [U_{11}, U_{10}, V_{11}, V_{10}, 1, 1, 1, 1]$ in the first iteration of Algorithm 1. This saves 13 multiplications and 1 squaring in the DBL function. In addition, in the first iteration, the function UPDATEDBL is free, since $f_n = f_d = 1$.

Table 3. Multiplication count of Miller loop operations for genus 2 curves of the form $\mathcal{C}: y^2 = x^5 + ax$ with $k \in \{8, 16, 24\}$ and $i = k/8$ [18].

	Case	C_{DBL}	$C_{DOUBLELINE}$	$C_{VERTICALLINE}$	$C_{UPDATEDBL}$
1st DBLSTEP	Case 1	$25\mathbf{m}_i + 5\mathbf{s}_i$	$4c\mathbf{m}_i$	0	0
	Case 2		$14c\mathbf{m}_i + 4\mathbf{m}_i + 1\mathbf{s}_i$	0	0
DBLSTEP	Case 1	$38\mathbf{m}_i + 6\mathbf{s}_i$	$4\mathbf{m}_i$	0	$1\mathbf{s}_k + 18\mathbf{m}_i$
	Case 2		$14c\mathbf{m}_i + 4\mathbf{m}_i + 1\mathbf{s}_i$	0	
	Case	C_{ADD}	$C_{ADDLINE}$	$C_{VERTICALLINE}$	$C_{UPDATEADD}$
ADDSTEP	Case 1	$37\mathbf{m}_i + 5\mathbf{s}_i$	$4\mathbf{m}_i$	0	$18\mathbf{m}_i$
	Case 2		$14c\mathbf{m}_i + 4\mathbf{m}_i + 1\mathbf{s}_i$	0	

Table 3 reports the cost of the operations that are executed in the DBLSTEP and ADDSTEP in the Miller algorithm, considering Remark 1, excluding the cost of the VERTICALLINE, λ_d and $u_3(D_2)$. Further, Table 3 considers both cases where the second input divisor is degenerate or general. The cost of the relevant functions is presented in terms of multiplications and squarings over $\mathbb{F}_{p^i}$, for $i = k/8$, where $k \in \{8, 16, 24\}$. Based on these assumptions, the cost for computing the Miller function via Algorithm 1 can be described by the formula:

$$
\begin{aligned}
\mathbf{C}_{\text{MILLER}} &= (\log_2(S) - 1)\mathbf{C}_{\text{DBLSTEP}} + (\text{hw}(S) - 1)\mathbf{C}_{\text{ADDSTEP}} + 1\mathbf{m}_k + 1\mathbf{i}_k \quad (10) \\
&= (\mathbf{C}_{\text{1STDBL}} + \mathbf{C}_{\text{DOUBLELINE}}) \\
&\quad + (\log_2(S) - 2)(\mathbf{C}_{\text{DOUBLELINE}} + \mathbf{C}_{\text{DBL}} + \mathbf{C}_{\text{UPDATEDBL}}) \\
&\quad + (\text{hw}(S) - 1)(\mathbf{C}_{\text{ADDLINE}} + \mathbf{C}_{\text{VERTICALLINE}} + \mathbf{C}_{\text{ADD}} + \mathbf{C}_{\text{UPDATEADD}}) \\
&\quad + 1\mathbf{m}_k + 1\mathbf{i}_k.
\end{aligned}
$$

When the NAF representation of S is used, we replace $\text{hw}(S)$ by $\text{hw}_{\text{NAF}}(S)$. In this cost, we also need to add some precomputations related to the second divisor D_2, which are required for the evaluation of the rational function $c_{T,D}(D_2)$. Specifically, we need $1\mathbf{m}_1 + 1\mathbf{s}_1$ when D_2 is a degenerate divisor and $13\mathbf{m}_1 + 3\mathbf{s}_1$ when it is a general divisor (see [18] for details).

4.2   Final Exponentiation

To compute the final pairing value we need to raise the output f of Miller's algorithm to the exponent $(p^k - 1)/r$. This is a computationally demanding operation and requires to employ certain tricks, originating from elliptic curve pairings (see for example [1,32,35]). When working with even embedding degrees, the key idea is to rewrite the above exponent as:

$$
\frac{p^k - 1}{r} = \left(p^{k/2} - 1\right) \cdot \frac{p^{k/2} + 1}{\Phi_k(p)} \cdot \frac{\Phi_k(p)}{r}, \quad \text{where} \quad \frac{\Phi_k(p)}{r} = \sum_{i=0}^{\varphi(k)-1} \lambda_i p^i, \quad (11)
$$

for some $\lambda_i \in \mathbb{Q}$. Raising f to the first two exponents is the "easy part", which can be efficiently computed using Frobenius exponentiations. Raising an element to the third exponent constitutes the "hard part". For the efficient computation of the hard part, we refer to the specific examples that are presented later in this section, since there is no standard method.

According to [35] there are different methods for optimizing the final exponentiation in elliptic curve pairings. In our examples we apply the LLL approach, which is a lattice-reduction technique on the exponent in base p, aiming at reducing the size of the coefficients of the base-p expansion. We argue that our final exponentiation formulas are likely to be further optimized using alternative techniques reported in [35], however, we leave this for future work.

4.3   Examples of Genus 2 Pairings

We study the application of pairings on the genus 2 curves described in Table 1 and calculate the cost of each pairing in terms of $\mathbb{F}_p$ multiplications. We use Table 4 to reduce multiplications and squarings to $\mathbb{F}_p$.

Table 4. Relative cost of field operations [32].

k	1	2	3	4	5	6	7	8	12	16	24
m_k	1m	3m	6m	9m	13m	18m	22m	27m	54m	81m	162m
s_k	1m	2m	5m	7m	13m	12m	22m	18m	36m	54m	108m
f_k	0	0	2m	2m	4m	4m	6m	6m	10m	14m	22m
s_k^{cyclo}						6m		12m	18m	36m	54m
i_k	25m	29m	37m		73m	59m	129m	69m	119m	159m	343m

Genus 2 Pairings on CP8-544. The CP8-544 curve $\mathcal{C} : y^2 = x^5 + 3x$ has a degree $\delta = 8$ twist represented by the curve with equation $\mathcal{C}^t : y^2 = x^5 + 3\lambda x$, where $\lambda = 3$. Since $m = \gcd(k, \delta) = 8$, we have $e = k/m = 1$. Observe that $p^e \bmod r = u$, where $\log_2(u) = 64$. In addition, u has NAF Hamming weight $\text{hw}_{\text{NAF}}(u) = 5$. Hence the twisted Ate pairing can be applied with an optimal Miller loop length of 64 iterations, which is given by the formula:

$$e_{\text{Ate}}^{\text{twist}}(D_1, D_2) = f_{u,D_1}(D_2)^{\frac{p^8-1}{r}},$$

where $D_1 \in J_{\mathcal{C}}(\mathbb{F}_p)[r]$ and $D_2 \in J_{\mathcal{C}}(\mathbb{F}_{p^8})[r] \cap \ker([\xi_8]\pi - [1])$. Using Eq. (10) and Tables 3 and 4, the total cost for computing the Miller function in case 1 is:

$$\mathbf{C}_{\text{MILLER}} = (\mathbf{C}_{\text{DOUBLELINE}} + \mathbf{C}_{\text{1STDBL}}) + 62(\mathbf{C}_{\text{DOUBLELINE}} + \mathbf{C}_{\text{DBL}} + \mathbf{C}_{\text{UPDATEDBL}})$$
$$+ 4(\mathbf{C}_{\text{ADDLINE}} + \mathbf{C}_{\text{ADD}} + \mathbf{C}_{\text{UPDATEADD}}) + 1s_8 + 1i_8 = 5498m.$$

In case 2 the corresponding cost is 7173m.

For the final exponentiation, the "easy part" requires $\mathbf{C}_{\text{EASYPART}} = 1f_8 + 1i_8 + 1m_8$ operations. For the "hard part", we follow the same approach as in Guillevic et al. [32] and write $\Phi_8(p)/r = 1 + (p + u)(p^2 + u^2)e$, where e is defined as:

$$e = (l_x^2 + 2l_y^2 + l_y + 1/8)u^4 + (l_x + l_y + 1/4)u^3 - (l_x + l_y - 1/8)u^2$$
$$- (l_y + 1)u + (l_x^2 + 2l_y^2)$$

Observe here that the computation of the "hard part" requires exponentiations by the lifts l_x, l_y. The reason for choosing $l_x = \text{0xa031}$ and $l_y = 1$ in CP8-544 is in order to reduce this cost. Since $\log_2(l_x) = 16$ and $\text{hw}(l_x) = 5$ we get:

$$1e_{l_x} = (\log_2(l_x) - 1)s_8^{\text{cyclo}} + (\text{hw}(l_x) - 1)m_8 = 276m$$

and $1e_{l_y} = 0$. This suggests that the cost for the hard part is:

$$\mathbf{C}_{\text{HARDPART}} = 16m_8 + 17s_8 + 2f_8 + 3e_u + 4e_{u_0} + 3e_{l_x} + 1i_8,$$

where $u_0 = u/4$ and

$$1e_u = (\log_2(u) - 1)s_8^{\text{cyclo}} + (\text{hw}(u) - 1)m_8 = 63s_8^{\text{cyclo}} + 4m_8 = 864m$$
$$1e_{u_0} = (\log_2(u_0) - 1)s_8^{\text{cyclo}} + (\text{hw}(u_0) - 1)m_8 = 61s_8^{\text{cyclo}} + 4m_8 = 840m$$

Therefore, the final exponentiation costs $\mathbf{C}_{\text{FINALEXPO}} = \mathbf{C}_{\text{EASYPART}} + \mathbf{C}_{\text{HARDPART}} = 7701\mathbf{m}$ and the total cost for the twisted Ate pairing on CP8-544 considering also precomputations is:

$$\mathbf{C}_{\text{TWISTEDATE},8} = \begin{cases} \mathbf{C}_{\text{PREC}} + \mathbf{C}_{\text{MILLER}} + \mathbf{C}_{\text{FINALEXPO}} = 13201\mathbf{m}, & \text{(case 1)} \\ \mathbf{C}_{\text{PREC}} + \mathbf{C}_{\text{MILLER}} + \mathbf{C}_{\text{FINALEXPO}} = 14890\mathbf{m}, & \text{(case 2)} \end{cases}$$

Genus 2 Pairings on KT16-447. We apply the HV pairings on KT16-447 with equation $\mathcal{C} : y^2 = x^5 + 7x$ and Jacobian $J_{\mathcal{C}}$ with embedding degree 16. Let $\mathbb{F}_{p^{16}} = \mathbb{F}_p[\omega]/\langle \omega^{16} - 7 \rangle$, where ω is the generator of $\mathbb{F}_{p^{16}}$ over $\mathbb{F}_p$, such that $\omega^8 = v$. Then for $\lambda = v$, the curve $\mathcal{C}^t : y^2 = x^5 + 7\lambda x$ is a degree $\delta = 8$ twist of $\mathcal{C}$. Note that for $i = 13$, we find that $s \equiv p^{13} \bmod r = u$, with $\log_2(u) = 32$ and $hw(u) = 4$. Hence the e_{Ate_i} pairing applies here for $i = 13$ and formula:

$$e_{\text{Ate}_{13}}(D_2, D_1) = f_{s,D_2}(D_1)^{\frac{p^{16}-1}{r}},$$

where $D_1 \in J_{\mathcal{C}}(\mathbb{F}_p)[r]$ and $D_2 \in J_{\mathcal{C}}(\mathbb{F}_{p^{16}}) \cap \ker([\xi_8]\pi - 1)$. Using Eq. (10) and Tables 3 and 4, the total cost for computing the Miller function in case 1 is:

$$\mathbf{C}_{\text{MILLER}} = (\mathbf{C}_{\text{DOUBLELINE}} + \mathbf{C}_{\text{1STDBL}}) + 30(\mathbf{C}_{\text{DOUBLELINE}} + \mathbf{C}_{\text{DBL}} + \mathbf{C}_{\text{UPDATEDBL}}) \\ + 3(\mathbf{C}_{\text{ADDLINE}} + \mathbf{C}_{\text{ADD}} + \mathbf{C}_{\text{UPDATEADD}}) + 1\mathbf{s}_{16} + 1\mathbf{i}_{16} = 8144\mathbf{m}.$$

In case 2 the corresponding cost is $10384\mathbf{m}$.

For the final exponentiation, the "easy part" costs $\mathbf{C}_{\text{EASYPART}} = 1\mathbf{f}_{16} + 1\mathbf{i}_{16} + 1\mathbf{m}_{16}$, while for the "hard part", $\Phi_{16}(p)/r = \lambda_0 + \lambda_1 p + \ldots + \lambda_7 p^7$, where:

$$(\lambda_0, \lambda_1, \lambda_2, \lambda_3, \lambda_4, \lambda_5, \lambda_6, \lambda_7) = ((u+1)^2 + 2u^4(u-1)^2, -8 - u^3\lambda_0, -u^3\lambda_1, u\lambda_0, \\ u\lambda_1, u\lambda_2, u\lambda_3, u\lambda_4).$$

This representation suggests that the "hard part" requires:

$$\mathbf{C}_{\text{HARDPART}} = 11\mathbf{m}_{16} + 6\mathbf{s}_{16} + 7\mathbf{f}_{16} + 11\mathbf{e}_s + 2\mathbf{e}_{s-1} + 1\mathbf{i}_{16},$$

where for the exponentiations by u and $u-1$ we have $1\mathbf{e}_u = 1359\mathbf{m}$ and $1\mathbf{e}_{u+1} = 1278\mathbf{m}$. Thus we obtain $\mathbf{C}_{\text{FINALEXPO}} = \mathbf{C}_{\text{EASYPART}} + \mathbf{C}_{\text{HARDPART}} = 19231\mathbf{m}$ and the total cost for the $e_{\text{Ate}_{13}}$ pairing on the KT16-447 curve taking into account the precomputations is

$$\mathbf{C}_{\text{ATE}_{13},16} = \begin{cases} \mathbf{C}_{\text{PREC}} + \mathbf{C}_{\text{MILLER}} + \mathbf{C}_{\text{FINALEXPO}} = 27377\mathbf{m}, & \text{(case 1)} \\ \mathbf{C}_{\text{PREC}} + \mathbf{C}_{\text{MILLER}} + \mathbf{C}_{\text{FINALEXPO}} = 29631\mathbf{m}, & \text{(case 2)} \end{cases}$$

Genus 2 Pairings on AFK16-767. We apply the same technique as in the previous example to AFK16-767 with equation $\mathcal{C} : y^2 = x^5 + 13x$, over $\mathbb{F}_p$. As before, we fix the extension field $\mathbb{F}_{p^{16}} = \mathbb{F}_p[\omega]/\langle \omega^{16} - 7 \rangle$, where $\omega^8 = v$ and for $\lambda = v$ the curve $\mathcal{C}^t : y^2 = x^5 + 13\lambda x$ is a degree $\delta = 8$ twist of $\mathcal{C}$. For $i = 13$ we find that $s \equiv p^{13} \bmod r = u$, with $\log_2(u) = 48$ and $\mathrm{hw}_{\mathrm{NAF}}(u) = 5$. Then for the total cost for the Miller function in case 1 we have:

$$\mathbf{C}_{\mathrm{MILLER}} = (\mathbf{C}_{\mathrm{DOUBLELINE}} + \mathbf{C}_{\mathrm{1STDBL}}) + 46(\mathbf{C}_{\mathrm{DOUBLELINE}} + \mathbf{C}_{\mathrm{DBL}} + \mathbf{C}_{\mathrm{UPDATEDBL}})$$
$$+ 4(\mathbf{C}_{\mathrm{ADDLINE}} + \mathbf{C}_{\mathrm{ADD}} + \mathbf{C}_{\mathrm{UPDATEADD}}) + 1\mathbf{s}_{16} + 1\mathbf{i}_{16} = 11957\mathbf{m}.$$

In case 2 the corresponding cost is $15221\mathbf{m}$.

For the final exponentiation, the "easy part" remains the same as KT16-447 and for the "hard part" we write $\Phi_{16}(p)/r = \lambda_0 + \lambda_1 p + \ldots + \lambda_7 p^7$, where:

$$(\lambda_0, \lambda_1, \lambda_2, \lambda_3, \lambda_4, \lambda_5, \lambda_6, \lambda_7) = \left(8 + (u+1)^2(1 + 2u^4 - 8u^5 + 8u^6), -(8 + \lambda_0 u^3),\right.$$
$$\left. u^3 \lambda_1, u\lambda_0, u\lambda_1, -u^4 \lambda_1, u^2 \lambda_0, u^2 \lambda_1\right).$$

Based on our implementation, the "hard part" requires:

$$\mathbf{C}_{\mathrm{HARDPART}} = 12\mathbf{m}_{16} + 6\mathbf{s}_{16} + 7\mathbf{f}_{16} + 13\mathbf{e}_s + 2\mathbf{e}_{s+1} + 1\mathbf{i}_{16},$$

where for the exponentiations by u and $u+1$ we have $1\mathbf{e}_u = 2016\mathbf{m}$ and $1\mathbf{e}_{u+1} = 1935\mathbf{m}$. Hence we find that $\mathbf{C}_{\mathrm{FINALEXPO}} = \mathbf{C}_{\mathrm{EASYPART}} + \mathbf{C}_{\mathrm{HARDPART}} = 31885\mathbf{m}$, which results in the total cost for the $e_{\mathrm{Ate}_{13}}$ pairing:

$$\mathbf{C}_{\mathrm{ATE}_{13},16} = \begin{cases} \mathbf{C}_{\mathrm{PREC}} + \mathbf{C}_{\mathrm{MILLER}} + \mathbf{C}_{\mathrm{FINALEXPO}} = 43685\mathbf{m}, & \text{(case 1)} \\ \mathbf{C}_{\mathrm{PREC}} + \mathbf{C}_{\mathrm{MILLER}} + \mathbf{C}_{\mathrm{FINALEXPO}} = 46963\mathbf{m}, & \text{(case 2)} \end{cases}$$

Genus 2 Pairings on AFK24-575 and AFK24-576. We apply the HV pairings on the curve AFK24-575 with equation $\mathcal{C} : y^2 = x^5 + 7x$, over $\mathbb{F}_p$. For $i = 11$ we find that $s \equiv p^{11} \bmod r = u$, with $\log_2(u) = 49$ and $\mathrm{hw}_{\mathrm{NAF}}(u) = 3$. Then for the total cost for the Miller function in case 1 we have:

$$\mathbf{C}_{\mathrm{MILLER}} = (\mathbf{C}_{\mathrm{DOUBLELINE}} + \mathbf{C}_{\mathrm{1STDBL}}) + 47(\mathbf{C}_{\mathrm{DOUBLELINE}} + \mathbf{C}_{\mathrm{DBL}} + \mathbf{C}_{\mathrm{UPDATEDBL}})$$
$$+ 2(\mathbf{C}_{\mathrm{ADDLINE}} + \mathbf{C}_{\mathrm{ADD}} + \mathbf{C}_{\mathrm{UPDATEADD}}) + 1\mathbf{s}_{24} + 1\mathbf{i}_{24} = 23763\mathbf{m}.$$

In case 2 the corresponding cost is $29713\mathbf{m}$.

For the final exponentiation, the "easy part" costs $\mathbf{C}_{\mathrm{EASYPART}} = 2\mathbf{f}_{24} + 1\mathbf{i}_{24} + 2\mathbf{m}_{24}$ "hard part" we write $\Phi_{16}(p)/r = \lambda_0 + \lambda_1 p + \ldots + \lambda_7 p^7$, where:

$$\lambda_4 = -1 + 2u - 3u^2 - 4u^3 - 2u^4, \lambda_5 = 8 - u\lambda_4, \lambda_6 = -u\lambda_5, \lambda_7 = -u\lambda_6,$$
$$\lambda_0 = u\lambda_7, \lambda_1 = -u\lambda_0, \lambda_2 = -u\lambda_1, \lambda_3 = -u\lambda_2$$

Based on our implementation, the "hard part" requires:

$$\mathbf{C}_{\mathrm{HARDPART}} = 13\mathbf{m}_{24} + 8\mathbf{s}_{24} + 11\mathbf{f}_{24} + 11\mathbf{e}_u + 1\mathbf{i}_{24},$$

where $1\mathbf{e}_u = 2916\mathbf{m}$. Hence we find that $\mathbf{C}_{\mathrm{FINALEXPO}} = \mathbf{C}_{\mathrm{EASYPART}} + \mathbf{C}_{\mathrm{HARDPART}} = 35037\mathbf{m}$, which results in the total cost for the $e_{\mathrm{Ate}_{13}}$ pairing:

$$\mathbf{C}_{\mathrm{ATE}_{11},24} = \begin{cases} \mathbf{C}_{\mathrm{PREC}} + \mathbf{C}_{\mathrm{MILLER}} + \mathbf{C}_{\mathrm{FINALEXPO}} = 58802\mathbf{m}, & \text{(case 1)} \\ \mathbf{C}_{\mathrm{PREC}} + \mathbf{C}_{\mathrm{MILLER}} + \mathbf{C}_{\mathrm{FINALEXPO}} = 64766\mathbf{m}, & \text{(case 2)} \end{cases}$$

Table 5. Comparison of proposed genus 2 pairings with elliptic curves at 128-bit and 192-bit security levels, in terms of $\mathbb{F}_p$-multiplications.

Genus	Case	Rep.	k	Construction	$\log_2(p)$	Precomp. (m)	Miller (m)	Final exp. (m)	Total (m)
128-bit security									
1	–	NAF	8	Cocks-Pinch [31]	544	–	4502	7056	11558
2	Case 1	NAF	8	CP8-544	544	2	5498	7701	13201
	Case 2					16	7173	7701	14890
	Case 1	Bin	16	KT16-447	447	2	8144	19231	27377
	Case 2					16	10384	19231	29631
192-bit security									
1	–	NAF	16	AFG16-765 [19]	765	–	9838	29322	39160
	–	NAF	24	BLS24-509 [19]	509	–	15345	24968	40313
2	Case 1	Bin	16	Ishii [36]	671	–	19913	32856	52769
	Case 1	NAF	16	AFK16-767	767	2	11957	31726	43685
	Case 2					16	15221	31726	46963
	Case 1	Bin	24	AFK24-575	575	2	23763	35037	58802
	Case 2					16	29713	35037	64766
	Case 1	Bin	24	AFK24-576	576	2	24864	40383	65249
	Case 2					16	31171	40383	71570

Similarly, we obtain the cost for AFK24-576:

$$C_{\text{ATE}_{11},24} = \begin{cases} C_{\text{PREC}} + C_{\text{MILLER}} + C_{\text{FINALEXPO}} = 65249\text{m}, & \text{(case 1)} \\ C_{\text{PREC}} + C_{\text{MILLER}} + C_{\text{FINALEXPO}} = 71570\text{m}, & \text{(case 2)} \end{cases}$$

4.4 Comparison with Elliptic Curve Pairings

In Table 5 we present the number of $\mathbb{F}_p$-multiplications required for the computation of our genus 2 pairings with embedding degrees 8, 16 and 24. We refer to our SageMath implementation [2] for verifying the correctness of the number of $\mathbb{F}_p$-multiplications. We also report the best instances of elliptic curve pairings for the same embedding degrees. Comparing the performance of the pairings in Table 5 from a theoretical perspective is not straightforward as different pairings operate on prime fields of different sizes. The only meaningful comparison can be made between the elliptic curve Cocks–Pinch pairing presented in [32] and our genus 2 CP8-544 instance, since the base field has the same size of 544-bits in both cases. In particular, the theoretical analysis shows that our genus 2 CP8-544 curve requires approximately 13% more $\mathbb{F}_p$-multiplications (for case 1) compared to the Cocks–Pinch elliptic curve for $k = 8$.

In order to compare pairings that operate on prime fields of different sizes, we follow the approach of Aranha et al. [1]. In particular, we assume an architecture with limbs of size 64-bits. Then elements in $\mathbb{F}_p$ can be represented with $\ell = 1 + \lfloor \log_2(p) \rfloor$-bits, split in $w = \lceil \ell/64 \rceil$ 64-bit machine-words. As stated in [1], if the Montgomery representation is assumed, a multiplication in $\mathbb{F}_p$ has complexity $O(2w^2 + w)$. Using this setup, we can translate the cost of an $\mathbb{F}_p$-multiplication over a prime p of size $w \times 64$-bits to the cost of a multiplication over a field of size 512-bits. In particular, we have the following conversions that are relevant to our cases, based on the size of the prime fields that we consider:

$$\text{for } w = 7: \quad 1\mathbf{m}_{448} = [(2 \cdot 7^2 + 7)/(2 \cdot 8^2 + 8)]\mathbf{m}_{512} = 0.772\mathbf{m}_{512}$$

$$\text{for } w = 9: \quad 1\mathbf{m}_{576} = [(2 \cdot 9^2 + 9)/(2 \cdot 8^2 + 8)]\mathbf{m}_{512} = 1.257\mathbf{m}_{512}$$

$$\text{for } w = 11: \quad 1\mathbf{m}_{704} = [(2 \cdot 11^2 + 11)/(2 \cdot 8^2 + 8)]\mathbf{m}_{512} = 1.860\mathbf{m}_{512}$$

$$\text{for } w = 12: \quad 1\mathbf{m}_{768} = [(2 \cdot 12^2 + 12)/(2 \cdot 8^2 + 8)]\mathbf{m}_{512} = 2.205\mathbf{m}_{512}$$

Using this formulas, we obtain the results in Table 6, representing the number of $\mathbf{m}_{512}$ multiplications required for each pairing.

Table 6. Cost estimates of genus 2 and elliptic curve pairings in terms of finite field multiplications, normalized w.r.t. a multiplication in $\mathbb{F}_p$ of size 512-bits.

Genus	Case	Rep.	k	Construction	$\log_2(p)$	Precomp. ($\mathbf{m}_{512}$)	Miller ($\mathbf{m}_{512}$)	Final exp. ($\mathbf{m}_{512}$)	Total ($\mathbf{m}_{512}$)
128-bit security									
1	–	NAF	8	Cocks-Pinch [31]	544	–	5659	8869	14528
2	Case 1	NAF	8	CP8-544	544	3	6911	9680	16594
	Case 2					20	9016	9680	18716
	Case 1	Bin	16	KT16-447	447	2	6287	14846	21135
	Case 2					12	8016	14846	22874
192-bit security									
1	–	NAF	16	AFG16-765 [19]	765	–	21693	64655	86348
	–	NAF	24	BLS24-509 [19]	509	–	15345	24968	40313
2	Case 1	Bin	16	Ishii [36]	671	–	37038	61112	98150
	Case 1	NAF	16	AFK16-767	767	4	26365	69956	96325
	Case 2					35	33562	69956	103553
	Case 1	Bin	24	AFK24-575	575	3	29870	44042	73915
	Case 2					20	37349	44042	81411
	Case 1	Bin	24	AFK24-576	576	3	31254	50761	82018
	Case 2					20	39182	50761	89963

The theoretical comparison in Table 6 shows that the most efficient genus 2 pairing option at 128-bit security is CP8-544, since it requires 22% less $\mathbf{m}_{512}$ multiplications compared to KT16-447 for case 1 and 18% less $\mathbf{m}_{512}$ multiplications in case 2. For $k = 16$, the elliptic curve AFG16-765 and the genus 2 curve AFK16-767 operate on prime fields where p fits in 12 machine-words. In this case, AFK16-767 requires only 10% more $\mathbf{m}_{512}$ multiplications (for case 1). Note also that the example of Ishii [36] requires 98150$\mathbf{m}_{512}$, while AFK16-767 requires 96325$\mathbf{m}_{512}$. Even with a smaller prime field, Ishii's pairing is less efficient than our AFK16-767. For 192-bit security, Table 6 shows that the most promising candidate is AFK24-575, since it requires less $\mathbf{m}_{512}$ multiplications than any other genus candidate at this security level.

5 Conclusion

We presented examples of efficient pairings on genus 2 curves at 128 and 192-bit security levels, by exploiting various speedups from the literature for both

genus 2 and elliptic curve pairings. We presented an instance of the twisted
Ate pairing applied on a 2-dimensional Jacobian with embedding degree 8 at
128-bit security, which is currently the most efficient genus 2 pairing in the
literature. Our theoretical cost estimates show that it is also competitive with
the state-of-the-art elliptic curve pairing presented in [31] for $k = 8$. For 192-bit
security, we presented instances of the Ate_i pairing on a 2-dimensional Jacobian
with embedding degrees 16 and 24, which are derived by our new families of
pairing-friendly jacobians with $k = 16$ (AFK16) and 24 (AFK24). Based on our
theoretical analysis, the Ate_i on the AFK24-575 genus 2 curve is the fastest
genus 2 pairing in the literature at 192-bit security. Our genus 2 pairings are
implemented in SageMath [2] in order to demonstrate their practicality.

Clearly, genus 2 pairings are less efficient than elliptic curve ones, however,
we believe that our work shrinks this gap. Given that genus 2 pairings are less
studied, we believe that our work might motivate researchers to study ways to
optimize our examples. One part that potentially allows further improvements
is the DBL and ADD steps in Miller's algorithm. It is not yet clear whether
we can apply different models for the DBL and ADD processes, as it is done in
the case of elliptic curves (e.g. using twisted Edwards or Jacobi quartic curves).
Additionally, the final exponentiation operation can be further optimized. An
improvement on the final exponentiation in addition to potential improvements
in DBL and ADD steps might speed up our genus 2 pairings and perhaps
outperform elliptic curve pairings in specific instances.

Acknowledgements. The authors acknowledge the financial support from the
Luxembourg National Research Fund (FNR) under the CORE project Privacy-
Preserving Tokenisation of Artworks –PABLO (C21/IS/16326754/PABLO) and the
INTER project Secure and Verifiable Electronic Testing and Assessment Systems –
SEVERITAS (INTER /ANR/20/14926102 ANR-20-CE39-009-03).

A   Generating Pairing-Friendly 2-Dimensional Jacobians

A.1   Cocks-Pinch Algorithm for 2-Dimensional Jacobians

Drylo's Cocks-Pinch algorithm with the modification of Guillevic et al. [32] is
described in Algorithm 2 (see also [16, Algorithm 8]).

A.2   Brezing-Weng Algorithm for 2-Dimensional Jacobians

Drylo's Brezing-Weng algorithm is described in Algorithm 3 (see also [16, Algorithm 18]).

Family 4 (BLS-analogue, Embedding Degree 12) Let $l = k = 12$, $s = 4$
and $d = 3$. Set $r(x) = \Phi_{12}(x)$, so that $w(x) = x$ is a primitive 12th root of unity
and $z(x) = 2x^2 - 1 \mapsto \sqrt{-3}$ in $L = \mathbb{Q}[x]/\langle r(x)\rangle$. Then Algorithm 3 for $i = 1$ and
$j = 3$ outputs the Frobenius polynomial:

$$\pi(x) = \zeta_4\left(X(x) + Y(x)\sqrt{-3}\right) = i\left(-\frac{x^3 - x^2 + 1}{2} + \frac{x^3 - x^2 - 2x - 1}{6}\sqrt{-3}\right),$$

Algorithm 2: COCKSPINCH($k, s, d, u_0, u_{\max}, s_r, s_p$)

Input: $k, s, d \in \mathbb{Z}_{>0}$, d: square-free, lower/upper bounds $u_0, u_{\max}$, sizes s_r, s_p.
Output: Prime r and $\alpha = \zeta_s \alpha_0$, s.t. $\alpha_0 \in \mathbb{Q}(\sqrt{-d})$ & $\alpha\overline{\alpha} \equiv 1 \bmod k$ is prime.

1   **for** $u \in \{u_0, \ldots, u_{\max}\}$ **do**
2   **if** $r = \Phi_k(u)$: *not prime* **then**
3   **if** $\lceil \log_2(r) \rceil = s_r$ **then**
4   **for** $i \in \{1, \ldots, k-1\}$ s.t. $\gcd(i,k) = 1$ **do**
5   **for** $j \in \{1, \ldots, k-1\}$ s.t. $j \mid k$ *and* $\mathbb{Q}(\zeta_j, \sqrt{-d})$: *CM-field* **do**
6             $\zeta_k \leftarrow u^i \bmod r, \zeta_s \leftarrow u^j \bmod r$
7             $x_0 \leftarrow (\zeta_s^{-1} + \zeta_s \zeta_k)/2 \bmod r$
8             $y_0 \leftarrow (\zeta_s^{-1} - \zeta_s \zeta^k)/(2\sqrt{-d}) \bmod r$
9   **if** (x_0, y_0) *does not satisfy System (3)* **then**
10               $y_0 \leftarrow -y_0$
11   **repeat**
12   Set: $x \leftarrow l_x r + x_0, y \leftarrow l_y r + y_0$, for lifts: $l_x, l_y \in \mathbb{Z}$,
13               $\alpha \leftarrow \zeta_s(x + y\sqrt{-d})$ and $p \leftarrow \alpha\overline{\alpha} = (x^2 + dy^2)/4$
14   **until** p: *is prime*, $p \equiv 1 \bmod k$, $x \neq 0$ *and* $\lceil \log_2(p) \rceil = s_p$

15 **return** (α, r)

Algorithm 3: MODIFIEDBREZINGWENG(k, s, d, L)

Input: $k, s, d \in \mathbb{Z}_{>0}$, d: square-free, a number field $L = \mathbb{Q}(\zeta_l)$, with
       $l = \text{lcm}(s, m, k)$, s.t. $\sqrt{-d} \in \mathbb{Q}(\zeta_m)$.
Output: A complete family $[\alpha, r]$ of simple, ordinary, pairing-friendly Jacobians
       with embedding degree k and discriminant d.

1   choose: $r \in \mathbb{Q}[x]$, s.t. $L \cong \mathbb{Q}[x]/\langle r(x) \rangle$
2   $u \mapsto \zeta_k, v \mapsto \zeta_s, z \mapsto \sqrt{-d}$ in $\mathbb{Q}[x]/\langle r(x) \rangle$
3   **for** $i \in \{1, \ldots, k-1\}$ s.t. $\gcd(i,k) = 1$ **do**
4   **for** $j \in \{1, \ldots, k-1\}$ s.t. $\gcd(j,k) > 1$ *and* $\mathbb{Q}(\zeta_j, \sqrt{-d})$: *CM-field* **do**
5       $X_0 \leftarrow (v^{-j} + v^j w^i)/2 \bmod r$, $Y_0 \leftarrow (v^{-j} - v^j w^i)/(2z) \bmod r$
6   **if** (X_0, Y_0) *does not satisfy System (6)* **then**
7         $Y_0 \leftarrow -Y_0$
8   **repeat**
9   choose lifts: $h_x, h_y \in \mathbb{Q}[x]$ and set $X \leftarrow h_x r + X_0, Y \leftarrow h_y r + Y_0$
10        $\pi \leftarrow \zeta_s(X + Y\sqrt{-d})$ and $p \leftarrow \pi\overline{\pi} = X^2 + dY^2$
11   find $a, b \in \mathbb{Z}$, s.t. $p(ax + b) \in \mathbb{Z}[x]$
12   **until** p: *represents primes*, $X \neq 0$

13 **return** $[\pi, r], a, b$

---

for which $p(x) = \pi(x)\overline{\pi}(x)$ is irreducible and integer-valued for every $x \equiv 1 \bmod 3$. The characteristic polynomial of Frobenius in $\mathbb{Z}[x, t]$ is defined as:

$$\chi(x, t) = t^4 + 2\left(p(x) - 6Y(x)^2\right)t^2 + p^2,$$

and we conclude that the pair $[\pi, r]$ represents a complete family of pairing-friendly Jacobians with $k = 12$.   □

Family 5 (FK-analogue, Embedding Degree 12) Let $l = k = 12$, $s = 4$ and $d = 3$. We choose the non-cyclotomic polynomial $r(x) = 36x^4 + 36x^3 + 18x^2 + 6x + 1$, which was used for the construction of the BN family of pairing-friendly elliptic curves [7]. Then $w(x) = 6x^2$ is a primitive 12th root of unity and $z(x) = -72x^3 - 36x^2 - 12x - 3 \mapsto \sqrt{-3}$ in $L = \mathbb{Q}[x]/\langle r(x) \rangle$. Applying Algorithm 3 for $i = 7$ and $j = 3$, we obtain the Frobenius polynomial:

$$\pi(x) = i \left(\frac{72x^3 + 42x^2 + 18x + 5}{2} - \frac{24x^3 + 18x^2 + 6x + 1}{2} \sqrt{-3} \right),$$

and the field polynomial $p = \pi(x)\overline{\pi}(x)$ is integer-valued and irreducible. The characteristic polynomial of Frobenius is the same as Example 4 and thus the pair $[\pi, r]$ represents a family of pairing-friendly Jacobians with $k = 12$.   □

References

1. Aranha, D.F., Fuentes-Castañeda, L., Knapp, E., Menezes, A., Rodríguez-Henríquez, F.: Implementing pairings at the 192-bit security level. In: Abdalla, M., Lange, T. (eds.) Pairing-Based Cryptography - Pairing 2012 - 5th International Conference, Cologne, Germany, May 16-18, 2012, Revised Selected Papers. Lecture Notes in Computer Science, vol. 7708, pp. 177–195. Springer (2012). https://doi.org/10.1007/978-3-642-36334-4_11
2. Arenas, M., Fotiadis, G.: Hyperelliptic curve pairings code (2024). https://doi.org/10.5281/zenodo.11172005
3. Balakrishnan, J., Belding, J., Chisholm, S., Eisenträger, K., Stange, K.E., Teske, E.: Pairings on hyperelliptic curves. In: Cojocaru, A., Lauter, K.E., Pries, R., Scheidler, R. (eds.) WIN - Women in Numbers - Research Directions in Number Theory, Fields Institute Communications, vol. 60, pp. 87–120. American Mathematical Society (2011)
4. Balasubramanian, R., Koblitz, N.: The improbability that an elliptic curve has subexponential discrete log problem under the Menezes - Okamoto - van-stone algorithm. J. Cryptology **11**(2), 141–145 (1998). https://doi.org/10.1007/s001459900040
5. Barbulescu, R., Duquesne, S.: Updating key size estimations for pairings. J. Cryptology **32**(4), 1298–1336 (2019). https://doi.org/10.1007/s00145-018-9280-5
6. Barreto, P.S.L.M., Lynn, B., Scott, M.: Constructing elliptic curves with prescribed embedding degrees. In: Cimato, S., Galdi, C., Persiano, G. (eds.) Security in Communication Networks, Third International Conference, SCN 2002, Amalfi, Italy, September 11-13, 2002. Revised Papers. Lecture Notes in Computer Science, vol. 2576, pp. 257–267. Springer (2002). https://doi.org/10.1007/3-540-36413-7_19

7. Barreto, P.S.L.M., Naehrig, M.: Pairing-friendly elliptic curves of prime order. In: Preneel, B., Tavares, S.E. (eds.) Selected Areas in Cryptography, 12th International Workshop, SAC 2005, Kingston, ON, Canada, August 11-12, 2005, Revised Selected Papers. Lecture Notes in Computer Science, vol. 3897, pp. 319–331. Springer (2005). https://doi.org/10.1007/11693383_22

8. Blake, I.F., Seroussi, G., Smart, N.P.: Advances in Elliptic Curve Cryptography, vol. 317. Cambridge University Press (2005)

9. Boneh, D., Franklin, M.K.: Identity-based encryption from the weil pairing. SIAM J. Comput. **32**(3), 586–615 (2003). https://doi.org/10.1137/S0097539701398521

10. Boneh, D., Lynn, B., Shacham, H.: Short signatures from the weil pairing. J. Cryptology **17**(4), 297–319 (2004). https://doi.org/10.1007/s00145-004-0314-9

11. Bowe, S.: BLS12-381: New zk-SNARK elliptic curve construction. https://electriccoin.co/blog/new-snark-curve/ (2017), march 11, 2017

12. Brezing, F., Weng, A.: Elliptic curves suitable for pairing based cryptography. Des. Codes Cryptogr. **37**(1), 133–141 (2005). https://doi.org/10.1007/s10623-004-3808-4

13. Brickell, E., Chen, L., Li, J.: A new direct anonymous attestation scheme from bilinear maps. In: Lipp, P., Sadeghi, A., Koch, K. (eds.) Trusted Computing - Challenges and Applications, First International Conference on Trusted Computing and Trust in Information Technologies, Trust 2008, Villach, Austria, March 11-12, 2008, Proceedings. Lecture Notes in Computer Science, vol. 4968, pp. 166–178. Springer (2008). https://doi.org/10.1007/978-3-540-68979-9_13

14. Cantor, D.G.: Computing in the Jacobian of a hyperelliptic curve. Math. Comput. **48**(177), 95–101 (1987)

15. Chen, L., Morrissey, P., Smart, N.P.: Pairings in trusted computing. In: Galbraith, S.D., Paterson, K.G. (eds.) Pairing-Based Cryptography - Pairing 2008, Second International Conference, Egham, UK, September 1-3, 2008. Proceedings. Lecture Notes in Computer Science, vol. 5209, pp. 1–17. Springer (2008). https://doi.org/10.1007/978-3-540-85538-5_1

16. Dryło, R.: Constructing pairing-friendly genus 2 curves with split Jacobian. In: Galbraith, S.D., Nandi, M. (eds.) Progress in Cryptology - INDOCRYPT 2012, 13th International Conference on Cryptology in India, Kolkata, India, December 9-12, 2012. Proceedings. Lecture Notes in Computer Science, vol. 7668, pp. 431–453. Springer (2012). https://doi.org/10.1007/978-3-642-34931-7_25

17. Dupont, R., Enge, A., Morain, F.: Building curves with arbitrary small MOV degree over finite prime fields. J. Cryptology **18**(2), 79–89 (2005). https://doi.org/10.1007/s00145-004-0219-7

18. Fan, X., Gong, G., Jao, D.: Efficient pairing computation on genus 2 curves in projective coordinates. In: Avanzi, R.M., Keliher, L., Sica, F. (eds.) Selected Areas in Cryptography, 15th International Workshop, SAC 2008, Sackville, New Brunswick, Canada, August 14-15, Revised Selected Papers. Lecture Notes in Computer Science, vol. 5381, pp. 18–34. Springer (2008). https://doi.org/10.1007/978-3-642-04159-4_2

19. Fotiadis, G.: A short-list of pairing-friendly curves resistant to the special TNFS at 192-bit security level. https://members.loria.fr/AGuillevic/siam-ag23-elliptic-curves-and-pairings-in-cryptography-minisymposium/ (2023), SIAM Conference on Applied Algebraic Geometry (AG23) Elliptic Curves and Pairings in Cryptography

20. Fotiadis, G., Konstantinou, E.: Ordinary pairing-friendly genus 2 hyperelliptic curves with absolutely simple Jacobians. In: Blömer, J., Kotsireas, I.S., Kutsia, T.,

Simos, D.E. (eds.) Mathematical Aspects of Computer and Information Sciences - 7th International Conference, MACIS 2017, Vienna, Austria, November 15-17, 2017, Proceedings. Lecture Notes in Computer Science, vol. 10693, pp. 409–424. Springer (2017). https://doi.org/10.1007/978-3-319-72453-9_33

21. Fotiadis, G., Konstantinou, E.: Generating pairing-friendly elliptic curve parameters using sparse families. J. Math. Cryptology **12**(2), 83–99 (2018). https://doi.org/10.1515/jmc-2017-0024

22. Fotiadis, G., Konstantinou, E.: TNFS resistant families of pairing-friendly elliptic curves. Theor. Comput. Sci. **800**, 73–89 (2019). https://doi.org/10.1016/j.tcs.2019.10.017

23. Fotiadis, G., Martindale, C.: Optimal TNFS-secure pairings on elliptic curves with composite embedding degree. IACR Cryptol. ePrint Arch. **2019**, 555 (2019). https://eprint.iacr.org/2019/555

24. Freeman, D.: A generalized brezing-weng algorithm for constructing pairing-friendly ordinary abelian varieties. In: Galbraith, S.D., Paterson, K.G. (eds.) Pairing-Based Cryptography - Pairing 2008, Second International Conference, Egham, UK, September 1-3, 2008. Proceedings. Lecture Notes in Computer Science, vol. 5209, pp. 146–163. Springer (2008). https://doi.org/10.1007/978-3-540-85538-5_11

25. Freeman, D., Scott, M., Teske, E.: A taxonomy of pairing-friendly elliptic curves. J. Cryptology **23**(2), 224–280 (2010). https://doi.org/10.1007/s00145-009-9048-z

26. Freeman, D., Stevenhagen, P., Streng, M.: Abelian varieties with prescribed embedding degree. In: van der Poorten, A.J., Stein, A. (eds.) Algorithmic Number Theory, 8th International Symposium, ANTS-VIII, Banff, Canada, May 17-22, 2008, Proceedings. Lecture Notes in Computer Science, vol. 5011, pp. 60–73. Springer (2008). https://doi.org/10.1007/978-3-540-79456-1_3

27. Freeman, D.M., Satoh, T.: Constructing pairing-friendly hyperelliptic curves using Weil restriction. J. Number Theory **131**(5), 959–983 (2011)

28. Frey, G., Rück, H.G.: A remark concerning m-divisibility and the discrete logarithm in the divisor class group of curves. Math. Comput. **62**(206), 865–874 (1994)

29. Galbraith, S.D., Hess, F., Vercauteren, F.: Hyperelliptic pairings. In: Takagi, T., Okamoto, T., Okamoto, E., Okamoto, T. (eds.) Pairing-Based Cryptography - Pairing 2007, First International Conference, Tokyo, Japan, July 2-4, 2007, Proceedings. Lecture Notes in Computer Science, vol. 4575, pp. 108–131. Springer (2007). https://doi.org/10.1007/978-3-540-73489-5_7

30. Granger, R., Hess, F., Oyono, R., Thériault, N., Vercauteren, F.: Ate pairing on hyperelliptic curves. In: Naor, M. (ed.) Advances in Cryptology - EUROCRYPT 2007, 26th Annual International Conference on the Theory and Applications of Cryptographic Techniques, Barcelona, Spain, May 20-24, 2007, Proceedings. Lecture Notes in Computer Science, vol. 4515, pp. 430–447. Springer (2007). https://doi.org/10.1007/978-3-540-72540-4_25

31. Guillevic, A.: A short-list of pairing-friendly curves resistant to special TNFS at the 128-bit security level. In: Kiayias, A., Kohlweiss, M., Wallden, P., Zikas, V. (eds.) Public-Key Cryptography - PKC 2020 - 23rd IACR International Conference on Practice and Theory of Public-Key Cryptography, Edinburgh, UK, May 4-7, 2020, Proceedings, Part II. Lecture Notes in Computer Science, vol. 12111, pp. 535–564. Springer (2020). https://doi.org/10.1007/978-3-030-45388-6_19

32. Guillevic, A., Masson, S., Thomé, E.: Cocks-pinch curves of embedding degrees five to eight and optimal ate pairing computation. Des. Codes Cryptogr. **88**(6), 1047–1081 (2020). https://doi.org/10.1007/s10623-020-00727-w

33. Guillevic, A., Singh, S.: On the alpha value of polynomials in the tower number field sieve algorithm. IACR Cryptol. ePrint Arch. **2019**, 885 (2019). https://eprint.iacr.org/2019/885

34. Guillevic, A., Vergnaud, D.: Genus 2 hyperelliptic curve families with explicit Jacobian order evaluation and pairing-friendly constructions. In: Abdalla, M., Lange, T. (eds.) Pairing-Based Cryptography - Pairing 2012 - 5th International Conference, Cologne, Germany, May 16-18, 2012, Revised Selected Papers. Lecture Notes in Computer Science, vol. 7708, pp. 234–253. Springer (2012). https://doi.org/10.1007/978-3-642-36334-4_16

35. Hayashida, D., Hayasaka, K., Teruya, T.: Efficient final exponentiation via cyclotomic structure for pairings over families of elliptic curves. IACR Cryptol. ePrint Arch. p. 875 (2020). https://eprint.iacr.org/2020/875

36. Ishii, M.: Pairings on hyperelliptic curves with considering recent progress on the NFS algorithms. In: Takagi, T., Wakayama, M., Tanaka, K., Kunihiro, N., Kimoto, K., Duong, D.H. (eds.) Mathematical Modelling for Next-Generation Cryptography: CREST Crypto-Math Project, pp. 81–96. Mathematics for Industry, Springer Singapore (2017). https://doi.org/10.1007/978-981-10-5065-7_5

37. Ishii, M., Inomata, A., Fujikawa, K.: A Construction of a twisted ate pairing on a family of Kawazoe-Takahashi curves at 192-bit security level and its cost estimate. In: Camp, O., Furnell, S., Mori, P. (eds.) Proceedings of the 2nd International Conference on Information Systems Security and Privacy, ICISSP 2016, Rome, Italy, February 19-21, 2016, pp. 432–439. SciTePress (2016). https://doi.org/10.5220/0005742304320439

38. Joux, A.: A one round protocol for tripartite Diffie-Hellman. J. Cryptology **17**(4), 263–276 (2004). https://doi.org/10.1007/s00145-004-0312-y

39. Kachisa, E.J.: Generating more Kawazoe-Takahashi genus 2 pairing-friendly hyperelliptic curves. In: Joye, M., Miyaji, A., Otsuka, A. (eds.) Pairing-Based Cryptography - Pairing 2010 - 4th International Conference, Yamanaka Hot Spring, Japan, December 2010. Proceedings. Lecture Notes in Computer Science, vol. 6487, pp. 312–326. Springer (2010). https://doi.org/10.1007/978-3-642-17455-1_20

40. Kawazoe, M., Takahashi, T.: Pairing-friendly hyperelliptic curves with ordinary Jacobians of type $y^2 = x^5 + ax$. In: Galbraith, S.D., Paterson, K.G. (eds.) Pairing-Based Cryptography - Pairing 2008, Second International Conference, Egham, UK, September 1-3, 2008. Proceedings. Lecture Notes in Computer Science, vol. 5209, pp. 164–177. Springer (2008). https://doi.org/10.1007/978-3-540-85538-5_12

41. Kim, T., Barbulescu, R.: Extended tower number field sieve: a new complexity for the medium prime case. In: Robshaw, M., Katz, J. (eds.) Advances in Cryptology - CRYPTO 2016 - 36th Annual International Cryptology Conference, Santa Barbara, CA, USA, August 14-18, 2016, Proceedings, Part I. Lecture Notes in Computer Science, vol. 9814, pp. 543–571. Springer (2016). https://doi.org/10.1007/978-3-662-53018-4_20

42. Lauter, K.E., Shang, N.: Generating pairing-friendly parameters for the CM construction of genus 2 curves over prime fields. Des. Codes Cryptogr. **67**(3), 341–355 (2013). https://doi.org/10.1007/s10623-012-9611-8

43. Menezes, A., Okamoto, T., Vanstone, S.A.: Reducing elliptic curve logarithms to logarithms in a finite field. IEEE Trans. Inf. Theory **39**(5), 1639–1646 (1993). https://doi.org/10.1109/18.259647

44. Milne, J.S.: Abelian varieties. In: Cornell, G., Silverman, J.H. (eds.) Arithmetic Geometry, pp. 103–150. Springer, New York, NY (1986). https://doi.org/10.1007/978-1-4613-8655-1_5

310   M. P. Arenas et al.

45. Oort, F.: Abelian varieties over finite fields. Nato Secur. Sci. Ser. D Inf. Commun. Secur. **16**, 123 (2008)
46. Zhang, F.: Twisted ate pairing on hyperelliptic curves and applications. Sci. China Inf. Sci. **53**(8), 1528–1538 (2010)
47. Zhao, C., Zhang, F., Huang, J.: A note on the ate pairing. Int. J. Inf. Sec. **7**(6), 379–382 (2008). https://doi.org/10.1007/s10207-008-0054-1

Same Values Analysis Attack
on Weierstrass Binary Elliptic Curves

Aubain Jose Mayeukeu[1]([✉])[ID] and Emmanuel Fouotsa[2][ID]

[1] Departement of Mathematics and Computer Science, The University of Dschang,
P.O Box 67, Dschang, Cameroon
mayeukeuaubainjose@gmail.com
[2] Center for Cybersecurity and Mathematical Cryptology, The University
of Bamenda, P.O.Box 39, Bambili, Cameroon
fouotsa.emmanuel@uniba.cm

Abstract. Public key Crystosystems based on Elliptic Curves are increasingly recommended, due to their small key size. However, they are vulnerable to a type of attack called Side Channel Attack (**SCA**). A Side Channel Attack on Elliptic Curve Cryptography (**ECC**) is an attack which exploits information like power consumption, current consumption and tries to obtain the secret key. Among Side Channel Attacks on **ECC**, we have the Same Values Analysis (**SVA**) which exploits the same intermediate values when adding or doubling points and use internal collision to recover the secret key. In this paper we study **SVA** on elliptic curves defined over binary fields. We study same-values points on Standards for Efficient Cryptography Group (**SECG**) recommended curves and the National Institute of Standard Technology (**NIST**) recommended curves with the computer algebra software Sagemath.

Keywords: Elliptic Curve Cryptography · Side Channel Attack · Same Values Power Analysis

1 Introduction

V. Miller [11] and N. Koblitz [8] introduced Elliptic Curve Cryptography. Several Side Channel Attacks have been defined on Elliptic Curve Cryptosystems such as Simple Power Analysis (SPA) [9]. This attack is based on the fact that the power consumption produced by a device implementing a scalar multiplication algorithm is different depending on whether point addition or point doubling is executed. **ECC** is vulnerable to SPA if one uses the Binary Method for scalar multiplication. To resist SPA it is recommended to use the Double-And-Add-Always Method or the Montgomery Method. However, even using these different methods for scalar multiplication, ECC is vulnerable to a more rigorous Side

---

This work was done when the first author visited the University of Bamenda Center for Cybersecurity and Mathematical Cryptology funded by the ARES Belgium Project.

S. Vaudenay and C. Petit (Eds.): AFRICACRYPT 2024, LNCS 14861, pp. 311–326, 2024.
https://doi.org/10.1007/978-3-031-64381-1_14

Channel Attack called Differential Power Analysis (DPA) [9]. Effective counter-measures of DPA are points randomization [3], curve randomization [7].

L. Goubin was interested to circumvent randomization and noticed that points with zero coordinates are not randomized, which motivated him to mount a DPA type attack based on these points. This attack is the Refined Power Analysis (RPA) [5]. N. Smart [14] analyzed the refined analysis attack of Gouvin and concluded that isogeny defence is an efficient countermeasure of RPA. Supposing that the base point for scalar multiplication is the point P on an elliptic curve E. Isogeny defence consists of finding an elliptic curve E_0 such that there is an isogeny $\phi : E \mapsto E_0$, and E_0 does not contain zero coordinate points. The image of the base point is the point $\phi(P)$. Now the new base point is the point $\phi(P)$ and the scalar multiplication is carried out this time rather on the elliptic curve E_0 and the resulting point is returned to the initial curve E through the dual isogeny of ϕ. The absence of points with zero coordinates on an elliptic curve does not make it immune to Side Channel Attack. Akishita and T.Takagi [1] have proposed an extension of the RPA which exploits the zero value register during scalar multiplication and recovers the secret key bit by bit. This attack is called Zero Value Point (ZVP) attack. Akishita and T.Takagi modified Smart's algorithm [14] and proposed isogeny defence as an effective countermeasure of ZVP on Standards for Efficient Cryptography Group (SECG) recommended curves. T. Izu and T. Takagi [6] proposed Exceptional Procedure Attack (EPA), which is a Side Channel Attack based on the fact that during the scalar multiplication, the addition or doubling of points is not done in affine coordinates, the conversion in affine coordinates will produce an error when the quantity for which the division occurs will be zero. V. Sedlacek et al. [13] proved that the RPA, ZVP attack EPA are the variants of the same attack [13]. C. Crepau and R. Kazmi have made an analysis of ZVP attack on binary elliptic curves [4]. They studied conditions of existence of zero value points (ZVP) on binary curves and verified with sagemath the presence of points that satisfied these conditions on National Institute of Standard Technology (NIST) recommended curves and SECG recommended curves and proved that some of these curves are ZVP resistant. They also investigated isogeny defence against ZVP attack on elliptic curves defined over binary fields. Cedric Murdica et al. proposed the Same Values Analysis (SVA) attack [12] on Weierstrass elliptic curves over finite fields of characteristic p such that $p > 3$. The SVA attack is an internal collision attack that exploits the same input during the same field operation (and identical side channel traces) during the implementation of scalar multiplication and try to recover the secret key. Arithmetic of elliptic curve over binary fields can be implemented more efficiently on computer systems.

In this work, we study conditions of the existence of same-values points for addition and doubling over binary Weierstrass elliptic curves. Our results verified with the computer algebra software sagemath show that all SECG and NIST standard curve are vulnerable to SVA attack. Arithmetic of elliptic curve over binary fields can be implemented more efficiently on computer systems. Elliptic curve over binary fields are often used in application where computational efficiency is crusial such as mobile devices, smart cards and other embedded systems. Standards like **NIST, SECG** include elliptic curves over binary fields among the recommended choices for cryptographic implementations.

This paper is organized as follows: in Sect. 2 we recall some properties of elliptic curves over binary fields, particularly elliptic curve scalar multiplication. In Sect. 3 we study Same Values Analysis attack on an elliptic curve defined over binary fields. In Sect. 4 we study same value points on SECG and NIST standardized curves with the computer algebra software Sagemath.

2   Ellipic Curves, Scalar Multiplication and Side Channel Attack

In this section, we recall some properties of elliptic curves defined over binary fields. In particular, we present the scalar multiplication algorithm and Side Channel Attack.

2.1   Elliptic Curves

Let $K = \mathbb{F}_p$ be a finite field, where p is prime. The Weierstrass form of an elliptic curve over K is described as:

$$E : y^2 + a_1 xy + a_3 y = x^3 + a_2 x^2 + a_4 x + a_6, \quad (a_i \in K)$$

, together with a rationnal point $\mathcal{O}$ called the point at infinity.

If $char(K) = 2$, the equation can be transformed to:

$$E : y^2 + xy = x^3 + Ax^2 + B, \quad (A, B \in K).$$

The set of points $P = (x, y)$ satisfying E, together with the point at infinity $\mathcal{O}$, is denoted by $E(K)$, which forms an abelian group, with $\mathcal{O}$ as the neutral element. In this case the opposite of a point $P = (x, y)$ is given by $-P = (x, x + y)$. For the addition of points $P_1 = (x_1, y_1)$ and $P_2 = (x_2, y_2)$, the sum $P_3 = P_1 + P_2 = (x_3, y_3)$ is computed as follows:

– If $P_1 \neq \pm P_2$ then

$$x_3 = \left(\frac{y_1 + y_2}{x_1 + x_2} \right)^2 + \left(\frac{y_1 + y_2}{x_1 + x_2} \right) + x_1 + x_2 + A,$$

and

$$y_3 = \left(\frac{y_1 + y_2}{x_1 + x_2} \right)^3 + \left(\frac{y_1 + y_2}{x_1 + x_2} \right)(x_2 + A + 1) + x_1 + x_2 + A + y_1.$$

– If $P_1 = P_2$ then

$$x_3 = \left(\frac{x_1 + y_1}{x_1}\right)^2 + \left(\frac{x_1 + y_1}{x_1}\right) + A,$$

and

$$y_3 = \left(\frac{x_1 + y_1}{x_1}\right)^3 + \left(\frac{x_1 + y_1}{x_1}\right)(x_1 + A + 1) + A + y_1.$$

The above addition formulae contain finite field inversions which are costly and can be avoided by changing the affine coordinates to other systems such as projective coordinates.

2.2 Elliptic Curve in Projective Coordinates over Binary Fields

The most efficient method for doubling of points and addition of points over binary fields was proposed in [10] by J. Lopez and R. Dahab. For their formula, they pass from affine coordinates to projective coordinates by perfoming the transformation $(x, y) \mapsto (X, Y, Z)$, with $x = X/Z$ and $y = Y/Z^2$ [4], the equation of the elliptic curve over these projective coordinates becomes:

$$Y^2 Z + a_1 XYZ + a_3 Y Z^2 = X^3 + a_2 X^2 Z + a_4 X Z^2 + a_6 Z^3,$$

and $\mathcal{O} = (0, \theta, 0)$ for some $\theta \in K^*$. In this work, we denote the addition of points on projective coordinates over binary fields by $\mathbf{add}^{\mathcal{P}}(P_1; P_2)$, and the doubling of point in projective coordinates over binary fields by $\mathbf{dbl}^{\mathcal{P}}(P_1)$. Let $P_1 = (X_1 : Y_1 : Z_1)$, $P_2 = (X_2 : Y_2 : Z_2)$ be two points over binary elliptic curve, and $P_1 + P_2 = P_3 = (X_3 : Y_3 : Z_3)$.
P_3 is computed as follows:

– If $P_1 \neq \pm P_2$ then $P_3 = \mathbf{add}^{\mathcal{P}}(P_1, P_2)$
with $X_3 = C^2 + H + G$, $Y_3 = HI + Z_3 J$, $Z_3 = F^2$, where:
$A_0 = Y_2 Z_1^2, A_1 = Y_1 Z_2^2, B_0 = X_2 Z_1, B_1 = X_1 Z_2, C = A_0 + A_1, D = B_0 + B_1,$
$E = Z_1 Z_2, F = DE, G = D^2(F + AE^2), H = CF, I = D^2 B_0 E + X_3,$
$J = D^2 A_0 + X_3.$
– If $P_1 = P_2$ then $P_3 = \mathbf{dbl}^{\mathcal{P}}(P_1)$
$Z_3 = Z_1^2 X_1^2, X_3 = X_1^4 + B Z_1^4, Y_3 = B Z_1^4 Z_3 + X.(A Z_3 + Y_1^2 + B Z_1^4).$

In both cases, the algorithms for the computation of P_3 are given in $\mathbf{add}^{\mathcal{P}}(P_1, P_2)$ and $\mathbf{dbl}^{\mathcal{P}}(P_1)$ [4]. The last columns of which algorithm corresponding to operation of the degree of Z_1 and Z_2. For example at the line 7 of the algorithm $\mathbf{dbl}^{\mathcal{P}}(P_1)$, A_5 is obtain by multiply X_1^2 and Z_1^2, $X_1^2 = x_1^2 Z_1^2$ that has 2 as the degree of Z_1, then $A_5 = X_1^2 Z_1^2 = x_1^2 Z_1^4$ that has 4 as the degree of Z_1. At the line 9 of algorithm $\mathbf{add}^{\mathcal{P}}(P_1, P_2)$, C is computed by adding $Y_2 Z_1^2$ and $Y_1 Z_2^2 =$, $Y_2 Z_1^2 = y_2 Z_1^2 Z_2^2$ and $Y_1 Z_2^2 = y_1 Z_1^2 Z_2^2$ the two ones have 2 as the degree of Z_1 and 2 as the degree of Z_2., then $C = Y_2 Z_1^2 + Y_1 Z_2^2 = (y_1 + y_2) Z_1^2 Z_2^2$. The most used coordinate systems are projective and Jacobian coordinates. C. Murdica et al. [12] used the implementation of addition and doubling in Jacobian coordinates for their attack [12]. In our work we agree to use projective coordinates on elliptic curves over binary fields. In projective coordinates let $P_1 = (Z_1 x_1 : Z_1^2 y_1 : Z_1)$ for some $Z_1 \in \mathbb{F}_{2^m}$. Now we recall different implementations of $\mathbf{add}^{\mathcal{P}}(P_1; P_2)$ point addition on Projective coordinates over binary fields and $\mathbf{dbl}^{\mathcal{P}}(P_1)$ point doubling on Projective coordinates over binary fields [4].

Algorithm:$\mathbf{dbl}^{\mathcal{P}}$ over Binary Fields

Input: $(P_1 \neq \mathcal{O}, c = B^{2^{m-1}})$

Output: $P_3 = (X_3, Y_3, Z_3) = 2P_1$

	Operation	Intermediate Values Computed	$deg(Z_1)$
1	$T_1 \leftarrow X_1, T_2 \leftarrow Y_1,$		
	$T_3 \leftarrow Z_1$		
2	$T_4 \leftarrow c$		
3	$T_3 \leftarrow T_3 \times T_3:$	$\{= Z_1^2 = A_1\}$	$(2 \leftarrow 1 \times 1)$
4	$T_4 \leftarrow T_3 \times T_4:$	$\{= c Z_1^2 = A_2\}$	$(2 \leftarrow 0 \times 2)\}$
5	$T_4 \leftarrow T_4 \times T_4:$	$\{= B Z_1^4 = A_4\}$	$(4 \leftarrow 2 \times 2)\}$
6	$T_1 \leftarrow T_1 \times T_1:$	$\{= X_1^2 = A_3\}$	$\{2 \leftarrow 1 \times 1)\}$
7	$T_3 \leftarrow T_1 \times T_3:$	$\{= X_1^2 Z_1^2 = Z_2 = A_5\}$	$(4 \leftarrow 2 \times 2)$
8	$T_1 \leftarrow T_1 \times T_1:$	$\{= X_1^4 = A_6\}$	$(4 \leftarrow 2 \times 2)$
9	$T_1 \leftarrow T_1 + T_4:$	$\{= X_1^4 + B Z_1^4 = X_2 = A_7\}$	$(4 \leftarrow 4 + 4)$
10	$T_2 \leftarrow T_2 \times T_2:$	$\{= Y_1^2 = A_8\}$	$(4 \leftarrow 2 \times 2)$
11	If $A \neq 0$		
	$T_5 \leftarrow A$		
12	$T_5 \leftarrow T_3 \times T_5$	$\{= A Z_2 = A_9\}$	$(4 \leftarrow 4 + 4)$
13	$T_2 \leftarrow T_5 + T_2$	$\{= A Z_2 + Y_1^2 = A_{10}\}$	$(4 \leftarrow 4 + 4)$
14	$T_2 \leftarrow T_2 + T_4:$	$\{= A Z_2 + Y_1^2 + B Z_1^4 = A_{11}\}$	$(4 \leftarrow 4 + 4)$
		or $\{= Y_1^2 + B Z_1^4 = A_{11}\}$	$(4 \leftarrow 4 + 4)$
15	$T_2 \leftarrow T_1 \times T_2:$	$\{= X_2(A Z_2 + Y_1^2 + B Z_1^4) = A_{12}\}$	$(8 \leftarrow 4 \times 4)$
		or $\{= X_2(Y_1^2 + B Z_1^4) = A_{12}\}$	$(8 \leftarrow 4 \times 4)$
16	$T_4 \leftarrow T_3 \times T_4:$	$\{= B Z_2 Z_1^4 = A_{13}\}$	$(8 \leftarrow 4 \times 4)$
17	$T_2 \leftarrow T_2 + T_4:$	$\{= B Z_2 Z_1^4 + X_2$	
		$(A Z_2 + Y_1^2 + B Z_1^4) = Y_2 = A_{14}\}$	$(8 \leftarrow 8 + 8)$
		or $\{= B Z_2 Z_1^4 + X_2$	
		$(Y_1^2 + B Z_1^4) = Y_2 = A_{14}\}$	$(8 \leftarrow 8 + 8)$
18	$X_2 \leftarrow T_1$		
19	$Y_2 \leftarrow T_2$		
20	$Z_2 \leftarrow T_3$		

Algorithm: add^P over Binary Field
Input: $(P_1 \neq \mathcal{O}, P_2 \neq \mathcal{O}, A, B)$
Output: $P_3 = (X_3, Y_3, Z_3) = P_1 + P_2$

Operation	Intermediate Values	$deg(Z_1)$, $deg(Z_2)$
1 $T_1 \leftarrow X_1, T_2 \leftarrow Y_1$		
$T_3 \leftarrow Z_1$		
2 $T_4 \leftarrow X_2, T_5 \leftarrow Y_2$		
$T_6 \leftarrow Z_2$		
3 $T_7 \leftarrow T_4 \times T_3$:	$\{= X_2 Z_1 = B_0\}$	$(1_1 1_2 \leftarrow 1_1 \times 1_2)$
4 $T_1 \leftarrow T_6 \times T_1$:	$\{= X_1 Z_2 = B_1\}$	$(1_1 1_2 \leftarrow 1_1 \times 1_2)$
5 $T_3 \leftarrow T_3 \times T_6$:	$\{= Z_1 Z_2 = E\}$	$(1_1 1_2 \leftarrow 1_1 \times 1_2)$
6 $T_3 \leftarrow T_5 \times T_7$:	$\{= Y_2 Z_1^2 = A_0\}$	$(2_1 2_2 \leftarrow 2_1 \times 2_2)$
7 $T_6 \leftarrow T_6 \times T_6$:	$\{Z_2^2\}$	$(2_2 \leftarrow 1_2 \times 1_2)$
8 $T_6 \leftarrow T_2 \times T_6$:	$\{= Y_1 Z_2^2 = A_1\}$	$(2_1 2_2 \leftarrow 2_1 \times 2_2)$
9 $T_2 \leftarrow T_3 + T_6$:	$\{= Y_2 Z_1^2 + Y_1 Z_2^2 = C\}$	$(2_1 2_2 \leftarrow 2_1 2_2 + 2_1 2_2)$
10 $T_4 \leftarrow T_1 + T_7$:	$\{= X_2 Z_1 + X_1 Z_2 = D\}$	$(1_1 1_2 \leftarrow 1_1 1_2 + 1_1 1_2)$
11 $T_5 \leftarrow T_4 \times T8$:	$\{D(Z_1 Z_2) = F\}$	$(2_1 2_2 \leftarrow 1_1 1_2 \times 1_1 1_2)$
12 $T_6 \leftarrow T_5 \times T_5$:	$\{= F^2 = Z_3\}$	$(4_1 4_2 \leftarrow 2_1 2_2 \times 2_1 2_2)$
13 $T_4 \leftarrow T_4 \times T_4$:	$\{= D^2\}$	$(2_1 2_2 \leftarrow 1_1 1_2 \times 1_1 1_2)$
14 $T_9 \leftarrow T_8 \times T_8$:	$\{= E^2\}$	$(2_1 2_2 \leftarrow 1_1 1_2 \times 1_1 1_2)$
15 $T_9 \leftarrow A \times T_8$:	$\{= AE^2\}$	$(2_1 2_2 \leftarrow 0 \times 2_1 2_2)$
16 $T_9 \leftarrow T_5 + T_9$:	$\{= AE^2 + F\}$	$(2_1 2_2 \leftarrow 2_1 2_2 + 2_1 2_2)$
17 $T_9 \leftarrow T_4 \times T_9$:	$\{= D^2(AE^2 + F) = G\}$	$(4_1 4_2 \leftarrow 2_1 2_2 \times 2_1 2_2)$
18 $T_1 \leftarrow T_2 \times\ T_2$:	$\{(Y_2 Z_1)^2 + (Y_1 Z_2)^2 = C^2\}$	$(4_1 4_2 \leftarrow 2_1 2_2 \times 2_1 2_2)$
19 $T_2 \leftarrow T_2 \times T_5$:	$\{CF = H\}$	$(4_1 4_2 \leftarrow 2_1 2_2 \times 2_1 2_2)$
20 $T_1 \leftarrow T_1 + T_2$:	$\{= C^2 + H\}$	$(4_1 4_2 \leftarrow 4_1 4_2 + 4_1 4_2)$
21 $T_1 \leftarrow T_1 + T_9$:	$\{= C^2 + H + G = X_3\}$	$(4_1 4_2 \leftarrow 4_1 4_2 + 4_1 4_2)$
22 $T_5 \leftarrow T_4 \times T_7$:	$\{= D^2 B_0\}$	$(3_1 3_2 \leftarrow 2_1 2_2 \times 1_1 1_2)$
23 $T_5 \leftarrow T_5 \times T_8$:	$\{= B_0 D^2 E\}$	$(4_1 4_2 \leftarrow 3_1 3_2 \times 1_1 1_2)$
24 $T_5 \leftarrow T_5 + X_2$:	$\{= B_0 D^2 E + X_3 = I\}$	$(4_1 4_2 \leftarrow 4_1 4_2 + 4_1 4_2)$
25 $T_8 \leftarrow T_4 + T_3$:	$\{= A_0 D^2\}$	$(4_1 4_2 \leftarrow 2_1 2_2 \times 2_1 2_2)$
26 $T_8 \leftarrow T_8 + T_2$:	$\{= A_0 D^2 + X_3 = J\}$	$(4_1 4_2 \leftarrow 4_1 4_2 + 4_1 4_2)$
27 $T_8 \leftarrow T_6 \times T_8$:	$\{= Z_3 J\}$	$(8_1 8_2 \leftarrow 4_1 4_2 \times 4_1 4_2)$
28 $T_2 \leftarrow T_2 \times T_5$:	$\{= HI\}$	$(8_1 8_2 \leftarrow 4_1 4_2 \times 4_1 4_2)$
29 $T_2 \leftarrow T_2 + T_8$:	$\{= HI + Z_3 J = Y_3\}$	$(8_1 8_2 \leftarrow 8_1 8_2 + 8_1 8_2)$

Elliptic Curve Cryptosystems are vulnerable to a Side Channel Attack that exploits the same intermediate values during the addition of points or doubling of points. This attack is called Same Values Analysis.

2.3 Review of the Same Values Analysis (SVA) Attack on Elliptic Curve Defined over Fields of Odd Characteristic

In this section, we review the principle of the SVA attack on an elliptic curve defined over fields of odd characteristic. This attack is based on the presence of equal intermediate values during the addition of points or during the doubling of points. Let us now recall the very important definitions for the attack.

Definition 1. *(Same Value point for **dbl**) [12] Let E be an elliptic curve over a finite field $\mathbb{F}_p$, and an algorithm of doubling **dbl**. A point $P = (x, y)$ in E is said to be a same values point relative to **dbl** if and only if any representation of*

P shows up same values among intermediate variables during the computation of the point $2P$ using the algorithm **dbl**.

Definition 2. *(Same Values points for* **add** *) [12] Let E be an elliptic curve over a finite $\mathbb{F}_p$, and an algorithm of addition* **add**. *The points $P_1 = (x_1, y_1)$, $P_2 = (x_2, y_2)$ in E are said to be same-values points relative to* **add** *if and only if any representation of P_1 and P_2 shows up an equality of intermediate values during the computation of point $P_1 + P_2$ using the algorithm* **add**.

In this work, we note a same value point by **SVP**. The condition for a point to be a same value point for the elliptic curve doubling is denoted by **SEDn** where n is an integer, whereas the condition for a point to be a same value point for the elliptic curve addition is denoted by **SEAn** where n is an integer.

SVA is an internal collision attack in which the attacker can force some points to have collision, that is to say they produce some identical intermediate values during the addition of points or doubling of points. The collision can be observed if same field operation produces the same output (and identical side channel traces) during the implementation of doubling of points or addition of points. The collision could be detected when a field operation (multiplication, addition, doubling or squaring) is performed several times with the same inputs. If the attacker is able to recognize same values, he could obtain information about the secret key and with several iterations he would obtain the secret key. Murdica et al. [12] have proven that if $E : y^2 = x^3 + ax + b$ is an elliptic curve defined over a finite field $\mathbb{F}_p$ with $p > 3$ is a prime, the special points that can produce the collision when doubling points in Jacobian coordinates are the points $P = (x, y)$ satisfying one of the conditions **(SED2)** $x = 1$, **(SED3)** $x^2 = y$ and **(SED15)** $2y = 3x^2$. Following the same principle they also proved that special points that can produce the collision when adding points in Jacobian coordinates are the points $P_1 = (x_1, y_1)$ and $P_2 = (x_2, y_2)$ satisfying the condition **(SEA9)** $y_2 - y_1 = x_2 - x_1$.

Recall the secret key is $d = (d_{n-1}....d_1 d_0)_2$. Suppose that the attacker already knows $d_{n-1}....d_{i+1}$ of d, the attacker can get d_i as follows:
He chooses a point P_0 which satisfy one of the conditions **(SED2)**, **(SED3)** or **(SED15)**, he computes the base point $P = ((d_{n-1}....d_{i+1})_2)^{-1}\text{Mod}[\#E(K)]P_0$, where $\#E(K)$ is the cardinality of the elliptic curve. The attacker sends the base point P to the targeted chip that computes the elliptic curve scalar multiplication using the fixed scalar d. If $d_i = 0$, the point P_0 will be doubled and the collision of power consumption will appear during the elliptic curve scalar multiplication. If the collision is not detectable then $d_i = 1$. The attacker can recursively recover all bits of d.

For more details of Same Values Analysis on elliptic curve over finite fields of odd characteristic we refer to [12].

3   Same Values Analysis on Binary Elliptic Curves

In this section, we study SVA on elliptic curve defined over binary fields. For the attack developed in this section, we use the formulas for adding points and doubling points in projective coordinates of Lopez and Dahab [10], the attack works also on other types of coordinates and others curve models. The formulas for addition of points and doubling of points must be known in advance because the attack is directly linked to these formulas. Firstly, we look for points admitting at least two identical intermediate values during addition of points or during doubling of points. We will then list among these points those which admit identical values during doubling or squaring, these points will allow us to detect collision during the implementation of addition or doubling algorithms. Let's now look at same value points for doubling of points.

3.1 Special Points of Same Values During Doubling

We recall that an elliptic curve over binary fields is defined as follows:

$$E : y^2 + xy = x^3 + Ax + B, \qquad \text{where } A, B \in \mathbb{K} = \mathbb{F}_{2^m}, \text{ where } m \text{ is a positive integer.}$$

Let $P_1 = (x_1, y_1)$ be a point on the elliptic curve E, in projective coordinates $P_1 = (Z_1 x_1 : Z_1^2 y_1 : Z_1)$ for some $Z \in \mathbb{F}_{2^m}$. Let $P_3 = (X_3 : Y_3 : Z_3) = 2P_1$.

Theorem 1 summarizes all conditions that a point will verify to be same value point for doubling on elliptic curve over a binary field.

Theorem 1. *Let E be an elliptic curve defined by the equation $y^2 + xy = x^3 + Ax^2 + B$ over a binary field $K = \mathbb{F}_{2^m}$, where m is a positive integer. The point $P_1 = (x_1, y_1) \in E$ is a same values point relative to the algorithm* $dbl^P(P_1)$ *if and only if one of the following conditions given below is satisfied:*

$c = 1$	(SED1)	$x_1 = 1$	(SED2)
$x_1^2 = c$	(SED3)	$x_1^2 = B$	(SED4)
$x_1^4 = B$	(SED5)	$x_1 = 0$	(SED6)
$y_1^2 + B = 0$	(SED7)	$Ax_1^2 + B = 0$	(SED8)
$y_1^2 + Ax_1^2 = B$	(SED9)	$y_1 = 0 \text{ or } y_1^2 + Ax_1^2 = 0$	(SED10)
$x_1^4 + x_1^2 + B = 0$	(SED11)	$x_1 = y_1$	(SED12)
$A = 1$	(SED13)	$(A+1)x_1^2 + y_1^2 = 0$	(SED14)
$B = 0$	(SED15)	$(A+1)x_1^2 + y_1^2 + B = 0 \text{ or } x_1^2 + y_1^2 + B = 0$	(SED16)
$x_1^2 = y_1$	(SED17)	$x_1^2 = A$	(SED18)
$x_1^4 + Ax_1^2 + y_1^2 = 0$	(SED19)	$x_1^4 + y_1^2 + B = 0 \text{ or } x_1^4 + Ax_1^2 + y_1^2 + B = 0$	(SED20)
$x_1^4 + y_1^2 + B = 0$	(SED21)	$x_1^4 + Ax_1^2 + B = 0$	(SED22)
$A = 0$	(SED23)	$Ax_1^4 + (1 + A)B = 0$	(SED24)
$(A+1)x_1^2 + y_1^2 + B = 0 \text{ or } x_1^2 + y_1^2 + B = 0$			(SED25)
$Bx_1^4 + x_1^4 y_1^2 + By_1^2 + Bx_1^2 + B^2 = 0 \text{ or } Ax_1^6 + x_1^4 y_1^2 + Bx_1^4 + B(A+1)x_1^2 + By_1^2 + B^2 = 0$			(SED26)

Proof. Let P be a point $P_1 = (x_1, y_1)$ on an elliptic curve E: $y^2 + xy = x^3 + Ax^2 + B$ over a binary field $K = \mathbb{F}_{2^m}$, where m is a positive integer. In projective coordinates, $x_1 = X_1/Z_1$, $y_1 = Y_1/Z_1^2$, in projective coordinates $P_1 = (X_1 : Y_1 : Z_1) = (Z_1 x_1 : Z^2 y_1 : Z_1)$. We have to check equalities between terms with the same degree of Z_1, and zero values between all terms. Let S_i denote the set of values which involve a term Z_1 with a degree i. When we look at the algorithm for point doubling on elliptic curve over a binary field in projective coordinates $dbl^P(P_1)$, we have:

1. $S_2 = \{Z_1^2 = A_1, cZ_1^2 = A_2, X_1^2 = A_3\}$.

2. $S_4 = \{BZ_1^4 = A_4, X_1^2Z_1^2 = A_5, X_1^4 = A_6, X_1^4 + BZ_1^4 = A_7, Y_1^2 = A_8, AZ_2 = A_9, AZ_2 + Y_1^2 = A_{10}, (AZ_2 + Y_1^2 + BZ_1^4) = A_{11}$ or $(Y_1^2 + BZ_1^4) = A_{11}\}$.

3. $S_8 = \{(X_2(AZ_2 + Y_1^2 + BZ_1^4)) = A_{12}$ or $(X_2(Y_1^2 + BZ_1^4) = A_{12}, BZ_2Z_1^4 = A_{13}, (BZ_2Z_1^4 + X_2(AZ_2 + Y_1^2 + BZ_1^4)) = A_{14}$ or $(BZ_2Z_1^4 + X_2(Y_1^2 + BZ_1^4)) = A_{14}\}$.

Equal values can only be found in the same set. By equating the terms of each subset two by two:

- For S_2:
  $A_1 = A_2$ gives $(SED1)$, $A_1 = A_3$ gives $(SED2)$, $A_2 = A_3$ gives $(SED3)$.
- For S_4:
  $A_4 = A_5$ gives $(SED4)$, $A_4 = A_6$ gives $(SED5)$, $A_4 = A_7$ gives $(SED6)$, $A_4 = A_8$ gives $(SED7)$, $A_4 = A_9$ gives $(SED8)$, $A_4 = A_{10}$ gives $(SED9)$, $A_4 = A_{11}$ gives $(SED10)$. $A_5 = A_6$ gives $(SED2)$ and $(SED6)$, $A_5 = A_7$ gives $(SED11)$, $A_5 = A_8$ gives $(SED12)$, $A_5 = A_9$ gives $(SED6)$ and $(SED13)$, $A_5 = A_{10}$ gives $(SED14)$, $A_5 = A_{11}$ gives $(SED16)$. $A_6 = A_7$ gives $(SED15)$, $A_6 = A_8$ gives $(SED6)$ and $(SED18)$, $A_6 = A_9$ gives $(SED6)$ and $(SED18)$, $A_6 = A_{10}$ gives $(SED19)$, $A_6 = A_{11}$ gives $(SED20)$ and $(SED21)$. $A_7 = A_8$ gives $(SED21)$, $A_7 = A_9$ gives $(SED22)$, $A_7 = A_{10}$ gives $(SED20)$, $A_7 = A_{11}$ gives $(SED17)$ and $(SED19)$. $A_8 = A_9$ gives the first part of $(SED10)$, $A_8 = A_{10}$ gives $(SED6)$ and $(SED23)$. $A_8 = A_{11}$ gives $(SED8)$ and $(SED15)$. $A_9 = A_{10}$ gives the second part of $(SED10)$, $A_9 = A_{11}$ gives $(SED7)$ and $(SED9)$. $A_{10} = A_{11}$ gives $(SED15)$ and $(SED8)$.
- For S_8:
  $A_{12} = A_{13}$ gives $(SED26)$, $A_{12} = A_{14}$ gives $(SED6)$, $(SED15)$ and $(SED24)$, $A_{13} = A_{14}$ gives $(SED25)$.

Several conditions of Theorem 1 can be verified by several points of large order. This should therefore be said that the **SVA** attack is a serious attacks. However, all the conditions of Theorem 1 will not allow the attack to be mounted. It would therefore be necessary to find the preceding conditions. This will be done with more details in the next section of this document. We are now interested in the conditions that two points must satisfy to be called same-values points for addition.

3.2 Special Points of Same Values During Addition

We recall that an elliptic curve over binary fields is defined as follows:

$$E : y^2 + xy = x^3 + Ax^2 + B, \qquad \text{where } A, B \in \mathbb{K} = \mathbb{F}_{2^m}, \text{ where } m \text{ is a positive integer.}$$

Let $P_1 = (x_1, y_1)$, and $P_2 = (x_2, y_2)$ be two points on E. In projective coordinates $P_1 = (Z_1x_1 : Z_1^2y_1 : Z_1)$, $P_2 = (X_2 : Y_2 : Z_2) = (Z_2x_2 : Z_2^2y_2 : Z_2)$ where $Z_1, Z_2 \in \mathbb{F}_{2^m}$. Let $P_3 = (X_3 : Y_3 : Z_3) = P_1 + P_2$

Theorem 2 summarizes all conditions that the points will verify to be same-values points for addition on an elliptic curve over a binary field in projective coordinates.

As for Theorem 1, all the conditions of Theorem 2 will not be useful to mount the SVA attack. It will subsequently be necessary to search for those which will allow an internal collision to be obtained. For the moment let's give all the conditions that two points must satisfy to be same-values points for addition.

Theorem 2. *Let E be an elliptic curve defined by the equation $y^2 + xy = x^3 + Ax^2 + B$ over a binary field $K = \mathbb{F}_{2^m}$, where m is a positive integer. The points $P_1 = (x_1, y_1)$, $P_2 = (x_2, y_2) \in E$ are same-values points relative to the algorithm $\mathbf{add}^P(P_1; P_2)$ if and only if one of the following conditions given below is satisfied:*

$x_1 = 0$	(SEA1)	$x_2 = 0$	(SEA2)
$x_1 + x_2 = 0$	(SEA3)	$x_1 + A = 0$	(SEA4)
$x_2 = 1$	(SEA5)	$x_1 = 1$	(SEA6)
$y_2 = 0$	(SEA7)	$y_1 = 0$	(SEA8)
$y_1 + y_2 = 0$	(SEA9)	$x_2 = y_2$	(SEA10)
$A = 1$	(SEA11)	$A = 0$	(SEA12)
$x_1 + x_2 + A =$	(SEA13)	$y_2(x_1 + x_2)^2 = (y_1 + y_2)^2$	(SEA14)
$y_2 = 1$	(SEA15)	$y_1 = 1$	(SEA16)
$y_2 = A$	(SEA17)	$y_1 = A$	(SEA18)
$y_1 = x_1 + x_2 + A$	(SEA19)	$y_2 = x_1 + x_2 + A$	(SEA20)
$y_1 = x_1 + x_2$	(SEA21)	$y_2 = x_1 + x_2$	(SEA22)
$y_1 = (x_1 + x_2)^2$	(SEA23)	$y_2 = (x_1 + x_2)^2$	(SEA24)
$x_1 + x_2 = y_1 + y_2$	(SEA25)	$(x_1 + x_2)^2 = y_1 + y_2$	(SEA26)
$y_1 + y_2 = A$	(SEA27)	$y_1 + y_2 = 1$	(SEA28)
$(y_1 + y_2) = y_2(x_1 + x_2)$	(SEA29)	$(y_1 + y_2) = x_2(x_1 + x_2)$	(SE30)
$(x_1 + x_2)^2 = (x_1 + x_2) + A$	(SEA31)	$(x_1 + x_2) + A = 1$	(SEA32)
$x_1 + x_2 = 1$	(SEA33)	$(x_1 + x_2)^2 = A$	(SEA34)
$(y_1 + y_2)^2 = x_2(x_1 + x_2)^2$	(SEA35)	$y_1 + y_2 = (x_1 + x_2) + A$	(SEA36)

$(y_1 + y_2)^2 + (x_1 + x_2)^2(x_1 + x_2 + A) = 0$ *(SEA 37)*

$(y_1 + y_2)^2 = (x_1 + x_2)^2(x_1 + x_2 + A)$ *(SEA 38)*

$(y_1 + y_2)^2 + (y_1 + y_2)(x_1 + x_2) = (x_1 + x_2)^2(x_1 + x_2 + A)$ *(SEA 39)*

$(y_1 + y_2) = (x_1 + x_2)(x_1 + x_2 + A)$ (SEA40)

$(x_1 + x_2)^2 = (y_1 + y_2)^2 + (y_1 + y_2)(x_1 + x_2) + (x_1 + x_2)^2(x_1 + x_2 + A)$ (SEA41)

$x_2(x_1 + x_2)^2 + (y_1 + y_2)^2 + (x_1 + x_2)^2(x_1 + x_2 + A) = 0$ (SEA42)

$y_2(x_1 + x_2)^2 + (y_1 + y_2)^2 + (x_1 + x_2)^2(x_1 + x_2 + A) = 0$ (SEA43)

$x_2(x_1 + x_2)^2 = (y_1 + y_2)^2 + (y_1 + y_2)(x_1 + x_2)$ (SEA44)

$y_2(x_1 + x_2)^2 = (y_1 + y_2)^2 + (y_1 + y_2)(x_1 + x_2)$ (SEA45)

$(x_1 + x_2)^2 = (y_1 + y_2)^2 + (y_1 + y_2)(x_1 + x_2)$ (SEA46)

$x_2(x_1 + x_2)^2 = (y_1 + y_2)^2 + (y_1 + y_2)(x_1 + x_2) + (x_1 + x_2)^2(x_1 + x_2 + A)$ (SEA47)

$y_2(x_1 + x_2)^2 = (y_1 + y_2)^2 + (y_1 + y_2)(x_1 + x_2) + (x_1 + x_2)^2(x_1 + x_2 + A)$ (SEA48)

$x_2(x_1 + x_2)^2 = y_2(x_1 + x_2)^2 + (y_1 + y_2)^2 + (y_1 + y_2)(x_1 + x_2) + (x_1 + x_2)^2(x_1 + x_2 + A)$ (SEA49)

$(x_1 + x_2)^2 = y_2(x_1 + x_2)^2 + (y_1 + y_2)^2 + (y_1 + y_2)(x_1 + x_2) + (x_1 + x_2)^2(x_1 + x_2 + A)$ (SEA50)

$(x_1 + x_2)^2 = x_2(x_1 + x_2)^2 + (y_1 + y_2)^2 + (y_1 + y_2)(x_1 + x_2) + (x_1 + x_2)^2(x_1 + x_2 + A)$ (SEA51)

$(y_1 + y_2)[x_2(x_1 + x_2)^2 + (y_1 + y_2)^2 + (y_1 + y_2)(x_1 + x_2) + (x_1 + x_2)^2(x_1 + x_2 + A)]$ (SEA52)

Proof. Let E be an elliptic curve defined by the equation $y^2 + xy = x^3 + Ax^2 + B$ over a binary field $K = \mathbb{F}_{2^m}$, where m is a positive integer. Given points $P_1 = (x_1, y_1)$, $P_2 = (x_2, y_2) \in E$, in projective coordinates $x_1 = X_1/Z_1$, $y_1 = Y_1/Z_1^2$, $x_2 = X_2/Z_2$, $y_2 = Y_2/Z_2^2$, in projective coordinates $P_1 = (X_1 : Y_1 : Z_1) = (Z_1 x_1 : Z_1^2 y_1 : Z_1)$, $P_2 = (X_2 : Y_2 : Z_2) = (Z_2 x_2 : Z_2^2 y_2 : Z_2)$ we have to check equalities between terms with the same degree of Z_1 and Z_2, and zero values between all terms. Let $S_{i,j}$ denote the set of values which involve a term Z_1 with a degree i and Z_2 with a degree j. When we look at the algorithm for point adding in binary curve, we have:

1. $S_{1,1} = \{X_2 Z_1 = S_1, X_1 Z_2 = S_2, Z_1 Z_2 = S_3, X_2 Z_1 + X_1 Z_2 = S_4\}$.
2. $S_{2,2} = \{Y_2 Z_1^2 = S_5, Y_1 Z_2^2 = S_6, Y_2 Z_1^2 + Y_1 Z_2^2 = S_7, F = S_8, D^2 = S_9, E^2 = S_{10}, AE^2 = S_{11}, AE^2 + F = S_{12}\}$.
3. $S_{3,3} = \{D^2 B_0\}$.
4. $S_{4,4} = \{F^2 = S_{13}, G = S_{14}, C^2 = S_{15}, CF = S_{16}, C^2 + H = S_{17}, C^2 + H + G = S_{18}, B_0 D^2 E = S_{19}, B_0 D^2 E + X_3 = S_{20}, A_0 D^2 = S_{21}, A_0 D^2 + X_3 = S_{22}\}$.
5. $S_{8,8} = \{Z_3 J = S_{23}, IH = S_{24}, IH + Z_3 J = S_{25}\}$.

Equal values can only be found in the same set. By equaling the terms of each subset two by two:

- For the set $S_{1,1}$:
  $S_1 = S_2$ gives $(SEA3)$, $S_1 = S_3$ gives $(SEA5)$, $S_1 = S_4$ gives $(SEA1)$, $S_2 = S_3$ gives $(SEA6)$, $S_2 = S_4$ gives $(SEA2)$, $S_3 = S_4$ gives $(SEA33)$.
- For the set $S2, 2$:
  $S_5 = S_6$ gives $(SEA9)$, $S_5 = S_7$ gives $(SEA8)$, $S_5 = S_8$ gives $(SEA22)$, $S_5 = S_9$ gives $(SEA24)$, $S_5 = S_{10}$ gives $(SEA15)$, $S_5 = S_{11}$ gives $(SEA17)$, $S_5 = S_{12}$ gives $(SEA20)$. $S_6 = S_7$ gives $(SEA7)$, $S_6 = S_8$ gives $(SEA21)$, $S_6 = S_9$ gives $(SEA23)$, $S_6 = S_{10}$ gives $(SEA16)$, $S_6 = S_{11}$ gives $(SEA18)$, $S_6 = S_{12}$ gives $(SEA19)$. $S_7 = S_8$ gives $(SEA25)$, $S_7 = S_9$ gives $(SEA26)$, $S_7 = S_{10}$ gives $(SEA28)$, $S_7 = S_{11}$ gives $(SEA27)$, $S_7 = S_{12}$ gives $(SEA36)$. $S_8 = S_9$ gives $(SEA3)$ and $(SEA33)$, $S_8 = S_{10}$ gives $(SEA33)$, $S_8 = S_{11}$ gives $(SEA13)$, $S_8 = S_{12}$ gives $(SEA12)$. $S_9 = S_{10}$ gives $(SEA33)$, $S_9 = S_{11}$ gives $(SEA34)$, $S_9 = S_{12}$ gives $(SEA31)$. $S_{10} = S_{11}$ gives $(SEA11)$, $S_{10} = S_{12}$ gives $(SEA32)$. $S_{11} = S_{12}$ gives $(SEA3)$.
- For the set $S_{4,4}$:
  $S_{13} = S_{14}$ gives $(SEA3)$ and $(SEA32)$, $S_{13} = S_{15}$ gives $(SEA23)$, $S_{13} = S_{16}$ gives $(SEA3)$ and $(SEA23)$, $S_{13} = S_{17}$ gives $(SEA47)$, $S_{13} = S_{18}$ gives $(SEA41)$, $S_{13} = S_{19}$ gives $(SEA3)$ and $(SEA5)$, $S_{13} = S_{20}$ gives $(SEA51)$, $S_{13} = S_{21}$ gives $(SEA3)$ and $(SEA15)$, $S_{13} = S_{22}$ gives $(SEA50)$. $S_{14} = S_{15}$ gives $(SEA38)$, $S_{14} = S_{16}$ gives $(SEA3)$ and $(SEA40)$, $S_{14} = S_{17}$ gives $(SEA39)$, $S_{14} = S_{18}$ gives $(SEA7)$ and $(SEA25)$, $S_{14} = S_{19}$ gives $(SEA3)$ and $(SEA4)$, $S_{14} = S_{20}$ gives $(SEA44)$, $S_{14} = S_{21}$ gives $(SEA3)$ and $(SEA20)$, $S_{14} = S_{22}$ gives $(SEA45)$. $S_{15} = S_{16}$ gives $(SEA9)$ and $(SEA25)$, $S_{15} = S_{17}$ gives $(SEA3)$ and $(SEA9)$, $S_{15} = S_{18}$ gives $(SEA3)$ and $(SEA40)$, $S_{15} = S_{19}$ gives $(SEA35)$, $S_{15} = S_{20}$ gives $(SEA45)$, $S_{15} = S_{21}$ gives $(SEA14)$, $S_{15} = S_{22}$ gives $(SEA43)$. $S_{16} = S_{17}$ gives $(SEA9)$, $S_{16} = S_{18}$ gives $(SEA37)$, $S_{16} = S_{19}$ gives $(SEA3)$ and $(SEA30)$, $S_{16} = S_{20}$ gives $(SEA42)$, $S_{16} = S_{21}$ gives $(SEA3)$ and $(SEA29)$, $S_{16} = S_{22}$ gives $(SEA43)$. $S_{17} = S_{18}$ gives $(SEA3)$ and $(SEA32)$, $S_{17} = S_{19}$ gives $(SEA44)$, $S_{17} = S_{20}$ gives $(SEA3)$ and $(SEA4)$, $S_{17} = S_{21}$ gives $(SEA45)$, $S_{17} = S_{22}$ gives $(SEA20)$. $S_{18} = S_{19}$ gives $(SEA47)$, $S_{18} = S_{20}$ gives $(SEA2)$ and $(SEA3)$, $S_{18} = S_{21}$ gives $(SEA48)$, $S_{18} = S_{22}$ gives $(SEA3)$ and $(SEA7)$.
  $S_{19} = S_{20}$ gives $(SEA39)$, $S_{19} = S_{21}$ gives $(SEA3)$ and $(SEA10)$ $S_{19} = S_{22}$ gives $(SEA49)$. $S_{20} = S_{21}$ gives $(SEA49)$ $S_{19} = S_{22}$ gives $(SEA3)$ and $(SEA10)$.

- For the set $S8, 8$:
  $S_{23} = S_{24}$ gives $(SEA52)$, $S_{23} = S_{25}$ gives $(SEA3)$, $(SEA9)$ and $(SEA47)$.
  $S_{24} = S_{25}$ gives $(SEA3)$ and $(SEA48)$.

3.3   Collision Power Analysis on Binary ECC Using Same-Values Points

The Theorems 1 and 2 allowed us to determine same-values points for addition of points on the one hand and doubling of points of other parts. These points are recognized by the existence of at least two equal intermediate values during addition of points or doubling of points. These same values are recovered without taking into account the operation field (addition, doubling, multiplication, square) which made it possible to obtain them. The collision will therefore be detected only if we have performed the same operation field several times. Among all conditions of Theorems 1 and 2, the conditions below give the result needed:

- **(SED2):** $x_1 = 1$, this condition implies that the power consumption during the computation of the **square** at the lines 3 and 6 of $\mathbf{dbl}^{\mathcal{P}}$ are the same.
- **(SED5):** $x_1^4 = B$, this condition implies that the power consumption during the computation of the **square** at the lines 5 and 8 of $\mathbf{dbl}^{\mathcal{P}}$ are the same.
- **(SED7):** $y_1^2 = B$, this condition implies that the power consumption during the computation of the **square** at the lines 5 and 10 of $\mathbf{dbl}^{\mathcal{P}}$ are the same.
- **(SED17):** $x_1^2 = y_1$, this condition implies that the power consumption during the computation of the **square** at the lines 8 and 10 of $\mathbf{dbl}^{\mathcal{P}}$ are the same.
- **(SEA25):** $x_1 + x_2 = y_1 + y_2$, this condition implies that the power consumption during the computation of the **square** at the lines 12 and 18 of $\mathbf{add}^{\mathcal{P}}$ are the same.
- **(SEA33):** $x_1 + x_2 = 1$, this condition implies that the power consumption during the computation of the **square** at the lines 13 and 14 of $\mathbf{add}^{\mathcal{P}}$ are the same.

3.4   Some Countermeasures of Same Values Analysis

About some efficient countermeasures against the **SVA** attack, we can speak about: Scalar Randomisation [3], Random Scalar Split [2], Isogeny Defense [1,14], Point Blinding [3].

Scalar Randomisation consists of replacing the secret scalar d when computing $d \times P$ by $d' = d + [r \# E(K)]$, where r is a random number. $[r \# E(K)] \times P = \mathcal{O}$ then $d' \times P = d \times P + [r \# E(K)] \times P = d \times P$.

Random Scalar Split is effective against **SVA**. That consists of precomputing $d_1 \times P$ and $d_2 \times P$ where $d = d_1 + d_2$, then $d \times P$ is computed as $d \times P = d_1 \times P + d_2 \times P$.

Point Blinding consists of selecting a random point R and precomputed $R \times P$, replacing the computation of $d \times P$ by that of $d \times (P + R)$, the value $R \times P$ is subtracted at the end of the computation.

Isogeny Defense: Isogeny defence against **SVA** attack consists of finding an elliptic curve E_0 such that there is an isogeny $\phi : E \mapsto E_0$, and E_0 does not contain same value points. The image of the base point is the point $\phi(P)$. Now the new base point is the point $\phi(P)$ and the scalar multiplication is carried out this time rather on the elliptic curve E_0 and the resulting point is returned to the initial curve E through the dual isogeny of ϕ.

Random Isomorphism Curve [7] against **SVA** attack consists of finding an elliptic curve E' such that there is an isomorphism $\psi : E \mapsto E'$, and E' does not contain same value points.

4 Same Values Analysis for Doubling on Standard Curve on Binary Fields

Finding special points to **SVA** attack is done in a similar way to finding special points for the **ZVP** attack. Like [1,4,12], we will only concentrate on finding special points for doubling algorithm.

- Special points which satisfy **(SED2)**: $x_1 = 1$ are points for which the x coordinate is a root of the polynomial $P(x) = x - 1$, we can find the roots of this polynomial on a binary field $\mathbb{F}_{2^m}$, where m is a positive integer and finding an intersection with the elliptic curve.
- Special points which satisfy **(SED5)**: $x_1^4 = B$ are points for which the x coordinate is a root of the polynomial $Q(x) = x^4 - B$, we can find the roots of this polynomial on a binary field $\mathbb{F}_{2^m}$ and finding an intersection with the elliptic curve.
- Special points which satisfy **(SED7)**: $y_1^2 = B$ are points for which the x coordinate is a root of the polynomial $L(x) = x^3 + Ax^2 - B^{2^{m-1}}x$, we can find the roots of this polynomial on a binary field $\mathbb{F}_{2^m}$, where m is a positive integer and finding an intersection with the elliptic curve.
- Special points which satisfy **(SED17)**: $x_1^2 = y_1$ are points for which the x coordinate is a root of the polynomials $M = x^4 - Ax^2 - B$, we can find the roots of this polynomial on a binary field $\mathbb{F}_{2^m}$, where m is a positive integer and finding an intersection with the elliptic curve.

To find the roots of these different polynomials as well as the intersecting points with the different elliptic curves we used sagemath and obtain the result we need.

For example the NIST recommended curve $K - 283$ of order n on a binary field $\mathbb{F}_{2^m}$ with:

$n = 0 \times 1fffffffffffffffffffffffffffffffffffffffe9ae2ed07577265dff7$ $f94451e061e163c61$ in hexadecimal

$A = 0 \times 00000000000000000000000000000000000000000000000000000000000000000000000000$,

$B = 0 \times 0000000000000000000000000000000000000000000000000000000000000000000000000001$

$m = 283$

- Points of the curve $K - 283$ with $P(x) = x - 1$ are $S_1 = (1 : 0 : 1)$ a point of order 4 and $S_2 = (1 : 1 : 1)$ a point of Order 4.
- Points of the curve with $Q(x) = x^4 - B$ are also $S_1 = (1 : 0 : 1)$ a point of order 4 $S_2 = (1 : 1 : 1)$ a point of order 4.
- Points of the curve with $M(x) = x^4 - Ax^2 - B$: $S_1 = (1 : 0 : 1)$ a point of order 4 $S_2 = (1 : 1 : 1)$ a point of order 4.
- Points of the curve with $L(x) = x^3 + Ax^2 - xB^{2m-1}$ $S_3 = (0 : 1 : 1)$ a point of order 2, $S_2 = (1 : 1 : 1)$ a point of order 4.

Table 1. SECG curves over $\mathbb{F}_{2^m}$ and **SVA** points from **dbl** - $\mathbb{F}_{2^m}$, where m is a positive integer.

Name of Curve	$x = 1$	$x^4 = B$	$y^2 = B$	$x^2 = y$	Curve Order	Execution Time
sect113r1	L	N	L, S	L	$2 \times n$	0.1656479835510254
sect113r2	L	N	L, S	N	$2 \times n$	0.11415243148803711
sect131r1	L	S	L, S	N	$2 \times n$	0.27272844314575195
sect131r2	N	S	S	N	$2 \times n$	0.09245753288269043
sect163k1	N	N	S	N	$4 \times n$	0.06290864944458008
sect163r1	N	N	S	L	$2 \times n$	0.20116949081420898
sect163r2	N	N	L, S	N	$2 \times n$	0.1479189395904541
sect193r1	L	S	L, S	N	$2 \times n$	0.4444913864135742
sect193r2	L	N	L, S	N	$2 \times n$	0.380489577838135
sect233k1	S	S	S	S	$4 \times n$	0.23964238166809082
sect233r1	L	N	S	L	$2 \times n$	1.6709847450256348
sect239k1	S	S	S	S	$4 \times n$	0.22464609146118164
sect283k1	S	S	S	S	$4 \times n$	0.1726086139678955
sect283r1	L	N	L	L	$2 \times n$	1.0795626640319824
sect409r1	N	N	S	N	$2 \times n$	0.3824753761291508
sect409k1	S	S	S	S	$4 \times n$	0.20759129524230957
sect571k1	S	S	S	S	$4 \times n$	0.8523068428039551
sect571r1	N	N	S	N	$2 \times n$	1.0717732906341553

Table 2. NIST curves over $\mathbb{F}_{2^m}$ and **SVA** points from **dbl** - $\mathbb{F}_{2^m}$, where m is a positive integer.

Name of Curve	$x = 1$	$x^4 = B$	$y^2 = B$	$x^2 = y$	Curve Order	Execution Time
K-163	N	N	S	N	$2 \times n$	055924415588378906
B-163	N	N	L, S	N	$2 \times n$	0.20136809349060059
B-233	L	N	S	L	$2 \times n$	1.7690699100494385
K-233	S	S	S	S	$4 \times n$	0.16431379318237305
B-283	L	N	L	L	$2 \times n$	1.126676321029663
K-283	S	S	S	S	$4 \times n$	0.2727367877960205
B-409	N	N	S	N	$2 \times n$	0.3601799011230469
K-409	S	S	S	S	$4 \times n$	0.31488513946533203
B-571	N	N	S	N	$2 \times n$	0.2166743278503418
K-571	S	S	S	S	$2 \times n$	0.6794748306274414

Tables 1 and 2 summarize **SVA** on Standard for Efficient Cryptography **SECG** and **NIST** curves over binary fields $\mathbb{F}_{2^m}$, where m is a positive integer. In the Table 1, n is a large prime number. Table 1 (respectively Table 2) contains in the first column the names of the different curves recommended by **SECG** (respectively **NIST**) The second to the fifth column of each table tells us if the recommended curve has same-values points verifying the condition cited above. We have indicated in Tables 1 and 2 by 'L' to signify that the curve has a same-values point of large order, 'S' to signify that the curve has a same-values point of small order, 'N' to signify that the curve do not have a same-values point which satisfy the condition aboved. L, S in the table signify that the curve have some point of large order and some point of small order that satisfy the condition aboved. In the last column of each table, we have mentioned execution time of our sage code to obtain same value point of which curve. For the execution, we have used an Intel core I7-6600UCPU@ 2.60GHZ with 19GiB of RAM. The code can be found in the github https://github.com/AJM030/Binary-Curves. git private repository.

Some curves which are **ZVP** resistant like **sect163k1**, **sect233r1**, **sect409r1**, **K-163**, **B-233**, **B-409** are **SVA**- vulnerable, all curves which are **ZVP** vulnerable are also **SVA**- vulnerable. If it is true that these two tables allow us to have a complete conclusion on the vulnerability of standard curves to the **SVA** attack, it should also be noted that these tables include a non-exhaustive list of same-values points because we are only interested in to doubling algorithm.

5 Conclusion

In this work, we studied the special points and same values analysis on elliptic curves over binary fields. We looked for these special points on NIST and SECG recommended curves, none of these curves do not resist same values analysis attack. SVA is therefore a more dangerous side channel attack on elliptic curves cryptosystems than the previous ones. If it is true that we focused only on the doubling algorithm for the search of same value points on standard curves, it was necessary to give conditions for obtaining same value points for the addition algorithm to allow a better understanding of the attack.

For future work, we want to study same values analysis attack on curves of genus 2 and isogeny defence on SVA over finite fields.

Acknowledgments. The authors thank the anonymous reviewers for their comments which enable to improve the quality of this article.

References

1. Akishita, T., Takagi, T.: Zero-value point attacks on elliptic curve cryptosystem. In: Boyd, C., Mao, W. (eds.) ISC 2003. LNCS, vol. 2851, pp. 218–233. Springer, Heidelberg (2003). https://doi.org/10.1007/10958513_17

2. Ciet, M., Joye, M.: (Virtually) free randomization techniques for elliptic curve cryptography. In: Qing, S., Gollmann, D., Zhou, J. (eds.) ICICS 2003. LNCS, vol. 2836, pp. 348–359. Springer, Heidelberg (2003). https://doi.org/10.1007/978-3-540-39927-8_32

3. Coron, J.-S.: Resistance against differential power analysis for elliptic curve cryptosystems. In: Koç, Ç.K., Paar, C. (eds.) CHES 1999. LNCS, vol. 1717, pp. 292–302. Springer, Heidelberg (1999). https://doi.org/10.1007/3-540-48059-5_25

4. Crépeau, C., Kazmi, R.A.: An analysis of ZVP-attack on ECC cryptosystems. Cryptology ePrint Archive (2012)

5. Goubin, L.: A refined power-analysis attack on elliptic curve cryptosystems. In: Desmedt, Y.G. (ed.) PKC 2003. LNCS, vol. 2567, pp. 199–211. Springer, Heidelberg (2003). https://doi.org/10.1007/3-540-36288-6_15

6. Izu, T., Takagi, T.: Exceptional procedure attack on elliptic curve cryptosystems. In: Desmedt, Y.G. (ed.) PKC 2003. LNCS, vol. 2567, pp. 224–239. Springer, Heidelberg (2003). https://doi.org/10.1007/3-540-36288-6_17

7. Joye, M., Tymen, C.: Protections against differential analysis for elliptic curve cryptography — an algebraic approach —. In: Koç, Ç.K., Naccache, D., Paar, C. (eds.) CHES 2001. LNCS, vol. 2162, pp. 377–390. Springer, Heidelberg (2001). https://doi.org/10.1007/3-540-44709-1_31

8. Koblitz, N.: Elliptic curve cryptosystems. Math. Comput. 48(177), 203–209 (1987)

9. Kocher, P., Jaffe, J., Jun, B.: Introduction to differential power analysis and related attacks (1998)

10. López, J., Dahab, R.: Fast multiplication on elliptic curves over $GF(2^m)$ without precomputation. In: Koç, Ç.K., Paar, C. (eds.) CHES 1999. LNCS, vol. 1717, pp. 316–327. Springer, Heidelberg (1999). https://doi.org/10.1007/3-540-48059-5_27

11. Miller, V.S.: Use of elliptic curves in cryptography. In: Williams, H.C. (ed.) CRYPTO 1985. LNCS, vol. 218, pp. 417–426. Springer, Heidelberg (1986). https://doi.org/10.1007/3-540-39799-X_31

12. Murdica, C., Guilley, S., Danger, J.-L., Hoogvorst, P., Naccache, D.: Same values power analysis using special points on elliptic curves. In: Schindler, W., Huss, S.A. (eds.) COSADE 2012. LNCS, vol. 7275, pp. 183–198. Springer, Heidelberg (2012). https://doi.org/10.1007/978-3-642-29912-4_14

13. Sedlacek, V., Chi-Domínguez, J.-J., Jancar, J., Brumley, B.B.: A formula for disaster: a unified approach to elliptic curve special-point-based attacks. In: Tibouchi, M., Wang, H. (eds.) ASIACRYPT 2021. LNCS, vol. 13090, pp. 130–159. Springer, Cham (2021). https://doi.org/10.1007/978-3-030-92062-3_5

14. Smart, N.P.: An analysis of Goubin's refined power analysis attack. In: Walter, C.D., Koç, Ç.K., Paar, C. (eds.) CHES 2003. LNCS, vol. 2779, pp. 281–290. Springer, Heidelberg (2003). https://doi.org/10.1007/978-3-540-45238-6_23

Cryptanalysis of a New Variant of the RSA Cryptosystem

Abderrahmane Nitaj[1]($\boxtimes$), Nurul Nur Hanisah Adenan[2],
and Muhammad Rezal Kamel Ariffin[2]

[1] Normandie Univ, UNICAEN, CNRS, LMNO, 14000 Caen, France
`abderrahmane.nitaj@unicaen.fr`
[2] Institute for Mathematical Research, Universiti Putra Malaysia,
43400 Serdang Selangor, Malaysia
`rezal@upm.edu.my`

Abstract. Let $N = pq$ be an RSA modulus which is the product of two balanced prime factors. In 2018, Murru and Saettone presented a variant of the RSA cryptosystem based on a cubic Pell equation in which the public exponent e and the private exponent d satisfy $ed \equiv 1 \left(\bmod \frac{(p^3-1)(q^3-1)}{(p-1)(q-1)} \right)$. In 2022, Cotan and Teşeleanu extended the scheme of Murru and Saettone and proposed a variant of the RSA cryptosystem where e and d satisfy the key equation $ed \equiv 1 \left(\bmod \frac{(p^n-1)(q^n-1)}{(p-1)(q-1)} \right)$ for any $n \geq 2$. Moreover, they presented an attack based on the continued fraction algorithm that factor N when $2 \leq n \leq 4$, $e = N^{n-1}$ and $d < N^{\frac{1}{4}}$. In this paper, we transform the key equation of the scheme of Cotan and Teşeleanu to a modular equation of the form $xH(y)+1 \equiv 0 \pmod{e}$, propose a new method to find the small solutions of this equation, and apply it to find d and to factor the modulus N when d is sufficiently small. The attack is based on Coppersmith's method and improves the bound on d from $d < N^{\frac{1}{4}}$ up to $d < N^{0.292(n-1)}$. Moreover, our method is valid for all $n \geq 2$.

Keywords: RSA · Factorization · Coppersmith's method · RSA variants

1 Introduction

In 1978, Rivest, Shamir, and Adleman [21] proposed RSA, one of the first public key cryptosystems. Since then, RSA has been used in various applications in cryptography, and has been extended and generalized in various forms. The main ingredients in RSA are an integer $N = pq$ which is the product of two large primes, a public exponent e, and a private exponent d. The exponents are related by the modular equation $ed \equiv 1 \pmod{(p-1)(q-1)}$. In parallel, several attacks have been proposed to break RSA, some are based on factoring algorithms, and others are based on algebraic methods. Since the factorization

S. Vaudenay and C. Petit (Eds.): AFRICACRYPT 2024, LNCS 14861, pp. 327–345, 2024.
https://doi.org/10.1007/978-3-031-64381-1_15

of large integers of the form $N = pq$ with balanced prime factors is infeasible, a lot of efforts have been deployed to gain information from the public key (N, e) that can be exploited. In 1990, Wiener [24] proposed an algebraic method based on the continued fraction algorithm to factor N using the key equation $ed \equiv 1 \pmod{(p-1)(q-1)}$, and the convergents of $\frac{e}{N}$ when $d < \frac{1}{3}N^{\frac{1}{4}}$. In 1999, Boneh and Durfee [2] improved the bound up to $d < N^{0.292}$ by using Coppersmith's method [5] and lattice basis reduction techniques, applied to the equation $ed \equiv 1 \pmod{(p-1)(q-1)}$. In 2004, Blömer and May extended the equation to $ex - k(p-1)(q-1) = y$, and showed that, by mixing the continued fraction algorithm and Coppersmith's method, one can factor N if $|x| < \frac{1}{3}N^{\frac{1}{4}}$ and $|y| < cN^{-\frac{3}{4}}e|x|$ for some constant $c < 1$. For more attacks on RSA, we refer to [1,7,13].

For efficiency and security reasons, several variants of RSA have been proposed. Some variants have a similar modulus $N = pq$, such as CRT-RSA [20], Rebalanced RSA [24], and KMOV [10], and other variants have different moduli, such as Multi-Prime RSA [4], Prime-Power RSA [23], and Prime-Power KMOV [3].

In 2018, Murru and Saettone [15], proposed another variant of RSA with a modulus $N = pq$, where the encryption and the decryption algorithms use the arithmetic of the cubic Pell curve with the equation $x^3 + cy^3 + c^2z^3 - 3cxyz \equiv 1 \pmod{N}$, where c is a cubic-non residue modulo N. In this scheme, the public exponent is an integer e, and the decryption exponent is the integer d satisfying $ed \equiv 1 \pmod{\psi_3(N)}$ with $\psi_3(N) = (p^2 + p + 1)(q^2 + q + 1)$. The scheme of Murru and Saettone has attracted much attention, and has been intensively cryptanalyzed in [16,18,19,22,25].

In 2022, Cotan and Teşeleanu [6] generalized the scheme of Murru and Saettone to any value of $n \geq 2$, where the public exponent e, and the decryption exponent d satisfy $ed \equiv 1 \pmod{\psi_n(N)}$ with $\psi_n(N) = \frac{(p^n-1)(q^n-1)}{(p-1)(q-1)}$. For $n = 3$, this retrieves the scheme of Murru and Saettone. Moreover, Cotan and Teşeleanu presented an attack on the new scheme that allows to find d and factor the RSA modulus when $d = N^\delta$, $e = N^\alpha$, and $\delta < \frac{1}{4}(2n-2\alpha-1)$. Typically, for $e \approx N^{n-1}$, that is $\alpha = n - 1$, the former bound becomes $d < N^{\frac{1}{4}}$. The attack of Cotan and Teşeleanu is based on the continued fraction algorithm, applied to $\frac{e}{\psi_{0,n}(N)}$, where $\psi_{0,n}(N)$ is an approximation of $\psi_n(N)$ that depends only on n and N. In case $\delta < \frac{1}{4}(2n - 2\alpha - 1)$, the private exponent d can be computed as a denominator of a convergent $\frac{k_0}{d_0}$ of $\frac{e}{\psi_{0,n}(N)}$. This leads to $\psi_n(N) = \frac{ed_0-1}{k_0}$. To find p and q using the system formed by $N = pq$ and $\psi_n(N) = \frac{(p^n-1)(q^n-1)}{(p-1)(q-1)}$, one has to solve a polynomial equation of degree $n - 1$, which is not easy when $n > 4$.

In this paper, we revisit the cryptanalysis of the scheme of Cotan and Teşeleanu for any $n \geq 2$ by applying Coppersmith's method [5] to find the small solutions d of the equation $ed - k\psi_n(N) = 1$. First, we show that $\psi_n(N)$ can be transformed into a polynomial in $p + q$ of the form

$$\psi_n(N) = (p+q)^{n-1} + a_{n-2}(p+q)^{n-2} + \ldots + a_1(p+q) + a_0,$$

where the coefficients $a_{n-2}, \ldots, a_1, a_0$ are integers depending only on n and N. Then, the equation $ed - k\psi_n(N) = 1$ can be transformed into a modular equation of the form $xH(y) + 1 \equiv 0 \pmod{e}$, where $H(y) = y^{n-1} + a_{n-2}y^{n-2} + \ldots + a_1 y + a_0$, with the solution $(x_0, y_0) = (k, p+q)$.

This motivates us to propose a new method to find the small solutions (x_0, y_0) of the modular equation $xH(y) + c \equiv 0 \pmod{e}$ when c is a small constant, $H(y)$ is a polynomial with integer coefficients and degree r, $|x_0| < N^\beta$, $|y_0| < N^\gamma$, $e = N^\alpha$, and $\beta < \alpha - \sqrt{r\alpha\gamma}$. We notice that the new method is significantly different from the one presented by Kunihiro [11] in 2012, while the results are similar.

We apply our method to solve the key equation $ed - k\psi_n(N) = 1$ in the scheme of Cotan and Teşeleanu [6], and to factor N if $d \leq N^\delta$ and $e \approx N^\alpha$ are such that

$$\delta < n - 1 - \frac{\sqrt{2}}{2}\sqrt{(n-1)\alpha}.$$

A straightforward calculation shows that the former bound is always better than the bound $\delta < \frac{1}{4}(2n - 2\alpha - 1)$ of Cotan and Teşeleanu. In the standard situation $e \approx N^{n-1}$, the new bound becomes

$$\delta < \frac{2 - \sqrt{2}}{2}(n-1) \approx 0.292(n-1),$$

which is clearly larger than the bound $\delta < \frac{1}{4}$ of Cotan and Teşeleanu.

The rest of the paper is organized as follows. In Sect. 2, we present some preliminaries. In Sect. 3, we propose new formulae for $\psi_n(N)$. In Sect. 4, we present our method to find the small solutions of the modular equation $xH(y) + c \equiv 0 \pmod{e}$. In Sect. 5, we apply our method to cryptanalyse the scheme of Cotan and Teşeleanu. We conclude the paper in Sect. 6.

2 Preliminaries

In this section, we present the scheme of Cotan and Teşeleanu, as well as some lemmas that will be used in the paper.

2.1 The Scheme of Cotan and Teşeleanu

Let $n \geq 2$ be an integer, and p a prime number. Let $\mathbb{F}_p$ be the finite field of p elements, and $r \in \mathbb{F}_p$ such that the polynomial $t^n - r$ is irreducible in $\mathbb{F}_p[t]$. The quotient field related to $t^n - r$ is defined by

$$\mathbb{A}_n(p) = \mathbb{F}_p[t]/(t^n - r) = \{a_0 + a_1 t + \ldots + a_{n-1}t^{n-1}, \ a_i \in \mathbb{F}_p\}.$$

If $a = \sum_{i=0}^{n-1} a_i t^i \in \mathbb{A}_n(p)$ and $b = \sum_{i=0}^{n-1} b_i t^i \in \mathbb{A}_n(p)$, then

$$a + b \equiv \sum_{i=0}^{n-1} (a_i + b_i) t^i \pmod{p},$$

$$ab \equiv \sum_{i=0}^{n-1} c_i t^i \pmod{p},$$

where

$$c_i \equiv \begin{cases} \displaystyle\sum_{j=0}^{i} a_j b_{i-j} + r \sum_{j=0}^{i+n} a_j b_{i-j+n} \pmod{p} & \text{if } i \leq n-2, \\ \displaystyle\sum_{j=0}^{n-1} a_j b_{n-1-j} \pmod{p} & \text{if } i = n-1. \end{cases}$$

The quotient field $\mathbb{A}_n(p)$ can be transformed into a projective form by setting $\mathbb{B}_n(p) = \mathbb{A}_n^*/\mathbb{F}_p^*$, so that the elements of $\mathbb{B}_n(p)$ are of the form

$$[1], \ [a_0 + t], \ [a_0 + a_1 t + t^2], \ \dots, \ [a_0 + a_1 t + \dots + a_{n-2} t^{n-2} + t^{n-1}].$$

The number of the different elements of $\mathbb{B}_n(p)$ is then

$$|\mathbb{B}_n(p)| = 1 + p + p^2 + \dots + p^{n-1} = \frac{p^n - 1}{p - 1}.$$

If e is a positive integer and $a \in \mathbb{B}_n(p)$, an exponentiation on $\mathbb{B}_n(p)$ can be defined by

$$a^e \equiv \underbrace{a \times a \cdots \times a}_{e \text{ times}} \pmod{p}.$$

Then, for any $a \in \mathbb{B}_n(p)$, and any positive integer k, one has

$$a^{k|\mathbb{B}_n(p)|} \equiv 1 \pmod{p}.$$

If q is another prime number, and $N = pq$, the former arithmetic is also valid for $\mathbb{B}_n(N)$. In particular, one has

$$|\mathbb{B}_n(N)| = \frac{(p^n - 1)(q^n - 1)}{(p - 1)(q - 1)}.$$

Moreover, for any $a \in \mathbb{B}_n(N)$, and any positive integer k, one has

$$a^{k|\mathbb{B}_n(N)|} \equiv 1 \pmod{N}.$$

The scheme of Cotan and Teşeleanu is composed by three algorithms.

- **Key generation.**
  1. Choose a positive integer $n \geq 2$, and a security size $\lambda > 0$.

2. Generate two distinct prime numbers p and q of size λ.
3. Compute $N = pq$ and $\psi_n(N) = \frac{(p^n-1)(q^n-1)}{(p-1)(q-1)}$.
4. Select an integer r such that $t^n - r$ is irreducible in $\mathbb{Z}/p\mathbb{Z}$, $\mathbb{Z}/q\mathbb{Z}$, and $\mathbb{Z}/N\mathbb{Z}$.
5. Select an integer e such that $\gcd(e, \psi_n(N)) = 1$, and compute $d \equiv e^{-1}$ (mod $\psi_n(N)$).
6. The public key is (N, n, r, e), and the private key is (N, n, r, d).

- **Encryption.**
    1. Represent the plaintext as $m = m_0 + m_1 t + \ldots + m_{n-2}t^{n-2} + t^{n-1}$.
    2. Compute $c \equiv m^e$ (mod N) using $t^n = r$.
    3. The ciphertext is c.
- **Decryption.**
    1. Compute $m \equiv c^d$ (mod N) using $t^n = r$.
    2. The plaintext is m.

2.2 Lattices and Coppersmith's Method

Let m and n be positive integers such that $m \leq n$. Let $u_1, \ldots, u_m$ be m linearly independent vectors of $\mathbb{R}^n$. The lattice $\mathcal{L}$ spanned by the basis $\{u_1, \ldots, u_m\}$ is formed by

$$\mathcal{L} = \left\{ v \in \mathbb{R}^n : v = \sum_{i=1}^{m} \lambda_i u_i, \lambda_i \in \mathbb{Z} \right\}.$$

The dimension of the lattice $\mathcal{L}$ is n, and its rank is m. In most applications, $m = n$, and the lattice is full-rank. The determinant of the lattice is $\det(\mathcal{L}) = \sqrt{\det(BB^t)}$ where B is the matrix formed by the entries of the basis, and B^t is its transpose.

Lattices are extensively used in cryptography for the design of new schemes because of the existence of several hard problems such as the Shortest Vector Problem (SVP), and the Closest Vector Problem (CVP). Another hard problem in lattices is the reduction of a basis. In 1982, Lenstra, Lenstra and Lovász [12] proposed an algorithm called LLL that approximates SVP, CVP, and outputs a basis with good properties.

Theorem 1 (LLL [12,14]). *Let $\mathcal{L}$ be a lattice that is constructed by a basis $(u_1, ..., u_\omega)$. The LLL algorithm produces a new basis $(b_1, \ldots, b_\omega)$ of $\mathcal{L}$ satisfying*

$$\|b_1\| \leq \ldots \leq \|b_i\| \leq 2^{\frac{\omega(\omega-1)}{4(\omega+1-i)}} \det(\mathcal{L})^{\frac{1}{\omega+1-i}},$$

for $i = 1, 2, \ldots, \omega$.

The LLL algorithm is also used in cryptanalysis, specifically in Coppersmith's method [5]. If $f(x_1, \ldots, x_n)$ is a polynomial in n variables, and N is a positive integer, Coppersmith's method is devoted to find the small solutions of the modular equation $f(x_1, \ldots, x_n) \equiv 0$ (mod N). Coppersmith's method is intensively used for the cryptanalysis of RSA and its variants. The following result is a cornerstone in Coppersmith's method.

Theorem 2 (Howgrave-Graham [8]**).** *Let* $F(x_1,\ldots,x_n) = \sum a_{i_1\ldots i_n} x_1^{i_1} \cdots x_n^{i_n} \in \mathbb{Z}[x_1,\ldots,x_n]$ *be a polynomial with at most* ω *monomials and norm*

$$\|F(x_1,\ldots,x_n)\| = \sqrt{\sum a_{i_1\ldots i_n}^2}.$$

If $|y_1| < X_1,\ldots,|y_n| < X_n$, *and*

$$F(y_1,\ldots,y_n) \equiv 0 \quad (\mathrm{mod}\ e^m),$$

$$\|F(X_1x_1,\ldots,X_nx_n)\| < \frac{e^m}{\sqrt{\omega}},$$

then $F(y_1,\ldots,y_n) = 0$ *holds over the integers.*

Coppersmith's method is heuristic, and depends on the following assumption which is widely used in cryptanalysis of RSA and its variants.

Assumption 1. *The lattice basis reduced by the LLL algorithm yields algebraically independent polynomials, and the common roots of these polynomials can be efficiently computed by the Gröbner basis technique, or by the resultant computation.*

2.3   Useful Lemmas

Let $N = pq$ be an RSA modulus with $q < p < 2q$. The following result gives the bounds for p, and q in terms of N (see [17]).

Lemma 1. *Let* $N = pq$ *be the product of two unknown integers with* $q < p < 2q$. *Then*

$$\frac{\sqrt{2}}{2}\sqrt{N} < q < \sqrt{N} < p < \sqrt{2}\sqrt{N}.$$

In the scheme of Cotan and Teşeleanu [6], the generalized totient function for $N = pq$ and $n \geq 2$ is

$$\psi_n(N) = \frac{(p^n - 1)(q^n - 1)}{(p-1)(q-1)}.$$

The following result from [6] is useful to approximate it.

Lemma 2. *For* $n \geq 2$, *let* $N = pq$ *and* $\psi_n(N) = \frac{(p^n-1)(q^n-1)}{(p-1)(q-1)}$. *Then*

$$\left(\frac{\sqrt{N}^n - 1}{\sqrt{N} - 1}\right)^2 < \psi_n(N) < \frac{\left(\sqrt{2N}\right)^n - 1}{\sqrt{2N} - 1} \cdot \frac{\left(\frac{\sqrt{2N}}{2}\right)^n - 1}{\frac{\sqrt{2N}}{2} - 1}.$$

The former result implies that $\psi_n(N)$ can be approximated by $\psi_n(N) \approx N^{n-1}$.

3   Formulae for $\psi_n(N)$

The following lemma shows that $\psi_n(N)$ can be expressed as a polynomial in $p+q$ with integer coefficients.

Lemma 3. *Let* $N = pq$ *and* $n \geq 2$. *Then there exist* $n-1$ *coefficients* $a_{n-2}, \ldots, a_0$ *depending only on* N *and* n *such that*

$$\psi_n(N) = (p+q)^{n-1} + \sum_{j=0}^{n-2} a_j (p+q)^j.$$

Proof. First, observe that

$$\psi_n(N) = \frac{p^n - 1}{p - 1} \frac{q^n - 1}{q - 1} = \left(p^{n-1} + p^{n-2} + \cdots + 1\right)\left(q^{n-1} + q^{n-2} + \cdots + 1\right),$$

which implies that $\psi_n(N)$ is an integer. Using the complex primitive roots, the factorization of $x^n - 1$ is

$$x^n - 1 = \prod_{j=0}^{n-1}\left(x - e^{2ij\pi/n}\right),$$

where $i^2 = -1$. We consider two cases.

Case 1. If $n = 2k+1$ with $k \geq 1$, then

$$x^n - 1 = (x-1)\prod_{j=1}^{k}\left(x - e^{2ij\pi/n}\right)\left(x - e^{-2ij\pi/n}\right).$$

Hence, using $N = pq$ and $S = p+q$, we get

$$\psi_n(N) = \frac{(p^n - 1)(q^n - 1)}{(p-1)(q-1)}$$

$$= \prod_{j=1}^{k}\left(p - e^{2ij\pi/n}\right)\left(p - e^{-2ij\pi/n}\right)\left(q - e^{2ij\pi/n}\right)\left(q - e^{-2ij\pi/n}\right)$$

$$= \prod_{j=1}^{k}\left(N - Se^{2ij\pi/n} + e^{4ij\pi/n}\right)\left(N - Se^{-2ij\pi/n} + e^{-4ij\pi/n}\right)$$

$$= \prod_{j=1}^{k}\left(S^2 - (N+1)\left(e^{2ij\pi/n} + e^{-2ij\pi/n}\right)S + N^2 + N\left(e^{4ij\pi/n} + e^{-4ij\pi/n}\right) + 1\right)$$

$$= S^{2k} + \sum_{j=0}^{2k-1} a_j S^j.$$

Hence $\psi_n(N) = S^{n-1} + \sum_{j=0}^{n-2} a_j S^j$ where a_j depends only on n and N.

Case 2. If $n = 2k$ with $k \geq 1$, then we use

$$x^n - 1 = (x-1)(x+1)\prod_{j=1}^{k-1}\left(x - e^{2ij\pi/n}\right)\left(x - e^{-2ij\pi/n}\right).$$

Again, using $pq = N$ and $S = p + q$, we get

$$\psi_n(N) = \frac{(p^n - 1)(q^n - 1)}{(p-1)(q-1)}$$

$$= (p+1)(q+1)\prod_{j=1}^{k-1}\left(p - e^{2ij\pi/n}\right)\left(p - e^{-2ij\pi/n}\right)\left(q - e^{2ij\pi/n}\right)\left(q - e^{-2ij\pi/n}\right)$$

$$= (S + N + 1)\times$$

$$\prod_{j=1}^{k-1}\left(N - Se^{2ij\pi/n} + e^{4ij\pi/n}\right)\left(N - Se^{-2ij\pi/n} + e^{-4ij\pi/n}\right)$$

$$= (S + N + 1)\times$$

$$\prod_{j=1}^{k-1}\left(S^2 - (N+1)\left(e^{2ij\pi/n} + e^{-2ij\pi/n}\right)S + N^2 + N\left(e^{4ij\pi/n} + e^{-4ij\pi/n}\right) + 1\right)$$

$$= S^{2k-1} + \sum_{j=0}^{2k-2} a_j S^j.$$

Hence $\psi_n(N) = S^{n-1} + \sum_{j=0}^{n-2} a_j S^j$ where a_j depends only on n and N. □

The following result gives a way to recursively compute $\psi_n(N)$.

Lemma 4. *Let $N = pq$ and $S = p + q$. Then $\psi_1(N) = 1$, $\psi_2(N) = N + 1 + S$, and for $n \geq 3$,*

$$\psi_n(N) = N^{n-1} + 1 + S\psi_{n-1}(N) - N\psi_{n-2}(N).$$

Proof. First, we have $\psi_1(N) = 1$, and $\psi_2(N) = (p+1)(q+1) = N + 1 + S$. For $n \geq 3$, we have

$$p^n + q^n = (p+q)\left(p^{n-1} + q^{n-1}\right) - pq\left(p^{n-2} + q^{n-2}\right)$$

$$= S\left(p^{n-1} + q^{n-1}\right) - N\left(p^{n-2} + q^{n-2}\right)$$

$$= S\left(N^{n-1} + 1 - (p-1)(q-1)\psi_{n-1}(N)\right)$$

$$\quad - N\left(N^{n-2} + 1 - (p-1)(q-1)\psi_{n-2}(N)\right)$$

$$= S\left(N^{n-1} + 1\right) - N\left(N^{n-2} + 1\right)$$

$$\quad - S(p-1)(q-1)\psi_{n-1}(N) + N(p-1)(q-1)\psi_{n-2}(N).$$

Then, for $n \geq 3$, we get

$$
\begin{aligned}
\psi_n(N) &= \frac{(p^n - 1)(q^n - 1)}{(p - 1)(q - 1)} \\
&= \frac{N^n + 1 - (p^n + q^n)}{(p - 1)(q - 1)} \\
&= \frac{N^n + 1 - S(N^{n-1} + 1) + N(N^{n-2} + 1)}{(p - 1)(q - 1)} + S\psi_{n-1}(N) - N\psi_{n-2}(N) \\
&= N^{n-1} + 1 + S\psi_{n-1}(N) - N\psi_{n-2}(N).
\end{aligned}
$$

This terminates the proof.   □

Lemma 4 can be used to find the first values for $\psi_n(N)$.

$$
\psi_2(N) = p + q + N + 1
$$
$$
\psi_3(N) = (p + q)^2 + (N + 1)(p + q) + N^2 - N + 1,
$$
$$
\psi_4(N) = (p + q)^3 + (N + 1)(p + q)^2 + (N^2 - 2N + 1)(p + q) + \\
N^3 - N^2 - N + 1,
$$
$$
\psi_5(N) = (p + q)^4 + (N + 1)(p + q)^3 + (N^2 - 3N + 1)(p + q)^2 + \\
(N^3 - 2N^2 - 2N + 1)(p + q) + N^4 - N^3 + N^2 - N + 1,
$$
$$
\psi_6(N) = (p + q)^5 + (N + 1)(p + q)^4 + (N^2 - 4N + 1)(p + q)^3 + \\
(N^3 - 3N^2 - 3N + 1)(p + q)^2 + (N^4 - 2N^3 + 3N^2 - 2N + 1)(p + q) + \\
N^5 - N^4 + N^3 + N^2 - N + 1.
$$

The following result shows that $\psi_n(N)$, expressed as a polynomial in $S = p + q$, has only integer coefficients.

Corollary 1. *Let $N = pq$, $S = p + q$, and $n \geq 2$. Then, the coefficients $a_{n-2}, \ldots, a_0$ in the polynomial*

$$
\psi_n(N) = (p + q)^{n-1} + \sum_{j=0}^{n-2} a_j (p + q)^j,
$$

are integers.

Proof. By Lemma 4, we have $\psi_1(N) = 1$, $\psi_2(N) = N + 1 + S$, and for $n \geq 3$,

$$
\psi_n(N) = N^{n-1} + 1 + S\psi_{n-1}(N) - N\psi_{n-2}(N).
$$

Recursively, this implies that $\psi_n(N)$, as a polynomial in S, has integer coefficients. Combining with Lemma 3, this shows that

$$
\psi_n(N) = (p + q)^{n-1} + \sum_{j=0}^{n-2} a_j (p + q)^j,
$$

where the coefficients a_j are all integers.   □

4   Solving the Equation $xH(y) + c \equiv 0 \pmod{e}$

In this section, we propose a new method to find the small solutions of the equation $xH(y)+c \equiv 0 \pmod{e}$ where c is a small constant, and $H(y)$ is a polynomial with integer coefficients and degree r. Notice that the equation $xH(y) + c \equiv 0 \pmod{e}$ was first studied by Kunihiro [11]. Here, we present a different approach which is different from the method of Kunihiro. Nevertheless, it produces similar results.

Theorem 3. *Let $N = pq$ be the product of two unknown prime factors with $q < p < 2q$. Let $H(y)$ be a monic polynomial with integer coefficients and degree r. Suppose that $xH(y) + c \equiv 0 \pmod{e}$ with $e = N^\alpha$, $|x| < N^\beta$, and $|y| < N^\gamma$. Then one can find x and y in polynomial time if $|c| < N^{\beta + r\gamma}$, $\alpha \geq r\gamma$, and*

$$\beta < \alpha - \sqrt{r\alpha\gamma}.$$

Proof. Let $H(y) = y^r + a_{r-1}y^{r-1} + \ldots + a_0 \in \mathbb{Z}[y]$. Consider the polynomial $f(x,y) = xH(y) + c$. We combine Coppersmith's method [5] and the extended strategy of Jochemsz and May [9] to solve the equation $f(x,y) \equiv 0 \pmod{e}$. Let m be a positive integer. For $0 \leq k \leq m$, we define the set

$$M_k = \bigcup \{x^i y^j \mid x^i y^j \text{ is a monomial of } f^m(x,y)$$

$$\text{and } \frac{x^i y^j}{(xy^r)^k} \text{ is a monomial of } f^{m-k}(x,y)\}.$$

The expansion of $f^m(x,y)$ shows that $x^i y^j$ is a monomial of $f^m(x,y)$ if

$$i = 0, \ldots, m, \quad j = 0, \ldots, ri.$$

From this, it follows that $x^i y^j$ is a monomial of $f^{m-k}(x,y)$ if

$$i = 0, \ldots, m - k, \quad j = 0, \ldots, ri.$$

Hence, when $x^i y^j$ is a monomial of $f^m(x,y)$, then $\frac{x^i y^j}{(xy^r)^k}$ is a monomial of $f^{m-k}(x,y)$ if $i = k, \ldots, m$, $j = rk, \ldots, ri$. Then, the monomials of M_k satisfy

$$x^i y^j \in M_k \text{ if } i = k, \ldots, m, \; j = rk, \ldots, ri.$$

This implies that

$$x^i y^j \in M_{k+1} \text{ if } i = k+1, \ldots, m, \; j = rk + r, \ldots, ri,$$

with the convention that $M_{m+1} = \{\}$. Then, for $0 \leq k \leq m$, we have $x^i y^j \in M_k \backslash M_{k+1}$ if

$$i = k+1, \ldots, m, \; j = rk, rk+1, \ldots rk + r - 1,$$
$$i = k, j = rk.$$

Define the following collection of polynomials

$$g_{k,i,j}(x,y) = \frac{x^i y^j}{(xy^r)^k} f(x,y)^k e^{m-k},$$

with $x^i y^j \in M_k \backslash M_{k+1}$. Since, for $0 \le k \le m$,

$$i - k = 1, \ldots, m - k, \ j - rk = 0, 1, \ldots r - 1,$$
$$i - k = 0, \ j - rk = 0.$$

then the polynomials $g_{k,i,j}(x,y)$ can be rewritten in the following form

$$g_{k,i,j}(x,y) = x^i y^j f(x,y)^k e^{m-k},$$
$$\text{for} \quad k = 0, \ldots m, \ i = 1, \ldots, m - k, \ j = 0, 1, \ldots, r - 1,$$
$$\text{and for} \quad k = 0, \ldots m, \ i = 0, \ j = 0.$$

Let $t \ge 0$ be an extra parameter to be optimized. In the list of the polynomials $g_{k,i,j}(x,y)$, we suppress the polynomials with $i = 0$, and add a few others in the form

$$g_{k,i,j}(x,y) = x^i y^j f(x,y)^k e^{m-k},$$
$$\text{for} \quad i = 0, j = 0, \ldots, \lfloor t \rfloor, \ k = \left\lfloor \frac{m}{t} \right\rfloor j, \ldots, m.$$

Since $xH(y) + c = xy^r + x\left(a_{r-1}y^{r-1} + \ldots + a_0\right) + c$, we set $xy^r + c = z$. Then $f(x,y) = F(x,y,z)$, and the polynomials $g_{k,i,j}(x,y,z)$ can be transformed into the following polynomials

$$G_{k,i,j}(x,y,z) = x^i y^j F(x,y,z)^k e^{m-k},$$
$$\text{for} \quad j = 0, 1, \ldots, r - 1, \ k = 0, \ldots m, \ i = 1, \ldots, m - k,$$
$$\text{or} \quad j = 0, \ldots \lfloor t \rfloor, \ k = \left\lfloor \frac{m}{t} \right\rfloor j, \ldots, m, \ i = 0,$$

where each term xy^r is replaced by $z - c$. Moreover, if we set $z_0 = x_0 y_0^r + c$, then we get

$$G_{k,i,j}(x_0, y_0, z_0) \equiv 0 \pmod{e^m}.$$

Assume that $|x_0| < X = N^\beta$, $|y_0| < Y = N^\gamma$, and $|c| < |x_0 y_0^r|$. Then $|z_0| = |x_0 y_0^r| + |c| < Z = 2N^{\beta+r\gamma}$.

We use the polynomials $G_{k,i,j}(x,y,z)$ to build a lattice $\mathcal{L}$ spanned by the coefficient vectors of the polynomials $G_{k,i,j}(Xx, Yy, Zz)$ where X, Y, and Z are positive integers satisfying

$$X \approx N^\beta, Y \approx N^\gamma, Z \approx 2N^{\beta+r\gamma}. \tag{1}$$

The rows of the matrix of the lattice are ordered following the lexical order of (k, i, j), that is $G_{k,i,j}(Xx, Yy, Zz) \prec G_{k',i',j'}(Xx, Yy, Zz)$ if $k < k'$, or if $k = k'$ and $i < i'$, or if $k = k'$, $i = i'$, and $j < j'$. Similarly, for the monomials, we set

Table 1. The matrix of the lattice for $m = 3$, $t = 1$ with the polynomial $H(y) = y^3 + a_2 y^2 + a_1 y + a_0$.

$G_{k,i,j}$	1	x	xy	xy^2	x^2	x^2y	x^2y^2	x^3	x^3y	x^3y^2	z	xz	xyz	xy^2z	x^2z	x^2yz	x^2y^2z	z^2	xz^2	xyz^2	xy^2z^2	z^3	yz^3
$G_{0,0,0}$	e^3	0	0	0	0	0	0	0	0	0	0	0	0	0	0	0	0	0	0	0	0	0	0
$G_{0,1,0}$	0	e^3X	0	0	0	0	0	0	0	0	0	0	0	0	0	0	0	0	0	0	0	0	0
$G_{0,1,1}$	0	0	e^3XY	0	0	0	0	0	0	0	0	0	0	0	0	0	0	0	0	0	0	0	0
$G_{0,1,2}$	0	0	0	e^3XY^2	0	0	0	0	0	0	0	0	0	0	0	0	0	0	0	0	0	0	0
$G_{0,2,0}$	0	0	0	0	e^3X^2	0	0	0	0	0	0	0	0	0	0	0	0	0	0	0	0	0	0
$G_{0,2,1}$	0	0	0	0	0	e^3X^2Y	0	0	0	0	0	0	0	0	0	0	0	0	0	0	0	0	0
$G_{0,2,2}$	0	0	0	0	0	0	$e^3X^2Y^2$	0	0	0	0	0	0	0	0	0	0	0	0	0	0	0	0
$G_{0,3,0}$	0	0	0	0	0	0	0	e^3X^3	0	0	0	0	0	0	0	0	0	0	0	0	0	0	0
$G_{0,3,1}$	0	0	0	0	0	0	0	0	e^3X^3Y	0	0	0	0	0	0	0	0	0	0	0	0	0	0
$G_{0,3,2}$	0	0	0	0	0	0	0	0	0	$e^3X^3Y^2$	0	0	0	0	0	0	0	0	0	0	0	0	0
$G_{1,0,0}$	0	0	0	★	0	0	0	0	0	0	e^2Z	0	0	0	0	0	0	0	0	0	0	0	0
$G_{1,1,0}$	0	★	0	0	★	0	0	0	0	0	0	XZe^2	0	0	0	0	0	0	0	0	0	0	0
$G_{1,1,1}$	0	0	★	0	0	★	0	0	0	0	0	0	$XYZe^2$	0	0	0	0	0	0	0	0	0	0
$G_{1,1,2}$	0	0	0	★	0	0	★	0	0	0	0	0	0	XY^2Ze^2	0	0	0	0	0	0	0	0	0
$G_{1,2,0}$	0	0	0	0	★	0	0	★	0	0	0	0	0	0	X^2Ze^2	0	0	0	0	0	0	0	0
$G_{1,2,1}$	0	0	0	0	0	★	0	0	★	0	0	0	0	0	0	X^2YZe^2	0	0	0	0	0	0	0
$G_{1,2,2}$	0	0	0	0	0	0	★	0	0	★	0	0	0	0	0	0	$X^2Y^2Ze^2$	0	0	0	0	0	0
$G_{2,0,0}$	0	★	0	0	★	0	0	0	0	0	★	0	0	0	0	0	0	eZ^2	0	0	0	0	0
$G_{2,1,0}$	0	0	★	0	0	★	0	0	0	0	0	★	0	0	0	0	0	0	XZ^2e	0	0	0	0
$G_{2,1,1}$	0	★	0	★	★	0	★	0	0	0	0	0	★	0	0	0	0	0	0	XYZ^2e	0	0	0
$G_{2,1,2}$	0	0	★	0	0	★	0	★	0	0	0	0	0	★	0	0	0	0	0	0	XY^2Z^2e	0	0
$G_{3,0,0}$	0	★	0	0	★	0	0	★	0	0	★	★	0	0	★	0	0	★	0	0	0	Z^3	0
$G_{3,0,1}$	0	★	★	0	★	★	★	0	★	0	0	★	★	★	★	★	★	★	★	★	★	0	YZ^3

$x^i y^j z^k \prec x^{i'} y^{j'} z^{k'}$ if $k < k'$, or if $k = k'$ and $i < i'$, or if $k = k'$, $i = i'$, and $j < j'$. In Table 1, we present an example of the matrix of the lattice for $m = 3$, $t = 1$, where the symbols $\star$ are non-zero entries.

By construction, the matrix of the lattice is left triangular. Its determinant is in the form

$$\det(\mathcal{L}) = X^{n_X} Y^{n_Y} Z^{n_Y} e^{n_e}. \tag{2}$$

We define

$$S(z) = \sum_{j=0}^{r-1} \sum_{k=0}^{m} \sum_{i=1}^{m-k} z + \sum_{j=0}^{\lfloor t \rfloor} \sum_{k=\lfloor \frac{m}{t} \rfloor j}^{m} \sum_{i=0}^{0} z.$$

Let $\tau \geq 0$ such that $t = m\tau$. To simplify the computations, we approximate $\lfloor t \rfloor \approx t$, and $\lfloor \frac{m}{t} \rfloor \approx \frac{m}{t}$. Then the dominant parts of the former parameters, as well as of the dimension ω of the lattice are

$$n_X = S(i) = \frac{1}{6} r m^3 + o(m^3)$$

$$n_Y = S(j) = \frac{1}{6} \tau^2 m^3 + o(m^3)$$

$$n_Z = S(k) = \frac{1}{6}(2\tau + r)m^3 + o(m^3) \tag{3}$$

$$n_e = S(m - k) = \frac{1}{6}(\tau + 2r)m^3 + o(m^3)$$

$$\omega = S(1) = \frac{1}{2}(\tau + r)m^2 + o(m^2).$$

Next, we combine Theorems 2 and 1 with $i = 3$ by setting

$$2^{\frac{\omega(\omega-1)}{4(\omega-2)}} \det(\mathcal{L})^{\frac{1}{\omega-2}} < \frac{e^m}{\sqrt{\omega}}.$$

In addition to (2), this gives

$$e^{n_e - m(\omega-2)} X^{n_X} Y^{n_Y} Z^{n_Z} < \frac{2^{-\frac{\omega(\omega-1)}{4}}}{(\sqrt{\omega})^{\omega-2}}. \tag{4}$$

Using (3) with $X = N^\beta$, $Y = N^\gamma$, $Z = N^{\beta+r\gamma}$, and $e = N^\alpha$, we get

$$\left(\frac{1}{6}(\tau + 2r) - \frac{1}{2}(\tau + r) \right) \alpha + \frac{1}{6} r\beta + \frac{1}{6} \gamma \tau^2 + \frac{1}{6}(2\tau + r)(\beta + r\gamma) < -\varepsilon_1,$$

where ε_1 is a small positive constant in terms of m and N. The former inequality can be simplified to

$$\gamma \tau^2 + 2(r\gamma - \alpha + \beta)\tau + r^2\gamma - r\alpha + 2r\beta < -\varepsilon_1 \tag{5}$$

where the optimal value for τ is $\tau_0 = \frac{\alpha - \beta - r\gamma}{\gamma}$. This value leads to two cases.

Case 1: Suppose that $\alpha \leq \beta + r\gamma$, that is $e \leq xy^r$. Then $\tau_0 \leq 0$, and we take $\tau = 0$ in (5). This leads to

$$\beta < \frac{1}{2}(\alpha - r\gamma) \leq \frac{1}{2}(\beta + r\gamma - r\gamma) = \frac{1}{2}\beta,$$

which is not possible for $\beta \geq 0$. Hence, in this situation, the method can not solve the equation $xH(y) + c \equiv 0 \pmod{e}$.

Case 2: Suppose that $\alpha > \beta + r\gamma$, that is $e > xy^r$. Then $\tau_0 > 0$, and plugging it in (5), we get

$$-\beta^2 + 2\alpha\beta - \alpha^2 + r\gamma\alpha < -\varepsilon_2,$$

for a small $\varepsilon_2 > 0$, which implies

$$\beta < \alpha - \sqrt{r\alpha\gamma}.$$

Moreover, we have to satisfy the condition $\alpha - \sqrt{r\alpha\gamma} \geq 0$. This is true if $r\gamma \leq \alpha$. Then, under the condition $r\gamma \leq \alpha$, we have

$$\beta < \min\left(\alpha - \sqrt{r\alpha\gamma}, \alpha - r\gamma\right) = \alpha - \sqrt{r\alpha\gamma}.$$

This terminates the proof.   □

5 A New Attack on the Scheme of Cotan and Teşeleanu

In this section, we consider the scheme of Cotan and Teşeleanu, and present a method to find the small solutions of the key equation of the scheme, namely $ed - k\psi_n(N) = 1$, where e is the public exponent, and $\psi_n(N) = \frac{(p^n - 1)(q^n - 1)}{(p-1)(q-1)}$.

5.1 The New Attack

Theorem 4. *Let $N = pq$ be the product of two unknown prime factors with $q < p < 2q$. Suppose that $ed - k\psi_n(N) = 1$ with $\psi_n(N) = \frac{(p^n - 1)(q^n - 1)}{(p-1)(q-1)}$, $e = N^\alpha$, and $d < N^\delta$. Then one can factor N in polynomial time if $\frac{n-1}{2} \leq \alpha \leq 2(n-1)$, and*

$$\delta < n - 1 - \frac{\sqrt{2}}{2}\sqrt{(n-1)\alpha}.$$

Proof. For $n \geq 2$, by Corollary 1, we have

$$\psi_n(N) = \frac{(p^n - 1)(q^n - 1)}{(p-1)(q-1)} = (p+q)^{n-1} + \sum_{j=0}^{n-2} a_j(p+q)^j,$$

with $a_j \in \mathbb{Z}$ for $j = 0, \ldots n - 2$. Let $H(y) = y^{n-1} + \sum_{j=0}^{n-2} a_j y^j$. Suppose that $e = N^\alpha$ is a public exponent satisfying $ed - k\psi_n(N) = 1$ with $d < N^\delta$. By Lemma 2, we have $\psi_n(N) > N^{n-1}$. Then

$$k = \frac{ed - 1}{\psi_n(N)} < \frac{ed}{\psi_n(N)} < N^{\alpha + \delta + 1 - n}.$$

The equation $ed - k\psi_n(N) = 1$ can be rewritten as $k\psi_n(N) + 1 \equiv 0 \pmod{e}$, or $xH(y) + 1 \equiv 0 \pmod{e}$ with the solution (x_0, y_0) satisfying $x_0 = k < N^{\alpha+\delta+1-n}$ and $y_0 = p + q < 3N^{\frac{1}{2}}$ by Lemma 1. One can then apply Theorem 3 with $r = n - 1$, $X = N^\beta = N^{\alpha+\delta+1-n}$ and $Y = N^\gamma = N^{\frac{1}{2}}$. It implies that one can find $k = x_0$ and $p + q = y_0$ if

$$\beta = \alpha + \delta + 1 - n < \alpha - \sqrt{\frac{1}{2}(n-1)\alpha},$$

that is

$$\delta < n - 1 - \frac{\sqrt{2}}{2}\sqrt{(n-1)\alpha}.$$

Note that the second condition in Theorem 3 is that $r\gamma \le \alpha$ which gives $\frac{n-1}{2} \le \alpha$. Also, we want $\delta \ge 0$. This is possible if $n - 1 - \frac{\sqrt{2}}{2}\sqrt{(n-1)\alpha} \ge 0$, that is if $\alpha \le 2(n-1)$. Under the former conditions, one can find the solutions (x_0, y_0) of the equation $xH(y) + 1 \equiv 0 \pmod{e}$. Then, using the solution (x_0, y_0) one can solve the system of equations $p + q = y_0$, $pq = N$. This leads to the factorization of N. $\square$

5.2 Comparison with Former Attacks

Comparison for $n = 3$. The original scheme of Murru and Saettone [15] corresponds to $n = 3$ in the scheme of Cotan and Teșeleanu, and has been intensively cryptanalyzed (see [16,18,19,22,25]). The key equation in this scheme is of the form $ed - k\psi_3(N) = 1$ with $\psi_3(N) = (p^2 + p + 1)(q^2 + q + 1)$, $d < N^\delta$, and $e = N^\alpha$. The attacks presented in [18,25] show that one can find d if $\delta < 2 - \sqrt{\alpha}$. If we apply Theorem 4 with $n = 3$, then the bound becomes $\delta < 2 - \sqrt{\alpha}$. This shows that the results presented in [25] is a special case of Theorem 4.

Comparison for $n = 2, 4$. In the scheme of Cotan and Teșeleanu [6], the key equation is $ed - k\psi_n(N) = 1$ with $\psi_n(N) = \frac{(p^n-1)(q^n-1)}{(p-1)(q-1)}$, $d < N^\delta$, and $e = N^\alpha$. In [6], the cryptanalysis is based on the continued fraction method. It shows that one can find d if $\log_2(d) < 0.5(n - \alpha - 0.5)\log_2(N)$, that is if $\delta < \frac{2n-1}{4} - \frac{1}{2}\alpha$. Moreover, the cryptanalysis leads to the value of $\psi_n(N)$, from which one has to find p and q using $N = pq$. This is infeasible for $n \ge 5$.

To compare the bound of Cotan and Teșeleanu with our bound in Theorem 4, we give an estimation of their difference Δ. We have

$$\Delta = n - 1 - \frac{\sqrt{2}}{2}\sqrt{(n-1)\alpha} - \left(\frac{2n-1}{4} - \frac{1}{2}\alpha\right)$$

$$= \frac{2n-3+2\alpha}{4} - \frac{\sqrt{2}}{2}\sqrt{(n-1)\alpha}$$

$$= \frac{4\alpha^2 + 4n^2 - 4\alpha - 12n + 9}{4\left(2n - 3 + 2\alpha + 2\sqrt{2}\sqrt{(n-1)\alpha}\right)}$$

$$= \frac{(2n-3)^2 + (2\alpha-1)^2 - 1}{4\left(2n - 3 + 2\alpha + 2\sqrt{2}\sqrt{(n-1)\alpha}\right)}.$$

For $n \geq 2$, we have $(2n - 3)^2 \geq 1$, and consequently, $\Delta \geq 0$. This shows that the bound in Theorem 4 is better than the bound of [6] for all $n \geq 2$.

On the other hand, in the case $e \approx \psi_n(N) \approx N^{n-1}$, that is $\alpha = n - 1$, the bound in [6] reduces to $\delta < \frac{1}{4}$, while the bound in Theorem 4 is

$$\delta < (n - 1) - \frac{\sqrt{2}}{2}\sqrt{(n - 1)\alpha} = (n - 1) - \frac{\sqrt{2}}{2}(n - 1) \approx 0.292(n - 1),$$

which is much larger than $\frac{1}{4}$.

In Table 2, we present a numerical comparison between the bound of [6], and the new bound for $e \approx \psi_n(N) \approx N^{n-1}$, that is $\alpha = n - 1$.

Table 2. Comparison of the bound in [6] with the bound in Theorem 4 for $\alpha = n - 1$.

n	$\delta_0 = \frac{2n-1}{4} - \frac{1}{2}\alpha$ in [6]	$\delta_1 = (n - 1) - \frac{\sqrt{2}}{2}\sqrt{(n - 1)\alpha}$ in Theorem 4	Difference $\Delta = \delta_1 - \delta_0$
2	0.25	0.292	0.042
3	0.25	0.585	0.335
4	0.25	0.878	0.628
5	0.25	1.171	0.921
6	0.25	1.464	1.214

5.3   Experimental Results

In this section, we present the results of the experiments performed to evaluate the effectiveness of our method as presented in Sect. 5.

We have implemented our method as described in Theorem 4 in Windows 11 environment on a computer with Intel(R) Core(TM) i5-8250U CPU 1.60 GHZ, 8.0 GO. To conduct the experiments, we used two random prime numbers p, q of various sizes up to 512 bits, computed $N = pq$ and $\psi_n(N) = \frac{(p^n-1)(q^n-1)}{(p-1)(q-1)}$ with $n = 4$. We then generated an integer $d = N^\delta$ with $\delta < 0.292(n - 1) = 0.876$ such that $\gcd(d, \psi_n(N)) = 1$, and computed $e = N^\alpha$ such that $e \equiv d^{-1} \pmod{\psi_n(N)}$. We applied the method described in Theorem 4 to solve the equation $xH(y) + 1 \equiv 0 \pmod{e}$ with

$$H(y) = y^3 + (N + 1)y^2 + (N^2 - 2N + 1)y + N^3 - N^2 - N + 1.$$

Table 3 shows the experimental results for various moduli $N = pq$ for $n = 4$ using Maple. While the theoretical bound is $d < N^{0.878}$ in Table 2, experimentally, we were able to solve the equation in all cases with $d < N^{0.6}$, and factor N.

Table 3. Experimental results for various bit-sizes with the method of Theorem 4 with the polynomial $H(y) = y^3 + (N+1)y^2 + (N^2 - 2N + 1)y + N^3 - N^2 - N + 1$.

$\log(N)$	δ	α	m	t	Dimension	Time (sec)
200	0.514	2.996	3	3	28	127
300	0.515	2.999	3	3	28	315
400	0.514	2.991	3	3	28	647
500	0.509	2.998	3	3	28	1022
600	0.509	2.994	3	3	28	1758
700	0.508	3.0	3	3	28	2406
800	0.508	2.999	3	3	28	3191
900	0.509	2.996	3	2	27	3304
1024	0.509	2.998	3	3	28	5394

As an example with $n = 4$, we take the following parameters

$$N = 59469611817647890278747665048\mathrm{3},$$
$$e = 1210287603449784439808424816354973084778899798691\mathrm{19}\backslash$$
$$888967275140135233008591517832528624837$$

Then, $e = N^\alpha$ with $\alpha \approx 2.991$, and the equation is $xH(y) + 1 \equiv 0 \pmod{e}$ with

$$H(y) = y^3 + (N+1)y^2 + (N^2 - 2N + 1)y + N^3 - N^2 - N + 1.$$

We take the bounds

$$X = N^{0.6} \approx 732111219179101370,$$
$$Y = N^{0.5} \approx 771165428540776,$$
$$Z = XY^3 + 1 \approx 33575285768213843410336590394708960869482\mathrm{33}\backslash$$
$$86772399963641349121.$$

We take $m = 4$, $t = 3$ so that the dimension of the lattice is $\omega = 28$. We construct the lattice $\mathcal{L}$ with the coefficients of the polynomials defined by

$$G_{j,k,i}(x, y, z) = x^i y^j F(x, y, z)^k e^{m-k},$$
$$\text{for} \quad j = 0, 1, \ldots, r-1, \ k = 0, \ldots m, \ i = 1, \ldots, m-k,$$
$$\text{or} \quad j = 0, \ldots \lfloor t \rfloor, \ k = \left\lfloor \frac{m}{t} \right\rfloor j, \ldots, m, \ i = 0.$$

Then, we reduce the lattice with the LLL algorithm, solve a system formed by three equations with Gröbner basis method, and find the solution

$$x_0 = 12323994910463208,$$
$$y_0 = 1610839209194556,$$
$$z_0 = 515119614145965267706175438038941277522864903785357956767841\mathrm{29}.$$

Note that $p + q = y_0$. Combining this with $N = pq$, we get

$$p = 1037808548596679,$$
$$q = 573030660597877,$$

which gives the factorization of N.

6 Conclusion

In this paper, we presented a new method to solve the modular equation $xH(y) + c \equiv 0 \pmod{e}$ where $H(y)$ is a monic polynomial with integer coefficients and degree $r \geq 1$. The method is based on Coppersmith's method. For $e = N^\alpha$, our new method finds the small solutions (x_0, y_0) satisfying $|x_0| < N^\beta$, $|y_0| < N^\gamma$ under the conditions $|c| < N^{\beta + r\gamma}$, and $\beta < \alpha - \sqrt{r\alpha\gamma}$. We applied our method to analyse the scheme of Cotan and Teşeleanu by solving the key equation $ed - k\psi_n(N) = 1$ where $\psi_n(N) = \frac{(p^n - 1)(q^n - 1)}{(p-1)(q-1)}$, when $d = N^\delta$ is such that $\delta < n - 1 - \frac{\sqrt{2}}{2}\sqrt{(n-1)\alpha}$. Our result is valid for any $n \geq 2$, and significantly improve the former cryptanalysis of the scheme of Cotan and Teşeleanu.

References

1. Boneh, D.: Twenty years of attacks on the RSA cryptosystem. Notices Amer. Math. Soc. **46**(2), 203–213 (1999)
2. Boneh, D., Durfee, G.: Cryptanalysis of RSA with private key d less than $N^{0.292}$. In: Stern, J. (ed.) EUROCRYPT 1999. LNCS, vol. 1592, pp. 1–11. Springer, Heidelberg (1999). https://doi.org/10.1007/3-540-48910-X_1
3. Boudabra, M., Nitaj, A.: A new generalization of the KMOV cryptosystem. J. Appl. Math. Comput. **57**(1–2), 229–245 (2018)
4. Collins, T., Hopkins, D., Langford, S., Sabin, M.: Public key cryptographic apparatus and Method. US Patent #5,848,159, Jan. 1997 (1997)
5. Coppersmith, D.: Small solutions to polynomial equations, and low exponent RSA vulnerabilities. J. Cryptol. **10**(4), 233–260 (1997)
6. Cotan, P., Teşeleanu, G.: Continued fractions applied to a family of RSA-like cryptosystems. In: Su, C., Gritzalis, D., Piuri, V. (eds.) Information Security Practice and Experience. ISPEC 2022. Lecture Notes in Computer Science, vol. 13620, pp. 589–605. Springer, Cham (2022). https://doi.org/10.1007/978-3-031-21280-2_33
7. Hinek, M.: Cryptanalysis of RSA and Its Variants. Chapman & Hall/CRC, Cryptography and Network Security Series, Boca Raton (2009)
8. Howgrave-Graham, N.: Finding small roots of univariate modular equations revisited. In: Darnell, M. (ed.) Cryptography and Coding 1997. LNCS, vol. 1355, pp. 131–142. Springer, Heidelberg (1997). https://doi.org/10.1007/BFb0024458
9. Jochemsz, E., May, A.: A strategy for finding roots of multivariate polynomials with new applications in attacking RSA variants. In: Lai, X., Chen, K. (eds.) ASIACRYPT 2006. LNCS, vol. 4284, pp. 267–282. Springer, Heidelberg (2006). https://doi.org/10.1007/11935230_18

10. Koyama, K., Maurer, U.M., Okamoto, T., Vanstone, S.A.: New public-key schemes based on elliptic curves over the ring $\mathbb{Z}_n$. In: Proceedings of CRYPTO 1991, Lecture Notes in Computer Science, vol. 576, pp. 252–266 (1991)
11. Kunihiro, N.: On optimal bounds of small inverse problems and approximate GCD problems with higher degree. In: Gollmann, D., Freiling, F.C. (eds.) ISC 2012. LNCS, vol. 7483, pp. 55–69. Springer, Heidelberg (2012). https://doi.org/10.1007/978-3-642-33383-5_4
12. Lenstra, A.K., Lenstra, H.W., Lovász, L.: Factoring polynomials with rational coefficients. Math. Ann. **261**, 513–534 (1982)
13. May, A.: Using LLL-reduction for solving RSA and factorization problems: a survey. In: Nguyen, P., Vallée, B. (eds.) LLL+25 Conference in Honour of the 25th Birthday of the LLL Algorithm. Springer, Berlin, Heidelberg (2007). https://doi.org/10.1007/978-3-642-02295-1_10
14. May, A.: New RSA vulnerabilities using lattice reduction methods. PhD Thesis, University of Paderborn (2003). https://digital.ub.uni-paderborn.de/ubpb/urn/urn:nbn:de:hbz:466-20030101205
15. Murru, N., Saettone, F.M.: A novel RSA-like cryptosystem based on a generalization of the rédei rational functions. In: Kaczorowski, J., Pieprzyk, J., Pomykała, J. (eds.) NuTMiC 2017. LNCS, vol. 10737, pp. 91–103. Springer, Cham (2018). https://doi.org/10.1007/978-3-319-76620-1_6
16. Nassr, D.I., Anwar, M., Bahig, H.M.: Improving small private exponent attack on the Murru-Saettone cryptosystem. Theor. Comput. Sci. **923**, 222–234 (2022)
17. Nitaj, A.: Another generalization of Wiener's attack on RSA. In: Vaudenay, S. (ed.) Africacrypt 2008. LNCS, vol. 5023, pp. 174–190. Springer, Heidelberg (2008). https://doi.org/10.1007/978-3-540-68164-9_12
18. Nitaj, A., Ariffin, M.R.B.K., Adenan, N.N.H., Abu, N.A.: Classical attacks on a variant of the RSA cryptosystem. In: Longa, P., Ràfols, C. (eds.) LATINCRYPT 2021. LNCS, vol. 12912, pp. 151–167. Springer, Cham (2021). https://doi.org/10.1007/978-3-030-88238-9_8
19. Nitaj, A., Ariffin, M.R.B.K., Adenan, N.N.H., Lau, T.S.C., Chen, J.: Security issues of novel RSA variant. IEEE Access **10**, 53788–53796 (2022)
20. Quisquater, J.J., Couvreur, C.: Fast decipherment algorithm for RSA public-key cryptosystem. Electron. Lett. **18**(21), 905–907 (1982)
21. Rivest, R., Shamir, A., Adleman, L.: A method for obtaining digital signatures and public-key cryptosystems. Commun. ACM **21**(2), 120–126 (1978)
22. Shi, G., Wang, G., Gu, D.: Further cryptanalysis of a type of RSA variants. In: Susilo, W., Chen, X., Guo, F., Zhang, Y., Intan, R. (eds.) Information Security. ISC 2022. Lecture Notes in Computer Science, vol. 13640. Springer, Cham (2022). https://doi.org/10.1007/978-3-031-22390-7_9
23. Takagi, T.: A fast RSA-type public-key primitive modulo $p^k q$ using Hensel lifting. IEICE Trans. **87-A**, 94–101 (2004)
24. Wiener, M.: Cryptanalysis of short RSA secret exponents. IEEE Trans. Inf. Theory **36**, 553–558 (1990)
25. Zheng, M., Kunihiro, N., Yao, Y.: Cryptanalysis of the RSA variant based on cubic Pell equation. Theoret. Comput. Sci. **889**, 135–144 (2021)

Lattice-Based Cryptography
Constructions

DiTRU: A Resurrection of NTRU over Dihedral Group

Ali Raya[1](✉), Vikas Kumar[2](✉), and Sugata Gangopadhyay[1](✉)

[1] Department of Computer Science and Engineering, Indian Institute of Technology
Roorkee, Roorkee 247667, India
{ali_r,sugata.gangopadhyay}@cs.iitr.ac.in
[2] Department of Mathematics, Indian Institute of Technology Roorkee,
Roorkee 247667, India
v_kumar@ma.iitr.ac.in

Abstract. NTRU-like cryptosystems are among the most studied lattice-based post-quantum candidates. While most NTRU proposals have been introduced over a commutative ring of quotient polynomials, other rings can be used. Noncommutative algebra has been endorsed as a direction to build new variants of NTRU a long time ago. The first attempt to construct a noncommutative variant was due to Hoffstein and Silverman motivated by more resistance to lattice attack. The scheme has been built over the group ring of a dihedral group. However, their design differed from standard NTRU and soon was found vulnerable to algebraic attacks. In this work, we revive the group ring NTRU over the dihedral group as an instance of the GR-NTRU framework.

Unlike many proposals of noncommutative variants in the literature, our work focuses on putting the scheme into practice. We clear all the aspects that make our scheme implementable by proposing an efficient inversion algorithm over the new setting of the noncommutative ring, describing the decryption failure model, and analyzing the lattice associated with our instantiation. Finally, we discuss the best-known attacks against our scheme and provide an implementation targeting 128-bit, 192-bit, and 256-bit levels of security as proof of its practicality.

Keywords: NTRU · noncommutative · post quantum · lattice-based

1 Introduction

The first NTRU cryptosystem was proposed early in 1996 by Hoffstein, Pipher, and Silverman [22]. Two decades of thorough cryptanalysis could not degrade the confidence in the hardness of NTRU assumption for well-chosen parameter sets. The hard problem of NTRU can be related to finding unusually short vectors in lattices of a particular structure(q-ary lattices), and in this regard, NTRU is classified as a lattice-based cryptosystem. Because of the efficiency and reasonable memory requirements of NTRU, different NTRU-like schemes have been proposed in the literature, resulting in a standard (IEEE-1363.1) [53] and

© The Author(s), under exclusive license to Springer Nature Switzerland AG 2024
S. Vaudenay and C. Petit (Eds.): AFRICACRYPT 2024, LNCS 14861, pp. 349–375, 2024.
https://doi.org/10.1007/978-3-031-64381-1_16

other competent candidates that progressed to the third round of NIST standardization process [8]. NTRU proposal inspired different NTRU-like designs that replace the underlying ring with other rings motivated by faster computations [30] or more resistance to some lattice attacks [40]. Noncommutativity has been endorsed as a promising direction for building NTRU-like schemes long ago [13]. Consequently, a few works in literature have introduced variants based on noncommutative algebra.

1.1 Related Work

Hoffstein and Silverman have introduced the first known noncommutative scheme [24] in literature based on the dihedral group, which was vulnerable to an attack by Coppersmith and Shamir [12]. The design of the key generation, encryption, and decryption procedures differs from the standard NTRU, and the attack by Coppersmith and Shamir exploits the fact that ciphertext is a pair of two elements from the ring. The attack applies a map on the first element and retrieves some information that helps recover the message from the second element. We refer the reader to the work by Truman [50] for a detailed analysis of this attack. Similarly, NNRU [52] and PairTRU [31] have been proposed as noncommutative analogs to NTRU operating over a matrix ring of $k \times k$ matrices of polynomials. The motivation behind these variants was to avoid lattice attacks; however, the schemes' design differs from NTRU, i.e., the public key in [31,52] is a pair of two elements from the underlying ring. Therefore, a thorough analysis of the hardness of the new assumption is required before establishing trust in the schemes.

Other works introduce noncommutative NTRU-like schemes from quaternion algebra where the lattice attacks are still applicable but harder to apply, according to the authors' claim. QTRU [40] is a noncommutative multi-dimensional NTRU-like scheme using quaternion algebra. The authors conclude that QTRU is four times slower than NTRU but more resistant to lattice attacks. BQTRU [6] is another example of a noncommutative scheme based on quaternion algebra with bivariate polynomials as the underlying ring. The design of BQTRU is inspired by QTRU, and the authors conclude that BQTRU can be faster than NTRU for equivalent levels of security if Genty's attack [18] is not applicable against the scheme. Further, Ling and Mendelsohn [38] introduced an interesting theoretical construction of an NTRU variant in quaternion algebras of bounded discriminant. The doubts related to these variants of NTRU arise from the poor analysis of the security of the associated lattices. For instance, none of these schemes analyze the behavior of the lattice reduction algorithms in practice. Moreover, the claim that Gentry's attack is not practically applicable to the associated lattices is not solid enough.

The Group ring NTRU or GR-NTRU [54] is an interesting proposal that generalizes NTRU to a group ring NTRU. In GR-NTRU, different schemes with an underlying hard assumption similar to that in the standard NTRU can be designed from the group ring $\mathbb{Z}G$, where $\mathbb{Z}$ refers to the integer ring and G is any abelian or nonabelian group.

1.2   Context

NTRU Hard Assumption: First NTRU scheme is defined over a truncated ring of polynomials $\mathcal{R}_q = \mathbb{Z}_q[x]/(x^N - 1)$ for prime N and modulo $q \in \mathbb{Z}$. The private key is a pair of polynomials $f, g \in \mathcal{R}_q$ with small coefficients (*ternary*) where f is an invertible polynomial. The public key is the polynomial calculated as $h := f^{-1} * g \in \mathcal{R}_q$. NTRU hard problem is formulated as: given h, find $f', g' \in \mathcal{R}_q$ (two polynomials with small coefficients) such that $f' * h = g'$ (mod q).

Knowing the public key h, there are mainly two paths to attack the problem: either by following an efficient search approach like Meet-in-the-Middle attack (MITM) [25,41,51] to find such pair (f', g'), or by mapping the problem of finding the private key into finding a short vector in a lattice built from the public key h using the lattice reduction algorithms [11,45].

NTRU Learning Problem. [44, 4.4.4]: is a relaxed variant of NTRU problem that assumes the attacker knows many samples of the public key h_i calculated using the same f but different g_i. The problem is formulated as: given $h_i := f^{-1} * g_i$ for $i \in \{1, 2, \ldots, m\}$, find f (or $x^k * f$ for some k). The NTRU learning problem has been studied to analyze a simplified NTRU problem [47]. It was believed to be hard and has been used to build some primitives like [1].

Recently, Kim and Lee [32] proposed a polynomial time attack that can break NTRU learning problem if the attacker knows N different h_i, where N refers to the extension degree of the ring $\mathcal{R}_q$. The attack exploits: ① The design of the NTRU variant that samples the private polynomial g with exactly d ones and d minus ones. ② The commutative algebra of the underlying ring $\mathcal{R}_q$.

The broad idea of the attack relies on the fact that $g_i * \bar{g}_i$, where $\bar{g}_i$ refers to the conjugate of g_i, always has a constant term c equal to the hamming weight of g_i. Therefore, for all the known h_i, and since the underlying ring is **commutative**, the attacker can build a system of linear equations of the form

$$constant(h_i * \bar{h}_i * f * \bar{f}) = c$$

This system has $f * \bar{f}$ as a root that can recover the private key in a polynomial time as described in [32]. Therefore, considering noncommutative algebras makes some algebraic attacks harder to apply, thus increasing the security of the cryptosystem constructed using them.

1.3   Our Work

Most of the noncommutative schemes in the literature have been proposed differently than the NTRU design, resulting in new schemes triggering doubts about the hardness of the new proposed assumptions. Other schemes have been introduced theoretically without clearing many aspects to make them implementable and practical.

In our work, we focus on clearing all the aspects of designing a noncommutative NTRU-like scheme based on the dihedral group. As an abbreviation, we call it DiTRU. For DiTRU, we not only discuss the theoretical foundation of the cryptosystem but also provide experiments in support of our results. Our contribution can be summarized in the following:

- **DiTRU, a noncommutative analog of NTRU:** We instantiate the GR-NTRU framework [54] using the noncommutative dihedral group for our cryptosystem. The selection of the dihedral group is motivated by its closeness to the cyclic group, which enables the extension of many results and implementation constructions over the cyclic group (i.e., the underlying group of standard NTRU) to the new setting of the noncommutative ring.
- **Inversion algorithm:** We propose an inversion algorithm that can check the invertibility and find the inverse of elements over the group ring RD_N. We provide a necessary and sufficient condition to check/find inverses over RD_N by relating the inversion problem to the problem of checking/inverting elements over RC_N (Theorem 2). Particularly, for $R = \mathbb{Z}_q$ and q is a power of two, one can construct the inverse with complexity $O(N^2)$.
- **Analysis of DiTRU lattice:** We show that even if the DiTRU lattice is vulnerable to one layer of Gentry's attack, one need not exactly double the order of the dihedral group to match the same hardness of the SVP over the cyclic group of order N. For precise analysis, we describe the probability of decryption failure for DiTRU over D_N (of order $2N$) compared to NTRU over C_N (of order N). We show that the blocksize needed to retrieve the private key for DiTRU is larger than that for NTRU when a negligible decryption failure is allowed. This result follows as the lattice gap for DiTRU lattice is greater even if the SVP is being solved over lattices of the same dimension.
  For moderate lattice dimensions, we provide an experiment supporting our claim. In our experiment, we identify the smallest blocksize *beta* required to retrieve a decryption key for DiTRU vs. NTRU lattices when the SVP is solved over the same dimension. Figure 1a summarizes the experimental results for moderate-size lattices, and Fig. 1b compares the estimated blocksize to retrieve the private key according to *2016-estimator* in higher dimensions. Our experiment's implementation and detailed documentation can be accessed at https://github.com/The-Isogeniest/DiTRU_blocksize_experiment.
- **Full-fledged cryptosystem:** We discuss the cost of the search, primal, hybrid, and other related attacks against DiTRU, and based on that, we define three sets of parameters targeting 128-bit, 192-bit, and 256-bit security levels defined by NIST. We provide a C reference implementation of DiTRU and compare it with the parameter sets of NTRU that achieve the same security level according to the evaluation criteria followed for DiTRU. The package can be accessed at https://github.com/The-Isogeniest/DiTRU. To the best of our knowledge, this is the first noncommutative analog to NTRU, accompanied by a full-package implementation as proof of its practicality.

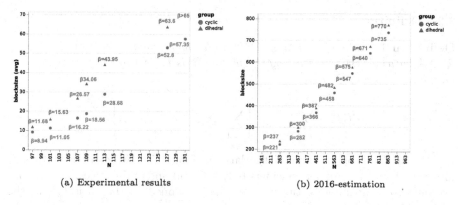

(a) Experimental results   (b) 2016-estimation

Fig. 1. Average blocksize needed to retrieve the key for DiTRU based on the dihedral group of order $2N$ after applying one layer of Gentry's attack vs. NTRU based on the cyclic group of order N. The experimental results are obtained for $q' = 512$ for NTRU lattice and q, achieving the same probability of decryption failure for DiTRU. While for 2016 estimation, the results are estimated for $(N, q') = (263, 1024), (367, 2048), (461, 2048), (563, 2048), (661, 2048), (761, 2048)$, and $(863, 2048)$ for NTRU and the equivalent parameters that achieve the same decryption failure for DiTRU. *2016-estimator* estimates that the gaps of the obtained blocksizes are $16, 18, 21, 24, 28, 31$, and 35, respectively.

1.4 Organization

We introduce preliminaries, NTRU, GR-NTRU in Sect. 2. Section 3 introduces DiTRU along with the inversion algorithm and the analysis of the associated lattice. In Sect. 4, we provide cryptanalysis considering the well-known attacks against DiTRU. The selected parameters are presented in Sect. 5 followed by the adopted design rationale and implementation details in Sect. 6. Finally, we conclude our work in Sect. 7.

2 Preliminaries

2.1 Notations

– Symbol $*$, wherever it occurs, denotes the multiplication of elements with respect to the underlying structure.
– $\mathbb{Z}$ denote the set of integers and $\mathbb{Z}_q = \{a \pmod{q} \mid a \in \mathbb{Z}, -q/2 < a \leq q/2\}$ for a positive integer q.
– G denotes a finite group, R denotes a commutative ring with unity and R^* be the group of units of R.
– Let $\mathbb{R}^n$ be the Euclidean space of dimension n, given a vector $\mathbf{v} = (v_1, v_2, \ldots v_n) \in \mathbb{R}^n$:
  • The Euclidean norm ℓ_2 is denoted $\|.\|$ and calculated as $\|\mathbf{v}\| = \sqrt{\sum_{i=1}^{n} v_i^2}$.
  • The ℓ–infinity norm ℓ_∞ is denoted $\|.\|_\infty$ and calculated as $\|\mathbf{v}\|_\infty = \max_{i=1}^{n} |v_i|$.

2.2   Definitions

Definition 1 *(Lattice). Let* $\mathbf{B} \in \mathbb{R}^{n \times m}$ *with independent rows* $\mathbf{b}_1, \mathbf{b}_2, \ldots, \mathbf{b}_n \in \mathbb{R}^m$. *A lattice* $\mathcal{L}(\mathbf{B})$ *generated by the matrix* $\mathbf{B}$ *is the set of integer linear combination of rows of* $\mathbf{B}$, *i.e.,*

$$\mathcal{L}(\mathbf{B}) = \sum_{i=1}^{n} \mathbb{Z}\mathbf{b}_i = \left\{ \sum_{i=1}^{n} z_i \mathbf{b}_i, \text{ where } z_i \in \mathbb{Z} \right\}. \tag{1}$$

We call $\mathbf{B}$ a basis matrix of the lattice. If $\mathbf{b}_i \in \mathbb{Z}^n$, we call the lattice an integral lattice. This paper considers only full-rank integral lattices, i.e., $n = m$. We refer to the volume of the parallelepiped spanned by the basis $\mathbf{b}_i$'s as the volume of the lattice defined as $det(\mathcal{L}(\mathbf{B})) = \sqrt{|det(\mathbf{BB}^T)|}$.

Definition 2 *(SVP). Given a lattice* $\mathcal{L}(\mathbf{B}) \subset \mathbb{R}^n$, *the Shortest Vector Problem (SVP) asks to find a non-zero vector* $\mathbf{v} \in \mathcal{L}(\mathbf{B})$ *such that* $\|\mathbf{v}\| \leq \|\mathbf{w}\|$ *for all non-zero vectors* $\mathbf{w} \in \mathcal{L}(\mathbf{B})$; *the length of the shortest vector in the lattice is denoted as* $\lambda_1(\mathcal{L}(\mathbf{B}))$.

A relaxed variant of the SVP called γ-SVP asks to find a short nonzero vector $\mathbf{x} \in \mathcal{L}(\mathbf{B})$ within an approximation factor $\gamma(n) \geq 1$ of the length of the shortest vector, i.e., $\|\mathbf{x}\| \leq \gamma(n)\lambda_1(\mathcal{L}(\mathbf{B}))$.

Definition 3 *(Gaussian heuristic). For a full rank lattice* $\mathcal{L}(\mathbf{B})$ *of dimension* d, *the estimation of the norm of the shortest vector according to the Gaussian heuristic is denoted as* $gh(\mathcal{L}(\mathbf{B}))$, *and calculated as*

$$gh(\mathcal{L}(\mathbf{B})) = \sqrt{d/2\pi e} \cdot \; det(\mathcal{L}(\mathbf{B}))^{1/d}. \tag{2}$$

Definition 4 *(Group ring). The group ring of a finite group* $G = \{g_i \mid i = 1, 2, \ldots, n\}$ *over* R *is the ring*

$$RG = \left\{ a = \sum_{i=1}^{n} \alpha_i g_i : \alpha_i \in R \quad for \quad i = 1, 2, \ldots, n \right\} \tag{3}$$

with the following operations: Let $a = \sum_{i=1}^{n} \alpha_i g_i, b = \sum_{i=1}^{n} \beta_i g_i \in RG$. *Then*

1. *Sum of* a *and* b *is* $\sum_{i=1}^{n} \alpha_i g_i + \sum_{i=1}^{n} \beta_i g_i = \sum_{i=1}^{n} (\alpha_i + \beta_i) g_i$.
2. *Product of* a *and* b *is* $\sum_{i=1}^{n} \alpha_i g_i * \sum_{i=1}^{n} \beta_i g_i = \sum_{i=1}^{n} \left(\sum_{g_h g_k = g_i} \alpha_h \beta_k \right) g_i$.

Definition 5 *(Coefficient vector). The coefficient vector of* $a = \sum_{i=1}^{n} \alpha_i g_i \in RG$ *is* $\mathbf{a} = (\alpha_1, \alpha_2, \ldots, \alpha_n) \in R^n$.

We use a and $\mathbf{a}$ to denote the group ring elements interchangeably depending on the context.

Definition 6 *(Matrix representation). The RG-matrix of $a = \sum_{i=1}^{n} \alpha_{g_i} g_i \in RG$ is defined as*

$$\mathbf{M}_{RG}(a) = \begin{pmatrix} \alpha_{g_1^{-1}g_1} & \alpha_{g_1^{-1}g_2} & \cdots\cdots & \alpha_{g_1^{-1}g_n} \\ \alpha_{g_2^{-1}g_1} & \alpha_{g_2^{-1}g_2} & \cdots\cdots & \alpha_{g_2^{-1}g_n} \\ \vdots & \vdots & \ddots & \vdots \\ \alpha_{g_n^{-1}g_1} & \alpha_{g_n^{-1}g_2} & \cdots\cdots & \alpha_{g_n^{-1}g_n} \end{pmatrix}. \tag{4}$$

The matrix representation of the group ring elements is unique and satisfies

$$\mathbf{M}_{RG}(a + b) = \mathbf{M}_{RG}(a) + \mathbf{M}_{RG}(b), \quad \mathbf{M}_{RG}(a * b) = \mathbf{M}_{RG}(a) * \mathbf{M}_{RG}(b) \tag{5}$$

for all $a, b \in RG$.

2.3 Lattice Basis Reduction

Given a publicly available *'bad'* basis with large and highly non-orthogonal vectors, a lattice reduction algorithm tries to find *'good'* basis consisting of reasonably short and orthogonal vectors that define the same lattice. LLL [37] is a famous example of a polynomial-time basis reduction algorithm that produces a good-reduced basis for low dimensions. Although LLL runs in polynomial time, the quality of the reduced basis degrades as the dimension of the lattice increases. BKZ [45], and its variants like BKZ2.0 [11] and Progressive BKZ [4] are generalizations of LLL that consider an additional parameter: the blocksize or β. The higher the value of β, the better the quality of the reduced basis and the higher the running time.

For a full rank lattice $\mathcal{L}(\mathbf{B})$ reduced with a blocksize β such that $\|\mathbf{b}_1\| \leq \|\mathbf{b}_2\| \leq \ldots \leq \|\mathbf{b}_d\|$, we give the following definitions:

Definition 7 *(Root Hermite factor). The root Hermite factor δ is defined via $\|\mathbf{b}_1\| = \delta^d \det(\mathcal{L}(\mathbf{B}))^{1/d}$ and can be estimated for larger β [10] as*

$$\delta = \left(\frac{\beta}{2\pi e} (\pi\beta)^{\frac{1}{\beta}} \right)^{\frac{1}{2(\beta-1)}}. \tag{6}$$

Definition 8 *(Geometric Series Assumption). The Geometric Series Assumption(GSA) estimates that $\|b_i^*\| \approx \delta^{-2}\|b_{i-1}^*\|$, where δ is the root Hermite factor.*

The exact blocksize required to find a short vector with norm $\|\mathbf{v}\|$ lying in a lattice $\mathcal{L}(\mathbf{B})$ is still an active area of research. A few estimators like *2016-estimator* [3] have been introduced to estimate the blocksize β needed to retrieve a short vector $\mathbf{v} \in \mathcal{L}$. 2016-estimator briefly states that BKZ with blocksize β can retrieve the vector $\mathbf{v}$ given that:

$$\sqrt{\beta/d}\|\mathbf{v}\| < \delta^{2\beta-d-1} \cdot \det(L)^{1/d}, \tag{7}$$

where δ indicates the root Hermite factor. The value of β and, therefore, the hardness of the problem increases with the increase of the lattice dimension d, and the lattice gap $\frac{\|v\|}{gh(\mathcal{L}(\mathbf{B}))}$. A further discussion regarding the cost of the SVP problem concerning DiTRU lattice with respect to enumeration and sieving regimes is given in Subsect. 4.2.

2.4   NTRU Cryptosystem

There are many variants of NTRU in literature. We discuss the key generation, encryption, and decryption of NTRU cryptosystem as described in [21].

Let N, p, q be positive integers such that N, p are prime numbers, $p \ll q$, and q is a power of 2. Let $\mathcal{R}$, $\mathcal{R}_p$, and $\mathcal{R}_q$ be the truncated ring of polynomials of degree N defined as

$$\mathcal{R} = \frac{\mathbb{Z}[x]}{(x^N - 1)}, \quad \mathcal{R}_p = \frac{\mathbb{Z}_p[x]}{(x^N - 1)}, \quad \mathcal{R}_q = \frac{\mathbb{Z}_q[x]}{(x^N - 1)}. \tag{8}$$

Let $\mathcal{T}_N$ be the space of all N length ternary polynomials with coefficients $-1, 0, 1$ and $\mathcal{T}_N(d_1, d_2)$ be the space of ternary polynomials with d_1 coefficients equal to 1, d_2 coefficients equal to -1, and the remaining coefficients equal to 0.

- **Key generation:** The NTRU private key is pair $(f, g) \in \mathcal{T}_N(d+1, d) \times \mathcal{T}_N(d, d)$, where $d = \lfloor N/3 \rfloor$ and f is invertible in $\mathcal{R}_p$ with inverse f_p as well as in $\mathcal{R}_q$ with inverse f_q. NTRU public key is computed as $h = f_q * g \in \mathcal{R}_q$.
- **Encryption:** A message $m \in \mathcal{R}_p$ is encrypted as $c = pr * h + m \in \mathcal{R}_q$, where r is sampled randomly from $\mathcal{T}(d, d)$.
- **Decryption:** First, compute $a = f * c \in \mathcal{R}_q$, then the decrypted message is retrieved as $m' = f_p * a \in \mathcal{R}_p$.

NTRU Lattice: The problem of finding the NTRU private key can be related to the SVP in a lattice of a certain form. Given the public information q, N and $h = f_q * g \pmod{q}$, construct the basis matrix for the lattice $\mathcal{L}(\mathbf{B_{cyclic}})$ as follows:

$$\mathbf{B_{cyclic}} = \begin{pmatrix} \mathbf{I}_N & \mathbf{H_{cyclic}} \\ \mathbf{0}_N & q\mathbf{I}_N \end{pmatrix}, \tag{9}$$

where $\mathbf{H_{cyclic}}$ is a right circulant matrix whose rows are the coefficient vectors of the polynomials $x^i * h$ for $i \in \{0, 1, \ldots, N-1\}$. The determinant of the lattice $\mathcal{L}(\mathbf{B_{cyclic}})$ is $det(\mathbf{B_{cyclic}}) = q^N$. Therefore, $gh(\mathcal{L}(\mathbf{B_{cyclic}})) = \sqrt{qN/\pi e}$.

While the norm of the private elements $(x^i * f, x^i * g)$ is approximately $\sqrt{4N/3}$ and $(x^i * f, x^i * g) \in \mathcal{L}(\mathbf{B_{cyclic}})$ since $(x^i * f) * h = x^i * g \pmod{q}$. Therefore, one expects (f, g) or its rotations to be the shortest vectors in the lattice $\mathcal{L}(\mathbf{B_{cyclic}})$ for large values of N.

2.5   Group Ring NTRU/GR-NTRU

There are various attempts in the literature to generalize NTRU. We find the GR-NTRU by Yashuda et al. [54], the most reasonable description for designing NTRU-like cryptosystems. We first describe NTRU as a cryptosystem based on a group ring to lay the path for introduction to GR-NTRU.

One can think of the ring $\mathcal{R} = \mathbb{Z}[x]/\left(x^N - 1\right)$ as the group ring of cyclic group $C_N = \langle x \mid x^N = 1 \rangle$ of order N over the ring of integers $\mathbb{Z}$. In other words, $\frac{\mathbb{Z}[x]}{(x^N-1)} \approx \mathbb{Z}C_N$. The matrix $\mathbf{H_{cyclic}}$ in Eq. 9 is $\mathbf{M}_{\mathbb{Z}C_N}(h)$, the $\mathbb{Z}C_N$-matrix of the public key h. The rest of the design criteria, as discussed in Sect. 2.4, follow naturally over the group ring $\mathbb{Z}C_N$.

One can change the cyclic group C_N with other groups to construct new variants of NTRU. This motivates the definition of GR-NTRU introduced in [54] as follows:

Definition 9 *(GR-NTRU). The GR-NTRU over a finite group G is a cryptosystem built over the group ring $\mathbb{Z}G$ with key generation, encryption, and decryption the same as NTRU except that the operations are performed over the rings $\mathbb{Z}G, \mathbb{Z}_pG$, and $\mathbb{Z}_qG$, where $p \ll q$ are positive integers.*

In general, deciphering the private key of GR-NTRU is also related to the shortest vector problem in lattices of particular structures associated with the underlying group ring. This paper focuses on GR-NTRU based on the integral group ring of dihedral group, which we call DiTRU.

3   DiTRU (GR-NTRU over dihedral group)

Let $D_N = \langle x, y \mid x^N = y^2 = 1, xy = yx^{N-1} \rangle$ be dihedral group of order $2N$. DiTRU is a GR-NTRU over the group ring

$$\mathbb{Z}D_N \approx \frac{\mathbb{Z}[x,y]}{(x^N - 1, y^2 - 1, xy - yx^{N-1})}. \tag{10}$$

Any element of the group ring $\mathbb{Z}D_N$ can be written in the form $f = f_0(x) + yf_1(x)$, where $f_0(x)$ and $f_1(x)$ are elements of the ring $\mathbb{Z}C_N \approx \mathbb{Z}[x]/(x^N - 1)$.

Let $h = h_0(x) + yh_1(x)$ be the public key of DiTRU corresponding to the private key $(f, g) = (f_0(x) + yf_1(x), g_0(x) + yg_1(x))$, and

$$\mathbf{H_{dihedral}} = \mathbf{M}_{\mathbb{Z}D_N}(h) \tag{11}$$

be the matrix representation of h. Since $\mathbf{f} * \mathbf{H_{dihedral}} = \mathbf{g} \pmod{q}$, DiTRU can be associated with the lattice $\mathcal{L}(\mathbf{B_{dihedral}})$ that contains (f, g), generated by the basis matrix

$$\mathbf{B_{dihedral}} = \begin{pmatrix} \mathbf{I}_{2N} & \mathbf{H_{dihedral}} \\ \mathbf{0}_{2N} & q\mathbf{I}_{2N} \end{pmatrix}. \tag{12}$$

It is discussed in [35] that $\mathbf{H_{dihedral}} = \begin{pmatrix} \mathbf{H_0} & \mathbf{H_1} \\ \mathbf{H_1} & \mathbf{H_0} \end{pmatrix}$, where $\mathbf{H_0}, \mathbf{H_1}$ are right and left circulant matrices whose first rows are the coefficient vectors $\mathbf{h_0}$ of $h_0(x)$ and $\mathbf{h_1}$ of $h_1(x)$, respectively.

Theorem 1 *([35, Thereom 5]). For all $0 \leq i \leq N-1$, the 'rotations' of private key (f, g) given by*

$$(x^i * f_0, x^{-i} * f_1, x^i * g_0, x^{-i} * g_1) \quad and \quad (x^i * f_1, x^{-i} * f_0, x^i * g_1, x^{-i} * g_0)$$

belong to the lattice $\mathcal{L}(\mathbf{B}_{\text{dihedral}})$.

3.1 Inversion Algorithm

There are works on characterizing units in dihedral group rings [39, 43]. However, all those classifications rely on group representation theory and are not easily implementable to construct units. Further, Hurley in [29] relates the invertibility of an element of the group ring RG with the invertibility of the associated RG-matrix over the ring R. However, this method of matrix inversion is inefficient for larger dimensions. Therefore, it becomes essential to look for alternative ways to check for units. In this section, we provide a time-effective algorithm to generate units in finite integral group rings of dihedral groups. Before discussing the main inversion algorithm, let us give the required definition and result.

Definition 10. *For $f(x) = f_0 + f_1 x + \ldots + f_{N-1} x^{N-1} \in RC_N$, the conjugate of $f(x)$ is defined as $\overline{f(x)} = f(x^{N-1})$. In the vector form, conjugate of $\mathbf{f} = (f_0, f_1, \ldots, f_{N-1})$ is $\overline{\mathbf{f}} = (f_0, f_{N-1}, f_{N-2}, \ldots, f_1)$.*

One can check that $\overline{\overline{u(x)}} = u(x)$, $\overline{u(x) \pm v(x)} = \overline{u(x)} \pm \overline{v(x)}$ and $\overline{u(x) * v(x)} = \overline{u(x)} * \overline{v(x)}$ for all $u(x), v(x) \in RC_N$.

Multiplication in RD_N: The relation $xy = yx^{N-1}$ between the generators of D_N gives that the product between two elements $f = f_0(x) + y f_1(x)$ and $g = g_0(x) + y g_1(x)$ of the group ring RD_N is

$$f * g = f_0(x) * g_0(x) + \overline{f_1(x)} * g_1(x) + y(f_1(x) * g_0(x) + \overline{f_0(x)} * g_1(x)). \quad (13)$$

Theorem 2 *(Necessary and sufficient condition). Let $f = f_0(x) + y f_1(x) \in RD_N$. Then, f is a unit in RD_N if and only if $c(x) = f_1(x) * \overline{f_1(x)} - f_0(x) * \overline{f_0(x)}$ is a unit in RC_N. Moreover, if $i(x)$ denotes the inverse of $c(x)$, then the inverse of f is given by*

$$f^{-1} = -\overline{f_0(x)} * i(x) + y f_1(x) * i(x). \quad (14)$$

Proof. From Eq. 13

$$f * f^{-1} = (f_0(x) + y f_1(x)) * (-\overline{f_0(x)} * i(x) + y f_1(x) * i(x))$$
$$= (f_1(x) * \overline{f_1(x)} - f_0(x) * \overline{f_0(x)}) * i(x) = 1$$

Since $c(x) * i(x) = 1$ therefore $\overline{c(x) * i(x)} = \overline{c(x)} * \overline{i(x)} = 1$. Using the commutativity of RC_N, we get $\overline{c(x)} = c(x)$. Hence, by the uniqueness of the inverse, $i(x) = \overline{i(x)}$. Now, consider

$$f^{-1} * f = (-\overline{f_0(x)} * i(x) + y f_1(x) * i(x)) * (f_0(x) + y f_1(x))$$
$$= (f_1(x) * \overline{f_1(x)} - f_0(x) * \overline{f_0(x)}) * \overline{i(x)} = 1$$

Conversely, suppose $f = f_0(x) + yf_1(x)$ is a unit in RD_N with inverse $f^{-1} = u(x) + yv(x)$. Then $f^{-1} * f = 1 + y0$ gives

$$f_0(x) * u(x) + \overline{f_1(x)} * v(x) = 1 \quad \text{and} \quad f_1(x) * u(x) + \overline{f_0(x)} * v(x) = 0.$$

Equivalently $\begin{pmatrix} f_0(x) & \overline{f_1(x)} \\ f_1(x) & \overline{f_0(x)} \end{pmatrix} \begin{pmatrix} u(x) \\ v(x) \end{pmatrix} = \begin{pmatrix} 1 \\ 0 \end{pmatrix}$. The uniqueness of the inverse in a group ring guarantees that the matrix $\begin{pmatrix} f_0(x) & \overline{f_1(x)} \\ f_1(x) & \overline{f_0(x)} \end{pmatrix}$ is invertible; therefore, its determinant $f_0(x) * \overline{f_0(x)} - f_1(x) * \overline{f_1(x)}$ is a unit in RC_N. Further,

$$\begin{pmatrix} f_0(x) & \overline{f_1(x)} \\ f_1(x) & \overline{f_0(x)} \end{pmatrix}^{-1} \begin{pmatrix} 1 \\ 0 \end{pmatrix} = \frac{1}{f_0(x) * \overline{f_0(x)} - f_1(x) * \overline{f_1(x)}} \begin{pmatrix} \overline{f_0(x)} & -\overline{f_1(x)} \\ -f_1(x) & f_0(x) \end{pmatrix} \begin{pmatrix} 1 \\ 0 \end{pmatrix}.$$

This gives that $u(x) = -\overline{f_0(x)} * i(x)$ and $v(x) = f_1(x) * i(x)$.   □

Algorithm 1: Inversion in RD_N

Input: $f = f_0(x) + yf_1(x) \in RD_N$
Output: $f^{-1} = u(x) + yv(x) \in RD_N$ an inverse of f, or a failure
1   $mul_1 \leftarrow f_0(x) * \overline{f_0(x)}$ /* product in RC_N */
2   $mul_2 \leftarrow f_1(x) * \overline{f_1(x)}$ /* product in RC_N */
3   $c(x) \leftarrow mul_2 - mul_1$ /* Coefficient-wise subtraction in R */
4   $i(x), found \leftarrow$ find-inverse-in-RC_N(c(x))
5   **if** *not found* **then**
6   ⌊ **return** *failure*

7   $u(x) \leftarrow -\overline{f_0(x)} * i(x)$ /* product in RC_N */
8   $v(x) \leftarrow f_1(x) * i(x)$ /* product in RC_N */
9   **return** $f^{-1} = u(x) + yv(x)$

Algorithm 1 relates the problem of finding the inverse of an element in RD_N to finding the inverse of an element in RC_N (line 4). Therefore, the cost of constructing the inverse in RD_N equals the cost of computing an inverse in RC_N plus $(4N^2 + N)$. In case $R = \mathbb{Z}_q$ for q prime or prime power, one can use an efficient algorithm to find the inverse for units in $\mathbb{Z}_q C_N$ as in [46], and therefore constructing units in $\mathbb{Z}_q D_N$ efficiently.

Corollary 1. *If $f = f_0(x) + yf_1(x)$ is a unit in RD_N then $f' = f_1(x) + yf_0(x)$ is also a unit in RD_N with inverse*

$$f'^{-1} = \overline{f_1(x)} * i(x) - y\overline{f_0(x)} * i(x) \tag{15}$$

where $i(x)$ is the inverse of $f_1(x) * \overline{f_1(x)} - f_0(x) * \overline{f_0(x)}$ in RC_N.

Since $f \in T(d+1, d)$ therefore $f_1(1) * \overline{f_1(1)} - f_0(1) * \overline{f_0(1)} \neq 0 \pmod 2$. Hence, for a prime N such that 2 is a primitive root modulo N, i.e., multiplicative order of 2 modulo N is $N-1$, the element $f_1(x) * \overline{f_1(x)} - f_0(x) * \overline{f_0(x)}$ is invertible in $\mathbb{Z}_q C_N$ with high probability and consequently f is invertible in $\mathbb{Z}_q D_N$ with high probability, where q is a power of 2 [20, Page 3].

3.2   Analysis of DiTRU Lattice

One-Layer of Gentry Attack: The dihedral group D_N for prime N has a composite order $2N$; therefore, one needs to consider if an extension of Gentry's attack [18] applies to the DiTRU lattice. Gentry's attack makes the problem of solving SVP easier by mapping the original lattice into smaller dimensional lattices through homomorphisms. In his original paper, Gentry elaborates his attack for a cyclic group of composite order 2^n for positive n. A similar one-layer attack can be extended to DiTRU lattice corresponding to D_N for prime N. If the vector corresponding to the private key $(\mathbf{f_0, f_1, g_0, g_1}) \in \mathcal{L}(\mathbf{B_h})$, then according to the homomorphisms defined in Fig. 2, $(\mathbf{f_0 + f_1, g_0 + g_1}) \in \mathcal{L}(\mathbf{B_{h_0+h_1}})$ and $(\mathbf{f_0 - f_1, g_0 - g_1}) \in \mathcal{L}(\mathbf{B_{h_0-h_1}})$. Therefore, it will be more beneficial for the attacker to find these images and build them back to get the original vector corresponding to the private key. Refer to [35] for a detailed discussion. One can think that the hardness of solving the SVP for the DiTRU lattice of order $2N$ is equivalent to that for a lattice built for a cyclic group of order N. However, for accurate hardness analysis, the lattice gap of the images of the short vector in the dimension-reduced lattices should be analyzed.

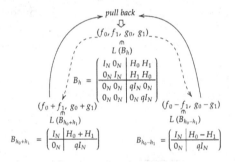

Fig. 2. One-layer of Gentry attack against DiTRU lattice

For a better understanding, we compare the hardness of the SVP for NTRU lattices based on C_N(order N) to that based on D_N(order $2N$) when an equal negligible decryption failure is allowed. Hence, we first introduce the estimation of the decryption failure for DiTRU before providing our analysis.

Decryption Failure: The probability of decryption failure can be estimated similarly to the discussion in [19]. For DiTRU based on a dihedral group of order $2N$ and designed according to the steps mentioned in section 2.4, a decryption failure occurs if the absolute value of any coefficients in $a = pr*g + m*f$ is greater than $t = q/2$. Therefore, if $g \in \mathcal{T}(d_g, d_g)$ and $d'_g \approx d_g/2$ (similar assumptions are considered for $f, r,$ and m), the probability of decryption failure is defined as

$$p_{dec}(t) = \text{Prob}(\ \|a\|_\infty \geq t), \tag{16}$$

and calculated as

$$p_{dec} = 2N * \texttt{erfc}(t/\sigma\sqrt{2}), \tag{17}$$

where $\sigma^2 = 8\left(\frac{p^2(d_r'd_g')+d_f'd_m'}{N}\right)$ and $\texttt{erfc}$ refers to the complementary error function. To prove the correctness of 17, we make the following valid assumptions:

Assumption 1. *Let $g = g_0(x) + yg_1(x)$ be elements of $\mathbb{Z}D_N$ such that $g \in \mathcal{T}(d_g, d_g)$, then for large N, we approximately expect that $g_0(x), g_1(x) \in \mathcal{T}(d_g', d_g')$ (similar assumptions are considered for f, r, and m).*

Assumption 2. *The coefficients of $g_0(x)$ are independent random variables taking the values 1 and -1 with probability d_g'/N, and 0 with probability $(N - 2d_g')/N$. Assuming the same for $g_1(x)$, $f_0(x)$, $f_1(x)$, $m_0(x)$, and $m_1(x)$.*

We know that a can be written as $a = a_0(x) + ya_1(x)$ for:

$$a_0(x) = p\left(r_0(x) * g_0(x) + \overline{r_1(x)} * g_1(x)\right) + m_0(x) * f_0(x) + \overline{m_1(x)} * f_1(x)$$

$$a_1(x) = p\left(\overline{r_0(x)} * g_1(x) + r_1(x) * g_0(x)\right) + \overline{m_0(x)} * f_1(x) + m_1(x) * f_0(x).$$

We give the discussion for $a_0(x)$; the same discussion can be translated to $a_1(x)$. Let X_j denote a coefficient in $a_0(x)$, then X_j is the sum of N terms as

$$X_j = \sum_{i=1}^{N} (p(z_{0_i} + z_{1_i}) + (w_{0_i} + w_{1_i})),$$

where z_{0_i}, z_{1_i}, w_{0_i}, and $\overline{w_{1_i}}$ denote the coefficient of $r_0(x) * g_0(x)$, $\overline{r_1(x)} * g_1(x)$, $m_0(x) * f_0(x)$, and $\overline{m_1(x)} * f_1(x)$, respectively. As a result, the variance

$$\sigma^2 = E(X_j^2) = \sum_{i=1}^{N} \left(p^2(E(z_{0_i}^2) + E(z_{1_i}^2)) + E(w_{0_i}^2) + E(w_{1_i}^2)\right)$$

$$= 2\left(p^2\frac{4d_r'd_g'}{N} + \frac{4d_f'd_m'}{N}\right) = 8\left(\frac{p^2(d_r'd_g') + d_f'd_m'}{N}\right). \tag{18}$$

For large N, we can apply the central limit theorem twice to estimate the probability, consequently

$$\texttt{Prob}(\,|X_j| \geq t) < \frac{2}{\sqrt{2\pi}}\int_{t/\sigma}^{\infty} e^{-x^2/2}dx \Rightarrow \texttt{Prob}(\,|X_j| \geq t) < \texttt{erfc}(t/\sigma\sqrt{2}). \tag{19}$$

Therefore, the probability of decryption failure can be conservatively estimated to have one coefficient or more, either in $a_0(x)$ or $a_1(x)$ with a value greater than t. Hence

$$p_{dec} = 2N * \texttt{erfc}(t/\sigma\sqrt{2}), \quad \text{for} \quad \sigma^2 = 8\left(\frac{p^2(d_r'd_g') + d_f'd_m'}{N}\right). \tag{20}$$

362 A. Raya et al.

Experimental Results: As Subsect. 3.2 mentions, the DiTRU lattice is vulnerable to one layer of Gentry's attack. To understand the hardness of reducing DiTRU lattices built over a dihedral group D_N of order $2N$, we experiment to figure out the minimum blocksize needed to retrieve a decryption key for moderate lattice dimensions; then, the results can be extended using simulators to estimate the blocksize for higher dimensions (Fig. 1b). For reference comparison, we compare the obtained blocksizes to those needed to reduce NTRU lattices over a cyclic group C_N of order N. For a negligible decryption failure, we set our experiment as the following:

- identify q', the modulo for cyclic NTRU, as the minimum power of 2 that satisfies a decryption failure probability p'_{dec} (as computed in [19]) equal to or smaller than the targeted.
- identify q, the modulo for DiTRU over D_N that gives an equal decryption failure p_{dec} compared to NTRU over C_N.
- for each parameter set for cyclic and dihedral, generate 100 random private keys, then build and publish the public key[1].
- for NTRU over the cyclic group, find the minimum blocksize β_{cyclic} needed to retrieve a decryption key (non-ternary and ternary).
- for DiTRU lattice:
  - apply one layer of Gentry's attack and build the lattices $\mathcal{L}(\mathbf{B}_{h_0+h_1})$ and $\mathcal{L}(\mathbf{B}_{h_0-h_1})$.
  - identify the smaller blocksize β_1 to get a non-ternary decryption key and β_2 the minimum blocksize to retrieve the ternary key.

We highlight that the experiment uses *progressive* BKZ with increasing blocksizes up to 65 with eight tours per blocksize and enumeration as an SVP-oracle. We ran the experiment depending on FPyLLL [49] as a Python wrapper to FPLLL [48] on a system Linux (Ubuntu 22.04.2 LTS) with Intel(R) Xeon(R) CPU E3-1246 v3 @ 3.50 GHz and 32 GB installed RAM. Furthermore, all the tested parameter sets are not in the overstretched regime of NTRU lattices, and the non-ternary decryption key is accepted if its norm is at most four times the original key.

Table 1. Average blocksizes needed to retrieve a decryption key checked experimentally (NTRU over cyclic group vs. DiTRU after one-layer of Gentry's attack.)

N	71	73	79	83	89	97	101	107	109	113	127	131
β_{cyclic}	2.28	2.48	3.02	3.64	5.22	8.94	11.05	16.22	18.56	28.68	52.8	57.35
β_1		2.62	2.95	3.54	4.94	7.06	11.62	15.59	25.47	32.75	43.1	63	-
β_2		2.87	3	3.88	5.06	7.18	11.68	15.63	26.57	34.06	43.95	63.6	-

---

[1] Starting from $N = 113$, the results are averaged over at least 20 trials (only) since the time taken by one trial becomes extensively high. For $N = 127$ with DiTRU lattice, we recorded the trials that found the key with $\beta \leq 65$.

Table 1 shows the experimental results tested for the corresponding N and $q' = 512$ for the NTRU over the cyclic group, and $q = 2 * \text{erfc}^{-1}(p'_{dec}/2N) * \sigma\sqrt{2}$ for DiTRU parameter sets where p'_{dec} is the probability of decryption failure in the case of the cyclic parameters. While the difference between the blocksizes may seem small, the gap in the running time is significantly large. For instance, for $N = 127$, the running time took an average of 626.6 core hours to retrieve the shortest vector in the case of DiTRU, while for NTRU, it took, on average, only 114.9 core hours.

4   Best Known Attacks

4.1   Search Attack

A DiTRU private key (f, g) is a ternary vector where $f = (f_0, f_1) \in \mathcal{T}_{2N}(d+1, d)$ and $g = (g_0, g_1) \in \mathcal{T}_{2N}(d, d)$ with $d \leq \lfloor 2N/3 \rfloor$. For convenience, let us denote $\mathcal{T}_{2N}(d+1, d)$ simply by $\mathcal{T}$. An attacker can brute force search for an $f' \in \mathcal{T}$ such that $f' * h \pmod q$ is short, possibly ternary. Therefore, the cost of a combinatorial search on DiTRU is given by

$$\frac{|\mathcal{T}|}{2N} = \frac{1}{2N}\binom{2N}{d}\binom{2N-d}{d+1}, \tag{21}$$

where we have divided by $2N$ to account for all the $2N$ rotations of f'. In fact, combinatorial meet-in-the-middle (MITM)[2] attacks by Odlyzko [25] and Howgrave et al. [27] with complexity $(|\mathcal{T}|/2N)^{0.5}$ (classically) and $(|\mathcal{T}|/2N)^{0.25}$ (quantumly) can be mounted by decomposing search space $\mathcal{T}$ into $\mathcal{T}' \oplus \mathcal{T}'$ such that $|\mathcal{T}'| = \sqrt{|\mathcal{T}|}$.

Knowing the fact that partial information about the secret key is veiled in smaller dimensional lattices $\mathcal{L}(\mathbf{B}_{h_0+h_1})$ and $\mathcal{L}(\mathbf{B}_{h_0-h_1})$ in the form of $(f_0 + f_1, g_0 + g_1)$ and $(f_0 - f_1, g_0 - g_1)$, spaces. Let

$$\mathcal{F}_N(d_1, d_2, d_3, d_4) = \left\{ f \in \mathbb{Z}^N \left| \begin{array}{l} f \text{ has } d_1 \text{ coefficients equal to } 1 \\ f \text{ has } d_2 \text{ coefficients equal to } -1 \\ f \text{ has } d_3 \text{ coefficients equal to } 2 \\ f \text{ has } d_4 \text{ coefficients equal to } -2 \\ \text{and other coefficients are } 0 \end{array} \right. \right\}, \tag{21}$$

and $\mathcal{F}_N \subset \mathbb{Z}^N$ be the space of all N length sequences with coefficients from the set $\{0, \pm 1, \pm 2\}$.

According to assumptions 1, 2, for any $f = (f_0, f_1) \in \mathcal{T}$, the attacker can expect with high probability that $f_0 + f_1, f_0 - f_1 \in \mathcal{S} = \mathcal{F}_N(d_1, d_2, d_3, d_4)$ with

$$d_1 = d_2 = \frac{d_f(N - d_f)}{N}, \quad d_3 = d_4 = \frac{d_f^2}{4N}.$$

---

[2] May [41] proposed an MITM attack on NTRU-type cryptosystems with a complexity $O(|\mathcal{T}|^{0.3})$(classic). However, it cannot be combined with hybrid attacks; therefore, we do not use it in our cost estimations.

Therefore, a brute force search with cost $O(|\mathcal{S}|)$ can be performed over the search space $\mathcal{S}$ to find private vectors in the lattices $\mathcal{L}(\mathbf{B}_{h_0+h_1})$ and $\mathcal{L}(\mathbf{B}_{h_0-h_1})$, where

$$|\mathcal{S}| = \binom{N}{d_1}\binom{N-d_1}{d_1}\binom{N-2d_1}{d_3}\binom{N-2d_1-d_3}{d_3}. \qquad (22)$$

Further, MITM attacks cost $\left(\frac{|\mathcal{S}|}{2N}\right)^{0.5}$ (classically) and $\left(\frac{|\mathcal{S}|}{2N}\right)^{0.25}$ (quantumly).

4.2 Cost of SVP Algorithms

Before discussing Primal and Hybrid attacks, we briefly introduce the cost of lattice reduction by an algorithm like BKZ. BKZ with blocksize β produces a $BKZ-\beta$ reduced basis by calling the SVP oracle in smaller lattices of dimension β. Enumeration and sieving are the most studied and used SVP oracles in the literature. The called oracle heavily affects the memory and time requirements for running the BKZ algorithm. Enumeration algorithms [16,42] solve the SVP with polynomial memory requirements and super-exponential time requirements while sieving algorithms [7,36] have exponential time and memory requirements. Kirshanova et al. [34] found experimentally that sieving starts outperforming enumeration from dimension 65 onwards. The best records for solving the SVP are over the sieving regime; however, the memory consumption is extensive for these algorithms. To give a conservative parameter selection, we consider the model described in [3] that assumes that the sieving algorithm works in the RAM model, i.e., the attacker can access any amount of the memory for free. The classical asymptotic estimation of the number of the operations according to this model of sieving is $\sqrt{3/2}^{\beta+o(\beta)} \approx 2^{0.292\beta+o(\beta)}$ classically [7] that can be brought down to $\approx 2^{0.265\beta+o(\beta)}$ by employing Grover's search [36]. However, a thorough analysis of the quantum asymptotic estimation in [2] shows that the result may be far from practicality. It is clear that the reduction cost increases with β, and therefore, from the attacker's perspective, it is beneficial to perform the reduction in the two lattices $\mathcal{L}(\mathbf{B}_{h_0+h_1})$ and $\mathcal{L}(\mathbf{B}_{h_0-h_1})$. Considering assumptions 1, 2, we expect

$$\|(f_0+f_1,g_0+g_1)\| \approx \|(f_0-f_1,g_0-g_1)\| \approx \sqrt{2}\sqrt{d_f+d_g}. \qquad (23)$$

Gaussian heuristic estimates the expected length of the shortest vector in lattices $\mathcal{L}(\mathbf{B}_{h_0+h_1})$ and $\mathcal{L}(\mathbf{B}_{h_0-h_1})$ to be

$$gh(\mathcal{L}(\mathbf{B}_{h_0+h_1})) = gh(\mathcal{L}(\mathbf{B}_{h_0-h_1})) = \sqrt{\frac{qN}{\pi e}}. \qquad (24)$$

Since $d_f, d_g \leq 2N/3$, and $q = O(N)$, the ratios

$$\frac{\|(f_0+f_1,g_0+g_1)\|}{gh(\mathcal{L}(\mathbf{B}_{h_0+h_1})} \approx \frac{\|(f_0-f_1,g_0-g_1)\|}{gh(\mathcal{L}(\mathbf{B}_{h_0-h_1})} \approx O\left(\frac{1}{\sqrt{N}}\right). \qquad (25)$$

Therefore, the vectors (f_0+f_1, g_0+g_1) and (f_0-f_1, g_0-g_1) and all their rotations are shortest vectors in the lattices $\mathcal{L}(\mathbf{B}_{h_0+h_1})$ and $\mathcal{L}(\mathbf{B}_{h_0-h_1})$, respectively, with a very high probability.

4.3   Primal Attack

We follow the methodology of **Core-SVP and GSA** to parameterize the proposed cryptosystem. The Core-SVP[3] is a conservative methodology of estimating the security that considers one call of the SVP oracle to be enough to solve the SVP. To estimate β according to this methodology, we model the behavior of BKZ according to the geometric series assumption (GSA, Definition 8), and depending on *2016-estimator* (Eq. 7), we find the required blocksize β that is the input for the sieving or enumeration model. In our case, we consider the sieving regime for security estimation.

4.4   Hybrid Attack

The MITM attack can be combined with the lattice reduction attack called the hybrid attack, introduced by Howgrave [26]. The basic idea is to reduce a (r_2-r_1) sized block $\mathbf{L}'$ of the matrix

$$\mathbf{B}_{\mathbf{H}'} = \left(\begin{array}{c|c} q\mathbf{I}_N & \mathbf{0}_N \\ \hline \mathbf{H}' & \mathbf{I}_N \end{array}\right) = \left(\begin{array}{c|c|c} q\mathbf{I}_{r_1} & 0 & 0 \\ \hline * & \mathbf{L}' & 0 \\ \hline * & * & \mathbf{I}_{2N-r_2} \end{array}\right). \tag{26}$$

In our case, $\mathbf{H}' = \mathbf{H}_0 + \mathbf{H}_1$ and $\mathbf{H}' = \mathbf{H}_0 - \mathbf{H}_1$. Let $\mathbf{U}'$ be an unimodular matrix such that $\mathbf{U}'\mathbf{L}'$ is reduced, and $\mathbf{Y}'$ be an orthogonal transformation such that $\mathbf{T}' = \mathbf{U}'\mathbf{L}'\mathbf{Y}'$ is a lower triangular matrix. Then, the lattice generated by the matrix

$$\mathbf{T} = \mathbf{U}\mathbf{B}_{\mathbf{H}'}\mathbf{Y} = \left(\begin{array}{c|c|c} \mathbf{I}_{r_1} & 0 & 0 \\ \hline 0 & \mathbf{U}' & 0 \\ \hline 0 & 0 & \mathbf{I}_{2N-r_2} \end{array}\right) \left(\begin{array}{c|c|c} q\mathbf{I}_{r_1} & 0 & 0 \\ \hline * & \mathbf{L}' & 0 \\ \hline * & * & \mathbf{I}_{2N-r_2} \end{array}\right) \left(\begin{array}{c|c|c} \mathbf{I}_{r_1} & 0 & 0 \\ \hline 0 & \mathbf{Y}' & 0 \\ \hline 0 & 0 & \mathbf{I}_{2N-r_2} \end{array}\right) \tag{27}$$

is isomorphic to the original lattice $\mathcal{L}(\mathbf{B}_{\mathbf{H}'})$. Therefore, $(g', f')\mathbf{Y}$ is a short vector in the resulting lattice, where $(g', f') = (g_0 + g_1, f_0 + f_1)$ for $\mathbf{H}' = \mathbf{H}_0 + \mathbf{H}_1$ and $(g', f') = (g_0 - g_1, f_0 - f_1)$ (or) for $\mathbf{H}' = \mathbf{H}_0 - \mathbf{H}_1$.

The diagonal entries of $\mathbf{T}$ are $\{q^{\alpha_0}, q^{\alpha_1}, \ldots, q^{\alpha_{2N-1}}\}$, where $\sum_{i=0}^{2N-1} \alpha_i = N$, $\alpha_i = 1$ for $i < r_1$, and $\alpha_i = 0$ for $i > r_2$. The matrix $\mathbf{L}'$ roughly obeys the geometric series assumption (GSA), and the rate of decrease of α_i can be estimated based on the Hermite root factor δ achieved by the lattice reduction algorithm. As calculated in [20]

---

[3] In NTRUPrime, the authors conclude that according to the submission to NIST standardization process, a cryptosystem achieves levels of security corresponding to AES-128, AES-192, and AES-256, if the classical (pre-quantum) Core-SVP model assign at least $2^{125}, 2^{181}$, and 2^{254}, respectively to the selected parameter sets.

$$\alpha_{r_1} = \frac{N - r_1}{r_2 - r_1} + (r_2 - r_1)\log_q(\delta), \quad \alpha_{r_2} = \frac{N - r_1}{r_2 - r_1} - (r_2 - r_1)\log_q(\delta) \qquad (28)$$

and α_i for $i \in [r_1, r_2]$ decrease almost linearly.

Let $K = 2N - r_2$; an attacker strives to balance the cost of combinatorial search over the K coordinates against the cost of the lattice reduction. An MITM search can be performed over the last K entries, and we assume that all collisions occur to have a conservative security estimation.

Let $\pi : \mathbb{Z}^N \to \mathbb{Z}^K$ be the projection onto the last K coordinates and

$$\mathcal{F}_\pi = \{\pi(v) : v \in \mathcal{S}\} \subset \mathbb{Z}^K. \qquad (29)$$

Since $f' \in \mathcal{S}$, therefore, the projected component of f' appears in $\mathcal{F}_\pi$, and the search can be performed with $O(\sqrt{|\mathcal{F}_\pi|})$ time and memory consumption. However, estimating $|\mathcal{F}_\pi|$ is not straightforward. Let

$$\mathcal{F}_\pi(a_1, a_2, a_3, a_4) = \left\{ v \in \mathcal{S} \; \middle| \; \begin{array}{l} \pi(v) \text{ has } a_1 \text{ coefficients equal to } 1 \\ \pi(v) \text{ has } a_2 \text{ coefficients equal to } -1 \\ \pi(v) \text{ has } a_3 \text{ coefficients equal to } 2 \\ \pi(v) \text{ has } a_4 \text{ coefficients equal to } -2 \\ \text{and other coefficients are } 0 \end{array} \right\}, \qquad (30)$$

and $P : \mathcal{F}_K \to \mathbb{R}$ be the probability mass function for the distribution induced on $\mathcal{F}_K$ by uniform and random sampling on $\mathcal{S}$ and projecting onto the last K coordinates. Then, the size of the search space $\mathcal{F}_\pi$ can be estimated as $2^{H(P)}$, where $H(P)$ is the Shannon entropy of P.

For every tuple (a_1, a_2, a_3, a_4), let us fix a representative $v_{(a_1,a_2,a_3,a_4)}$ of the set $\mathcal{F}_\pi(a_1, a_2, a_3, a_4)$. Since the space $\mathcal{S}$ is symmetric under coordinate permutations therefore $P(\pi(v)) = P(\pi(v_{(a_1,a_2,a_3,a_4)}))$ for all $v \in \mathcal{F}_\pi(a_1, a_2, a_3, a_4)$. The probability of every representative is given by

$$P\left(\pi(v_{(a_1,a_2,a_3,a_4)})\right) = \frac{1}{K_{(a_1,a_2,a_3,a_4)}} \frac{|\mathcal{F}_\pi(a_1,a_2,a_3,a_4)|}{|\mathcal{S}|}, \qquad (31)$$

where

$$K_{(a_1,a_2,a_3,a_4)} = \binom{K}{a_1}\binom{K - a_1}{a_2}\binom{K - a_1 - a_2}{a_3}\binom{K - a_1 - a_2 - a_3}{a_4},$$

$$|\mathcal{F}_\pi(a_1,a_2,a_3,a_4)| = K_{(a_1,a_2,a_3,a_4)} \times \binom{N-K}{d_1 - a_1}\binom{N-K-d_1+a_1}{d_1-a_2} \times \binom{N-K-2d_1+a_1+a_2}{d_3-a_3}$$

$$\binom{N-K-2d_1-d_3+a_1+a_2+a_3}{d_3-a_4}.$$

Thus, the entropy of P is

$$\begin{aligned} H(P) &= -\sum_{v \in \mathcal{F}_K} P(v)\log_2 P(v) = -\sum_{v \in \mathcal{S}} P(\pi(v))\log_2 P(\pi(v)) \\ &= -\sum_{\substack{0 \le a_1, a_2 \le d_1 \\ 0 \le a_3, a_4 \le d_3}} K_{(a_1,a_2,a_3,a_4)} P\left(\pi(v_{(a_1,a_2,a_3,a_4)})\right)\log_2 P\left(\pi(v_{(a_1,a_2,a_3,a_4)})\right). \end{aligned}$$

Considering the rotations, the search space size can be further decreased by a factor of $2N$, and the log base 2 complexity of the hybrid MITM search is $\xi(H(P) - \log_2(2N))$ where $\xi = 0.5(0.25)$ classically (quantumly).

In order to resist the hybrid attack and achieve a security level equal to λ, for each fixed K we must have

$$\log_2 \text{(hybrid attack cost)} \quad \text{or} \quad \log_2 \text{(lattice reduction cost)} \geq \lambda \qquad (32)$$

where the root Hermite factor δ satisfies $\alpha_{r_2} \geq \log_q(4)$. Equivalently,

$$\log_2(\delta) \leq \frac{N - r_1}{(2N - K - r_1)^2} \log_2 q - \frac{2}{2N - K - r_1}. \qquad (33)$$

For hybrid attack cost estimation, we find an optimal K that balances and minimizes the maximum of both costs in 32.

4.5   Subfield Attack

As mentioned earlier, the standard NTRU lattice does not include only the vector corresponding to the secret key (f, g) but also all the vectors corresponding to the rotations $(x^i * f, x^i * g)$ for $0 \leq i \leq n$ where n is the group order. All these rotations form a dense sublattice(i.e., lattice with many exceptionally short vectors). Finding a basis for this dense sublattice is called Dense Lattice Discovery (DSD). For large values of q, Kirchner and Fouque [33] observed that DSD happens before the event of finding a short vector in the lattice, and therefore, the SVP becomes easier to solve. Under this condition, the NTRU cryptosystem is called *overstretched*. A refined analysis by Ducas and Woerden [15] shows that an NTRU-like cryptosystem becomes overstretched when the value of q approximately exceeds $0.004 * n^{2.484}$ for $n > 100$. Similarly, for DiTRU, the associated lattice does not include only the vector corresponding to the key (f_0, f_1, g_0, g_1), but also all the rotations of the form $(x^i * f_0, x^{-i} * f_1, x^i * g_0, x^{-i} * g_1)$ and $(x^i * f_1, x^{-i} * f_0, x^i * g_1, x^{-i} * g_0)$ for $0 \leq i \leq N$ where $n = 2N$ is the group order. Even after applying one layer of Gentry's attack, the two lattices $\mathcal{L}(\mathbf{B}_{h_0 + h_1}), \mathcal{L}(\mathbf{B}_{h_0 - h_1})$ contain dense sublattices corresponding to the images of the private key and its rotations according to the homomorphism defined in Fig. 2. Consequently, the estimation [15] remains valid for N that defines the dihedral group D_N. Obviously, one can notice that the selected parameter sets in Table 3 are not in the *overstretched* regime. Therefore, the subfield attack is not applicable to our parameters.

4.6   Coppersmith and Shamir Attack

We discuss the attack by Coppersmith and Shamir [12] on the first noncommutative version of NTRU over the dihedral group ring by Hoffstein and Silverman [23], and its inapplicability to DiTRU. The old cyptosystem is built over the subring $R_0 = \{\alpha \in \mathbb{Z}D_N : \alpha y = y\alpha\}$. The private key is (f, ω) where $f \in R_0$

with coefficients from the interval $\left(-\frac{q-1}{2}, \frac{q-1}{2}\right]$ and $\omega \in \mathbb{Z}D_N$ is an element with ternary coefficients. The public key is constructed as $h = pf * \omega * F$ (mod q), where $f * F = 1$ (mod q). The ciphertext of any ternary message $m \in \mathbb{Z}D_N$ is a pair (e, E) computed as $e = \phi * h * \phi' + \psi (\text{mod} q)$ and $E = \Psi * h + m(\text{mod} q)$, where $\phi, \phi' \in R_0$, and $\psi \in \mathbb{Z}D_N$ are ternary elements with $\psi = \Psi$ (mod p). First, one can observe that any attack on this cryptosystem to recover the secret key from the public key or the message from the ciphertext is not applicable in the case of DiTRU or, in general, GR-NTRU, as the design of Hoffstein and Silverman's scheme, i.e., key generation and encryption-decryption, is entirely different from DiTRU.

Coppersmith and Shamir broke this cryptosystem using a subset $\{\alpha \in \mathbb{Z}D_N : \alpha y = -y\alpha\}$ and a linear map $\theta : \mathbb{Z}_q D_N \to \mathbb{Z}_q D_N$ that is identity on R_0 and maps R_1 to itself. An attacker tries to find an alternative ω' with small coefficients such that $\theta(h) = p\omega'$. Then, applying θ to e helps recover ψ and consequently, the message. An elaborate discussion on the Coppersmith attack regarding the construction of such a θ and finding ω' is provided in [50]. However, in the case of GR-NTRU, the ciphertext is given by $e = pr * h + m(\text{mod} q)$, and any map θ that recovers r breaks the standard NTRU. Therefore, DiTRU, by design, is not vulnerable to this attack.

5   Parameter Selection

According to NIST's definition of the level of security, we propose three parameter sets for levels 1,3 and 5. The parameters for DiTRU in Table 2 are selected according to the cost of the previous attacks with $\xi = 0.5(0.25)$ for the classical (quantum) cost of the meet-in-the-middle search and considering the maximum depth of the quantum circuit to be 2^{96} when one is performing the quantum search.

Table 2. Core-SVP cost against DiTRU parameter sets

security level	(N, d, q)	Classical						Quantum					
		primal attack		hybrid attack				primal attack		hybrid attack			
		β	cost	K	β	cost		β	cost	K	β	cost	
128	(541, 234, 2048)	445	**130**	164	524	153		445	**118**	155	545	144	
192	(797, 530, 4096)	660	**193**	217	800	234		660	**175**	203	832	220	
256	(1039, 478, 4096)	882	**258**	318	1057	309		882	**234**	300	1099	291	

For the sake of accurate comparison, we describe the parameter sets of NTRU in Table 3 that achieve the same level of security according to the same evaluation criteria followed for DiTRU.

Table 3. Core-SVP cost against NTRU parameter sets

security level	(N, d, q)	Classical						Quantum					
		primal attack		hybrid attack				primal attack		hybrid attack			
		β	cost	K	β	cost		β	cost	K	β	cost	
128	(587, 195, 2048)	456	133	166	438	**128**		456	121	156	454	**120**	
192	(863, 159, 2048)	701	205	298	658	**192**		701	186	282	684	**181**	
256	(1109, 369, 4096)	893	261	331	883	**258**		893	**237**	311	915	242	

6   Design Rationale

We follow a design rationale similar to the one used in the NTRUEncrypt submission that designs the encryption scheme as a partially correct probabilistic public key scheme (PPKE). One can notice that the design of the PPKE in Fig. 3 is identical to that used in standard NTRU, while the only difference is changing the underlying ring to the noncommutative group ring of the dihedral group. Therefore, similar to standard NTRU, the CPA security of the PPKE is based on the hardness of the NTRU assumption. We provide a CCA-2 secure implementation of the proposed PPKE scheme for DiTRU using the NAEP transformation [28][4]. It can be converted into KEM following similar steps as given in [9, Algorithm 9,10].

KeyGen(*seed*)

1. Instantiate Sampler with $\mathcal{L}_f$ and *seed*
2. do f ← Sampler until f is invertible modulo q
3. Instantiate Sampler with $\mathcal{L}_g$ and *seed*
4. g ← Sampler
5. h ← 3g * f_q (mod q)
6. return f, h

Encrypt(h,m,*coins*)

1. Instantiate Sampler with $\mathcal{L}_r$ and *coins*
2. r ← Sampler
3. t = r * h(mod q)
4. Instantiate Sampler with $\mathcal{T}'$ and HASH(t)
5. m_{mask} ← Sampler
6. m' = m − m_{mask}(mod p)
7. c = t + m'(mod q)
8. return c

Decrypt(f,c)

1. m' = c * f(mod p)
2. t = c − m'(mod q)
3. Instantiate Sampler with $\mathcal{T}'$ and HASH(t)
4. m_{mask} ← Sampler
5. m = m' + m_{mask}(mod p)
6. return m

Fig. 3. A PPKE scheme for DiTRU

*: product over the group ring $\mathbb{Z}D_N$ modulo q and p.

Sampler: randomly samples an element unique to the seed from the input space.

$$\mathcal{L}_f := \{1 + 3\mathbf{F} : \mathbf{F} \in \mathcal{T}_{2N}(d_f + 1, d_f)\}, \quad \mathcal{L}_g := \mathcal{T}_{2N}(d_g, d_g), \quad \mathcal{L}_r := \mathcal{T}_{2N}(d_r, d_r), \quad \mathcal{T}' := \mathcal{T}_{2N},$$

---

[4] Our implementation is based on NTRU submissions to the first and third round of NIST competition with the required modifications to the dihedral group setup.

where $d_g = \lfloor 2N/3 \rfloor$ and $d_r = d_f$. The decryption failure probability, according to the considered design criteria, is given by Eq. 17 with $\sigma^2 = 2\left(\frac{d_r d_g + d_f d_m}{N}\right)$ and $t = \frac{q-2}{2p}$.

Table 4 records the memory requirements and the average cycle counts for the recommended parameter sets of DiTRU, while Table 5 compares the implementation costs for DiTRU vs. NTRU while encrypting/decrypting messages of the same length(for every level of security, the length of the polynomial corresponding to the message is the order of the dihedral group multiplied by the order of the cyclic group). The results are measured on a device with the same specification mentioned in Subsect. 3.2 on a single core, TurboBoost, and hyperthreading disabled. We compiled the code using GCC version 4:11.2.0-1ubuntu1 with **no** optimization flags enabled.

Table 4. Memory requirements and implementation cost for DiTRU parameters

DiTRU2048_541				DiTRU4096_797				DiTRU4096_1039			
size (in bytes)		cpu cycles (ref)		size (in bytes)		cpu cycles (ref)		size (in bytes)		cpu cycles (ref)	
sk:	217	gen:	83063049	sk:	319	gen:	178993352	sk:	416	gen:	301007142
pk:	1488	enc:	12653184	pk:	2391	enc:	26350252	pk:	3117	enc:	43440107
ct:	1488	dec:	23848004	ct:	2391	dec:	50365994	ct:	3117	dec:	83684000

Table 5. DiTRU vs. NTRU implementation cost (average CPU cycles)

Security level	Key Generation			Encryption			Decryption		
	DiTRU	NTRU	ratio	DiTRU	NTRU	ratio	DiTRU	NTRU	ratio
128	83063049	67573991	1.23	7477322227	4509252772	1.65	14088417108	8267862833	1.70
192	178993352	144771971	1.24	23400674192	13256355697	1.77	44737178607	24807462541	1.80
256	301007142	237913501	1.26	48268245887	27633654748	1.75	92916097739	52110865556	1.78

One can notice from Table 5, the efficiency of our inversion algorithm for DiTRU. Further, the cost of encryption/decryption is less than two times that of NTRU for equivalent levels of security, even though the underlying algebra is noncommutative for DiTRU.

7   Final Remarks

This paper introduces DiTRU, a noncommutative analog of NTRU as GR-NTRU instantiated over the dihedral group. Our work focuses on clearing all the aspects that make the scheme practical. As a result, we provide a full-package cryptosystem accompanied by a detailed cryptanalysis. The security evaluation considers the one layer of Gentry's attack due to the algebraic structure of the dihedral group ring. Avoiding the one-layer of Gentry's attack means that lower values of N can achieve the same level of security, thereby improving the time and memory requirements of DiTRU. One way to achieve this could be twisting the multiplication of the group ring, resulting in a generalized form of group rings called twisted group rings. We briefly discuss the concept of twisted group rings.

Definition 11 *(2-cocycle). A map* $\lambda : G \times G \rightarrow R^*$ *is called a 2-cocycle if satisfies* $\lambda(1,1) = 1$ *and* $\lambda(g_1 g_2, g_3)\lambda(g_1, g_2) = \lambda(g_1, g_2 g_3)\lambda(g_2, g_3)$ *for all* $g_1, g_2, g_3 \in G.$

Definition 12 *(Twisted group ring). A twisted group ring* $R^\lambda G$ *of group* G *over the ring* R *corresponding to the 2-cocycle* λ *is same as the group ring* RG *as in definition 4 but with a twisted multiplication given by*

$$\sum_{i=1}^{n} \alpha_i g_i * \sum_{i=1}^{n} \beta_i g_i = \sum_{i=1}^{n} \left(\sum_{g_h g_k = g_i} \alpha_h \beta_k \lambda(g_h, g_k) \right) g_i. \tag{34}$$

If we twist the dihedral group ring $\mathbb{Z}_q D_N$ with the 2-cocycle $\lambda : D_N \times D_N \rightarrow \mathbb{Z}_q^*$ defined as

$$\lambda(y^k x^i, y^l x^j) = \begin{cases} -1, & \text{for } i,j \in \{0,1,\ldots,N-1\} \text{ and } k = l = 1 \\ 1, & \text{otherwise} \end{cases}$$

then, the elements in the twisted group ring $\mathbb{Z}_q^\lambda D_N$ have the matrix representation of the form

$$\mathbf{H} = \begin{pmatrix} \mathbf{H}_0 & \mathbf{H}_1 \\ -\mathbf{H}_1 & \mathbf{H}_0 \end{pmatrix}. \tag{35}$$

To our understanding, it is not possible to reduce $\mathbf{H}$ into integral matrices of smaller dimensions such that the corresponding lattices contain short vectors carrying partial information about the secret key. One homomorphism that we can think of is $\mathbf{H} \rightarrow \mathbf{H}_0 \pm i\mathbf{H}_1$ where $i = \sqrt{-1}$, but then the smaller matrices have complex entries, and to apply lattice reduction algorithms, one again needs to map these complex matrices to larger dimensional real matrices. Moreover, the matrix representation of elements in the ring $\mathbb{Z}_q[x]/(x^N + 1)$ is also the same as for $\mathbf{H}$. Therefore, if one can reduce $\mathbf{H}$ into the desired form, then possibly the same reduction can be applied in the case of $\mathbb{Z}_q[x]/(x^N + 1)$. However, it is known that the polynomial $x^N + 1$ does not factor over $\mathbb{Z}_q$ into smaller degree polynomials with small norm [5]. This is why the ring $\mathbb{Z}_q[x]/(x^N + 1)$ is used in some cryptographic designs like [14,17]. Although we have selected our parameters considering one layer of Gentry's attack, twisting the underlying algebra can prevent the dimension reduction. This idea seems promising but needs a rigorous analysis and thus is left as future work.

References

1. Agrawal, S., Pellet-Mary, A.: Indistinguishability obfuscation without maps: attacks and fixes for noisy linear FE. In: Canteaut, A., Ishai, Y. (eds.) EURO-CRYPT 2020. LNCS, vol. 12105, pp. 110–140. Springer, Cham (2020). https://doi.org/10.1007/978-3-030-45721-1_5

2. Albrecht, M.R., Gheorghiu, V., Postlethwaite, E.W., Schanck, J.M.: Estimating quantum speedups for lattice sieves. In: Moriai, S., Wang, H. (eds.) ASIACRYPT 2020. LNCS, vol. 12492, pp. 583–613. Springer, Cham (2020). https://doi.org/10. 1007/978-3-030-64834-3_20

3. Alkim, E., Ducas, L., Pöppelmann, T., Schwabe, P.: Post-quantum key {Exchange-A} new hope. In: 25th USENIX Security Symposium (USENIX Security 16), pp. 327–343 (2016)

4. Aono, Y., Wang, Y., Hayashi, T., Takagi, T.: Improved progressive BKZ algorithms and their precise cost estimation by sharp simulator. In: Fischlin, M., Coron, J.-S. (eds.) EUROCRYPT 2016. LNCS, vol. 9665, pp. 789–819. Springer, Heidelberg (2016). https://doi.org/10.1007/978-3-662-49890-3_30

5. Avanzi, R., et al.: CRYSTALS-Kyber algorithm specifications and supporting documentation. NIST PQC Round (2020). https://csrc.nist.gov/Projects/post-quantum-cryptography/post-quantum-cryptography-standardization/round-3-submissions

6. Bagheri, K., Sadeghi, M.R., Panario, D.: A non-commutative cryptosystem based on quaternion algebras. Des. Codes Cryptogr. **86** (2018). https://doi.org/10.1007/s10623-017-0451-4

7. Becker, A., Ducas, L., Gama, N., Laarhoven, T.: New directions in nearest neighbor searching with applications to lattice sieving. In: Proceedings of the Twenty-Seventh Annual ACM-SIAM Symposium on Discrete Algorithms, pp. 10–24. SIAM (2016)

8. Chen, C., et al.: NTRU: algorithm specifications and supporting documentation. NIST (2020). https://csrc.nist.gov/Projects/post-quantum-cryptography/post-quantum-cryptography-standardization/round-3-submissions

9. Chen, C., Hoffstein, J., Whyte, W., Zhang, Z.: NIST PQ submission: ntruencrypt a lattice based encryption algorithm. NIST (2017)

10. Chen, Y.: Réduction de réseau et sécurité concrete du chiffrement completement homomorphe (Ph. D. thesis) (2013)

11. Chen, Y., Nguyen, P.Q.: BKZ 2.0: better lattice security estimates. In: Lee, D.H., Wang, X. (eds.) ASIACRYPT 2011. LNCS, vol. 7073, pp. 1–20. Springer, Heidelberg (2011). https://doi.org/10.1007/978-3-642-25385-0_1

12. Coppersmith, D.: Attacking non-commutative NTRU. Technical report, IBM research report, April 1997. Report (2006). https://dominoweb.draco.res.ibm.com/d102d0885e971b558525659300727a26.html

13. Coppersmith, D., Shamir, A.: Lattice attacks on NTRU. In: Fumy, W. (ed.) EURO-CRYPT 1997. LNCS, vol. 1233, pp. 52–61. Springer, Heidelberg (1997). https://doi.org/10.1007/3-540-69053-0_5

14. Ducas, L., Durmus, A., Lepoint, T., Lyubashevsky, V.: Lattice signatures and bimodal gaussians. In: Canetti, R., Garay, J.A. (eds.) CRYPTO 2013. LNCS, vol. 8042, pp. 40–56. Springer, Heidelberg (2013). https://doi.org/10.1007/978-3-642-40041-4_3

15. Ducas, L., van Woerden, W.: NTRU fatigue: how stretched is overstretched? In: Tibouchi, M., Wang, H. (eds.) ASIACRYPT 2021. LNCS, vol. 13093, pp. 3–32. Springer, Cham (2021). https://doi.org/10.1007/978-3-030-92068-5_1

16. Fincke, U., Pohst, M.: Improved methods for calculating vectors of short length in a lattice, including a complexity analysis. Math. Comput. **44**(170), 463–471 (1985)

17. Fouque, P.A., et al.: FALCON: fast-fourier lattice-based compact signatures over NTRU. Technical report (2018). https://www.di.ens.fr/~prest/Publications/falcon.pdf

18. Gentry, C.: Key recovery and message attacks on NTRU-composite. In: Pfitzmann, B. (ed.) EUROCRYPT 2001. LNCS, vol. 2045, pp. 182–194. Springer, Heidelberg (2001). https://doi.org/10.1007/3-540-44987-6_12

19. Hirschhorn, P.S., Hoffstein, J., Howgrave-Graham, N., Whyte, W.: Choosing NTRUEncrypt parameters in light of combined lattice reduction and MITM approaches. In: Abdalla, M., Pointcheval, D., Fouque, P.-A., Vergnaud, D. (eds.) ACNS 2009. LNCS, vol. 5536, pp. 437–455. Springer, Heidelberg (2009). https://doi.org/10.1007/978-3-642-01957-9_27

20. Hoffstein, J., Pipher, J., Schanck, J.M., Silverman, J.H., Whyte, W., Zhang, Z.: Choosing parameters for NTRUEncrypt. In: Handschuh, H. (ed.) CT-RSA 2017. LNCS, vol. 10159, pp. 3–18. Springer, Cham (2017). https://doi.org/10.1007/978-3-319-52153-4_1

21. Hoffstein, J., Pipher, J., Silverman, J.: An Introduction to Mathematical Cryptography, 1st edn. Springer Publishing Company, New York (2008). Incorporated. https://doi.org/10.1007/978-0-387-77993-5

22. Hoffstein, J., Pipher, J., Silverman, J.H.: NTRU: a ring-based public key cryptosystem. In: Buhler, J.P. (ed.) ANTS 1998. LNCS, vol. 1423, pp. 267–288. Springer, Heidelberg (1998). https://doi.org/10.1007/BFb0054868

23. Hoffstein, J., Silverman, J.: A non-commutative version of the NTRU public key cryptosystem. It was for a while available at (1997). http://www.tiac.net/users/ntru/NTRUFTP.html

24. Hoffstein, J., Silverman, J.H.: A non-commutative version of the NTRU public key cryptosystem. unpublished paper, February 1997

25. Hoffstein, J., Silverman, J.H., Whyte, W.: Meet-in-the-middle attack on an NTRU private key. Technical report, NTRU Cryptosystems, July 2006. Report (2006)

26. Howgrave-Graham, N.: A hybrid lattice-reduction and meet-in-the-middle attack against NTRU. In: Menezes, A. (ed.) CRYPTO 2007. LNCS, vol. 4622, pp. 150–169. Springer, Heidelberg (2007). https://doi.org/10.1007/978-3-540-74143-5_9

27. Howgrave-Graham, N., Silverman, J.H., Whyte, W.: A meet-in-the-middle attack on an NTRU private key. NTRU cryptosystem Technical report #004. (2003). https://www.securityinnovation.com/uploads/Crypto/NTRUTech004v2.pdf

28. Howgrave-Graham, N., Silverman, J.H., Whyte, W.: Choosing parameter sets for NTRUEncrypt with NAEP and SVES-3. In: Menezes, A. (ed.) CT-RSA 2005. LNCS, vol. 3376, pp. 118–135. Springer, Heidelberg (2005). https://doi.org/10.1007/978-3-540-30574-3_10

29. Hurley, T.: Group rings and rings of matrices. Int. J. Pure Appl. Math. 31, 319–335 (2006). https://www.researchgate.net/publication/228928727_Group_rings_and_rings_of_matrices

30. Jarvis, K., Nevins, M.: ETRU: NTRU over the eisenstein integers. Des. Codes Crypt. 74(1), 219–242 (2015). https://doi.org/10.1007/s10623-013-9850-3

31. Karbasi, A.H., Atani, S.E., Atani, R.E.: PairTRU: pairwise Non-commutative Extension of the NTRU public key cryptosystem. Int. J. Inf. Secur. Sci. 8, 1–10 (2018)

32. Kim, J., Lee, C.: A polynomial time algorithm for breaking NTRU encryption with multiple keys. Des. Codes Cryptogr. 1–11 (2023).https://doi.org/10.1007/s10623-023-01233-5

33. Kirchner, P., Fouque, P.-A.: Revisiting lattice attacks on overstretched NTRU parameters. In: Coron, J.-S., Nielsen, J.B. (eds.) EUROCRYPT 2017. LNCS, vol. 10210, pp. 3–26. Springer, Cham (2017). https://doi.org/10.1007/978-3-319-56620-7_1

34. Silverman, J.H., Pipher, J., Hoffstein, J.: An Introduction to Mathematical Cryptography. UTM, Springer, New York (2008). https://doi.org/10.1007/978-0-387-77993-5

35. Kumar, V., Raya, A., Gangopadhyay, S., Gangopadhyay, A.K.: Lattice attack on group ring NTRU: the case of the dihedral group (2023). https://doi.org/10.48550/arXiv.2309.08304

36. Laarhoven, T.: Search problems in cryptography: from fingerprinting to lattice sieving. Phd thesis, Eindhoven University of Technology (2015). https://research.tue.nl/en/publications/search-problems-in-cryptography-from-fingerprinting-to-lattice-si

37. Lenstra, A.K., Lenstra, H.W., Lovász, L.: Factoring polynomials with rational coefficients. Math. Ann. **261**(ARTICLE), 515–534 (1982). https://doi.org/10.1007/BF01457454

38. Ling, C., Mendelsohn, A.: NTRU in quaternion algebras of bounded discriminant. In: Johansson, T., Smith-Tone, D. (eds.) Post-Quantum Cryptography. PQCrypto 2023. LNCS, vol. 14154, pp. 256–290. Springer, Cham (2023). https://doi.org/10.1007/978-3-031-40003-2_10

39. Makhijani, N., Sharma, R., Srivastava, J.: Units in finite dihedral and quaternion group algebras. J. Egypt. Math. Soc. **24**(1), 5–7 (2016). https://doi.org/10.1016/j.joems.2014.08.001

40. Malekian, E., Zakerolhosseini, A., Mashatan, A.: QTRU : a lattice attack resistant version of NTRU PKCS based on quaternion algebra. IACR Cryptology ePrint Archive **2009** (2009). https://eprint.iacr.org/2009/386

41. May, A.: How to meet ternary LWE keys. In: Malkin, T., Peikert, C. (eds.) CRYPTO 2021. LNCS, vol. 12826, pp. 701–731. Springer, Cham (2021). https://doi.org/10.1007/978-3-030-84245-1_24

42. Micciancio, D., Walter, M.: Fast lattice point enumeration with minimal overhead. In: Proceedings of the Twenty-Sixth Annual ACM-SIAM Symposium on Discrete Algorithms, pp. 276–294. SIAM (2014)

43. Miyata, T.: On the units of the integral group ring of a dihedral group. J. Math. Soc. Jpn. **32**(4) (1980)

44. Peikert, C.: A decade of lattice cryptography. Found. Trends® Theor. Comput. Sci. **10**(4), 283–424 (2016)

45. Schnorr, C.P.: A hierarchy of polynomial time lattice basis reduction algorithms. Theor. Comput. Sci. **53**(2–3), 201–224 (1987). https://doi.org/10.1016/0304-3975(87)90064-8

46. Silverman, J.H.: Almost Inverses and Fast NTRU Key Creation. NTRU Cryptosystems Technical report #14 (1999)

47. Singh, S., Padhye, S.: Cryptanalysis of NTRU with n public keys. In: 2017 ISEA Asia Security and Privacy (ISEASP), pp. 1–6 (2017). https://doi.org/10.1109/ISEASP.2017.7976980

48. Development team, T.F.: FPLLL, a lattice reduction library, Version: 5.4.4 (2023). https://github.com/fplll/fplll

49. Development team, T.F.: FPYLLL, a Python wraper for the fplll lattice reduction library, Version: 0.5.9 (2023). https://github.com/fplll/fpylll

50. Truman, K.R.: Analysis and Extension of Non-Commutative NTRU. PhD dissertation, University of Maryland (2007). https://drum.lib.umd.edu/handle/1903/7344

51. van Hoof, I., Kirshanova, E., May, A.: Quantum key search for ternary LWE. In: Cheon, J.H., Tillich, J.-P. (eds.) PQCrypto 2021 2021. LNCS, vol. 12841, pp. 117–132. Springer, Cham (2021). https://doi.org/10.1007/978-3-030-81293-5_7

52. Vats, N.: NNRU, a noncommutative analogue of NTRU (2009). https://arxiv.org/abs/0902.1891
53. Working Group of the C/MM Committee and others: IEEE P1363.1 Standard Specification for Public-Key Cryptographic Techniques Based on Hard Problems over Lattices (2009)
54. Yasuda, T., Dahan, X., Sakurai, K.: Characterizing NTRU-variants using group ring and evaluating their lattice security. IACR Cryptol. ePrint Arch., p. 1170 (2015). http://eprint.iacr.org/2015/1170

Guidance for Efficient Selection of Secure Parameters for Fully Homomorphic Encryption

Elena Kirshanova[1], Chiara Marcolla[1], and Sergi Rovira[2(✉)]

[1] Technology Innovation Institute, Abu Dhabi, United Arab Emirates
[2] Pompeu Fabra University, Barcelona, Spain
sergi.rovira@upf.edu

Abstract. The field of Fully Homomorphic Encryption (FHE) has seen many theoretical and computational advances in recent years, bringing the technology closer to practicality than ever before. For this reason, practitioners from neighbouring fields such as machine learning have sought to understand FHE to provide privacy to their work. Unfortunately, selecting secure and efficient parameters in FHE is a daunting task due to the many interdependencies between the parameters involved. In this work, we solve this problem by moving away from the standard parameter selection procedure, introducing formulas which provide secure and optimal parameters for any lattice-based scheme. We build our formulas from a strong theoretical foundation based on cryptanalysis against LWE.

Keywords: Fully Homomorphic Encryption · Parameter Selection · Learning With Errors · Primal attacks · Bounded Distance Decoding

1 Introduction

With the advancements of future-generation networking technologies like cloud services, artificial intelligence applications, Internet of Things, and edge computing, concerns about data privacy are increasing significantly. Homomorphic encryption serves as a solution for preserving privacy during data processing, allowing computations on encrypted data without the need for decryption. More specifically, Fully Homomorphic Encryption (FHE) schemes define ciphertext operations corresponding to computations on the underlying plaintext as additions or multiplications [1, 16, 44, 45].

The first FHE scheme was introduced in 2009 by Gentry [32]. Gentry provided a method for constructing a general FHE scheme from a scheme with limited but sufficient homomorphic evaluation capacity. Since then, several FHE constructions have been proposed, being BGV [14], BFV [13, 30], TFHE [19, 20], and CKKS [17, 18], the most well-known schemes in the field.

The security of most FHE schemes is based on the presumed intractability of the (decision) Learning with Errors (LWE) problem, [49], and its ring variant

S. Vaudenay and C. Petit (Eds.): AFRICACRYPT 2024, LNCS 14861, pp. 376–400, 2024.
https://doi.org/10.1007/978-3-031-64381-1_17

(RLWE), [42]; the latter version is often preferred for efficiency reasons. Informally, decisional LWE consists in distinguishing equations $\{(a_i, b_i = s \cdot a_i + e_i)\}_i$ mod q, perturbed by small noise e_i (also called error), from uniform random tuples from $\mathbb{Z}_q^n \times \mathbb{Z}_q$.[1] To guarantee a correct decryption, the noise added has to be small. Indeed, roughly speaking, if the error surpasses the modulus q, it can result in a wrap-around effect, altering the decrypted output. Therefore, maintaining a limited noise level and computing a tight bound of the error's size is essential for ensuring the recovery of the plaintext.

The problem arising from lattice-based constructions is that the noise grows whenever an homomorphic operation is performed. In particular, it grows exponentially when homomorphic multiplications are computed. To increase the number of supported operations, we could increase the ciphertext modulus q. However, a larger modulus also decreases the security level of the underlying scheme, requiring a larger LWE dimension n to keep the same security level, which comes at the cost of efficiency.

This required trade-off between security (small q) and error margin (large q) illustrates the challenge of identifying an optimal set of parameters for a given FHE scheme. Such a balancing process, called *parameter estimation*, is one of the main issues that need to be addressed to make FHE practical.

In this work, we deduce precise and closed-form formulas for parameter selection of LWE-based schemes. Our approach to parameter selection greatly simplifies the development and deployment of FHE-based privacy-preserving applications. That is, we provide a fast methodology to easily choose secure parameters without the need to understand the underlying cryptanalytic details or the interdependencies between the parameters.

Related Works. Several efforts have been made by the FHE community to address the challenge of facilitating the deployment of FHE among researchers and practitioners and to select an optimal set of parameters. For instance, some FHE compilers, which are high-level tools that aim at abstracting the technical APIs exposed by FHE libraries, allow a sort of automatic parameter generation (for *specific* FHE schemes) according to some predefined requirements [44,55]. Some examples are ALCHEMY [23], Cingulata [15], EVA [25] and SEALion [29]. For more details of supported schemes and the methodology behind automatic parameter selection in FHE compilers, we refer the reader to [55].

Moreover, Bergerat *et al.* [10] proposed a framework for efficiently selecting parameters in TFHE-like schemes. Mono *et al.* [47] developed an interactive parameter generator for the levelled BGV scheme that supports arbitrary circuit models and Biasioli *et al.* [11] extended [47] to the BFV scheme.

Finally, important steps have been made to address parameter selection, providing methods and formulas for *any* FHE schemes. For instance, the Homomorphic Encryption Standard [3] provides upper limits on the size of the ciphertext

---

[1] While in FHE literature n is often referred to as polynomial degree, having in mind Ring-LWE based constructions, in this work we refer to n as to LWE dimension, as we do not utilize any algebraic properties of Ring-LWE.

378   E. Kirshanova et al.

modulus for certain security levels λ and dimension n in the form of lookup tables, using the Lattice Estimator[2] [5]. Moreover, in [47], the authors proposed a compact formula that computes the hardness of LWE for given dimension n, modulus q, the standard deviation of secret distribution σ_s, and σ_e – the standard deviation of the error distribution. Yet, as emphasised in the invited talk of Paillier [48], these efforts are still insufficient to provide an efficient easy-to-use tool for secure parameter selection.

Our Contribution. In this paper, we present a novel method for determining optimal parameters for any FHE scheme, focusing on the *macro* level, namely n, q, σ_s, σ_e and λ. To achieve this, starting with the theoretical foundation of lattice attacks, we introduce formulas that select these macro parameters. Concretely, our contributions are the following.

1. We consider the most relevant lattice attacks (for FHE parameters) and derive closed and precise formulas of their running times as functions of n, q, σ, and λ.
2. These formulas enable us to express the LWE dimension n as a function of $\lambda, q, \sigma_e, \sigma_s$, giving a way to choose, for a desired security level λ, an appropriate n. We verify our formulas by running extensive experiments with the Lattice Estimator [5]. By creating a large dataset of points that relates n, q, σ, λ, we are able to fine-tune our formulas to make sure that lower-order terms in the derived expressions are of the correct form and, hence, provide accurate estimates for broad parameter sets.
3. We provide Python scripts that implement these formulas, and we specify the best practices for using them. The scripts are publicly available on our Github repository[3].

Our analysis considers two types of lattice algorithms: the so-called bounded distance decoding attack and the unique Shortest Vector Problem attack. We chose these two as currently they are the most efficient attacks whose correctness was not refuted. Efficient dual attacks that can outperform the attacks we consider here, at the time of writing, do not offer correctness [28].

Comparison with Related Work. In [10], the authors build a framework to efficiently find optimal parameters for TFHE-like schemes. Their methodology relies on a *security oracle*, which given the parameters n, q, λ and σ_s, outputs the minimal σ_e that guarantees security λ. In practice, this oracle is constructed as a linear approximation. Our methodology deviates considerably from their approach. The main difference is that our formulas do not come solely from empirical results but from the analysis of the main lattice attacks. The point of contact of the two works is the use of the Lattice Estimator to build a database and the use of a fitting function. However, while [10] uses the fitting function to build the totality of their formula, our use is solely for optimizing lower-order terms.

---

[2] The Lattice Estimator (https://github.com/malb/lattice-estimator) is the successor of the LWE Estimator, which is a software tool to determine the security level of LWE instances under various attacks proposed until the present time.
[3] https://github.com/sergiorovira/fastparameterselection.

We want to highlight that our formulas provide not only an alternative to the existing procedures of parameter selection in FHE but also a faster paradigm. That is, using a script-based strategy (such as running the Lattice Estimator for different sets of parameters) is inefficient since the only way to obtain suitable parameters is trial and error, which can mean checking hundreds of cases until the optimal parameters are found. Using a look-up table of pre-computed values is, of course, faster but also limited since it might not accommodate all possible needs that arise when selecting parameters for FHE schemes. This approach is used in the vast majority of FHE libraries [8,40,53]. Using a formula-based method, we get the best of both approaches. Namely, we can get optimal parameters for any given application instantly. Another advantage of using formulas is that we can understand the behaviour of the parameters in relation to each other, allowing us to easily check if the parameters we are using are optimal. Finally, it is worth mentioning that our formulas are applicable to *any* construction based on the hardness of LWE and not only to FHE schemes.

To conclude, our approach significantly accelerates the parameter selection process, offering a practical and efficient tool for researchers and practitioners deploying FHE in real-world applications.

2 Preliminaries

2.1 Notation

For a positive integer q, we denote by $\mathbb{Z}_q = \mathbb{Z}/q\mathbb{Z}$ the ring of integers modulo q. For $n \geq 1$, denote by $\mathbb{R}^n$ the real vector space. For a vector $\mathbf{x}$, both $\mathbf{x}_i$ and $\mathbf{x}[i]$ denote either the i-th scalar component of the vector or the i-th element of an ordered finite set of vectors. Matrices are denoted by bold capital letters. We denote by $\|\mathbf{x}\|$ the Euclidean norm of $\mathbf{x}$. By $\mathbf{A}^t$ we denote the transpose of $\mathbf{A}$.

2.2 Mathematical Background

Let $\mathbf{B} = (\mathbf{b}_1, \ldots, \mathbf{b}_k)$ be linearly independent vectors in $\mathbb{R}^n$, then we can define the *lattice* $\mathcal{L}(\mathbf{B})$ generated by $\mathbf{B}$ as the set of all integer linear combinations of elements of $\mathbf{B}$:

$$\mathcal{L} = \mathcal{L}(\mathbf{B}) = \Big\{ \sum_{i=1}^{k} \gamma_i \mathbf{b}_i : \quad \gamma_i \in \mathbb{Z}, \mathbf{b}_i \in \mathbf{B} \Big\}.$$

If $k = n$, the lattice is said to be *full rank*. We will be concerned with integral lattice, i.e., $\mathcal{L} \subset \mathbb{Z}^n$. An integral lattice $\mathcal{L}$ is called q-ary if $q\mathbb{Z}^n \subset \mathcal{L} \subset \mathbb{Z}^n$. The determinant of a lattice $\mathcal{L}$ defined by a basis $\mathbf{B}$ is $\det(\mathcal{L}) = \sqrt{\det(\mathbf{B}^t\mathbf{B})}$ and is independent of the choice of basis.

For basis vectors $\mathbf{b}_i$, we write $\mathbf{b}_i^\star$ for the corresponding Gram-Schmidt vectors. Concretely, the i-th Gram-Schmidt vector $\mathbf{b}_i^\star$ is the projection of $\mathbf{b}_i$ orthogonally to the subspace $\mathrm{Span}_{\mathbb{R}}(\mathbf{b}_1, \ldots, \mathbf{b}_{i-1})$. We denote such projecting operator

π_i. We write $\mathbf{B}_{[i,j]}$ to denote the matrix whose columns are $\{\pi_i(\mathbf{b}_i), \ldots, \pi_i(\mathbf{b}_j)\}$. It generates (a projective) sublattice of dimension $j - i + 1$. We will make use of the fact that $\det(\mathcal{L}(\mathbf{B})) = \prod_{i=1}^{n} \|\mathbf{b}_i^\star\|$.

The *minimum distance* or the *first successive minimum* of lattice $\mathcal{L}$, denoted by $\lambda_1(\mathcal{L})$, is the Euclidean norm of a shortest non-zero vector in $\mathcal{L}$: $\lambda_1(\mathcal{L}) = \min\{\|\mathbf{v}\| : \mathbf{v} \in \mathcal{L}, \mathbf{v} \neq \mathbf{0}\}$. The i-th successive minimum $\lambda_i(\mathcal{L})$ is the smallest $r > 0$ such that $\mathcal{B}(\mathbf{0}, r)$ contains i linearly independent vectors of $\mathcal{L}$, where $\mathcal{B}(\mathbf{0}, r)$ is a ball in $\mathbb{R}^n$ of radius r centered at $\mathbf{0}$. The successive minima are independent of the basis choice.

The *Gaussian Heuristic* predicts $\lambda_1(\mathcal{L})$ for an n-dimensional lattice $\mathcal{L}$:

$$\lambda_1(\mathcal{L}) \approx \frac{\sqrt{n}}{\sqrt{2\pi e}} (\det(\mathcal{L}))^{1/n}.$$

Hard Problems on Lattices. There are several fundamental problems related to lattices, the following ones are relevant to this work.

The *Shortest Vector Problem (SVP)* asks to find $\mathbf{v} \in \mathcal{L}$ such that $\|\mathbf{v}\| = \lambda_1(\mathcal{L})$.

In the promise variant of SVP, the so-called *unique SVP (uSVP)*, we are guaranteed that the first successive minimum is $\gamma > 1$ times smaller than the second minimum λ_2. We are asked to find $\mathbf{v} \in \mathcal{L}$ such that $\|\mathbf{v}\| = \lambda_1(\mathcal{L})$.

The *Closest Vector Problem (CVP)* asks to find $\mathbf{v} \in \mathcal{L}$ closest to a given target vector $\mathbf{t} \in \mathbb{R}^n$.

Given a lattice $\mathcal{L}$ and a target vector $\mathbf{t}$ close to the lattice, the *Bounded Distance Decoding (BDD)* problem asks to find $\mathbf{v} \in \mathcal{L}$ closest to the target $\mathbf{t}$ with the promise that $\|\mathbf{t} - \mathbf{v}\| \leq R$, where $R \ll \lambda_1(\mathcal{L})$.

Discrete Gaussian Distribution. For a vector $\mathbf{v}$ and any $\sigma > 0$, define $\rho_\sigma(\mathbf{v}) = \exp(-\pi\|\mathbf{v}\|^2/(2\pi\sigma^2))$. For a lattice $\mathcal{L}$, the *discrete Gaussian probability distribution* with standard deviation σ^4 is defined with the probability density function

$$\mathcal{D}_{\mathcal{L},\sigma}(\mathbf{v}) = \frac{\rho_\sigma(\mathbf{v})}{\sum_{\mathbf{x} \in \mathcal{L}} \rho_\sigma(\mathbf{x})}.$$

2.3   Lattice Reduction

Lattice reduction aims at improving the quality of a lattice basis. In this work, we are interested in the lattice reduction algorithm called BKZ (short for Block-Korkine-Zolotarev, [50]). Together with a lattice basis, it receives as input an integer parameter β (called the *block size*) that governs the quality of the output basis and the runtime. Here by 'quality' we mean the Euclidean norm of the

---

[4] Notice that the variance of a Discrete Gaussian and a Continuous Gaussian does not match when $\sigma \leq 0.6$. In this paper we use the same parameter for both since we always work with $\sigma > 0.6$.

shortest vector in the basis output by BKZ. Concretely, BKZ run with block size β on a lattice $\mathcal{L}$ of rank n, returns a basis containing a lattice vector $\mathbf{b}_1$ of norm

$$\|\mathbf{b}_1\| = \delta_\beta^n \cdot \det(\mathcal{L})^{1/n}, \tag{1}$$

where δ_β is known as the root Hermite-factor and can be expressed in terms of β as

$$\delta_\beta = (((\pi\beta)^{1/\beta}\beta)/(2\pi e))^{\frac{1}{2(\beta-1)}} \approx \left(\frac{\beta}{2\pi e}\right)^{\frac{1}{2\beta}}, \tag{2}$$

where the approximation holds for large β's such that $(\pi\beta)^{1/\beta} \approx 1$.

The BKZ-β algorithm works by calling multiple times an algorithm for SVP on sublattices of dimension β. In [34] it is shown that after poly(n) many number of SVP calls, the guarantee defined in Equation (1) is achieved. Hence, the running time of BKZ is determined by the complexity of SVP in β dimensional lattices. The asymptotically fastest algorithm for SVP is due to Becker-Gama-Ducas-Laarhoven [9] that outputs a shortest vector in an n-dimensional lattice in time $2^{0.292n+o(n)}$. We choose this running time (ignoring the $o()$-term) as the measure of SVP hardness. Further, for a more concrete complexity of BKZ-β on an n-dimensional lattice we set the running time of BKZ as

$$T_{\mathrm{BKZ}}(\beta, n) = 2^{0.292\beta} \cdot 8n \cdot 16.4, \tag{3}$$

which is the choice adopted by [12,26,31]. The correcting constant of 16.4 obtained experimentally [9]. The concrete choice of $T_{\mathrm{BKZ}}(\beta, n)$ is called the core-SVP model [6]. Our results are easy to adapt to other existing choices of $T_{\mathrm{BKZ}}(\beta, n)$.

In addition to Eq. 1, BKZ quality guarantees extend (heuristically) to norms of Gram-Schmidt vectors of the returned basis. It is formulated in Geometric Series Assumption. All known lattice estimators [5,24] rely on this assumption.

Definition 1 (Geometric Series Assumption (GSA), [51]). *The norms of Gram-Schmidt vectors of a BKZ-β reduced basis satisfy*

$$\|\mathbf{b}_i^\star\| = \alpha^{i-1}\|\mathbf{b}_1\|,$$

where $\alpha = \delta_\beta^{\frac{-2n}{n-1}} \approx \delta_\beta^{-2} \approx \beta^{-1/\beta}$.

Babai's Algorithm. For one of the attacks considered in this work, we need an efficient BDD solver: Babai's algorithm [7]. Its running time is polynomial in the lattice dimension. In a BDD instance, we are given a lattice basis $\mathbf{B}$ and the target $\mathbf{t}$. Assume for simplicity that the coordinates of $\mathbf{t}$ are independent Gaussians with standard deviation σ (case of LWE). Informally, the success probability of Babai depends on the relation between $\|\mathbf{b}_i^\star\|$ and σ: if $\|\mathbf{b}_n^\star\| > \sigma$, the success probability is constant, while if $\|\mathbf{b}_1^\star\| = \sigma$, the success probability is super-exponentially low (in the lattice dimension). We will be concerned with the first case (constant success probability) formally defined in the next claim. We use the formulation from [35].[5]

Lemma 1 ([35, **Lemma 4**]). *Let the sequence* $\|\mathbf{b}_1^\star\|, \ldots, \|\mathbf{b}_n^\star\|$ *follow GSA, and let* $\mathbf{t}$ *be a vector with coordinates distributed as independent Gaussians with standard deviation* σ. *The success probability of Babai's algorithm is* $1 - o(1)$, *if* $\|\mathbf{b}_n^\star\| > \sigma (\log n)^{1/2+\varepsilon}$ *for fixed constant* $\varepsilon > 0$.

2.4   The Learning with Errors Problem

The Learning with Errors problem (LWE) was introduced by Regev in [49]. The LWE problem is parametrized by an integer n, modulus q (not necessarily prime), an error distribution $\chi_e : \mathbb{Z}_q \to \mathbb{R}^+$ with standard deviation σ_e, and a secret distribution $\chi_s : \mathbb{Z}_q \to \mathbb{R}^+$ with standard deviation σ_s.

Definition 2 (The Learning with Errors (LWE) problem). *Given a vector* $\mathbf{b} \in \mathbb{Z}_q^m$ *and a matrix* $\mathbf{A}$ *taken uniformly at random from* $\mathbb{Z}_q^{m \times n}$, *the search version of the LWE problem consists in finding an unknown vector* $\mathbf{s} \in \mathbb{Z}_q^n$ *such that*

$$\mathbf{A}\,\mathbf{s} + \mathbf{e} = \mathbf{b} \bmod q,$$

where $\mathbf{e} \in \mathbb{Z}_q^m$ *is sampled coordinate-wise from an error distribution* χ_e, *and* $\mathbf{s}$ *is sampled coordinate-wise from* χ_s. *In other words, the goal is to find a vector* $\mathbf{s} \in \mathbb{Z}_q^n$ *given a list of* m *noisy equations from*

$$\mathcal{A}_{\mathbf{s},\chi_e,\chi_s} = \{(\mathbf{a}_i, b_i = \langle \mathbf{a}_i, \mathbf{s}\rangle + e_i) \in \mathbb{Z}_q^n \times \mathbb{Z}_q : \mathbf{a}_i \xleftarrow{\$} \mathbb{Z}_q^n, e_i \leftarrow \chi_e, \mathbf{s}_i \leftarrow \chi_s\}.$$

Often in FHE constructions, we have $\chi_s \in \{\mathcal{U}_3, \mathcal{U}_2\}$, the uniform distribution on $\mathbb{Z}_3$ (called *ternary secret* LWE) or on $\mathbb{Z}_2$ called (*binary secret* LWE). For the error, we are concerned with discrete Gaussian distribution centered in 0 with standard deviation $\sigma_e = 3.19$ [3].

There exist several versions of LWE: Ring-LWE [42,54] and Module-LWE [39]. These are mainly used for efficiency reasons, security-wise these versions, at the time of writing, are believed to be equivalent to 'plain' LWE. Therefore, all our results extend to these other versions, in particular to Ring-LWE, the most relevant variant in the FHE context.

3   Deriving LWE Dimension for Required Security Level

On Chosen Algorithms. We focus on *primal* attacks on LWE, and do not consider the so-called dual attacks. First, the recent discoveries [28] of failing heuristics employed in efficient dual attacks [33,46] invalidate the claimed complexities.

---

[5] Even though in [35, Lemma 4] the authors talk about *continuous* Gaussian, the result holds for the discrete Gaussian too.

Despite of ongoing attempts to bring dual attacks back into play [27], no complete algorithm is presented that outperforms primal attacks. While other potentially less efficient versions of dual attacks have not been invalidated, the primal attacks perform better on the parameters considered in this work. Second, dual attacks seem to be much harder to implement: we are not aware of an existing implementation of a competitive dual attack.

We neither consider here the so-called *hybrid* attacks [2,36]. These are relevant for sparse secret LWE, i.e., for cases when the Hamming weight of the secret is less than $n/2$. The analysis of these attacks is left for future work.

We receive on input an LWE instance $(\mathbf{A}, \mathbf{b} = \mathbf{As} + \mathbf{e}) \in \mathbb{Z}_q^{m \times n} \times \mathbb{Z}_q^m$, where $\mathbf{s}$ follows the distribution χ_s with standard deviation σ_s, and $\mathbf{e}$ follows the distribution χ_e with standard deviation σ_e. We now describe in details the two attacks: BDD and uSVP, derive accurate formulas for their complexities, and finally reverse these formulas to express n as a function of q, σ_e, σ_s, and the desired security level λ.

3.1   The BDD Attack

While the BDD attack on LWE has been known for years [41], we did not find a reference that aligns well the Lattice Estimator [5], hence we first describe the attack, then derive its running time and reverse the runtime expression for the desired parameters, e.g., the LWE dimension n.

The search LWE problem is an average-case BDD problem for the $(m + n)$−dimensional q-ary lattice

$$\mathcal{L}_{\mathsf{bdd}} = \{\mathbf{v} \in \mathbb{Z}^{n+m} \mid [\mathbf{A}|\mathbf{I}_m]\mathbf{v} = 0 \bmod q\},$$

with the target vector $(\mathbf{0}, \mathbf{b}) \in \mathbb{Z}^n \times \mathbb{Z}^m$. To see this, consider a basis for this lattice over $\mathbb{Z}^{m+n}$ given by the columns of the matrix

$$\mathbf{B}_{\mathsf{bdd}} = \begin{pmatrix} \mathbf{I}_n & 0 \\ \mathbf{A} & q\mathbf{I}_m \end{pmatrix}.$$

From the LWE equation $\mathbf{As} + \mathbf{e} = \mathbf{b} - \mathbf{k} \cdot q$ for some $\mathbf{k} \in \mathbb{Z}^m$, we know that

$$\mathbf{B}_{\mathsf{bdd}} \cdot (\mathbf{s}, \mathbf{k})^t = (\mathbf{s}, \mathbf{b} - \mathbf{e})^t = (\mathbf{s}, -\mathbf{e})^t + (\mathbf{0}, \mathbf{b})^t.$$

The lattice $\mathcal{L}_{\mathsf{bdd}}$ is with high probability of full rank $m + n$ (since $\mathbf{A}$ has full column rank n with high probability) and the determinant of $\mathcal{L}_{\mathsf{bdd}}$ is $\det(\mathcal{L}_{\mathsf{bdd}}) = q^m$. The Gaussian Heuristic suggests that

$$\lambda_1(\mathcal{L}_{\mathsf{bdd}}) \approx \frac{\sqrt{m+n}}{2\pi e} \cdot q^{\frac{m}{m+n}}.$$

Further, the vector $(\mathbf{0}, \mathbf{b})$ is at distance $\|(\mathbf{s}, \mathbf{e})\| \approx \sqrt{n\sigma_s^2 + m\sigma_e^2} \ll \lambda_1(\mathcal{L}_{\mathsf{bdd}})$ from $\mathcal{L}_{\mathsf{bdd}}$, hence we have a BDD instance $(\mathcal{L}_{\mathsf{bdd}}, (\mathbf{0}, \mathbf{b}))$.

In cases were $\sigma_s < \sigma_e$, one can 're-balance' the contribution of $\mathbf{s}, \mathbf{e}$ into the distance $\sqrt{n\sigma_s^2 + m\sigma_e^2}$ by scaling the $\mathbf{I}_n$ part of B_{bdd} by $\zeta = \max\{1, \lfloor \sigma_e/\sigma_s \rceil\}$, that is we perform the attack on $\mathbf{B}_{\mathrm{bdd}} = \begin{pmatrix} \zeta\mathbf{I}_n & 0 \\ \mathbf{A} & q\mathbf{I}_m \end{pmatrix}$. Even though it increases the distance of the target to the lattice, it also scales $\det(\mathcal{L}_{\mathrm{bdd}})$ by a factor ζ^n, which in turn increases $\lambda_1(\mathcal{L}_{\mathrm{bdd}})$ and hence the decoding properties of $\mathcal{L}_{\mathrm{bdd}}$. For FHE parameters, the secret $\mathbf{s}$ is often binary or ternary, in which cases $\zeta = \sigma_e/(1/2) = 2\sigma_e$ or $\zeta = \sigma_e/(\sqrt{2/3}) = \sqrt{3/2}\sigma_e$.

Denote for simplicity $d := m + n$, the dimension of $\mathbf{B}_{\mathrm{bdd}}$. The bounded distance decoding algorithm [41] works in three steps. In Step 1, we run a BKZ-β lattice reduction algorithm on $\mathbf{B}_{\mathrm{bdd}}$. Denote the output basis by $\mathbf{B}'_{\mathrm{bdd}}$. The goal of BKZ is to obtain a basis with the property

$$\lambda_1(\mathbf{B}'_{\mathrm{bdd},[d-\eta,d]}) < \|\pi_{d-\eta}((\mathbf{s},\mathbf{e}))\|$$

for $0 \leq \eta < d$ as small as possible. Under the Gaussian Heuristic and the approximation $\|\pi_{d-\eta}((\mathbf{s},\mathbf{e}))\| \approx \sigma_e\sqrt{\eta}$, the above inequality can be rewritten as

$$\frac{\sqrt{d}}{2\pi e} \det\left(\mathbf{B}'_{\mathrm{bdd},[d-\eta+1,d]}\right)^{1/d} < \sigma_e\sqrt{\eta}. \qquad (4)$$

This condition means that the orthogonal projection of our short vector $(\mathbf{s},\mathbf{e})$ on $\mathrm{Span}_{\mathbb{R}}(\mathbf{b}_1,\ldots,\mathbf{b}_{d-\eta+1})$ is shorter than the shortest vector in the projected lattice $\mathbf{B}'_{\mathrm{bdd},[d-\eta+1,d]}$ given by the basis $(\pi_{d-\eta+1}(\mathbf{b}'_{d-\eta+1}),\ldots,\pi_{d-\eta+1}(\mathbf{b}'_d))$. In the LWE setting, GSA suggests that for small η's the left-hand side of Ineq. (4) is always larger than the right-hand side. Although both sides decrease for decreasing η, the left-hand side does it faster (again, due to GSA) and at some point Ineq. (4) is satisfied.

This implies that running an SVP solver on $[\mathbf{B}'_{\mathrm{bdd},[d-\eta+1,d]}|\pi_{d-\eta+1}((\mathbf{0},\mathbf{b}))]$ will find the *projection* $\pi_{d-\eta+1}((\mathbf{s},\mathbf{e}))$ of our secret. This SVP call constitutes the second step of the algorithm. Notice that we call SVP on a rank-(η) lattice generated by $[\mathbf{B}'_{\mathrm{bdd},[d-\eta+1,d]}|\pi_{d-\eta+1}((\mathbf{s},\mathbf{e}))]$.

The third step of the attack 'lifts' the found projected vector $\pi_{d-\eta+1}((\mathbf{s},\mathbf{e}))$ using Babai's algorithm on the 'remaining' part of the lattice $\mathbf{B}'_{\mathrm{bdd},[1,d-\eta+1]}$, which is a sublattice of $\mathbf{B}'_{\mathrm{bdd}}$ generated by its first $(d-\eta+1)$ vectors. The norms of Gram-Schmidt vectors of this sublattice, $\|\mathbf{b}_1^\star\|,\ldots\|\mathbf{b}_{d-\eta+1}^\star\|$ satisfy

$$\|\mathbf{b}_i^\star\| \geq \lambda_1(\mathbf{B}'_{\mathrm{bdd},[i,d]}) \geq \sigma_e\sqrt{d-i}, \quad i \leq d-\eta+1,$$

where the first inequality comes from the fact that $\mathbf{b}_i^\star \in B'_{\mathrm{bdd},[i,d]}$, and the second is due to Ineq. (4). Applying Lemma 1 to $\mathbf{B}'_{\mathrm{bdd},[1,d-\eta+1]}$ gives constant probability of Babai algorithm to output $(\mathbf{s},\mathbf{e})$.

Runtime analysis of BDD. Let us now analyse the runtime of this attack. Among the three steps of the BDD attack, the most expensive ones are the first step

(BKZ-β) and the second (SVP in dimension η). It is optimal to balance these two steps.

The runtime of BKZ-β on a d-dimensional lattice as given in Eq. 3 is $T_{\text{BKZ}}(\beta, d) = 2^{0.292\beta} \cdot 8d$, while the runtime of SVP on η-dimensional lattice is $T_{\text{SVP}}(\eta) = 2^{0.292\eta}$. The two runtimes differ only by the $\log(8d)$ factor, hence we expect $\beta \approx \eta$ to be optimal. Indeed, running the estimator confirms this choice.

The required β can be derived from Ineq. (4). Concretely, using GSA and the BKZ-β guarantee on $\|\mathbf{b}'_1\|$, we compute

$$\det\left(\mathbf{B}'_{\text{bdd},[d-\eta+1,d]}\right) = \prod_{i=d-\eta+1}^{d} \|\mathbf{b}^\star_i\| = \prod_{i=d-\eta+1}^{d} \delta_\beta^{d-1-2i} (\det \mathbf{B}_{\text{bdd}})^{\frac{1}{d}} = \delta_\beta^{-\eta(d-\eta+2)} \cdot (q^m \zeta^n)^{\frac{\eta}{d}}.$$

From now on we use the approximation $\beta \approx \eta$ and work with β only. Here we notice that in LWE one is free to choose the number of samples m, which in turn affects the lattice dimension d. Minimizing the expression $\delta_\beta^{-\eta(d-\eta+2)} \cdot (q^m \zeta^n)^{\frac{\eta}{d}}$ with respect to d, yields optimal $d = \sqrt{\frac{n \ln(q/\zeta)}{\ln \delta_\beta}}$. From Ineq. (4) and Eq. 2, we obtain the following expression for β as a function of d, q, σ_e, ζ:

$$\beta \geq \frac{d \ln\left(\frac{\beta}{2\pi e}\right)}{\ln\left(\frac{\beta}{2\pi e}\right) + 2\ln\left(\frac{q}{\sigma_e \sqrt{2\pi e}}\right) - 2\frac{n}{d}\ln\left(\frac{q}{\zeta}\right)}. \tag{5}$$

Asymptotically, assuming ζ, σ_e are constants and $\ln q \geq \ln \beta$, the above inequality is of the form $\beta / \ln(\beta) \geq \frac{d}{\ln(q)}$. Solutions for such inequality do not have closed form expressions[6], however, one can check that they all belong to $\Theta\left(\frac{n}{\ln(q)} \ln\left(\frac{n}{\ln q}\right)\right)$ given the optimal choice for d. The experiments suggest that the constant inside the Θ-notation is around 2. In the later section such constant will be found by interpolation. We use this asymptotic expression for the terms $\ln\left(\frac{\beta}{2\pi e}\right)$ appearing on the right-hand side of the inequality. Plugging-in the optimal value for d gives us finally the lower bound on β, treated as equality:

$$\beta = \frac{2n \ln q \ln\left(\frac{n \ln(n/\ln q)}{\pi e \ln q}\right)}{\left(\ln\left(\frac{n \ln(n/\ln q)}{\pi e \ln q}\right) + \ln\left(\frac{q}{2\pi e \cdot \sigma_e \sigma_s}\right)\right)^2}. \tag{6}$$

Having β (and optimal d), we obtain the expression for the security level λ achieved by the LWE parameters n, q, σ_e, σ_s:

$$\lambda = \log(T_{\text{BKZ}}(\beta, n), 2) = 0.292\beta + \log(8d, 2) + 16.4. \tag{7}$$

In the next section, we show that this formula gives very close results to the Lattice Estimator predictions, and hence we can use it to express the LWE dimension n.

---

[6] The solutions can be expressed via the Lambert-W function https://en.wikipedia. org/wiki/Lambert_W_function. However, using the bounds for this function or using our estimates results in the same asymptotic behavior of the solutions.

Expressing n. Expressing n via $\lambda, q, \sigma_e, \sigma_s$ using Eq. 5 and the approximation $\ln(\beta) \approx \ln(\lambda/0.292)$, we obtain

$$n = \frac{\lambda \cdot \left(\ln \left(\frac{\lambda}{0.584\pi e} \right) + \ln \left(\frac{q}{2\pi e \cdot \sigma_e \sigma_s} \right) \right)^2}{0.584 \ln(\lambda/(0.584\pi e)) \ln(q)} - \texttt{non\_leading\_order\_term}, \qquad (8)$$

where `non_leading_order_term` is omitted due to its size and can be found in the scripts from our Github repository. In the next section, we provide experimental evidence of our formula's accuracy and a more compact expression for n.

3.2   The uSVP Attack

Another approach to evaluate the hardness of LWE is to model the problem of finding a unique shortest vector (uSVP) in a lattice closely related to $\mathcal{L}_{\text{bdd}}$ [4,6]. The uSVP attack extends $\mathcal{L}_{\text{bdd}}$ by embedding the vector $\mathbf{b}$ in it [37] :

$$\mathcal{L}_{\text{uSVP}} = \{\mathbf{v} \in \mathbb{Z}^{d+1} \mid [\mathbf{A}|\mathbf{I}_m| - \mathbf{b}]\mathbf{v} = 0 \bmod \ q\},$$

where as before $d = m + n$, later we optimize for d. The lattice $\mathcal{L}_{\text{uSVP}}$ admits the following basis matrix (written column-wise):

$$\mathbf{B}_{\text{uSVP}} = \begin{pmatrix} \zeta\mathbf{I}_n & \mathbf{0} & \mathbf{0} \\ \mathbf{A} & q\mathbf{I}_m & \mathbf{b} \\ \mathbf{0} & \mathbf{0} & 1 \end{pmatrix},$$

where again $\zeta = \max\{1, \lfloor \sigma_e/\sigma_s \rceil\}$ is the scaling constant to "balance" the $\mathbf{s}$ and $\mathbf{e}$ components of the shortest vector $(\zeta\mathbf{s}| - \mathbf{e}| - 1) \in \mathcal{L}_{\text{uSVP}}$. The constant 1 in the lattice is again a conventional practical choice [4].

The primal uSVP attack consist of running the BKZ lattice reduction algorithm [50,52] on the aforementioned basis of $\mathcal{L}_{\text{uSVP}}$. The estimates [4,6] predicts that BKZ succeeds in finding $(\zeta\mathbf{s}| - \mathbf{e}| - 1)$ if

$$\sqrt{\beta/(d)}\|(\zeta\mathbf{s}| - \mathbf{e}| - 1)\| \approx \sqrt{\beta}\sigma_e \leq \delta^{2\beta-(n+m+1)} \det(\mathcal{L}_{\text{uSVP}})^{1/d}.$$

From the shape of the basis $\mathbf{B}_{\text{uSVP}}$ of $\mathcal{L}_{\text{uSVP}}$, computing its volume (from now on we ignore the +1 in the dimension of $\mathcal{L}_{\text{uSVP}}$ and simplify it to $\dim(\mathcal{L}_{\text{uSVP}}) = n + m =: d$) leads to

$$\sqrt{\beta}\sigma_e \leq \delta^{2\beta-(d)} \cdot \zeta^{\frac{n}{d}} \cdot q^{1-\frac{n}{d}}. \qquad (9)$$

Now let us obtain a closed form for β as a function of the LWE parameters. The following derivations are rather technical, the reader may jump directly to Eq. 12 for the final result.

As in case of BDD, an attacker is allowed to choose m – the number of LWE samples to build the lattice from. As our objective is to reach the condition above for as small β as possible (the lower the β is, the easier is the attack) we aim at finding m that maximizes the right-hand size of Inequality (9). The maximum is achieved for $d = \sqrt{\frac{n \ln(q/\zeta)}{\ln \delta_\beta}}$. Substituting it in the Inequality (9) and taking logarithms leads to the success condition:

$$2\beta \ln \delta - 2\sqrt{n \ln(q/\zeta \ln \delta)} + \ln(q/\sigma_e) - \frac{1}{2} \ln \beta \geq 0.$$

Using the approximation $\ln(\delta) \approx \frac{\ln(\beta/(2\pi e))}{2\beta}$, obtain the condition on β (we keep the constants as they turn out to matter for the final result):

$$\beta \geq \frac{2n \ln(q/\zeta) \ln(\beta/(2\pi e))}{\ln^2(q\sqrt{\beta}/(2\pi e \sigma_e))}.$$

For the FHE parameters, the modulus q is chosen to be much larger than n and m and hence, larger than β. Therefore, asymptotically, the right-hand side of the inequality above belongs to $\Theta\left(\frac{n}{\ln q} \ln\left(\frac{n}{\ln q}\right)\right)$. This leads us to (again, as in BDD, the equation below is rather the inequality giving the lower bound on successfully β):

$$\beta = \frac{2n \ln(q/\zeta) \ln\left(\frac{n \ln(n/\ln q)}{2\pi e \ln(q/\sigma_e)}\right)}{\ln^2\left(\frac{q\sqrt{n \ln(n/\ln(q/\sigma_e))/\ln q}}{2\pi e \sigma_e}\right)} \tag{10}$$

Comparing this result with Eq. 6, we notice that asymptotically both expressions for β in BDD and in uSVP attack match.

Substituting Eq. 10, obtain the expression for λ

$$\lambda = 0.292\beta + \ln\left(8\sqrt{\frac{2n \ln(q/\zeta)\beta}{\ln(\beta/(2\pi e))}}\right) + 16.4. \tag{11}$$

Expressing n. Analogously to BDD, we express n as a function of $\lambda, q, \sigma_e, \sigma_s$:

$$n = \frac{\lambda \cdot \left(0.5 \ln(\lambda/0.292) + \ln\left(\frac{q}{2\pi e \cdot \sigma_e}\right)\right)^2}{0.584 \ln(\lambda/(0.584\pi e)) \ln(q\sigma_s/\sigma_e)} - \texttt{non\_leading\_order\_term}, \tag{12}$$

where **non_leading_order_term** is omitted and can be found in our Github repository.

4   Fine-Tuning and Verification

4.1   Our Methodology

As we have detailed in the previous section, during the derivation of our formulas, several simplifications had to be made in order to express the security parameter λ via LWE parameters, and, inversely, the LWE dimension n via $\lambda, q, \sigma_e, \sigma_s$. Although our formulas perform very well 'by default', we can optimize them and compensate for the loss in accuracy coming from the simplifications via a fitting function. The idea is to add certain parameters to our formulas and then learn them by using a list of points computed from the Lattice Estimator [5] and a fitting function. We remark that the simplifications only have a noticeable effect on the non-leading terms, and they perform very well by 'default'. Thus, the correction done via the fitting function can be understood as fixing these terms.

Database. The database used to verify our formulas has been constructed as follows. Fix $\sigma_e = 3.19$. Given a range of values for q, a range for LWE dimension n and $\sigma_s \in \{\mathcal{U}_2, \mathcal{U}_3\}$, we run the Lattice Estimator to obtain the security level of the corresponding points. It is worth noticing that $\sigma_s = \mathcal{U}_2$ is employed in TFHE-like schemes where $2^{10} \leq n \leq 2^{11}$, while $\sigma_s = \mathcal{U}_3$ is utilized in the other schemes (BGV, BFV and CKKS), where the dimension n is much bigger, i.e. $n \leq 2^{16}$. We have selected various parameter sets providing different security levels to validate our formulas exhaustively. Following common practice in the FHE literature we populate our database with parameters offering at least 80 bits of security [21,22,43]. Table 1 shows the number of points that we considered.

Table 1. Number of points (in our database) used to verify our formulas divided by secret distribution. Half of them correspond to the output of the lattice Estimator for uSVP and the other half for BDD.

σ_s	Range of n	Range of $\log q$	σ_e	Num. points
$\mathcal{U}_2$	$[2^{10}, 2^{11}]$	$[20, 64]$	3.19	42962
$\mathcal{U}_3$	$[2^{10}, 2^{15}]$	$[10, 1600]$	3.19	5282

Classification and Curation. Given the database, we classify the points per security level. It is important to notice that, given a security level, not all points need to be considered since most of them will never be used in practice. The considered points follow this criterion:

- Fix a LWE dimension n, we consider the point (n, q) with the biggest possible q. We can perform more computations with a bigger q.
- Fix a modulus q, we will only consider the point (n, q) with the smallest possible n. We have higher efficiency with a smaller n.

Verification. The verification step consists of plotting the curated points against our optimized formulas. Since we provide formulas derived from the attacks against uSVP and BDD, we verify each formula separately against the points where the security level corresponds to that attack.

Fine-tuning. After creating our database by running the Lattice Estimator as explained above, we do the following:

1. We refine the resulting formulas (Eqs. (7), (8), (12) and (11)) by incorporating additional variables. Using *coupled optimization*[7], we determine the optimal

---

[7] Specifically, we use the LMFIT Minimizer class: https://lmfit.github.io/lmfit-py/fitting.html.

values for these variables to ensure that our parameterized functions follows the data points generated with the Lattice Estimator, i.e., accurately reflects the security level estimation.

2. Finally, we provide a further simplification of these formulas, explicitly depending on the macro variables n, λ and q. Note that in this case, the variables found using the coupled optimization technique are intrinsically dependent on the secret distribution χ_s (and so on ζ).

4.2   Verification of uSVP Security Level, Eq. 11

Starting from Eq. 11 and using the process explained above, the resulting function for λ (considering the uSVP attack) is

$$\lambda = A\beta + B\ln\left(\frac{2n\ln(q/\zeta)\beta}{\ln(\beta/(2\pi e))}\right) + C, \tag{13}$$

where

$$A = 0.28862 \quad B = 1.33981 \quad C = 5.61427 \quad \text{if } \chi_s = \mathcal{U}_2$$
$$A = 0.296208 \quad B = 0.800603 \quad C = 12.09086 \quad \text{if } \chi_s = \mathcal{U}_3.$$

Now, our aim is to express Eq. 13 in a simplified form that explicitly depends on the variables n and q.

Let define $x = n/\ln q$, $k_1 = \frac{1}{2\pi e}$ and $k_2 = \frac{1}{2\pi e\sigma_e} = \frac{k_1}{\sigma_e}$, then since $\ln(q/\zeta) \approx \ln(q/\sigma_e) \approx \ln(q)$, we have that Eq. 10 can be approximate as

$$\beta \geq \frac{2n\ln(q/\zeta)\ln(k_1 x\ln x)}{\ln^2(k_2 q\sqrt{x\ln x})} \approx \frac{2n\ln q(\ln(x\ln x) - 2.8)}{(\ln q + 0.5\ln(x\ln x) - 4)^2}.$$

Considering n, q such that the security level is between 80 and 130, we have that $\ln q + 0.5\ln(x\ln x) - 4 \approx \ln q$. So

$$\beta \approx 2x\left(\ln(x) + \ln(\ln(x)) - 2.8\right). \tag{14}$$

Substituting Eq. 14 in Eq. 13 we have:

$$\lambda \approx 2A\ln\left(\frac{n}{\ln q} + \ln\left(\ln\left(\frac{n}{\ln q}\right)\right) - 2.8\right)\frac{n}{\ln q} + B\ln\left(\frac{2n\ln(q/\zeta)\beta}{\ln(\beta/(2\pi e))}\right) + C$$
$$\approx A'\ln\left(k_3\frac{n}{\ln q}\right)\frac{n}{\ln q} + B\ln\left(\frac{2n\ln(q)\beta}{\ln(\beta)-2.8}\right) + C$$
$$\approx A'\ln\left(k_3\frac{n}{\ln q}\right)\frac{n}{\ln q} + B\ln(4n^2 k_4) + C,$$

where k_3 and k_4 are small constants since if we consider n, q such that the security level is between 80 and 130,

$$k_4 = \frac{\ln x + \ln\left(\ln x\right) - 2.8}{\ln(2x) + \ln\left(\ln x + \ln\left(\ln x\right) - 2.8\right) - 2.8} \approx 1.$$

Using coupled optimization, we find the following

$$\lambda \approx A \ln \left(\frac{Bn}{\ln q} \right) \frac{n}{\ln q} + C \ln n + D \tag{15}$$

$A = 0.445309 \ \ B = 1.486982 \ \ C = 0.950115 \ \ D = 11.21416 \ \ \text{if } \chi_s = \mathcal{U}_2$
$A = 0.833542 \ \ B = 0.154947 \ \ C = 1.469823 \ \ D = 18.09877 \ \ \text{if } \chi_s = \mathcal{U}_3.$

The comparison results between the output of the Lattice Estimator and our formulas (Eqs. (13) and (15)) are presented in Tables 2 ans 3, demonstrating the effectiveness of our approach in accurately estimating security levels.

In Fig. 1 we pictured the data points of the Lattice Estimator and our formula proposed in Eq. 15.

Table 2. Comparison between the security level provided by our formulas (Eqs. (13) and (15)) and the Lattice Estimator with with $\sigma_s = \mathcal{U}_2$.

	$n = 2^{10}$				$n = 2^{11}$		
$\log q$	Estimator	(13)	(15)	$\log q$	Estimator	(13)	(15)
20	172	172	172	37	191	191	188
24	142	142	142	46	151	150	149
25	136	136	136	50	137	137	136
26	130	130	130	53	129	129	128
27	125	125	125	54	126	127	126
28	120	120	120	57	119	119	119
30	112	112	112	62	110	109	109
33	101	101	101	67	100	101	101
37	90	90	90	74	90	91	91
42	79	79	80	84	80	80	80

Table 3. Comparison between the security level provided by our formulas (Equations (13) and (15)) and the Lattice Estimator with $\sigma_s = \mathcal{U}_3$.

	$n = 2^{10}$				$n = 2^{15}$		
$\log q$	Estimator	(13)	(15)	$\log q$	Estimator	(13)	(15)
16	231	230	233	650	179	180	180
18	204	203	202	760	151	151	151
19	193	191	190	810	140	141	140
25	143	141	137	880	128	129	128
27	132	129	126	930	121	121	121
28	126	124	121	1000	112	112	112
30	117	115	112	1050	106	107	106
32	109	107	104	1200	93	93	93
43	80	78	76	1400	80	80	80
48	71	70	68	1500	74	75	75

4.3 Verification of BDD Security Level, Eq. 7

Starting from Eq. 7 and using the couple optimization, the resulting function for λ (considering the BDD attack) is

$$\lambda \approx A\beta + B\ln\left(\frac{2n\beta\ln(q/\zeta)}{\ln(\beta)}\right) + C. \tag{16}$$

where

$$A = 0.358587 \;\; B = 0.005 \;\;\;\;\;\;\; C = 27.56968 \;\; \text{if } \chi_s = \mathcal{U}_2.$$
$$A = 0.337349 \;\; B = 1.712118 \;\; C = 0.000003 \;\; \text{if } \chi_s = \mathcal{U}_3$$

In Figs. 2 and 3 we pictured the data points of the Lattice Estimator and our formula proposed in Eq. 16.

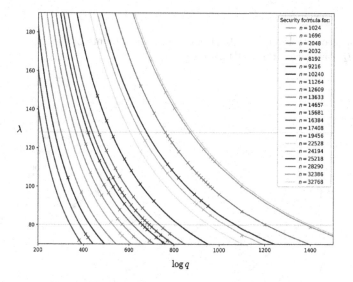

Fig. 1. The security formula (Eq. 15) with data points of the Lattice Estimator for $\chi_s = \mathcal{U}_3$ considering the uSVP attack.

From the Lattice Estimator outputs considered in this paper, we observed that for binary secret, the BDD attack always outperforms uSVP, although by a non-significant amount. Indeed, as our formulas suggest, the two attacks have very close runtimes.

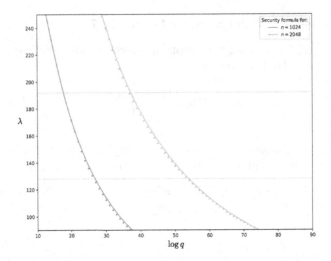

Fig. 2. The security level formula (Eq. 16) with data points of the Lattice Estimator for $\chi_s = \mathcal{U}_2$ considering the BDD attack.

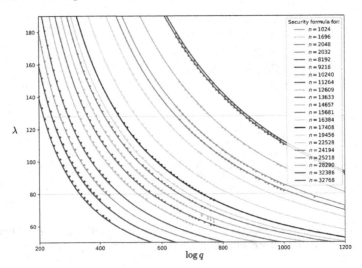

Fig. 3. The security formula (Eq. 16) with data points of the Lattice Estimator for $\chi_s = \mathcal{U}_3$ considering the BDD attack.

4.4   Verification of the LWE Dimension via uSVP, Eq. 12

Considering Eq. 15 and setting $x = n/\ln q$, we have

$$\lambda \approx A \ln(Bx)\frac{n}{\ln q} + C \ln x + C \ln \ln q + D.$$

Table 4. Comparison between the LWE dimension provided by our formula Eq. 17 and the Lattice Estimator with secret distribution $\mathcal{U}_2$. Est_n represents the n selected as input parameter for the Lattice Estimator. Est_λ represents the output security level provided by the Estimator given $\log q$, Est_n and the corresponding distribution.

$\log q$	Est_λ	Est_n	(17)	$\log q$	Est_λ	Est_n	(17)
$\lambda \approx 80$				$\lambda \approx 100$			
42	80	1024	1039	34	100	1024	1041
58	80	1408	1428	46	102	1408	1429
71	80	1728	1743	57	100	1728	1734
84	80	2048	2056	67	100	2048	2034
$\lambda \approx 110$				$\lambda \approx 120$			
31	110	1024	1038	28	123	1024	1042
42	112	1408	1426	39	121	1408	1424
52	111	1792	1747	48	121	1792	1749
61	112	2048	2063	57	121	2048	2074
$\lambda \approx 128$				$\lambda \approx 140$			
27	128	1024	1043	24	144	1024	1034
37	128	1408	1425	34	140	1408	1424
45	129	1728	1742	41	143	1728	1748
54	128	2048	2072	49	142	2048	2073

Table 5. Comparison between the LWE dimension provided by our formula Eq. 17 and the Lattice Estimator with secret distribution $\mathcal{U}_3$. Est_λ represents the output security level provided by the Estimator given $\log q$, Est_n and the corresponding distribution.

	$n = 2^{10} = 1024$			$n = 2^{15} = 32768$	
$\log q$	Est_λ	(17)	$\log q$	Est_λ	(17)
43	80	1063	1400	80	32801
34	102	1060	1100	101	32592
32	109	1062	1000	112	32809
29	122	1070	930	121	32908
27	132	1073	880	128	32890
25	143	1070	810	140	33012

Thus,

$$n \approx \left(\frac{\lambda - C\ln x - C\ln\ln q - D}{A\ln(Bx)} \right)\ln q \approx \left(\frac{\lambda + k_1 \ln\ln q}{k_2 \ln(x) + k_3} + k_4 \right)\ln q$$

where k_i are some constants. Since x appears only in the logarithm, we can consider the leading term of Eq. 15 approximating $x \approx a\lambda + b$, where a, b are some constants. Thus, using couple optimization, we obtain

$$n \approx \left(\frac{\lambda + A\ln(\ln q)}{B\ln(\lambda) + C} + D \right)\ln q, \tag{17}$$

A = −1.142080 B = 0.231197 C = 1.106616 D = −0.233138 if $\chi_s = \mathcal{U}_2$
A = −1.073049 B = 0.278319 C = 0.931202 D = 0.792882   if $\chi_s = \mathcal{U}_3$.

The comparison results between the output of the Lattice Estimator and our formula (Eq. 17) are presented in Tables 4 and 5, demonstrating the effectiveness of our approach in accurately estimating security levels.

In Fig. 4, we pictured the data points of the Lattice Estimator for uSVP attack and our formula proposed in Eq. 17.

4.5   Verification of the LWE Dimension via BDD, Eq. 8

We approximate Eq. 8 using coupled optimization techniques obtaining

$$n = \left(A\frac{\lambda}{\ln \lambda} + B\ln(\ln q) + C\right)\ln q + D, \tag{18}$$

A = 2.463040 B = 3.426581   C = −24.92487 D = 128.0417   if $\chi_s = \mathcal{U}_2$
A = 2.368303 B = −0.676307 C = −4.104371 D = −19.11047 if $\chi_s = \mathcal{U}_3$.

The comparison results between Eq. 18 and the output of the Lattice Estimator are presented in Tables 6 and 7. In Fig. 4, we show the data points of the Lattice Estimator for the uSVP attack and Eq. 17.

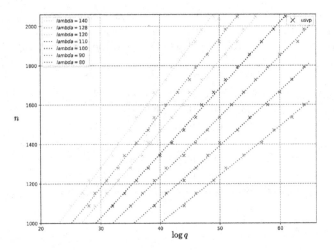

Fig. 4. Comparison between Eq. 17 and the data points output by the Lattice Estimator for $\chi_s = \mathcal{U}_2$, considering the uSVP attack. (Color figure online)

Table 6. Comparison between the LWE dimension n provided by Eq. 18 and the Lattice estimator with $\chi_s = \mathcal{U}_2$, for the BDD attack. Est_n represents the n selected as the input parameter for the Lattice Estimator. Est_λ represents the output security level provided by the Estimator given $\log q$, Est_n and the corresponding distribution.

$\log q$	Est_λ	Est_n	(18)	$\log q$	Est_λ	Est_n	(18)
	$\lambda \approx 80$				$\lambda \approx 100$		
42	80	1024	1039	34	100	1024	1041
58	80	1408	1428	46	102	1408	1429
71	80	1728	1742	57	100	1728	1734
84	80	2048	2056	67	100	2048	2034
	$\lambda \approx 110$				$\lambda \approx 120$		
31	110	1024	1038	28	123	1024	1041
42	112	1408	1426	39	121	1408	1424
52	111	1792	1748	48	121	1792	1749
61	112	2048	2062	57	121	2048	2073
	$\lambda \approx 128$				$\lambda \approx 140$		
27	128	1024	1042	24	144	1024	1034
37	128	1408	1424	34	140	1408	1424
45	129	1728	1742	41	143	1728	1748
54	128	2048	2072	49	142	2048	2072

Table 7. Comparison between the LWE dimension n provided by our formulas (Eq. 18) and the Lattice Estimator with $\chi_s = \mathcal{U}_3$, for the BDD attack. Est_λ represents the output security level provided by the Estimator given $\log q$, Est_n and the corresponding distribution.

$n = 2^{10} = 1024$			$n = 2^{15} = 32768$		
$\log q$	Est_λ	(18)	$\log q$	Est_λ	(18)
43	79	1066	1450	77	33351
34	101	1055	1150	97	33136
32	108	1055	1050	106	32929
29	120	1042	930	121	33034
27	129	1043	870	129	32805
25	140	1039	810	140	32943

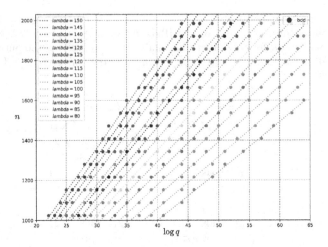

Fig. 5. The LWE dimension n (Eq. 18) with data points of the Lattice Estimator for $\chi_s = \mathcal{U}_3$ for the BDD attack.

4.6 Comparison with [10]

In [10], the authors detail a framework to find optimal parameters for applications built from TFHE-like schemes. They find parameters which are both secure and provide correctness of computation for the underlying cryptographic task. Their method relies on a *security oracle*, which given n, q, λ and σ_s outputs the minimal σ_e that guarantees security λ. In practice[8], this oracle is constructed as a linear approximation. Their methodology is the following. Fix $\log q = 64$, $\sigma_s = \mathcal{U}_2$ and security level λ. Given a range of values for σ_e, iterate over different values of n to find the minimum n for which the Lattice Estimator outputs security level λ. The output is then a collection of points $\{(n^i, \sigma_e^i)\}_i$ which can be linearly interpolated, obtaining parameters a, b. The oracle corresponds to the function $\mathcal{F}(n) = 2^{\lceil a \cdot n + b \rceil}$. Our methodology deviates considerably from [10]. The main difference is that our formulas do not come solely from empirical results but from the mathematical descriptions of the attacks against uSVP and BDD. A more detailed comparison can be found in the extended version of the paper [38].

4.7 How to Use Our Results in Practice

We provide our formulas that relate the macro parameters $n, q, \sigma_e, \sigma_s, \lambda$ as a tool in our Github repository[9]. Our code emulates the workflow of the Lattice Estimator for the uSVP and BDD attacks. That is, given n, q, σ_s and σ_e, one can use our tool to obtain a close approximation of the security level λ, without the need to run the Estimator. Moreover, given λ, q, σ_s and σ_e our tool can be used

---

[8] See https://github.com/zama-ai/concrete/tree/main/tools/parameter-curves.
[9] https://github.com/sergiorovira/fastparameterselection.

to obtain a n equal to or close to the optimal value for the given parameter set. Once the user has greatly narrowed down their possible choices of parameters using our tool, the recommended practice is to check them against the Estimator. Notice that our tool targets *security* and does not take into account *correctness* of computation. That is, we provide a shortcut to finding secure parameters for FHE schemes at the macro level. These parameters will not guarantee the correctness of computation as this will depend on the circuit being evaluated and the chosen FHE scheme.

5   Conclusion

We provided a pioneering methodology to obtain closed formulas for the security level of LWE as a function of the LWE dimension n, modulus q, standard deviations of secret σ_s, and error σ_e. From these formulas, we can express n as a function of q, σ_s, σ_e and the security level λ. We have extensively tested and verified our formulas against empirical data obtained from the Lattice Estimator [5].

The results obtained in this work significantly accelerate the parameter selection process of any LWE-based encryption scheme. We use them to build a practical and efficient tool for researchers and practitioners deploying FHE in real-world applications. Unlike the current slow, cumbersome and rigid parameter selection process of FHE parameters, our formulas open the door to a fast, user-friendly and easily adaptable paradigm.

We are positive that the methodology detailed in this work provides a good starting point for the derivation of q and/or σ_e as functions of the remaining parameters. We leave this task for future development of our tool.

Acknowledgement. The third listed author was supported by the Spanish Ministry of Science and Innovation under Grant Agreement No RTI2018-102112-B-I00.

References

1. Acar, A., Aksu, H., Uluagac, A.S., Conti, M.: A survey on homomorphic encryption schemes: theory and implementation. ACM Comput. Surv. (CSUR) **51**(4), 1–35 (2018)
2. Albrecht, M.R.: On dual lattice attacks against small-secret LWE and parameter choices in HElib and SEAL. In: Advances in Cryptology – EUROCRYPT 2017, pp. 103–129 (2017)
3. Albrecht, M.R., et al.: Homomorphic encryption security standard. Technical Report, HomomorphicEncryption.org , Toronto, Canada, November 2018
4. Albrecht, M.R., Göpfert, F., Virdia, F., Wunderer, T.: Revisiting the expected cost of solving uSVP and applications to LWE. In: Advances in Cryptology–ASIACRYPT 2017, pp. 297–322 (2017)
5. Albrecht, M.R., Player, R., Scott, S.: On the concrete hardness of learning with errors. J. Math. Cryptology **9**(3), 169–203 (2015)

6. Alkim, E., Ducas, L., Pöppelmann, T., Schwabe, P.: Post-quantum key exchange: a new hope. In: Proceedings of the 25th USENIX Conference on Security Symposium, pp. 327–343 (2016)
7. Babai, L.: On Lovász' lattice reduction and the nearest lattice point problem. Combinatorica **6**(1), 1–13 (1986)
8. Badawi, A.A., et al.: OpenFHE: open-source fully homomorphic encryption library. Cryptology ePrint Archive, Paper 2022/915 (2022)
9. Becker, A., Ducas, L., Gama, N., Laarhoven, T.: New directions in nearest neighbor searching with applications to lattice sieving. In: SODA 2016, pp. 10–24. SIAM (2016)
10. Bergerat, L., et al.: Parameter optimization and larger precision for (T)FHE. J. Cryptol. **36**(3), 28 (2023)
11. Biasioli, B., Marcolla, C., Calderini, M., Mono, J.: Improving and automating BFV parameters selection: an average-case approach. Cryptology ePrint Archive, Paper 2023/600 (2023)
12. Bos, J.W., et al.: CRYSTALS - Kyber: A CCA-secure module-lattice-based KEM. In: 2018 IEEE EuroS&P, pp. 353–367 (2018)
13. Brakerski, Z.: Fully homomorphic encryption without modulus switching from classical GapSVP. In: Advances in Cryptology – CRYPTO 2012, pp. 868–886 (2012)
14. Brakerski, Z., Gentry, C., Vaikuntanathan, V.: (Leveled) fully homomorphic encryption without bootstrapping. ACM Trans. Comput. Theor. (TOCT) **6**(3), 1–36 (2014)
15. Carpov, S., Dubrulle, P., Sirdey, R.: Armadillo: a compilation chain for privacy preserving applications. In: Proceedings of the 3rd International Workshop on Security in Cloud Computing, pp. 13–19 (2015)
16. Cheon, J.H., et al.: Introduction to homomorphic encryption and schemes. In: Protecting Privacy through Homomorphic Encryption, pp. 3–28 (2021)
17. Cheon, J.H., Han, K., Kim, A., Kim, M., Song, Y.: A full RNS variant of approximate homomorphic encryption. In: Cid, C., Jacobson Jr., M. (eds.) Selected Areas in Cryptography - SAC 2018, SAC 2018, LNCS, vol.11349, pp. 347–368. Springer, Cham (2019). https://doi.org/10.1007/978-3-030-10970-7_1
18. Cheon, J.H., Kim, A., Kim, M., Song, Y.: Homomorphic encryption for arithmetic of approximate numbers. In: Advances in Cryptology – ASIACRYPT 2017, pp. 409–437 (2017)
19. Chillotti, I., Gama, N., Georgieva, M., Izabachène, M.: Faster fully homomorphic encryption: bootstrapping in less than 0.1 seconds. In: Cheon, J., Takagi, T. (eds.) Advances in Cryptology - ASIACRYPT 2016, ASIACRYPT 2016, LNCS, vol. 10031, pp. 3–33. Springer, Berlin (2016). https://doi.org/10.1007/978-3-662-53887-6_1
20. Chillotti, I., Gama, N., Georgieva, M., Izabachène, M.: TFHE: fast fully homomorphic encryption over the torus. J. Cryptol. **33**(1), 34–91 (2020)
21. Costache, A., Smart, N.P.: Which ring based somewhat homomorphic encryption scheme is best? In: Sako, K. (ed.) CT-RSA 2016. LNCS, vol. 9610, pp. 325–340. Springer, Cham (2016). https://doi.org/10.1007/978-3-319-29485-8_19
22. Costache, A., Smart, N.P.: Homomorphic encryption without gaussian noise. Cryptology ePrint Archive, Paper 2017/163 (2017)
23. Crockett, E., Peikert, C., Sharp, C.: Alchemy: a language and compiler for homomorphic encryption made easy. In: Proceedings of the 2018 ACM SIGSAC Conference on Computer and Communications Security, pp. 1020–1037 (2018)

24. Dachman-Soled, D., Ducas, L., Gong, H., Rossi, M.: LWE with side information: attacks and concrete security estimation. In: Micciancio, D., Ristenpart, T. (eds.) CRYPTO 2020. LNCS, vol. 12171, pp. 329–358. Springer, Cham (2020). https://doi.org/10.1007/978-3-030-56880-1_12

25. Dathathri, R., Kostova, B., Saarikivi, O., Dai, W., Laine, K., Musuvathi, M.: EVA: an encrypted vector arithmetic language and compiler for efficient homomorphic computation. In: Proceedings of the 41st ACM SIGPLAN Conference on Programming Language Design and Implementation, pp. 546–561 (2020)

26. Ducas, L., et al.: CRYSTALS-Dilithium: a lattice-based digital signature scheme. IACR Trans. Cryptographic Hardware Embed. Syst. **2018**(1), 238–268 (2018)

27. Ducas, L., Pulles, L.N.: Accurate score prediction for dual-sieve attacks. Cryptology ePrint Archive, Report 2023/1850 (2023)

28. Ducas, L., Pulles, L.N.: Does the dual-sieve attack on learning with errors even work?. In: Handschuh, H., Lysyanskaya, A. (eds.) Advances in Cryptology - CRYPTO 2023, CRYPTO 2023, LNCS, vol. 14083, pp- 37–69. Springer, Cham (2023). https://doi.org/10.1007/978-3-031-38548-3_2

29. van Elsloo, T., Patrini, G., Ivey-Law, H.: SEALion: a framework for neural network inference on encrypted data. arXiv preprint arXiv:1904.12840 (2019)

30. Fan, J., Vercauteren, F.: Somewhat practical fully homomorphic encryption. IACR Cryptology ePrint Archive (2012)

31. Fouque, P.A.: FALCON: fast-fourier lattice-based compact signatures over NTRU. Submission NIST's Post-quantum Crypt. Standardization Process **36**(5), 1–75 (2018)

32. Gentry, C.: A fully homomorphic encryption scheme, vol. 20. Stanford university Stanford (2009)

33. Guo, Q., Johansson, T.: Faster dual lattice attacks for solving LWE with applications to CRYSTALS. In: Tibouchi, M., Wang, H. (eds.) ASIACRYPT 2021. LNCS, vol. 13093, pp. 33–62. Springer, Cham (2021). https://doi.org/10.1007/978-3-030-92068-5_2

34. Hanrot, G., Pujol, X., Stehlé, D.: Analyzing blockwise lattice algorithms using dynamical systems. In: Advances in Cryptology – CRYPTO 2011, pp. 447–464 (2011)

35. Herold, G., Kirshanova, E., May, A.: On the asymptotic complexity of solving lwe. Des. Codes Cryptography **86**(1), 55–83 (2018)

36. Howgrave-Graham, N.: A hybrid lattice-reduction and meet-in-the-middle attack against NTRU. In: Advances in Cryptology - CRYPTO 2007, pp. 150–169 (2007)

37. Kannan, R.: Improved algorithms for integer programming and related lattice problems. In: Proceedings of the Fifteenth Annual ACM Symposium on Theory of Computing, pp. 193–206 (1983)

38. Kirshanova, E., Marcolla, C., Rovira, S.: Guidance for efficient selection of secure parameters for fully homomorphic encryption. Cryptology ePrint Archive, Paper 2024/1001 (2024). https://eprint.iacr.org/2024/1001

39. Langlois, A., Stehlé, D.: Worst-case to average-case reductions for module lattices. Des. Codes Cryptography **75**(3), 565–599 (2015)

40. Lattigo. http://github.com/ldsec/lattigo

41. Liu, M., Nguyen, P.Q.: Solving BDD by enumeration: an update. In: Dawson, E. (ed.) CT-RSA 2013. LNCS, vol. 7779, pp. 293–309. Springer, Heidelberg (2013). https://doi.org/10.1007/978-3-642-36095-4_19

42. Lyubashevsky, V., Peikert, C., Regev, O.: On ideal lattices and learning with errors over rings. In: Gilbert, H. (ed.) Advances in Cryptology – EUROCRYPT 2010, pp. 1–23 (2010)

43. Ma, S., Huang, T., Wang, A., Wang, X.: Accelerating BGV bootstrapping for large p using null polynomials over $\mathbb{Z}_{p^e}$. Cryptology ePrint Archive, Paper 2024/115 (2024)

44. Marcolla, C., Sucasas, V., Manzano, M., Bassoli, R., Fitzek, F.H., Aaraj, N.: Survey on fully homomorphic encryption, theory, and applications. Proc. IEEE **110**(10), 1572–1609 (2022)

45. Martins, P., Sousa, L., Mariano, A.: A survey on fully homomorphic encryption: an engineering perspective. ACM Comput. Surv. (CSUR) **50**(6), 1–33 (2017)

46. MATZOV: Report on the security of LWE: improved dual lattice attack, April 2022. https://zenodo.org/records/6412487

47. Mono, J., Marcolla, C., Land, G., Güneysu, T., Aaraj, N.: Finding and evaluating parameters for BGV. In: El Mrabet, N., De Feo, L., Duquesne, S. (eds.) Progress in Cryptology - AFRICACRYPT 2023. AFRICACRYPT 2023. LNCS, vol. 14064, pp. 370–394. Springer, Cham (2023). https://doi.org/10.1007/978-3-031-37679-5_16

48. Paillier, P.: Invited talk: recent advances in homomorphic compilation. https://youtu.be/phWYLwlPTY0?si=gwcf8svL6tOYcizv

49. Regev, O.: On lattices, learning with errors, random linear codes, and cryptography. In: Proceedings of the Thirty-Seventh Annual ACM Symposium on Theory of Computing, pp. 84–93 (2005)

50. Schnorr, C.P.: A hierarchy of polynomial time lattice basis reduction algorithms. Theoret. Comput. Sci. **53**(2), 201–224 (1987)

51. Schnorr, C.P.: Lattice reduction by random sampling and birthday methods. In: Alt, H., Habib, M. (eds.) STACS 2003, pp. 145–156 (2003)

52. Schnorr, C.P., Euchner, M.: Lattice basis reduction: improved practical algorithms and solving subset sum problems. Math. Program. **66**(1–3), 181–199 (1994)

53. Microsoft SEAL (release 3.4). https://github.com/Microsoft/SEAL, October 2019, microsoft Research, Redmond, WA

54. Stehlé, D., Steinfeld, R., Tanaka, K., Xagawa, K.: Efficient public key encryption based on ideal lattices. In: Matsui, M. (ed.) ASIACRYPT 2009. LNCS, vol. 5912, pp. 617–635. Springer, Heidelberg (2009). https://doi.org/10.1007/978-3-642-10366-7_36

55. Viand, A., Jattke, P., Hithnawi, A.: SoK: fully homomorphic encryption compilers. In: 2021 IEEE Symposium on Security and Privacy (SP), pp. 1092–1108. IEEE Computer Society (2021)

Lattice-Based Cryptography
Cryptanalysis

Finding Dense Submodules
with Algebraic Lattice Reduction

Alexander Karenin[1,2]([⊠]) and Elena Kirshanova[1,2]

[1] Technology Innovation Institute, Abu Dhabi, UAE
{alexander.karenin,elena.kirshanova}@tii.ae
[2] I.Kant Baltic Federal University, Kaliningrad, Russia

Abstract. We prove an algebraic analogue of Pataki-Tural lemma
(Pataki-Tural, *arXiv:0804.4014, 2008*) – the main tool in analysing
the so-called *overstretched* regime of NTRU. Our result generalizes this
lemma from Euclidean lattices to modules over any number field enabling
us to look at NTRU as rank-2 module over cyclotomic number fields with
a rank-1 dense submodule generated by the NTRU secret key.

For Euclidean lattices, this *overstretched* regime occurs for large moduli q and enables to detect a dense sublattice in NTRU lattices leading to faster NTRU key recovery. We formulate an algebraic version of
this event, the so-called Dense Submodule Discovery (DSD) event, and
heuristically predict under which conditions this event happens. For that,
we formulate an algebraic version of the Geometric Series Assumption –
an heuristic tool that describes the behaviour of algebraic lattice reduction algorithms. We verify this assumption by implementing an algebraic
LLL – an analog of classical LLL lattice reduction that operates on the
module level. Our experiments verify the introduced heuristic, enabling
us to predict the algebraic DSD event.

Keywords: NTRU · Cryptoanalysis · LLL algorithm · Module lattices

1 Introduction

Modern lattice based cryptographic constructions, including the recent standards [6,12,14], rely on hard problems on module lattices, i.e., lattices that are
modules over the rings of integers of number fields.

Let K be a number field and $\mathcal{O}_K$ be its ring of integers. In this work we
focus on cyclotomic number fields of power-of-two conductor f, that is $K =
\mathbb{Q}[x]/(x^d + 1)$, $\mathcal{O}_K = \mathbb{Z}[x]/(x^d + 1)$ for $d = f/2$. For $n \geq 1$, an $\mathcal{O}_K$-module
$M \in K^n$ is a finitely generated set of vectors from K^n stable under addition
and multiplication by elements from $\mathcal{O}_K$. Any module admits a representation
$M = \sum_{i=0}^{n-1} \mathbf{b}_i \cdot \mathfrak{b}_i$, where $\mathbf{b}_i \in K^n$ are K-linearly independent and $\mathfrak{b}_i$ are non-zero
fractional ideals.

One of the cryptographically interesting example of a module arises from the
NTRU key equation [15] $h = g\phi^{-1} \bmod q$, where q is some integer, ϕ, g are

© The Author(s), under exclusive license to Springer Nature Switzerland AG 2024
S. Vaudenay and C. Petit (Eds.): AFRICACRYPT 2024, LNCS 14861, pp. 403–427, 2024.
https://doi.org/10.1007/978-3-031-64381-1_18

elements from $\mathcal{O}_K$ with small coefficients, and ϕ is invertible. When given h as a public key (with (ϕ, g) being a secret key), the secret key recovery of the NTRU cryptosystem translates into the problem of finding a short vector (ϕ, g) in the module $M_{\mathsf{NTRU}} = \begin{pmatrix} 1 \\ h \end{pmatrix} \mathcal{O}_K \oplus \begin{pmatrix} 0 \\ q \end{pmatrix} \mathcal{O}_K$. The recovery of (ϕ, g) from h is called the NTRU Problem.

Any module $M \subset K^n$ forms a lattice in $\mathbb{C}^{nd}$ under the canonical embedding. Up until now the NTRU problem has been treated as a problem in Euclidean lattice over $\mathbb{C}^{2d}$ (in fact, over $\mathbb{Z}^{2d}$): indeed, the NTRU problem can be seen as a problem of finding a short vector in an integral lattice $\mathcal{L}_{\mathsf{NTRU}}$ of dimension $2d$ [10], without taking into account any module structure.

Dense Sublattices in NTRU. Specific to NTRU is the property that the secret (ϕ, g) forms what is called a dense d-dimensional sublattice $\mathcal{L}_{\phi,g} \subset \mathcal{L}_{\mathsf{NTRU}}$. This is due to the fact that $x^i \phi h = x^i g, 0 \leq i < d$, and hence the embeddings of $(x^i \phi, x^i g)$ are also in $\mathcal{L}_{\mathsf{NTRU}}$ and they are all short and linearly independent. Hence, the sublattice $\mathcal{L}_{\phi,g}$ generated by these rotations is dense.

It has been observed [1,11,19] that for sufficiently large modulus q, called the *overstretched* NTRU regime, lattice basis reduction [26] finds a basis for $\mathcal{L}_{\phi,g}$ significantly faster than predicted by the analysis for key recovery (ϕ, g). The detection of a basis of $\mathcal{L}_{\phi,g}$ when reducing $\mathcal{L}_{\mathsf{NTRU}}$ is called *Dense Submodule Discovery (DSD)*. Ducas and van Woerden [11] showed that DSD happens for $q = \Omega(d^{2.484})$.

In order to show the existence of the *overstretched* regime in NTRU, [11,19] used the so-called Pataki-Tural result [25, Lemma 1]. Informally, it gives a lower bound on the volume of sublattices relative to the shape of a basis of the full lattice. Due to the presence of the dense $\mathcal{L}_{\phi,g}$, its volume becomes smaller than the "expected" smallest volume of a sublattice in $\mathcal{L}_{\mathsf{NTRU}}$, causing a contradiction to the Pataki-Tural result. Kirchner-Fouque [19] argue that lattice reduction somehow detects this event, while Ducas-van Woerden [11] explain why and under which conditions this overstretched regime happens.

Our Contributions. In this work we ask whether all these results can be translated to the algebraic setting. Indeed, M_{NTRU} contains a rank-1 dense *submodule* $\begin{pmatrix} \phi \\ g \end{pmatrix} \mathcal{O}_K$. To study the hardness of finding this dense submodule in M_{NTRU}, we contribute with the following results.

1. We formulate a generalization of Pataki-Tural lemma in the algebraic setting. We prove an analogous result that provides a lower bound on the volume of submodules with respect to the geometry of the full module. The translation of the result from 'classical' setting to the algebraic one is not straightforward: first, we are working with *pseudobases* (not bases), second, the norms we are dealing with are not Euclidean but algebraic; and third, some of the relevant tools like computation of the Hermite Normal Form in a form of *a matrix* is not available for modules.

2. We develop an algebraic analogue of the so-called Geometric Series Assumption (GSA) – an heuristic that dictates the geometry of a reduced lattice basis.

3. We combine the GSA with our algebraic version of Pataki-Tural lemma which provides us with a tool to analyze the *algebraic DSD* event – the Dense Submodule Discovery. This enables us to analyse NTRU modules from the algebraic perspective.

4. In order to validate our heuristics we need an algorithm for algebraic lattice reduction. That is, a reduction that provides guarantees not on Euclidean norms of basis vectors, but on their algebraic norms. Kirchner, Espitau, and Fouque describe in [17,18] a version of an LLL algorithm for free modules over cyclotomic fields. Lee et al. [22] give a complete generalization of LLL to $\mathcal{O}_K$-modules for arbitrary fields K. However, this later result seems hard to implement in practice as it requires costly precomputations on high dimensional Euclidean lattices. Due to the lack of working algebraic lattice reduction[1], we implemented a version of algebraic LLL. We provided some tricks to speed up our implementation and with that we were able to verify our algebraic GSA and our analysis for the Dense Submbodule Discovery event. Our code is available at https://github.com/mooninjune/AlgebraicLLL.

Comparison to Classical DSD. Our experiments show that so far algebraic techniques are inferior to classical lattice reduction techniques in the tasks of detecting DSD event in practice. Concretely, our implementation of algebraic LLL requires larger moduli q to succeed in detecting DSD event rather than classical BKZ [26] reduction. In order to be competitive with classical lattice reduction tools, algebraic techniques require an algorithm that finds short lattice vectors in the algebraic norm, which is so far not available. However, we believe that the theoretical tools developed in this work are independent from the development of practical algebraic reduction techniques.

2 Preliminaries

We use bold capital letters to denote matrices, bold letters for vectors, Gothic letters for ideals. The transposition of a matrix $\mathbf{B}$ is denoted as $\mathbf{B}^T$, and for matrices over $\mathbb{C}$, we denote with † their transposition and conjugation. The j-th element of i-th column of $\mathbf{B}$ is denoted as $\mathbf{b}_i[j]$.

Lattices. A lattice is a free $\mathbb{Z}$-module with its field of scalars being $\mathbb{R}$ or $\mathbb{C}$. We describe a lattice by its bases written as columns of a matrix $\mathbf{B} \in \mathbb{C}^{m \times n}$, where m is the dimension of the ambient space and n is the rank of the lattice. Each lattice of rank more than 1 has an infinite amount of bases. If $\mathbf{B}$ and $\mathbf{B}'$ are two $m \times n$ matrices corresponding to the two bases of the same lattice then one can

---

[1] The available LLL PARI-GP implementation from https://espitau.github.io/fastlll.html described in [17] does not seem to terminate on a 31-bit modulus q, $d = 2^6, 2^7$ within reasonable time frame.

write $\mathbf{B}' = \mathbf{B} \cdot \mathbf{U}$ for a unimodular matrix $\mathbf{U} \in \mathbb{Z}^{n \times n}$. The *determinant* of a lattice with a basis $\mathbf{B}$ is $\det\left(\mathbf{B}^{\dagger} \cdot \mathbf{B}\right)^{1/2}$.

The *ith successive minima* of a lattice $\mathcal{L}$ is denoted by $\lambda_i(\mathcal{L})$ and is the least radius r such that the ball centered at the origin contains at least i linearly independent vectors. The Euclidean norm of a shortest nonzero vector is $\lambda_1(\mathcal{L})$.

The problem of finding a nonzero lattice vector $\mathbf{v} \in \mathcal{L}$ such that it is no longer than $\gamma \cdot \lambda_1(\mathcal{L})$ for a given $\gamma \geqslant 1$ is considered to be hard in general. This problem is called the *approxSVP problem* (approximate Shortest Vector). For $\gamma = 1$, the problem is known as SVP. Let $\mathbf{t} \in \mathbb{R}^m$ be a vector with $\mathbf{u} \in \mathcal{L}$ being closest to $\mathbf{t}$. The *approxCVP problem* (approximate Closest Vector Problem) asks to find $\mathbf{v} \in \mathcal{L}$ given $\mathbf{t} \in \mathrm{Span}_{\mathbb{R}}(\mathcal{L})$ such that $\|\mathbf{t} - \mathbf{v}\| \leq \gamma \cdot \|\mathbf{t} - \mathbf{u}\|$. For $\gamma = 1$, the problem is called CVP.

Number Fields. Let K be a number field of degree d and $\mathcal{O}_K$ be its ring of integers. The number field K has r_1 real embeddings and $2r_2$ complex embeddings into $\mathbb{C}^d$ with $r_1 + 2r_2 = d$. We denote them as σ_i for $0 \leqslant i < d$. There are two ways to embed elements from K. The canonical (Minkowski) embedding $\mathcal{F}$ of an element $k \in K$ into $\mathbb{C}^d$ is defined as the vector $(\sigma_i(k))_{0 \leqslant i < d}$. The coefficient embedding of an element $k = \sum_{l<d} c_l \cdot \zeta^l \in K$ into $\mathbb{R}^d$ is defined as the vector $(c_0, \ldots, c_{d-1})$.

For $k \in K$, the field norm is defined as $\mathcal{N}(k) = \prod_{\sigma_i} \sigma_i(k)$. For a fractional ideal $\mathfrak{a} \subset K$ its norm $\mathcal{N}(\mathfrak{a})$ is defined as the cardinality of the factor-ring $K/\mathfrak{a}$. The trace $\mathrm{Tr}(k)$ of k is defined as $\sum_{\sigma_i} \sigma_i(k)$. Both norm and trace of an element $k \in K$ are in $\mathbb{Q}$. Let L be a subfield of a number field K. The relative norm $\mathcal{N}_{K/L}(k)$ for some $k \in K$ is defined as the determinant (over L) of the linear map: $K \to K : x \mapsto k \cdot x$. The trace of this linear map (over L) is denoted as $\mathrm{Tr}_{K/L}(k)$ and is called the relative trace. An $\mathcal{O}_K$ element of algebraic norm ± 1 is called a unit. The set of all $\mathcal{O}_K$ units forms a multiplicative group called the unit group.

For a given fractional principal ideal $\mathfrak{a}$ the problem of finding $a \in K$ such that $a \cdot \mathcal{O}_K = \mathfrak{a}$ is called the Principal ideal Problem (PIP). For cyclotomic fields it can be solved classically in sub-exponential time [2] and in polynomial time using quantum computers [4].

We define $K_{\mathbb{R}}$ as the tensor product $K \otimes_{\mathbb{Q}} \mathbb{R}$. We write $K_{\mathbb{R}}^+$ as the subset of $K_{\mathbb{R}}$ with nonnegative coordinates under the canonical embedding. We can take the square root of $k \in K_{\mathbb{R}}^+$ by applying it coordinate-wise after the canonical embedding. For $k \in K_{\mathbb{R}}$, its conjugation $\bar{k} \in K_{\mathbb{R}}$ is well-defined since $K_{\mathbb{R}} \subset \mathbb{C}^d$.

The ring of integers $\mathcal{O}_K$ is a lattice of rank d under the canonical embedding. The absolute value of the discriminant of K, denoted Δ_K, is the squared volume of $\mathcal{O}_K$, namely $\Delta_K = |\det(\sigma_i((\mathbf{b}_j)))_{i,j}|^2$ for any $\mathbb{Z}$-basis $\{\mathbf{b}_j\}_j$ of $\mathcal{O}_K$.

For $n \in \mathbb{N}^+$, K^n is a vector space equipped with Hermitian inner product $\langle \mathbf{u}, \mathbf{v} \rangle_{K_{\mathbb{R}}} = \sum (\mathbf{u})_i \cdot \overline{(\mathbf{v})}_i, 0 \leqslant i < n$ where $\bar{\mathbf{v}}$ denotes the conjugation over $K_{\mathbb{R}}$ applied to $\mathbf{v}$ component-wise. For an intermediate field $L \subset K$, we define $\|k\|_{K/L} = (\mathrm{Tr}_{K/L}(k \cdot \bar{k}))^{1/2}$ and $\|k\| = \|k\|_{K/\mathbb{Q}}$. The Euclidean norm of vector $\mathbf{v}$ over $\mathbb{Q}$ is defined as $\|\mathbf{v}\| = \mathrm{Tr}_{K/\mathbb{Q}}(\langle \mathbf{v}, \mathbf{v} \rangle_{K_{\mathbb{R}}})^{1/2}$. The algebraic norm $\mathbf{v} \in K^n$

is defined as $\mathcal{N}(\langle \mathbf{v}, \mathbf{v} \rangle_{K_\mathbb{R}})^{1/2}$. By abuse of notations, we write $\langle \mathbf{a}, \mathbf{b} \rangle := \langle \mathbf{a}, \mathbf{b} \rangle_{K_\mathbb{R}}$ when $\mathbf{a}, \mathbf{b} \in K^n$. The canonical embedding of $\mathbf{v} = (v_0, \ldots, v_{n-1}) \in K^n$ if defined as $\mathcal{F}(\mathbf{v}) = (\mathcal{F}(v_0), \ldots, \mathcal{F}(v_{n-1})) \in \mathbb{C}^{nd}$. A matrix $\mathbf{U} \in \mathcal{O}_K^{n \times n}$ is called unimodular if $\mathcal{N}(\det \mathbf{U}) = \pm 1$.

Vectors $\mathbf{v}_0, \ldots, \mathbf{v}_{n-1}$ are said to be $K_\mathbb{R}$-*linearly independent* if there is no nontrivial linear combination with the coefficients $c_i \in K_\mathbb{R}$ such that $\sum c_i \cdot \mathbf{v}_i = 0$.

Cyclotomic Number Fields. Let $\zeta \in \mathbb{C}$ be an f-th root of unity for some $f \in \mathbb{N}$. The number field $K = \mathbb{Q}(\zeta)$ is called the f-th cyclotomic field. Its ring of integers $\mathcal{O}_K$ coincides with $\mathbb{Z}[\zeta]$ and admits the orthogonal integral basis $\{1, \zeta, \ldots, \zeta^{d-1}\}$ under the coefficient embedding. Its degree is given by $d = \varphi(f)$ for φ being the Euler totient function. Cyclotomic fields of degree d that is a power of two are called power-of-2 cyclotomic fields. In that case we have $\lambda_1(\mathcal{O}_K)$ is $\sqrt{d}$. For a power-of-2 cyclotomic field K of degree d, as the direct consequence of [29, Proposition 2.1], we have that $\log |\Delta_K| = d \cdot \log(d)$.

To bound the algebraic norm of a cyclotomic number field element, we need the following lemma which sometimes being referred to as the algebraic-geometric inequality.

Lemma 1. *Let K be a cyclotomic field. Then for all $k \in K$:*

$$\mathcal{N}(k) \leqslant d^{-d/2} \cdot \|k\|^d$$

Algebraic Lattices. A projective $\mathcal{O}_K$ module M of rank n is defined as $M = \mathfrak{b}_0 \cdot \mathfrak{b}_0 \oplus \ldots \oplus \mathfrak{b}_{n-1} \cdot \mathfrak{b}_{n-1}$, where all $\mathfrak{b}_i$'s are $K_\mathbb{R}$-linearly independent and $\mathfrak{b}_i$'s are fractional nonzero ideals. We will be focusing on the case $\mathfrak{b}_i = \mathcal{O}_K, \forall i$.

A tuple of pairs $((\mathbf{b}_0, \mathfrak{b}_0), \ldots, (\mathbf{b}_{n-1}, \mathfrak{b}_{n-1}))$ is called a pseudobasis of M. If an algebraic module admits a pseudobasis with all ideals equal to $\mathcal{O}_K$, the module is said to be free. In that case we refer to $\mathbf{b}_i$'s as just a basis. We can represent a (pseudo)basis as a matrix over K with $\mathbf{b}_i$'s being its columns, and an ordered set of n fractional ideals. Let $\mathbf{B}$ be such a matrix. The ideal $\det_K M = \sqrt{\det(\mathbf{B}^\dagger \cdot \mathbf{B})} \cdot \prod_i \mathfrak{b}_i$ is called the determinant of M. In the special case of a free module, we have $\det_K M = \sqrt{\det(\mathbf{B}^\dagger \cdot \mathbf{B})} \cdot \mathcal{O}_K$.

An algebraic module M endowed with the inner product $\langle \mathbf{v}, \mathbf{u} \rangle$ for every $\mathbf{v}, \mathbf{u} \in M$ is called an *algebraic lattice* $\mathcal{L}$. The rank of an algebraic lattice is its rank as a module. An algebraic lattice $\mathcal{L}$ of rank n forms a lattice over $\mathbb{C}^{nd}$ under the canonical embedding, e.g., $\mathcal{F}(\mathcal{L}) = \{\mathcal{F}(\mathbf{v}) \mid \mathbf{v} \in \mathcal{L}\} \subset \mathbb{C}^{nd}$ is a lattice. The determinant of $\mathcal{L}$ is $\det \mathcal{L} = \Delta_K^{n/2} \cdot \mathcal{N}(\det_K(M))$. Any submodule of M with the same inner product is called an *algebraic sublattice*.

An algebraic lattice can have infinitely many pseudobases so it is crucial to determine a criteria which tells if two pseudobases represent the same module. For this task we use the definition given in [9, Proposition 1.4.2].

Proposition 1. *Two algebraic lattices given by $((\mathbf{a}_0, \mathfrak{a}_0), \ldots, (\mathbf{a}_{n-1}, \mathfrak{a}_{n-1}))$ and $((\mathbf{b}_0, \mathfrak{b}_0), \ldots, (\mathbf{b}_{n-1}, \mathfrak{b}_{n-1}))$ form the same lattice if and only if there exists an invertible matrix $\mathbf{U} \in K^{n \times n}$ such that $\mathbf{B} = \mathbf{A}\mathbf{U}$, every $\mathbf{u}_i[j] \in \mathfrak{a}_j \cdot \mathfrak{b}_i^{-1}$ and $\mathbf{u}_i'[j] \in \mathfrak{a}_i^{-1} \cdot \mathfrak{b}_j$ for $\mathbf{u}_i'$ being columns of the inverse matrix $\mathbf{U}' = \mathbf{U}^{-1}$ for $0 \leqslant i < n$. When the module is free, the determinant of such $\mathbf{U}$ is an $\mathcal{O}_K$ unit.*

We shall make use of the following definition of a primitive vector from K^n.

Definition 1 (Primitive vector). *Let* **B** *be a basis of an algebraic lattice. A vector* **v** *of that lattice with coefficients* $(c_0, \ldots, c_{n-1})$ *with respect to the basis* **B** *is said to be primitive if* $\bigoplus_{0 \leqslant i < n} c_i \cdot \mathcal{O}_K = \mathcal{O}_K$.

This definition is correct in the sense that if a vector is primitive with respect to a given basis of an algebraic lattice, then it is primitive for every other basis.

The algebraic minimum of an algebraic lattice $\mathcal{L}$ is defined as

$$\lambda_1^{\mathcal{N}}(\mathcal{L}) = \inf_{\mathbf{v} \in \mathcal{L} \setminus \{0\}} \mathcal{N}(\mathbf{v}).$$

The problem of finding a vector $\mathbf{v} \in \mathcal{L}$ that is a $\gamma_{\mathcal{N}}$ approximation of $\lambda_1^{\mathcal{N}}(\mathcal{L})$ for $\gamma_{\mathcal{N}} \geqslant 1$ is called the *algebraic approxSVP problem*. The algebraic minimum can be bounded using the Euclidean minima both from below and above [22, Lemma 2.2].

Gram-Schmidt Orthogonalization. Let $\mathbf{B} \in K^{m \times n}$ be a basis of some lattice $\mathcal{L}$. The Gram matrix of **B** is defined as $\mathbf{G} = \mathbf{B}^\dagger \cdot \mathbf{B}$. It contains the information about the Hermitian inner product between every basis vector.

The Gram Schmidt vectors $\{\mathbf{b}_i^*\}_i$ for a basis $\mathbf{B} = \{\mathbf{b}_i\}_i$ are defined as:

$$\mathbf{b}_i^* = \mathbf{b}_i - \sum_{k < i} \frac{\langle \mathbf{b}_i, \mathbf{b}_k^* \rangle}{\langle \mathbf{b}_k^*, \mathbf{b}_k^* \rangle} \cdot \mathbf{b}_k^* \quad \text{for } 0 \leqslant i < n. \tag{1}$$

Following the LLL algorithm described in [24], we set $r_{i,i} = \langle \mathbf{b}_i^*, \mathbf{b}_i^* \rangle \in K_{\mathbb{R}} \subset \mathbb{R}^+$ for every $i < n$ and $\mu_{i,j} = \frac{\langle \mathbf{b}_i, \mathbf{b}_k^* \rangle}{\langle \mathbf{b}_k^*, \mathbf{b}_k^* \rangle}$ for $i \geqslant j$. Then, $\mu_{i,j} = r_{i,j}/r_{j,j}$ for $i > j$, and

$$r_{i,j} = \langle \mathbf{b}_i, \mathbf{b}_j \rangle - \sum_{k=0}^{j-1} \mu_{j,k} \cdot r_{i,k}, \quad i > j. \tag{2}$$

As the cyclotomic fields are CM-fields, we have that Gram-Schmidt vectors are over K^n and all $\mu_{i,j}, r_{i,j}$ are in K. The projection of a vector **v** on a vector **u** is defined as: $\pi_{\mathbf{u}}(\mathbf{v}) = \frac{\langle \mathbf{v}, \mathbf{u} \rangle}{\langle \mathbf{u}, \mathbf{u} \rangle} \cdot \mathbf{u}$. We shall make use of basis vectors projected orthogonally to the vector space spanned by $\{\mathbf{b}_0^*, \ldots \mathbf{b}_{i-1}^*\}$. We denote such projection as $\pi_i(\mathbf{v}) = \mathbf{v} - \sum_{j < i} \pi_{\mathbf{b}_j^*}(\mathbf{v})$.

Closely related to Gram-Schmidt orthogonalization is QR-decomposition: for $\mathbf{B} \in \mathcal{O}_K^{m \times n}$, there exist matrices $\mathbf{Q} \in \mathcal{O}_K^{m \times m}$ and $\mathbf{R} \in \mathcal{O}_K^{m \times n}$ such that $\mathbf{B} = \mathbf{Q} \cdot \mathbf{R}$ and **R** is upper triangular and **Q** is orthonormal. The diagonal entries of the R-factor are given by $r_{i,i}^{1/2}$, off-diagonal entries are $\left(r_{i,j} \cdot r_{j,j}^{1/2} \right)$ for $i > j$.

Classical LLL. We call non-algebraic LLL algorithms classical, and by classical lattices we mean lattices defined over $\mathbb{R}^n$ with no underlying module structure.

A basis $\mathbf{B} \in \mathbb{R}^{m \times n}$ of a rank m lattice $\mathcal{L} \subset \mathbb{R}^n$ is δ-LLL reduced if for all $0 \leqslant i < n, 0 \leqslant j < m$ and some $1/4 < \delta < 1$ the following conditions are met:

$$\mu_{i,j} \leqslant 1/2 \quad \text{(Size reducedness)},$$
$$\delta \pi_i(\mathbf{b}_i) \leqslant \pi_i(\mathbf{b}_{i+1}) \quad \text{(Lovász condition)}.$$

Classical LLL reduction can be computed in time $\text{poly}(n, \log \max_i \{\|\mathbf{b}_i\|\})$ [23].

BKZ Reduction. In this work we rely on classical BKZ lattice reduction algorithm [8,26,28]. We do not focus on the details of the algorithm, but use the following facts about the quality of its output. BKZ algorithm has an important integral parameter $\beta \geqslant 2$ called *blocksize* that controls the quality of the output basis. BKZ algorithm outputs shorter vectors than the LLL algorithm, but requires more time to terminate. The runtime of the BKZ algorithm is at least exponential in β.

The quality of a reduced basis is usually studied using so-called log-profile originally introduced by Schnorr in [27].

Definition 2. *Let* $\mathbf{B} \in \mathbb{Z}^{m \times n}$ *be a basis of some lattice* $\mathcal{L}$. *The vector* $\mathbf{p} = (\log(\|\mathbf{b}_0^*\|), \ldots, \log(\|\mathbf{b}_{n-1}^*\|))$ *is called the log-profile of* $\mathbf{B}$.

In this work we focus on a special case of lattices called q-ary. An n-dimensional lattice $\mathcal{L} \subset \mathbb{Z}^n$ is called q-ary for some $q \in \mathbb{N}, q > 1$ if $q \cdot \mathbb{Z}^n \subset \mathcal{L}$. In this work we will consider the case of lattices that admit a basis with profile $\mathbf{p}$ given by

$$\mathbf{p} = (\overbrace{\log q, \ldots, \log q}^{n/2}, \overbrace{0, \ldots, 0}^{n/2}).$$

The BKZ output quality relates the decay of $\mathbf{p}_i = \log(\|\mathbf{b}_i^*\|)$ using the value $\alpha_\beta \approx \left(\frac{\dim(\mathcal{L})}{2\pi e} \cdot \det(\mathcal{L})^{\frac{2}{\dim(\mathcal{L})}} \right)^{1/(\beta-1)}$. That is, α_β controls the slope of the log-profile of the basis output by BKZ. The following heuristic, called Z-shape Geometric Series Assumption (ZGSA), provides a fairly accurate prediction of this log-profile for large enough $\beta' s$.

Heuristic 1 ([11, Heuristic 2.8]). *Let* $\mathbf{B} \in \mathbb{Z}^{n \times n}$ *be a basis of an n-dimensional q-ary lattice (for n even) with its log-profile given by*

$$\mathbf{p} = (\overbrace{\log q, \ldots, \log q}^{n/2}, \overbrace{0, \ldots, 0}^{n/2})$$

After BKZ-β reduction called on $\mathbf{B}$ *the profile vector* $\mathbf{p}'$ *of a resulting reduced basis is given by*

$$\mathbf{p}'_i = \begin{cases} \log q, & i \leqslant n/2 - n' \\ \log q \cdot (1 - \frac{i - n/2 + n'}{2n'}), & n/2 - n' < i < n/2 + n' - 1 \\ 0, & i \geqslant n/2 + n' - 1, \end{cases} \quad (3)$$

for $n' = (1 + \ln q / \ln \alpha_\beta)/2$.

2.1 Algebraic Lattice Reduction

Below we give a definition of an algebraically LLL reduced basis following [22, Definition 3.1].

Definition 3 (LLL reduced basis). *A pseudobasis* $(\mathbf{B}, \{\mathfrak{b}_i\}_i)$ *of an algebraic lattice is said to be* α-*LLL reduced for some real* $\alpha > 1$ *if* $\alpha \cdot \mathcal{N}(r_{i+1,i+1} \cdot \mathfrak{b}_{i+1}) \geqslant \mathcal{N}(r_{i,i} \cdot \mathfrak{b}_i)$.

Recall that $r_{i,i} = \|\mathbf{b}_i^*\|_{K_{\mathbb{R}}}^2$. The purpose of LLL is to bound the decay in the norms of $r_{i,i}$. As in the classical LLL, it is achieved by finding a short vector in some rank-2 sublattice and replacing $\mathbf{b}_i^*$ with this short vector. The difference to the classical case is that we are interested in the *algebraic norm* rather than the Euclidean norm.

To study the behavior of the algebraic LLL algorithm we generalize the concept of the log-profile which carries information about algebraic properties of bases and is a measure of reducedness.

Definition 4. *Let* $(\mathbf{B} \in K^{m \times n}, \{\mathfrak{b}_i\}_i)$ *be a pseudobasis of an algebraic lattice. Let* $\mathbf{Q} \cdot \mathbf{R}$ *be its QR-decomposition. Consider* $\{r_{i,i}^{1/2} \in K_{\mathbb{R}}^+ \subset \mathbb{R}^+\}$, *the set of diagonal elements of* $\mathbf{R}$. *The ordered set* $\mathbf{p}((\mathbf{B}, \{\mathfrak{b}_i\}_i)) = \{\log(|r_{i,i}| \cdot \mathcal{N}(\mathfrak{b}_i))/2\}_{0 \leqslant i < n}$ *is called the log-profile of* $\mathbf{B}$.

In the case when $K = \mathbb{Q}$ this definition coincides with Definition 2. Notice that $\sum_{i=0}^{n-1} \mathbf{p}_i((\mathbf{B}, \{\mathfrak{b}_i\}_i)) = \log(\mathcal{N}(\det \mathbf{B}) \cdot \prod_{i=0}^{n-1} \mathcal{N}(\mathfrak{b}_i))$. Together with the condition $\alpha \cdot \mathcal{N}(r_{i+1,i+1}) \geqslant \mathcal{N}(r_{i,i})$ this guarantees that the log-profile on an LLL reduced basis cannot decrease too rapidly.

2.2 NTRU Modules

The NTRU problem asks to find $\phi, g \in \mathcal{O}_K$ such that ϕ is invertible in $\mathbb{Z}[X]/(q, X^d + 1)$ and the coefficients of both ϕ, g are chosen uniformly at random[2] from $\{-1, 0, 1\}$ under the coefficient embedding, when given

$$h = g \cdot \phi^{-1} \mod q. \tag{4}$$

Algebraic NTRU Lattice. The NTRU problem can be viewed as finding a short element in the rank-2 $\mathcal{O}_K$-module defined as

$$M_{\mathsf{NTRU}} = \begin{pmatrix} 1 \\ h \end{pmatrix} \mathcal{O}_K \oplus \begin{pmatrix} 0 \\ q \end{pmatrix} \mathcal{O}_K. \tag{5}$$

In particular, we have $(\phi, g) \in M$ since $\begin{pmatrix} 1 \\ h \end{pmatrix} \phi + \begin{pmatrix} 0 \\ q \end{pmatrix} k_q = \begin{pmatrix} \phi \\ g \end{pmatrix}$ for some $k_q \in \mathcal{O}_K$

that satisfies $h = g\phi^{-1} + qk_q$. Furthermore, $M_{\phi,g} = \begin{pmatrix} \phi \\ g \end{pmatrix} \mathcal{O}_K \subset M_{\mathsf{NTRU}}$ is a

---

[2] Several versions of NTRU with varying Hamming weights of ϕ, g exist [7], our results extend to these other versions too.

so-called *dense* rank-1 submodule of M_{NTRU}. It has been observed in [1] (and further studied in [11,19]) that for sufficiently large q finding a basis for this dense submodule is easier than the recovery of (ϕ, g). In that case for a large enough blocksize β, the BKZ algorithm recovers a basis of the dense submodule. When this happens, such event is called *the DSD event*. Precisely,

Definition 5. *The dense submodule Discovery. Let* $\mathbf{B} \in \mathbb{Z}^{n \times n}$ *be a* $\mathbb{Z}$-*basis of an NTRU module. We define the DSD as an event when BKZ-β called on* $\mathbf{B}$ *returns a basis* $[\mathbf{M}|\mathbf{B}']$ *for* $\mathbf{B}', \mathbf{M} \in \mathbb{Z}^{n \times (n/2)}$ *and a module spanned by* $\mathbf{M}$ *contains the secret vector* $(\mathbf{f}, \mathbf{g})$ *corresponding to the coefficient embedding of* (ϕ, g).

The NTRU modules viewed as a $\mathbb{Z}$-lattices are q-ary. The larger q is, the easier it is to recover $M_{\phi,g}$ (for a fixed d). Note that once a basis for this dense rank-1 submodule is found, one can focus on finding (ϕ, g) in this smaller dimensional rank-1 submodule. Experiments suggest [20] that indeed in practice the problem of finding (ϕ, g) is not significantly harder than obtaining a basis for $M_{\phi,g}$ in the case of a sufficiently large q.

In [19] the authors combine Heuristic 1 with the Pataki-Tural lemma [25, Lemma 1] to obtain a criteria to deduce which BKZ blocksize β is sufficient to trigger the DSD event on NTRU lattices. A more precise statement following the same arguments can be found in [11, Claim 2.12]:

Heuristic 2 ([11, Claim 2.12]). *Let* $\mathcal{L}_q$ *be an NTRU lattice of dimension 2d over* $\mathbb{Z}$ *with a dense submodule* $\mathcal{L}_{\phi,g}$. *Under the ZGSA, BKZ-β triggers the DSD event if:*

$$\det \mathcal{L}_{\phi,g} < q^{\frac{n'-1}{2}} \cdot \alpha_\beta^{-\frac{1}{2}(n'-1)^2},$$

where $n' = (1 + \ln q / \ln \alpha_\beta)/2$.

The asymptotic analysis provided in [11] suggests that the DSD event (as per definition above) precedes the recovery of the secret vector for $\log q \geqslant d^{2.783+o(1)}$. The NTRU modules with q satisfying this inequality are called *overstretched*. For fixed values of $\det \mathcal{L}_{\phi,g}$ and d, Heuristic 2 suggests that the larger q is, the smaller β is required to trigger the DSD event. The value of blocksize β sufficient to trigger the DSD event is estimated as $\tilde{\Theta}(d/\log(q)^2)$ where $\tilde{\Theta}(f(x))$ means that there exist some constant $c \geqslant 0$ such that $f(x) = O(f(x) \cdot |\log f(x)|^c)$.

3   Pataki-Tural Lemma for Modules

In this section we are generalising the concept of DSD events to the algebraic setting. As in the classical case the DSD event should lead to a discovery of a smaller rank sublattice that still contains the required short vector. This will reduce the search problem to an easier one. We start our study of algebraic DSD events with introducing the algebraic analogues of necessary lemmas. After that we describe a technique that allows us to descend NTRU modules defined over a number field K to a some proper subfield $L \subset K$ in Sect. 3.1. In Sect. 3.2 we formulate an algebraic analogue of ZGSA and, after all necessary tools are developed, generalize the definition of DSD events to the algebraic setting. All these results combined yield an estimator for algebraic DSD.

Lemma 2. *Let $\mathcal{L}$ be an algebraic lattice in K^m given by a pseudobasis $(\mathbf{B}, \{\mathfrak{b}_i\}_{i<n})$. Let $\mathcal{P}$ be rank-k algebraic sublattice. Then there exists an ordered set $\{\mathbf{y}_i\}_{i<k}$ of linearly independent vectors of $\mathcal{P}$ such that:*

$$\mathbf{y}_{k-1} \in \text{Span}\{\mathbf{b}_i\}_{0\leqslant i \leqslant n-1}, \ldots, \mathbf{y}_0 \in \text{Span}\{\mathbf{b}_i\}_{0\leqslant i\leqslant n-k}, \text{ and}$$
$$\mathbf{y}_{k-1} \notin \text{Span}\{\mathbf{b}_i\}_{0\leqslant i\leqslant n-2}, \ldots, \mathbf{y}_0 \notin \text{Span}\{\mathbf{b}_i\}_{0\leqslant i\leqslant n-k-1}.$$

Proof. Without loss of generality all $\mathbf{b}_i \in \mathcal{O}_K^m$ and all $\mathfrak{b}_i \subset \mathcal{O}_K$, otherwise we can scale $\mathcal{L}$ accordingly.

Let $\mathbf{X} \in K^{m\times k}$ be a rank-k matrix with its columns $\mathbf{x}_i \in \mathcal{P}$. Each $\mathbf{x}_\kappa$ is a $\mathcal{O}_K$-linear combination of $\mathbf{b}_j$ for $0 \leqslant j < n$. More precisely, for all $\kappa < k, j < n$ there exist $u_{\kappa,j} \in \mathfrak{b}_j \subset \mathcal{O}_K$ such that we can write

$$\mathbf{x}_\kappa = \sum_{0\leqslant j<n} u_{\kappa,j} \cdot \mathbf{b}_j, \quad 0 \leqslant \kappa < k.$$

In matrix from the equation above can be written as $\mathbf{X} = \mathbf{B} \cdot \mathbf{U}$ for $\mathbf{X} \in K^{m\times k}, \mathbf{U} \in \mathcal{O}_K^{n\times k}, \mathbf{B} \in K^{m\times n}$.

Every $\mathcal{O}_K$-linear combination of vectors $\mathbf{x}_0, \ldots, \mathbf{x}_{k-1}$ is also a vector from $\mathcal{P}$ as it holds that $\zeta^i \mathbf{x}_j \in \mathcal{P}$ for ζ – a primitive root of K, any $i \in \mathbb{Z}$ and any $0 \leq j \leq k-1$. Hence $\mathcal{L}(\mathbf{X}, \{\mathcal{O}_K\}^k)$ is a free submodule of $\mathcal{P}$.

Next we apply a transformation to $\mathbf{U}$ reminiscent to the column-echelon form for Euclidean lattice bases. Notice that any transformation of the columns of $\mathbf{U}$ given by $\mathbf{u}_\kappa \leftarrow \alpha \cdot \mathbf{u}_\kappa + \beta \cdot \mathbf{u}_\ell$ for some $\alpha, \beta \in \mathcal{O}_K, \alpha \neq 0, \kappa \neq \ell$ sends $\mathbf{x}_\kappa$ to $\alpha \cdot \mathbf{x}_\kappa + \beta \cdot \mathbf{x}_\ell$ accordingly. In addition, any such transformation preserves both the rank of $\mathbf{X}$ and the inclusion $\mathcal{L}(\mathbf{X}, \{\mathcal{O}_K\}^k) \subset \mathcal{P}$ (since every $\mathbf{B} \cdot \mathbf{u}_\kappa \in \mathcal{O}_K^m$ remains to be a linear $\mathcal{O}_K$ combination of vectors from $\mathcal{P}$). Any permutation of the columns preserves the module and, thus, the inclusion as well.

Now we mimic the column-echelon form computation algorithm for $\mathbf{U}$ in Algorithm 3.1. On input $\mathbf{U} \in \mathcal{O}_K^{n\times k}$, it returns $\mathbf{T} \in \mathcal{O}_K^{n\times k}$ such that the following inclusions hold

$$\mathcal{L}(\mathbf{BUT}, \{\mathcal{O}_K\}^k) \subseteq \mathcal{L}(\mathbf{X}, \{\mathcal{O}_K\}^k) \subseteq \mathcal{P}.$$

The routine is described in Algorithm 3.1. It takes $\mathbf{U}$ as an input and uses a subroutine $\text{LNE}(\mathbf{u}) = \max\{i \mid \mathbf{u}[i] \neq 0\}$ that returns the index of the last nonzero element of a vector $\mathbf{u}$.

The algorithm iterates for $\ell = m-1, \ldots, m-k$ (corresponding to rows) and $\kappa = \ell-1-(m-k), \ldots, 0$ (corresponding to columns). At a fixed ℓ we sort the first ℓ columns such that the indices of the last nonzero entry of consequent columns do not decrease. Now it holds that either the new value of $\mathbf{u}_{\ell-(m-k)}[\ell]$ is nonzero, or the entire ℓ-th row is zero. The latter situation can only occur if $\text{rank}\mathbf{U} < k$ which contradicts the rank of $\mathbf{X}$. By applying the transformation described in Line 6 of Algorithm 3.1, we can ensure that for all $0 \leqslant \kappa < \ell - (m-k)$ we have $\mathbf{u}_\kappa[\ell] = 0$ by solving the equation $\alpha\mathbf{u}_\kappa[\ell] + \beta\mathbf{u}_{\ell-(m-k)}[\ell] = 0$ for arbitrary α and β from $\mathcal{O}_K$ with $\alpha \neq 0$. Once the outer loop over ℓ is finished, we obtain

Algorithm 3.1. Echelon Form for Algebraic lattices

Input: $\mathbf{U} \in K^{m \times k}$ – a matrix for $k \leqslant m$ of rank k.
Output: $\mathbf{T} \in K^{m \times k}$ – an upper-triangular matrix.

1: **for** $\ell = m - 1, \ldots, m - k$ **do**
2:     Sort $\{\mathbf{u}_0, \ldots, \mathbf{u}_{\ell-(m-k)}\}$ in non decreasing order of $\mathrm{LNE}(\mathbf{u}_i)$.
3:     **if** $\mathbf{u}_{\ell-(m-k)}[\ell] \neq 0$ **then**
4:         **for** $\kappa = \ell - 1 - (m - k), \ldots, 0$ **do**
5:             Find $\alpha, \beta \in \mathcal{O}_K, \alpha \neq 0$ such that $\alpha \mathbf{u}_\kappa[\ell] + \beta \mathbf{u}_{\ell-(m-k)}[\ell] = 0$
6:             $\mathbf{u}_\kappa := \alpha \cdot \mathbf{u}_\kappa + \beta \cdot \mathbf{u}_{\ell-(m-k)}$
7: **return** $\mathbf{T} = (\mathbf{u}_0, \ldots, \mathbf{u}_{k-1})$

---

an upper triangular $\mathbf{T}$ which can be expressed as $\mathbf{U} \cdot \mathbf{W}$ for some $\mathbf{W} \in \mathcal{O}_K^{k \times k}$ corresponding to k linear combinations of the vectors from $\mathbf{X}$.

Consider the ordered set $\{\mathbf{y}_i = \mathbf{X} \cdot \mathbf{W}_i = \mathbf{B} \cdot \mathbf{T}_i\}_{0 \leqslant i < k} \subset \mathcal{P}$. Each $\mathbf{y}_i = \sum_{\kappa=0}^{n-1} \mathbf{t}_i[\kappa] \cdot \mathbf{b}_\kappa$. By construction of $\mathbf{T}$ last $\max(0, k - i - 1)$ coordinates of $\mathbf{t}_i$ are zero which implies $\mathbf{y}_i = \sum_{\kappa=0}^{n-k+i} \mathbf{t}_i[\kappa] \cdot \mathbf{b}_\kappa$ for some nonzero $\mathbf{t}_i[n - k + i]$. Such $\{\mathbf{y}_i\}_{0 \leqslant i < k}$ satisfy the statement of the lemma since each $\mathbf{y}_i$ is a $\mathcal{O}_K$-linear combination of exactly $n - k + i$ first vectors of $\mathbf{B}$.   □

Now we need a tool to transform k linearly independent vectors of a module $\mathcal{L}$ into a pseudobasis that preserves the algebraic norms of Gram-Schmidt vectors. We use the following lemma for this task.

Lemma 3 ([13, Theorem 4]). *Let $\mathcal{L} \subset K^m$ be a rank-n algebraic lattice. Let $\{\mathbf{s}_i\}_i$ be a full rank set of vectors in $\mathcal{L}$. Then there exists a pseudobasis $(\mathbf{B}, \{\mathfrak{b}_i\})$ of $\mathcal{L}$ such that for all $i < n$: $\mathbf{b}_i \in \mathcal{L}, \mathbf{b}_i \in \mathrm{Span}\{\mathbf{s}_j\}_{j \leqslant i}, \mathbf{b}_i^* = \mathbf{s}_i^*$.*

To prove the main theoretical result of this section we need the following technical lemma.

Lemma 4 ([9, Theorem 1.2.35]). *Let $\mathcal{L} \subset K^m$ be an algebraic lattice of rank n. Let $\mathcal{P}$ be its algebraic sublattice of rank $k \leqslant n$. Then there exist pseudobases $(\mathbf{X}, \{\mathfrak{x}_i\}_{i<n})$ of $\mathcal{L}$ and $((\mathbf{x}_i), \{\mathfrak{d}_i \mathfrak{x}_i\}_i)_{n-k<i<n-1}$ of $\mathcal{P}$ for some $\mathbf{X} \in K^{m \times n}$, fractional ideals $\mathfrak{x}_i$ and integral ideals $\mathfrak{d}_i$ such that:*

$$\mathcal{L} = \bigoplus_{0 \leqslant i < n} \mathfrak{x}_i \cdot \mathbf{x}_i \quad and \quad \mathcal{P} = \bigoplus_{n-k \leqslant j < n} \mathfrak{d}_j \cdot \mathfrak{x}_j \cdot \mathbf{x}_j. \tag{6}$$

The Euclidean norm of a vector cannot increase after an orthogonal projection. Similarly, the algebraic norm cannot increase after the orthogonal projection over $K_\mathbb{R}$ which is stated in the following claim.

Claim 1. *For all vectors $\mathbf{u}, \mathbf{v} \in K_\mathbb{R}^n$ such that $\mathbf{u} \perp \mathbf{v}$ we have $\mathcal{N}(\mathbf{u} + \mathbf{v}) \geqslant \max\{\mathcal{N}(\mathbf{u}), \mathcal{N}(\mathbf{v})\}$. This also implies $\mathcal{N}(\mathbf{v}) \geqslant \mathcal{N}(\pi_\mathbf{w}(\mathbf{v}))$ for all $\mathbf{w} \in K_\mathbb{R}^n$.*

Proof. Consider mutually orthogonal $\mathbf{u}, \mathbf{v} \in K_\mathbb{R}^n$ and construct the matrix $\mathbf{B} \in K_\mathbb{R}^{n \times 2}$ with first column being $\mathbf{u}$ and the second one being $\mathbf{v}$. Perform the QR-factorization $\mathbf{B} = \mathbf{Q} \cdot \mathbf{R}$. Now we have an upper triangular $\mathbf{R} \in K_\mathbb{R}^{2 \times 2}$. Since $\mathbf{u} \perp$

$\mathbf{v}$ we have that $\mathbf{R}$ is also diagonal. In addition $\mathcal{N}(\mathbf{u}) = \mathcal{N}(\mathbf{r}_0)$ and $\mathcal{N}(\mathbf{v}) = \mathcal{N}(\mathbf{r}_1)$ implying $\mathcal{N}(\mathbf{u} + \mathbf{v}) = \mathcal{N}(\mathbf{r}_0 + \mathbf{r}_1)$. The latter is $\mathbf{r}_0[0] \cdot \bar{\mathbf{r}}_0[0] + \mathbf{r}_1[1] \cdot \bar{\mathbf{r}}_1[1] \in K_{\mathbb{R}}^+$ – a sum of two non-negative real numbers. Hence $\mathcal{N}(\mathbf{r}_0 + \mathbf{r}_1) \geqslant \max\{\mathcal{N}(\mathbf{r}_0), \mathcal{N}(\mathbf{r}_1)\}$ which gives the first part of the claim.

To prove the second part of the claim we rewrite $\mathbf{v} = \pi_{\mathbf{w}}(\mathbf{v}) + p \cdot \mathbf{w}$ for some $p \in K_{\mathbb{R}}$. We have $\pi_{\mathbf{w}}(\mathbf{v}) \perp \mathbf{w}$ which implies $\mathcal{N}(\mathbf{v}) \geqslant \max\{\mathcal{N}(\pi_{\mathbf{w}}(\mathbf{v})), \mathcal{N}(p \cdot \mathbf{w})\} \geqslant \mathcal{N}(\pi_{\mathbf{w}}(\mathbf{v}))$. $\square$

For us to proceed we need to connect the Gram-Schmidt vectors of some projective lattice $\mathcal{L}(\mathbf{D}) = \pi_{n-k}(\mathcal{L}(\mathbf{B}))$ with those of $\mathcal{L}(\mathbf{B})$. For this we prove Lemma 5.

Lemma 5. *Let $\mathbf{B} \in K^{m \times n}$ and $\mathbf{U}' \in K^{k \times k}$ be a rank-n and rank-k matrices respectively with $\mathbf{D} = \pi_{n-k}([\mathbf{b}_{n-k}, \ldots, \mathbf{b}_{n-1}]) \cdot \mathbf{U}'$. Let $\mathbf{B}^*, \mathbf{D}^*$ be a matrix of Gram-Schmidt vectors for $\mathbf{B}$ and $\mathbf{D}$ respectively. Suppose also that $\mathbf{d}_\kappa \in \mathrm{Span}\{\mathbf{b}_j^*\}_{n-k \leqslant j \leqslant n-k+\kappa}$ and $\mathbf{d}_\kappa \notin \mathrm{Span}\{\mathbf{b}_j^*\}_{n-k \leqslant j \leqslant n-k+\ell}$ for $\ell < \kappa$. Then $\mathbf{d}_\kappa^* = \mathbf{u}_\kappa'[\kappa] \cdot \mathbf{b}_{n-k+\kappa}^*$.*

Proof. Let $\{\mathbf{d}_\kappa^*\}_{0 \leqslant \kappa < k}$ be the Gram-Schmidt vectors of $\{\mathbf{d}_\kappa\}_{0 \leqslant \kappa < k}$. We have

$$\mathrm{Span}\{\mathbf{d}_\iota^*\}_{\iota < \kappa} = \mathrm{Span}\{\mathbf{d}_\iota\}_{\iota < \kappa} = \mathrm{Span}\{\pi_{n-k}(\mathbf{b}_{n-k+\iota})\}_{\iota < \kappa} = \mathrm{Span}\{\mathbf{b}_{n-k+\iota}^*\}_{\iota < \kappa}$$

Since for $\kappa < k$ we have $\mathbf{d}_\kappa^* \in \mathrm{Span}\{\mathbf{b}_{n-k+\iota}^*\}_{\iota \leqslant \kappa}$ is an orthogonal projection away from $\mathrm{Span}\{\mathbf{b}_{n-k+\iota}^*\}_{\iota < \kappa}$ it lies in $\mathrm{Span}\{\mathbf{b}_{n-k+\iota}^*\}_{\iota \leqslant \kappa} \cap \mathrm{Span}\{\mathbf{b}_{n-k+\kappa}^*\} = \mathrm{Span}\{\mathbf{b}_{n-k+\kappa}^*\}$. Then we can write $\mathbf{d}_\kappa^* = \mathbf{d}_\kappa - \sum_{\iota=0}^{\kappa-1} \left(\frac{\langle \mathbf{d}_\kappa, \mathbf{d}_\iota^* \rangle}{\langle \mathbf{d}_\iota^*, \mathbf{d}_\iota^* \rangle} \cdot \mathbf{d}_\iota^* \right)$ as

$$\frac{\langle \mathbf{d}_\kappa - \sum_{\iota=0}^{\kappa-1} \left(\frac{\langle \mathbf{d}_\kappa, \mathbf{d}_\iota^* \rangle}{\langle \mathbf{d}_\iota^*, \mathbf{d}_\iota^* \rangle} \cdot \mathbf{d}_\iota^* \right), \mathbf{b}_{n-k+\kappa}^* \rangle}{\langle \mathbf{b}_{n-k+\kappa}^*, \mathbf{b}_{n-k+\kappa}^* \rangle} \cdot \mathbf{b}_{n-k+\kappa}^* =$$

$$\frac{\langle \mathbf{d}_\kappa, \mathbf{b}_{n-k+\kappa}^* \rangle}{\langle \mathbf{b}_{n-k+\kappa}^*, \mathbf{b}_{n-k+\kappa}^* \rangle} \cdot \mathbf{b}_{n-k+\kappa}^* = \qquad \text{Since } \langle \mathbf{d}_\iota^*, \mathbf{b}_{n-k+\kappa}^* \rangle = 0,\ 0 \leq \iota \leq \kappa - 1$$

$$\frac{\langle \sum_{i=0}^{k} \mathbf{u}_\kappa'[i] \pi_{n-k}(\mathbf{b}_{n-k+i}), \mathbf{b}_{n-k+\kappa}^* \rangle}{\langle \mathbf{b}_{n-k+\kappa}^*, \mathbf{b}_{n-k+\kappa}^* \rangle} \cdot \mathbf{b}_{n-k+\kappa}^* =$$

$$\frac{\langle \sum_{i=0}^{k} \left(\mathbf{u}_\kappa'[i] \mathbf{b}_{n-k+i} - \mathbf{u}_\kappa'[i] \left(\sum_{j=0}^{n-k-1} \frac{\langle \mathbf{b}_{n-k+i}, \mathbf{b}_j^* \rangle}{\langle \mathbf{b}_j^*, \mathbf{b}_j^* \rangle} \cdot \mathbf{b}_j^* \right) \right), \mathbf{b}_{n-k+\kappa}^* \rangle}{\langle \mathbf{b}_{n-k+\kappa}^*, \mathbf{b}_{n-k+\kappa}^* \rangle} \cdot \mathbf{b}_{n-k+\kappa}^* =$$

$$\frac{\langle \sum_{i=0}^{k} \mathbf{u}_\kappa'[i] \mathbf{b}_{n-k+i}, \mathbf{b}_{n-k+\kappa}^* \rangle}{\langle \mathbf{b}_{n-k+\kappa}^*, \mathbf{b}_{n-k+\kappa}^* \rangle} \cdot \mathbf{b}_{n-k+\kappa}^*. \qquad \text{Since } \langle \mathbf{d}_\iota^*, \mathbf{b}_{n-k+\kappa}^* \rangle = 0,\ 0 \leq \iota \leq \kappa - 1$$

Overall,

$$\mathbf{d}_\kappa^* = \frac{\langle \sum_{i=0}^{k} \mathbf{u}_\kappa'[i] \mathbf{b}_{n-k+i}, \mathbf{b}_{n-k+\kappa}^* \rangle}{\langle \mathbf{b}_{n-k+\kappa}^*, \mathbf{b}_{n-k+\kappa}^* \rangle} \cdot \mathbf{b}_{n-k+\kappa}^*. \tag{7}$$

Since $\langle \mathbf{u}_\kappa'[i] \mathbf{b}_{n-k+i}, \mathbf{b}_{n-k+\kappa}^* \rangle$ is non-zero only for $i = \kappa$, Eq. (7) implies $\mathbf{d}_\kappa^* = \mathbf{u}_\kappa'[\kappa] \cdot \mathbf{b}_{n-k+\kappa}^*$. $\square$

The following result is an analogue of [25, Lemma 1] generalized to the setting of algebraic lattices. In the classical setting it shows that the determinant of any rank-k lattice $\mathcal{P}$ of a lattice $\mathcal{L}$ cannot exceed the product of k least norms of Gram-Schmidt vectors of *any* basis of $\mathcal{L}$. To prove the analogous result for the case when $\mathcal{P}$ and $\mathcal{L}$ are algebraic, we first consider an arbitrary submodule $\mathcal{P} \subset \mathcal{L}$ and construct its overlattice $\mathcal{L}'$ that is "primitive", that is all ideals of the pseudobasis of $\mathcal{L}'$ satisfy $\mathfrak{d}_j = \mathcal{O}_K$ for $n - k \leqslant j < n$ in the context of Lemma 4. This is done to reduce an amount of the ideals considered during the proof to simplify it. We then consider the projection $\pi_{n-k}(\mathcal{L}')$ with respect to a fixed basis of $\mathcal{L}$ and deduce relations between the pseudobases of each member of the chain $\mathcal{L} \supseteq \mathcal{L}' \supseteq \mathcal{P}$ and $\pi_{n-k}(\mathcal{L}')$. These inclusions enable us to argue on the lower bound on $\mathcal{N}(\det \mathcal{P})$.

Theorem 1. *Let* $(\mathbf{B}, \{\mathfrak{b}_i\}_i)$ *be a pseudobasis of an algebraic lattice* $\mathcal{L}$ *and* $\mathbf{B}^*$ *its Gram-Schmidt vectors. Let* $\mathcal{P}$ *be a rank k algebraic sublattice of* $\mathcal{L}$*. Then*

$$\mathcal{N}(\det \mathcal{P}) \geqslant \min_{\substack{J \subset \{0,\ldots,n-1\} \\ |J|=k}} \prod_{k \in J} \mathcal{N}(\mathbf{b}_j^*) \cdot \mathcal{N}(\mathfrak{b}_i).$$

Proof. For $\mathcal{L}$ and its submodule $\mathcal{P}$, there exist pseudobases $(\mathbf{X}, \{\mathfrak{x}_i\}_{i<n})$ of $\mathcal{L}$ and $((\mathbf{x}_j)_j, \{\mathfrak{d}_j \cdot \mathfrak{x}_j\}_j)_{n-k \leqslant j < n}$ of $\mathcal{P}$ as in Lemma 4. Without loss of generality we can assume that all $\mathfrak{x}_i$ are integral. Since all $\mathfrak{d}_j \subset \mathcal{O}_K$, we have

$$\mathcal{P} \subset \bigoplus_{n-k \leqslant j < n} \mathfrak{x}_j \cdot \mathbf{x}_i := \mathcal{L}'.$$

The latter is a sublattice of $\mathcal{L}$ and an overlattice for $\mathcal{P}$, so proving the statement for such $\mathcal{L}'$ suffices.

Invoking Lemma 2 on $\mathcal{L}$ and its sublattice $\mathcal{L}'$, we obtain a set $\{\mathbf{v}_\kappa\}_{\kappa < k}$ of k linearly independent vectors of $\mathcal{L}'$ such that $\mathbf{v}_\kappa \in \mathrm{Span}\{\mathbf{b}_i\}_{0 \leqslant i \leqslant n-k+\kappa}$ and $\mathbf{v}_\kappa \notin \mathrm{Span}\{\mathbf{b}_i\}_{0 \leqslant i \leqslant n-k+\kappa-1}$ for all $0 \leqslant \kappa < k$.

We then apply Lemma 3 to $\mathcal{L}'$ and $\{\mathbf{v}_\kappa\}_{\kappa < k}$ to obtain a pseudobasis $(\mathbf{C}, (\mathfrak{c}_\kappa))$ of $\mathcal{L}'$ such that

$$\mathbf{c}_\kappa \in \mathrm{Span}\{\mathbf{v}_j\}_{j \leqslant \kappa} \subseteq \mathrm{Span}\{\mathbf{b}_j\}_{j \leqslant n-k+\kappa}; \ \mathbf{c}_\kappa \notin \mathrm{Span}\{\mathbf{v}_j\}_{j < \kappa} \subseteq \mathrm{Span}\{\mathbf{b}_j\}_{j < n-k+\kappa}$$
(8)

Since both $\mathbf{X}$ and $\mathbf{B}$ define the same module $\mathcal{L}$, we have $\mathbf{X} = \mathbf{B} \cdot \mathbf{W}$ for some $\mathbf{W} \in K^{n \times n}$. Decompose $\mathbf{W} = [\mathbf{W}_L \mid \mathbf{W}_R]$, where $\mathbf{W}_R \in K^{n \times k}$ consists of the last k columns of $\mathbf{W}$. The last k columns of $\mathbf{X}$, denoted by $\mathbf{X}_R$ can be now expressed as $\mathbf{X}_R = \mathbf{B} \cdot \mathbf{W}_R$, hence $((\mathbf{X}_R, \mathfrak{x}_{n-k+\kappa})_{\kappa < k})$ is a pseudobasis of $\mathcal{L}'$.

Similarly, consider $\mathbf{M} \in K^{k \times k}$ such that $\mathbf{X}_R \cdot \mathbf{M} = \mathbf{C}$. Since $(\mathbf{C}, \{\mathfrak{c}_\kappa\}_\kappa)$ and $(\mathbf{X}_R, (\mathfrak{x}_{n-k+\kappa}))$ are pseudobases of the same lattice $\mathcal{L}'$, we have that $\mathbf{M}$ is a transformation matrix and hence $\mathbf{m}_i[\ell] \in \mathfrak{x}_\ell \cdot \mathfrak{c}_i^{-1}$ by Proposition 1. It holds that

$$\mathbf{B} \cdot \mathbf{W}_R \cdot \mathbf{M} = \mathbf{X}_R \cdot \mathbf{M} = \mathbf{C}.$$
(9)

Consider the entries $\mathbf{u}_i[j]$ of $\mathbf{U} := \mathbf{W}_R \cdot \mathbf{M} \in K^{n \times k}$. We want to show that $\mathbf{u}_i[j] \in \mathfrak{b}_j \mathfrak{c}_i^{-1}$. Indeed, we have that $\mathbf{u}_i[j] = \sum_{\ell=0}^{k-1} \mathbf{w}_\ell[j] \cdot \mathbf{m}_i[\ell]$. For $\ell < n$ the fact that $\mathbf{W}$ is a transformation matrix implies that we have inclusions $\mathbf{w}_\ell[j] \in \mathfrak{b}_j \cdot \mathfrak{x}_\ell^{-1}$ and $\mathbf{m}_i[\ell] \in \mathfrak{x}_\ell \cdot \mathfrak{c}_i^{-1}$, again by Proposition 1. From here, $\mathbf{w}_\ell[j] \cdot \mathbf{m}_i[\ell] \in \mathfrak{b}_j \cdot \mathfrak{c}_i^{-1}$ for $0 \leqslant i < k$ and $0 \leqslant j < n$. Hence,

$$\mathbf{u}_i[j] \in \mathfrak{b}_j \mathfrak{c}_i^{-1} \quad \text{for all } 0 \leqslant i < \kappa, 0 \leqslant j < n. \tag{10}$$

Thanks to Eq. (9), we have that $\mathbf{c}_\kappa = \sum_{j=0}^{n-1} \mathbf{u}_\kappa[j] \cdot \mathbf{b}_j$ for the aforementioned $\mathbf{U} \in K^{n \times \kappa}$. For $j > \kappa$ the value of $\mathbf{u}_\kappa[j] \cdot \mathbf{b}_j$ is zero since otherwise the corresponding $\mathbf{c}_\kappa$ would not be in $\mathrm{Span}\{\mathbf{v}_j\}_{j \leqslant \kappa}$. Thus, we can rewrite

$$\mathbf{c}_\kappa = \sum_{j=0}^{n-k+\kappa} \mathbf{u}_\kappa[j] \cdot \mathbf{b}_j \quad \text{for} \quad \mathbf{u}_\kappa[j] \in \mathfrak{b}_j \cdot \mathfrak{c}_\kappa^{-1} \quad \text{and} \quad \mathbf{u}_{n-k+\kappa}[j] \neq 0,$$

where the last condition is due to $\mathbf{c}_\kappa \notin \mathrm{Span}\{\mathbf{v}_j\}_{j < \kappa}$.

Now let us consider the projected lattice $\pi_{n-k}(\mathcal{L}')$, where π_{n-k} projects orthogonally to $\mathrm{Span}\{\mathbf{b}_i^*\}_{i \leqslant n-k-1}$. Then for $0 \leqslant \kappa < k$ the pseudobasis of $\pi_{n-k}(\mathcal{L}')$ is given by $(\mathbf{D}, (\mathfrak{c}_\kappa)) = ((\pi_{n-k}(\mathbf{c}_\kappa))_\kappa, (\mathfrak{c}_\kappa))$. Since the projections $\pi_{n-k}(\mathbf{b}_i)$ are zero for $i < n - k$ we can write $\mathbf{D}$ as $\pi_{n-k}([\mathbf{b}_{n-k}, \ldots, \mathbf{b}_{n-1}]) \cdot \mathbf{U}'$ where $\mathbf{U}' \in K^{k \times k}$ consists of last k rows of $\mathbf{U}$. Hence $(\pi_{n-k}(\mathbf{c}_\kappa))_\kappa$ can be explicitly written as:

$$\mathbf{d}_0 = \mathbf{u}_0'[n-k] \cdot \pi_{n-k}(\mathbf{b}_{n-k}),$$
$$\mathbf{d}_1 = \mathbf{u}_1'[n-k] \cdot \pi_{n-k}(\mathbf{b}_{n-k}) + \mathbf{u}_1[n-k+1] \cdot \pi_{n-k}(\mathbf{b}_{n-k+1}),$$

$$\vdots$$

$$\mathbf{d}_{k-1} = \sum_{j=0}^{k-1} \mathbf{u}_{k-1}'[n-k+j] \cdot \pi_{n-k}(\mathbf{b}_{n-k+j})$$

for $\mathbf{d}_\kappa$ being the columns of $\mathbf{D}$ From these last equations it follows that

$$\mathbf{d}_\kappa^* \in \mathrm{Span}\pi_{n-k}\{\mathbf{b}_i^*\}_{n-k \leqslant i \leqslant n-k+\kappa} = \mathrm{Span}\{\mathbf{b}_{n-k+\iota}^*\}_{0 \leqslant \iota \leqslant \kappa} \tag{11}$$

$$\mathbf{d}_\kappa^* \notin \mathrm{Span}\pi_{n-k}\{\mathbf{b}_i^*\}_{n-k \leqslant i \leqslant n-k-1} = \mathrm{Span}\{\mathbf{b}_{n-k+\iota}^*\}_{0 \leqslant \iota \leqslant \kappa-1} \tag{12}$$

Thus, the rank of $\mathbf{U}'$ is k. Hence, we can apply Lemma 5 to $\mathbf{B} \in K^{m \times n}, \mathbf{U}' \in K^{k \times k}$, and $\mathbf{D}$, which yields

$$\mathbf{d}_\kappa^* = \mathbf{u}_\kappa'[\kappa] \cdot \mathbf{b}_{n-k+\kappa}^*. \tag{13}$$

Next we want to prove that $\forall \kappa < k : \mathcal{N}(\mathbf{c}_\kappa^*) \geqslant \mathcal{N}(\mathbf{d}_\kappa^*)$ Notice that

$$\mathbf{c}_\kappa^*, \mathbf{d}_\kappa^* \in \mathrm{Span}\{\mathbf{b}_j^*\}_{0 \leqslant j \leqslant n-k+\kappa} \ \forall \kappa < k, \tag{14}$$

where first inclusion is due to Eq. (8) and the second is by Eq. (11). By definition, $\mathbf{d}_\kappa = \pi_{n-k}(\mathbf{c}_\kappa)$. Due to Eqs. (11) to (14)

$$\mathbf{u}_\kappa'[\kappa] \cdot \mathbf{b}_{n-k+\kappa}^* = \mathbf{d}_\kappa^* = \pi_{n-k+\kappa}(\mathbf{d}_\kappa) = \pi_{n-k+\kappa}(\pi_{n-k}(\mathbf{c}_\kappa)) = \pi_{n-k+\kappa}(\mathbf{c}_\kappa).$$

The latter is $\pi_{n-k+\kappa}(\mathbf{c}_\kappa^*) + \pi_{n-k+\kappa}\left(\sum_{\iota=0}^{\kappa-1} \frac{\langle \mathbf{c}_\kappa, \mathbf{c}_\iota^* \rangle}{\langle \mathbf{c}_\iota^*, \mathbf{c}_\iota^* \rangle} \cdot \mathbf{c}_\iota^*\right)$ where the second summand is zero by Eq. (14). Thus, $\mathbf{c}_\kappa^* = \pi_{n-k+\kappa}(\mathbf{c}_\kappa^*) + \mathbf{w}$, where $\mathbf{w} \in \mathrm{Span}\{\mathbf{b}_i^*\}_{0 \leqslant i < n-k+\kappa}$. Claim 1 applied to $\mathbf{c}_\kappa^* = \mathbf{d}_\kappa^* + \mathbf{w}$ gives us $\mathcal{N}(\mathbf{c}_\kappa^*) \geqslant \mathcal{N}(\mathbf{d}_\kappa^*)$.

Combining the definition of $\mathcal{L}' = \mathcal{L}(\mathbf{D}, \{\mathfrak{c}_\kappa\}_{\kappa<k})$ and Eq. (13) we get

$$\det \pi_{n-k}(\mathcal{L}') = \prod_{\kappa=0}^{k-1} \mathcal{N}(\mathbf{d}_\kappa^* \cdot \mathfrak{c}_\kappa) = \prod_{\kappa=0}^{k-1} \mathcal{N}(\mathbf{b}_{n-k+\kappa}^* \cdot \mathbf{u}_\kappa'[\kappa] \cdot \mathfrak{c}_\kappa).$$

Recall that all $\mathbf{u}_\kappa[n - k + \kappa] \in \mathfrak{b}_{n-k+\kappa} \cdot \mathfrak{c}_\kappa^{-1}$ as shown in Eq. (10). Then

$$\prod_{\kappa=0}^{k-1} \mathcal{N}(\mathbf{b}_{n-k+\kappa}^* \cdot \mathbf{u}_\kappa[n - k + \kappa] \cdot \mathfrak{c}_\kappa) \geqslant \prod_{\kappa=0}^{k-1} \mathcal{N}(\mathbf{b}_{n-k+\kappa}^*) \cdot \mathcal{N}(\mathfrak{b}_{n-k+\kappa} \cdot \mathfrak{c}_\kappa^{-1} \cdot \mathfrak{c}_\kappa);$$

$$\det \pi_{n-k}(\mathcal{L}') \geqslant \prod_{\kappa=0}^{k-1} \mathcal{N}(\mathbf{b}_{n-k+\kappa}^*) \cdot \mathcal{N}(\mathfrak{b}_{n-k+\kappa}) \geqslant \min_{\substack{J \subset \{0,\dots,n-1\} \\ |J|=k}} \prod_{j \in J} \mathcal{N}(\mathbf{b}_j^*) \cdot \mathcal{N}(\mathfrak{b}_j).$$

This implies $\det(\mathcal{L}') = \prod_{\kappa=0}^{k-1} \mathcal{N}(\mathbf{c}_\kappa^*) \cdot \mathcal{N}(\mathfrak{c}_\kappa) \geqslant \prod_{\kappa=0}^{k-1} \mathcal{N}(\mathbf{d}_\kappa^*) \cdot \mathcal{N}(\mathfrak{c}_\kappa) = \det \pi_{n-k}(\mathcal{L}')$. Hence $\det \mathcal{L}' \geqslant \det \pi_{n-k}(\mathcal{L}')$. Summing up, the following chain of inequalities proves the result:

$$\det \mathcal{P} \geqslant \det \mathcal{L}' \geqslant \det(\pi_{n-k}(\mathcal{L}')) \geqslant \min_{\substack{J \subset \{0,\dots,n-1\} \\ |J|=k}} \prod_{k \in J} \mathcal{N}(\mathbf{b}_j^*) \cdot \mathcal{N}(\mathfrak{b}_i).$$

$\square$

3.1 Descending to Subfields

The problem of finding short vectors (in the algebraic norm) in a rank-2 module over a number field K can be reduced to the problem of finding a short vector in a rank-$2d'$ module defined over a subfield $L \subset K$ with $[K : L] = d'$ and $\zeta \in L$ such that $K = L[\zeta]$. We would make use of this method while studying the behaviour of our algebraic lattice reduction algorithm on the NTRU modules defined in Sect. 2.2.

Let K and $L \subset K$ be two number fields of a relative degree $d' = [K : L]$. Concretely, we have:

$$\mathcal{O}_K = \mathcal{O}_L \oplus \zeta \mathcal{O}_L \oplus \dots \oplus \zeta^{d'-1} \mathcal{O}_L. \tag{15}$$

As a consequence, the module $M = \mathbf{b}_0 \cdot \mathcal{O}_K + \mathbf{b}_1 \cdot \mathcal{O}_K$ decomposes over $\mathcal{O}_L$ as:

$$\left(\mathbf{b}_0 \cdot \mathcal{O}_L \oplus \zeta \mathbf{b}_0 \cdot \mathcal{O}_L \oplus \dots \oplus \zeta^{d'-1}\mathbf{b}_0 \cdot \mathcal{O}_K\right) \oplus$$
$$\left(\mathbf{b}_1 \cdot \mathcal{O}_L \oplus \zeta \mathbf{b}_1 \cdot \mathcal{O}_L \oplus \dots \oplus \zeta^{d'-1}\mathbf{b}_1 \cdot \mathcal{O}_K\right),$$

yielding a basis of M viewed as a free $\mathcal{O}_L$-module of rank $2d'$. We refer to this process as descending (into the subfield L).

Formally, in order to descend from fields and their subfields we define the descend procedure. It represents a rank-n $\mathcal{O}_K$ module given by matrix $\mathbf{B} \in K^{m \times n}$ as a rank-$(n \cdot d')$ module over subfield L with the small relative degree $[K : L]$. It returns the $md' \times nd'$ matrix over L representing the basis of the initial module over the subfield L up to a certain permutation of the coordinates.

3.2 Predicting DSD Events

All NTRU modules always admit a free basis. Let $\mathbf{B}_{\mathrm{NTRU}} \in K^{2 \times 2}$ be an $\mathcal{O}_K$-basis of an NTRU module defined over a power-of-two cyclotomic field $L \subset K$. As discussed in Sect. 3.1 we can descend a basis of any free module to some subfield of K. Let $\mathbf{B}$ be a basis of an NTRU module of rank $n = 2 \cdot [K : L]$ over a number field $L \subset K$ for which one has a small index $n' = [K : L]$. We would like to deduce how the log-profile $\mathbf{p} := (\log(\mathcal{N}(r_{i,i}) \cdot \mathcal{N}(\mathfrak{b}_i)))_{i<n}$ of an LLL reduced basis of $\mathcal{L}(\mathbf{B})$ will look like. We heuristically assume that the α-LLL reduced basis of $\mathcal{L}(\mathbf{B})$ admits a profile of a special form. There are two horizontal regions at the beginning and the end of the profile and a central line connecting those two flat regions. The slope of this line is controlled by α. We introduce an algebraic analogue of Heuristic 1 as follows.

Heuristic 3 (AZGSA). *Let L be a number field of degree d. Let $\mathbf{B}$ be an α-LLL reduced $\mathcal{O}_L$ basis of a rank-n NTRU module for some $\alpha > 0$. Let $\mathbf{p}$ be a log-profile of $\mathbf{B}$. Then we have:*

$$\mathbf{p}_i = \begin{cases} d \log q, & i \leqslant n/2 - n' \\ d \log q \cdot (1 - \frac{i - n/2 + n'}{2n'}), & n/2 - n' < i < n/2 + n' - 1 \\ 0, & i \geqslant n/2 + n' - 1, \end{cases} \quad (16)$$

for $n' = 1/2 + d \log d / \log \alpha$.

For fixed n, d, the larger $\log q$ is, the greater $\min_{J \subset \{0,\ldots,n-1\} : |J| = n/2} \sum_{j \in J} \mathbf{p}_j$ is. For sufficiently large $\log q$ the AZGSA would contradict Theorem 1. This observation allows us to introduce the algebraic Dense Submodule Discovery event as follows.

Definition 6 (Algebraic DSD event). *Let $B \in \mathcal{O}_L^{n \times n}$ be an $\mathcal{O}_L$-basis for some NTRU module for an even $n \in \mathbb{N}$. We define the DSD as an event when an algebraic lattice reduction algorithm called on $\mathbf{B}$ returns a pseudobasis $([\mathbf{M}|\mathbf{B}'], \{\mathfrak{m}_i\}_{i<n/2} \cup \{\mathfrak{b}'_i\}_{n/2 \leqslant i < n})$ for $\mathbf{B}', \mathbf{M} \in \mathcal{O}_L^{n \times (n/2)}$ and a module spanned by $(\mathbf{M}, \{\mathfrak{m}_i\}_{i<n/2}))$ contains the secret vector $(\mathbf{f}, \mathbf{g})$.*

As in the classical case we postulate that for reasonably large modulus q the DSD event occurs meaning that we find a rank-$(n/2)$ submodule that contains $(\mathbf{f}, \mathbf{g})$. For simplicity we introduce the heuristic predicting the conditions for the algebraic LLL algorithm to trigger the DSD event assuming that the output of the algorithm is a free basis meaning all $\mathfrak{m}_i = \mathfrak{b}_j = \mathcal{O}_K$.

Heuristic 4 (Condition for algebraic DSD event). *Let* **B** *be an α-LLL reduced basis of a rank-n algebraic NTRU module over a power-of-2 cyclotomic field L for some $\alpha > 0$. Then* **B** *contains a basis of a dense rank-$(n/2)$ sublattice $\mathcal{L}'$ containing $(\mathbf{f}, \mathbf{g})$ as soon as:*

$$\log \mathcal{N}(\det(\mathcal{L}')) < \left(\frac{n'-1}{2}\right) \log q^{\deg L} - \frac{(n'-1)^2}{2} \log \alpha \qquad (17)$$

for $n' = 1/2 + d \log d / \log \alpha$.

In order to make an algebraic DSD event estimator, we rewrite Eq. (17) as $\log q > \frac{2 \log \mathcal{N}(\det(\mathcal{L})) + (n'-1)^2 \log \alpha}{(n'-1) \deg L}$. This view enables us to say, for given NTRU parameters d, n and a parameter α, for which $\log q$ the DSD event occurs.

4   Algebraic LLL

To confirm our theoretical result on the DSD event prediction we first need an implementation of an algebraic LLL. For this we implement a variant of an algebraic LLL from [22] restricted to the case of free bases (that is all ideals of a pseudobasis are $\mathcal{O}_K$). For the implementation details we refer the reader to the full version of this article [16].

As the classical LLL does, our algorithm relies on a short vector search in (algebraic) lattices of rank 2. Once a vector $\mathbf{v}_i = w_0 \cdot \mathbf{b}_i + w_1 \cdot \mathbf{b}_{i+1}$ with a short projection against $\mathbf{b}_0^*, \dots, \mathbf{b}_{i-1}^*$ is found, we insert it into the basis. For classical lattices, if we want to update a basis of $\mathcal{L}$ by inserting a vector $\mathbf{v}$ in it, we need to check the primitivity of $\mathbf{v}$ first. A vector $\mathbf{v}$ of a classical lattice $\mathcal{L}$ is called primitive if its coefficients $(c_0, \dots, c_{n-1})$ w.r.t. a given basis admit $\tau = \gcd(c_0, \dots, c_{n-1})$ being an unit. If $\tau \neq 1$, we can always insert $\mathbf{v}/\tau$. Unfortunately, this is not the case for algebraic lattices since $\mathcal{O}_K$ is not a gcd domain in general. This issue can potentially be resolved by finding a unimodular basis transformation that modifies the basis such that it contains the desired vector. Such an approach works in practice but *cannot be proven* to succeed theoretically since some vectors cannot be inserted into a free basis of a given lattice. We study this phenomenon closer in Sect. 5.3.

To predict a DSD event one needs to predict the value of α – the parameter responsible for the quality of algebraic reducedness. In this section we focus on studying two phenomena that can affect this value observed in practice. The first one is the situation when the algorithm has found an algebraically shorter vector, but is unable to insert it without altering the module and simultaneously keeping the basis free. The second one is the quality of the BKZ algorithm as an algebraic approxSVP oracle.

4.1   Inserting a Short Vector

LLL starts by considering projective lattices of the form $\pi_i([\mathbf{b}_i, \mathbf{b}_{i+1}])$. It finds a short (in the algebraic norm) vector $\mathbf{s}'$ in every such 2-dimensional lattice and inserts $\mathbf{s}$ into the initial lattice basis. Such insertions take place until the basis is LLL reduced. Each of these insertions is equivalent to applying a transformation given by an unimodular matrix $\mathbf{W} \in \mathcal{O}_K^{2 \times 2}$ such that $\mathbf{w}_0 \cdot [\mathbf{b}_i, \mathbf{b}_{i+1}] = w_0 \mathbf{b}_i + w_1 \cdot \mathbf{b}_{i+1} = \mathbf{s}$ where $\pi_i(\mathbf{s}) \in \mathcal{L}(\pi_i([\mathbf{b}_i, \mathbf{b}_{i+1}]))$ to $[\mathbf{b}_i, \mathbf{b}_{i+1}]$.

Given w_0 and w_1, the construction of a such $\mathbf{W}$ boils down to solving the Bézout equation $\mu w_0 + \nu w_1 = 1$. Given two coprime ideals $\mathfrak{a} = w_0 \cdot \mathcal{O}_K$ and $\mathfrak{b} = w_1 \cdot \mathcal{O}_K$, there exist two elements $a \in \mathfrak{a}, b \in \mathfrak{b}$ such that $a + b = 1$ [9, Proposition 1.3.1] which gives a solution to the mentioned Bézout equation.

Recall that we define the primitivity of $\mathbf{v}$ with coefficients $(c_0, \ldots, c_{n-1})$ w.r.t. a basis of $\mathcal{L} \subset K^n$ as (see Definition 1): $\mathbf{v}$ is primitive if and only if $\sum_{i<n} c_i \cdot \mathcal{O}_K = \mathcal{O}_K$. The rationale behind this definition follows from the Laplace expansion formula which suggests that the determinant of any $n \times n$ unimodular matrix with its first row equal to $(c_0, \ldots, c_{n-1})$ lies in $\sum_{i<n} c_i \cdot \mathcal{O}_K$. If this sum is not $\mathcal{O}_K$, it is impossible to obtain a unimodular matrix with $(c_0, \ldots, c_{n-1})$ being its first column.

Assume, we found a short vector with coefficient vector $\mathbf{w} = (w_0, w_1)$ (we will be inserting only in rank-2 modules, hence the dimension of $\mathbf{w}$). We need to find $\nu, \mu \in \mathcal{O}_K$ such that the following matrix is unimodular:

$$\mathbf{W} = \begin{pmatrix} w_0 & \nu \\ w_1 & \mu \end{pmatrix} \in \mathcal{O}_K^{2 \times 2}.$$

Since (w_0, w_1) are the coordinates of a short vector w.r.t. a given basis, it is expected that the new inserted vector has a smaller *algebraic* norm than the replaced vector. This procedure can only insert primitive vectors.

Overall, the fact that the algebraic LLL algorithm sometimes fails to insert non primitive vectors is leveraged down by a complex of measures: the PIP solver and processing several insertion candidates. Since the complete failures of our algorithm due to inability to insert a vector are rare, we can ignore their effect on the value of α observed in practice for the algebraic LLL algorithm. This observation is also backed up experimentally in Sect. 5.3.

4.2   Quality of Algebraic ApproxSVP Oracle

A good approxSVP oracle does not necessarily yield a good algebraic approxSVP oracle. The algebraic norm of a vector can be bounded from above with Lemma 1 which for a module

$$M = \begin{pmatrix} r_{0,0} \\ 0 \end{pmatrix} \cdot \mathcal{O}_K \oplus \begin{pmatrix} r_{1,0} \\ r_{1,1} \end{pmatrix} \cdot \mathcal{O}_K,$$

gives $\lambda_1^{\mathcal{N}}(M) \leqslant d^{-d/2} \cdot \lambda_1(M)^d$. This, assuming that the algebraic oracle is imperfect and has an approximation factor $\gamma_{\mathcal{N}}$, leads to $\gamma_{\mathcal{N}}^{2d} 2^d |\Delta_K|$ as a choice for α.

However, our experiments show that this upper bound is rather imprecise. Our best fit in practice is obtained with $\gamma_{\mathcal{N}} = 1/2$. This happened because the bound in Lemma 1 is loose and a vast majority of actual short module vectors do not reach this upper bound. Hence in our ZGSA simulator we use the experimentally derived value of $\alpha = 2^{-d}|\Delta_K|$. This adjustment correlates with the actual log-profiles well and allows us to predict DSD events on NTRU lattices.

It is also worth noting that the algebraic approach has limitations. In particular, finding a small norm element in a field, does not guarantee that its Euclidean norm will be sufficiently small. The relation between the algebraic norm (over K) of v and the Eucledian norm of the corresponding vector $\mathbf{v}$ is given by the inequality from Lemma 1. Thus, minimizing $\mathcal{N}_{K/\mathbb{Q}}(\mathbf{v})$ does not necessarily entail minimizing $\|\mathbf{v}\|$. Vectors $\mathbf{v}$ that are the shortest possible in the algebraic norm, will correspond to somewhat short $\mathbf{v}$ w.r.t. the Euclidean norm, but not necessarily *the shortest possible*.

5   Experiments

We implemented a version of algebraic LLL in SageMath 9.8. For the algebraic approxSVP oracle we call the FPYLLL [28] library. The implementation accompanying our work and the experimental data can be found at https://github.com/mooninjune/AlgebraicLLL. In all our experiments we use an AMD EPYC 7742 processor with 2 TB of RAM. Each EPYC is equipped with 128 physical cores that, with parallelization, give 256 threads. This number of cores was used to run multiple parallel experiments.

5.1   ZGSA Accuracy

One of the most prominent example of algebraic lattices in cryptography are modules that come from the module-LWE problem [21]. Modern lattice-based post-quantum signature and encryption standards [6,12,14] rely on the hardness of this problem. Given $m > k \geq 0$ and a modulus $q > 1$, sample $k \cdot m$ elements $(a_{0,0}, \ldots, a_{0,k-1}, \ldots, a_{m-1,0}, \ldots, a_{m-1,k-1})$ uniformly at random from $\mathcal{O}_K/q\mathcal{O}_K$. Consider a rank-$(m + k)$ module with an $\mathcal{O}_K$-basis given by the columns of the following matrix $\mathbf{B} \in \mathcal{O}_K^{(m+k)\times(m+k)}$:

$$\mathbf{B} = \begin{pmatrix} q & \cdots & 0 & a_{0,0} & \cdots & a_{k-1,0} \\ \vdots & \ddots & \vdots & \vdots & \ddots & \vdots \\ 0 & \cdots & q & a_{m-1,0} & \cdots & a_{k-1,m-1} \\ 0 & \cdots & 0 & 1 & \cdots & 0 \\ \vdots & \ddots & \vdots & \vdots & \ddots & \vdots \\ 0 & \cdots & 0 & 0 & \cdots & 1 \end{pmatrix}. \tag{18}$$

For $\mathbf{B}$ as above, the module-LWE problem can be formulated as the closest vector problem on the module lattice generated by $\mathbf{B}$ with the guarantee that the solution is unique. Hence, we are interested in the behaviour of lattice reduction algorithms on such bases.

We run our algebraic LLL on modules defined by bases $\mathbf{B}$ (with $k = m$) and monitor how the profile, that is the sequence $\{\mathcal{N}(r_{i,i})\}_i$ as per Definition 4 with the ideals of the pseudobasis being $\mathcal{O}_K$, changes. We plot these profiles in Fig. 1 and compare the profiles to Heuristic 3. By the shape of **B** given in Eq. (18), the input profile consists of the first k q-ary vectors and the last $r_{i,i}$ for $k \leq i < 2k$ are 1. As expected, after the LLL reduction, the profiles becomes 'flatter' and resembles the predicted profiles quite accurately. This situation is analogous to the behaviour of the classical lattice profiles after the execution of a classical LLL algorithm.

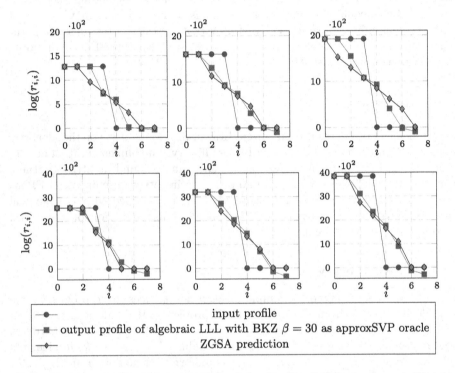

Fig. 1. Algebraic profiles for q-ary modules defined in Eq. (18) for $k = m = 4$. We take cyclotomic fields of conductor $f = 64$ for the top figures, and $f = 128$ for the bottom figures. Profiles are averaged over 20 different modules. From left to right: we choose q to be primes of 20-, 25-, 30-bits.

5.2   NTRU Modules

Concrete Estimations. To compare the predictions of Heuristic 4 with practice, we consider NTRU modules M over a cyclotomic field K of a conductor f as in Eq. (5). We descend the bases of these modules twice obtaining corresponding modules of rank 8 over a filed $L \subset K$ for a degree $\deg L = (\deg K)/4$. We launch our LLL algorithm on such bases and detect the recovery the dense sublattice containing $(\mathbf{f}, \mathbf{g})$.

Our estimator predicts that algebraic LLL recovers such dense sublattice at $\log_2 q = 12.8$ for $f = 32$, $\log_2 q = 16.1$ for $f = 64$, and $\log_2 q = 20.1$ for the conductor $f = 128$. The comparison between our predictions with the experimental data is given in Table 1. Our experiments confirm the predictions: the success rate for the predicted $\log q$ is close to 1 for cases $f = 32, 64$.

Table 1. Percentage of DSD events on various algebraic LLL reduced NTRU lattices. For $f \in \{32, 64\}$ the BKZ block size is 25 and 50 for $f = 128$.

$f = 32$		$f = 64$		$f = 128$	
$\log_2 q$	Success rate, %	$\log_2 q$	Success rate, %	$\log_2 q$	Success rate, %
12.5	80	16.0	90	20.0	0
13.0	100	16.5	100	20.5	30
13.5	100	17.0	100	21.0	75
14.0	100	17.5	100	21.5	95
14.5	100	18.0	100	22.0	100

A minor but still visible discrepancy with the predictions appears in the case of $f = 128$. This phenomenon occurs due to the following issue. For 128-th cyclotomic field we are forced to launch an algebraicSVP oracle on submodules of dimension 128 over $\mathbb{Z}$. Using the BKZ algorithm with large block sizes becomes rather expensive, so we use block size at most 50 which affected the quality of the oracle, but made our extensive experiments feasible. A minor adjustment $\gamma_\mathcal{N}$ to 0.55 gives a prediction $\log q = 21.2$ which resembles the actual situation more precisely.

In order to estimate for which q the DSD event occurs for the *classical LLL algorithm*, we ran the DSD estimator from [11] for the block size set to 2. The comparison of the least moduli sufficient to trigger the DSD events both in classical and the algebraic settings are presented in Table 2. The data illustrates that the algebraic DSD events occur for larger moduli than in the classical case.

Table 2. Predicted $\log q$ sufficient to trigger a DSD event on NTRU modules: our LLL vs. classical one.

Field conductor f	32	64	128
$\log q$ for classic LLL	5.95	10.4	14.85
$\log q$ for algebraic LLL	12.8	16.1	20.1

We used the FPyLLL implementation of BKZ-50 algorithm [28] for an algebraic approxSVP oracle inside the algebraic LLL. This block-size is significantly greater than the block sizes required to detect dense sublattice using classical lattice reduction.

For the NTRU ,modules over the 512-th cyclotomic field we ran classical BKZ reduction and compared the average block sizes required to trigger the DSD event. The results are presented in Table 3. It shows that, while we relied on the BKZ with the block size 50 to reduce the algebraic modules, the reduction could be performed by means of the classical algorithms with significantly smaller blocksizes. In order to make algebraic LLL competitive with the classical lattice reduction, a faster algebraic approxSVP oracle is needed. If such an oracle exists and can be efficiently implemented in polynomial time, our proposed algorithm can compete with the classical LLL at triggering the DSD events at least for mentioned parameters. We leave the question of existence of such oracle open.

Table 3. Average β_{BKZ} that triggers a DSD event on NTRU modules over 512-th cyclotomic field with parameter q.

$\log_2 q$	20.0	20.5	21.0	21.5	22.0
β_{BKZ}	2.5	2.3	2.2	2.0	2.0

5.3   Insertion Failures

A short vector with coefficients (c_0, c_1) will be inserted into a dimension-2 lattice basis if $c_0 \cdot \mathcal{O}_K + c_1 \cdot \mathcal{O}_K = \mathcal{O}_K$. Let us now discuss how restrictive this condition is. In our implementation of the algebraic LLL algorithm we 1)call BKZ reduction which returns many short vectors, and 2) try to leverage the condition using a PIP solver. However, there exist rank-2 $\mathcal{O}_K$-modules with the property that none of their free bases contains the shortest (again, in the Euclidean norm) vector. We now explicitly describe such modules.

Let M be given by

$$M = \begin{pmatrix} r_{0,0} \\ 0 \end{pmatrix} \cdot \mathcal{O}_K \oplus \begin{pmatrix} r_{1,0} \\ r_{1,1} \end{pmatrix} \cdot \mathcal{O}_K, \tag{19}$$

for some $r_{0,0}, r_{1,0}, r_{1,1} \in K_{\mathbb{R}}$. Such modules arise, for example, when we look at R-factors of algebraic rank-2 modules.

Suppose that a shortest vector in the module defined by Eq. (19), is $\mathbf{v} = (s, 0)^T$. As the second coordinate of $\mathbf{v}$ is zero, we have that the intersection $M \cap (K_{\mathbb{R}} \times \{0\})$ is $\begin{pmatrix} r_{0,0} \\ 0 \end{pmatrix} \cdot \mathcal{O}_K$. It may, however, happen that $s \cdot \mathcal{O}_K \neq r_{0,0} \cdot \mathcal{O}_K$. In this case $(s, 0)$ cannot be inserted as a basis vector of M while keeping it a basis (not pseudobasis).

This example relies on the fact that the principal ideals of number fields might not have their shortest element in the Euclidean norm being a generator. We perform some experiments to see how often this situation arises in practice.

For that we generate "random" principal ideals in cyclotomic fields of conductors 32 and 64. The concept of "randomness" in the ideal class group is given in [5], where the authors describe a random walk in the so-called Arakelov class group. We do not give the details of this random walk here, but refer the reader to [5] and to our implementation https://github.com/mooninjune/AlgebraicLLL.

The result of a walk is an ideal $\mathcal{I}$. We check if it is principal (this step makes the experiments hard to extend to large fields). If the ideal turns out to be principal, we run classical enumeration on its (scaled) basis in order to find its shortest nonzero vector $\mathbf{s}$. We then compute how often $\mathcal{I} \neq s\mathcal{O}_K$, where s is such that its coefficient embedding is $\mathbf{s}$. The results of the experiments are given in Table 4. These results suggest that an Euclidean SVP oracle does not guarantee a solution to SVP in the algebraic norm.

Table 4. Percentage of principal ideals not generated by their shortest (in Euclidean norm) element. We run 500 experiments per field.

Field conductor	% ideals not generated by their shortest element
32	69.4
64	70.2

Yet not all is lost when the candidate for insertion is not primitive. In case $c_0 \cdot \mathcal{O}_K + c_1 \cdot \mathcal{O}_K = \tau \cdot \mathcal{O}_K$ for some $\tau \in \mathcal{O}_K$, we can insert $\mathbf{v}/\tau$ into the basis since now $\mathbf{v}/\tau$ is primitive. Finding τ is known as the Principal Ideal Problem (PIP) that asks to find, for a given principal ideal (in an $\mathcal{O}_K$-basis), its generator. Known algorithms for this problem are subexponential in Δ_K assuming Generalized Riemann Hypothesis [2,3]. However, for some number fields of not so large degree solving PIP is efficient in practice.

Of course, we do not know a priori that $c_0 \cdot \mathcal{O}_K + c_1 \cdot \mathcal{O}_K$ is principal. However, as we have precomputed the class group for fields of conductor up to 128, this check is efficient in practice. On fields of conductor 256 and higher, the algorithm from [3] fails on non-principal inputs, which can be detected.

References

1. Albrecht, M., Bai, S., Ducas, L.: A subfield lattice attack on overstretched NTRU assumptions. In: Robshaw, M., Katz, J. (eds.) CRYPTO 2016. LNCS, vol. 9814, pp. 153–178. Springer, Heidelberg (2016). https://doi.org/10.1007/978-3-662-53018-4_6
2. Biasse, J.F.: Subexponential time relations in the class group of large degree number fields. Adv. Math. Commun. 8(4), 407–425 (2014)
3. Biasse, J.-F., Espitau, T., Fouque, P.-A., Gélin, A., Kirchner, P.: Computing generator in cyclotomic integer rings. In: Coron, J.-S., Nielsen, J.B. (eds.) EUROCRYPT 2017. LNCS, vol. 10210, pp. 60–88. Springer, Cham (2017). https://doi.org/10.1007/978-3-319-56620-7_3

4. Biasse, J.F., Song, F.: Efficient quantum algorithms for computing class groups and solving the principal ideal problem in arbitrary degree number fields. In: Proceedings of the Twenty-Seventh Annual ACM-SIAM Symposium on Discrete Algorithms, pp. 893–902. SIAM (2016)

5. de Boer, K., Ducas, L., Pellet-Mary, A., Wesolowski, B.: Random self-reducibility of ideal-SVP via Arakelov random walks. In: Micciancio, D., Ristenpart, T. (eds.) CRYPTO 2020. LNCS, vol. 12171, pp. 243–273. Springer, Cham (2020). https://doi.org/10.1007/978-3-030-56880-1_9

6. Bos, J.W., et al.: CRYSTALS - Kyber: a CCA-secure module-lattice-based KEM. In: 2018 IEEE EuroS&P, pp. 353–367 (2018)

7. Chen, C., et al.: PQC round-3 candidate: NTRU. Technical report (2019). https://ntru.org/f/ntru-20190330.pdf

8. Chen, Y., Nguyen, P.Q.: BKZ 2.0: better lattice security estimates. In: Lee, D.H., Wang, X. (eds.) ASIACRYPT 2011. LNCS, vol. 7073, pp. 1–20. Springer, Heidelberg (2011). https://doi.org/10.1007/978-3-642-25385-0_1

9. Cohen, H.: Advanced Topics in Computational Number Theory, vol. 193. Springer, Heidelberg (2012)

10. Coppersmith, D., Shamir, A.: Lattice attacks on NTRU. In: Fumy, W. (ed.) EUROCRYPT 1997. LNCS, vol. 1233, pp. 52–61. Springer, Heidelberg (1997). https://doi.org/10.1007/3-540-69053-0_5

11. Ducas, L., van Woerden, W.: NTRU fatigue: how stretched is overstretched? In: Tibouchi, M., Wang, H. (eds.) ASIACRYPT 2021. LNCS, vol. 13093, pp. 3–32. Springer, Cham (2021). https://doi.org/10.1007/978-3-030-92068-5_1

12. Ducas, L., et al.: CRYSTALS-Dilithium: a lattice-based digital signature scheme. IACR Trans. Cryptogr. Hardw. Embedded Syst. **2018**(1), 238–268 (2018)

13. Fieker, C., Stehlé, D.: Short bases of lattices over number fields. In: Hanrot, G., Morain, F., Thomé, E. (eds.) ANTS 2010. LNCS, vol. 6197, pp. 157–173. Springer, Heidelberg (2010). https://doi.org/10.1007/978-3-642-14518-6_15

14. Fouque, P.A., et al.: FALCON: fast-Fourier lattice-based compact signatures over NTRU (2018). https://www.di.ens.fr/~prest/Publications/falcon.pdf

15. Hoffstein, J., Pipher, J., Silverman, J.H.: NTRU: a ring-based public key cryptosystem. In: Buhler, J.P. (ed.) ANTS 1998. LNCS, vol. 1423, pp. 267–288. Springer, Heidelberg (1998). https://doi.org/10.1007/BFb0054868

16. Karenin, A., Kirshanova, E.: Finding dense submodules with algebraic lattice reduction. Cryptology ePrint Archive, Paper 2024/844 (2024). https://eprint.iacr.org/2024/844

17. Kirchner, P., Espitau, T., Fouque, P.A.: Algebraic and Euclidean lattices: optimal lattice reduction and beyond. Cryptology ePrint Archive, Paper 2019/1436 (2019). https://eprint.iacr.org/2019/1436

18. Kirchner, P., Espitau, T., Fouque, P.-A.: Fast reduction of algebraic lattices over cyclotomic fields. In: Micciancio, D., Ristenpart, T. (eds.) CRYPTO 2020. LNCS, vol. 12171, pp. 155–185. Springer, Cham (2020). https://doi.org/10.1007/978-3-030-56880-1_6

19. Kirchner, P., Fouque, P.-A.: Revisiting lattice attacks on overstretched NTRU parameters. In: Coron, J.-S., Nielsen, J.B. (eds.) EUROCRYPT 2017. LNCS, vol. 10210, pp. 3–26. Springer, Cham (2017). https://doi.org/10.1007/978-3-319-56620-7_1

20. Kirshanova, E., May, A., Nowakowski, J.: New NTRU records with improved lattice bases. In: Johansson, T., Smith-Tone, D. (eds.) PQCrypto 2023. LNCS, vol. 14154, pp. 167–195. Springer, Cham (2023). https://doi.org/10.1007/978-3-031-40003-2_7

21. Langlois, A., Stehlé, D.: Worst-case to average-case reductions for module lattices. Des. Codes Crypt. **75**(3), 565–599 (2015)
22. Lee, C., Pellet-Mary, A., Stehlé, D., Wallet, A.: An LLL algorithm for module lattices. In: Galbraith, S.D., Moriai, S. (eds.) ASIACRYPT 2019. LNCS, vol. 11922, pp. 59–90. Springer, Cham (2019). https://doi.org/10.1007/978-3-030-34621-8_3
23. Lenstra, A.K., Lenstra, H.W., Lovász, L.: Factoring polynomials with rational coefficients. Math. Ann. **261**(ARTICLE), 515–534 (1982)
24. Nguyen, P., Stehlé, D.: An LLL algorithm with quadratic complexity. SIAM J. Comput. **39**, 874–903 (2009)
25. Pataki, G., Tural, M.: On sublattice determinants in reduced bases. arXiv preprint arXiv:0804.4014 (2008)
26. Schnorr, C.: A hierarchy of polynomial time lattice basis reduction algorithms. Theor. Comput. Sci. **53**, 201–224 (1987)
27. Schnorr, C.P.: Lattice reduction by random sampling and birthday methods. In: Alt, H., Habib, M. (eds.) STACS 2003. LNCS, vol. 2607, pp. 145–156. Springer, Heidelberg (2003). https://doi.org/10.1007/3-540-36494-3_14
28. The FPLLL Development Team: FPyLLL, a Python wrapper for the FPLLL lattice reduction library, Version: 0.6.1 (2023). https://github.com/fplll/fpylll
29. Washington, L.C.: Introduction to Cyclotomic Fields. Graduate Texts in Mathematics, vol. 83. Springer, New York (1982). https://doi.org/10.1007/978-1-4684-0133-2

The Cool and the Cruel: Separating Hard Parts of LWE Secrets

Niklas Nolte[1]($\boxtimes$), Mohamed Malhou[1], Emily Wenger[1], Samuel Stevens[2], Cathy Li[3], François Charton[1]($\boxtimes$), and Kristin Lauter[1]

[1] FAIR, Meta, Menlo Park, CA, USA
{nolte,mmalhou,ewenger,fcharton,klauter}@meta.com
[2] Ohio State University, Columbus, OH, USA
stevens.994@osu.edu
[3] University of Chicago, Chicago, IL, USA
cathyli@uchicago.edu

Abstract. Sparse binary LWE secrets are under consideration for standardization for Homomorphic Encryption and its applications to private computation [20]. Known attacks on sparse binary LWE secrets include the sparse dual attack [5] and the hybrid sparse dual-meet in the middle attack [19], which requires significant memory. In this paper, we provide a new statistical attack with low memory requirement. The attack relies on some initial lattice reduction. The key observation is that, after lattice reduction is applied to the rows of a q-ary-like embedded random matrix **A**, the entries with high variance are concentrated in the early columns of the extracted matrix. This allows us to separate out the "hard part" of the LWE secret. We can first solve the sub-problem of finding the "cruel" bits of the secret in the early columns, and then find the remaining "cool" bits in linear time. We use statistical techniques to distinguish distributions to identify both cruel and cool bits of the secret. We recover secrets in dimensions $n = 256, 512, 768, 1024$ and provide concrete attack timings. For the lattice reduction stage, we leverage recent improvements in lattice reduction (flatter [34]) applied in parallel. We also apply our new attack to RLWE with 2-power cyclotomic rings, showing that these RLWE instances are much more vulnerable to this attack than LWE.

Keywords: Learning With Errors · R-LWE · Sparse secrets

1 Introduction

Lattice-based cryptosystems are attractive candidates for Post-Quantum Cryptography (PQC), standardized by NIST in the 5-year PQC competition (2017–2022) and by the Homomorphic Encryption community [3,17]. Special parameter choices, such as binary, ternary, binomial, or Gaussian secrets, small error, or small *sparse* secrets, are often made to improve efficiency or functionality.

N. Nolte, M. Malhou and E. Wenger—Equal Contribution.
F. Charton and K. Lauter—Co-Senior authors.

S. Vaudenay and C. Petit (Eds.): AFRICACRYPT 2024, LNCS 14861, pp. 428–453, 2024.
https://doi.org/10.1007/978-3-031-64381-1_19

Homomorphic Encryption (HE) implementations routinely assume small error and sparse binary or ternary secrets [3,16], and the NIST-standardized Kyber schemes assume small secret and small error (binomial distribution) [17].

Although these implementation choices may weaken security of the lattice-based cryptosystems, surprisingly few concrete results and benchmarks exist to quantify the actual time and resources required to attack systems with sparse secrets and small error. Over the last few decades, the lattice cryptography community has developed theoretical predictions of time and resources needed to attack lattice-based cryptosystems in general by studying and improving lattice reduction algorithms, such as LLL, BKZ, BKZ2.0 with various strategies such as sieving, early abort etc. [18,25,36]. To estimate the performance of these algorithms, the community relies on the LWE Estimator [9], but these estimates are often inaccurate for special parameter choices and for parameter sizes that can be tested in practice. While some attacks on sparse secrets have been proposed, such as the Sparse dual attack [5] and the Hybrid Sparse Dual Meet-in-the-Middle attack [19], general benchmarks for measuring attacks on small sparse secrets have not yet been developed. Existing benchmarks, such as the Darmstadt Lattice Challenges [13] are not relevant, since they do not cover such parameter choices.

Our Contribution. Given the potentially widespread adoption of lattice cryptosystems with sparse, small secrets, more work is needed to assess their hardness. To that end, we provide a new tool for attacking sparse small secrets, based on the observation that lattice reduction with certain parameters separates secrets into "cruel bits", corresponding to unreduced data which is hard to analyze, and "cool bits" that can be recovered in linear time once the hard bits are known. This leads us to define an attack on sparse small secrets, in three stages:

1. initial partial lattice reduction in parallel;
2. brute force recovery of a small number of hard, cruel bits;
3. statistical recovery of cool bits, and the secret.

We provide concrete experimental results for our attack, demonstrating its efficacy on LWE instances with sparse binary secrets in dimension $n \leq 768$. Furthermore, we show how this attack applies to both LWE and RLWE instances, with RLWE instances being much more vulnerable. We believe this attack should be taken into account whenever sparse secrets are being proposed, since a significant fraction of secrets are vulnerable to it (see Table 6), and we hope it provides a helpful practical benchmark for future research.

High-Level Attack Idea. Our key observation is that, for an LWE instance $(\mathbf{A} \in \mathbb{Z}_q^{m \times n}, b \in \mathbb{Z}_q^m)$, lattice reduction of q-ary embedded matrices of the form

$$\mathbf{\Lambda} = \begin{pmatrix} 0 & q\mathbf{I}_n \\ \omega\mathbf{I}_m & \mathbf{A} \end{pmatrix}, \tag{1}$$

produces a reduced matrix $\mathbf{A}'$ with a non-uniform distribution of variances over its columns; see Sect. 3 for details. Specifically, the variance of the first

n_u columns of $\mathbf{A}'$ is unaffected by lattice reduction. We call the bits of the secret in the first n_u columns "cruel" (unreduced). The other $n_r = n - n_u$ columns of the matrix have significantly reduced variance, and we call the secret bits corresponding to these columns the "cool" bits. The number of unreduced and reduced columns of $\mathbf{A}'$, n_u and n_r, depends on the overall lattice reduction quality and the penalty parameter ω, which controls a trade-off between reduction and error variance after reduction.

Our attack leverages this observation to reduce the original LWE problem to one with higher error on only the "cruel" entries in $\mathbf{A}$, by essentially ignoring the "cool" bits. If the error introduced by the ignored bits is sufficiently small, a secret guess s^* where only the first n_u bits are correct can be identified with sufficient statistics. The remaining (cool) bits can then be recovered one by one.

Table 1. Successful LWE secret recovery attacks leveraging our cruel/cool observation for various n/q settings. The timings do not include time for parallelized lattice reduction.

n	$\log_2 q$	Hamming Weight	Time (Sec)
256	12	12	3865
512	28	12	2417
	41	60	376
768	35	12	1,291
1024	50	17	6,395

Table 1 presents parameter settings and timings for successful recovery of sparse binary secrets, and demonstrates the benefits of cruel-cool bit separation in non-trivial LWE settings (see Table 6 for additional results). In these examples, Hamming weights were selected so that secret recovery from reduced matrices only takes a small amount of compute. We choose those settings because the lattice reduction step is theoretically least well understood, whereas the rest of the attack can be understood better theoretically (see Sect. 5) and does not need extensive experimentation. For example, for dimension $n = 512$ and $\log_2 q = 41$, our attack recovers binary secrets with Hamming weight 60 in about 6 min on one GPU. This does not include the time spent on lattice reduction to prepare the data, which is about 12 h/matrix (see Table 4). Table 1 also shows successful secret recovery for larger dimensions, such as $n = 768$ and $\log_2 q = 35$, for binary secrets with Hamming weight 12, in roughly 22 min using 20 GPUs.

RLWE Attack. Our attack can also be applied in the Ring-LWE setting. When the ring is a 2-power cyclotomic ring defined by the polynomial $x^n + 1$, where $n = 2^k$, then the RLWE samples corresponding to a polynomial RLWE sample, $(a(x), b(x) = a(x) \cdot s(x) + e(x))$ can be described via a skew-circulant matrix, A_{circ}; see Sect. 7 for details. When the matrix has this structure, we can rotate the "cruel bits" around (without redoing any lattice reduction) by inspecting samples from only certain indices of circulant matrices. This greatly increases our chances of recovering the secret and makes attacking the 2-power cyclotomic RLWE problem clearly easier than generic LWE. We give concrete timings for the RLWE setting, estimate the average speed-up over LWE, and show the improved success rate in Sect. 7.

Outline of the Paper. Section 2 describes related work. Section 3 presents our attack in detail. Section 4 explains the lattice reduction step for processing LWE samples to use in the attack. Section 5 contains the statistical analysis of the attack, including an estimate for number of samples needed. Section 6 presents our concrete secret recovery results and performance of comparable attacks. Section 7 adapts the attack to the RLWE setting.

2 Related Work

Albrecht et al. [6] classify attacks on LWE broadly into primal [7,28,29] and dual [5,30] attacks. Some primal attacks reduce search-LWE (see Sect. 3 for definition) to the unique shortest vector problem (uSVP) and solve this via lattice reduction [8]. Others employ a combination of lattice reduction and Bounded Distance Decoding (BDD) [28]. The goal of dual attacks is to solve Decision-LWE (see Sect. 3) by reducing it to the Shortest Integer Solution (SIS) problem [1], further reduced into the problem of finding short vectors in the dual lattice defined by $\{x \in \mathbb{Z}_q^m | Ax = 0 \mod q\}$.

Hybrid Attacks. The notion of hybrid attacks was introduced in 2007 by [24], who proposed combining lattice reduction and meet-in-the-middle (MITM) attacks against NTRUEncrypt. [14] extended this idea to binary-error LWE. A collection of such hybrid attacks have been proposed for different LWE settings. [11] provide a succinct overview in their Table 1. [35] succeeded in applying a hybrid attack to settings of sparse ternary secrets with small error via a primal attack strategy. [5] was the first work to combine the notions of hybrid attacks in the dual lattice for sparse binary and ternary secrets and small error. The attack benefits from optimizing a trade-off between success probability by guessing parts of the secret and performing the costly lattice reduction on the now lower-dimensional lattice. [19] improved upon [5] by using MITM for the guessing part. [23] optimized further by recognizing an inefficiency in the matrix multiplication during the guessing and considered small, non-sparse secrets. [11] extended this line of attack to arbitrary secrets and find that "hybrid dual attacks [usually] outperform [non-hybrid] dual attacks regardless of the secret distribution".

Our Work. In contrast to (but not necessarily incompatible with) work in hybrid attacks, our attack performs partial lattice reduction on full-sized lattices arising from different subsets of available LWE samples. Our lattice reduction uses a scaling (or penalty) parameter ω similar to the one in [5,10], and its utility is discussed in Sect. 4. Our key insight, the non-uniformity over coordinates in the reduced basis, naturally splits the problem into two parts (in this case the "cruel" and "cool" bits), reminiscent of a hybrid attack.

Table 2. Notation used in this paper.

Symbol	Description
q	The modulus of the LWE problem considered
n	Problem dimension (the dimension of vectors $\mathbf{a}$ and $\mathbf{s}$)
n_u	The number of unreduced (aka cruel) entries in $\mathbf{a}$
n_r	Number of reduced (aka cool) entries in $\mathbf{a}$. $n = n_u + n_r$
$\mathbf{s}$	The unknown secret, used to construct $b = \mathbf{a} \cdot \mathbf{s} + e$
$\mathbf{s}^*$	A candidate secret, not necessarily correct
h	The Hamming weight of the secret (number of 1 bits)
h_u	The Hamming weight of the n_u unreduced bits of the secret
h_r	The Hamming weight of the n_r reduced bits of the secret ($h = h_u + h_r$)
σ_u	The standard deviation of unreduced entries in $\mathbf{a}$ (equal to $\frac{q}{\sqrt{12}}$)
σ_r	The standard deviation of reduced entries in $\mathbf{a}$
σ_e	The standard deviation of error (amplified by reduction)
$\sigma(x)$	The standard deviation of the random variable x
ρ	The reduction factor of pre-processing, i.e. the ratio $\frac{\sigma(\mathbf{RA})}{\sigma(\mathbf{A})}$
m	The number of LWE samples (reduced or unreduced)
ω	The penalty used during reduction
$a:b$	integer range $[a,b)$, used for indices
$\mathbf{X}_{*,i}$	ith column of $\mathbf{X}$

3   The Attack

The Learning With Errors (LWE) problem, first introduced by Regev [33], can be stated in 2 forms. The Search-LWE problem is: given a random matrix $\mathbf{A} \in \mathbb{Z}_q^{m \times n}$, a secret vector $\mathbf{s} \in \mathbb{Z}_q^n$, and an error vector $\mathbf{e} \in \mathbb{Z}_q^m$ (usually sampled from some small error distribution), find $\mathbf{s}$, given $\mathbf{A}$ and

$$\mathbf{b} = \mathbf{A} \cdot \mathbf{s} + \mathbf{e} \mod q, \tag{2}$$

where m denotes the number of LWE samples, n is the lattice dimension, and q is the modulus. In the related Decision-LWE problem, the objective is not to find the secret vector $\mathbf{s}$, but to distinguish between two distributions: given a random matrix $\mathbf{A} \in \mathbb{Z}_q^{m \times n}$ and a vector $\mathbf{b} \in \mathbb{Z}_q^m$, decide whether $\mathbf{b}$ is drawn from the distribution $\mathbf{A} \cdot \mathbf{s} + \mathbf{e} \mod q$ for some secret vector $\mathbf{s} \in \mathbb{Z}_q^n$ and error vector $\mathbf{e} \in \mathbb{Z}_q^m$, or whether $\mathbf{b}$ is drawn from the uniform random distribution over $\mathbb{Z}_q^m$. [33] showed that for q of size polynomial in n, there is a reduction from Search-LWE to Decision-LWE. See Table 2 for notation used in the paper.

We introduce a new attack on the LWE problem for sparse binary secrets, i.e. $\mathbf{s} \in \{0,1\}^n$, with h, the Hamming weight (number of 1s in $\mathbf{s}$), small. The attack leverages an observation about the shape of reduced LWE matrices to separate the hard and easy parts of the secret. It works as follows.

Attack Part 1: Lattice Reduction. We begin by applying lattice reduction to (the rows of) an embedding $\mathbf{\Lambda} \in \mathbb{Z}_q^{(m+n)\times(m+n)}$ of the data:

$$\mathbf{\Lambda} = \begin{pmatrix} 0 & q\mathbf{I}_n \\ \omega\mathbf{I}_m & \mathbf{A} \end{pmatrix} \tag{3}$$

The reduction finds a linear transformation $[\mathbf{C}, \mathbf{R}]$ such that $\mathbf{\Lambda}^r = [\mathbf{C}, \mathbf{R}]\,\mathbf{\Lambda} = [\omega\mathbf{R}\mathbf{I}_m, q\mathbf{C}\mathbf{I}_n + \mathbf{R}\mathbf{A}]$. We extract the transformation matrix $\mathbf{R} = \mathbf{\Lambda}^r_{*,0:m}/\omega$, which corresponds to the row and column operations performed to transform the matrix A into its reduced form. $\mathbf{R}$ is applied to both $\mathbf{A}$ and $\mathbf{b}$ to create reduced sample pairs. For ease of notation, we will refer to $\mathbf{RA}$ as $\mathbf{A}$ or "reduced $\mathbf{A}$" and $\mathbf{Rb}$ as $\mathbf{b}$ throughout the text, and otherwise specify "original" pairs.

Reduction algorithms trade off the error on the reduced LWE pairs for the norm of the rows in reduced $\mathbf{A}$. The "penalty parameter" ω controls this trade-off, where higher ω causes less norm and variance reduction, but also less error amplification. Details of lattice reduction can be found in Sect. 4.

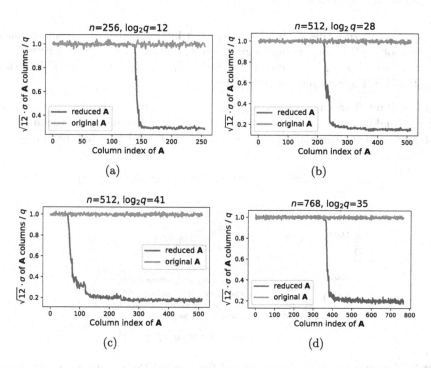

Fig. 1. The standard deviation of elements within each column of the $\mathbf{A}$ matrix before and after reduction (and extraction from the q-ary embedding) for various n/q settings. The first n_u unreduced columns (left half of the figures) correspond to the "cruel" bits of the secret, while the remaining $n_r = n - n_u$ are the "cool" bits. This phenomenon is distinct from the "z-shape" exhibited by the Gram-Schmidt orthogonalized rows of a q-ary lattice before and after lattice reduction [4,24] (see Appendix A.3 for details).

Attack Part 2: Identify Cruel and Cool Bits. The key observation of this attack is that the resulting reduced **A** samples all share a reduction pattern:

> **Key observation:** *The first n_u elements of each sample vector $\mathbf{A}_{*,0:n_u}$ remain unreduced and retain their uniform distribution over $\mathbb{Z}_q$, and all subsequent $n_r = n - n_u$ elements of $\mathbf{A}_{*,n_u:n}$ are heavily reduced.*

To illustrate this key observation, we plot the standard deviation over columns in **A** against the column index in Fig. 1 for various n and $\log_2 q$ settings. This observation of cruel and cool bits inspires the following hypothesis:

> **Hypothesis:** For any row **a** of reduced matrix **A**, the n_r last entries contribute comparatively little to the overall dot product $\mathbf{a} \cdot \mathbf{s}$. Thus, for a sparse enough secret, the Decision-LWE may be solvable without correctly guessing the n_r secret bits.

In other words, this shape resulting from lattice reduction means we only need to solve LWE on a smaller dimension $n_u < n$. In essence, *we separate out the hard part of the LWE secret at the cost of increased error.* We validate this hypothesis in the remainder of this paper.

Attack Part 3: Secret Guessing. Next, we leverage statistical properties of the cool and cruel regions to guess the secret. Figure 2 shows a histogram of the distribution of the residuals of reduced data $\mathbf{a} \cdot \mathbf{s} - b \mod q$ (in blue) and $\mathbf{a} \cdot \mathbf{s}^* - b$

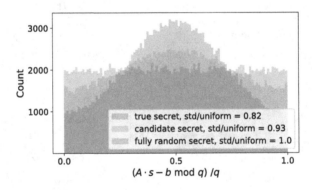

Fig. 2. Histogram of 4 million samples of the residual $(\mathbf{a} \cdot \mathbf{s}^* - b) \mod q$ (centered and normalized) for reduced data and different secret guesses $\mathbf{s}^*$ ($n = 512$, $\log_2 q = 41$, $h = 20$). The three histograms correspond to three different guesses. Blue corresponds to the true secret, orange to the secret candidate where the first $n_u = 75$ entries are guessed correctly, and green to a random secret with $h = 20$. The numbers in the legend correspond to sample standard deviation relative to uniform standard deviation $\frac{q}{\sqrt{12}}$. (Color figure online)

mod q (in orange), where s^* shares the first n_u entries with s and has all other n_r elements set to 0. Green corresponds to a random guess for the secret with equal hamming weight. The orange and the green distributions are distinct, enabling us to detect the correctness of the first n_u bits in the secret without knowing the others. Given the size of the error on the reduced LWE problem, so far we have not found a more efficient attack for guessing the first n_u secret bits than brute force. One could think of using one of the hybrid attack strategies outlined in the related work on the cruel part, but we leave this for future work.

Given a secret guess s^* with correct n_u cruel bits, the n_r remaining cool bits can be recovered easily, given enough samples. One fast method is greedy recovery, presented in Algorithm 1. It works as follows: start with a candidate secret s^* which shares the first n_u cruel bits with s and has all other n_r bits set to 0. Starting with the first cool bit, flip that bit of s^* to 1. Then calculate if this flip increases the standard deviation of the resulting $a \cdot s^* - b \mod q$ (over m reduced samples (a, b)). If so, flip it back to 0 and move to the next bit. Note the standard deviation here is a practical proxy for a proper statistical test. Section 3.1 expands on this. Intuitively, greedy recovery works because every correct bit flipped to 1 will reduce the orange distribution in Fig. 2 closer to the blue and every wrong one will introduce more noise, sending it closer to the green.

Algorithm 1. Greedy recovery of cool bits

1: **for** $i \in n - n_r : n$ **do**
2:     $s^*[i] \leftarrow 0$
3:     $\sigma_0 \leftarrow \sigma(a \cdot s^* - b \mod q)$
4:     $s^*[i] \leftarrow 1$
5:     $\sigma_1 \leftarrow \sigma(a \cdot s^* - b \mod q)$
6:     **if** $\sigma_0 \leq \sigma_1$ **then**
7:         $s^*[i] \leftarrow 0$
8:     **else**
9:         $s^*[i] \leftarrow 1$
10:    **end if**
11: **end for**

Otherwise, one can employ more principled gradient-free optimization methods, like simulated annealing. Annealing works better with limited data, but is slower. The best choice depends on the setting. All methods work efficiently due to the reduced variance of the corresponding entries in A.

3.1 Practical Considerations

Implementation. As described in detail in Sect. 4, we sample views of the $4 \cdot n$ sized lattice defined by the LWE samples and reduce them individually, forming a large set of reduced LWE samples for use in the attack, following [26, 27].

After identifying the cool and cruel bits, secret recovery runs in two parts: first, guessing the cruel secret bits on the reduced LWE problem with large error, then the recovery of the full secret via Algorithm 1.

We use brute force enumeration for cruel secret bit recovery. All code is implemented in Python, and we employ GPU acceleration via `pytorch` [31]. Batches of secret candidates are continuously sent to the device and evaluated on a suitable amount of data to distinguish the residuals $\mathbf{A} \cdot \mathbf{s}^* - \mathbf{b} \mod q$ if the true (part of the) secret was found, see the orange histogram in Fig. 2. Since our brute force is perfectly parallelizable, we can distribute the work to an arbitrary number of GPUs or CPUs. Candidate secrets are enumerated in ascending Hamming weight, and a record of the top-k candidates, according to a metric defined below, are evaluated at constant intervals throughout the enumeration. Evaluation involves running Algorithm 1 and then checking if the resulting secret produces nearly correct $(\mathbf{A}, \mathbf{b})$ pairs. The evaluation frequency can be traded off against the amount of data used during enumeration and k, the number of candidates kept in the top-k set.

Candidate Evaluation. The metric by which candidate secrets are sorted can involve any test that distinguishes from uniformity in the residual, but in practice it must be fast. Most non-parametric tests like Kolmogorov-Smirnov or Kuiper involve calculating a Cumulative Distribution Function (CDF) and thus sort the data, which is slow. A likelihood ratio test is generally more powerful, but evaluating such a test on a distribution modulo q involves evaluation over multiple "wraps" around the modulus. Under certain assumptions, detailed in Sect. 5, the distribution we aim to distinguish from uniform is a mod-Gaussian involving an infinite sum:

$$f(x) \propto \sum_{k=-\infty}^{\infty} \mathcal{N}(x; \mu + k \cdot q, \sigma^2). \tag{4}$$

Even with suitable truncation, the runtime of a likelihood ratio test will at best be $O(N \cdot K)$ with N samples and truncation to K elements of the sum. [23] also explores a way of specifically distinguishing modular Gaussians via a periodic aggregation metric $Y = \sum_{i=1}^{N} \exp(2\pi i X_i)$, see their Algorithm 2. We thought, since both distributions, uniform and mod-Gaussian are fully defined by their first two moments and have their mean fixed to the same value, a direct comparison of the second moment suggests itself as a simple but powerful distinguishing method. Thus, we choose the direct variance comparison described in Algorithm 1 due to its simplicity and computational efficiency. Empirically, we found that it was similarly powerful to a Kuiper test, and more than 5x faster in the settings considered.

Other Performance Considerations. Values of $\mathbf{A}, \mathbf{b}$ are of the order of q and thus large in the considered scenarios. However, high precision is not needed during the enumeration and evaluation, since all precision is drowned out by the large error. Since modern GPUs work best with 16-bit floating point numbers, we scale all values down to a range appropriate for those representations. We also employ `pytorch` compilation to alleviate some of the overhead of python being an interpreted language. This feature compiles, optimizes and fuses tensor operations, giving a 2-3x speed improvement over the default eager execution.

Our implementation can evaluate roughly 5 billion secrets of dimension $n = 512$ through an NVIDIA V100 GPU in about 1 h during the brute force search. The greedy secret recovery step is fast and runs infrequently. Additional speedups can be had with additional optimizations, such as the use of dedicated CUDA kernels. Additionally, our attack does not yet exploit the recursive search space structure trick from [23].

4   Lattice Reduction

Here, we briefly describe the lattice reduction techniques used to produce the data in our attacks. Classical lattice reduction algorithms, such as LLL, BKZ, BKZ2.0 [18,25,36] seek to reduce the size of vectors in a lattice. Attacks on LWE such as the uSVP and dual attacks use lattice reduction algorithms to find the shortest vector, or a *short enough* vector, in a specifically constructed lattice. Our attack leverages lattice reduction methods, but instead of attempting to find a single very short vector, we use reduced lattices as data for a distinguishing attack. For our attack, we apply lattice reduction techniques to the embedded matrix in Eq. (3).

Lattice reduction can be viewed as finding an integer-valued transformation matrix $\mathbf{R}$ which, when multiplied by $\mathbf{A}$ modulo q, reduces the Frobenius norm of $\mathbf{A}$. Given LWE samples in the form of a matrix $\mathbf{A}$ and a vector $\mathbf{b} = \mathbf{A} \cdot \mathbf{s} + \mathbf{e}$, we can use lattice reduction to reduce the entries of the matrix $\mathbf{A}$, yielding $\mathbf{R}\mathbf{A}$. Then the corresponding LWE samples are $(\mathbf{R}\mathbf{A}, \mathbf{R}\mathbf{b} = \mathbf{R}\mathbf{A} \cdot \mathbf{s} + \mathbf{R}\mathbf{e})$. Because $\mathbf{R}$ is applied to the noisy vector $\mathbf{b}$ as well, the initial noise in $\mathbf{b}$ is increased by the magnitude of the elements in $\mathbf{R}$.

For this attack, it is not always beneficial to reduce as much as possible, but rather to trade off reduction quality with the magnitude of the error $\mathbf{R}\mathbf{e}$ introduced by the reduction via the parameter ω. Intuitively, the stronger the reduction, the higher the error. The error magnitude determines the width of the blue and orange distributions in Fig. 2. Section 5 expands on the theory which describes this trade-off.

4.1   Our Reduction Methods

Generating Sufficient LWE Data. Our attack relies on the ability to distinguish distributions from uniform, and successful distinguishing requires sufficient data. Details are discussed in Sect. 5 below. An attacker might not have access to enough samples to run our attack in a real world scenario. However, subsampling comes to the rescue [27]. From an initial number of m_0 samples, one can select a subset of m_1 samples, create a new $\mathbf{A}$ matrix, embed it in Λ, and perform lattice reduction. This can be done many times, up to $\binom{m_0}{m_1}$ times. This technique "inflates" the number of samples usable for this attack dramatically, at the cost of reduction of many matrices corresponding to different sub-lattices.

The SALSA Picante [27] attack, which proposed this sub-sampling method, eavesdrops $4n$ LWE samples, then sub-samples n samples at a time and applies lattice reduction to $2n \times 2n$ q-ary matrices. Instead, here we sub-sample $m = \text{round}(0.875n)$ from $4n$ LWE samples. We then form q-ary matrices of size $(m + n) \times (m + n)$ and reduce them.

Reduction Algorithms. We leverage 3 different algorithms in our lattice reduction step: BKZ2.0 [18], flatter [34], and polish [15]. Each algorithm has strengths and weaknesses, and combining them maximizes the strengths of each. BKZ2.0 provides strong reduction, but is slow for large block size and high dimensional lattices. In contrast, flatter is fast and can reduce lattices with $n \geq 512$ and large q, but only has reduction performance analogous to LLL. The polish algorithm runs at the end of a flatter or BKZ2.0 loop [26] and "polishes" by iteratively orthogonalizing matrices. It provably produces strictly decreasing vector norms when run, is implemented in C, and runs very fast.

Measuring Performance. We measure lattice reduction performance via ρ, the ratio of the standard deviation of the entries of the reduced lattice to the expected standard deviation of the entries of a random lattice:

$$\rho = \frac{\sigma(\mathbf{A})}{\sigma(\mathbf{A}_{\text{initial}})} = \frac{\sigma(\mathbf{A})}{\frac{q}{\sqrt{12}}}, \tag{5}$$

with $\sigma(\mathbf{A})$ the standard deviation of all entries of $\mathbf{A}$, and $\sigma(\mathbf{A}_{\text{initial}})$ the unreduced, original LWE sample matrix that follows a uniform distribution. When $\rho = 1$, lattice reduction did not succeed. When $\rho \ll 1$, a significant reduction in lattice norms has been achieved. Our attack depends crucially on ρ, since it determines the number of cruel bits in the secret.

Interleaved Reduction Strategy. Empirically, we found that combining these three algorithms gave the best reduction performance, in terms of both time and quality. flatter sometimes gets "stuck" and cannot further reduce a given lattice, particularly for smaller q. In these instances, "interleaving" BKZ2.0 and

Table 3. Comparing performance of 3 preprocessing methods for $n = 512$ and varying $\log_2 q$: flatter only, flatter-initialized BKZ (e.g. flatter $\rightarrow$ BKZ) and Interleaving. Each entry in the table reports ρ/hours. **Bold** indicates most reduction ρ with ties broken by shortest time.

$\log_2 q$		20	22	24	26	28	30	32	35	38
$\omega = 4$	Interleave	**0.77/12**	**0.75/12**	0.72/14	**0.69/10**	**0.67/14**	**0.64/24**	**0.57/52**	**0.50/55**	**0.44/56**
	flatter→BKZ	0.81/92	0.79/92	0.76/ 92	0.75/114	0.97/72	0.65/109	0.63/55	0.60/63	0.58/60
	flatter only	0.97/72	0.97/72	**0.72/2**	0.7/3	0.68/4	0.68/5	0.58/54	0.58/132	0.46/94
$\omega = 10$	Interleave	**0.80/11**	**0.77/14**	**0.74/14**	**0.71/14**	**0.68/13**	**0.66/13**	**0.59/53**	**0.53/54**	0.47/57
	flatter→BKZ	0.81/93	0.80/93	0.78/93	0.76/114	0.76/92	0.97/72	0.65/50	0.62/55	0.58/58
	flatter only	0.97/72	0.97/72	0.97/72	0.72/2	0.69/3	0.68/7	0.62/74	0.58/130	**0.46/98**

flatter provided a higher quality reduction while helping flatter jump out of these minima (see Table 3 for a comparison of different ways of combining flatter and BKZ2.0). Our interleaving algorithm starts each reduction run with several rounds of flatter and declares a "stall" when flatter runs 3 times but produces an average reduction in ρ of less than 0.001. Then, the reduction runs BKZ2.0, and when BKZ2.0 stalls, it switches back to flatter and repeats until the reduction converges. polish runs after each BKZ2.0 or flatter step.

Early Termination. To increase the number of reduced LWE matrices produced from a single lattice reduction run, we leverage an early termination strategy. When the standard deviation reduction ratio ρ stalls , we export the reduced matrix, then sub-sample a new $(m + n) \times (m + n)$ q-ary matrix from the initial set of n LWE samples and start again. This better leverages available compute.

4.2 Final Datasets

We apply the interleaved reduction strategy described above on the 5 different parameter sets. The number of cruel bits, n_u, is strongly correlated with the reduction factor ρ: better reduction (lower ρ) yields fewer cruel bits. Because brute-forcing the n_u bits is the bottleneck for our attack, we optimize the lattice reduction configuration to maximize reduction. Reduction is trivially parallelizable, since each matrix can be processed on a different core, but is slower for larger dimensions n and moduli q.

Table 4. Datasets used in concrete attacks. β_1 and β_2 are block sizes used in lattice reduction. σ_e is the ratio of standard deviation mod q of the magnified error **Re** to standard deviation of uniform distribution mod q. n_u is the number of cruel bits. We define any bits with standard deviation greater than $\frac{1}{2}\sigma(A_{\text{initial}})$ as cruel bits.

Inputs					Outputs			
n	$\log_2 q$	β_1, β_2	ρ	Hrs/Matrix	σ_e	n_u	$\rho^2 n$
256	12	35, 40	0.769	15	0.952	143	151.3
512	28	18, 22	0.677	12	0.692	228	234.6
512	41	18, 22	0.413	13	0.337	75	87.3
768	35	18, 22	0.710	15	0.938	373	387.1
1024	50	18, 22	0.704	36	0.827	495	506.1

4.3 Quality of Reduction and Our Attack

Experimentally we observe that the number of cruel bits, n_u, is roughly $\rho^2 n$. The data sets presented in Table 4 confirm this observation. Intuitively, this makes sense when assuming column independence and that the standard deviation of the cool bits σ_r is much smaller than that of the cruel bits σ_u:

$$\sigma_{\text{total}}^2 = \frac{1}{n}(n_u \cdot \sigma_u^2 + n_r \cdot \sigma_r^2) \approx \frac{1}{n}(n_u \cdot \sigma_u^2) \qquad (6)$$

During our experiments we usually find $\sigma_r < 0.3\sigma_u$.

5 Statistical Tests and Analysis

Three statistical tests must be performed during the attack: testing whether a brute force guess of the cruel bits is correct, testing whether cool bits are zero or one (in Algorithm 1), and testing a full secret guess. The first two tests are performed on reduced LWE samples, obtained during the pre-processing phase. The third involves a simple check of residuals on the original LWE sample and will not be discussed here. We elaborate on the statistical properties of these tests, estimate the number of samples needed, and illustrate our results with concrete attack statistics.

5.1 Testing Brute-Forced Guesses of the Cruel Bits

Suppose a guess of the cruel bits was made, and let $\mathbf{s}^*$ be the secret guess derived by setting all cruel bits to their guessed values and all cool bits to zero. We are given m reduced LWE samples $(\mathbf{a}, b)$, with the same secret $\mathbf{s}$, error e and reduction factor ρ. We consider the random variable $x = \mathbf{a} \cdot \mathbf{s}^* - b = \mathbf{a} \cdot (\mathbf{s}^* - \mathbf{s}) - e \mod q$, centered to $(-\frac{q}{2}, \frac{q}{2})$. Our intuition from Sect. 3 is that the standard deviation of x (calculated on m reduced samples) will be lowest when all cruel bits are correctly predicted.

More precisely, let n be the problem dimension and n_u the number of cruel bits. Over reduced LWE samples $(\mathbf{a}, b)$, the n_u first coordinates of $\mathbf{a}$, which correspond to the cruel bits, have standard deviation $\sigma_u = \frac{q}{\sqrt{12}}$ (the standard deviation of the uniform distribution). The standard deviation σ_r of the n_r remaining coordinates of $\mathbf{a}$ (the cool bits) can be derived from the reduction factor ρ and n_u under the assumption that all coordinates of $\mathbf{a}$ are independent after reduction, as follows:

$$\rho^2 \sigma_u^2 = \frac{n_u}{n} \sigma_u^2 + \frac{n_r}{n} \sigma_r^2, \tag{7}$$

and therefore

$$\sigma_r = \sqrt{\frac{\rho^2 n - n_u}{n_r}} \sigma_u. \tag{8}$$

Applying these formulas to the examples in Table 4, we have:

- $\sigma_r = 0.27\sigma_u$ for $n = 256$ and $\log_2 q = 12$ ($\rho = 0.769$ and $n_u = 143$)
- $\sigma_r = 0.15\sigma_u$ for $n = 512$ and $\log_2 q = 28$ ($\rho = 0.677$ and $n_u = 228$)
- $\sigma_r = 0.17\sigma_u$ for $n = 512$ and $\log_2 q = 41$ ($\rho = 0.413$ and $n_u = 75$)
- $\sigma_r = 0.19\sigma_u$ for $n = 768$ and $\log_2 q = 35$ ($\rho = 0.710$ and $n_u = 373$)
- $\sigma_r = 0.14\sigma_u$ for $n = 1024$ and $\log_2 q = 50$ ($\rho = 0.703$ and $n_u = 495$)

When all cruel bits are correctly predicted, and if h_r is the number of ones in the n_r cool bits of the secret (a known value since the Hamming weight of the secret is known), the variance of x is $\sigma_{\mathcal{G}_q}^2(x) = F_q(h_r \sigma_r^2 + \sigma_e^2)$, with $F_q(v)$

the variance of a centered Gaussian modulo q (which we call $\mathcal{G}_q$) with variance v and a modular operation. We assume independence in the reduced samples and therefore a Gaussian distribution of x before the modulo operation, so the Central Limit Theorem (CLT) holds.

When some cruel bits are incorrect, the residual distribution becomes almost indistinguishable from uniform, because even one incorrect cruel bit significantly increases the Gaussian variance.

Samples Needed for Cruel Bit Recovery. We now derive M, the number of reduced samples needed to verify cruel bit guesses, and consequently the amount of pre-processing resources needed for our attack. Since in practice the distribution of residuals is indistinguishable from uniform over $[0, q]$ when the cruel bits are incorrectly chosen, we frame the task of identifying correct cruel bits as distinguishing from uniform. As describe in Sect. 3.1, we do so by measuring the variance. First, we calculate $\hat{\sigma}^2(x)$ over M reduced samples via

$$\hat{\sigma}^2 = \frac{1}{M} \sum_{i=0}^{M-1} x_i^2. \tag{9}$$

We can construct a lower confidence bound ι for the variance under the null hypothesis of uniformity, assuming a Gaussian distribution of $\hat{\sigma}^2$ under the CLT:

$$\iota(\alpha, M) = \sigma_{\mathcal{U}_q}^2 + G^{-1}(\alpha) \cdot \sqrt{\frac{\sigma_{\mathcal{U}_q^2}^2}{M}} = \sigma_{\mathcal{U}_q}^2 + G^{-1}(\alpha) \cdot \sqrt{\frac{\sigma_{\mathcal{U}_q}^2}{M} \cdot \frac{q^2 - 4}{15}}, \tag{10}$$

where G^{-1} is the percent point function of $\mathcal{N}(0, 1)$ and $\sigma_{\mathcal{U}_q}^2$ (resp. $\sigma_{\mathcal{U}_q^2}^2$) is the distribution variance of x (resp. x^2) under the null hypothesis of uniformity. α is the false negative error, i.e. the probability of rejecting a true null hypothesis. Since we are brute-forcing a large number of possible solutions, the false negative error α should be small (i.e. $\alpha <$ the inverse of the number of secret candidates).

Given α and β false positive error (the probability of failing to reject a false null hypothesis), we can estimate the minimum number of samples needed for our attack to succeed with probability $\approx 1 - \beta$ using CLT (see Sect. A.2 for more details):

$$M(\alpha, \beta) = \left[\frac{G^{-1}(\alpha)\sigma_{\mathcal{U}_q^2} + G^{-1}(\beta)\sigma_{\mathcal{G}_q^2}}{(\sigma_{\mathcal{G}_q}^2 - \sigma_{\mathcal{U}_q}^2)} \right]^2 \tag{11}$$

where $\sigma_{\mathcal{G}_q}$ resp. $\sigma_{\mathcal{G}_q^2}$ is the standard deviation of x resp. x^2 when $x \sim \mathcal{G}_q$ i.e. discrete centered Gaussian mod q. Table 5 gives concrete calculations of M for various h secrets.

These results indicate that in the easiest settings (e.g. $n = 512$) a few thousand reduced samples are enough to test cruel bit guesses. For $n = 256$, a few tens of thousands of reduced pairs are needed. As indicated in Sect. 3.1, the amount of data used can be traded off by running the cool bit estimation and subsequent secret check more often.

Table 5. Number of reduced samples M needed in the statistical test for false negative error $\alpha = 2^{-128}$ and false positive error $\beta = 10^{-5}$ for LWE settings specified by n, $\log_2 q$, n_u, and secret Hamming weight h. The Worst Case number of samples corresponds to the case where all the 1s in the secret are in the reduced region $h_r = h$, whereas the Average case assumes the average number of 1s in that region, which is the fraction $\frac{n_r}{n}h$. Because overall lattice reduction depends on both n and $\log_2 q$, problem difficulty, and thus M, does not monotonically increase with respect to only n.

n	$\log_2 q$	n_u	h	Worst case M $(h_r = h)$	Average case M $(h_r = \frac{n_r}{n}h)$
256	12	143	12	5.67×10^4	1.12×10^4
512	28	228	20	3.29×10^3	1.66×10^3
512	41	75	60	1.98×10^4	1.02×10^4
768	35	373	20	3.13×10^4	9.74×10^3
768	35	373	64	6.21×10^6	1.47×10^5
1024	50	495	15	2.37×10^3	1.35×10^3

5.2   Testing Cool Bit Predictions

Once the cruel bits have been guessed, we can use Algorithm 1 to recover the cool bits of the secret one bit at a time. As before, we will estimate the standard deviation of $x = \mathbf{a} \cdot \mathbf{s}^* - b$ over a sample of reduced LWE pairs, but the cruel bits in our guess $\mathbf{s}^*$ are now assumed to be correct. For each cool coordinate, k, we compare two guesses, $\mathbf{s}_0^*$ and $\mathbf{s}_1^*$, which agree with the secret on the $k - 1$ first characters, are zero on the $n - k$ characters, and have their k-th bit set to 0 and 1 respectively. If the k-th bit is zero, $x_0 = \mathbf{a} \cdot \mathbf{s}_0^* - b$ should have a lower standard deviation than $x_1 = \mathbf{a} \cdot \mathbf{s}_1^* - b$.

Suppose that all the cruel bits and the $k - 1$ first cool coordinates have been correctly guessed, and there are h^* one bits to be discovered in the remaining cool coordinates. Let the null hypothesis be $H_0 : \mathbf{s}_k = 0$ and the alternative hypothesis: $H_1 : \mathbf{s}_k = 1$. The residual $x_0 = \mathbf{a} \cdot \mathbf{s}_0^* - b$ has in both cases variance $\sigma_0^2 = F_q(h^*\sigma_r^2 + \sigma_e^2)$. Under H_0 the variance of $x_1 = \mathbf{a} \cdot \mathbf{s}_1^* - b$ will be $\sigma_{+1}^2 = F_q((h^* + 1)\sigma_r^2 + \sigma_e^2) > \sigma_0^2$. Under H_1 the variance of x_1 is $\sigma_{-1}^2 = F_q((h^* - 1)\sigma_r^2 + \sigma_e^2) < \sigma_0^2$.

In each iteration k of Algorithm 1, our objective is to determine whether the difference in estimated variance, denoted as $\delta(\sigma^2) := \hat{\sigma}^2(x_1) - \hat{\sigma}^2(x_0)$, is more closely aligned with $\sigma_{+1}^2 - \sigma_0^2 > 0$ or $\sigma_{-1}^2 - \sigma_0^2 < 0$. To achieve this, we estimate the variance difference using enough samples. Without the need for optimal threshold tuning, we reject the null hypothesis if the variance difference $\delta(\sigma^2)$ is negative, and accept it otherwise.

6   Recovery Results

In this section we provide concrete performance results for our attacks. We run the attack as described in Sect. 3.1 for different LWE parameter settings and

Table 6. Concrete attacks on different secrets. n = dimension, $\log_2 q$ = modulus size, h = Hamming weight of the secret. h_u = # cruel bits equal to 1. % and cumulative % show the percentage of hamming weight h secrets which have h_u cruel bits (or fewer). All attacks run on 1 GPU, except the toughest settings on 20 GPUs in parallel.

n	$\log_2 q$	h	h_u	% (cum. %)	Samples Used	Time (1 V100 GPU)
256	12	12	4	6.7 (9.5)	200K	28 s
		12	5	14.1 (23.6)		84 s, 241 s
		12	6	21.2 (44.8)		3865 s, 4098 s
		12	7	23.0 (67.8)		23229 s, 26229 s
512	28	12	3	9.5 (13.9)	200K	29 s
		12	4	17.5 (31.4)		70 s
		12	5	22.7 (54.0)		2417 s, 3510 s
512	41	60	7	16.6 (53.6)	1M	376 s, 341 s
		60	8	15.5 (69.1)		1555 s
768	35	10	3	13.1 (19.5)	200K	165 s, 168 s
		10	4	21.7 (41.2)		269 s, 745 s
		12	4	13.5 (22.1)		607 s, 688 s
		12	5	20.5 (42.6)		1291 s (scaled to 20 GPUs)
1024	50	10	3	13.2 (20.0)	100K	59 s, 64 s
		13	4	10.2 (16.0)		1304 s
		17	5	5.8 (9.1)		6395 s (scaled to 20 GPUs)

report results in Table 6. After reduction, the running time depends almost entirely on the amount of enumeration that has to be done on the cruel bits. Enumeration is done in ascending hamming weight on those bits. We extend the secret to the cool bits via the greedy algorithm, every 40M secret candidates, or whenever completing the enumeration on one hamming weight.

All times reported in Table 6 include the compilation time during the first run over a secret, which is of the order of 10 s, and loading data, also of the order of 10 s. For some hamming weights, we report multiple timings to illustrate that the process is somewhat noisy, mostly depending on where in the enumeration the secret happens to be. For the settings with higher hamming weights ($h = 60$), we use 200k samples for the brute force attack and 1M for the greedy attack. For the lower hamming weights, we use 10k–30k samples for the brute force attack and 200k for the greedy part. Recall that samples are generated via the pre-processing step explained in Sect. 4.1, so the raw number of samples needed for each attack is always $4n$. Also note that attacks are run on 1 V100 GPU in general, using 20 GPUs in parallel only for the hardest cases.

Existing Attacks. For completeness, we compare the performance of our attack to prior work. The hybrid dual meet-in-the-middle (MiTM) attack is most similar to ours [19], but options for comparison are limited, since no concrete performance results are provided in [19]. Some concrete performance results are given for related attacks, but [8] only considers $n \leq 110$, $\log q = 11$, while [32] considers $n \leq 100$, $\log q = 8$. Thus, we choose two routes for comparison. First, we compare against estimated cost of the hybrid dual MiTM estimate from the LWE estimator tool [9][1], and then we compare against a recent concrete attack implementation for sparse secret LWE proposed in [21]. The latter has code available[2] and claims to be fast. It provides a MITM attack in Python for the $n = 256$, $\log q = 12$ setting and a modified uSVP/BDD attack for larger parameters.

Table 7. Claimed attacks for comparison from [9] and [21]. Estimates from [9] do not represent actual secret recovery, only predictions. Estimates given in terms of ROP = estimated number of required operations for attack, Repeats = # of times attack must run to succeed with probability 0.99999, Total Cost = total estimated ROP for this attack, omitting storage costs. For the code from [21], '-' indicates no success after running for 3 weeks on our hardware.

LWE setting (n, q, h)	Dual Hybrid MiTM [9]			Ducas et al. [21]
	ROP	Repeats	Total Cost	Time (sec)
$(256, 12, 12)$	$2^{52.7}$	$2^{14.5}$	$2^{67.2}$	200
$(512, 28, 12)$	$2^{48.6}$	$2^{10.6}$	$2^{59.2}$	-
$(512, 41, 60)$	$2^{50.6}$	$2^{8.6}$	$2^{59.2}$	-
$(768, 35, 12)$	$2^{49.1}$	$2^{10.6}$	$2^{59.7}$	-
$(1024, 50, 17)$	$2^{50.9}$	$2^{11.1}$	$2^{61.0}$	-

Table 7 reports comparison results. For the estimator [9], we report the estimated number of operations and the number of attack repeats required to achieve a $1 - 10^{-5}$ probability of success (to match our α, β levels in Sect. 5). We note that the ROP metric reported by the estimator is a crude estimate for runtime, since it refers to the number of comparisons or operations necessary for the attack to run, which does not easily translate to time measurements. For example, if it means $(\mathbf{Z}/q\mathbf{Z})$ ring operations then one should multiply by the cost of a multiplication modulo q, naively $(\log q)^2$, or if it means ciphertext operations then one should multiply by the cost of polynomial multiplications modulo q, etc.

For the attack reported in [21], we find that it does not succeed and does not recover secrets in the dimensions >256 reported in this paper and in [26]. The attack ran for up to 3 weeks in all cases where dimension >256 (on the same hardware as our attack). No secrets were recovered and in some cases the jobs crashed after running for days/weeks. This claimed attack and code was also presented in [2], without verifying the code or the fact that it does not recover secrets in the dimensions (>256) we attack.

---

[1] https://github.com/malb/lattice-estimator, commit 00ec72ce.
[2] https://github.com/lducas/leaky-LWE-Estimator/tree/human-LWE/human-LWE.

7   2-Power Cyclotomic Ring-LWE

Our attack can also be applied in the 2-power cyclotomic Ring-LWE setting. Ring-LWE (RLWE) is a special case of LWE where the LWE samples are represented more compactly as polynomials in a polynomial ring. Not all instances of Ring-LWE are hard, as was shown in [22]. But 2-power cyclotomic rings are not vulnerable to the attack of [22], so those are the rings proposed for standardized use in Homomorphic Encryption [3,12].

Consider the 2-power cyclotomic ring defined by the polynomial x^n+1, where $n = 2^k$: $R_q = \mathbb{Z}_q[x]/(x^n + 1)$. Then the RLWE samples $(a(x), b(x) = a(x) \cdot s(x) + e(x))$ can be described via a skew-circulant matrix, $\mathbf{A}_{circ}$. If $a(x) = a_0 + a_1 x + ... + a_{n-1}x^{n-1}$, then using the embedding $\mathbf{a} = (a_0, a_1, \ldots, a_{n-1})$:

$$\mathbf{A}_{\text{circ}} = \begin{bmatrix} a_0 & -a_{n-1} & -a_{n-2} & \cdots & -a_1 \\ a_1 & a_0 & -a_{n-1} & \ddots & -a_2 \\ \vdots & a_1 & a_0 & \ddots & -a_{n-1} \\ a_{n-1} & \ddots & & \ddots & a_0 \end{bmatrix}$$

and $\mathbf{b}_{\text{circ}} = \mathbf{A}_{\text{circ}}\mathbf{s} + \mathbf{e}$ where $\mathbf{s}$ and $\mathbf{e}$ are the vector representations of $s(x)$ and $e(x)$ respectively. When the matrix has this structure, we can rotate the "cruel bits" around (without redoing any lattice reduction) by constructing datasets composed of elements from certain indices in the matrix As Appendix Fig. 4 shows, shifting increases our chances of recovering the secret, since we can rotate the cruel region essentially for free. Rotating around, we may find a rotation of the cruel region with only a few cruel (active) bits. We can then run our attack on this new, easier problem. This ability to shift the cruel region makes the RWLE problem clearly easier than generic LWE, with respect to our attack.

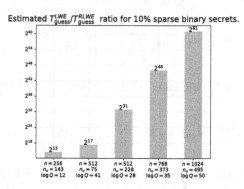

Fig. 3. Exhaustive search cost ratio for LWE versus RLWE as defined in Eq. (13) and Eq. (14) assuming a fixed 10% binary secret sparsity. The values of n_u are obtained experimentally.

More formally, RLWE cruel bit shifting works as follows. After running reduction on the original RLWE polynomials $a(x)$, we have reduced samples, $\mathbf{A} \in \mathbb{Z}_q^{m \times n}$, where $\mathbf{A} = \mathbf{R} \mathbf{A}_{\text{circ}}$ for some $\mathbf{R} \in \mathbb{Z}^{m \times n}$. We can shift-negate the reduced samples k times to get new samples $(\mathbf{A}^{\leftarrow k}, \mathbf{b}^{\leftarrow k})$ (see Sect. A.1). The attack for RLWE brute forces n sliding windows $[k, k + n_u \mod n)$ simultaneously (or any other number of windows by using a higher sliding step). Exhaustive search only requires checking up to $h_u^{(1)} = \min_{0 \le i < n} h_{n_u,i}(\mathbf{s})$ hamming weight where

$$h_{n_u,i}(\mathbf{s}) = \sum_{j=i}^{i+n_u-1[n]} s_j \tag{12}$$

$h_{n_u,i}(\mathbf{s})$ represents the Hamming weight of a specific segment of the secret vector $\mathbf{s}$, starting at position i and of length n_u. When $i = 0$, this notation aligns with our previous use of h_u to denote the Hamming weight of the first n_u elements of $\mathbf{s}$. Similarly, when $n_r = n - n_u$, $h_{n_r,n_u}(\mathbf{s})$ aligns with our previous use of h_r to denote the Hamming weight of the last $n_r = n - n_u$ elements of $\mathbf{s}$.

To evaluate the speed up of the RLWE attack, we estimate the cost of the brute force component while assuming equal cost of lattice reduction for LWE and RLWE. Let $c \cdot M(h_r(s), \alpha, \beta)$ represent the cost of checking a secret candidate using $M(h_r(s), \alpha, \beta)$ samples, where c is a constant accounting for the computational cost of each verification. Let $T_{\text{guess}}^{\text{LWE}}$ be the average time complexity of the exhaustive search for LWE, assuming we sweep through secret candidates in ascending Hamming weight order:

$$T_{\text{guess}}^{\text{LWE}} = \mathbb{E}_s \left[c \cdot M(h_r(s), \alpha, \beta) \sum_{k=0}^{h_u(s)} \binom{n_u}{k} \right]$$

Using the same number of samples $M = M(h_r(s), \alpha, \beta)$ for each secret candidate:

$$T_{\text{guess}}^{\text{LWE}} = c \cdot M \cdot \sum_{k=0}^{h} \binom{n_u}{k} \mathbb{P}(h_u(s) \ge k) \tag{13}$$

Contrast this with the RLWE case, where we have $\mathbb{P}(h_u^{(1)} \le \frac{h n_u}{n}) = 1$ so that:

$$T_{\text{guess}}^{\text{RLWE}} = n \cdot c \cdot M \cdot \sum_{k=0}^{\lfloor \frac{h n_u}{n} \rfloor} \binom{n_u}{k} \mathbb{P}(h_u^{(1)} \ge k) \tag{14}$$

In Fig. 3, we estimate the ratio of these costs. The distribution of $h_u(s)$ with fixed total hamming weight h follows a hyper-geometric distribution when the secret bits are from a Bernoulli distribution, while the $h_u^{(1)}$ distribution is computed empirically.

We conduct several experiments comparing LWE with RLWE, using identical secrets. The results of these experiments, for parameters $n = 256$, $n = 512$ and

Table 8. RLWE/LWE Attack times for $n = 256, h = 12, \log q = 12, n_u = 145$, run on 10 randomly sampled secrets. Actual time is the empirical time of the attack. Estimated time is computed via the formula: $T_{\text{guess}}^{\text{LWE}} = b + a \sum_{k=0}^{h_u(s)} \binom{n_u}{k}$ and $T_{\text{guess}}^{\text{RLWE}} = n(b + a \sum_{k=0}^{h_u^{(1)}} \binom{n_u}{k})$ for RLWE. $h_u(s) = $ # cruel bits of the secret, and $h_u^{(1)}$ is the minimum hamming weight over all windows of length n_u. We use $56K$ samples for cruel bit recovery and $200K$ for Algorithm 1.

Secret	LWE			RLWE		
	Estimated time (sec)	Actual time (sec)	$h_u(s)$	Estimated time	Actual time	$h_u^{(1)}(s)$
1	2.33×10^1	2.21×10^1	3	5.86×10^3	4.83×10^3	2
2	4.60×10^2	5.24×10^2	5	1.18×10^5	1.73×10^5	5
3	2.09×10^5	–	7	1.18×10^5	1.48×10^5	5
4	2.09×10^5	–	7	9.77×10^3	1.20×10^4	4
5	2.09×10^5	–	7	9.77×10^3	1.15×10^4	4
6	3.66×10^6	–	8	9.77×10^3	1.26×10^4	4
7	3.66×10^6	–	8	9.77×10^3	1.19×10^4	4
8	5.65×10^7	–	9	5.97×10^3	4.12×10^3	3
9	5.65×10^7	–	9	1.18×10^5	1.33×10^5	5
10	7.81×10^8	–	10	5.86×10^3	4.74×10^3	2

Table 9. Attack times vs. estimated costs for $n = 512, n_u = 75, h = 60, \log q = 41$ (in seconds) for 10 random secrets sorted by # cruel bits in the secret. We use $40K$ samples for cruel bit recovery and $1.5M$ for Algorithm 1

Secret	LWE			RLWE		
	Estimated time (sec)	Actual time (sec)	$h_u(s)$	Estimated time	Actual time	$h_u^{(1)}(s)$
1	6.88×10^2	5.95×10^2	6	1.82×10^5	7.74×10^4	4
2	3.98×10^3	3.93×10^3	7	1.82×10^5	7.68×10^4	4
3	3.45×10^4	–	8	3.52×10^5	1.08×10^5	6
4	2.82×10^5	–	9	1.95×10^5	1.15×10^6	5
5	2.06×10^6	–	10	1.82×10^5	4.64×10^4	4
6	2.06×10^6	–	10	1.81×10^5	–	2
7	1.36×10^7	–	11	1.82×10^5	–	4
8	8.06×10^7	–	12	1.81×10^5	4.43×10^4	3
9	4.36×10^8	–	13	1.82×10^5	–	4
10	9.88×10^9	–	15	1.81×10^5	4.67×10^4	2

$n = 1024$, are presented in Tables 8, 9, and 10. Each table row corresponds to a distinct secret s, and the columns detail the actual/estimated time costs for the LWE/RLWE attacks, along with the number of cruel bits in the secret. In the tables, Actual Time is the empirically measured duration of the attack, while the Estimated Time is estimated using an approximation $T_{\text{guess}}^{\text{LWE}} = b + a \sum_{k=0}^{h_u(s)} \binom{n_u}{k}$. This estimate provides an idea of the time required to attack a secret when h_u is large.

Table 10. Attack times vs. estimated times for $n = 1024, h = 20, \log q = 50, n_u = 495$ (in seconds) for 10 random secrets sorted by # cruel bits in the secret. We use $10K$ samples for cruel bit recovery (scaled to 4 GPUs) and $100K$ for Algorithm 1

Secret	LWE			RLWE		
	Estimated time (sec)	Actual time (sec)	$h_u(s)$	Estimated time	Actual time	$h_u^{(1)}(s)$
1	6.34×10^9	–	8	1.51×10^9	–	6
2	6.34×10^9	–	8	2.01×10^7	2.01×10^7	5
3	3.45×10^{11}	–	9	1.71×10^6	4.78×10^5	3
4	3.45×10^{11}	–	9	1.51×10^9	–	6
5	3.45×10^{11}	–	9	1.06×10^{11}	–	7
6	1.68×10^{13}	–	10	1.06×10^{11}	–	7
7	1.68×10^{13}	–	10	1.51×10^9	–	6
8	1.68×10^{13}	–	10	1.06×10^{11}	–	7
9	3.02×10^{16}	–	12	1.51×10^9	–	6
10	1.13×10^{18}	–	13	1.90×10^6	3.14×10^6	4

For RLWE attacks, time is multiplied by n since n brute force attacks are run, although they can be run simultaneously. The final row of Table 8 provides the average values across all secrets. As can be seen, the RLWE attack is significantly faster on average, with the ratio of average times being $\sim 10^3$ for $n = 256$ and 5×10^3 for $n = 512$, but converge to the theoretical values in Fig. 3 when estimated on more secret samples. The RLWE advantage can also be seen in the values of $h_u^{(1)}(s)$ which are much smaller than $h_u(s)$.

8   Discussion and Future Work

We have presented an attack on Learning With Errors in the setting of sparse binary secrets. Our key insight is the reduction of the LWE problem to one of smaller dimension via lattice reduction and sufficient subsampling. We discuss the attack empirically and theoretically and highlight actual successful attacks for dimension up to $n = 1024$. We leave several important tasks as future work.

Improving Upon Combinatorial Scaling in Reduced Problem. We use brute force to solve the smaller LWE problem (e.g. in the cruel region). This is the crudest way to solve this problem, albeit perfectly parallelizable. The guessing parts of hybrid attack strategies of related work could speed up enumeration. One related way in which we already exploit this is in the 2-cyclotomic RLWE setting. But of course, the rotation (or more generally, permutation) of the cruel bit region can of course be done on the LWE settings as well. We did not elaborate on that (hybrid) approach because it requires re-reduction of lattices.

Balancing Reduction and Secret Recovery Costs. Currently, our attack runs lattice reduction until it stalls for a given n/q setting, then runs secret recovery for the highest h that can be achieved in reasonable time. In the future, our attack should balance the reduction and enumeration costs given the setting of concern, also depending on how hybrid attacks will be employed.

Recovering the Cool Bits. As Sect. 5.2 demonstrates, cool bit recovery is somewhat sample-inefficient, because Algorithm 1 must distinguish between $F_q(k\sigma_r^2 + \sigma_e^2)$ and $F_q((k+1)\sigma_r^2 + \sigma_e^2)$. This difference tends to be small when k is large, and σ_e is large, compared to σ_r, necessitating more samples. This suggests an additional consideration for the lattice reduction phase: balancing the amount of reduction achieved and the noise added in the process. When reduction factor ρ is smaller, σ_r is smaller, resulting in fewer cruel bits and easier recovery. On the other hand, a smaller ρ means a larger σ_e, necessitating more data during the attack. We leave the quantitative analysis of this relationship as future work.

A Appendix

A.1 Rotating Reduced Short 2-Cyclotomic RLWE Vectors

Consider the R_q-endomorphism ϕ defined by $\phi : a \mapsto xa$. We establish its counterpart in the canonical embedding as:

$$\Phi(A) = AX, \quad \forall A \in \mathbb{Z}^{m \times n},$$

where X is defined as $X = \mathrm{Circ}(x_{\mathrm{vec}})^\top$, with Circ denoting the skew-circulant and x being the degree 1 polynomial whose vector representation is given by $x_{\mathrm{vec}} = (0, 1, 0, \dots, 0) \in \mathbb{Z}^n$. We further introduce the notation $\Phi_k(A)$ to denote the k-fold composition of Φ, i.e., $\Phi^k(A) = \Phi \circ \Phi \circ \cdots \circ \Phi$. If $A_{\mathrm{circ}} = \mathrm{Circ}(a)$, then A_{circ} and X commute: $XA_{\mathrm{circ}} = A_{\mathrm{circ}}X$. This is due to the associativity in the ring R_q. This allows us to have new samples $(A^{\to k}, b^{\to k})$ by shift-negating the reduced samples k times:

$$A^{\to k} := AX^k = \Phi_k(A) \quad \text{and}$$

$$
\begin{aligned}
A^{\to k}s &= RA_{\mathrm{circ}}X^k s \\
&= RX^k A_{\mathrm{circ}} s \\
&= RX^k(A_{\mathrm{circ}}s + e) - RX^k e \\
&= \Phi_k(R)b_{\mathrm{circ}} - \Phi_k(R)(e)
\end{aligned}
$$

So by defining $b^{\to k} := R^{\to k}b_{\mathrm{circ}}$, $(A^{\to k}, b^{\to k})$ are LWE samples with secret s.

We illustrate empirically how sub-selecting samples from different indices of the circulant matrix affects h_u in Fig. 4. When we sub-sample elements when $k = 0$ (e.g. no shifting), $h_u = 16$ for a $n = 256$ $\log q = 12$, $h = 16$ problem. However, sub-sampling elements at $k = 124$ yields $h_u = 4$, a much easier secret.

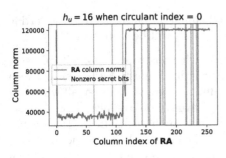 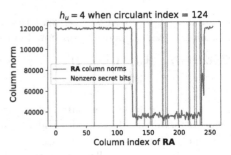

Fig. 4. Effect of shifting the RLWE circulant matrix on number of h_u secret bits, for $n = 256$, $\log_2 = 12$, $n_u = 143$, $h = 20$.

A.2   Minimum Sample Requirement for Hypothesis Testing

We examine two centered discrete distributions, namely $\mathcal{U}_q := Uniform(\mathbb{Z}_q)$ and $\mathcal{G}_q := Discrete\ Gaussian(0, \sigma_{\mathcal{G}}^2) \mod q$ where $\sigma_{\mathcal{G}}^2 = h_r \sigma_r^2 + \sigma_e^2$ and $\sigma_{\mathcal{G}_q}^2 = F_q(\sigma_{\mathcal{G}}^2)$.

The variance of x^2 when x is uniform is $\sigma_{\mathcal{U}_q^2}^2 = \sigma_{\mathcal{U}_q}^2 \frac{q^2 - 4}{15}$. For the discrete Gaussian $\mod q$, the variance of x^2: $\sigma_{\mathcal{G}_q^2}^2 = \mathbb{E}_{\mathcal{G}_q}(x^4) - \mathbb{E}_{\mathcal{G}_q}(x^2)^2$ is approximated. Let x be a sample drawn from either of the two aforementioned distributions. We also consider M samples x_i drawn from the same distribution as x. To differentiate between the two distributions, we conduct a statistical test with the following null and alternative hypotheses:

$$\textbf{H0:}\ \sigma^2(x) = \sigma_{\mathcal{U}_q}^2 \quad \textbf{H1:}\ \sigma^2(x) = \sigma_{\mathcal{G}_q}^2$$

We consider the unbiased variance estimator for a known 0 mean: $\hat{\sigma}_M^2 = \frac{1}{M}\sum_{i=0}^{M-1} x_i^2$. The threshold $\iota(\alpha, M)$ is set so that the type-1 error: $\alpha = \mathbb{P}_{\mathcal{U}_q}(\hat{\sigma}_M^2 < \iota(\alpha, M)) = \mathbb{P}(\hat{\sigma}_M^2 < \iota(\alpha, M)|x \sim \mathcal{U}_q)$ is given. Using Central Limit Theorem and solving for $\iota(M, \alpha)$

$$\alpha = \mathbb{P}(\hat{\sigma}_M^2 < \iota|x \sim \mathcal{U}_q) = \mathbb{P}\left(\sqrt{\frac{M}{\sigma_{\mathcal{U}_q^2}^2}}(\hat{\sigma}_M^2 - \sigma_{\mathcal{U}_q}^2) < \sqrt{\frac{M}{\sigma_{\mathcal{U}_q^2}^2}}(\iota - \sigma_{\mathcal{U}_q}^2)|x \sim \mathcal{U}_q\right)$$

$$\approx \mathbb{P}\left(\mathcal{G}(0,1) < \sqrt{\frac{M}{\sigma_{\mathcal{U}_q^2}^2}}(\iota - \sigma_{\mathcal{U}_q}^2)\right) = G\left(\sqrt{\frac{M}{\sigma_{\mathcal{U}_q^2}^2}}(\iota - \sigma_{\mathcal{U}_q}^2)\right)$$

Which results in the equation:

$$\iota(M, \alpha) = \sigma_{\mathcal{U}_q}^2 + G^{-1}(\alpha)\frac{\sigma_{\mathcal{U}_q^2}}{\sqrt{M}} \tag{15}$$

Doing the same for the type-2 error given $\iota(M, \alpha)$ and solving for M:

$$\beta = \mathbb{P}(\hat{\sigma}_M^2 \geq \iota(M, \alpha)|x \sim \mathcal{G}_q) \approx G\left(\sqrt{\frac{M}{\sigma_{\mathcal{G}_q^2}^2}}(\sigma_{\mathcal{G}_q}^2 - \iota(M, \alpha))\right)$$

By substituting $\iota(M, \alpha)$ by its expression in Eq. (15), we have:

$$M = \left[\frac{G^{-1}(\alpha)\sigma_{\mathcal{U}_q^2} + G^{-1}(\beta)\sigma_{\mathcal{G}_q^2}}{(\sigma_{\mathcal{G}_q}^2 - \sigma_{\mathcal{U}_q}^2)} \right]^2$$

A.3 Our Observation and the Q-ary Lattice Z-Shape

Prior work has observed a "z-shape" in q-ary lattices in the context of the hybrid attack [4,24]. This classic z-shape is exhibited by the Gram-Schmidt orthogonalized rows of a q-ary lattice (see left plot of Fig. 5, orange before reduction, blue after). This is distinct from the behavior we observe in the columns of **A** after reduction (see right plot of Fig. 5 in blue).

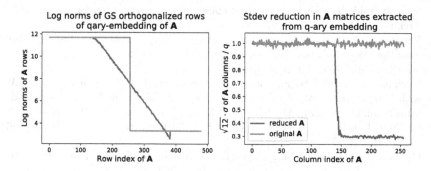

Fig. 5. (Color figure online).

References

1. Ajtai, M.: Generating hard instances of lattice problems. In: Proceedings of the 28th Annual ACM Symposium on Theory of Computing (1996)
2. Albrecht, M.: An update on lattice cryptanalysis, vol. 1. The dual attack on LWE. In: Real World Crypto RWPQC 2024 talk (2024)
3. Albrecht, M., et al.: Homomorphic encryption standard. In: Lauter, K., Dai, W., Laine, K. (eds.) Protecting Privacy through Homomorphic Encryption, pp. 31–62. Springer, Cham (2021). https://doi.org/10.1007/978-3-030-77287-1_2
4. Albrecht, M., Ducas, L.: Lattice attacks on NTRU and LWE: a history of refinements. Cryptology ePrint Archive (2021)
5. Albrecht, M.R.: On dual lattice attacks against small-secret LWE and parameter choices in HElib and SEAL. In: Coron, J.-S., Nielsen, J.B. (eds.) EUROCRYPT 2017. LNCS, vol. 10211, pp. 103–129. Springer, Cham (2017). https://doi.org/10.1007/978-3-319-56614-6_4
6. Albrecht, M.R., et al.: Estimate all the LWE, NTRU schemes! Cryptology ePrint Archive, Paper 2018/331 (2018). https://eprint.iacr.org/2018/331

7. Albrecht, M.R., Fitzpatrick, R., Göpfert, F.: On the efficacy of solving LWE by reduction to unique-SVP. Cryptology ePrint Archive, Paper 2013/602 (2013). https://eprint.iacr.org/2013/602

8. Albrecht, M.R., Göpfert, F., Virdia, F., Wunderer, T.: Revisiting the expected cost of solving uSVP and applications to LWE. In: Takagi, T., Peyrin, T. (eds.) ASIACRYPT 2017. LNCS, vol. 10624, pp. 297–322. Springer, Cham (2017). https://doi.org/10.1007/978-3-319-70694-8_11

9. Albrecht, M.R., Player, R., Scott, S.: On the concrete hardness of learning with errors. J. Math. Cryptol. (2015). https://eprint.iacr.org/2015/046

10. Bai, S., Galbraith, S.D.: Lattice decoding attacks on binary LWE. In: Susilo, W., Mu, Y. (eds.) ACISP 2014. LNCS, vol. 8544, pp. 322–337. Springer, Cham (2014). https://doi.org/10.1007/978-3-319-08344-5_21

11. Bi, L., Lu, X., Luo, J., Wang, K., Zhang, Z.: Hybrid dual attack on LWE with arbitrary secrets. Cryptology ePrint Archive, Paper 2021/152 (2021). https://eprint.iacr.org/2021/152

12. Bossuat, J.P., Cammarota, R., Cheon, J.H., Chillotti, I., Curtis, B.R., et al.: Security guidelines for implementing homomorphic encryption. Cryptology ePrint Archive (2024)

13. Buchmann, J., et al.: Creating cryptographic challenges using multi-party computation: the LWE challenge. In: Proceedings of the 3rd ACM International Workshop on ASIA Public-Key Cryptography (2016)

14. Buchmann, J., Göpfert, F., Player, R., Wunderer, T.: On the hardness of LWE with binary error: revisiting the hybrid lattice-reduction and meet-in-the-middle attack. In: Pointcheval, D., Nitaj, A., Rachidi, T. (eds.) AFRICACRYPT 2016. LNCS, vol. 9646, pp. 24–43. Springer, Cham (2016). https://doi.org/10.1007/978-3-319-31517-1_2

15. Charton, F., Lauter, K., Li, C., Tygert, M.: An efficient algorithm for integer lattice reduction. SIAM J. Matrix Anal. Appl. **45**(1), 353–367 (2024)

16. Chen, H., Han, K.: Homomorphic lower digits removal and improved FHE bootstrapping. In: Nielsen, J.B., Rijmen, V. (eds.) EUROCRYPT 2018. LNCS, vol. 10820, pp. 315–337. Springer, Cham (2018). https://doi.org/10.1007/978-3-319-78381-9_12

17. Chen, L., Moody, D., Liu, Y.K., et al.: PQC Standardization Process: Announcing Four Candidates to be Standardized, Plus Fourth Round Candidates. US Department of Commerce, NIST (2022). https://csrc.nist.gov/News/2022/pqc-candidates-to-be-standardized-and-round-4

18. Chen, Y., Nguyen, P.Q.: BKZ 2.0: better lattice security estimates. In: Lee, D.H., Wang, X. (eds.) ASIACRYPT 2011. LNCS, vol. 7073, pp. 1–20. Springer, Heidelberg (2011). https://doi.org/10.1007/978-3-642-25385-0_1

19. Cheon, J.H., Hhan, M., Hong, S., Son, Y.: A hybrid of dual and meet-in-the-middle attack on sparse and ternary secret LWE. IEEE Access **7**, 89497–89506 (2019)

20. Cheon, J.H., Kim, A., Kim, M., Song, Y.: Homomorphic encryption for arithmetic of approximate numbers. In: Takagi, T., Peyrin, T. (eds.) ASIACRYPT 2017. LNCS, vol. 10624, pp. 409–437. Springer, Cham (2017). https://doi.org/10.1007/978-3-319-70694-8_15

21. Ducas, L., Postlethwaite, E., Sotakova, J.: SALSA Verde vs. The Actual State of the Art (2023), https://crypto.iacr.org/2023/rump/crypto2023rump-paper13.pdf

22. Elias, Y., Lauter, K.E., Ozman, E., Stange, K.E.: Provably weak instances of Ring-LWE. In: Gennaro, R., Robshaw, M. (eds.) CRYPTO 2015. LNCS, vol. 9215, pp. 63–92. Springer, Heidelberg (2015). https://doi.org/10.1007/978-3-662-47989-6_4

23. Espitau, T., Joux, A., Kharchenko, N.: On a hybrid approach to solve small secret LWE. Cryptology ePrint Archive, Paper 2020/515 (2020). https://eprint.iacr.org/2020/515

24. Howgrave-Graham, N.: A hybrid lattice-reduction and meet-in-the-middle attack against NTRU. In: Menezes, A. (ed.) CRYPTO 2007. LNCS, vol. 4622, pp. 150–169. Springer, Heidelberg (2007). https://doi.org/10.1007/978-3-540-74143-5_9

25. Lenstra, H.J., Lenstra, A., Lovász, L.: Factoring polynomials with rational coefficients. Math. Ann. **261**, 515–534 (1982)

26. Li, C., Wenger, E., Allen-Zhu, Z., Charton, F., Lauter, K.: SALSA VERDE: a machine learning attack on learning with errors with sparse small secrets. In: Proceedings of NeurIPS (2023)

27. Li, C.Y., et al.: Salsa Picante: a machine learning attack on LWE with binary secrets. In: Proceedings of ACM CCS (2023)

28. Lindner, R., Peikert, C.: Better key sizes (and attacks) for LWE-based encryption. In: Kiayias, A. (ed.) CT-RSA 2011. LNCS, vol. 6558, pp. 319–339. Springer, Heidelberg (2011). https://doi.org/10.1007/978-3-642-19074-2_21

29. Liu, M., Nguyen, P.Q.: Solving BDD by enumeration: an update. In: Dawson, E. (ed.) CT-RSA 2013. LNCS, vol. 7779, pp. 293–309. Springer, Heidelberg (2013). https://doi.org/10.1007/978-3-642-36095-4_19

30. Micciancio, D., Regev, O.: Lattice-based cryptography. In: Bernstein, D.J., Buchmann, J., Dahmen, E. (eds.) Post-Quantum Cryptography, pp. 147–191. Springer, Heidelberg (2009). https://doi.org/10.1007/978-3-540-88702-7_5

31. Paszke, A., Gross, S., Massa, F., et al.: Pytorch: an imperative style, high-performance deep learning library. In: Proceedings of NeurIPS (2019)

32. Postlethwaite, E.W., Virdia, F.: On the success probability of solving unique SVP via BKZ. In: Garay, J.A. (ed.) PKC 2021. LNCS, vol. 12710, pp. 68–98. Springer, Cham (2021). https://doi.org/10.1007/978-3-030-75245-3_4

33. Regev, O.: On lattices, learning with errors, random linear codes, and cryptography. In: Proceedings of the Thirty-Seventh Annual ACM Symposium on Theory of Computing (2005). https://dblp.org/rec/journals/corr/cs-DS-0304005.bib

34. Ryan, K., Heninger, N.: Fast practical lattice reduction through iterated compression. In: Handschuh, H., Lysyanskaya, A. (eds.) CRYPTO 2023. LNCS, vol. 14083. Springer, Cham (2023). https://doi.org/10.1007/978-3-031-38548-3_1

35. Son, Y., Cheon, J.H.: Revisiting the hybrid attack on sparse and ternary secret LWE. Cryptology ePrint Archive, Paper 2019/1019 (2019). https://eprint.iacr.org/2019/1019

36. The FPLLL Development Team: FPLLL, a lattice reduction library, Version: 5.4.4 (2023). https://github.com/fplll/fplll

Author Index

S. Vaudenay and C. Petit (Eds.): AFRICACRYPT 2024, LNCS 14861, p. 455, 2024.
https://doi.org/10.1007/978-3-031-64381-1

Printed in the United States
by Baker & Taylor Publisher Services